THE PAPERS OF
WOODROW WILSON

VOLUME 15
1903-1905

SPONSORED BY THE WOODROW WILSON
FOUNDATION
AND PRINCETON UNIVERSITY

THE PAPERS OF

WOODROW WILSON

ARTHUR S. LINK, *EDITOR*

DAVID W. HIRST AND JOHN E. LITTLE

ASSOCIATE EDITORS

JEAN MACLACHLAN AND SYLVIA E. FONTIJN

CONTRIBUTING EDITORS

M. HALSEY THOMAS, *CONSULTING EDITOR*

JOHN M. MULDER, *EDITORIAL ASSISTANT*

Volume 15 · 1903-1905

PRINCETON, NEW JERSEY

PRINCETON UNIVERSITY PRESS

1973

INTRODUCTION

THE opening of this volume finds Wilson beginning the second year of his presidency of Princeton University. His apprenticeship behind him, Wilson now moves boldly to institute several significant reforms. First he wrests the power of appointment of faculty members from the Curriculum Committee of the Board of Trustees and vests it in his own and the faculty's hands. Second, he organizes the teaching staff into well-defined departments, thereby ending a long-standing administrative anarchy. Next, as chairman of the faculty Committee on the Course of Study, Wilson undertakes a thoroughgoing revision of the undergraduate course of study. It was one of the notable curricular reforms in the history of higher education in the United States and a milestone in the development of Princeton University. Throughout, it should be emphasized, Wilson is acting in accord with an educational philosophy formerly inchoate and now coming to first maturity in his mind.

A notable feature of this volume is the variety of the documents that it contains. There are sermons, addresses on educational theory and method, and annual reports to the Board of Trustees either hitherto not printed or not easily found. The diary that Wilson kept from January 1 through February 13, 1904, is printed herein for the first time, as are letters and other materials relating to the most controversial and difficult act of his early Princeton presidency—his dismissal of Arnold Guyot Cameron as Woodhull Professor of French. Mrs. Wilson made a highly eventful two-month tour of Italy in the spring of 1904. Her letters to her husband detail a vivid view of the Italy of that day, while Wilson's letters to her reveal much about his personal life and the ongoing affairs of the university. Of particular interest also are the numerous "begging" letters that he wrote in a successful effort to meet a serious deficit in the university's budget and others that reveal his leading role in the architectural development of Princeton.

Readers are again reminded that *The Papers of Woodrow Wilson* is a continuing series; that persons, institutions, and events that figure prominently in earlier volumes are not re-identified in subsequent ones; and that the Index to each volume gives cross references to fullest earlier identifications. We also reiterate that it is our practice to print texts *verbatim et literatim*, repairing words and phrases only when necessary for clarity or ease of reading, and that we make silent corrections only of obvious typographical errors in typed copies.

We are grateful to Mrs. Bryant Putney of Princeton University Press for continued help in copyediting, and to Miss Marjorie Sirlouis and Colonel James B. Rothnie, U.S.A., Ret., for deciphering Wilson's shorthand.

THE EDITORS

Princeton, New Jersey
July 8, 1972

CONTENTS

Introduction, vii
Illustrations, xvii
Abbreviations and Symbols, xix

The Papers, September 18, 1903–February 6, 1905

ILLUSTRATIONS

Following page 292

TEXT ILLUSTRATIONS

ABBREVIATIONS

AL	autograph letter
ALI	autograph letter initialed
ALS	autograph letter(s) signed
CCL	carbon copy of letter
CCLI	carbon copy of letter initialed
EAW	Ellen Axson Wilson
Hw	handwriting, handwritten
HwL	handwritten letter
sh	shorthand
TCL	typed copy of letter
TCLI	typed copy of letter initialed
TCLS	typed copy of letter signed
TLS	typed letter signed
T MS.	typed manuscript
TR	typed report
TRS	typed report signed
TS	typed signed
WW	Woodrow Wilson
WWhw	Woodrow Wilson handwriting, handwritten
WWhw MS.	Woodrow Wilson handwritten manuscript
WWhwRS	Woodrow Wilson handwritten report signed
WWshLS	Woodrow Wilson shorthand letter signed
WWT MS.	Woodrow Wilson typed manuscript
WWTCL	Woodrow Wilson typed copy of letter
WWTCLS	Woodrow Wilson typed copy of letter signed
WWTLS	Woodrow Wilson typed letter signed

ABBREVIATIONS FOR COLLECTIONS
AND LIBRARIES

Following the National Union Catalog
of the Library of Congress

CtY	Yale University
DLC	Library of Congress
FTU	University of Tampa
MB	Boston Public Library
MdHi	Maryland Historical Society
MH	Harvard University
MoSHi	Missouri Historical Society
MWC	Clark University
NcD	Duke University
NHi	New York Historical Society
NIC	Cornell University
Nj	New Jersey State Library
NjR	Rutgers University
NN	New York Public Library
OCHP	Historical and Philosophical Society of Ohio
PHi	Historical Society of Pennsylvania

PPAmP	American Philosophical Society
RSB Coll., DLC	Ray Stannard Baker Collection of Wilsoniana, Library of Congress
TxU	University of Texas
UA, NjP	University Archives, Princeton University
ViHi	Virginia Historical Society
ViU	University of Virginia
WC, NjP	Woodrow Wilson Collection, Princeton University
WHi	State Historical Society of Wisconsin
WP, DLC	Woodrow Wilson Papers, Library of Congress
WWP, UA, NjP	Woodrow Wilson Papers, Archives, Princeton University Library

SYMBOLS

[Sept. 24, 1903]	publication date of a published writing; also date of document when date is not part of text
[*Nov. 29, 1903*]	latest composition date of a published writing
[[Nov. 5, 1903]]	delivery date of a speech if publication date differs

THE PAPERS OF

WOODROW WILSON

VOLUME 15

1903-1905

THE PAPERS OF
WOODROW WILSON

From William Church Osborn[1]

Dear President Wilson   Garrison N.Y.   Sept. 18/03

There is apparently a feeling abroad, that the Princeton spirit is setting more strongly towards buildings than towards scholarship, or, at least, that the teaching force has hardly developed side by side with our architecture and especially in the first two years of the course.

If you should share this feeling and think that it would be desirable to add to the teaching staff, I should be glad to help by paying $1200 or $1500 for a tutorship in Freshman & Sophomore English.[2] I would probably pay the same sum next year, though I do not wish to definitely commit myself. Perhaps you think some other branch is in greater need; if so, I hope that you will not hesitate to speak of it.

May I also ask you not to use my name in this connection. This is not modesty, but results from a very practical experience of the number of "noes" that must be said, if the left hand learns that the right hand sometimes opens.

I trust that you have had a refreshing summer & remain
                         Cordially yours   Wm. Church Osborn

ALS (WP, DLC).
[1] A.B., College of New Jersey, 1883; LL.B., Harvard, 1888. Member of the New York law firm of Dexter, Osborn, and Gillispie and brother of Henry Fairfield Osborn.
[2] Wilson's reply is missing, but, as W. C. Osborn to WW, April 26 and 28, 1904, reveal, Osborn contributed $1,500, which Wilson at once used to employ Horace Meyer Kallen and Daniel Lindsey Thomas as Instructors in English.

From Archibald Clinton Harte

                         Young Men's Christian Association.
My dear Dr. Wilson: Mobile, Alabama   Sept. 18th., 1903.

I hardly suppose you will remember me: I, of course, know you as I was a '92 man at Wesleyan.

Last year when Mr. Murfee of Marion and Mr. Petrie of the Alabama Polytechnic Institute at Auburn[1] had a conference with reference to bringing great educators to our state to help us, we, every one of us, hoped we might secure you.

Mr. Murfee tells me, that there is some probability of your coming this fall.[2] I trust if you do, we may have the pleasure of having you in Mobile. We will get our college men together and give you a rousing time and will bring you as good an audience as can be had in any city.

College sentiment is growing among us, and each year more of our young men are going to college.

This year over fifty of the members of our association have gone, many of them to the great universities of the country.

We formed during the vacation a college men's association, the object being to make college life appeal to the young men of our city, and our expressed purpose is to get one hundred men to go to college from our city each year. You will help us in this and in many other ways if you will come to us.

Mr. P. J. Hamilton, who was a member of your class at Princeton, is the chairman of our library committee. He is not at present in the city, but I know if he were here he would write you a much stronger invitation than I could write.

Hoping to see you this fall, I am

Most sincerely yours,   A. C. Harte   General Secretary.

TLS (WP, DLC).

[1] Hopson Owen Murfee, Assistant Superintendent of the Marion, Alabama, Military Institute, and George Petrie, Professor of History and Latin, Alabama Polytechnic Institute, Auburn, Ala.

[2] See H. O. Murfee to WW, Aug. 6, 1902, Vol. 14. Wilson did not go to Alabama in the autumn of 1903. As subsequent documents will disclose, he did plan an extensive tour of the state for the spring of 1904, which he had to cancel because of illness in his family.

A News Item

[Sept. 24, 1903]

OPENING EXERCISES.

The University Formally Opened
with Exercises Yesterday Afternoon.

The exercises attendant upon the opening of the University were held at three o'clock yesterday afternoon in Marquand Chapel. President Wilson was unavoidably absent on account of a congestion of the throat which made it impossible for him to speak. In his absence Dean Fine presided. Dr. Henry van Dyke read a passage from the Scripture and then offered the prayer. After some announcements by Dean Fine and the singing of a hymn, the exercises were concluded with the benediction by Dr. van Dyke.

Printed in the *Daily Princetonian*, Sept. 24, 1903.

To Harry Augustus Garfield

Princeton, New Jersey.

My dear Mr. Garfield: 25 September, 1903.

I do not wonder that you are surprised at the contents of the clipping which you sent me from the Cleveland Leader,[1] and, of course, it has put you in an embarrassing position, which I sincerely regret.

The statement that I was to announce your election to a chair in Princeton was an invention of the reporter, because, of course, I am not at liberty to announce it until the Trustees have acted; but I find that the rumor is everywhere that you are coming,— which just proves that when a man as well-known as yourself is concerned, matters of this sort are almost impossible of concealment.

I do not myself know just how to treat the matter. I am, of course, glad to acknowledge to every one who asks me that it is true that you are coming, and every one who hears it expresses the greatest gratification; but as far as I am concerned, the proprieties of the situation demand, I dare say, that I should observe a becoming reticence. That does not relieve your difficulty, however, and I am distressed that it should have caused you inconvenience. Perhaps the best thing to do is simply to say that you have been asked to come to Princeton, and expect to accept when the matter is put in formal shape.

I have just reached home, and am looking forward with pleasure to the time when I may welcome you here.

Very cordially yours,   Woodrow Wilson

TLS (H. A. Garfield Papers, DLC).

[1] It is missing, but it was a clipping of a brief news item on the front page of the *Cleveland Leader*, Sept. 23, 1903, with the dateline, "Princeton, N. J., September 22," and the headline, "H. A. GARFIELD ELECTED TO CHAIR OF POLITICS AT PRINCETON UNIVERSITY," and saying that Garfield's appointment would be announced on September 23.

From George William Patterson[1]

Dear Sir: Montgomery, Ala., Sept. 25, 1903.

You may possibly have some difficulty in recalling me to your mind, as our acquaintance has been very slight. I was one of your fathers students in Clarksville,[2] and it was at his house that I first had the pleasure of meeting you.[3]

I have been informed that we may have the pleasure of a visit from you at some time during the present session. I write to express my gratification over the prospect, and to assure you of my earnest desire to make that visit pleasant to you. I consider that our city will be most fortunate in having you here, and our people cannot fail to be both pleased and profited in hearing you.

For the sake of the tender feelings that bind me to your father's memory, as well as for the deep interest I feel in your own work, it would give me great pleasure to be your host while you are in Montgomery.

If you have already promised your presence to any one, can you not at least give Mrs. Patterson and myself the pleasure of having you with us for either dinner or tea?

I understand that both the time and the circumstances of your visit are still in an uncertain state, but I would like you to know that my home is open to you. Also, if there is any way in which I can be of service in arranging for your visit, I would be glad if you would command me.

A member of your Faculty, Professor [Edward G.] Elliott, was a member of the church I served in Tennesee,[4] and he and all the members of his family are my valued friends. I should be glad to be remembered to him.

Mr. F. P. Glass,[5] of our city, whom you know, is one of the Elders in my present charge, and it was he who informed me of the possibility of your visiting Montgomery.

I congratulate you on the bright prospects of increasing prosperity in the work of the noble institution of which you are the head.

While not an Alumnus of Prinseton, I have always been deeply interested in the work done there, and hope to be able to send my boy thither as a student, when the proper time comes.[6]

Please think of me as one deeply interested in your proposed visit to Montgomery, and as willing to do every thing possible to further its success.

Very truly yours,   G. W. Patterson.

TLS (WP, DLC).

1 Pastor of the First Presbyterian Church of Montgomery, Ala.

2 That is, at Southwestern Presbyterian University, from which he received the B.A. degree in 1887 and at which he took courses in the Theological Department in 1889.

3 Probably in the summer of 1886, when Wilson and his wife made an extended visit to Wilson's parents in Clarksville, Tenn.

4 The Presbyterian Church of Murfreesboro, of which he was pastor from 1893 to 1901.

5 Franklin Potts Glass, born Centreville, Bibb County, Ala., June 7, 1858. A.B., College of New Jersey, 1877. Founded the *Bibb Blade*, a weekly newspaper, in 1880. Bought the *Selma Daily Times* in 1881 and served as its editor to 1885. Purchased a half interest in the *Montgomery Advertiser* in 1886 and was its general manager and a frequent editorial contributor until 1915. He became editor-in-chief, vice-president, and part owner of the *Birmingham News* in 1910 and remained with it until 1920. Was part owner and editorial director of the *St. Louis Star*, 1923-25. In 1927 he returned to Montgomery, bought a majority interest in the *Advertiser*, and was its president and publisher until his death. President of the American Newspaper Publishers Association, 1918-20. A friend of Wilson's from college days and later his strong political supporter, Glass sent two of his sons, Franklin Purnell Glass and John Purnell Glass, to Princeton. Died Jan. 10, 1934.

6 In fact, Patterson's son did not attend Princeton.

A News Item

[Sept. 28, 1903]

ANNUAL RECEPTION

To the Freshmen, Given by Philadelphian Society Saturday Night.

The annual reception of the Philadelphian Society to the Freshman class, was held in Murray-Dodge Hall from 7.30 to 10 o'clock Saturday evening. Benjamin O. Satterthwaite [Satterwhite] 1904, President of the Society, welcomed the entering men in behalf of the Philadelphian Society and of Princeton.

President Wilson was unable to be present because of illness, but in a letter he expressed his sympathy with the interests of the University and greeted the men just entering Princeton. Professor John Finley, who is now President of the College of the City of New York, welcomed the men in behalf of the faculty. He urged all to build up character, to work hard and to do their best cheerfully in all things. . . .

Printed in the *Daily Princetonian*, Sept. 28, 1903.

From Ellen Axson Wilson[1]

My own darling,   Baltimore   Sept 29 1903

I reached here safely at 5.13 yesterday and found Madge[2] & Margaret at the station, Madge having decided to exchange her ticket and go home with me. I have a very comfortable little boarding-place just across the street from Fensal Hall. Margaret is looking *very* well and happy and seems to be already quite in love with the life.

We are having a happy time together. I am writing from her room now having neglected to bring any ink or paper myself.

She spent yesterday evening with me; I saw her this morning at chapel at ten; and after that of course she was busy until afternoon. Madge & I spent the rest of the morning calling upon Mrs. Bird and Florence.[3] Madge had reported Mrs. Reid[4] as still away but while Florence & I were talking she went down there & found she had returned last night.

The girls, I regret to say, give me a "tea" this afternoon at 4.30, robbing me of the afternoon which I had meant to spend with Margaret—seeing about her gown & hat. But I must try and be grateful for their good intentions. Tonight I dine with them in hall & tomorrow night with Florence & Miss Bedinger.[5] Margaret Hoyt[6] is expected tomorrow.

I am very well—the weather is glorious, & it is delightful to see my dear little girl again; but I sure am homesick for you, my darling! I am perfectly spoiled by this summer when we were always together.

But it is time for me to stop & go back and dress for the tea. I don't have any too much time all alone with Margaret, so I havn't felt it right to write a *long* letter,—after all I am to see you very soon again. Dear love to all.

Your devoted little wife   Eileen.

ALS (WC, NjP).
  [1] She had gone to Baltimore to visit her daughter, Margaret, who had just matriculated at the Woman's College of Baltimore (now Goucher College).
  [2] Her sister, Margaret Randolph Axson.
  [3] Sarah Baxter (Mrs. William Edgeworth) Bird and Mrs. Wilson's first cousin, Florence Stevens Hoyt, who was teaching English at the Bryn Mawr School in Baltimore.
  [4] Edith Gittings (Mrs. Harry Fielding) Reid.
  [5] Maria Voorhees Bedinger, who taught mathematics at the Bryn Mawr School.
  [6] Margaret Bliss Hoyt, sister of Florence Stevens Hoyt.

To Ellen Axson Wilson

My own darling,   Princeton, 30 Sept., 1903

Your dear letter of yesterday has made me very happy this morning. You do not give your address, but I will send this in Margaret's care(!)

I find that I cannot come down to-morrow. An engagement has turned up here which it would be wrong for me to neglect,—an engagement made last Spring.[1] But I will come on Friday, arriving at 12:25. Alas, this means another day without you, and my heart aches with the novel loneliness; but I see no right way to avoid it. No doubt, too, you are finding enough to keep you busy another day. I know it will add to dear Margaret's happiness, at least.

Your letter is very sweet, my pet. I am so glad that Margaret is getting so soon the zest of the thing and that the first trial of it all is wearing off. She is a plucky, splendid little woman.

Sister[2] took Jessie in to Dr. Arnold[3] again yesterday and reports him very well pleased indeed with her progress. He says it is evident and most satisfactory. I went in to Finley's inauguration;[4] but stayed only to the morning's exercises. The day was chilly and I was afraid to stand out-of-doors at the laying of the corner-stone in the afternoon. We sat from eleven till a quarter past two and heard thirteen speeches! I was utterly worn out and bored, but took no harm. Finley's own address was excellent and spoken better than I ever heard him speak.

My cold goes away very reluctantly, but it goes, and by the end of the week ought to be gone. I am taking good care of myself.

Ah, how I love you and long for you! You are more indispensable to me than ever, and more dear.

Deepest love to Margaret and to Madge.

Your own   Woodrow

ALS (WC, NjP).
[1] He had promised to address the Philadelphian Society. See the news report printed at Oct. 2, 1903.
[2] Annie Wilson (Mrs. George, Jr.) Howe.
[3] John P. Arnold, M.D., 127 South 18th St., Philadelphia.
[4] As President of the College of the City of New York.

An Announcement

[Sept. 30, 1903]

ST. PAUL'S SOCIETY RECEPTION.

The annual reception of the St. Paul's Society to the Episcopalians, in the Freshman class, will be held this evening, at the Society's room on Mercer street, at eight o'clock. All Episcopalians in the entering class should be present. President Woodrow Wilson, Dr. A. B. Baker, Rector of Trinity Church, and Mr. Officer,[1] Curate, will address the meeting.

Printed in the *Daily Princetonian*, Sept. 30, 1903.
[1] The Rev. Harvey Officer.

Notes for a Religious Talk

St. Paul's Society—30 Sept., 1903
Philad. Soc'y, Nov. '06

"We are unprofitable servants: we have done that which was our duty to do." Luke XVII., 10.

The Bible so often reverses our own moral judgments

The very idea of a Society like this, to do more than our individual duty

But the tendency of our ordinary associations (relations) to do no more than our bounden duty

Trades Unions

The undergraduate code

The code of the *employee* in general

Philanthropy and *work* drifting apart.

Our standard as university men

To obtain light *and* diffuse it?

Citizens of a *spiritual* world.[1]

WWhw MS. (WP, DLC).
[1] No newspaper report of this address has been found.

A News Report of a Religious Talk

[Oct. 2, 1903]

PRESIDENT WILSON ADDRESSES
PHILADELPHIAN SOCIETY.

President Woodrow Wilson addressed the first regular weekly meeting of the Philadelphian Society in Murray Hall last evening. He read a part of the seventh chapter of Romans and took as his text the closing clause: "We should serve in newness of spirit and not in the oldness of the letter." He said in part:

No man realizes what college is until it is over and then he who goes about with his face over his shoulder instead of looking forward to the future, shows weakness and will ultimately fail. Those who go to college because they are bidden and study for the same reason, "serve in the oldness of the letter." There are two sides to every life, the spiritual and the intellectual, which are inseparable. The law of the spirit is the law of the mind, and the soul and the mind dwell together in the spirit.

President Wilson took as an illustration of his text the two types of employees, the one working every moment of his time whether he is watched or not, the other keeping busy only when under the eye of his superior. The former serves in the newness of the spirit, the latter, in the oldness of the letter.

The spirit of scholarship is in the spirit of faith. The history of civilization has shown how darkness has reached [receded] with the advance of knowledge.

Printed in the *Daily Princetonian*, Oct. 2, 1903.

St. Paul's Society, — 30 Sept., 1903
Philad. Soc'y, Nov. '06

"We are unprofitable servants: we have done that which was our duty to do." Luke XVII., 10.

The Bible so often reverses our own moral judgments

The very idea of a Society like this, to do more than our individual duty

But the tendency of our ordinary as- sociations (relations) to do no more than our bounden duty

Trades Unions
The undergraduate code
The code of the employer in general

Philanthropy and work drifting apart.

A page of Wilson's notes for his address at the annual reception for Epis- copalians in the Freshman class.

From Franklin Potts Glass

My Dear Wilson: Montgomery, Ala.   2 Oct. '03

It is understood that you are to come South before very long, that you are to include Montgomery in your itinerary, and that you are to be my guest while here. Now for details.

I have seen President Abercrombie of the State University at Tuskaloosa,[1] and he promised me to write you there. President

Thach of the State Polytechnic Institute at Auburn[2] tells me he has invited you to visit that institution & Rev. Mr. Anderson of this place tells me you have agreed to visit the Marion Military Institute.

Now I do not know whether you are going to be able to spare the time to Alabama for all these visits. I hope you can, for each one of them would be advantageous to Princeton, and I take it that, entre nous, your trip this way will be largely to give P. some artistic and much needed advertising. However, I would like to know your plans and your wishes, so that I may fall in with them and do whatever may appear desirable to make your stay in Alabama as pleasant and profitable as possible. Can you now fix approximate dates for your visit? Have you any suggestions to make as to what you would prefer in any detail? Please advise me fully, and be perfectly free to command me in any respect. You have had considerable experience in handling yourself on these trips, and you must have some clear ideas as to what should and should not be done. In connection with your visit to Montgomery I want to secure as full an attendance of all the alumni in Alabama as possible. There is not a large number of them, but most of them will average very well with Princetonians elsewhere in the country.

So write me as soon as you can spare the time all the information you can at present give me.

Frank[3] is back in his Sophomore work now. He did not work as hard last year as he ought, and he has some conditions. I have been trying to get a coal of fire on his back all Summer, but I am not sure I have succeeded. He does very well in Math., but not so well in Latin, Greek and German. This Summer I had him at work as a reporter, to keep him busy, and to teach him journalism, and he took deep interest in it. He is sober, moral and promising. But he does not appreciate scholarship sufficiently to stir his will and keep him steadily at work. I fear he cares more for the Club he makes, the style he lives in, the tone of his associates, and for athletics, than for the mental equipment he needs for life. I am afraid I have preached myself out with him. I wish you would send for him, talk over his standing and work, and try to win him with your magnetism into harder application. He tells me he has never availed himself of your kind invitations to visit you at any time: he seems to think some of his fellows would accuse him of "bootlicking"—that old bugbear that existed in our day, too. But if you can find a way to ask him around, when you can have the opportunity to talk to him, I believe it would do him much good.

My regards to Mrs. Wilson.

Sincerely Yours   Frank P. Glass

ALS (WP, DLC).
    [1] John William Abercrombie, President of the University of Alabama.
    [2] Charles Coleman Thach.
    [3] Franklin Purnell Glass, at this time a member of the sophomore class at Princeton, who was eventually graduated with the Class of 1907.

An Announcement About Plans for 1903-1904

[Oct. 3, 1903]

President Wilson has returned to Princeton in excellent health, having spent the summer in Europe. With Mrs. Wilson he visited Scotland, England, France and Switzerland, being away from July 1st to September 22nd. During this year he does not intend to leave Princeton any more than is necessary in the line of his official duty. He expects to remain here and give his attention more particularly to the pressing tasks of his office. Among other things, he has in mind the work of readjustment of the courses of study. . . . The President's only important outside engagement to be announced at present is for the Founder's Day celebration at the Carnegie Institute at Pittsburgh, on November 5th, at which he is to be the orator.[1]

Printed in the *Princeton Alumni Weekly*, IV (Oct. 3, 1903), 6-7.
    [1] A news report of this affair is printed at Nov. 6, 1903, the text of Wilson's address at Nov. 5, 1903.

James Mark Baldwin to the Board of Trustees of Princeton University

Gentlemen,   Princeton, Oct. 4, '03.

I beg to tender my resignation of the Stuart Chair of Psychology in the University—the resignation to take effect as may be the will of the Board in view of the arrangement made with the President for the current term as follows—

I have agreed to conduct my courses as heretofore, for the first half-year, except the course in Required Junior Psychology, which I am not to give. I have suggested to the President that I am willing to do this for the half-year, provided I be allowed a half-year's salary less the amount paid for the substitute in the Junior

Psychology. I am not to receive full salary elsewhere (at the Johns Hopkins University) until the second half-year.

I wish to express my sense of gratitude to the President and Board of Trustees, and to the former President, the Rev. Dr. Patton, under whose recommendation I came to Princeton, for the great consideration and kindness which they have never failed to show me; and for the generous response so often made to my requests, both personal and collegiate. And I can not, in this slight expression, pass over the fact that the degree of success that has attended my efforts, in the class room and in the larger circle outside, has been in great measure due to the intelligent interest and sympathy, joined to the active aid, given me by Ex-President Patton. As President, his relation to the Department was ideal, both for wisdom and for encouragement, and I count it to exemplify the remarkable fitness for his high position which made his administration an unequalled one in the history of Princeton.

With regret that I find it necessary to accept a call elsewhere, for the sake of facilities and conditions which can not be realized here, and with pleasant memories of my ten years of service, believe me, Gentlemen,

Yours most respectfully,   J. Mark Baldwin

TLS (Trustees' Papers, UA, NjP).

From the Minutes of the Princeton University Faculty

5 p.m.   October 7, 1903.

The Faculty met, the President presiding. The minutes of the meeting of September 23 were read and approved.

The President announced the following changes in Committees: To the Committee on Attendance in place of Messrs. A. H. Wilson and Priest were appointed Messrs. Gillespie and C. A. Robinson: to the S. S.[1] Committee on Examinations and Standing in place of Professor Rockwood, Professor Lovett was appointed Chairman and Professor Harris was added.

The following statement concerning the pecuniary aid given to students was presented by the President, approved and ordered inserted in the Catalogue:

In order that deserving students of insufficient means may be enabled to secure a college education, it is customary for the Faculty to remit the sum of one hundred dollars per annum from the charge for tuition and public room fee of students in the

Academic Department who present satisfactory testimonials as to scholarship and character and proof that the assistance is absolutely needed.

Remission is granted in all cases for one year, and will be continued if the following conditions have been complied with:

1. If the recipient has maintained a stand in one of the first three groups of his class.

2. If he has been regular in attendance at his college exercises and free from censure or discipline.

3. If he has practised strict economy. A student whose college bill for the previous year has exceeded $350.00 will be considered able to pay full tuition.

These conditions also apply to applicants who have been students in the University for one year or more.

The amount of tuition remitted is to be regarded as a loan to be repaid to the University when it can be done without serious financial embarrassment.

For application blanks and further information apply to Mr. Charles W. McAlpin, Secretary of the University. . . .

"Minutes of the University Faculty of Princeton University Beginning September, 1902 Ending June 1914," bound minute book (UA, NjP).
1 That is, the School of Science.

A News Report

[Oct. 10, 1903]

MASS MEETING.

Dean West and Prof. Cameron Speak in Behalf of Whig and Clio Hall.

The annual mass meeting in the interest of the American Whig and Cliosophic Societies was held at eight o'clock last evening in Murray Hall. President Wilson presided at the meeting and made a short address of welcome in which he said that it was with great pleasure that he accepted the invitation to preside over the meeting, for one never loses his enthusiasm when once he has become a member of either Hall. President Wilson then introduced Dean West of the Cliosophic Society. Dean West said that it took a full, busy, college course, to teach one the value of the halls, and he regretted that more men did not learn their value. He especially emphasized the great benefit obtained from debating, and he said that frankness, generosity, and cheerfulness were gained through the intellectual comradeship of debating.

He added that the two principal things gained in a college course were definiteness and decision. The curriculum work should give us definiteness, but decision and firmness are best gained through the halls.

Printed in the *Daily Princetonian*, Oct. 10, 1903.

A News Report

[Oct. 15, 1903]

INAUGURATION OF PRESIDENT PATTON.

The exercises in connection with the inauguration of the Reverend Francis Landey Patton, D.D., LL.D., as president of the Princeton Theological Seminary, were held yesterday at 11 o'clock, in the First Presbyterian Church. The academic procession, consisting of the Board of Directors of the Seminary, the Trustees and Faculty of the Seminary and of the University, the invited guests, the alumni, and the student body, started from Miller Chapel[1] at half-past ten o'clock. Among the guests of the Seminary was Governor Murphy of New Jersey. . . .

Following the services in the First Presbyterian Church, a banquet was held in Stuart Hall. The Hon. Elmer Ewing Green presided, and speeches were made by the Rev. Theodore L. Cuyler '41, President Wilson '79, President George B. Stewart of Auburn Theological Seminary, and the Rev. Charles R. Erdman '87 ['86].

Printed in the *Daily Princetonian*, Oct. 15, 1903.
[1] At Princeton Theological Seminary, as was Stuart Hall, mentioned later in this account.

From Hopson Owen Murfee

Dear Sir: Marion, Alabama   19 October 1903

We regret to learn through your letter of the 17th that it will be impossible for you to make a trip through the South in November and to address our boys, but we are glad to know that you will come in April of next year.

The special work which we are endeavoring to do here is to train the representative boys of the South for such universities as Princeton, and we earnestly desire to bring to our boys the living words of distinguished representatives of the great universities. When only a boy I had the privilege of hearing you speak at the University of Virginia. Your words on that occasion have exerted a lasting influence on my life.[1]

Since undertaking the work here, I have wished that you might address our boys; and I rejoice to know that you will bring them a message next April.

Our boys are already deeply indebted to Princeton through Dr. Lovett's visit. His words touching the efforts of our boys in self-government have been a source of great encouragement and inspiration to them. We thank you for sending him to us, and we thank you for the honor of your intended visit.

Very sincerely yours   H. O. Murfee
Assistant Superintendent

TLS (WP, DLC).
  1 When Wilson addressed the Society of Alumni of the University of Virginia on June 12, 1895. A synopsis of his address is printed at that date in Vol. 9.

From John Howell Westcott, with Enclosure

Dear Woodrow: [Princeton, N.J.]   Oct 19, 1903

You asked me a few days ago to frame a suggestion for a "classical curriculum," one of a dozen or more to be framed.¹ I find it necessary to assume some unit for courses & have taken a 2 or 4 hour basis for the lower, & a 3 hour one for the upper years.

I have decided to make my suggestion purely as my own, not modified by the views of anyone else. It is probably not as good as it might be made by such modifications, but it is rather what you might well have—an independent proposition from each one of us. I feel that my scheme is very crude, but it embodies my main ideas, viz: that there should not be many subjects pursued at once, & that there should be quantity enough of some few things to make them really "worth while."

If you don't like this at all, or if you wish to suggest modifications, I shall be glad to talk on the subject at your convenience.

Yrs faithfully   J. H. Westcott

ALS (WP, DLC).
  1 This is presumably the first response to Wilson's request to certain professors that they outline what they considered to be ideal curricula for students concentrating in their subjects. It is also the first documentary evidence that Wilson had set in motion the discussions and plans that would culminate in the adoption by the faculty of a new course of study in the spring of 1904. All extant replies to Wilson's request will be printed.

A Suggestion for a Classical Curriculum

Curriculum in Classics

Freshman (as now)

Greek	4	4
Latin	4	4
Math	4	4
English	2	2
French or German	2	2
Hygiene	1	1

Sophomore

Greek	4		4
Latin	4		4
Mod. Lang. (one or two)*	4(2)		4(2)
English	2		2
Math or Chemistry**	2	Logic or Chemistry	2**

I think Logic & Chemistry & Physics should be taken by all students whatsoever their "School." Logic & Chemistry will, therefore, appear a second time in a place where they may be taken by those who omit either in Sophomore year.

I have omitted History from Soph. year. I don't take much stock in history courses in general—but I think Greek & Roman history should be entrance requirements—& if the subjects are taught they should be taught as part of the Greek & Latin courses. The entrance examination also should be part of the examination in Classics.

Junior

Classics	6 (to 9)	Classics	6 (to 9)
Physics	3	Hist. Philos	3
Pol. Econ	3	Gen. Jurisprudence	3

Then if only 6 hrs are taken in
Classics—one of the following

Ethics	3	Psychology	3
Mod Lang	3	Mod Lang	3
English	3	English	3

* May take one 4 hrs—or two each 2 hrs, or only one, 2 hrs.
** Both if only 2 hrs are taken in Mod. Langs. I encourage large amount of Mod. Lang. in order to enable students to use German & French books in Classical Study.

I think all students whatsoever should take Hist. of Philos. & General Jurisprudence[.] Probably also Pol. Economy—of this I am not quite so sure: but under present circumstances my doubt is very slight.

I should give them another chance at Ethics & Psychology in Senior Year.

Senior

Classics   6 (to 15)   6 (to 15[)]

Make up the remainder of 15 hrs (if any) from the following: not more than 2 courses in one category.

1. Philosophy
   Ethics, Psychology, Logic—elementary courses for beginners—advanced courses for those who have previously taken general courses.
   Metaphysics
   Lucretius might be classified as Latin or as philosophy.
2. Jur. & Pol.
   All courses exc. such as require preparation not previously obtained by the student in question
   Rom. Law, classified as Latin or Jur & Pol.
3. History: any courses—but not more than one in modern history—providing antecedent preparation is had—if such is needed.
4. Archaeology incl. "Art" and Architecture
5. Indo-Iranian & Sanskrit.
6. Semitics—? This is not germane to Classics—but one intending to enter the ministry might specialize in Greek & also wish to begin Hebrew in college.
7. Modern Languages—in French & German advanced courses. May be elementary in Italian & Spanish.
8. Physical Science
   (Can't include math. wh. has been dropped at the end of Freshman or middle of Soph year)
   Physics   advanced
   Chemistry   "   (but for any who omitted it in Soph. year, a general course)
   Astronomy   gen. elementary course
   Geology   "   "   "
   Biology   "   "   "

Hw memorandum (WP, DLC).

To George Sibley Johns[1]

My dear Johns: Princeton, New Jersey.   20 October, 1903.

You may be sure that if I would do it for anybody, I would do for you what you request and send you a contribution to the special edition which the Post Dispatch has planned as its twenty-fifth anniversary number.

But in the first place you have asked me to do what I have no gift for at all. When I have tried things of this sort they have been as jejune and flat as possible; and in the second place I should get myself into deep trouble. I have declined I should say 15 or 20 requests of this sort, and if I yielded now I should be without defense for the future. I couldn't plead that I have a special friend on the staff of the Post Dispatch.

As for backing your request for a few lines from Mr. Cleveland, I know better than to try that. Mr. Cleveland has to be dealt with in a particular way, and hates above all things to have any pursuasion or influence brought to bear upon him. I feel quite sure that if he has anything to say, he will take pleasure in saying it, and if he doesn't care to write anything nothing would make him do so. This is the result of my study of a very strong man.

Will you not be kind enough to express to Mr. O'Neill,[2] who has also written to me as Editor of the Anniversary Number,[3] my sincere appreciation and regret, and believe me, in spite of my refusal,   Always faithfully yours,   Woodrow Wilson

TLS (G. S. Johns Papers, MoSHi).
    1 Princeton 1880; editor of the St. Louis *Post-Dispatch*. Johns and Wilson were close friends as undergraduates. Johns was a reporter on the *Princetonian* while Wilson was managing editor and succeeded Wilson in that post.
    2 Frank R. O'Neill, reporter on the St. Louis *Post-Dispatch*.
    3 His letter is missing.

Henry Burchard Fine to the Board of Trustees' Committee on Morals and Discipline

Gentlemen: PRINCETON UNIVERSITY, October 21, 1903.

With your permission I will not at this time discuss in any general way the irregularities of our undergraduates in respect to morals and conduct. I have not as yet had time properly to inform myself as to the situation, to say nothing of contriving methods for its improvement. I may say, however, that I begin my career as Dean with the conviction that the situation is not by any means a discouraging one, on the contrary, that we have as fine and clean a body of undergraduates as any in the land and that to keep them clean, as orderly as is necessary, and properly attentive to their college duties, we do not need new and more stringent rules and regulations, but the strict and fair enforcement of the rules we already have. I shall endeavor to enforce our rules in this spirit; but any hopes that I have of proving a useful Dean rest less on this determination than on a feeling, which I trust may not prove unfounded, that I may reach and in some measure control by personal influence those of the undergraduates who are prone to go wrong through negligence or weakness. I am well aware that in so large a body of young men there must be some who are essentially vicious. There is but one proper method of dealing with such men. They must be dismissed finally as soon as they are discovered. But most of the students reported for misconduct are not essentially bad, they are merely indolent, careless and weak. It should be possible to reach them by personal influence, for they are, for the most part, truthful, good tempered, fair minded and very responsive to friendly interest and sympathy.

I proceed to enumerate the few cases in which thus far I have been called upon to administer discipline. I shall then make a brief report on the operation of our rules of scholarship and on the results of this years matriculation.

I DISHONESTY IN THE ENTRANCE EXAMINATIONS

To put a check on cheating in our entrance examinations, the Faculty decided a year ago to exclude permanently from entrance to Princeton any student who should be found guilty of this offense. A warning to this effect was printed at the top of all the question papers set in June and September. Notwithstanding this warning, we found it necessary to reject, because of dishonesty in their examinations, eight candidates in June and three in September.

To this number must be added an undergraduate who took one of the entrance examinations this fall to remove an entrance condition. He has been finally dismissed from college for copying from the paper of one of the entering freshmen.

II DRINKING

Thus far the Proctor[1] has not reported to me any case of intoxication on the part of an undergraduate. At my request he has given me the names of several students who have fre-

[1] John William Topley.

quently been observed drinking to excess and these men I have admonished.

At the opening of the term and on Saturday nights since then we have been disturbed by a few recent graduates more or less intoxicated and very noisy, but the Proctor has as yet discovered no drunken undergraduates among them. I am not as yet prepared to offer suggestions as to the solution of the problem of graduate misdemeanors in Princeton, but it is of vital importance that we discover some means of checking this abuse.

Last year the town ordinance which requires that all drinking places be closed by eleven o'clock at night was strictly enforced except in the case of the Grill Room of the Princeton Inn. I have urged the Mayor, Mr. Robinson,[2] to enforce the ordinance in this case also. I may add that this is quite in accordance with the wishes of Mr. Lee,[3] the Proprietor of the Inn.

III HAZING

So far as I have been able to learn either from the Proctor or from other sources, there has as yet been no serious case of hazing. The "horsing" of the freshmen, that is, making them take off their hats, run through the streets, and so on, ceased, as is the student custom, after the freshmen-sophomore base-ball game, and since that time the relations of the two lower classes has seemed to be altogether amicable.

IV BASE-BALL BON FIRE

On the evening of October 7th. the base-ball victory over Yale[4] was celebrated by a bon fire about the cannon. On securing my consent to their having this bon fire, the Captain and Manager of the Base-Ball Team[5] promised to do what they could to prevent the stealing of fences and other combustible articles from the people of the town. As a consequence, only a little damage of this sort seems to have been done and the Base-Ball Manager is at present collecting money to meet all reasonable demands for its reparation.

V ATTENDANCE

Some forty or fifty of the students returned to college this fall without having done the "pensums" assigned them by the Ab-

2 Harvey L. Robinson, Mayor of Princeton Borough.
3 Edwin H. Lee, Manager.
4 Princeton won the baseball championship in 1903 by defeating Yale 7 to 6 in the third and deciding game of the spring series on June 13, 1903.
5 Clyde Garfield Stevens '04 and Wilbur Fisk Preston '04, respectively.

sence Committee for excessive absence during the last session. I instructed the Committee to allow these delinquents two weeks within which to do these tasks, with a promise of suspension if they chose to be recalcitrant. All but three responded to this stimulus and these three are at present under suspension.

Thus far in the present term the student attendance at Chapel and at recitations has been very good.

VI SCHOLARSHIP

In the Academic Department, after the mid-year's examinations last February, every student who was deficient in as much as half his work, was dropped from his class, as is required by our rules of Scholarship. The Committee on Examinations and Standing refused to consider the trivial excuses which students in this strait usually have at command. The effect on the work done by the students in the second term was most salutary; for after the June examination, though the rule was again strictly enforced, it was found necessary to drop but twelve students (as against twenty-eight dropped in February) namely, seven sophomores, four freshmen and one special.

The showing in the School of Science is much less satisfactory. In February twenty-eight men were dropped, in June twenty-seven. Of these twenty-seven, eleven were B.S. men (two sophomores and nine freshmen), eleven were C[ivil]. E[ngineering]. men (two juniors and nine freshmen), and five were specials. I may add that in February the School of Science Committee on Examinations and Standing did not enforce the rule for dropping students with the same strictness as the Academic Committee.

The Faculty has recently voted to abandon the practice of "demoting" students who have back conditions. It caused great irritation among the students effected [affected] by it, and with good reason, since it really misrepresented their college standing.

On considering the cases of some of the men dropped in February, the Academic Committee on Examinations and Standing came to feel very strongly the practical injustice of dropping a student for a whole year because of failure in the studies of a half year, and they obtained the consent of the Academic Faculty to an arrangement under which a dropped student may by industry make his degree in February after the graduation of the class from which he was dropped. In a later report I shall be able to give some account of the practical workings of this new arrangement.

VII MATRICULATION

The total number of new students enrolled this fall and present in Princeton is 435, as against 403 last year. They are distributed among the several classes as indicated in the following table, in which, for purposes of comparison, I have entered the corresponding figures for last year.

An examination of this table will show that there has been a falling off in the Academic entrance, but an increase in the School of Science entrance great enough to more than offset this loss.

Nearly one-half of the entering freshmen are Presbyterians and nearly one-quarter of them are Episcopalians. The rest are scattered among no less than nineteen denominations and a small body who avow no church connection. It is interesting to observe that this year as last, there are fourteen Catholics among the entering students.

About one-half of the freshmen are communicants of the churches with which they are connected. Among the Presbyterian students the proportion of communicants is greater than this, being sixty per cent.

It is noticeable this year as last that the percentage of communicants among the Academic is much higher than among the School of Science freshmen.

	1903	1902
Freshmen Academic	167	190
B.S.	131	100
C.E.	75	51
Total	373	341
New Specials Acad.	14	15
" " S.S.	27	31
" Seniors Acad.	5	3
" " S.S.	1	1
" Juniors Acad.	4	6
" " S.S.	1	0
" Sophomores Acad.	6	5
" " S.S.	4	1
Grand total	435	403

Respectfully submitted, H. B. Fine,
Dean of the Faculty.

TRS (Trustees' Papers, UA, NjP).

From John William Abercrombie

Dear Sir: University, Ala., Oct. 21, 1903.

I am informed by Mr. F. P. Glass, of the Montgomery Advertiser, that you will make a trip south during the month of November, and I write to express the hope that you will be able to visit the University of Alabama and, if agreeable, deliver an address before the student body. While I am not provided with an appropriation to cover an honorarium for this service, I know that a visit and an address from you would be highly appreciated by our faculty and students.

If you find it convenient to accept this invitation, please let me know when to expect you, that due notice may be given to all concerned. Your institution is represented in our faculty, and every member of the faculty would be delighted at your coming.

Hoping to receive a favorable reply, I am,
Yours very truly,   John W. Abercrombie, President.

TLS (WP, DLC).

From the Minutes of the Board of Trustees of Princeton University

[Oct. 21, 1903]

SALARY OF PROFESSOR BALDWIN

RESOLVED that $500 of the salary of Professor Baldwin be paid to Professor Hibben for taking Professor Baldwin's regular classes for the first term and that the balance of one half his salary, being $1200, be paid to Professor Baldwin. . . .

"Minutes of the Trustees of Princeton University, June 1901-Jan. 1908," bound minute book (UA, NjP).

To Harry Augustus Garfield

Princeton, New Jersey.
My dear Mr. Garfield: 22 October, 1903.

I have great pleasure in informing you that our Board of Trustees yesterday elected you Professor of Politics with a most hearty unanimity. It caused the greatest satisfaction that you had consented to accept, and you have now this additional ground for knowing how warm your welcome will be.

I hope that you are still thinking of coming to Princeton next month. It will be a great pleasure to have you here as soon as possible.

With warm regard,

Cordially yours,   Woodrow Wilson

TLS (H. A. Garfield Papers, DLC).

From David Ruddach Frazer[1]

My dear Dr. Wilson,   Newark, N. J.   10/23/03.

Should you feel called upon to reply, I certify you in advance I will be very careful how I put pen to paper in the future.

I write now to say that I have no sympathy with Dr. Craven's captious criticisms & his quasi attack, "in re, Garfield."[2]

It was hard for me to keep seat & silence in Curriculum Comm. & I should have surely relinquished the one & broken the other in Board Meeting—but—as you know—I had to attend to ecclesiastical concerns. . . .

I am sure our Board, unanimously & cordially, endorsed your sensible & only possible posture in the Garfield matter. Had not a strict constructionist, always smelling for mice, been chairman, the unpleasant episode of Garfield would not have occurred. I beg that you will not let it burden you for one second. I am glad I could not get a show at our Senior Trustee & my once-fellow-Newark Pastor[3] for I surely would not have put things in as sweet a form as they were to the Curr. Comm. & as, I discount, they were before the Board.

I have little money, less mind, but lots of muscle when my friends need it. Go on, repeat Garfield when the occasion requires, & never debate as to the muscle command of

Yours always,   D. R. Frazer.

ALS (WP, DLC).
   [1] Pastor of the First Presbyterian Church of Newark since 1883 and a member of the Curriculum Committee of the Board of Trustees.
   [2] Obviously, Dr. Craven, the senior trustee and long-time chairman of the heretofore powerful Curriculum Committee, had been very upset by Wilson's failure to obtain that body's prior approval of Garfield's appointment. Indeed, there is no evidence that Wilson had even discussed the possibility of Garfield's appointment with the Curriculum Committee at its meeting in June 1903.
   Wilson's initiative in offering the chair to Garfield represented a turning point in the history of Princeton University. It had been President Patton's practice carefully to obtain the Curriculum Committee's approval of professorial appointments. Indeed, on some occasions he nominated two or three candidates and permitted the committee to make the choice. In the future, as in the Garfield case, Wilson (after conferring with departmental heads and other concerned professors) made appointments on his own responsibility and then submitted them, pro forma, to the Curriculum Committee for its approval.

[3] Craven had been pastor of the Third Presbyterian Church of Newark from 1854 to 1887.

A News Report of the Laying of the Cornerstone of Seventy-Nine Hall

[Oct. 24, 1903]

The corner-stone of the new '79 Dormitory was laid last Friday afternoon, about twenty-five members of the class being present. The Rev. Dr. A. W. Halsey, President of the class, began the ceremonies with the Lord's Prayer, in which the class joined. William B. Isham read the list of papers placed in the corner-stone (inside a copper box) and President Wilson formally laid the stone, making a brief address on Class Sentiment. Then there were cheers for the class and for the University, and a closing prayer. In the evening they had a dinner at the Inn, having as guests Mr. Morris, the architect, and Mr. [Gutzon] Borglum, the sculptor who is modelling the grotesques and carvings.

Here is a list of the things deposited in the corner-stone: Class programme at the inauguration of President Wilson, Oct. 24-25, 1902; copy of Presidents of the College of New Jersey and Princeton University; copy of the Princetonian of June 11, 1879; copy of the Nassau Herald of June, 1879; copy of the Sexennial Record of the Class of '79; circular on the new dormitory, copies of which were sent to all members of the class, April 25, 1903; circulars on the corner-stone, copies of which were sent to all members of the class, Oct. 1, 1903; menu of a dinner given at the Princeton Inn, March 12, 1897, in honor of President Wilson,[1] with "The Works of President Wilson"; copy of President Wilson's address, Princeton for the Nation's Service; circulars on the graduation of the Class of '79; copy of the Vicentennial Souvenirs of the Class of '79; copy of the Quindecennial Record of the Class of '79. The trowel used in laying the corner-stone is a very handsome one, and bears this inscription:

WITH THIS TROWEL WOODROW WILSON LAID THE CORNER-STONE OF THE BUILDING ERECTED BY THE CLASS OF '79

The walls of the new dormitory are now nearing the top of the second story, and it is hoped to have them under roof by the first of the year. The building is to be completed next spring, in time for its formal presentation to the University at the 157th Commencement. An appropriate feature of the carvings will include several tiger heads among the bosses in the archway under the tower.

Printed in the *Princeton Alumni Weekly*, IV (Oct. 24, 1903), 64-65.
  [1] A news report of this affair is printed at March 18, 1897, Vol. 10.

From David Benton Jones

My dear Mr. President: Chicago   October 24th, 1903.

I was sorry to leave Princeton without having a few moments with you further entirely in the way of encouragement.

From the little I was able to see Princeton from the inside has certainly been regenerated. This in so brief a time is a great accomplishment. I fully realize that there is still much to do but I am convinced that the one thing needful has been done and in due time I am also convinced that all things needful will be added unto you.

As I see it there is hardly a chance that you or anybody else can do anything in the way of money for the next two or three years.[1] Anyone familiar with the industrial situation will I think confirm what I say. I hope Mr. Palmer[2] saw you. He promised to do so, and I feel sure that he will confirm the above statement. I am making this statement to you in order that it may not be an element of discouragement to you. I shall not regard it as an element to trouble about if absolutely no progress is made in the way of an endowment for the next two or three years.

The fact is that during the past ten years Princeton has stood entirely too much aloof from knowing or caring what the world outside was about. It will take time and hard work to convince it that Princeton is not only aware of its needs but is prepared to meet them even in the direction of practical efficiency which fundamentally, of course, involves sound judgement and sound character.

If taken hold of by the proper persons I feel quite confident that an emergency fund amounting to say a hundred thousand dollars a year could be secured which would hold good until the industrial situation improved and possibly longer. This could be done by getting ten Alumni who would give $5,000 a year each and twenty who would give $2,500 each. I do not believe that a plan of this kind would at all interfere with the prospect later on of getting large sums, even if there should be a prospect of the larger sums coming from some members of the subscribers to this emergency fund.[3]

It is not necessary for you to make any reply to this letter. I am sending it merely to give you my impressions of Princeton and to indicate my anxiety that some steps should be taken to make visible and evident the regeneration of the moral and intellectual side which has taken place. I shall be very glad to talk this matter over with you in December so please do not burden yourself with a reply of any kind.

Very sincerely yours   David B. Jones.

TLS (WP, DLC). P.S. omitted.

¹ The monetary expansion that had begun in December 1900 reached its peak in September 1902, when the market entered a twenty-three-month contraction. In the autumn of 1902, the ratio of cash reserves to net deposits in New York City banks was lower than at any time since 1883. Although Secretary of the Treasury Leslie M. Shaw took steps which added $57,000,000 to the money market, he could not prevent further contraction. During the past two years, Wall Street syndicates had underwritten stock promotions with loans from New York banks. As the tension increased in November and December 1902, the banks began to call in the loans, causing heavy liquidation in the stock market. In a "rich man's panic," the market broke under the sales of high-grade stocks and bonds. United States Steel stopped its dividends on common stock; railroads could not borrow on usual terms; and some production companies and financial houses went under. Lasting until August 1904, the contraction was followed by a vigorous and protracted expansion. See Milton Friedman and Anna J. Schwartz, *A Monetary History of the United States, 1867-1960* (Princeton, N. J., 1963), pp. 151-52.

² Stephen S. Palmer, prominent New York capitalist.

³ As numerous subsequent documents will reveal, Wilson adopted this suggestion with alacrity and, as it turned out, success.

From George McLean Harper and Williamson Updike Vreeland

Dear Dr. Wilson: [Princeton, N. J.] October 26, 1903

In accordance with your request, we submit the following suggestions regarding a Modern Language Group, & some further remarks on the arrangement of courses in the modern languages for students electing other groups:

We make a general recommendation that three hours a week be the time allowed for all the modern language courses. The plan we propose is made on the assumption that this will be the allotment.

THE MODERN LANGUAGE GROUP

Freshman Year

1. Students electing this group shall continue through Freshman year to study the modern language (French or German) in which they have passed for entrance.
2. They shall pursue through Freshman year the study of the

other language (French or German). This they shall do in a division for beginners.

3. In case they have passed the entrance requirements in both languages, they shall take both the *regular* Freshman courses.

4. If they have qualified for higher courses than those of Freshman year (i.e. by fulfilling the advanced requirements in one or both languages) they shall be admitted to the courses for which they shall be deemed fit.

5. In any case, they shall have 3 hrs. of French & 3 hrs. of German throughout the year.

6. Students who *begin* French or German in Freshman year shall continue pursuing courses in that language for at least two years.

Sophomore Year   Modern Language Group

Students electing this group shall, in addition to the modern language *begun* in Freshman year, take one & may take two, but not more than two, of the following languages: French, German, Italian, & Spanish. Thus in Sophomore year a student of this group would have either six or nine hours a week of modern languages.

Junior Year

Students electing this group shall take two and may take three, but not more than three, of the following courses.

French Literature French Language German Literature German Language Italian Spanish	Under any of these heads more than one course might be offered if the teaching force is sufficient. The courses in French Language & German Language might be either philological or practical (i.e. advanced work in grammar & composition for men who expect to teach).

Thus in Junior year a student of this group will have six hours & may have nine hours, but not more than nine, of modern languages.

Senior Year

Students electing this group shall take at least nine hours & may take fifteen hours, of modern foreign languages.

Suggestions regarding modern language work for students *not* electing the Modern Language Group

Freshman Year

1. The modern language in which a student passes at entrance should be continued through Freshman year.

2. Students passing at entrance in French B or German B should be admitted to the Sophomore course in the language.
3. In case candidates pass in both French & German (as they may now do for admission to the School of Science) they should continue both languages through Freshman year.

Sophomore Year

While it is in most cases desirable that the modern language offered for entrance & pursued through Freshman year should be continued through Sophomore year, we do not feel prepared to recommend more than that an elective course in French be open to students who have completed the work of Freshman year in that language, & an elective course in German be open to students who have completed the work of Freshman year in German.

Junior Year

1. A course in French literature & a course in German literature should be open as electives to students who have qualified to pursue them. Ordinarily this should mean that the French course should be open to students who had entered college with French & pursued French courses through Freshman & Sophomore years; & so for the German. Nevertheless, in exceptional cases, students who had omitted the Sophomore course might be admitted if their previous record were excellent.
2. There should be an opportunity for Juniors to begin French, German, Italian or Spanish. Students in Junior year electing beginners' Italian or Spanish could enter the classes opened in those subjects to men of the Modern Language Group in Sophomore year. Juniors electing beginners' French or German could enter the classes opened in those subjects to men of the Modern Language Group in Freshman year.

Senior Year

1. There should be at least one course in French & German open to Seniors not electing the Modern Language Group—a course based upon & in advance of the Junior Course.
2. If in his Senior year a student who has begun French or German in his Junior year wishes to continue that study, he should be allowed to elect the course for which the department concerned deems him fit, & this should count as one of his Senior electives.
3. Seniors who wish to continue the Italian or Spanish begun in Junior year should be allowed to take the second year course in that language & have it count as a Senior elective.

Apart from the suggested change to a three-hour base, our recommendations would not necessarily involve an increase of teaching time, except for the four beginners' courses, viz.: French & German in Freshman year, Italian & Spanish in Sophomore year. Students electing the Modern Language Group & other students taking one or more modern language courses would generally be found in the same divisions.

Yours respectfully,   Geo. M. Harper
W. U. Vreeland

ALS (WP, DLC).

To Morgan Poitiaux Robinson[1]

My dear Sir: Princeton, New Jersey. 30 October, 1903.

In reply to your letter of October 27,[2] I would say that my judgment is altogether against the suggestion you make that students should wait upon the tables.

Such services are often rendered by the men in the New England colleges, but it seems to me that the matter is entirely different where menial service of that kind is ordinarily rendered by negroes. There would I think be an inevitable loss of self respect associated with such work.

As to your question about myself, I can only express my astonishment that such a story ever got abroad. I was fortunate enough to be so situated that I did not have to undertake any work at all for my support until after my graduation in Law. If I had been oblige[d] to undertake it, I am sure I should not have resorted to menial work of that kind. I have the highest respect and admiration for the men who earn their own education by work outside, but I think it is every man's duty to choose the sort of work which will maintain his self-respect and social standing.

Very truly yours,   Woodrow Wilson

TLS (ViHi).
   [1] Robinson, born in 1876, had taken courses at the University of Virginia from time to time since 1894 and was graduated from that institution in 1905.
   [2] It is missing.

From Henry Cooper Pitney, Jr.

Dear Doctor Wilson: Morristown, N. J.   Nov. 4, 1903.

Since I received your telegram of June 30[1] we have done nothing toward printing your address of February 22.[2]

The Officers of the Association do not wish to publish any-thing which you did not say or do not authorize. But they are embarrassed by having nothing to publish, and they will have to make some explanation to our numerous members who are still expecting to read your address in print.

It is a pity that the faults in the stenographer's notes should entirely defeat the publication. We have due respect for your re-quest not to publish.

And we do not ask or expect you to re-write the address. But if you could supply to us some matter which you had already revised, and would authorize for publication, I think you would do justice to yourself and would gratify our members. Is it not possible to arrange this?

I had expected to see you at Princeton within the last month. But having failed to reach Princeton I am compelled to address you by this letter.

Very truly yours,   [H. C. Pitney, Jr.]

CCL (Washington Association of N. J., Morristown, N. J.).
    [1] It is printed at June 30, 1903, Vol. 14.
    [2] Actually, the address was delivered on February 23, 1903; see the steno-graphic report printed at that date in *ibid*.

An Address[1]

[[Nov. 5, 1903]]

THE STATESMANSHIP OF LETTERS

Statesmanship is the guidance of the opinion and purpose of a nation in the field of political action. The man of letters also deals with opinion and therefore with purpose; but we are in-clined to deny him kinship with the statesman because he seems to stand remote from the field of concerted action. We have estab-lished in our minds a sort of antithesis between what is literary and what is practical, and have come to assume that there is no guidance in letters for the man of affairs. But the fact is not so. If letters guide the thought and lead the imagination they are an intimate part of the stuff the statesman deals with. Men have been subtly formed and singularly dominated by what they read, and those who form their reading for them are more truly their masters than their statesmen are. It behooves us to look into this matter, question some of the antitheses we have set up, and see life as it is.

    [1] A news report of the affair at which Wilson delivered this address is printed as the following document.

The atmosphere of our time is not literary. The man of letters is made to feel by the challenges of the modern world that he must justify his existence, must prove himself not idle and bent upon a mere self-pleasing use of his faculties, but seriously and serviceably at work on what will advance the world's business. We live in an atmosphere of practical endeavor, in which men are apt to feel that the only achievements are those of practical success. In such an atmosphere letters seem a thing of idleness —the poem for music and fancy, the tale for pastime, the essay for entertaining comment, and books not packed with information are called upon to justify their existence in a busy world.

The educator feels this very keenly. He is asked on all hands why lads should be made to study mere letters in a world which needs above all else practical skill and a knowledge of affairs, and is met with raised eyebrows and a skeptical smile when he replies that they must be made to study letters just because it is necessary that they should have a "knowledge of affairs." Men do not know affairs chiefly by contact with them; they know them much more by report of them. No man comes into contact with enough of the great experiences of the world to form in his own mind a complete view of life or a complete rule of conduct. Most of his knowledge he takes from the talk of the world about him, from the tradition of his elders and the experience of his comrades, from what he hears and reads and has report of; and the true object of some letters is to do with some touch of completeness and system what rumor and the passing narrative and the chance tale of personal experience and the imperfect tradition do piecemeal and incompletely. Letters are the mirror of life.

The object of all study is collation, abstraction, the analytic and synthetic treatment of thought and fact and event. The poem which is a mere fancy does not stick in the mind and govern it; but the poem which really speaks an actual human experience with a voice of unmistakable authenticity, with a tone and penetration which once for all reveal the heart to itself, serves the man who reads it like a personal experience, and makes his mind thereafter the more delicate instrument for the interpretation of his own life.

We are apt to contrast science with letters, and to suppose that the difference between them is that science handles concrete facts whereas letters handle only figments of the mind; but the business of both science and letters in their higher range is the same. They seek not the record of single objects or emotions, but the origin of objects and emotions. Their process is one of interpretation. What the one interprets is as occult as what the other interprets; it is also as real. The books of interpretation, which are not books of science, are books which seek the broad and general view, or else search out the hidden emotion and reveal the secret springs of action in such a way that each man who reads can see himself revealed in mood or circumstance, and see the map of life spread out before him.

Literature, if you conceive it broadly enough, is the conspectus of affairs outside the narrow path of what is merely technical or of the hand, and the literature of which this is true is the literature of science no less than the literature of the imagination. Masters of science like Huxley have the touch of interpretation and illumination no less than masters of the imagination like Browning. It is as much the function of letters to show the relation of scientific thought and principle to the rest of human thinking and to the validity of human experience as to show the relation of man to nature and of men to one another in respect of the things that govern conduct and rule the emotions.

And so books have ever been the most efficient and direct instruments of education. Education, roughly speaking, is in three kinds. The object of one sort of education is to make practical, efficient men, fitted to carry forward the skilled processes of life and industry; and this sort of education every nation should look to and provide for the great masses of the men who are to attempt the material undertakings of its life. The object of another sort of education is to make literate citizens, fitted to form judgments in affairs, to vote, to choose from among their neighbors those who shall be fit to govern. This is the sort of education which we have ever sought to provide in our common schools, in order that men might be prepared in sufficient numbers to carry out the difficult and delicate work of self-government. A third sort of education is intended to make those who take it fit to lead, to give them the general, inclusive, instructed view of life which shall have for its object no one occupation but the varied life of society itself. This higher sort of education is, by economic necessity only for the few—for a few chosen, however, not by birth, but by ambition, by opportunity, by the compulsion of gifts of initiative, by the dictates of that higher sort of necessity which puts a social compulsion upon men to stand at the front and offer themselves as guides. Its object is to make men experts in the relations of things.

Certainly no men ever stood in greater need than we do of leadership and the comprehensive thinking which interprets life.

As the almost infinite complexity and unlimited scope of modern undertakings has made captains of industry necessary, and captains of labor, so also has it made it necessary that there should be captains of the mind capable of a sort of statesmanship in thinking.   [Applause.]

There need be but little wonder that the confusion and quick changeful movement of the modern stage has baffled those who would seek to decipher the complete plot of the play; but after all the very difficulty of the task of interpretation ought to hearten rather than daunt the minds which are abroad in search of adventure. We are come upon a new thirteenth century, a new age of discovery, where the voyage is not by the old seas or across unknown continents in search of fabulous cities, but out upon the great shadowy main of the mind's life, where the battle is being fought for existence in the maintenance of ideals, for the deciphering of morals, for the clearing away of doubts and alarms; where, when the battle is over, a day of high anticipations shall dawn, and men shall see again the visions of belief, feel again the certitude of hope.

This captaincy upon the great high seas of intellectual enterprise is what I mean by the statesmanship of letters, that mastery of interpretation which shall penetrate the motives and the policies of the modern mind. When all is said and done, man is a spirit, and lives not by what he does, but by what he thinks and hopes. His satisfactions when they are not merely momentary, are of the spirit, and he has not steadied himself until he has interpreted his life in a way that will bring to him some consistent plan of achievement.

Among books, as among men, there is every variety of force and weakness, of capacity and inaptitude. There is the literature of the mere fancy, the literature of mere narration, the literature of power. I would not have you think that the writer of books is less steadily in search of reality than the builder of states, or the conductor of great material enterprises, or the man who is in the midst of action. Neither would I have you mistake the real elements of power. Power, in its last analysis, is never a thing of mere physical force; the power that lasts has as its center the just conception to which men's judgments assent, to which their hearts and inclinations respond. An unjust thing is ever ephemeral; it cannot outlast any age of movement or inquiry. The action of the world, if you will but watch it in the long measure, is always based upon right thinking, and the thinker must always walk at the front and show the way.

The man of letters has conceived his function too narrowly who does not see this. He stands in the midst of a world full of debate, of questions, of keen longings, of ardent endeavor. If he is wise and wishes to see life as it is he will take his share in the multifarious business which proceeds about him; and yet he will hold himself a little apart so that his scrutiny may have wider scope than that of other men, take more elements within its range —so that he may be sufficiently detatched [detached] not to be caught in the temporary swirl of emotion or the ephemeral current, and may have the judgment of an onlooker rather than of an absorbed participant.

It is not necessary that he should debate always the greater questions or seek always the larger and more universal aspects of what passes before him. It is sufficient, oftentimes, if he but clarify for the minds of those about him some one element of experience or feeling. He may not always be able to see the distances, but he must always be able to see what does come within his vision clearly and steadily, so that he may interpret it and make it seem what it really is to those who heed his words.

And I suppose that in using this description of the man of letters I have used terms which would need to be but little changed to describe the statesman. He too must be an actor on the stage and stand in the midst of life; and yet he too must walk apart and reflect upon the permanent and universal elements that lie within the transactions he takes part in, else his judgment will not be fit for guidance; he will not see coolly enough how these elements must be combined in order to attain the next step of progress or amelioration. He must first interpret the life about him before he undertakes to handle it, and the books he reads should quicken and facilitate that interpretation. He is a partner with the man of letters in the great undertaking of understanding and so serving the men who surge about him. He must know their destiny and their interests and their abiding motives better than they do, and serve them with a certain disinterested mastery like a man who solves a problem rather than like a man who furthers an interest.

We have been told again and again that literature is the criticism of life, but we do not often enough go to the bottom of what that means. It means that the office of literature is to enable men to understand their lives better, to use their lives more nobly, to endure more heroically and strive more hopefully. Without letters men could know nothing of the universal brotherhood of mankind, could conceive nothing of humanity as a whole, could love nothing but what they themselves saw and handled and coveted. It is worth while in the midst of a material age to enumerate just what are the specific offices which the greater books perform for us.

In the first place, they collect the scattered data of experience and set them in a common scheme which may serve us as a sort of map of the mind's territory and of the heart's domain, bringing their data from far and wide, not merely from the life of to-day, but also from the past; elucidating the incidents of the long journey by which men have come into the present time, with many accidents, many adventures, many tragic mishaps, always learning, too often forgetting; and when these things are set down we find our own lives grow clearer in the light of them, are instructed what to fear and what to look forward to, have it made clear to us what the tasks are which are set for our own hands. It clears away unnecessary alarms, rebukes unreasonable hopes and makes of us sober captains of our own fortunes.

The books of power do not stop there; they organize, also, the material which they collect, set it in the relation of cause and effect, draw it together in such system as will not only elucidate what has happened but also suggest to the mind what must next be undertaken. There is a profound saying of Cardinal Newman's that the final test of a trained mind is its ability to see how propositions stand related to each other; and it is undoubtedly the function of the literature of power to show how experiences stand related to each other in originative connection, so that there is thinking latent in the very order in which its conceptions are set forth.

And so it is the privilege of great writers no less than of great leaders upon the field of affairs to guide just because of their scope and the fine convincing order in which their conceptions move. Those who pore upon their pages are drawn into the current of their own movement, and go forward to a goal determined for them. It is this power to guide which entitles the greater sort of writing to be called the literature of power. It takes hold upon the mind as the greater sort of oratory does, entering not merely the ear to please it but also the heart itself to quicken it as the source of action. Great books have changed men's lives and altered the current of history. Great statesmen have ever fed upon great thinking. Thinkers stand at their elbows, as unmistakably of their own craft, seeking the same things that they seek; and the nation whose literature has sunk to inefficiency cannot expect to see its men masterful upon the field of action. [Applause.]

And it would be an error to suppose that literature in this kind was the product of any one class of writers or even of those writers deliberately bent upon the exposition of life and motive. I have found more in the poets that lay bare the minds of nations and the great forces of history than is to be found in the systematic writers upon affairs; and the historian is often more instructive when he draws near to poetic feeling in his exposition of events than when he narrates with cool, dispassionate tone and careful system. The novelist is often the best expounder of morals and the best historian of manners, and the essayist, should he have but moving force enough, may stand alongside the orator as the persuasive debator of policies and of the fortunes of nations.

There is even a sort of statesmanship in the finer masters of physical science. They handle the matter of their thought, not like mere expounders standing in the laboratory, but like men of creative imagination, seeming to divine what they cannot prove. Slow minds are fecundated by their quick flashes of suggestion, and the elaborate crop of laboratory experiments is produced because other minds have explored the regions which lie beyond experiment. This is the statesmanship of science; this is the influence which produces progress and induces that movement of mind which makes conquests of new regions of knowledge.

You will not be surprised to learn that my most immediate and vivid interest in this theme comes from the fact that it seems to me to have a direct application to the problems of higher education, which must ever be among the chief themes of a nation's interest. In order to greatness a people must have intellectual as well as material power; and not intellectual power only, but intellectual variety as well. We confuse our minds with regard to education by insisting upon thinking of all kinds of education at once, and discussing them as if they constituted but a single theme. Undoubtedly a profound knowledge of the processes of nature is necessary to the material greatness of an industrial people; undoubtedly the education which gives them skill of hand and acquaintance with all the means by which advancements in the practical arts are to be attained, making them masters of every craft, is an indispensable necessity. Schools of technical training are not only desirable but indispensable, and the greater part of the education which a nation attempts must be of that kind, because that is the sort of education most universally needed—needed, I mean, by the largest number of persons. But we are not to stop there, and we are not to put our minds in confusion by placing that sort of education in competition or contrast with that which has for its object, not technical skill, but sheer enlargement of the mind, not training for a special occupation, but training for the more general tasks which include many callings in their single view. The nation must have spiritual success as well as material success; and some men somewhere must devote their energies to laying before as many young minds as may be induced to resort to them the library of the world's full range of thinking and experience. The minds which they touch and enlarge will not be withdrawn from the field of practical success, but will be put into it with such a view of what lies before them as will fit them to get out of it the sort of achievement which will widen the whole aspect of every piece of business which they touch.

By "laying before young minds the library of the world's thinking and experience" I mean not merely the classics of the world's literature, not merely the books of power which I have already attempted to describe, but also the books which contain record of the kind of thinking which underlies every process of the modern industrial world. Abstract science, by which I mean the science of the investigator whose object is not a commercial product, but the discovery of the laws of nature and the exploration of every process which reveals nature in operation, must go before the practical application of the laws of nature in the factory and the shop. The laboratory is the place of generation. I do not mean the laboratory which lies alongside the factory to test and improve its processes, but the laboratory which lies within the university, whose workers never think from morning to night of what may happen to be the practical results of the matters they investigate. Abstract science, seeking nature for her own sake, is the mother of all practical achievement in the industrial arts; and the lads who are to supply the nation with real greatness are those who are made ready to supply it with new conceptions, and broad and valid ways of thinking, and an enthusiasm for the paths of pure truth.

My conception, therefore, of the higher education is a conception broad enough to embrace the whole field of thought, the whole record of experience; but what I emphasize about it is that it is withdrawal from the main motives of the world's material endeavor. I maintain that it is part of the statesmanship of mind that there should ever a certain seclusion of mind precede the struggle of life, a certain period of withdrawal and abstraction, when no particular skill is sought, no definite occupation studied, no single aim or ambition dwelt upon, but only a general preliminary orientation of the mind. It is a process by which the young mind is, so to say, laid alongside of the mind of the world, as nearly as may be, and enabled to receive its strength from the nourishing mother of us all, as Anteus received his strength from contact with the round earth. [Applause.]

There is something very subtle about the strength of a nation; its affections are as important in the making of its character as its practical aptitudes, its ideals as significant as its achievements. No doubt self-interest plays a chief part in the ambitions of every people and shows itself in ways no more admirable in a nation than in an individual; but just because a nation is compounded of many minds, not all of which have the same selfish objects, the unselfish motives which lift character to a purer air play, also, a part in its career. I am sure that, as we look back on the history of our own nation, we are proud of nothing so much as of the high ideals which we conceive to have been a moving force in all that we have attempted and achieved. We have loved liberty, not only because we would ourselves be free, if we might, from the more vexatious trammels of government, but also because we wished to show other nations a fortunate way to happiness, a certain way by which to rid themselves of tyranny and injustice. It may be that politicians in Washington had their own selfish interests to serve in bringing us to blows with Spain and in sweeping the foreign dominions of the Spanish Crown under our own rule; but the consciences of the vast majority of us are void of offense in that great matter. We know that our pulses beat high in that war because we truly believed ourselves to be defending peoples who were trodden upon and degraded by corrupt and selfish governors. We kept faith with Cuba, and we mean, with God's help, to keep faith also with the people of the Philippine Islands, by serving them and ameliorating their condition, by showing them the way to liberty without plundering them or making them our tools for a selfish end. It is the consciousness of such purpose that gives us self-respect and lends reality to our hopeful visions of the future. [Applause.]

What we really love about our nation, in short, is its character, not its wealth. Wealth, even national wealth, viewed as a means to national greatness, it is not an end but a means. We wish to be strong in order to show ourselves great, and our greatness lies, not in our strength, but in our use of it. It is no simple matter, therefore, that we should studiously fill the land with men who have been given a broad outlook upon the field of affairs and of thought. It is a central part of our statesmanship that we should have men constantly in training amongst us to take the broad view and be masters, not only of a single task, but also of the sort of thinking which will include past and present, and dwell as much upon the general interest as upon individual advantage.

You will ask, no doubt, whether I think that the universities of the country are really supplying us with men of this kind. I reply without hesitation that they are supplying us with some men of this kind, but that it is to be doubted whether they are supplying us with as many as came out of the smaller, simpler colleges of sixty years ago.

The reason seems to be two-fold. In the first place the greater universities with their crowding hosts of young men do not afford the individual student that direct, personal contact with the most stimulating of his instructors which used to be the chief means of transmitting intellectual impulse and the suggestions of character. In the second place the modern university undertakes a multitude of studies rather than a system of instruction; it scatters its effort and is obliged for the most part to devote itself to the communication of information rather than to the exposition of small and comparatively simple bodies of thought such as used to be the theme of the class-room.

It is not possible in the short range of four years to give a man the complete outfit of knowledge which he will need for the undertakings of the world, but it is possible to stimulate him to the best uses of his mind and to impart to him methods of thought, impulses of investigation, habits of candid inquiry, and a knowledge of the sources of information which will make him a real master of the information which subsequent observation, reading and experience will bring him. It is in the light of thought[s] such as these that the methods of our university instruction must, it seems to me, be reconsidered. This is plainly a question of the leadership of mind.

I have defined statesmanship as the guidance of the opinion and purpose of a nation in the channels of political action, and the statesmanship of letters is the determination of that general air of opinion and that general inclination of impulse which are the medium in which the political leader must work his effects. The statesmanship of education must similarly be the determination of inclinations and the development of powers fit for the best uses of society. It must make men who are in the best sense of the term cultivated, who have eyes open to see the real character of men and events and hearts trained to a catholic sympathy.

I have not claimed statesmanship in the field of mind for the greater men of letters in order to ask your indulgence for them, in order to beg a more widespread appreciation of the services they render us, but merely to point out to you forces which will take care of themselves. Letters which are nursed into existence will not be of the proper hardy growth. Men of letters must fight for themselves as the merchant fights for himself and the manufacturer and the political leader, and only dominant intelligence, timely intelligence, intelligence which familiarizes itself with the conditions of the struggle and accepts them, can avail to make letters great in any community. The moral of what I urge is that the mastery among any people must, whether we wish it so or not, be with those who think and with those who command our emotions. A single gust of misled passion might sweep away the accumulated wealth of a generation; but it cannot change the essential nature of man. Wealth is preserved and wisely used when there is sobriety of purpose and coolness of temper and a grave way of action; but these great traits are produced by immaterial forces which differ in their characteristics from those which are the creators of wealth.

You have only to examine any financial crisis to see that the moral elements predominate in it and determine its character. A financial crisis does not arise because of a sudden there is less money or less property or less capacity in the community, but because trust has received a sudden chill; and confidence is chilled, not always because men have been too hopeful, because they have expected impossible things and have acted rashly in the heat of a speculative fever, but more often because the hopefulness of the time has been taken advantage of by men who deliberately trade in what they know to be of no value, because, amidst a multitude of legitimate undertakings, illegitimate, fraudulent proposals are plausibly commended to those who are for the moment excited by seeing everything turn to gold under their touch. This is but another way of saying that knowledge and honesty are the ballast of all business and that character is the only safeguard against disaster.   [Applause.]

A nation's books and essays and tales and poems and editorials play no small part in the creation of the conditions with which the business man must deal. They exalt or discredit, they enforce or weaken honesty of mind and uprightness of purpose; they are of the subtle breath that pervades the whole tone of thought and conversation and may breed men or charlatans. You may not take your writers seriously, you may regard them as merely companions of your leisure moments, and fancy that you turn to them only for relaxation or entertainment; but they are working upon your fortunes unawares, and are, in spite of you, like intimates who have the confidence of your private ear. Though you may not be aware of it, you put more confidence in what they have written than you put in the counsel of a friend. The very quietness of the page impresses you; there is no distracting tone of the voice or trick of manner or intonation to lead your attention away from what is said to what influences the person who is saying it.

Take your historians, for example. Did you never reflect how invariably they have the last word upon your affairs? The statesman plays his public part amidst his opponents in the field of party strife, works his partial will, and disappears; and then judgment is passed upon him and your opinion of him is made up for you, not by another man of action in the midst of such affairs as he dealt with, but by a quiet student sitting apart in a room where business has never been transacted. He forms your notions of your country's past and gives those notions reality to your present men of action. Their policy looks back to the events as he has recited them, and you have in his conclusions a statesmanship which dominates all policies to come.

Think, too, of the epic and moving force that has been in all that was written to urge forward the settlement and use of this great continent which we have occupied: the building up of communities and states upon it, the shaping of the laws which rule our lives, the statement of the liberties which we cherish. The rough frontier which has been always at our front has got its glamour, not from the men who made it, but from the men who described it and idealized it, and gave us some conception of its significance in the written narration, the spoken oration, the swinging tone of some natural song.

Look, moreover, at the part letters have played in the field of political statesmanship itself. What would the constructive work of men like Hamilton and Madison have been had they not given it ideal and imperishable expression in the papers of the "Federalist?" What would we really know of the character of Washington if we could not read his grave letters and the elevated sentences of his public papers, full of a deep, abstract philosophy of politics and history? How could the spirit of nationality amongst us have received its conscious life had not Webster, more literary man than man of action, spoken his immortal reply to Hayne? How could the issues of the war have been settled had they not first been defined by Mr. Calhoun's pen, which traced theories like lines of light, fixed them in characters which no man could mistake or stumble at? You turn to your books to find out both what we are and what we have been, and there is, when a generation is gone, no other source of light.

This is what I call the statesmanship of letters, this clarification of meanings, this permanent record and sure transmission of past impulses and intentions, this informing of the mind and the affections, this government of the spirits of men from the written page. It is men's spirits that the statesman governs; he reigns in their affections because they admire him, because they trust him, because they have some belief that he is wise and far-sighted and adequately informed, and his ally in what he undertakes is always the written and printed word. This is the significance of the old, familiar saying that the man who is permitted to write a nation's songs can afford to let who may please make its laws: what they love and utter with the freedom of the song will determine whom they will follow, more than any statute or any precept of the law-giver.

America will be great among the nations only in proportion as she finds an adequate voice in letters for the best impulses and purposes that are in her. She will not be known until she is understood; and her wealth will not interpret her, or her physical power, or the breadth of her uncounted acres, or anything that she has builded; but only such revealing speech as will hold the ear and command the heed of other nations and of her own people. Our thinkers must assist her to know herself. Her actions, even, will not speak unequivocally for her. They, too, must get their interpretation from her living voice. Her writers must inform her statesmen, and then, if her statesmen be not themselves men of letters, must in turn interpret her statesmen to herself and to the world. There is no need that letters should be defended in America or exalted; they have ever had their due meed of praise amongst us, and will always be sure of the power to which the gifts of her writers entitle them; but it is of some moment that we should once and again state to ourselves in this definite fashion exactly what part it is that our literature and our literary education, our books and our aptitudes in the sort of catholic culture which produces the best books, play in our life. I have likened this part of statesmanship itself, and it is this that I mean and which I have sought to exalt as the statesmanship of letters. [Great applause.][2]

Printed in *The Eighth Celebration of Founder's Day at the Carnegie Institute Pittsburgh Thursday, November 5, 1903* (Pittsburgh, n.d.), pp. 7-21.
  [2] There is a WWTC, with WWhw additions and emendations, together with a brief outline of this address, in WP, DLC.

A News Report of an Address in Pittsburgh

[Nov. 6, 1903]

Announcement of the death of Mrs. Mary E. Schenley[1] was made yesterday afternoon to an audience which crowded Carnegie Music Hall, by President William N. Frew of the Board of Trustees of the Carnegie Institute. The death and its announcement cast a profound gloom over the audience, and when Mr. Frew told the audience a gasp of surprise and pity swept audibly through the hall. . . .

The announcement was made at the close of the annual Founder's Day celebration. For the eighth time the trustees of the Institute prepared to celebrate Founder's Day, which has been held each year since the Carnegie Institute opened, to commemorate the inception of one of the greatest gifts the city of Pittsburg ever received. . . .

The stage of the music hall was banked with shimmering green rows of palms. Back against the wall and great organ huge palms towered high, while similar palms terraced down until they stood about three feet high, possibly 15 feet from the rear wall. Immediately in front of the palms were rows of chairs for the trustees, and in front of them was a row of six chairs for the speakers. A great bunch of vari-colored chrysanthemums stood well forward on the stage in a large vase. A small reading desk was placed near the front of the stage, and here the speakers stood. . . .

President Woodrow [Wilson] of Princeton University delivered the principal address of the day. . . . He talked on "The Statesmanship of Letters." Dr. Wilson graduated from Princeton University in 1878 [1879] and in less than 25 years has risen to the presidency of that great institution of learning. He is a man of great brain power, but the most striking thing about him and his address yesterday was the simplicity of everything.

Dr. Wilson wore the conventional frock coat, but he wore it with an air in great contrast to the man of society. His diction was beautiful in its simplicity. Throughout his address there was not a word of more than three syllables. His delivery was the simplest, and he spoke clearly and distinctly, in a rather loud tone, and with perfect enunciation. This trinity of simplicities in a man so noted and of such high standing was generally commented upon in the audience. . . .

When President Wilson arose to speak he was accorded an ovation that showed he was no stranger to many in the audience. His voice was so clear that he was heard in all parts of the large auditorium, and the interest in what he had to say was evident from the first in the complete attention given him. Throughout his address applause was given as he made each telling point, and at its close he was forced to rise again.

Printed in the *Pittsburg Dispatch*, Nov. 6, 1903; editorial headings omitted.

[1] Mary E. Carson (Mrs. Edward W. H.) Schenley died in London on November 5, 1903. She had married a British army officer at the age of sixteen and spent most of the rest of her life in England. However, she made numerous benefactions to her native city of Pittsburgh, including the 500-acre tract which is now Schenley Park.

An Announcement

[Nov. 7, 1903]

UNIVERSITY NOTICES. . . .

SERVICES PREPARATORY TO COMMUNION.

A service, preparatory to the communion service in Marquand Chapel to-morrow, will be held in Dodge Hall at 4.15 p.m. It is expected that Pres. Wilson will conduct the meeting.

Printed in the *Daily Princetonian*, Nov. 7, 1903.

To John Grier Hibben and Jenny Davidson Hibben

Princeton, Saturday afternoon,

My dear Jack and Mrs. Hibben,   8 Nov., 1903.

What I really wanted to say to you to-day stuck in my throat through shyness.

I have been permitted these last years of our delightful friendship to see upon so many sides your ideal relationship to one another (as ideal as may be in this world) that I may, I hope, without presumption, claim a special right to congratulate you both upon the anniversary[1] of a marriage which has brought you so much happiness and your friends so deep and continual a satisfaction. "The Hibbens" are always thought of together. They are delightful apart and each is as individual as the other; but they are complete and perfect together! May all the rest of their lives be wrought of the same incomparable happiness!

Always faithfully & affectionately   Woodrow Wilson

ALS (photostat in WC, NjP).
1 Their sixteenth.

To Henry Cooper Pitney, Jr.

Princeton, New Jersey.

My dear Mr. Pitney: 9 November, 1903.

In reply to your letter of November 4, I would say that with the best intentions in the world, I really do not see how I am to comply with the request for something which you can publish in place of the address which I delivered last Feb[r]uary before the Washington Association. It is out of the question for me to write another address: I cannot make anything intelligible out of the stenographer's notes, and I have nothing of the same kind with which I could furnish you. I very earnestly beg that you will explain by circular to the members of the Association that owing to an unfortunate inability to get an accurate report of an extemporaneous address, you are unable to lay before them in print my address of last Feb[r]uary. This seems to be the only possible solution of the difficulty.

You will remember that before I delivered the address last Feb[r]uary, I informed you that it would not be from manuscript, and that while I was perfectly willing that you should publish what I said, it would be necessary to that end that you provide a stenographer capable of reporting the address verbatim. I know that you engaged the best stenographer at your command, but the fact is that he signally failed in reporting the address, for what reason I do not know, possibly because of some too great rapidity of utterance on my part. Unfortunate as the fact is, it is a fact, and I see no way of remedying it. As much as I regret the inconvenience to which you have been put, I do not see that I can be held responsible for the result.

Very truly yours,   Woodrow Wilson

TLS (Washington Association of N. J., Morristown, N. J.).

Henry Cooper Pitney, Jr., to the Members of the Washington Association of New Jersey

Morristown, N. J.   Nov. 10, 1903.

The address delivered by Woodrow Wilson, Ll.D., at Head-Quarters on February 23, 1903 was extemporaneous. A stenographer was employed to report the address. But we unfortunately failed to get a complete and accurate report. And after the report was submittted to Doctor Wilson he repeatedly declared that he was unable to revise it for publication, and he therefore distinctly requested us not to publish the address.

Every effort has been made to revise the report for publication. But we have nothing we can publish with the authority and consent of Doctor Wilson.

With regret, we therefore refrain from publishing anything to represent Doctor Wilson's address.

H. C. Pitney, Jr.,   Secretary.

CCL (Washington Association of N. J., Morristown, N. J.).

To Abel McIver Fraser[1]

Princeton, New Jersey.

My dear Mr. Frazer: 11 November, 1903.

I fear that you must often have wondered why I did not reply to your kind letter of June 29, which I found awaiting me on my return from Europe.[2] I hope that you have divined the true reason. I have waited in the hope that I might see my way clear to accept the very attractive invitation which it conveys.

The deeper I get into my work as President of Princeton, however, the more unmistakably apparent it becomes that I cannot undertake addresses of the character which you suggest. Only an historical discourse would be suitable for the occasion for which you are planning, and I know perfectly well that it would be impossible for me to write an address of that kind.

I have come to this conclusion with the greatest regret. I have a feeling of most loyal affection for Virginia and for the place of my birth, and I know that it would have gratified my father very much to have me undertake a service of this sort. I hope that you will be kind enough to let me know the date you finally fixed upon for the celebration, in order that I may if possible at least give myself the pleasure of being present.[3]

With much appreciation,

Very sincerely yours,   Woodrow Wilson

TLS (WP, DLC).
1 Pastor of the First Presbyterian Church of Staunton, Va., 1893-1931, and President of Mary Baldwin College, 1923-29.
2 It is missing, but Dr. Fraser had asked Wilson to give an address on the occasion of the centennial of the First Presbyterian Church of Staunton.
3 As WW to A. M. Fraser, Oct. 20, 1904, discloses, Wilson was unable to attend.

To Robert Bridges

Princeton, New Jersey.

My dear Bobbie:　　　　　　　　　　　11 November, 1903.

I would have answered your letter of November 2 sooner had I not been obliged to leave home for Pittsburgh.

I am declining as many invitations as possible this winter, but I would be willing to address the Men's Association of the Brick Church[1] if their meetings did not fall on Monday evenings. It is simply impossible for me to get to the city on Monday evenings because it would involve the neglect of my classes here, and I do not feel at liberty to sacrifice them. Please explain this to Mr. Smith, and tell him how sincerely sorry I am that it should be so. I realize how interesting an opportunity I am missing.

I am hoping before very long to get into New York with leisure enough to drop in to see you.

　　　　　　Always affectionately yours,　Woodrow Wilson

TLS (WC, NjP).
1 That is, the Brick Presbyterian Church of New York.

To William Butler Duncan[1]

Princeton, New Jersey.

My dear Mr. Duncan:　　　　　　　　　11 November, 1903.

Your son was kind enough to hand me your note of October 22,[2] urging upon me the acceptance of the invitation of the St. Andrew's Society for the evening of November 30.[3]

I have taken the liberty of keeping the letter for some time, in order to make sure that I would be free to go. I am happy to find that I shall be, and have just written to the Secretary of the Society accepting the invitation. It will give me great pleasure to reply to the toast which you suggest, namely, "Tle [The] land we live in."

I greatly appreciate your cordial letter, and shall look forward to the occasion with the greatest interest.[4]

　　　　　　Very sincerely yours,　Woodrow Wilson

TLS (WC, NjP).

¹ President and Chairman of the Board of Directors of the Mobile & Ohio Railroad Company, who lived in New York.
² It is missing.
³ Interestingly, November 30, 1903, fell on a Monday.
⁴ A news report of this affair is printed at Dec. 1, 1903.

An Announcement

[Nov. 12, 1903]

RECEPTION AT PROSPECT.

President and Mrs. Wilson will hold a reception this evening from 8 to 10 o'clock, at their home, Prospect, for the purpose of meeting the class of 1907.

Printed in the *Daily Princetonian*, Nov. 12, 1903.

Henry Cooper Pitney, Jr., to Jonathan William Roberts[1]

My Dear Sir: Morristown, N. J.   Nov. 14, 1903.

The inclosed letter, of Nov. 9 from Woodrow Wilson, shows that it is hopeless to think further of publishing anything with his consent. I therefore submit also a draft of circular announcing that his address will not be published.[2] Please criticise the circular fully. . . .

Very respectfully,   [Henry C. Pitney, Jr.]

CCL (Washington Association of N. J., Morristown, N. J.).
¹ Born in 1821, he was a retired New York dry goods merchant who lived in Morris Plains, N. J.; President of the Washington Association of New Jersey and of the New Jersey Historical Society.
² That is, a copy of his letter to the members of the Washington Association of New Jersey, Nov. 10, 1903.

Jonathan William Roberts to Henry Cooper Pitney, Jr., with Enclosure

My dear Mr. Pitney   Morris Plains N. J.   Nov 14 1903

I endorse your circular in whole, but cannot but feel that it is a little too mild, and send for your consideration a suggestion in a little different form which may possibly be of aid in your final draft.[1] I think Wilsons letter to you unworthy of the President of Princeton University and would not have been written in like circumstances by any of his Predecessors in that high office. It is a silly subterfuge of the southern man of today. . . .

Very truly Yours   Jonathan W. Roberts

ALS (Washington Association of N. J., Morristown, N. J.).
  1 The Editors have not found a copy of the circular that Pitney finally distributed to the members of the Washington Association of New Jersey.

ENCLOSURE

Jonathan William Roberts to the Members of the Washington Association of New Jersey

The address delivered by Woodrow Wilson, L.L.D. February 23rd 1903, was extemporaneous, and although the stenographer failed to give a perfectly accurate report of that address, the report when submitted to Doctor Wilson for the customary revision, was we believe, in its essential features, fairly correct.

Every effort has been made to obtain from Doctor Wilson a copy of the address, or something akin that we could publish, or else his revision of our report, and although he has been repeatedly urged, he has positively declined to do anything in the matter or to extend to us any aid in our unfortunate dilemma, and further distinctly requests us not to publish the address in any way.

We are therefore compelled to make, and send to you this explanation, in place of the published address that was promised you, and which you are entitled to receive.

HwL (Washington Association of N. J., Morristown, N. J.).

To Arnold Guyot Cameron

My dear Professor Cameron,   Princeton, 18 Nov. 1903

I have, as you will readily believe, devoted a great deal of serious thought, since our conversation about your salary, to the subject of your relations to the University,—with the sincere desire, let me assure you, to do you full justice and take no step that might mortify you or put you into a false position such as might injure your prospects in your profession.[1]

AL (WP, DLC).
  1 This fragmentary letter is the first documentary evidence relating to what was to develop into a bitter personal controversy, the most acrimonious of the early years of Wilson's presidency of Princeton University.
  Arnold Guyot Cameron, Princeton 1886, had been a Professor of French at Princeton since 1897 (for a biographical sketch of him, see the Minutes of the Trustees of Princeton University printed at June 13, 1898, n. 8, Vol. 10). His father, Henry Clay Cameron, Princeton 1847, had taught Greek at Princeton for half a century prior to his retirement in 1902 and had also served the college

at various times as registrar, librarian, and clerk of the faculty. Woodrow Wilson as a sophomore in 1876 had been highly critical of the elder Cameron for his anti-southern views and his "very stupid" conduct of recitations in Greek (see Wilson's shorthand diary for Sept. 11 and 15, 1876, Vol. 1). There are no further comments on the Camerons in the Wilson Papers until Guyot Cameron's marriage in June 1899. The conduct of Cameron's parents in refusing even to speak to the new bride provoked Wilson into making, in a letter to his wife, a scathing attack on the elder Camerons. He was sympathetic to the plight of Guyot and his bride, but his comments on Guyot Cameron as a "mimic man" showed pity rather than any admiration (see EAW to WW, June 26 and July 3, 1899, and WW to EAW, July 16, 1899, all in Vol. 11).

Wilson's fragmentary letter of November 18, 1903, makes it clear that he was at this time considering removing Cameron from the faculty, which he had the power to do under authority of the resolution of the Board of Trustees printed at October 21, 1902, Vol. 14. However, Wilson did not complete his letter and obviously decided to postpone action in the matter.

A memorandum by Cameron's classmate and close friend, Wilson Farrand, and interviews conducted by Henry Wilkinson Bragdon with former Princeton faculty members and other contemporaries shed a great deal of light on the reasons for Wilson's low opinion of Cameron as a teacher and faculty member. George McLean Harper recalled that Cameron was a popular lecturer whose courses were crowded. "The difficulty was," Harper added, "that he would not work with the department in organizing his courses; his lectures concerned everything, were rambling discourses on life in general." Williamson Updike Vreeland remembered Cameron as "brilliant in some ways, hypersensitive." "He was impossible to get along with," Vreeland continued. "His classes were amusing; he told stories; he talked about all sorts of topics; but he seldom taught any French." Harper and Vreeland, both at this time and later, were strong admirers and supporters of Wilson. However, William Francis Magie, who later became a severe critic of Wilson, also had a very adverse recollection of Cameron as a teacher, characterizing him as "hardly less than insane." "He gave nonsensical lectures," Magie added, "and had a bizarre manner."

Wilson clearly shared these opinions. For example, according to Magie, he said that Cameron was a "mountebank" ("a perfectly accurate description," Magie said). Farrand reported that Wilson said that Cameron was "a charlatan and a mountebank." Moreover, citing a remark in the classroom by Cameron that women were good only for raising bread, babies, and hell, Wilson told Farrand that Cameron's lectures "went beyond the bounds of decency."

Wilson took up the Cameron case again in the spring of 1904. On March 24, 1904, he wrote to his wife, then in Italy, that he had gone to New York on the previous day to consult with John Lambert Cadwalader, an Alumni Trustee, about Cameron, and that Cadwalader had advised him to proceed with the dismissal. But Wilson was agonizing a good deal over the decision, for in the same letter he said that he remembered his earlier promise not to do "*anything*" until Mrs. Wilson had returned from Italy. However, her homecoming was delayed two weeks, and at some time during the late spring of 1904, probably in early June, Wilson, in an interview at Prospect, asked Cameron to resign, offered him an additional year of employment in which to seek a new position, and promised to keep the whole matter quiet. Characteristically, Cameron became highly excited and "in his excitement . . . said things which should not have been said, and which might make the continuance of relations impracticable" (W. Farrand to WW, June 9, 1904). Among other things, Cameron said that Wilson's action was an "iniquitous proceeding," and that he, Cameron, would publish the facts to the world. According to Farrand, Wilson said that Cameron became so insulting that he withdrew the offer of an additional year and ordered Cameron from the house.

The affair came to its climax in early June and during the commencement period from June 10 to June 15, 1904. Wilson Farrand's letter to Wilson of June 9, 1904, indicates that Farrand had interceded with Wilson on Cameron's behalf a few days earlier. While Farrand reluctantly accepted the necessity for Cameron's ultimate dismissal, he suggested that it was still possible for Wilson to renew his offer of an extra year, and he added that he and Cameron's other friends would guarantee his good behavior during this period. While professing that his objective was to avoid any further public unpleasantness, Farrand warned that Cameron had considerable support among alumni and students and that his summary dismissal would lead to a "manifestation that will surprise you, and that will do harm." (See also R. T. H. Halsey to WW, June 10, 1904.)

Farrand visited Wilson a second time, probably during the early part of commencement week. Many of the undergraduates, Farrand said, had heard the news of the dismissal and were planning to hold a torchlight parade of protest. He thought that he could persuade them to cancel the parade if Wilson would permit Cameron to stay on another year. Wilson refused to strike any bargain, saying that he had been insulted in his own house and could not let the insult pass. Refusing to give up, Farrand induced the undergraduates to cancel their parade and also persuaded Cameron to sign a letter of apology to Wilson which he, Farrand, drafted. As Wilson's letter to Farrand of June 17 indicates, Wilson accepted the apology and said that Cameron could have the additional year. By so doing, however, he earned no credit with the Camerons. Believing that the best defense was a strong counterattack against Wilson and his motives, they pursued their anti-Wilson campaign all through the summer with members of the Board of Trustees, undergraduates, alumni, members of Cameron's Class of 1886, and townspeople. (See J. W. Alexander to WW, Sept. 8, 1904.)

Whatever further agitation of the affair may have taken place during Cameron's final year of teaching at Princeton, 1904-1905, there is no reflection of it in the contemporary documentary record. No letter of resignation by Cameron is to be found in the Trustees' Papers or the Wilson Papers, and the only reference to his departure in the Minutes of the Board of Trustees is an incidental mention in the Report of the Committee on Finance on June 12, 1905, stating that Professor Vreeland's salary was to be raised, "the increase to be derived from the salary of A. Guyot Cameron, who resigns." The only public mention of his departure was the following sentence in the *Daily Princetonian*, September 28, 1905: "Arnold Guyot Cameron, Ph.D., Princeton, has resigned."

Cameron's dismissal proved genuinely tragic for himself and his family. Unlike many college professors of his era, he was not a man of independent means. He never again held a full-time teaching position. In his autobiographical report to the Class of 1886 in 1911, he stated candidly that he had been "out of a job" for six years. At that time his family included four children, the eldest being eleven years of age; and a final child was about to be born. In later years he became a writer on financial affairs and held a variety of positions, none of them for any considerable period of time, with financial publications, including the *Wall Street Journal* and the *National Financial News*. Cameron continued to reside in Princeton, but up to the time of his death on July 29, 1947, he remained bitterly unreconciled to Princeton University. It is said that he never set foot on the campus after his dismissal.

For the sources of this note, in addition to the contemporary letters cited above and printed in this and preceding volumes of this series, see Wilson Farrand, memorandum on the Cameron affair, undated but written probably in May 1942, in the W. Farrand Papers, NjP; and Henry Wilkinson Bragdon, reports of interviews with Wilson Farrand, Dec. 20, 1939; George McLean Harper, July 3, 1939; William Francis Magie, June 12, 1939; and Williamson Updike Vreeland, March 27, 1940, all in NjP. See also the autobiographical statements by Cameron in *After Twenty-Five Years: Class Record of 1886, 1886-1911* (Princeton, N. J., n.d.), pp. 18-21; and in *After Forty Years, 1886-1926* (n.p., n.d.), pp. 23-24. In addition to their biographical value, both of these very rambling communications are suggestive of the highly eccentric personality of their author.

To Harry Augustus Garfield

Princeton, New Jersey.

My dear Mr. Garfield: 19 November, 1903.

I shall not want the notes on politics and on constitutional government,[1] which I sent you, before the second term. It will suit me perfectly to have you bring them back in December, and I would rather not on the whole trust them to the mail, safe as that is.

I am sincerely glad that you felt so welcome in Princeton, and realized that friends and not strangers were awaiting you. Certainly the feeling of everybody is already that of cordial friendship both towards you and Mrs. Garfield, and we all look forward with the greatest pleasure to your coming.

Cordially and faithfully yours,   Woodrow Wilson

TLS (H. A. Garfield Papers, DLC).
¹ The Politics notes are printed at March 5, 1898, Vol. 10, those for Constitutional Government at Sept. 19, 1898, Vol. 11.

From Charles Williston McAlpin

[Princeton, N. J.]
My dear Dr. Wilson: November 19, 1903.

I find the following recommendation to the Board in the Report of the Committee on the Curriculum made June 8, 1903, and adopted by the Trustees:

"That the President of the University be authorized to organize the work of the Faculty under departments and departmental heads at his discretion, and that he be authorized to do this even when it may prove necessary to create departments which shall include instructors on both the Academic and Scientific sides of the University."

I remain,

Very sincerely yours,   [C. W. McAlpin] Secretary

CCL (McAlpin File, UA, NjP).

A Memorandum

[c. Nov. 20, 1903]
Departmental Organization   November, 1903¹

I. *Duties of Heads of Departments:*

    1. To call and preside over all meetings of the Department.

    2. To effect joint counsel upon all points which concern the Dept. as a whole, particularly with regard to the co-ordination of courses, changes in the Course of Study, and the distribution of duties among the several members of the Dept.

    3. To speak for the Dept. in all administrative dealings with the President of the University

    4. To represent the Dept. in all nominations of instructors and in all proposals made to the Faculty with regard to

the institution of new or the modification of old courses of instruction.

5. To perform such other duties in connection with the work of the Dept. as the President of the University may assign to him.

II. *Departments and Heads*:

    I.   Philosophy. Prof. Alexander Thomas Ormond

    II. History and Politics. Prof. Winthrop More Daniels

    III. Art and Archaeology.

    IV. Classics.   Prof. Andrew Fleming West

    V.   Mathematics. " Henry Burchard Fine

    VI. English   " Theodore Whitefield Hunt.

    VII. Modern Languages. Prof. Williamson Updike Vreeland

    VIII. Natural Sciences.   " William Berryman Scott

    IX. Physics. Prof. Cyrus Fogg Brackett

    X. Chemistry. " Fred Neher

    XI. Astronomy " Charles Augustus Young.[2]

WWhw memorandum (WP, DLC).

[1] This memorandum was Wilson's first setting down of a plan for the rationalization of the chaotic and anarchical arrangement of departments and subdivisions which prevailed at Princeton at this time. In 1903, the Academic Department consisted of the Department of Philosophy, which included not only Moral and Mental Philosophy (including Psychology), but also History, Jurisprudence and Politics, Political Economy and Sociology, Archaeology and the History of Art, and Architecture; the Department of Language and Literature, which included all languages and literatures, ancient and modern; and the Department of Mathematics and Natural Sciences, which included all sciences, both physical and biological. The School of Science overlapped greatly in subject matter with the Academic Department. The former was divided into Departments of Science, Civil Engineering, and Electrical Engineering. There was no formal organization by subject matter within all these large departments or their subdivisions, each professor in theory being subject only to the authority of the President of the University. In practice, a kind of informal cooperation and hierarchical organization had grown up among members of each of the subject matter fields, such as, for example, Wilson's own subdivision of Jurisprudence and Politics.

The restructuring was also a necessary preliminary to the new course of study about which Wilson was beginning to think seriously, since, as he already contemplated, upperclassmen under the new plan would concentrate their work in particular departments organized according to subject matter. A third and no less important objective was the complete integration of those departments of the School of Science not concerned with engineering into the university's academic structure and curriculum.

[2] For Wilson's announcement of the new plan of departmental organization, see his report to the Board of Trustees printed at Dec. 10, 1903.

From Harper and Brothers

Dear Sir: New York City   November 23, 1903.

Replying to your favor of the 21st inst., we beg to advise you that we have contemplated changing the form of the subscription edition of your "History of the American People," but before doing so we wish to dispose of the small stock which we have on hand of the present edition bound in blue cloth.

Our announcement to the effect that there are very few sets of this edition left was made because the new edition will be different.

We have not found the subscription set difficult to dispose of but think that it will sell better in the new binding of red leather. It is found necessary with subscription books to issue them from time to time in a different binding and at a different price in order that the interest of the public may be continued. It is our opinion that for many years we will have a satisfactory sale of your History.   Very truly yours,   Harper & Brothers.

TLS (WP, DLC).

A News Report

[Nov. 23, 1903]

HILL SCHOOL CLUB DINNER.

The Hill School Club held its annual dinner at the Inn on Saturday evening. In addition to the members of the club, there were present eighteen guests, including President Woodrow Wilson, Professor [John] Meigs and other masters of the Hill School, and the men from the school who expect to enter Princeton next fall.

L. M. Adsit 1904, president of the club, acted as toast master, and among those who spoke were President Wilson, Professor Meigs, and Mr. [Michael F.] Sweeney, of the Hill School. After these speeches, J. R. Truesdale 1904, sang several solos, and also led in the singing of several Princeton and Hill School songs.

Printed in the *Daily Princetonian*, Nov. 23, 1903.

A News Item

[*Nov. 29, 1903*]

PRINCETON MAY GET A LAKE.

PRINCETON, N. J., Nov. 29.—A report from Philadelphia this morning to the effect that Andrew Carnegie intends to make an artificial lake near Princeton and present it to the university is but a revival of a story spread abroad last Spring. At that time Mr. Carnegie sent his confidential agent, a Mr. Butler,[1] to Princeton. He looked into the matter and secured some options, but nothing further came of it. The site of the proposed lake is near the Delaware and Raritan Canal, and comprises a large area of swamp land.

Mr. Butler was in town again last week and took up some of the options he had secured last Spring, but made no statement to university authorities. President Wilson this afternoon said no direct offer of a lake had been made to him.[2]

Printed in the *New York Times*, Nov. 30, 1903; one editorial heading omitted.

1 Howard Russell Butler, Princeton 1876, artist and lawyer of New York. Butler managed the intricate negotiations for acquiring the land necessary to create what would become Lake Carnegie and supervised most of the construction work. A small collection of his papers relating to Lake Carnegie is in NjP. For Butler's own account, see "The History of the Lake," *Princeton Alumni Weekly*, v (April 29, 1905), 489-92.

2 For further details, see the news reports printed at Dec. 5, 1903; Nov. 30, 1904; and Jan. 6 and 19, 1905. See also the report of the dedication ceremonies printed at Dec. 8, 1906, Vol. 16.

A Newspaper Report of an After-Dinner Speech

[Dec. 1, 1903]

WILSON AND CARNEGIE TO ST. ANDREW'S SONS

Speaking before the members of the St. Andrew's Society of the State of New York, gathered at their one hundred and forty-seventh annual banquet at Delmonico's last evening, Andrew Carnegie and President Woodrow Wilson of Princeton University moved four hundred hearers to cheers time and time again.

It was most distinctly a Scotch banquet, from decorations to speeches, and in the spoken words as in the swirl of bagpipe and strain of Scotch airs was breathed the spirit of the country whose native heather each guest wore in his buttonhole.

President Woodrow Wilson had for a subject "The Land We Live In," and as he announced his toast, he called out a cheer by adding in the same breath, "For 'tis not that we love Scotland less, but America more."

"It is a land of confusing variety," he said when the applause had subsided. "We meet a new kind of American thing every day and our powers of generalization are taxed to the point of failure in trying to define the American type.

"It's a curious thing how in politics we may discern the same distrust as we approach a Presidential election. Politicians don't know what to think; they can't reckon what is going to happen because of the surging independence of thinking in these United States. There's a vigor, variety, and initiative in the country, although we don't find so much of it here in this immediate section, where we're all naturally highly conventional and wear the same kind of clothes, where the cut of our jibs is so much the same, and we are constitutionally uneasy because there is a place called Kansas.

"We have been taught to believe that all men in this country are created free and equal; but when we have departed a little from the creation I don't know what we will be, for it even seems that some of our friends can just go out West and come back so changed that we don't know them.

"I suppose that there is no private right of interpretation of the Constitution. But I must confess that some of us just now seem to put a private interpretation upon international law. And I fancy we feel a little worried about it, after all, and if we weren't too big to be questioned, that we might be put through our paces.

"And for the matter of that we may be yet if we keep on, like a big man who was bullying a little one, until the victim, past the point of all sufferance, yells out: 'I know you're bigger than I am, but if you don't stop I'll get a step ladder and lick you.'[1]

"My old friend Prof. Archibald Hodge of Princeton[2] didn't believe in Democracy, and he used to give voice to his feeling in this respect, particularly in the remark that we would never reach the height of Democracy until we had a negro woman as President of the United States."

Then, in a more serious turn, Dr. Wilson went on: "Yet, with all this variety, there is one impressive thing in this country, and that thing is the extraordinary force of the majority. Another force is the power of accumulated fact. Yesterday's history is not questioned tomorrow, and we are pushed on and on until the accomplished fact becomes so nearly doctrine that we say that we who question this history of yesterday are even become of doubtful patriotism.

"And because of this I feel that one of the requisite things is that we should cultivate hardness enough of fibre to stand when it is necessary and right, against the crowd. We forget that there is much more patriotism in having the audacity to differ from the majority than in running before the crowd; we forget that in the resistance of the minority some of the biggest things in our own history have been accomplished, and the man who looks on the Stars and Stripes and doesn't hold a right to say nay to his neighbor, even if the neighbor is of the larger party, has forgotten the history of his country."[3] (Applause.)

Andrew Carnegie eloquently bore tribute to "The Land o' Cakes." . . .

Other speakers were W. Butler Duncan, who presided; the Rev. Dr. George C. Lorimer,[4] Job E. Hedges,[5] and George T. Wilson[6] of the Pilgrims of America.

Printed in the *New York Times*, Dec. 1, 1903; some editorial headings omitted.
[1] An obvious reference to President Roosevelt's tacit support of the Panamanian revolt against Colombia on November 3, 1903, the precipitate recognition of the Republic of Panama by the United States on November 6, and the signing of the Hay-Bunau-Varilla Treaty on November 18.
[2] The Rev. Dr. Archibald Alexander Hodge, Princeton 1841, long-time professor at Princeton Theological Seminary.
[3] There is a brief WWhw outline of this talk, dated Nov. 30, 1903, in WP, DLC.
[4] The Rev. Dr. George Claude Lorimer, pastor of the Madison Avenue Baptist Church of New York.
[5] Job Elmer Hedges, Princeton 1884, at this time practicing law in New York.
[6] Third Vice-President of the Equitable Life Assurance Society of New York.

John David Davis to Moses Taylor Pyne

My dear Pyne,   Saint Louis.   Dec. 2, 1903

Will you kindly report to the Trustees that the Committee have decided that it is inadvisable to make an exhibit at the Worlds Fair[1] next year in view of the fact that Prest Wilson deemed it inexpedient to make an exhibit upon a basis of only $3000.00 being raised therefor.

I wrote Prof West that I would try & raise $3000.00 if the University would make an exhibit on the lines suggested by Prof. Rogers[2] the Chief of the Dept. of Education & in reply I received a telegram from Prof West on Nov. 13, 1903 reading— "The President does not deem it advisable to prepare an exhibit." I thereupon surrendered the space reserved for Princeton & it has now been allotted to the University of Virginia.

In view of the fact that Prest Wilson did not favor making an exhibit even if I could collect the sum of $3000.00 I did not consider it necessary to endeavor to have the Committee meet before abandoning the project. Thanking you very much for the trouble you have taken in the matter in my absence, & regretting my inability to be present at the meeting of the Trustees on Thursday I remain   Sincerely yours   Jno D Davis

ALS (Trustees' Papers, UA, NjP).
[1] That is, the Universal, or Louisiana Purchase, Exposition to be held in St. Louis in 1904.
[2] Howard Jason Rogers, formerly Deputy State Superintendent of Public Instruction of New York.

A News Report of an Address on Civic Patriotism

[*Dec. 3, 1903*]

PASSAIC CIVIC DINNER.

Woodrow Wilson Talks.

Passaic, N. J., Dec. 3.—An especially successful civic dinner was given at the Acquackanonk Club in this city, to-night, for President Woodrow Wilson of Princeton University. It was attended by three hundred well known men of Passaic and other cities in New-Jersey. The dinner was given by the civic committee of the Passaic Board of Trade. Mayor Charles M. Howe was the toastmaster. Others at the guest table were Dr. Wilson, Justice [Francis] Scott, of the Court of Common Pleas, United States Senator [John] Kean, Brigadier General B. W. Spencer, N.J. N.G., and Mayor [John] Hinchliffe of Paterson. Each of these made a short address after Dr. Wilson had spoken.

An autograph letter of regret from President Roosevelt[1] was read. It was as follows:

I am sorry that it will not be possible for me to accept the courteous invitation which you extend to me to attend the Passaic Civic banquet on December 3.

I should be more than pleased to be with you on that occasion, and to listen to the address of Dr. Wilson on "Civic Patriotism." We have before us many grave problems to solve and many important things to do, and if we are to be successful in the solving and the doing, the one absolutely essential quality which we must bring to every problem, and to every deed, and without which true success is impossible, is intense Americanism—to be American in heart, in soul, in spirit and in purpose.

I am sure that this gathering of your citizens cannot fail to be fruitful of good. I thank you for the invitation.

President Wilson, speaking on "Civic Patriotism," realized, he said, the great difficulty of defining the meaning of patriotism since it is a meaning instinct with the strongest feeling, and feeling is always difficult of definition, but that, after all, patriotism is not a mere sentiment; it is a principle of action, it is an energy of character, which manifests itself and seeks its object beyond the narrow circle of self-interest; it is a thoughtful energy which looks beyond self for its satisfaction. He said in part:

Patriotism has always manifested itself at its best in the larger sort of natures; among that more noble class of men who feel that their duty is not done, their power of character not satisfied, until they have found something larger than their own affairs to spend it upon. This large and noble sort of energy breeds the sentiment which we call patriotism, but that sentiment is not based in mere feeling, it is based in character.

At different periods of our national history patriotism has undoubtedly worn different aspects because seeking different objects. When the life of the nation was simple, and its main object merely the physical mastery of the continent and the building of new communities upon it, patriotism went with the swing of the ax upon the frontier and the crack of the borderer's rifle in the forest and young men were the most serviceable servants of progress and development, but, with the increasing complexity of our life, even patriotic duty grew less simple. It was harder to see it expressed in items of conduct; the things to be handled were invisible and intangible; institutions, habits of life, schemes of law, the great combinations of commerce and manufacture, and the international relationships of a great world power. Our present tasks, far from being obvious and suitable for mere rough strength, have become delicate and difficult, requiring nicety of thought, a purged temper, a just self-restraint, and we shall get the thoughtful energy which we need for their accomplishment only by understanding our day and deliberately knowing it and seeing it in the complex details of our daily lives.

It is the singularity of our polity that it rests upon a common understanding for its objects, a common intelligence, a common morality that each community carries, and carries virtually alone, its separate part in the great undertaking of self-government. Each community is either self-governed or self-demoralized, self-disordered. De Tocqueville, even in his simpler day, saw that institutions, free as ours, and yet complex and difficult, required extraordinary "variety of information and excellence of discretion" on the part of the people, that it pre-supposed information and capacity of quite unprecedented compass and flexibility. Every man among us, therefore, is put upon his honor to understand and serve the community in which he lives, and the only true patriotism is that which is local in its rootage— vital patriotism begins at home; it is not a vague interest, spread out over the whole affairs of a whole nation, but a direct and definite identification of feeling and purpose with the interests of one's home and neighbors.

It would be natural to ask whether it were possible to breed a motive which shall control the conduct; that is, whether one can deliberately cultivate patriotism? It is clear that it is quite possible to do so; motive is the child of interest, and it is perfectly possible to cultivate an interest— an interest in your own affairs, which will breed a selfish motive, or an interest in the affairs of your community, which will beget an unselfish motive, and the conditions under which this can be done are worth understanding. You cannot touch the life of a nation directly; you must touch and move it indirectly by thought and motive where you are. You can deliberately acquaint yourself with the conditions existing around you, and can embark, if you will, upon every local enterprise that promises betterment.

This community will never awake to its own betterment and best development through any abstract motive of duty, but only through a concrete image of its own life and interests, through a sort of ardent and enduring self-consciousness. You will find that there is mixed with all patriotic motives a certain pride in the past of the community, a consciousness of what it has been and is, and a desire for its distinction as a whole. The revival of historical study in our day in respect of the history of localities particularly, of neighborhoods, of countrysides, is full of hope for the creation of the better sort of local self-consciousness and ambition. There is hope also in the mere fact that our populations are beginning to become more stationary, less restless and nomadic; that we are being compelled both individually and as communities to take permanent local rootage, and live upon our affection for particular groups of friends and neighbors.

Distrust the patriotism of a man who is always spending his feeling upon some distant object, whose energy does not seek the nearest duty, but the more remote. Every citizen who is thoughtful of the welfare of his country should seek to see and understand his nearest duty and to do it with all thoughtfulness, and yet without impatience.

Patience is indeed, though one of the most difficult, yet one of the most indispensable virtues in a polity like our own, for the essence of that polity is consultation, movement not singly or in chosen groups, but in the mass and multitude, so that in whatever we think or purpose we must carry masses of men with us, and so we need the sort of patience which is full of hope and equally full of persistence. We need constant and frank talk also about affairs local and national—full, uncolored information, courage to select and use the right arguments and push the right motives. Every effort is worth while which leads even to the slightest betterment, and no discouragement of temporary failure ought to hold us back from the long fight to put the knowledge and the practice of what is right at the front at all times and in every contest.

Printed in the New York *Daily Tribune*, Dec. 4, 1903; some editorial headings omitted.
1 T. Roosevelt to C. M. Howe, Nov. 25, 1903, T. Roosevelt Papers, DLC.

Two Letters from Cyrus Hall McCormick

My dear Woodrow: [Chicago]   December 4, 1903.

Your speech in New York[1] has created quite an enthusiasm and I congratulate you on the impression which you made. As I have seen only a few brief notices of the speech may I ask whether it is to be put in permanent form, and if so if I can have some copies. If this has not been done or is not to be done where can I find the best account of the speech? There are several here who would like to see some note of it.

When I was in New York I spoke to C. C.[2] about the matter of the building fund[3] and expect to write to Barringer and Vanuxem to see Waller[4] on the subject of their subscriptions. It is really aggravating to have men like Barringer and Vanuxem retreating from the promises which it was understood clearly they had made, and thus throwing the burden on other men. I am in hopes that by the proper pressure and keeping our patience we will, between now and next June, be able to secure the payments from both of these men.

I am,   Very sincerely yours,   Cyrus H McCormick.

1 That is, Wilson's address to the St. Andrew's Society of the State of New York on November 30, 1903. See the news report printed at Dec. 1, 1903.
2 Cornelius Cuyler Cuyler '79.
3 That is, for Seventy-Nine Hall.
4 Daniel Moreau Barringer, Louis Clark Vanuxem, and James Breckinridge Waller, all members of the Class of 1879.

My dear Woodrow: [Chicago]   December 4, 1903.

Enclosed I hand you a printed statement[1] describing the very interesting step which the stockholders of the McCormick Harvesting Machine Company have taken on the occasion of the winding up of that Company when the business was passed over to the new Company.[2] I think it will interest you to see the terms upon which this plan has been worked out, after much thought and study, and I feel sure that the way in which it has been received by all classes of the employes of the McCormick Company will show the wisdom of the actions taken.

Yours sincerely,   Cyrus H. McCormick.

CCL (C. H. McCormick Papers, WHi).
   [1] It is missing.
   [2] That is, upon the formation of the International Harvester Co. by the amalgamation of the McCormick Harvesting Machine Co. and several other firms that manufactured farm machinery, about which see John A. Garraty, *Right-Hand Man: The Life of George W. Perkins* (New York, 1960), pp. 126-42.

From Winthrop More Daniels

My dear Wilson: Princeton, Dec. 4, 1903.

Next Wednesday evening, and also on the Wednesday evening following, I have charge of the Debating Class; and shall therefore, in all probability, be absent from the meeting of the Curriculum Com.[1]—unless Covington can run the debate by himself. In case I am absent, will you kindly suggest that the proposed schedules which make Economics a prescribed study be,—at least tentatively,—considered in the light of a proposed elementary course of 3 hours per week *running through both terms*. This would give it the same amount of time as the General Physics course. Two years ago I endeavored to convince Dr. Patton that such an extension of time was necessary. I submitted evidence from Yale and Harvard to show that in both places they allotted that amount of time to their respective courses in General Economics. The same is true of Cornell, and indeed of most of the larger colleges, even in the West. I enclose herewith Taussig's description of the Harvard course.[2] The letter from Yale I have unfortunately lost or mislaid. I am writing Ormond a line also, asking him in the construction of his Jr. schedule for the Philosophical Group to bear in mind this possibility of a "*3 hr.-per-week—both-terms*"—course in General Economics.

Very sincerely yours,   W. M. Daniels

ALS (WP, DLC).
   [1] He meant the Committee on the Course of Study, of which Wilson was chair-

man. This is the first evidence that the committee had begun systematically to meet and plan the new curriculum.

2 This communication from Frank William Taussig, Henry Lee Professor of Political Economy at Harvard, is missing.

From Robert Jenkins Nevin[1]

Dear Sir,   Dec. 4th 1903—N.Y.

As Executor of the Estate of my late mother, Martha J. Nevin of Lancaster Penna, I beg to present to Princeton University an original portrait of the Revd. Gilbert Tennant, which I think she would have preferred to have so disposed of.

This portrait was given to my mother many years ago by the late Yeates Cunningham of Lancaster Penna, in whose family it had come down as a valued possession. Mr. Cunningham was I believe the last of his line.[2]

Very truly yours   R. J. Nevin

ALS (Trustees' Papers, UA, NjP).
1 Rector of the Protestant Episcopal Church in Rome, Italy.
2 The portrait, attributed to Gustavus Hesselius, now hangs in Prospect, the faculty club of Princeton University.

A News Report

[Dec. 5, 1903]

PRINCETON LAKE.

The projected lake, long talked of, appears to be assuming definite shape. The purchases of the needed land have quite generally been consummated, good prices being paid in every instance. Some of the land needed has been donated by owners of adjoining property. J. J. Cross, an engineer of wide repute, has made the surveys. As mapped out, a dam near Kingston, the exact site not yet determined, but probably a little way east of the brook crossing the highway, on the Kingston road, will impound the waters of the Millstone river and of Stony Brook to the causeway bridge on Washington Road. The lake will follow the line of Stony Brook eastward until its junction with the Millstone at the Aqueduct, where the river runs in a northerly direction toward Kingston. Necessarily the lake will not be very deep, for its southerly and easterly boundary must be for a large part of its length the Delaware and Raritan Canal, which also crosses the river at the Aqueduct. The sheet of water will be near three miles long and of varying width, from a few hundred to a thousand feet in width.

Mr. Carnegie's name has been associated with the project from the beginning, it being generally understood that the expense of its construction will be entirely borne by him. It has been necessary in some cases to purchase entire farms in order to secure the meadow lands to be flooded by the lake. In such cases a syndicate of generous Princeton men has supplied the money for the purchase of the lands not actually needed for lake purposes.

It is rumored that contractors are making estimates on the work to be done, and that in the early spring operations will begin and be pushed to a speedy conclusion.

Printed in the *Princeton Press*, Dec. 5, 1903.

An Announcement

[Dec. 5, 1903]

UNIVERSITY BULLETIN. . .

7.10 p.m. [Dec. 6] 1904 class prayer meeting, in upper west room, Dodge Hall, [to be] led by President Wilson.[1]

Printed in the *Daily Princetonian*, Dec. 5, 1903.
[1] There was no report of this talk in the local newspapers, but for it Wilson used the notes printed at April 4, 1895, Vol. 9.

To Cyrus Hall McCormick

My dear Cyrus: Princeton, New Jersey. 7 December, 1903.

Thank you for your kind letter of December 4. I quite agree with you in your feeling about Barringer and Vanuxem. I must believe that they are under some misapprehension and that the matter will clear itself up.

I suppose the speech in New York to which you allude is the one which I made recently at the Saint Andrew's Society dinner. It was only a fifteen minute, after dinner speech, and I am quite surprised that it attracted so much attention. I do not think that it was reported at all. I have not seen any newspaper which contained it.

I have also received the interesting "Announcement by the Stock-holders of the McCormick Harvesting Machine Company," and have examined it with a great deal of interest. I congratulate you on the way in which the new arrangements are being put into effect.

Cordially and faithfully yours, Woodrow Wilson

TLS (WP, DLC).

To John Hampden Chamberlayne Bagby[1]

My dear Sir: Princeton, New Jersey.   8 December, 1903.

I do not wonder that you have been incredulous of the statement made to you with regard to our seniors being required to make public addresses.

When I was an undergraduate we had what we called "Senior chapel stage." The senior class was divided into speaking sections, and once a week one section of the class delivered speeches in the college chapel, always before a decent audience. But that was a mere exercise in English and elocution, and was soon afterward discontinued, I do not know why, its discontinuance having fallen when I was away. Nothing of its kind has taken its place, and now no public addresses are required of seniors except three or four public orations assigned as honors at Commencement.

Very sincerely yours,   Woodrow Wilson

TLS (ViHi).

[1] Professor of Physics and Astronomy at Hampden-Sydney College.

A Report of an After-Dinner Speech

[Dec. 10, 1903]

SOUTHERN SOCIETY DINNER

Nearly 400 exiles from Dixie Land gathered at the eighteenth annual dinner of the Southern Society, held last night at the Waldorf-Astoria, and besides the members of the society and their guests the boxes overlooking the ballroom, in which the banquet was spread, were crowded with their wives and daughters and sisters, who joined in the singing of "Dixie," and applauded the speakers. . . .

The first speaker of the evening was Prof. Woodrow Wilson. In speaking on "The Southerner in the North" he said:

"All we Southerners here to-night illustrate the true American spirit of not living where we were born. But, after all, we men of the South have given an advantage to the country through the mixture of blood in coming to the North. The real question, after all, is nationality, the getting to understanding alike and thinking alike, and the mixture of blood is the best process of promoting National life. I wish even that every young man who goes to college may go as far away from home as possible in order that there may be brought about a mixture of feeling and thought.

"The thinking in the South and in the West is done nearer to nature than the thinking that is being done in the East. We have got to get down to thinking not in lithographed securities, but in crops; not in stock quotations, but in the products of the earth. We have been matching lithographed paper for the resources of the companies issuing that paper, and that has led to some very peculiar results here in the New York financial world recently.

"What is it that the Southerner has contributed to the North? In the first place the Southern man has contributed a unique individuality. The trouble is that up here every man's jib is likely to be cut like every other man's jib. There is nothing so powerful here as the instinct to be like everybody else. One of the Southerner's characteristic[s] is his distinctive opinion. I would rather he kept that, although he bases it on prejudice. I am so tired of this indifference and poise of the people of the North. I do not believe that strong lives were ever lived by men who were without ardor of opinion. The danger of our democracy is the eternal yielding to the fear of being thought a singular person.

"One private virtue which the Southerner ought to practice is the keeping alive in his home here in the North the memories and traditions of the old white people of the South of the old days. If those days are bygone days we are responsible for it. I believe if we return to the old ideals of chivalry and honor we can verify our pedigree as in no other way."[1] (Applause.)

Printed in the *New York Times*, Dec. 10, 1903; one editorial heading omitted.
[1] There is a brief WWhw outline of this talk, dated Dec. 9, 1903, in WP, DLC.

To the Board of Trustees of Princeton University

Princeton, December 10, 1903.

GENTLEMEN OF THE BOARD OF TRUSTEES:

I am gratified, in looking back over the fourteen months which have elapsed since my last report, to find that I can lay before you a statement of the condition of the University which is on the whole very encouraging. It is my own impression and the impression of my colleagues in the Faculty that there is manifest among the students of the University a slowly increasing soberness and diligence in their studies, a growing sense of responsibility, a frank readiness to submit to all fair and reasonable discipline; and we are convinced that it is only necessary to give the courses of study a new and more coherent organization and greater vitality of method to lift the intellectual work of the University to the highest level of interest and energy for which we can hope with our present force and equipment.

The report of the Dean of the University at the October meeting of the Board[1] shows how marked an improvement has been noticed in the examinations, at least on the academic side of the University. Only half as many men came under discipline for failure at the June examinations as at the examinations in February. On the scientific side there was not the same improvement,—partly because our entrance requirements admit men insufficiently prepared, or rather insufficiently matured, for the severe test of such courses as that in civil engineering; partly because the rules of the University with regard to the standards to be maintained at examinations have not been as firmly and consistently enforced on the scientific as on the academic side. This latter ground of difference will presently disappear, and we shall then be in a much better position to judge what additional requirements for entrance or what new adaptations in methods of instruction we ought to adopt to put the scholarship of the two sides of the University upon the same footing of efficiency.

Of the material growth of the University you have all been witnesses: a great gymnasium has been added by the generosity of our alumni and friends, a fine heat and light plant has been put at our disposal by the public spirited generosity of the group of gentlemen who have established the University Power Company, and the Class of '79 is pushing towards completion a new dormitory, now partially under roof, which the contractors confidently expect to finish before the close of the present university year. Every month sees something done to put our buildings and grounds into more perfect repair or to add some touch of greater beauty or convenience to them. The cost of maintenance and improvement is for the present very great and constitutes a serious and quite disproportionate drain on our income, but it is confidently hoped that when we have once put our property into a condition of thorough repair and serviceability it will be possible to maintain it for considerably less than we are now spending.

We have been so unfortunate as to lose from our Faculty by resignation two of its most conspicuous members,—men whom we could ill afford to lose,—Professor John Huston Finley, of the Department of Politics, who left us to assume the Presidency of the College of the City of New York, and Professor James Mark Baldwin, of the Department of Philosophy, who has accepted the headship of a new department in Johns Hopkins University, which is meant to afford him special opportunities to follow his favorite lines of research. Professor Finley had taken a singu-

---

[1] It is printed at Oct. 21, 1903.

larly strong hold alike upon the minds and upon the affections of the undergraduates, and had endeared himself to all of us as not only a man of the finer sort of force and influence but also a most loyal friend and colleague. Professor Baldwin put all his students under the stimulus of an original mind, contributed a touch of enthusiasm to the advanced work in Psychology, and himself made Princeton one of the centres of psychological investigation and theory. I deeply regret the necessity which took such men from us.

I hope to be able at the next meeting of the Board to nominate for Professor Baldwin's chair a man who may confidently be expected to restore to the department the full efficiency which, in our first disappointment, it seemed in danger of losing permanently by the departure of so eminent a scholar. The vacancy created by Professor Finley's withdrawal has already been filled by the election of Mr. Harry Augustus Garfield, of Cleveland, Ohio, whose acceptance of the place assures the maintenance of the best traditions of the department. Mr. Garfield has won a reputation for character and ability at the bar of Cleveland, and a reputation for public spirit and for sagacity and capacity in affairs in connection with movements to reform city government and to put the consular service of the United States upon a footing of professional efficiency, which have brought him the warm admiration of thoughtful and observant men all over the country. He has studied his profession like a scholar and followed it like a man of affairs, and contributes to our working force in the University both character and achievement.

Those of us who directly handle the affairs of the University know that it grows like a living thing, almost in spite of us and in ways which sometimes seem independent of our control. In reality, however, its vital forces need our constant guidance; and at no time has this been more apparent than it is now. The Faculty is not conveniently organized either for instruction or for business and the course of study has by mere incidental growth lost system. The curriculum has become a variety of studies, but has almost entirely lost its character as a course of study. The Faculty Committee on the Course of Study, of which I have the pleasure of being chairman, has taken up the work of reconstruction with great seriousness, and we are holding weekly meetings to push the business forward, regarding it as preliminary to all the plans of the University for the next generation.

Notwithstanding our earnest diligence in the matter, we shall, I fear, have to ask you to be very patient in awaiting the result.

It is too complex a piece of business to be finished before the end of the present academic year, if, indeed, we are fortunate enough to finish it within that time. The chief earnest of our success lies in the fact that we are agreed upon the necessity and upon the method. We are agreed that the academic Freshman year should be left substantially as it is, a year in which all our new students, coming from all parts of the country and from all sorts of preparatory schools, may be whipped into shape for the work of the years which are to follow. If we make any attempt to modify it we will probably add to it a preliminary science course adapted to serve as a general introduction to the group of sciences from which the student will be called upon to choose his studies in Sophomore, Junior, and Senior years. Beyond freshman year we are planning to open to the student a choice among no less than ten courses of study.

It is our purpose to build each of these courses around some one substantial body of studies: one, for example, around the distinctively philosophical courses, one around the courses in history and politics, one around the classical studies, one around the English language and literature, one around the mathematical studies, one around the natural sciences, others around the physical sciences, etc. But each "Group," as we shall call it, though its emphasis will lie upon some one body of studies, to which the student may be said to be giving his special attention, will be made, so far as possible, symmetrical by the prescription of other studies which will round it out and give it the character of a liberal discipline. Every scientific group, for example, will be rounded by prescribed literary and philosophical studies, every literary or philosophical group by prescribed scientific courses, so that each group may be in itself, as it were, a well-considered liberal curriculum.

The variety of our courses of instruction will, we hope, enable us to do this without making any given group too rigid or too narrow. We see no reason why we may not give to the student a certain range of choice of coures [courses] within the particular group he selects. But we have not yet got far enough into the details of our work to see exactly how this purpose is to be expressed in practice.

It is our strong conviction that the A.B. and B.S courses should be drawn together into a common system, and we confidently expect to be able when we have worked out the groups of study on the academic side of the University to open a majority of the groups thus constructed to the candidates for the degree of Bachelor of Science, adding, it may be, to our scheme a few groups specially adapted to their requirements where their studies sharply diverge, by their own choice, from those of the candidates for the degree in Arts. Such changes will do away with all that is artificial in our present distinction between the School of Science and the Academic Department of the University. The greater part of that distinction is now, as the result of many accidents of growth and development, purely artificial, and we shall gain much in facility and efficiency by closely uniting the two sides in respect of the studies which they have in common.

Such changes will no doubt render the present organization of the body of instructors into three faculties[2] awkward and antiquated; but I shall not suggest any change of administrative organization in this respect until the courses of study are worked out and we are able to judge upon considering them as a whole what methods and machinery of administration would be likely to prove most serviceable and convenient.

There is, however, no such reason for delaying the reorganization of the teaching force of the University for the purpose of instruction which the Board was kind enough to authorize me to effect by the resolution passed at its June meeting. It has long seemed desirable to draw all instructors in the same or similar branches of study together, whether separated by the artificial line between the School of Science and the Academic Department or not, into departments, and to place each department under the chairmanship of a head. I have, therefore, organized the following departments: I. Philosophy; II. History and Politics; III. Art and Archæology; IV. Classics; V. Mathematics; VI. English; VII. Modern Languages; VIII. The Natural Sciences; IX. Physics; X. Chemistry; XI. Astronomy.[3] Over each of these, except the department of Art and Archæology, which is for the present to remain without a complete organization, I have placed a Chairman: over the department of Philosophy, Professor Alexander Thomas Ormond; over the department of History and Politics, Professor Winthrop More Daniels; over the department of Classics, Professor Andrew Fleming West; over the department of Mathematics, Professor Henry Burchard Fine; over the department of English, Professor Theodore Whitefield Hunt; over the

---

[2] That is, the University, Academic, and Scientific faculties.

[3] Perhaps owing to the impending retirement of Professor Charles Augustus Young (he retired in June 1905), a separate Department of Astronomy was dropped before the new plan of organization went into operation in the autumn of 1904. At the same time, the projected Department of Natural Sciences was divided into two departments, Geology and Biology, with William Berryman Scott as chairman of both.

department of Modern Languages, Professor Williamson Updike Vreeland; over the department of Natural Science, Professor William Berryman Scott; over the department of Physics, Professor Cyrus Fogg Brackett; over the department of Chemistry, Professor Fred Neher; and over the department of Astronomy, Professor Charles Augustus Young.

I have thought it best that, for the present at any rate, the appointment of the heads of departments should be from year to year. I have defined the duties of the head of a department as follows:

1. To call and preside over meetings of the department.

2. To effect joint counsel in the department upon all points which concern it as a whole, particularly with regard to the coördination of courses, changes in the course of study, and the distribution of duties among the several members of the department.

3. To speak for the department in all administrative dealings with the President of the University.

4. To represent the department in all nominations of instructors and in all proposals made to the Faculty with regard to the institution of new or the modification of old courses of instruction.

5. To perform such further duties in connection with the work of the department as the President of the University may assign him.

The estimate of income and expenditure made by the Treasurer of the University in his annual budget statement shows a probable deficit of several thousand dollars on the academic side and probably something over two thousand dollars surplus on the School of Science side. The number of students entering the School of Science this year for the first time exceeds the number entering the Academic Department of the University; the large majority of those who enter the School of Science pursue the courses which lead to the degree of Bachelor of Science; and the courses which the candidates for that degree select lie, at any rate in the upper years, rather more on the academic than on the scientific side, both sides of the University being open to them. No doubt, when the courses of study are reconstructed upon the plan I have already outlined it will be still harder, still more a mere arbitrary process, to distinguish between academic and scientific students, except in respect of the degree they are seeking. Candidates for the degree in science will in perhaps the majority of cases be pursuing the same courses with candidates for the degree in arts. These circumstances make it seem worth while to reconsider our budget in such a way as to devote the funds of the School of Science, so far as they will suffice, entirely to the support of strictly scientific courses, and those of the Academic Department to the support of the literary, linguistic, and philosophical studies, for the sake alike of economy and of convenience.

No readjustment of the funds, however, would make the present income of the University adequate to its existing needs. The necessity for increased endowments becomes more painfully manifest every day to those of us who are engaged in the actual work of administration. If the present condition of the money market and of the industries of the country makes the raising of such endowment as we need for the time being impracticable, it will, I think, be necessary for us to raise an emergency fund for the purpose of meeting current deficits and tiding us over a time of actual embarrassment.[4]

WOODROW WILSON

Printed document (WP, DLC).
[4] There is a WWsh draft of this report, dated Dec. 10, 1903, in WP, DLC.

Henry Burchard Fine to the Board of Trustees' Committee on Morals and Discipline

Gentlemen: PRINCETON UNIVERSITY, December 10, 1903.

I beg leave to submit the following report for the period which has elapsed since the last meeting of the Board of Trustees:

I DRINKING

Since my last report four students have been reported to me for intoxication. Two of these men had never before been reported for drinking, and to the Discipline Committee of the Faculty it seemed a sufficient penalty that I should admonish them and write to their parents. The remaining two had been reported before, to Dean Winans, the one twice and the other once, and we decided to suspend both of them until the Christmas holidays, or for periods of nine and six weeks respectively. I have no other serious cases of discipline to report.

II ATTENDANCE

As you are doubtless aware, a student is allowed a certain gratuity of recitation absences each quarter and a separate gratuity of Chapel absences.

As stated in our rules, the penalty for unexcused absences in excess of the gratuity is a pensum, or extra work assigned by the Instructor in whose course the largest number of absences have occurred, the work to be done by a tutor chosen by the Instructor.

The penalty for unexcused Chapel absences in excess of the gratuity is a reduction of the next quarter's gratuity if the excess is less than five, suspension if it is five or more.

In recent years, however, it has become the practice to make a pensum the penalty for an excess of Chapel absence, also to punish a student who has continued to absent himself from recitations after the assignment of a pensum, or who fails to do this pensum within the allotted time, by giving him a second pensum, instead of suspending him as was intended when the rules were adopted.

I found that the Chairman of the Committee on Attendance and the Registrar were convinced that this practice had seriously impaired the effectiveness of our rules and we therefore agreed to abandon it and to enforce the rules in their original form.

Furthermore, to put a check on the prodigal and careless use of the gratuity, we decided, except in cases of prolonged illness, to deduct from the gratuity of each student one-third the number of his excused absences.

These changes in the mode of administering our rules seem to have had a good effect, for in the quarter which closed at Thanksgiving day I have had to suspend but two students, both of them for failure to do their pensums within the allotted time.

None of us thinks, however, that we have yet found a thoroughly satisfactory solution of the difficult problem of irregularity of attendance.

III SCHOLARSHIP

We have endeavored to watch the class room work of the two lower classes closely enough to discover what students were falling so far behind, through negligence or lack of ability, as to be in danger of failing to pass the February examinations. The Freshmen of both Departments have been distributed among division officers whose duty it is to exercise some sort of personal supervision over the men assigned to them. Moreover, the Instructors of this class have already met twice, at intervals of a month, to review the roll, and in each instance they have reported to me the names of all students who were found to be below the passing mark in as much as half their work. I have seen all these men personally, and have written their parents regarding the situation.

There has been one such review of the roll of the Sophomore class, followed by personal interviews with me and letters home.

I am in hopes that these measures may have some effect in keeping the students attentive to their work. I may cite as one small piece of evidence, that of twelve Academic Freshmen, reported to me at the first reading of the roll, but four were reported at the second reading. These letters home are distasteful to the students, but parents seem grateful for them.

I am desirous of applying similar methods to the Junior and Senior classes so far as this is practicable, and at my request the Faculty has voted that the Instructors of these classes are hereafter to make such tests of the term work of their students as will enable them, about the middle of each term, to send me the names of all men whose work for the first half of the term has been below the passing mark. If I can obtain this information, I shall be able to warn all students who are seriously behind in their studies and shall no doubt be able to save some men who would otherwise be dropped from their classes.

Respectfully submitted,   H. B. Fine

TRS (Trustees' Papers, UA, NjP).

From the Minutes of the Board of Trustees of Princeton University

[Dec. 10, 1903]

ACTION IN THE MATTER OF ABSENCE FROM MEETINGS
OF TRUSTEES LAUGHLIN AND COWEN

The absence of Trustee Laughlin[1] from eight consecutive meetings of the Board and of Trustee Cowen[2] from four consecutive meetings of the Board having been reported in accordance with Section 7 of Chapter I of the By-Laws, it was, on motion of Mr. John A. Stewart, duly seconded,

> RESOLVED that action in the case of Mr. Laughlin be laid on the table and that the President be requested to take such steps in the matter as he may deem advisable.[3]

On motion of Mr. James W. Alexander, duly seconded, the following preamble and resolutions were adopted:

WHEREAS by Section 7, Chapter I, of the By-Laws of Princeton University, it is provided that

> "If any Trustee shall be absent from four consecutive stated meetings of the Board, his seat shall be regarded

as vacated, save by a special vote of the Board to the
contrary."

And whereas it appears from the minutes of the Board that the
Hon. John K. Cowen has been absent from four consecutive
meetings of the Board,

RESOLVED that the operation of the By-Laws aforesaid be
suspended in the case of Mr. Cowen, and that his seat be
and the same is not regarded as vacated, and

RESOLVED further that the attention of Mr. Cowen be
called by the President to the action of the Board. . . .[4]

[1] James Laughlin, Jr., of Pittsburgh, elected an Alumni Trustee in 1901.
[2] John Kissig Cowen of Baltimore, former President of the Baltimore & Ohio
Railroad, elected a Life Trustee in 1887, who was in very poor health at this time.
[3] See WW to H. H. Laughlin, Jan. 16, 1904. James Laughlin, Jr., was suffering
from some form of mental illness.
[4] See WW to J. K. Cowen, Jan. 16, 1904.

Notes for a Religious Address[1]

11 Dec., 1903[2]

Second Presbyterian Church, Philadelphia
13 Dec., 1903

The Church and Society.
  The salvation of Society, and of the individual by that means.
  Hence the *institutional church*, reaching out after men in their
    ordinary activities.
Spiritualizing life vs.
  Rationalizing religion. The former a more vital process than
    the latter. The everyday, business rationalization of life
    produces *a hunger for the mystery*
How spiritualize life?
  By example of *helpfulness*, disinterested counsel;
  By example of *unselfishness*;
  By example of *love* as a *principle* of action and coherence
  By example of *loyalty*, to an *ideal* embodied in *a person*.
Hence *a nursery* of motives wh. are *social*, moralizing, liberat-
    ing, keeping alive the integrating forces, the vital saps of
    the body politic.
And the *preaching* which comes out of all this? The preaching
    wh. reveals the spiritual content of life,—*the way of Christ
    among men.*

WWhw MS. (WP, DLC).
[1] A news report of this address is printed at Dec. 14, 1903.
[2] Wilson's composition date.

A News Item About a Speaking Engagement

[Dec. 12, 1903]

President Wilson '79 has accepted an invitation to speak at the annual dinner of the Princeton Club of Philadelphia, on the 18th.[1] On account of the unusual pressure of work at home, the President feels obliged to decline invitations for alumni reunions this year, but he is making an exception in the case of the Philadephia dinner, because he was prevented, by his father's death, from keeping his engagement last year, for the large reception arranged in his honor by the Philadelphia alumni.

Printed in the *Princeton Alumni Weekly*, IV (Dec. 12, 1903), 188.
[1] A news report of this affair is printed at Dec. 19, 1903.

An Address on Education[1]

[[Dec. 12, 1903]]

THE COLLEGE COURSE AND METHODS OF INSTRUCTION.

It gives me great pleasure to meet this association, and I feel the more freedom in speaking to you, because I have chosen a subject big enough to give room to turn in. There ought to be plenty to say about the college course and methods of instruction. The difficulty is not to find something to say, but to arrive at conclusions and to speak in a way that would be fairly representative of the present movement of opinion in this field.

This is the field in which there is, perhaps, the greatest movement of opinion. It seems to me that when we speak of the course of study, we are speaking of a thing, which at present does not exist. The trouble with the present college arrangement is, that there is no course of study anywhere that I can discover, except in one or two places where they are so poor that they must have a course of study. I was speaking not long ago at a banquet of the graduates of the University of Virginia—I myself have studied at that university and feel the affection of an alumnus for it—I was telling them that, while it was true that they, under the inspiration of Thomas Jefferson, introduced a free elective system at the University of Virginia before it was thought of elsewhere, it was also true that they had been so poor that they had never been able to give more than enough courses to qualify a man for grad-

[1] Delivered at a dinner meeting of the Schoolmasters' Association of New York and Vicinity at the Hotel St. Denis in New York.

uation, and that therefore all that they could say to their student was: Here is a circle of studies; you can enter the circle at any point, but you must complete the circle before you graduate. This is not the present system of free election. The present system of free election is to set before the student a confusing variety of studies, a bill of fare which he could not possibly eat through with digestion; a bill of fare which he could not possibly go through with in four years, no matter how hardy his digestion or how great his diligence, and then, spreading this confusing variety before him, say: We offer you no suggestions. You are younger than we are, and therefore know more than we do, and therefore we ask you to make your own choice and to follow your own course in the studies you shall pursue. We know that you were born with inclinations and tastes; we invite you to follow those inclinations and tastes. We would not question what God has created. He has created in you a predilection; follow it.

How am I to follow a predilection, an appetite with regard to dishes that I have never tasted? How am I to know which is the best thing, unless I choose merely according to the color, according to the odor, according to the appearance, according to the ease with which they can be got at? I know that as a matter of fact, the method of choice where there are systems of free election, is very interesting indeed. The student first of all selects those courses which, through previous acquaintance with the lecturer or by rumor among his fellow students, he knows to be the most interesting, those which are the most inviting; those which, now that he is free from the trammels of the school-room, look most like the studies of grown-up and liberated men. And by the time he has completed his sophomore year, he has completed all the studies of which he hears this pleasant report. During his junior and senior years, you see in him a blasé young gentleman who has tasted all the good things and who is now taking something else simply because he must, feeling the attitude towards life that was said at one time to prevail at Oxford: that there is nothing new and nothing true and no matter. And the last two years are years of lost impetus, instead of being the years of accumulating power and interest. Just in proportion to the variety of choice in an absolutely free system of election, is the confusion of the student and the unsatisfactory result, if the student be not a boy of uncommon discretion and of uncommon acquaintance with the real objects of his own life.

There was a time when the parts were not reversed between the young and the old. There was a time when it was supposed that a man who had studied a great deal knew more than a man who had not studied at all. We have for a time reversed those parts. You know how it is in a great many of our schools. It has been wittily said recently, that what is now said to the children in many of our schools is: "What studies would you like your teacher to study for you?" You know that in most of our schools the teachers are unspeakably over-worked and the children not worked at all. They are worked in the sense in which you work a bag which you are constantly filling. They are worked in the sense of being constantly worked upon. But they are not worked in the sense of being made to exercise any initiative of their own or to attack alone any of the difficulties of the subjects which they are studying. They are not taught to swim in the good old-fashioned manner of being put into the water and then left in sufficiently deep water to swallow an uncomfortable amount or else keep their heads above water.

The real difficulty, then, is that there is no course of study, because by a course of study, I mean a course laid out, a course measured, a course surveyed, a course determined. That is the only thing I understand by the word course. And if there is not a course of study, you have your choice between one of two things: either the absolute freedom of the pupil to choose for himself, or else a very elaborate system of advice, which the student may or may not take. If he must take the advice, why then you have a course of study for each man. If he need not take the advice, then there is no course of study at all.

I was talking not long ago with two gentlemen, both of them eminent men now, who graduated where there was an absolutely free election of studies and who in spite of that freedom had learned a great deal. Each of these gentlemen has several sons. They concurred in this statement: "When those boys grow up, we are going to look for a college to which to send them in which the whole course of study is prescribed." "Why?" I asked. "Because," they said, "of our own experience, in our own observation as undergraduates, we know that we were saved only by a merciful Providence from the dispersion of our faculties, and we do not believe that it is safe to trust all boys to the mere mercy of Providence. We suspect that it might be dangerous to trust our boys to start life without discipline."

For the thing which we have left out in leaving out courses of study is discipline. I am ready to say, that it is better to discipline a boy on useless studies, than merely to fill him with the information contained in useful studies. I believe that the great virtue of the process is its disciplinary virtue. I always compare a course of study in my own mind with a gymnasium. It is very interesting how inconsistent people are. They will admit that a gymnasium is a practical thing, that is to say that it is useful for boys to go in and exercise their muscles in a gymnasium. But I take it that there are very few boys who expect to do the double trapeze with their partners after they go into business. Most of the things that you do in a gymnasium are things that you will never dream of doing afterwards, and never have a chance to do afterwards. You are not doing the specific things which represent the movement of muscle which is to take place in your profession after you have left school. You are not acquiring a particular skill of hand, or a particular dexterity of force with the view of using that particular skill or dexterity for a definite object. You are simply getting your muscles in such shape, with such power of sinew and blood in them, that you can use them afterwards for anything you please, and that you may have a fit physical instrument for living your life. The object of study, it seems to me, is for the most part exactly the same, I mean of undergraduate study. It is to get the mind in such muscular and athletic shape that you can do anything with it afterwards that your life makes necessary. It is to get power of endurance, power of application, rapidity of movement, the quickness of sight which is necessary for rapidity of movement: all of that ease and poise and force which constitute real power in life. The real man in the field of affairs is the man of ready adaptation, of powers which meet a new situation as readily as they survive an old situation: and the men of initiative are the only men of success.

Very well, then: if you simply teach men tasks, you do nothing towards contributing to their power of initiative. Every man gets his power of initiative in spite of somebody else, not by the assistance of somebody else. That is what I mean. You don't give me power of initiative by instructing me what I should do in certain circumstances; because, if those circumstances arise, and I do what you told me, the initiative still is yours. I gain initiative by being put upon my own resources and finding out what to do without suggestion from anybody. That is what I understand by initiative. And if with an instinct of initiative, I have not the readiness, the poise, the resource, the strength of mind that I can get by training, then it is somebody's fault if somebody tried to train me. I have seen many a pitiful spectacle of young men who had gone through college without any training, who had the instinct of initiative, the instinct of leadership, and yet no capacity for carrying any task forward, because they had no muscle for the difficult part, no intellectual muscle.

I do not think that it is fancy, I do not think that it is merely my own feeling that the free elective system is a mistake, which makes me believe that there is a strong reaction in this country against that system in the colleges. And if there is a strong reaction in this country against the free elective system, there is another reaction that particularly affects you, and that is against the too great dispersion, if I may call it so, of the school course, a trying to teach too many things; the trying to prepare boys for any part of the miscellaneous programme which is to be offered to them after they get into college. The result of that has been to throw upon the schools a burden which they cannot carry, I mean, without very rich endowments. For example, when you try to prepare men for college in physics and chemistry, you cannot do so without very much better laboratories than most schools can afford. You cannot prepare them for that work without laboratories, merely out of books. And the experience of all colleges is, that the men who are admitted on examination in chemistry and physics have to be taught chemistry and physics over again; not because the school-master has not been intelligent, but because he has not had the time and the means to teach physics or chemistry in the way in which they ought to be taught. So that in every instance that I have inquired into, instead of going one step forward after the boy enters in physics or chemistry, he has to start at the beginning of them. In other words, the college teacher does not gain anything at all by requiring chemistry or physics for entrance: he has to begin as if the boy did not have chemistry or physics. I say again that I do not believe, and I have not met anybody that does believe, that this is because of the ignorance or incompetence of the school-teacher. It is because the conditions of teaching in the school and the means of teaching in the school are not proper for that purpose.

If, therefore, free election is being doubted now as a proper policy for the college, miscellaneous programmes for the school are to come under examination and revision, and we are to come to the question, Is not there some one definite body of preparation which will prepare pupils for the various lines which they are expected to pursue in college? I believe, that in the next generation, we are going to find out a great deal more than we know now about the necessary body of preparatory studies,—just as I believe that we are going to find out a good deal in the college circle about the necessary body of required studies,—the necessary back-bone, the necessary substance of every course, no matter which way the student turns.

For it seems to me that the only substitute for the modern free elective system is an election between several courses of study. You cannot, with the modern wealth of subjects of study, have *a* course of study in a college, that is to say, only one. There are too many things to study: there are too many routes through the field of knowledge. All that you can do is to make those routes definite routes, survey them, know the country through which they run, see to it that the country they run through is really representative of modern culture; that the outlooks from those routes are really the outlooks of modern life. So what is before us as a substitute for the free elective system is a system of election between various curricula. It has seemed to me that the wisest thing to do, for example, would be to take each substantial body of studies and group it, as a curriculum, around some central study of that body. Let us take one of the sciences; for example, take chemistry, and make a curriculum in which chemistry was more emphasized than anything else, so that the taste and predilection and inbred capacity of the student could be consulted to this extent, that, if his bent is scientific, if his taste is for chemistry, he can take this curriculum in which chemistry has the most prominent place; and in which, as the course develops, it is directed so that it makes the proper connections with the other sciences, and ultimately issues in a year of free scientific study: but that, during the first year, and the second year, and in part during the third year, you should prescribe studies to accompany chemistry, in order that there may be in this chemical course something like a liberal curriculum.

To be more specific, it would seem wisest that every scientific group of studies should be supplemented by literary and philosophical studies, so that the man should get some notion of those other important paths of knowledge: that in every group of study in which the classics predominated, there should be science as well as philosophy, a very substantial piece of science, a very important opportunity to view the world of modern scientific research. That, you will observe, is simply a way of saying, that there should be as many courses of study as there are important subjects of study, and that for each important subject there should be a course in which it predominates; but that after the student has made his choice of his predominating interest, the men who are older than he and have seen the world of letters longer than he shall tell him what is necessary for him to do besides that, in order to get a liberal education. It seems to me just as if, granted you had money enough, and preferred a certain sort of study, you were to establish a college with a curriculum in which that sort of study predominated. But you should be liberal enough in your endowment to make it a liberal course and not confine it to that study. Multiply colleges of that sort, and you have a greater college, a greater undergraduate organization, in which these various curricula are offered as branching courses of travel.

Of course, time would fail to go into any sort of detail: moreover, I do not think that detail in discussions of this sort is serviceable, because I believe that every college in this country must take its own course. The deadliest thing that could happen would be that all the colleges of this country should be alike. When I am told that we ought to do certain things at Princeton because they are done elsewhere, I always reply: "That depends upon what we *are* at Princeton. If our means are suitable to that, if our conditions can be adjusted to that, if our instructors are fitted for that, why then very likely we ought to do that, if it is good in itself. But we must do the thing which we can do best." It would be absurd for me to go on the stage as an operatic singer. While I think that operatic singing is one of the pleasures of life, (at any rate for those who listen, and I dare say for those who sing,) I don't think that I am obliged, and every other man who has some voice is obliged, to prepare for the operatic stage. That may be an extreme illustration, but nevertheless it illustrates, though extremely, the point I am making, that colleges, if they have any force at all, are as individual as persons; that if they are not as individual as persons, they ought to be; and that the student ought to go to the college whose individuality is what he needs. I have told the alumni of Princeton that there are a great many boys whom I don't want sent to Princeton, because if sent there, they will be sent under false pretenses, expecting to find what they do not find; that there is a particular kind of thing done at Princeton; and that the boy who wants that kind of thing ought to be sent there, and only the boy who wants that kind of thing. Just as soon as you recognize that principle of differentiation between colleges, you will vitalize the educational field of this country as it has never been vitalized before. We have been simply trying to make all of our colleges alike, with the result that we have deprived most of them of individuality and most of them of force.

There was a good deal in what Mr. Garfield said in the familiar quotation, that to his mind a college consisted of a log on one end of which sat Mark Hopkins and on the other end of which sat a student. It was Mr. Garfield's way of expressing the notion of the individuality of Williams College, due to the individuality, the intellectual and the spiritual individuality of the man Mark Hopkins. While it is not possible now-a-days, I dare say, to give our more complicated university organizations the stamp of one individual mind, it is possible to give them the stamp, the indelible stamp of traditions which are made by generations of individuals, and to let it be known what each particular institution stands for. Then we shall have enriched the country with respect of education, as we enrich the country in respect of gain, by every man's exercising his own faculties according to his own gift.

Now after we have determined that—I do not mean to say that I have determined it for you, but that I have determined it for myself—we are not through with the business. If we are dissati[s]fied with the free elective system, and find a good substitute, that is merely the beginning of something else; the rest of it is in the methods of instruction, because the best system is only as good as the teachers who conduct it. That is the reason why some people with a great deal of individuality get so impatient of the study of pedagogical method. And pedagogical method, in the last analysis, is most suitable for the person who has no method of his own. It is a means of supplying persons of unoriginal minds and very slight force of personality with a means of livelihood. Every school wants teachers whose method is themselves, whose success dwells in something that nobody ever described or analyzed, which proceeds from the interior spiritual forces of the individual. But we cannot get a whole faculty of persons of that sort. The Lord has been a little niggardly, let us say, in making persons of that kind: and therefore, we must discuss questions of method. We must employ persons who are not a method unto themselves. We must have some directing purpose and way of work which will dominate the individual more or less, unless the individual is so big that he cannot be dominated.

That leads me to ask: What ought to be the methods of study in a college? I am not now discussing universities, I am discussing the undergraduate question entirely. What ought to be the method of study in a college? You know that the college teacher has stuck as closely as he could in all these years of change to the recitation method, by getting a number of youngsters in one room with a particular text or a particular set of exercises to be tested upon, and getting them up one by one, or making conversational groups of them, in order to find out what they have done with that book or task. The objection to that is, that it makes no difference between the college and the school, and I have invariably found that the school-boy who comes to college is resentful of being kept at recitations for a couple of years, before he gets any sort of emancipation and is thrown upon his own resources. He doesn't see what he has gained by leaving school and getting to college. He doesn't see the difference between school and college, and I don't blame him, because so far forth there is no difference between the school and the college. I am ready to admit, as an interesting subject of discussion, that it may be a question whether there ought to be a difference between school and college in those early years; but I take it that most of us would say that there ought to be, or else that the school ought to be kept on a couple of years longer, and the college not begin until a couple of years later; that the school kind of work ought to be done by the school, and not by the college; that not to draw the line here is a confusion of words, a confusion of methods, a confusion of field.

Supposing that you agree with me on that point, that the method of the school ought not to run on indefinitely into the college, I ask: What is the reason why you feel that judgment? Why is not the recitation a proper college function? For the reason that I have already tried, in the best part of what I have said, to make evident—the recitation does not mature the pupil. It is a process by which the teacher seeks to put something into the pupil, something that is in himself, or something that was in the text-book until he began the process of transferring it to the student. The recitation, as far as the student is concerned, is for the most part a receptive process. It is a means of finding out whether the student has swallowed something or not, and knows what he has swallowed; whether he has been aware of the passage of this thing down his gullet and has analyzed the taste of it, so that he can tell what it is like. And that is all that the recitation process usually amounts to. There are some teachers of genius enough to set the minds of the students agoing, to have an independent way in a recitation, but not in any recitation that I ever attended. And that being the process, there is no maturing going on. The boy is growing older from month to month and from year to year; but he is not growing any less of a boy from month to month and from year to year, so far as his intellectual processes are concerned. He is finding out more about the world and its phenomena; he is learning more of what the world has thought about, and of the validity of the world's thought; but all that by way of receiving instruction, by way of following the teacher whose hand he holds along certain ways, where he does not see anything that the teacher does not point out. Moreover, you will see that just because it is a receptive process, it is not a process which encourages or imparts initiative to the student.

I heard something of a school the other day which I must say I applauded thoroughly. It would be regarded as a very belated school, but it was an exceedingly effective school. In arithmetic, for example, when a pupil had a difficulty, the teacher never helped him out. The teacher selected another pupil who had solved that problem and made that other pupil tell the one who could not solve it how it was to be solved, which put the pupil who had solved it to his best, naturally so; but put the pupil who had not solved the problem at a disadvantage that no boy wants to be put at, that of being taught by another fellow no bigger and older than himself. And those small chaps drove themselves not to have any unsolved problems, and they sat up at night—most parents are against their children sitting up at night: but I don't see how they are going to study if they don't—those children sat up at night, and worked that arithmetic, and they knew that there was no salvation for them outside of that book and the processes of their own minds. The consequence was that they prodded their own minds and insisted that their own minds should wake up and do the thing. That is not the way, I understand, with most schools. It was not the way of the school I attended. I was looked upon with great sympathy, if I could not do or solve a problem, and it was supposed that it was the fault of my father or of my grandfather, that there was something hereditary about it. It was said: "Why, the poor little chap, his brain cells are not made that way." Now there was a school right alongside of mine, I mean the one I attended, where the brain cells were stimulated by blows laid upon the cuticle, and it was extraordinary how hereditary tendencies were overcome by that simple process. The sensitiveness of the exterior covering with which we are endowed leads to a great assimilation of the mind.

I believe that the only study that ever does anybody any good is the study that he does for himself, and not the study that the teacher does for him. That is the only process by which initiative can be communicated to the human race by processes of education. Look at the processes of education of the poor little chaps that do not go to school. Look at the keenness, look at the readiness, look at the resource of some of the little children in our slums, who have to shift for themselves from the time they can crawl, and you will see what the processes of the world's school are. No pity, no assistance, no suggestion; just take the elements that lie under your mind and solve the problem for yourself. Of course it would be out of the question deliberately to carry the process to that pitiless extent; but nevertheless nature teaches us how to force the intellectual growth, because the intellectual growth is forced by that process, and those boys at five years are smarter than the coddled boys at fifteen. There must be something in that suggestion of nature. The recitation, therefore, I take it, is not a process that ought to be continued any longer than is absolutely necessary in the college, and I think there might be some revision of the methods of the recitation in the school.

Now as to the lecture. I suppose that you do not have to lecture very much, and therefore you do not know how futile an exercise it is. I have to lecture a great deal, and my conscience is a good deal damaged on that account, because I know perfectly well that lecturing is not the way to communicate a great subject of study. I know exactly what happens in a lecture. The men come in, and if they feel like it, they pay you a good deal of attention. They don't feel like it, unless you fight and get hold of them. The hardest thing that I have to do is to lecture to a college class. I had a great deal rather lecture to a room full of Pundits, who came there to hear me, than a college class which is there for the hundredth time to hear me; who know just where I am in the subject, just what is coming next; know just the way I am going to treat it, just how many times I am going to diverge and relieve the tedium of the hour with a story; know just my attitude towards the subject, just the range of my vocabulary. They cannot be surprised, they cannot be ravished by any eloquence that they have not heard before. And you have simply got to get down to business and get into communication with those fellows or quit. I know that it is not easy to quit, because the college prescribes that the exercise should be at least fifty minutes long; and some men go along notwithstanding the fact that they have not captured the men. The result is not noise or confusion necessarily, but a great attention to the windows and to the ceiling, and to the rest which was not completed the night before, and the thoughts are everywhere but on the lecture. I have often told the men in my classes that they can do anything that is quiet, but that there are men present who want to listen, and they must not disturb them.

Seriously, the lecture is at best a mere intellectual entertainment for the hour; and if you cannot do anything but lecture, as with classes of four or five hundred men you cannot, then it simply means that so many times a week you offer these young gentlemen as much intellectual entertainment as you can give them, and then about the week before examination time, they apply themselves to discover what it has all been about, or at any rate to get enough of it *pro forma* into their heads to make it appear that they did not know what it was about when it comes to the examination. That is not a proper way to communicate a great subject of study. I have heard men plod through lectures, plod through courses of lectures, which, if they had been printed, would have been very much inferior to almost any book on the subject that they might have put into the students' hands, and which were shorter than any book. You cannot deliver a whole book in a course of lectures, if it has anything in it, and it would have been a good deal better, so far as communication of the subject was concerned, to say about the week before the examination: "I expect you to get down to work and to read that book and to be ready to be examined on it." They would get more out of it than out of their lectures, in the week which they devoted to that interesting occupation.

What is the lecture for, then? I believe that lecturing is a very important academic function. I believe that it is one of the most important, but it is not for the purpose of communicating bodies of knowledge. It is for three several purposes. In the first place, it is for what I might call the general orientation of the student's mind with regard to a great field of study. Take any great field of study, and the student ought to be carried over its greatest topics and shown its major geographical relations, and made to feel the significance of the questions which arise in the course of the examination of that great body of study. You cannot stop long enough to answer the questions which are raised; but you may raise the questions, and having raised the questions, you may show how interesting—how stimulating it would be, and illuminating, if, answering all these questions, you could put the answers together and make a system of knowledge with regard to that particular subject. It is what, on the other side of the water, they call the encyclopedia of the subject, the great outlines, the *grundriss*, the ground-plan, so as to show what the building must be when it is erected, the architect's plan for the building of knowledge. That is one thing. But you cannot examine students on that, at least it is not very useful to examine them on it afterwards. That is simply for the purpose of enabling them to understand where they are, when they attempt the study of any particular part of a great subject.

But that is not the most important object of lectures. There is another function of the lecturer, it seems to me more important, and that is the function of stimulation. It is always a disadvantage to a lecturer to have persons who are listening take notes, because the minute you take notes, you release yourself from the hold that the lecturer has on you. The best thing that a lecturer can do for you is simply to get hold of you and keep hold of you, hold your mind, as it were, in solution, in the atmosphere of that subject for fifty minutes, so that afterwards you cannot get all of the fascination and suggestion of that great topic out of your head. You will know that, having touched this thing, you have touched something that lives, not something that is dead; that you have not touched a mere abstract and ghostly thing, but something that has its immediate connections with the validity of the processes of the mind and the observation of the phenomena of nature, and that you are a better cultured person in the world for having found out that there was power and life in that thing. That is what the lecturer is chiefly for.

But don't you see that very few lecturers can be used for that purpose, because very few lecturers are able to take fire, even from subjects which burn, and unless the lecturer can glow, he cannot communicate any heat? You cannot communicate what you have not. And if you are not yourself afire with the subject, nobody else will be the least excited about it, unless indeed he comes there already on fire, unless indeed he is already acquainted with the subject and can himself radiate a little bit of heat where he sits. But the lecturer who can take fire, the speaker who is combustible, is the rare artist. Most speakers are absolutely incombustible: they are asbestos, and you cannot use them for this purpose. You can use them for the first thing that I have named, the large, scholarly, calm exposition of the greater areas of some great subject. You can use them for that. Many a quiet man who has no fire in him is the very soul of lucidity in what he says. It is cool, it is clear. The atmosphere is not stimulating, but you can see any distance, and it is wholesome and useful to live a little while in that atmosphere and walk a little while with that calm directing mind. That is another function; that is not the one I am now talking about.

Then there is another function yet for the college lecturer, and that is the function of example. It seems to me that every college student ought to have some scholar stand up before him, and taking a small piece of a great subject, go through it with the utmost painstaking detail, being careful at every step to show where he got his detail and what the processes are by which he built up that nice correlated structure. In other words, there ought, for every class in every subject, to be some one man who can show the processes of research by his own example, take some scholarly piece of work that he has done himself, and anatomize it before the class, show it in its parts, show it in its pulses, show it in all the things which gave it form and gave it growth, so that they shall have the admirable advantage of one who sees an artist take his work apart, and show how every piece of it was put into relation with every other piece by honest painstaking labor, which contained in itself some artistic idea, always had the whole, an ideal, a complete vision before it, and was always working with infinite painstaking towards that thing. I never knew, for my part, the beauty of scholarship, the ideal of scholarship, until I heard a really great scholar do something like that. I had supposed that scholarship, the ideal of scholarship, was all horrid drudgery: but to have the horrid drudgery eliminated by a mind evidently great, evidently not petty, evidently seeking the greater relations of the little thing that it was studying, take it and hold it up to the light and turn it about until you could see just what it was and just what it contained, was to see revealed the inspiration of scholarship. Some people suppose that scholars, research students, are men without red corpuscles in their blood; that they sit in rooms apart, and do these dull tasks because they do not feel like doing anything more interesting; whereas it takes the reddest kind of blood to do that sort of thing, to resist the evident temptations of action, to resist the attractions of the electric air that is out of doors, and the free movement of men in the world, and to have so intense a vision of something that no man ever saw that you are willing day in and day out to pursue it in the quiet of a room where no man ever cheers you and where no man ever assists you. That is a great deal harder than any piece of business that ever resulted in the acquisition of millions of money. You have to pursue the quiet vision in order to do a thing of that sort; and when the youngster has once caught sight of the beauty and of the dignity of that sort of thing, he is going to see that scholarship has something in it that is worth coveting.

Those three functions, it seems to me, are the only functions of the college lecturer. I should say, if we could make an ideal college arrangement, that you ought to put the first man before a comparatively small group of students, to show them the outline of a great subject. You ought to put the man, however, who can put fire into a subject into the biggest hall you have, and let anybody come who wants to, with the sign on the door that Dr. Moody used to suggest for the spiritual improvement of his hearers: "This Place To Let With Power." That ought to be the sign on the door of that lecturer: "This Place Open; Power Supplied." Then the third man ought to lecture before very small groups of students, whom he has trained to be interested in the particular phases of some subject.

There is, therefore, no place for the lecturer who merely tries to communicate information by means of a lecture. Of course the millennium is some distance off yet, and the worst of it is, that to do anything in this world (apparently whether it be an ideal or not)—to do anything but save your soul, requires money. Fortunately, salvation is without money and without price, which reminds me of the retort of a vestryman of my acquaintance to a pewholder who was complaining of the pew rents. He said: "My friend, you are laboring under a misapprehension: salvation is free, but religion is extremely expensive." We all know the validity of that remark; so is education extremely expensive. And one may wish that he could do ideal things, but you can't do ideal things without the cash, and therefore I am simply holding up to you, not what I wish you to understand me to promise that I am going to do, but what I would do if I could, and because I believe that those are the objects at which to aim.

But after you have settled the function of the recitation by almost determining that it has no function at all, and the function of the lecture by proving that most lectures now given are of no use whatever, then what are you going to do? If the ordinary man cannot lecture to a class, and if you do not want anybody to hold a recitation, what are you going to do with your pupils? How will you employ them to keep them out of mischief? How do anything which will offset foot-ball? Why, it seems to me that the thing to do is to say to each young man: "We are going to supply you with all the kinds of assistance that we can, but here are certain subjects which you must learn. Now we are not particularly interested how you learn them, provided you learn them; but there is going to be a day of judgment, when we are going to find out whether you have learned them or not. This place is a pleasant place to live in and you are welcome here. There are a great many interesting men here, to whom we will give you free access for suggestion of any kind and for guidance of various sorts. It will probably be best that you should have stated appointments with them for the advice which you are going to get. But for the rest, all that they are going to do is to supply you laboratories in which you can make your experiments, libraries in which you can find your books, and say to you, at a certain period of the year, 'We are going to find out whether you know a certain subject or not, and we are not going to take any excuses at all.' If you do not, you will be without excuse in this place. Here are laboratories and libraries of books and men from whom you can get any sort of advice which is pertinent to the job you have in hand. It is not like turning you loose without assistance and saying, 'Learn this subject.' Here is a place prepared for learning this subject, with the apparatus supplied, the apparatus of specially trained men, specially selected books, specially prepared instruments; now learn the subject, or if you don't, get out, because that is what this place is for; and if you don't use this place for that purpose, this is not the place for you. You may be a nice fellow, but there are a great many other places in the world where nice fellows are welcome."

In the hope that not all of you have heard the witty remark of my predecessor in the Presidency of Princeton, I will tell you what he said to an anxious mother who brought her boy and placed him specially under his care. He said: "Madam, we guarantee satisfaction or return the boy." And I think that is all that we can do, guarantee satisfaction or return the boy. The beauty of this arrangement, in my judgment, would be this: that every man being put upon his own resources, no man any longer being obliged to look upon himself as a boy in leading strings, study would acquire a dignity which it never had before. We are not without proof in this matter. In every subject of study where the attempt has been made of setting the student independent tasks, like the preparations of papers on individual phases of the subject, and where he has been turned loose in the library without any further assistance than the names of the books in which he is most likely to find assistance, those tasks have always been the tasks best done,—the tasks from which the student really finds out that he has a mind and that it is a pleasure to use it.

Sometimes, when I go through the campus at Princeton at night, and see the brilliant display of lighted windows, I know perfectly well what is going on in those rooms. I have lived in those rooms myself, and the report—credible rumor—brings me word that the same thing goes on now that went on then. There is some studying, there is a lot of good fellowship, there is a lot of fun: but take the whole line of dormitories through, and except where here and there the lamp of an advanced student burns, they have not found out what fun it is to use their minds; that the best fun in the world is to do something hard with the mind, and do it successfully, and that they would go to bed after mid-night *without* a headache, when perhaps some of the practices they now attempt send them to bed after mid-night *with* a headache. And I have told the boys that my ambition was, if possible, before I die, to bring them within sight of the time when those lights would burn for another purpose, and when there would be more fun in those rooms than there is now. I would not undertake the job, if I thought I was going to deprive them of pleasure; but I know, and you know, and any man who has used his mind knows, that they have not discovered the real pleasure of life, and that if you can put them in the way of that discovery, they will be your debtors for the rest of their lives, and that those will be happier rooms than they are now. That is the fine thing that impels a teacher. He has treasure on board, if he can make the persons with whom he consorts know that it is treasure, and value it as such. Now whether that dream can be realized or not, depends upon a great many things, but it is the only dream worth dreaming. I do not want to teach anybody for his mental and spiritual correction. I do not understand that it is my duty to punish other people's sons. Unless I am doing something which they ought to want and which they will see some of these days as the thing they ought to want, why, then I ought to go into some more honorable profession. We are all on the wrong tack, if that vision is not the right vision. You know that some parents regard schools as places to which to send their children to get rid of them, and that we are expected simply to take care of them during the time that they are allotted to us. But I do not want that task, and I have learned this, that if you take young fellows into your confidence, into your counsels and let them know what you are after, they are willing to co-operate with you, unless they find that what you are after is to make them have an unpleasant time. Some of the severest men in the faculties that I have been connected with have been the most popular men, provided always they were what the boy very significantly calls "white," and provided they were no respecters of persons, provided that they did not have any personal animus in the task that they imposed upon another, as if they took a dislike to him and wanted to make him work harder than anybody else: who were even-handed, fair, and after merely one object, namely, to make that class learn a particular thing. When that is known to be the temper of the instructor, no kind of pressure can make him unpopular, unless of course he is born under some unhappy star. Unless the teacher has some uncommon, repulsive quality or repellant quality, mere rigor of process is perfectly safe so far as popularity is concerned. Popularity is not an object in itself, I must admit, but popularity is a pretty good weather-vane. There are different ways of getting it, and some ways are not good ways. Nevertheless, the unpopular teacher (I do not mean temporarily unpopular, but the teacher who has been unpopular with class after class), needs looking into. He ought to be examined for his Christian character. No Christian ought to be day in and day out disliked. There ought to be some effulgence from him which is agreeable to some eye, and he ought not to go on indefinitely repelling persons, whom he cannot instruct, if he thus repel.

You will see then where I have landed. I have dissolved all method, you will say. I have said that there is no method except to tell an individual that he must learn a certain subject. Well now, is not that a method? And is not that the only method that can be adopted, in view of the fact that no two of us are made alike? The thing that will stimulate one mind will not stimulate another mind. That is just the truth of the matter. I have found this: that almost invariably when I had the delightful experience of being thanked by some pupil for what I had done for him, it turned out that he was thanking me for something I had done outside of the class room, something that I had done for him as a man. After having talked with him and found out what he needed, then I could sometimes draw out of my own experience something that comforted him, that stimulated him, that made him see more plainly than he had seen before what the course of his life ought to be. And that sort of counsel is the only method, and this sort of method is the only one that permits of that sort of counsel: that you look your teachers up when you want their counsel and leave them alone when you don't want their counsel. That means that the teacher must be at the disposal of the student most of the twenty-four hours of the day. But then that is what he is there for.

A colleague of mine[2] visited Oxford not long ago, and was talking with a gentleman there, who was one of the tutors of Baliol College.[3] Baliol College is the honor college, that is to say the

[2] Probably Andrew F. West, who spent six weeks studying the Oxford college system in the autumn of 1902. See A. F. West to WW, July 17, 1902, n. 1, Vol. 14.
[3] He was probably James Leigh Strachan-Davidson (1843-1916), Classical Tutor and Senior Dean of Balliol College.

college where men are not taken in residence unless they mean to read for honors; mere pass men are not taken. It is therefore a college of hard students. By the same token, this gentleman's life was absolutely devoted to teaching. There was hardly an hour of the twenty-four that he could call his own. In spite of that, he has won a fame for historical knowledge which has crossed the water and reached many of us on this side. He has abilities which would undoubtedly have fitted him to make a great individual reputation as an historian. Knowing that, my colleague asked him if he did not regret all these years, for he is now past sixty, that he had spent in absolute devotion to teaching the various generations of youngsters who had come up to Baliol College. "Regret it?" he said. "How could I regret it? Look at what has ensued. Look at some of the men who have been my pupils." And he picked out the men like Lord Curzon, and Sir Alfred Milner, and Mr. Ritchie,[4] who are now the governors of the British Empire. He said: "Those men were not only my pupils, but they never make an important decision in their lives, that they do not first come up to Oxford to see me." And he answered, "Do you suppose that I regret that?"—Don't you remember the young man, the hero—(a somewhat stiff hero I will admit) in Lady Rose's Daughter,[5] who testified that he did not know he had a soul until he came into contact with his tutor at Oxford, and that by associating with that quiet man, who knew nothing of affairs and cared nothing, he first discovered his responsibility to his fellow-men, and that is what gave him the troublesome conscience that he carried the rest of his life, the feeling that he ought not to enter upon a great estate, for example, without devoting himself to the welfare of the tenants on that estate, and that the greatest misfortune that could come to a man would be to have great power and no conscience? He got that, he said, from his tutor at Oxford. He is a fictitious character, but he was not built upon a fictitious fact. He was drawn by Mrs. Ward from the men, without number, who have found their souls at Oxford University. Now I venture to say that no man ever found his soul in a recitation or at a lecture. The only thing that discovers your soul for you is to touch another soul; it is when life touches life. It is when the tinder touches the flame that the thing happens which is the vital thing in the life of every man. I need not tell you, ladies and gentlemen, that I

[4] Wilson was probably referring to Richmond Thackeray Ritchie, at this time Secretary of the Political Department of the India Office, who, in fact, attended Trinity College, Cambridge, not Balliol.

[5] Mary Augusta Arnold (Mrs. Humphry) Ward, Lady Rose's Daughter (London and New York, 1903).

came not prepared with a formal discourse, but merely to put out to you, as it came into my mind, the line of thought that is running through the mind of every college man in these days, and to suggest to you what possibly we may hope will be, either while we live or when we are dead, the solution of a great matter.

Printed in *Eleventh Annual Report of the Schoolmasters' Association of New York and Vicinity*[,] *1903-1904* [New York, 1904], pp. 45-65.

A News Report of a Religious Address in Philadelphia

[Dec. 14, 1903]

HEAD OF PRINCETON TALKS OF SOCIETY

Dr. Woodrow Wilson Discusses Its Relation to the Modern Church

"The Church and Society," was the subject of an address delivered by Dr. Woodrow Wilson, president of Princeton University, at the services in connection with the one-hundred-and-sixtieth anniversary of the Second Presbyterian Church, Walnut and Twenty-first streets, yesterday morning.

Dr. Wilson made a strong plea for greater unselfishness in modern life, through which alone society could be regenerated. The modern idea of society, he said, was that it is an organic whole with an existence of its own apart from that of the individuals which went to make it up. The late Herbert Spencer had written of society in the terms applied to physical organisms, as though it were an actual living body.

"We are becoming accustomed," he said, "to look upon individuals as not independent of the character of their surroundings, and urge environment as an excuse for their offenses and shortcomings. While there is much truth in this, nevertheless the supremacy of the individual will to its surroundings is the very basis of society. There can be no responsibility without this independence of the will, no law, no coercive power. We cannot grow as a nation unless the individual is held responsible for all that he does.

"At the same time the salvation of the individual is made largely dependent on the salvation of society, and this can only be done by co-operation and mutual helpfulness. Co-operation makes for lofty ideals. There is the key, there the clue, to the method that is to spiritualize society.

"Strange as it may seem, with every attempt that has been made to rationalize religion, there has been a corresponding effort to spiritualize society. In proportion to the rationalization of religion the power of the pulpit has decreased, while in proportion to the spiritualization of society the power of the Church has grown.

"The Church is called to a great mission which is to keep the sap in the body politic. It is called upon to keep alive the social instinct which is the instinct of unselfishness and co-operation. The sympathy of the Church with society is the highest expression of the Church's life, and the application of these principals [principles] of her spirit alone can save society from sordidness and greed."

Printed in the Philadelphia *Inquirer*, Dec. 14, 1903; one editorial heading omitted.

A News Report of a Talk to the Philadelphia Y.M.C.A.

[Dec. 14, 1903]

WOODROW WILSON TALKS TO MEN

Addresses the Y.M.C.A. Meeting in the Garrick Theatre

More than 2000 men crowded into the Garrick Theatre yesterday afternoon to hear Woodrow Wilson, President of Princeton University, in a gospel talk.

The service was under the auspices of the Central Young Men's Christian Association, and was presided over by Secretary [Herbert K.] Caskey. Rev. Dr. Charles Wood[1] introduced Dr. Wilson. There was music by a sextette of trumpets and Mrs. Zaidee Townsend Stuart, soprano of the Second Presbyterian Church.

President Wilson warned the men against leading lives of selfish enjoyment or making strife after money or power their ideals.

"The only true happiness," he said, "is to be found in loving and serving God and man.

"Why, some ask, should a man do right when it is sweet to do wrong, and when every impulse of his being draws him to do wrong? Yet the only dignity and nobility of man is in doing right. This is not only Christian but pagan teaching. We must ask ourselves whether our instinct or our conscience is going to be preeminent. There are only two motives in life, one of self-aggrandizement, the other of service. Self-aggrandizement is summed up in two words—money and power."

Dr. Wilson said neither of these was satisfying when a man came to die. The only way he can satisfy the faculties of his life is by service—to be in right relationship with other people, and particularly in right relationship with God. The nobility of service is the nobility of love—not self-pleasing love, but the love which embraces all.[2]

Printed in the Philadelphia *Public Ledger*, Dec. 14, 1903.
  [1] Pastor of the Second Presbyterian Church of Philadelphia and a trustee of Princeton University.
  [2] For this address, Wilson used the notes printed at Nov. 2, 1899, Vol. 11.

To Frederick Paul Keppel[1]

My dear Sir: Princeton, New Jersey. 15 December, 1903.

I must apologize for the delay in replying to your official communication of November 12[2] with regard to the application of the Universities of Virginia, Minnesota and Nebraska to be admitted to the Association of American Universities.[3] It has been due to my repeated absence from home.

It does not seem to me necessary that the Executive Committee should meet in order to determine the question of these admissions; and I take it for granted that no vote at all is necessary upon the case of the University of Minnesota, whose application has been withdrawn.

Our own vote would be in favor of the admission of the University of Virginia;[4] but I do not think we should feel prepared as yet to vote for the admission of the University of Nebraska.[5]

In response to your letter of December 12,[6] I would say that we shall take pleasure in appointing a delegate to attend the next meeting of the Association, and I will see to it that you and Mr. Stokes[7] are both notified of the choice.

              Very truly yours,   Woodrow Wilson

TLS (ViU).
  [1] Secretary of Columbia University and Secretary of the Association of American Universities for 1903-1904.
  [2] It is missing.
  [3] The Association of American Universities was founded in February 1900 "for the purpose of considering matters of common interest relating to graduate study." Its original members consisted of fourteen institutions engaged in graduate instruction: the University of California, Catholic University of America, the University of Chicago, Clark University, Columbia, Cornell, Harvard, the Johns Hopkins, Stanford, the University of Michigan, the University of Pennsylvania, Princeton, the University of Wisconsin, and Yale.
  [4] The constitution of the Association provided that additional institutions might be admitted at the annual conference, on invitation of the Executive Committee, endorsed by a three-fourths vote of the members. Up to 1904, no new members had been added to the original fourteen, and several proposals for expanding the membership had been defeated. The University of Virginia was elected to membership at the next meeting of the Association, on February 19, 1904.
  [5] The University of Nebraska was not admitted to membership until 1909.
  [6] It is missing.
  [7] Anson Phelps Stokes, Jr., Secretary of Yale University.

To Charles Williston McAlpin

Princeton, New Jersey.

My dear Mr. McAlpin: 16 December, 1903.

Here is a letter[1] which I am sure will excite your interest and sympathy. Is there not a fund in the hands of the Treasurer of the University which is intended to be given out as loans to men who can some day return the money? If there is anything available for this young man, I should feel inclined to advise that he be given a chance to finish his course.

If you will kindly return this letter when you have read it with an indication whether anything can be done or not, I should like to answer it personally.

Always faithfully yours,   Woodrow Wilson

TLS (McAlpin File, UA, NjP).
  [1] It is missing, but see McAlpin's reply, printed as the following document.

From Charles Williston McAlpin

[Princeton, N. J.]

My dear Dr. Wilson: December 17, 1903.

I have received your letter of the 16th inst. enclosing a letter from Mrs. Graham[1] in reference to Mr. E. L. Burrell.[2] I hope to make a fuller report to you the first of the week, but have learned from the Treasurer that thus far Mr. Burrell has not paid any of his present term bill which amounts to $168. During the first two weeks of the term he boarded at the Nassau Hotel paying $7.00 per week and since that time has boarded at a $6.00 club; his stand last year was in the fourth general group.

Mr. Duffield has just told me that there is a fund of $130.00 available for loaning, the loan to be repaid within a year.

I return Mrs. Graham's letter.

Sincerely yours,   [C. W. McAlpin] Secretary.

CCL (McAlpin File, UA, NjP).
  [1] The Editors have been unable to identify her.
  [2] Edward Louis Burrell '04.

A Newspaper Report of an Address to the Philadelphia Alumni

[Dec. 19, 1903]

LIVE TIGER A GUEST AT PRINCETON FEAST

Two hundred and fifty Princeton graduates, the largest number ever assembled at a banquet, honored their Alma Mater and praised the prowess of her football team in Horticultural Hall last night. The feast was given by the Princeton Club, into which was merged two years ago the Princeton Alumni Association of Philadelphia, which previous to that had held similar celebrations for thirty-eight consecutive years.

For the first time a live tiger graced the occasion, and proved to be, in a certain sense, the most remarkable guest. He had been loaned from a menagerie, and he was hungry—but he didn't get anything to eat. He is a magnificent royal Bengal, with broad, rich hued stripes. The tumult and the turmoil, the shriek of the brass horns of the musicians and the clash of the cymbals, interested him greatly—yet he was not invited to dine. He paced, with short, fretful strides, his narrow cage behind the toastmaster's seat, and the smoke of the viands tantalized him. But none of the fleshpots went to him. It became an old story. The Nassau yell grew tiresome to him. He pricked up his ears and lashed his tail at first, but very soon he decided that it was all a hollow farce. . . .

President Wilson spoke to the toast of "Princeton." Rising amid cheers, he said:

"I am sincerely glad to be here to-night. I know that you are all thinking chiefly of the men who are sitting at the other end of these tables. I mean, of course, of the football team. I am sincerely glad to pay my tribute, not merely to the football victory,[1] as such, but to the character of the men who won it. A victory obtained in that way, and by such fellows, is double in its value, because, after all, the value of a football team to a university is that it represents a certain sort of stalwart achievement and character. The men who won it may be forgotten as individuals, but not if the promise of that kind of victory is fulfilled. Its results will be very great, for it is a promise of the capacity to lead and to organize men for a victory, which is not selfish, which is not for the individual, but for the university.

"The morale which is indicated by such a victory is well worth talking about. You know how very hard the game of football has become; how much sacrifice is required to play in a leading position—in any position at all on the team. There are many men every year who go into the game, not because they enjoy the sport, but because they love the university and believe they can best serve it by playing.

"The beauty of this victory is that it was a victory of brains and character over muscle. It was really the muscle of the mind that won. I wish it were proper to pay a tribute to individual members of the team. I suppose most of the fellows at the university think that my time is entirely given to seeing to it that they get through their examinations, but I assure you that I am deeply engrossed also in seeing what the football teams do. I know that every man who admires this team as I admire it would prefer that I refrain from picking out individuals, and that we should admire it as a whole.

"I am proud of all sides of the university. I should feel that I had not well represented the football team unless I had told you something that they specially love, and that is the university itself.

"Our aim is to produce not only such splendid men as those whose praise you are singing to-night, but also men who will do conspicuous service in every high calling. There never was a time when careful thinking and courageous speech were more needed in this country than they are at this moment."

President Wilson mentioned Senator Hoar and Grover Cleveland as examples of the great moral influence of men who are not afraid to speak their mind on public questions at any and all times. The reference to the former President was greatly cheered.

When the speaker closed the alumni sang a refrain in his honor to the air of "Mr. Dooley."[2]

Other speakers were L. Irving Reichner, David T. Marvel, George R. Wallace and Professor J. B. Fine.

Printed in the Philadelphia *Public Ledger*, Dec. 19, 1903; two editorial headings omitted.
[1] Princeton defeated Yale, 11 to 6, on November 14, 1903.
[2] See n. 1 to the news report printed at Dec. 13, 1902, Vol. 14.

From James Mark Baldwin, with Enclosure

Dear Dr. Wilson,   Princeton, N. J., Dec. 22, '03.

I am availing myself of your kindness in offering to state the matter of my honorarium to Mr. Pyne, and enclose herewith the letter I have written out asking you to lay it before him with your own explanations. With it I send the letters from you (in copy) to which my text refers. I hope you have the letter I wrote you after the Board meeting, to which yours of the 26th. Oct. is a reply.[1]

As I surmise the whole misunderstanding turns on our different constructions of the phrases we used. But technically no special arrangement went into effect until after my resignation; and I was in the employ of the university on full salary up to that date (Oct. 1).

Pray be assured that my "argumentations" are as friendly as frank; and if I seemed "strenuous," even a bit, this morning it was due to my surprise, so fully did I understand the thing in my sense.   Faithfully yours,   J. Mark Baldwin

TLS (WP, DLC).
   ¹ Wilson's letters are missing, but Baldwin summarizes them in his letter to Pyne.

E N C L O S U R E

James Mark Baldwin to Moses Taylor Pyne

Dear Mr. Pyne,   Princeton, N. J.   Dec. 22, '03.

At the suggestion of Pres. Wilson, I draw up the following statement presenting my understanding of the arrangement for my honorarium for lecturing in the University during the current term (Oct. 1 to the mid-year examinations.)

I sent to the board of Trustees a statement of the agreement made conversationally with Pres. Wilson, in the note which contained my resignation to take effect on Oct. 1st—as I had proposed and all along understood it: to wit, after my resignation I was to remain in the department and give my usual lectures, for the special sum of $1200., being my regular salary for the full half year—the period to begin Oct. 1 after my resignation had taken effect, as I had already been paid up to Oct. 1—or $1700. less the amount $500. paid to Prof. Hibben for taking one of my courses. In order to be clear on the point as to when the arrangement was to begin, I explained to Dr. Wilson that it required payment for a full half year, which by calendar would extend beyond February, but that I could not undertake the work for less as my time was so broken up by going every week to Baltimore. Also when I was notified by Dr. Wilson (see his letter of Oct. 24, of which I enclose copy),¹ I wrote my understanding that the "half-year" for which the compensation was to be $1200. was to begin Oct. 1. He replied in the note (copied herewith) under date Oct. 26, accepting my understanding as correct.

It now seems that he understands that the period of my term of work under this agreement was to begin July 1st. and not Oct. 1st., and that consequently $850.00 received by me before my resignation took effect is to be counted in the $1200. due me for this term. This is a complete surprise to me and I am not able to accept it as a settlement of the matter. After effecting the arrangement here I informed the Johns Hopkins authorities that

my salary for the summer months was paid, and so my honorarium there—half salary only—did not begin until Oct.[,] the date
when I understood my special honorarium was to begin at Princeton. If the amount received in the summer is to go for salary this
fall, then it leaves me no salary at all for the summer!—and
this I can not afford.

I have given at very great inconvenience, five hours a week
in Princeton, and it goes on until Feb. I intended to make it plain
that the amount named, $1200., was a very moderate compensa-
tion; and at any rate it was the least sum for which I could continue the lectures. I shall accordingly have to make this my final
statement of the matter to the University.

Yours very truly   (signed) J. Mark Baldwin.

Kindly presented by Pres. Wilson.

TCL (WP, DLC).
[1] This and the subsequently mentioned enclosure are missing.

From Nicholas Murray Butler

My dear Sir: New York, December 22, 1903

On behalf of the Administrative Board charged with the general oversight and control of the International Congress of Arts
and Science, to be held in connection with the Universal Exposition at St. Louis, beginning on September 19, 1904,[1] I have the
honor to tender you an earnest invitation to accept a designation
as one of the seven divisional speakers.

The enclosed pamphlet[2] contains an outline of the organization
of the International Congress showing the seven divisions, the
twenty-four departments, and the one hundred and twenty-nine
sections into which the field of knowledge has been classified
for the purposes of the Congress. The seven divisional addresses
will be delivered on the opening day of the Congress, September
19, and it is expected that each divisional address will deal with
the inner unity of the general subject-matter included under the
division.

The authorities of the Exposition have invited the most distinguished scholars of Europe to be present and participate in
this International Congress, and already acceptances have been
received from about one hundred and twenty-five of those to
whom invitations were extended. It may, therefore, be said with
truth that at this International Congress the presence of the most
distinguished company of scholars, European and American,

ever brought together, is assured. The cooperation of the various learned and scientific associations has been asked and given, and the Administrative Board look forward with confidence to a gathering which will represent all that is highest and best in the world's scholarship, and that will exercise a potent influence on the intellectual life of the American people.

It is proposed that the divisional addresses shall be from forty-five minutes to one hour in length. An honorarium sufficient to cover travelling expenses has been voted by the Exposition authorities, and will be paid to each of the speakers. Elaborate provisions for the entertainment of the guests are being made by the Exposition authorities, and there is every reason to expect a most agreeable, as well as a most profitable, gathering at St. Louis.

I have the honor to urge upon you the acceptance of our most cordial invitation to deliver the divisional address in Division B, Historical Science. An inspection of the enclosed detailed classification will give a more complete view of the field which your divisional address would be expected to include in its survey.

Asking for an early, and I trust favorable, reply,[3]

I am,

Respectfully yours,   Nicholas Murray Butler
President

TLS (WP, DLC).
[1] About the Congress, see WW to Hugo Münsterberg, March 18, 1903, n. 1, Vol. 14.
[2] It is missing.
[3] As N. M. Butler to WW, Jan. 2, 1904, discloses, Wilson accepted at once. His address, "The Variety and Unity of History," is printed at Sept. 20, 1904.

From James Mark Baldwin

Dear Dr. Wilson,   Princeton, N. J., Dec. 23, '03

Not knowing whether the note just received was written before or after our conversation today—I may say that I fully understand now that Mr. Duffield was quite in accord with your intention, and I shall tell him so.

As to the matter itself you now have my statement to Mr. Pyne. The more I think of it the more I feel sure you will use your good offices—and that with some sense of the humor of the situation— to have the matter adjusted: the more when I say that I declined to take earlier the Hopkins salary at the rate of $5000. a year in order not to discommode you here by so abrupt an action, in beginning there at once. I am on half salary there until March 1. If the chacque [cheque] for $850. was up to Oct. (as the receipt reads) then I am working here (on your interpretation), five hours a week, the whole term, for $350. I should never have agreed to this; and I think you will remember my explanation that the arrangement should contemplate the academic half-year (beginning Oct. 1) and not the calendar half-year.

All this simply as further personal explanation.

Yours very truly,   J. Mark Baldwin

TLS (WP, DLC).

From Moses Taylor Pyne

My dear Woodrow: Princeton, N. J.   December 24, 1903.

I have your favor of the 23rd inst. regarding claim of Prof. Baldwin in which he is without question mistaken. The understanding was, that as he was to give up part of his classes during the first half of the current academic year, his place being taken by Prof. Hibben, and to discontinue entirely at the end of the first half of the year, he was to receive half of his salary, less $500.00 which Hibben was to take for doing half of his work. This was very clear in my mind and in the minds of the Committee,[1] as well as in your mind, because we have only a certain amount of money out of which to pay the salary for the whole year, and as the salary for the second half of the year will have to be paid to his successor, there would be no money available for the salary for the second half of the year were Prof. Baldwin to be paid more than one-half a year's salary.

This idea was so strongly in the minds of the whole Committee and of the Board, that the resolution was possibly drawn a little carelessly. It reads as follows:

"On motion of President Wilson, $500. of the salary of Prof. Baldwin was ordered to be paid to Prof. Hibben for taking Prof. Baldwin's required classes for the first term. The balance of one half the year's salary to be paid to Prof. Baldwin, making a total of $1 200 to be paid him."

Of course, Prof. Baldwin having drawn part of his $1,200 salary, might consider that the resolution referred to the salary after the first of October, as it was approved by the Board about the 20th of October, but in this he is entirely wrong. The intention was to pay him one half a year's salary less the amount he paid Prof. Hibben for doing part of his work, and there is no money available for paying any more, nor is it intended any more shall be paid. The salary was supposed to refer to the whole year and not from the 1st of October to the 1st of February.

With best wishes for a Merry Christmas to you and yours, believe me,   Very sincerely yours,   M. Taylor Pyne

TLS (WP, DLC).

1 That is, the Committee on Finance of the Board of Trustees.

From James Mark Baldwin

Dear Dr. Wilson,   Princeton, N. J., Dec. 24, '04 [1903].

I have your letter and am very sorry that I can not accept your view. If you will be good enough to return the papers I sent I shall myself forward them to Mr. Pyne.

On your own showing the "half-year," beginning July 1st.—the regular quarterly payment day,—would only go up to Jan. 1, and there would be no salary for the rest of this term.

I shall therefore have to consider my lecturing & other work absolutely finished from this date, much as I regret it. If I could afford it I should waive the "contract" in the interests of cordiality; but I see no method of having an interpretation of our essential difference except by someone not ourselves.

Yours very truly,   J. Mark Baldwin

TLS (WP, DLC)

To James Mark Baldwin

REPLY (Copy)

My dear Professor Baldwin,   [Princeton, N. J., Dec. 25, 1903]

I have read your letter of yesterday with not a little pain and regret. I am afraid that you will some day see, when the heat of your present displeasure has passed off, that you have put yourself in a very false position.

I assure you, however, that I have no desire to put any obstacle in the way of your acting in the way you think most just and honorable, and I shall leave the decision as to when your work here is to close entirely with yourself. One of the courses you were conducting was brought to an end, I understand, some two or three weeks ago, almost at mid-term.

I am sorry that I cannot return to you the papers for Mr. Pyne which you sent me. I forwarded them to him yesterday. His address is No. 52 Wall St.

Very truly Yours,   Woodrow Wilson

WWTCLS typed on J. M. Baldwin to WW, Dec. 24, 1903.

From James Mark Baldwin, with Enclosure

Dear Dr. Wilson,   Princeton, N. J.   Dec. 26, '03.

Your note of yesterday is received. I enclose an additional word to Mr. Pyne which I mail direct to him this morning.

I have not terminated any course in the University. My work has in all respects gone regularly forward and my classes are expecting me to return and fulfil the regular schedule hours after the holidays. I am at a loss to know what you refer to.[1]

As you have seen no way to accept my direct assurance that you were violating the explicit terms of a contract as I understand it, nor to suggest any way by which we may not be brought into direct conflict, I am hereby informing you, since you refer to my leaving Princeton, that while before I considered it a local separation, I must now feel it to be, while your administration lasts, a moral parting of the ways.

Yours very truly,   J. Mark Baldwin

[1] I shall take it kindly if you will correct your informant in this matter of my conduct of my courses, and also any others who may have been similarly misinformed.

TLS (WP, DLC).

E N C L O S U R E

James Mark Baldwin to Moses Taylor Pyne

Dear Mr. Pyne: Princeton, N. J., Dec. 26, 03.

Pres. Wilson has forwarded to you his correspondence with me, and my letter to you, in the matter of the payment of my honorarium for the present term.

I wish to add to those papers the following statements.

I explicitly told Pres. Wilson that under the arrangement effected the period contemplated was to begin after my resignation took effect (Oct. 1) and explained to him in the original conversation before the Trustees met that the "half-year" meant the academic term.

I consider the proper way to deal with such a genuine misunderstanding would be to courteously adjust the matter on some basis of fair settlement: as for example the fact that for taking over one of my courses another Professor has received $500.; for the two courses left in my hands the same established rate might have been adopted as a way out of our unfortunate disagreement.

As however the matter has now gone to you, I beg to say that I am myself finding it impossible to consider the subject further. I am hereby absolutely severing my connection in every way with the University, forwarding this to Pres. Wilson by the same mail: and declining to meet any further classes. I find it impossible to become involved in a controversy which involves opposition to Pres. Wilson before his own board of Trustees, and which I fancy in the process of settlement would only lead to further complications. I shall however have to make the entire correspondence available to the whole body of trustees and faculty—depositing it with the Secretaries of those bodies, inasmuch as my abrupt change of plan as to lecturing will need so much justification.

Yours sincerely,   Signed J. Mark Baldwin

I need not add my dear Pyne that the whole business makes me heavy in spirit.

TCLS (WP, DLC).

To John Grier Hibben and Jenny Davidson Hibben

My dear Jack and Mrs. Hibben,   Princeton, 28 Dec., 1903

I can't tell you how touched and pleased I was when I opened the little package this morning and found that you have chosen Thomas A Kempis's *Imitation of Christ* as my birthday present. I am glad that you thought me worthy of such a gift, and my spirit one which its sweet counsels would reach and strengthen. It is a subtle evidence of your affection for me which will make me all the more anxious to *be* what you deem me.

Always   Your devoted friend,   [Woodrow Wilson]

AL (photostat in WC, NjP).

From George McLean Harper

[Princeton, N. J.]

My dear Mr. President: December 28, 1903

You may remember that I once told you I might ask for a year's leave of absence, to begin next June. I have decided not to apply for this at present, & lest my former remark should stand in the way of anyone else in the English department, I now write to let you know.

It is probable, however, that I shall desire to go abroad for a year, in June 1905. Literary work which I have planned[1] will require residence for some months in England, & no doubt my teaching will, by that time, need the freshening that nothing else can give.

I was to have had a year's leave of absence in 1900-01, but gave it up, in consequence of my transfer to the English department.[2] Since coming to Princeton as an instructor, in 1889, I have had no leave of absence, except that I was allowed, several times, by making arrangements for my classes, to sail for Europe a few days or weeks before the close of the college year, & on one occasion to return a month late in the fall.

If you cannot give me any assurance at present that this request will meet with your approval, I beg you at least to make a note of it & let it receive all possible consideration. To me more than to most men, I imagine, foreign study has been a principal means of intellectual development & is one of the most cherished joys of life. By June 1905, I shall have built up & given two Junior, one Senior, & one or two graduate courses in English, which will then need to be enriched by much reading & to a large extent rewritten.[3]

Very sincerely yours,   Geo. M. Harper

ALS (WP, DLC).

[1] Research that would culminate in his *William Wordsworth: His Life, Works and Influence* (2 vols., London and New York, 1916).

[2] Harper, Woodhull Professor of Romance Languages, was elected by the trustees to the Holmes Professorship of Belles Lettres and English Language and Literature in March 1900, For Wilson's comment on the transfer, see WW to EAW, March 8, 1900, Vol. 11.

[3] In fact, Harper did not receive his leave of absence until 1907.

Notes for an Address of Welcome

29 December, 1903

Words of Welcome—American Philosophical Association[1]

Sincere pleasure of welcome.

Princeton always known a place of sound religion (fortunately, even though too often by way of confusion with the Sem.) but, perhaps, not often enough as the natural theatre of sound thinking—as the basis, not of sincere and righteous conduct merely, but also of all valid knowledge

Our theory: an education of the *thinking and perceiving faculties* rather than of the more *utilitarian aptitudes.*

Our philosophers: Witherspoon—Edwards—McCosh. Great men rather than great constructive philosophers, so far as their work at Princeton was concerned, breeding an atmosphere of manliness.

We recognize Philosophy as the preeminent discipline in which all other disciplines find at once their authentication and their crown.

We, therefore, bid you feel at home at Princeton.

Reception at "Prospect."

WWhw MS. (WP, DLC).

¹ The American Philosophical Association met in Princeton, December 29-31, 1903. Wilson delivered his address of welcome on the afternoon of December 29, and he and Mrs. Wilson gave a reception at Prospect for the members in the evening of that same day. For brief accounts of this conference, see the *Proceedings of the Third Meeting of the American Philosophical Association, Princeton University, December 29, 30 and 31, 1903* . . . (Lancaster, Pa., 1904), pp. 176-78, and the *Princeton Alumni Weekly*, IV (Jan. 9, 1904), 219-20.

From Moses Taylor Pyne, with Enclosure

My dear Woodrow: Princeton, N. J.   December 29, 1903.

I have your favor and am amazed by Baldwin's position. I can say, as I wrote before, that there might be a slight ambiguity in the resolution as drawn up, but this is the answer that I have sent to him.   Very sincerely yours,   M. Taylor Pyne

TLS (WP, DLC).

ENCLOSURE

Moses Taylor Pyne to James Mark Baldwin

My dear Prof. Baldwin: New York, December 29, 1903.

I have your two favors of the 22nd and 26th insts. regarding the arrangement made by the Board of Trustees with respect to your salary, and am very sorry that you should have misunderstood their action. This is what the Finance Committee passed unanimously and recommended to the Board, and which the Board confirmed and passed, to wit:

For the first half of the current year, beginning August 1st, it being understood that you were to give one-half your time to Princeton and the other half to Johns Hopkins, you were to be paid the full half year's salary, just as if you had done the full amount of work for that period, less, however, $500.00 which was to be paid to Prof. Hibben for supplementing your work.

It was never supposed or intended by the Board or the Finance Committee that this half year's payment should begin October 1st, the half year always being counted from August 1st to January 31st.

I am extremely sorry that this misunderstanding should have occurred, but I know that this was the act and intention of the Board.   Yours very sincerely,   signed MTP

TCLI (WP, DLC).

From James Waddel Alexander

Dear Mr. President,   [New York, c. Dec. 29, 1903]

I take no interest in this further than to turn it over to you in whom I have absolute confidence.   James W. Alexander

ALS written on J. M. Baldwin to J. W. Alexander, Dec. 28, 1903, TLS and ALS (WP, DLC). Enc.: J. M. Baldwin to M. T. Pyne, Dec. 26, 1903, TCL (WP, DLC).

To James Waddel Alexander

                                                Princeton, N. J.
My dear Mr. Alexander: 31 December, 1903.

The only thing that it seems worth while to say about Professor Baldwin's statements to you is that they are essentially false and misleading.

The long and short of the story is that he tried to get three quarters' pay for a half year. He joined the University in the autumn of 1893, beginning work in September of that year. He received salary, however, from the 1st July, 1893, receiving on the 1st October of that year a full quarter's salary before he had entered upon the work of the University. If his resignation was to take effect this year, it would naturally have taken effect on the 1st July, 1903. He stipulated, however, that it should take effect on the 1st October and that he should receive a half year's salary for a half year's work, less $500 which was to be paid to some one for taking the heaviest and only burdensome course on his list.

It now seems that his expectation was to receive $850, a quarter's salary, from the 1st July to the 1st October; and then after the 1st October to receive a half year's salary less $500. This would have made his total salary for the academic half year beginning July 1st $2050, exclusive of the $500 paid for a substitute. Inclusive of that $500, it would have made his salary for the half year $2550.

I could never, of course, have assented to any such arrangement, and never did assent to it. The arrangement authorized at my suggestion by the Finance Committee and the Board is clearly recorded on the minutes both of the Committee and of the Board, and speaks for itself.

I make this statement not for Baldwin's sake, who has won only my contempt, but for your own. Thank you very much indeed for forwarding his letters to me. I appreciate every evidence of your confidence.   Always faithfully yours,   W. W

CCLI (WP, DLC).

A Desk Diary

[Jan. 1-Dec. 31, 1904]

National 1904 Diary with WWhw entries of engagements and appointments.

Bound desk diary (WP, DLC).

To Frank Thilly[1]

Princeton, N. J.

My dear Professor Thilly: 1 January, 1904.

We were all of us sincerely sorry that you could not be present at the very interesting meetings of the American Philosophical Association, which have just come to a close here; and we are particularly sorry that the cause should have been illness in your family.

It was my intention to write you this morning to ask if it would be possible and convenient for you to meet me in St. Louis some time next week for a short conference; but a sudden turn for the worse in a cold of long standing has put me in bed with something like the grippe, and I see very plainly that it would not be wise for me to take the journey I had planned so soon. It occurs to me to ask, therefore, whether it would be possible for you, as soon as the circumstances at your home seem to permit, to come to Princeton, at the expense of the University, of course, in order that I may see you?

You know, I suppose, that Professor James Mark Baldwin has recently resigned from our Faculty to accept a position at the Johns Hopkins University, and we are, of course, looking about for a successor. I find myself a good deal hampered by my lack of acquaintance with the chief philosophical students of the country, and I see no other way of remedying the lack than to go as frankly about making their acquaintance as possible. The government at Princeton is such that I have not the right to offer the place to any one independently of the action of the Board of Trustees. My power is one of nomination, and the Committee of the Board, which has charge of such matters, generally expects that more than one name will be presented to them, in order that their choice will be more than nominal if they should choose to make it so.[2] In these circumstances it seems to me imperative that I should throw myself upon the indulgence of the gentlemen I wish to see, and ask them to be generous to me in the matter of interviews. It is not possible by correspondence to explain with entire satisfaction all the circumstances and conditions of a place such as Professor Baldwin has held, and I feel that an interview, particularly an interview at Princeton, would do more than any number of letters could to enable you to judge whether, in case I would be able to offer you the chair, you would be willing to consider the call.

If you should be able to come and start before there will be time for another letter, pray telegraph me of the day of your coming.

I feel that I am asking a great deal of you, but I am sure that you will appreciate the quandary of a man suddenly thrown on his back.

    With much regard,
        Very sincerely yours, Woodrow Wilson

TLS (Wilson-Thilly Corr., NIC).
[1] Born Cincinnati, Aug. 18, 1865, A.B., University of Cincinnati, 1887; Ph.D., University of Heidelberg, 1891. Fellow and Instructor in Philosophy, Cornell University, 1891-93. Professor of Philosophy, University of Missouri, 1893-1904. Stuart Professor of Psychology, Princeton, 1904-1906. Professor of Philosophy, Cornell, 1906-26; Sage Professor of Philosophy, 1926-34; Dean of the College of Arts and Sciences, 1915-21. Author, editor, and translator of many works on philosophy. Died Dec. 28, 1934.
[2] In making this statement, Wilson was simply leaving the door open for consideration of other candidates. As subsequent documents will show, he made the offer to Thilly, and Thilly accepted it, well before the next meeting of the Curriculum Committee in March 1904. And when that meeting occurred, Wilson nominated only Thilly as Baldwin's successor.

From Wilson's Diary for 1904

Friday, January 1, 1904

Spent the day in bed, my cold of three weeks' standing having taken a new hold upon me, with neuralgia,—something new for me

Read Weyman's *Long Night*,[1] a good story for a dreary day in bed.

Letter to Prof. Frank Thilly, Columbia, Mo., written (dictated) and despatched, inviting him to come to see me here,—*in re* vacancy in philosophical dept.

Hw entry in bound diary entitled *The Standard Diary 1904* (WP, DLC).
[1] Stanley John Weyman, *The Long Night* (London and New York, 1903).

Saturday, January 2, 1904

Rose after breakfast and came down stairs, feeling a good deal
better, tho. still with some neuralgia.

Long interview with Mr. H. W. Green about Baldwin's behaviour
in regard to his salary. He quite agreed that B's conduct in the
matter had been extraordinary and altogether inexcusable.

Took lunch in the study

After lunch Hibben came in, just back fr. spending New Year's
in Elizabeth, for a long comfortable talk about the meeting of
the Philosophical Ass'n, candidates for the vacancy, &c.

Rest of afternoon, business, bills, &c.

Evening, reading Morley's *Life of Mr. Gladstone*[1] and playing
games with the children and Sister A[nnie].

[1] John Morley, *The Life of William Ewart Gladstone* (3 vols., London and New
York, 1903).

From Nicholas Murray Butler

My dear President Wilson: New York   January 2, 1904

On returning from the West I have your kind letter of the 26th,
and am very much gratified to learn that you accept our invitation to deliver the address in Division B, Historical Science, in
the International Congress of Arts and Science at St. Louis in
September next.

The other divisional speakers are the following:

A—Normative Science—Prof. Royce of Harvard

C—Physical Science—Alexander Agassiz of Newport

D—Mental Science—Pres. Stanley Hall of Clark University

E—Utilitarian Sciences—Pres. Jordan of Stanford University

F—Social Regulation—Justice Oliver Wendell Holmes of the
U. S. Supreme Court

G—Social Culture—Dr. W. T. Harris, U. S. Commissioner of
Education

Faithfully yours,   Nicholas Murray Butler

TLS (WP, DLC).

From Wilson's Diary for 1904

Sunday, January 3, 1904

Did not go to church, fearing the effect of the snow and the wind (zero last night) on my nose and throat

Read Morley's Gladstone

West came in at noon for a little chat, and after him Hibben and Dulles. Mrs. Hibben did not get back (from the opera in N.Y.) till after 10 last night and had kept her bed this morning, not coming out at all

Ellen, Margaret, and Nellie went to church,—Madge to the service at St. Paul's.

Fraülein Clara Bohm came in to dinner,—Margaret went over to the Hibbens' to dine

Afternoon: worked a little while at the rearrangement of my books; talked with Florence Hoyt and Ellen in the sitting room; read a few chapters of Thomas A'Kempis.

Mrs. Hibben came in at about half past five, Jack at a little after six and stayed until about twenty-five minutes of seven, when they went off to take tea with West.

Evening: talk with sister A. about her business affairs and plans, and *Gladstone* till bedtime, with another bit of A'Kempis to put a good taste in my mouth.

Monday, January 4, 1904

Morning: Letters, errands, odds and ends of business. Florence Hoyt left for Balto. on the 8.24 A.M. train.

After lunch, a long interview with Ormond about the vacancy in Psychology. He had taken a strong fancy to Moore of Chicago[1] and had to be talked to at great length to be restored to a view of the whole field. Said he had written to Howison of California[2] to inquire more particularly about Stratton[3]

Went down to power house to see why steam heat had been turned off. To make new connexions.

From 4.25 to 5.30 at the Hibbens, where I saw both Jack and Mrs. Hibben.

Evening: meeting, in the study (because of my cold) of Committee on Course of Study, to consider groups (*curricula*) of study.

Adopted (provisionally) Group in Classics,—the third adopted.

Little Gladstone, no A Kempis.

[1] Addison Webster Moore, Associate Professor of Philosophy at the University of Chicago.

From James Waddel Alexander

Dear Dr. Wilson,   [New York]   Jan 4, 1904.

Thank you for the letter about Baldwin. It wasn't necessary. If Psychology produces such effects, then no Psychology for me. A good riddance to bad rubbish, even concealed under an Oxford cap.[1] I am afraid Mark (Heaven save the mark!) is disappointed that he didn't ruin Princeton by deserting it while your back was turned. From your analysis of his salary grab, it would seem that he even makes a poor trade-mark. Did he want to be our President? If so, he was wide of the mark. It's Wilson, that is all. There is one thing certain, we need no *re*-Mark.

Yours ever   James W Alexander

ALS (WP, DLC).
1 In 1900, Baldwin had received the first honorary degree in science—the D.Sc.—ever conferred by Oxford University.

From Wilson's Diary for 1904

Tuesday, January 5, 1904

Intensely cold,—thermometer said to have registered this morning ten degrees below zero.

Margaret set off for college on the 8.24 A.M. train, Ellen going to the station with her and coming back nearly frozen.

Mr. Wightman[1] confined to Infirmary with weeping cold. Wrote my own letters. Accepted invitation to speak at mass meeting in Washington, Jan'y 12, on international arbitration. To lunch that day w. Mr. Gilman.[2]

Went on an errand to the bank about noon, and found the clear, frosty air delightful.

After lunch, by the study fire, Ellen read me some of the little essays Jessie has written, as exercises, for Stockton, and I found them full of true unstrained effects and a real literary flavour. Was especially struck by translations from Heine and Vergil (the Aeneid) and a criticism, (or, rather, appreciation) of *Pride and Prejudice*, to which she is specially attached

At 4.30 found Jack gone to N.Y. and Mrs. Hibben excused because of a very painful trouble w. her teeth.

Evening: Ellen and I had long talk beside study fire on means
of giving me sufficient relaxation and mental stimulus amidst
my miscellaneous and distracting administrative duties! Jack
came in for a smoke and talk wh. I greatly enjoyed.

[1] McQueen Salley Wightman '04, Wilson's part-time student secretary.
[2] For some unknown reason, Wilson did not fulfill this engagement.

Wednesday, January 6, 1904

Cold somewhat moderated, Wightman back at his work.
A day of routine and odds and ends
Went to bed at 8.30 w. a distressing headache

Thursday, January 7, 1904

At breakfast received the shocking news of the death of Ruth
Cleveland fr. diphtheria. Wrote a note of heartfelt sympathy to
Mr. Cleveland and myself carried it to the house, the butler
receiving it thr. a bare crack in the door. Until yesterday morning the child was supposed to have only a case of tonsilitis, and
only yesterday did it appear, fr. the examination of a "culture"
fr. the throat, that it was diphtheria. She died about 3 this
morning, the dreadful disease attacking the heart, as usual.
This distressing event clouded our spirits for the whole day. At
5 Ellen and I went over and sat with the Hibbens for an hour
or more, and our talk was almost wholly of the loss, its incidents, its effects on Mrs. Cleveland. Almost the only diversion
fr. this sad vein came fr. reading a most engaging letter fr.
Professor Thilly, of the University of Missouri,—whom we
have been considering for the Baldwin vacancy,—showing him
to be a man after our own hearts. The letter was to Creighton[1]
and sent on by him to Hibben.
In the evening finished the first volume of the interminable
Gladstone, and read a bit of A'Kempis.

[1] James Edwin Creighton, Sage Professor of Logic and Metaphysics at Cornell
University.

Friday, January 8, 1904

A drear, chill morning, with a fine drizzle of snow,—rendered
memorably drear by Ruth Cleveland's funeral. Only Mr. Cleveland went to the grave, attended by Dr. Bryant[1] and by Finley,
West, H. van Dyke, and Hibben as pall bearers. Miss Finley,[2]

Mrs. Hibben, Mrs. McClenahan,[3] Mrs. Fine, Fisher[4] and Ned.
Howe[5] had filled the grave, and surrounded it with green
things and flowers—working in the numbing cold since 9
o'clock (the body arrived about 10.45)—and the flowers tum-
bled in upon the casket, when it was lowered, in beautiful profusion. Mr. Bartlett[6] conducted the ceremony.

Called at the Hibbens' at 5 and found them reacting fr. the
strain and inclined to return to natural moods and topics.

Evening: Conference w. Daniels about History-Economics Group
for the Committee on the Course of Study next Monday evening, fr. wh. I shall be obliged to be absent.[7]

[1] Joseph Decatur Bryant, M.D., of New York, long-time friend of Grover
Cleveland.
[2] Anna J. Finley, a sister of John Huston Finley who taught at Miss Fine's
School.
[3] Bessie Lee (Mrs. Howard) McClenahan, wife of the Assistant Professor of
Physics.
[4] Probably Frederick Fisher, employed by the university as a "mechanician."
[5] Edward Howe, President of the Princeton Bank.
[6] The Rev. Maitland Vance Bartlett, Stated Supply of the First Presbyterian
Church of Princeton.
[7] For the reason, see Wilson's diary entry for Jan. 11, 1904.

Saturday, January 9, 1904

New secretary this morning, J[ulian]. B[onar]. Beaty, '06—Wightman having gone to New York for Sunday, to be with his
brother. B. a likeable sort of fellow, but weak in spelling.

Day of routine.

Called at the Hibbens' at 5 and found them very much more
nearly restored to their usual mood and tone

Sunday, January 10, 1904

Paul van Dyke preached in the chapel on the survival of faith
after the distruction of illusions. Did not *quite* hit the attention
of the men, tho. it was, on the whole, an excellent sermon

A note fr. Miss Ricketts informed us that she had a sore throat
and thought it more prudent that she sh. not see the Hibbens
and us. She is nervous about the fact that the doctor has been
coming to the house after seeing a case of diphtheria.

Ellen and I called at the Hibbens, as usual, at 4, and at 5 walked
part of the way with them to the Clevelands'—where Mrs. H.
was going for the first time since the funeral,—the doctor having given his sanction.

Monday, January 11, 1904

Lecture, 10.30, on "Contracts."[1] Momo Pyne in (Baldwin)

At one Mrs. [Crawford Howell] Toy, of Cambridge, came, to spend the day and evening with us,—as alert and full of (half artful) charm as ever. Always draws me on to talk at my best

From 3.30–5 took Mrs. Toy about to see Princeton and the university buildings. I think the power plant, tucked away under its terrace, struck her more than anything else.

At dinner, Mrs. Toy, Mrs. Hibben, Jack, and Dr. Littmann,[2] besides sister, Madge, and ourselves. A very bright, interesting circle, our pleasure much added to by songs, chiefly Scottish, very naturally and sweetly sung by Mrs. Toy, after dinner, just before we broke up.

[1] In his course, Outlines of Jurisprudence.
[2] Richard Ludwig Enno Littmann, Lecturer on Semitic Philology at Princeton.

Tuesday, January 12, 1904

Mrs. Toy off at 9.05 A.M., Ellen accompanying her to Rwy station.

Day of routine. Kept in my office till quarter of 5 on business that might have been finished before 3 if academic men were only prompt in movement and brief in statement!

Five to 6.35 at the Hibbens'.

From Winthrop More Daniels, with Enclosure

My dear Wilson: Princeton, N. J.   Jan. 12, 1904.

Enclosed I send a tabulated diagram of the plans (proposed and adopted) in the general group of *History and Economics*. We met in the Classical Seminar where the lights go out at 10 p.m: and so had time to consider only the History and Economics group. The History and Politics group comes up at the next meeting. I will call and explain the various concessions that had to be made to secure the Committee's approval of the plan.

Yours very truly,   W. M. Daniels.

ALS (WP, DLC).

ENCLOSURE

A Plan for a History and Economics Curriculum

General Group: History and Economics.

	Plan Proposed.			*Plan Adopted*	
	Soph. Year.			*Soph. Year*	
6.	Latin and Greek	6	6	Latin. Greek. Math (All three or any two at student's option)	6
2	German or French	2	2	German or French	2
3	History/Logic	3	3	History/Logic	3
2	English	2	2	English	2
3	Physics	3	3	Physics	3
16		16	16		16
	Junior Year			*Junior Year.*	
3	Economics	3	3	Economics	3
4	History	4	6	History and Politics	6
4	Politics	4			
2	Hist. Phil.	2	3	Hist. of Phil.	3
2	An Elective	2	3(4)	Electives (1 three-hour or 2 two-hour courses)	3(4)
15		15	15 *or* 16		16 *or* 15
	Senior Year			*Senior Year*	
6	Economics	6	6	Economics	6
6	History	6	3	History *or* Politics	3
2	Hist Phil	2	6	Any 2 three-hour electives	6
14		14	15		15

Hw memorandum (WP, DLC).

To Alexander Van Rensselaer

[Princeton, N. J.]

My dear Mr. Van Rensselaer: 13 Jan'y, '04

It is particularly hard, as I need hardly tell you, to ask money of a friend, and especially of a generous friend who will find a refusal of the request,—if a refusal should be necessary,—both difficult and distasteful; but my responsibilities and the needs of the University give me no choice in the matter, and I must throw myself on your indulgence.

It seems quite certain that we shall at the end of the year have to face a deficit, on the academic side of the budget, of between $6,000 and $10,000,—not because our resources have decreased, but because our necessary expenses and permanent obligations have increased. Just because the deficit seems to be attributable to permanent and not to temporary causes it seems unwise to resort to our friends and backers for the mere sum of the deficit. We ought to make an effort, and ought to see to it that the effort is successful, to obtain a sum by subscription which will, so to say, capitalize the deficit.[*1] Several men,—Robert Garrett of Baltimore, for example, and Mr. Stephen Palmer,—who have themselves offered to become subscribers, have suggested that we try to raise a subscription list of $100,000 a year for three years, which would enable us to spend $10,000 of the amount subscribed each year and at the end of the three years have enough invested to yield $10,000. This would tide us over the present period of financial depression and would set our treasury on a sound footing again.

The gentlemen I have named, and four or five others, have agreed to give $5,000 apiece, on the understanding that they shall be at liberty to withdraw after any one of the three payments. Pyne and Cuyler and I have been working on a scheme, which was discussed at the last meeting of the Finance Committee and mentioned, you will perhaps remember, at the last meeting of the Board last month, and it has seemed best, if possible, to obtain $5,000 subscriptions, so as to make the number of subscribers as small as may be, and the general solicitation of money as limited as possible; but the needs of the University are too pressing and too immediate to permit us to make that an essential feature of the plan. We shall be glad to accept subscriptions in any amount, even at the expense of a general advertisement of our deficit.[*]

I know that I need never press this matter upon you in accents of a beggar, much as I am concerned to have it go through to a successful issue. You hold the interests of the University as much at heart as I do, and I am sure that you will help if it is possible. I can only beg that you will pardon the official beggar of the University for thus attacking you.

With warmest regards to Mrs. Van Rensselaer and all the members of your household,
        Always,
                Cordially and Faithfully yours   Woodrow Wilson.

Transcript of WWshLS (WP, DLC).
¹ See WW to J. L. Cadwalader, Jan. 14, 1904.

To James Hay Reed   (*Personal*)

My Dear Judge Reed: [Princeton, N. J., c. Jan. 13, 1904]

I hate above all things to write a begging letter to a generous man like you, who will feel the force of it more than most men would; but in the present circumstances of the University I seem to have no choice in the matter.

It is needless to tell you that this is not a time propitious for large gifts by way of an endowment. It has seemed to all of us that it would be folly to press just now for the endowments we stand in such sore need of. And yet we must have money. We are looking forward to having a deficit in our budget at the end of the year of quite $10,000; and that not because of extraordinary expenses falling upon us this year which are not likely to fall upon another year so much as because of the inevitable and normal growth of expenditure with the growth of the University. We must meet this expenditure and must look forward to meeting it again and again.

It seems to us unwise to simply collect the actual sum needed, and spend it, with the practical certainty that we shall have to ask for a like sum next year and the year after, until the present blight is off the money market. We have therefore resolved to raise the sum and capitalize it too, by soliciting subscriptions of $5,000 a year for three years, and getting enough subscribers to make the total subscription $100,000.00. That would enable us to invest a sum of $90,000.00 a year, and so at the end of three years have enough invested to yield $10,000.

We do not feel like asking anyone to bind himself upon so large a scale for the whole period of three years: We are asking only that we be promised the sum each year upon the understanding that after any one of the payments the subscriber, if he finds it necessary, may withdraw.

We may have to take smaller sums than $5,000, but several men have offered us that sum, and we should like, if possible, to limit the subscription to a small circle of our immediate

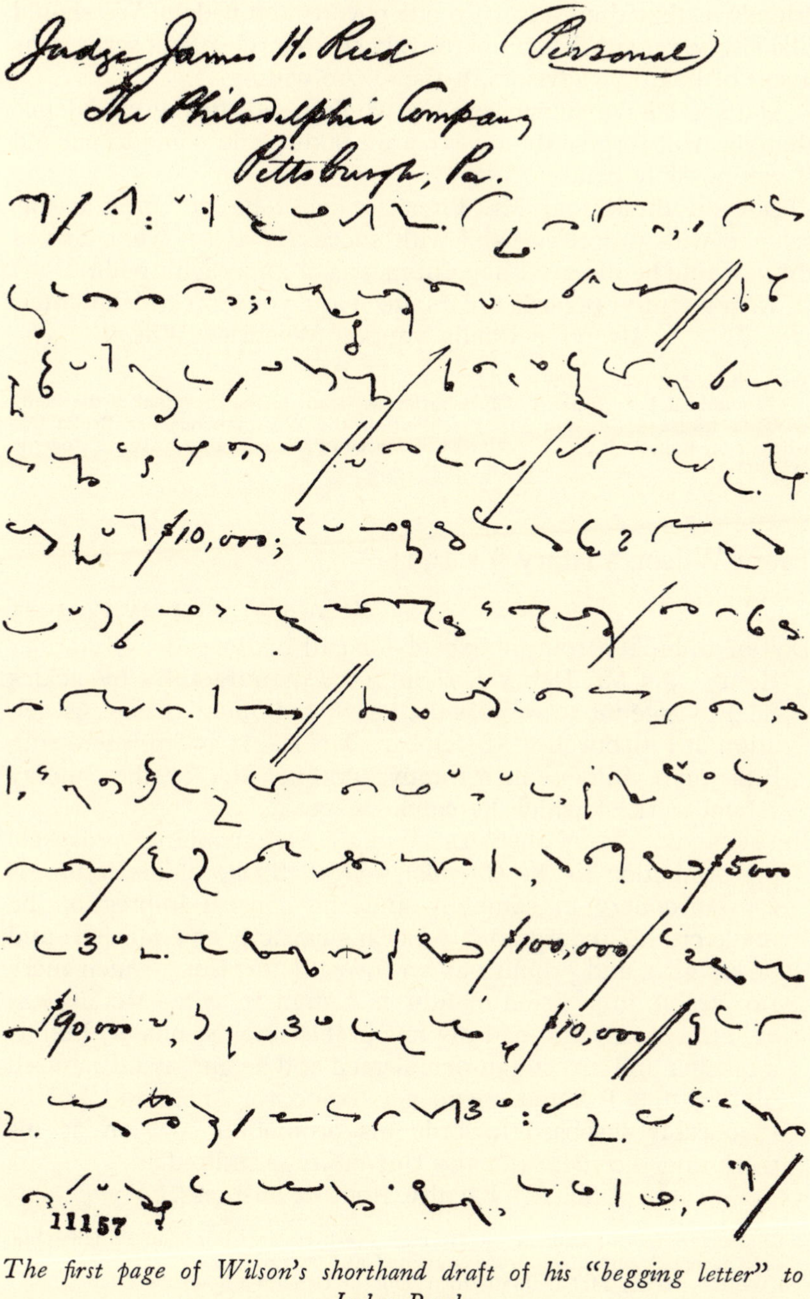

Judge James H. Reid   (Personal)
    The Philadelphia Company
        Pittsburgh, Pa.

[shorthand text]

$10,000;

$500

$100,000

$90,000

$10,000

11157

The first page of Wilson's shorthand draft of his "begging letter" to Judge Reed.

friends, rather than advertise our poverty too widely. We should like also to regard the comparatively small circle of subscribers as a sort of board of advisors, if they were willing.

You see I have shown you my whole hand, in the confidence that you will forgive the liberty I am taking and come to our aid if you possibly can.

Do you think that Mr. Pitcairn[1] could be drawn into this scheme with propriety (and with success)? If so, what do you think would be the most hopeful means of approaching him?

With warmest regards to Mrs. Reed and your son and daughter,
Always cordially yours,   Woodrow Wilson

Transcript of WWshLS (WP, DLC).
[1] Probably Robert Pitcairn of Pittsburgh, assistant to the President of the Pennsylvania Railroad Co. and Vice-President of the Westinghouse Air Brake Co., whose son, Robert, Jr., had received the degree of Civil Engineer from Princeton in 1898.

From Wilson's Diary for 1904

Wednesday, January 13, 1904

Day of unbroken routine except for call of Rev. Mr. Alexander Henry[1] and Mr. Henry J. Heinz (the manufacturer of pickles &c.) to urge me to address the Pa. State Sunday School Association at Pittsburgh next October.[2] Mr. Heinz a [an] interesting little man, full of an attractive enthusiasm for the Sunday school work of which he came to speak.

Interview w. McCay about Dr. Wm. H. McLauchlan's[3] prospects for promotion in the Chemistry Dept. Spoke of his fondness for buffoonery in company and the general impression he made on the undergraduates; of his capacity as a teacher; and of his gifts and promise as an investigator. Got a much more favourable impression of him as a man fr. what McCay was able to tell me, and had my favourable impressions of him as a teacher and investigator confirmed and heightened. Promised McCay that I would *try* to get $1200 for McL. and w'd be favourably disposed towards his promotion so soon as his work and the means of the University permitted.[4]

5 P.M. School of Science Faculty. Routine business.

[1] Princeton 1870, pastor of the Hermon Presbyterian Church of Philadelphia.
[2] He accepted, and his address is printed at Oct. 13, 1904.
[3] William Henry McLauchlan, Instructor in General Chemistry.
[4] McLauchlan was not promoted and left Princeton in 1905.

From Theodore Roosevelt

My dear Mr. Wilson: [Washington] January 13, 1904

If the chance comes and I can appoint Captain Landon,[1] subject to the claims of some others who have been a long time on the list, it will give me real pleasure to do so.[2]

With regard,   Sincerely yours,   Theodore Roosevelt

TLS (Letterpress Books, T. Roosevelt Papers, DLC).

[1] Francis Griswold Landon, Princeton 1881, captain in the Seventh Regiment, New York National Guard, and Republican member of the New York Assembly, 1901-1903.

[2] Wilson's letter in support of Landon is missing. However, President Roosevelt appointed him Third Secretary of the Embassy in Berlin in 1905. He served as Second Secretary of the Embassy in Vienna, 1905-1907, and was afterward active in the Republican party in New York State.

To John Lambert Cadwalader

My dear Mr. Cadwalader: [Princeton, N. J.] 14 Jan'y, '04

It is much harder to beg money of friends,—and particularly generous friends, oddly enough, than of a stranger, but my duty, unhappily, lies that way, and I am not at liberty to shirk it.

Possibly you will remember a statement which I made to the Board at its last meeting about the expected deficit in the budget at the end of the year and the plan that was being considered to meet it. It will amount to between \$6,000 and \$10,000, and it is evidently not a mere temporary deficiency due to extraordinary expenses or special obligations falling upon us this year but a permanent measure of expenditure, due to increasing demands of maintenance and instruction. It seems unwise, therefore, simply to ask for the sum of the deficit itself by way of subscription. We ought, if possible, to obtain a sum by subscription which will, so to say, capitalize the deficit.

(Copy letter to Mr. Van R. * to *)

I know that you will help us in this case, as in all others, if you can, and that you will not feel that any apology on my part, for bringing it to you, is necessary; at the same time I want to express to you the reluctance I feel to make such demands upon friends who are already devoting so much valuable effort to the service of the University. I must give myself the pleasure, too, of expressing the deep gratification we all feel that we can resort to you for aid and counsel and our deep sense of obligation we are already under to you.

As always

Cordially and faithfully yours   Woodrow Wilson.

Transcript of WWshLS (WP, DLC).

To James Henry Lockhart[1]

My dear Mr. Lockhart: [Princeton, N. J.]   14 Jan. '04

Since our conversation at the Duquesne Club[2] and my delightful glimpse of you at the Association of the Western Clubs[3] I feel that I can speak to you of the many matters of the University with the utmost frankness and with perfect assurance of your sympathy and indulgence. I will not apologize, therefore, for bringing to your attention our plan for meeting the immediate needs of the University, or for asking you to give it your most careful consideration.

The present state of the money market and the uneasiness which must always precede a presidential campaign have made us feel that it would not be wise to press just now our larger plans for the endowment of the University,—the plans which I discussed with you in our conversation at the Duquesne Club. But we cannot sit still and do nothing because, while the resources of the University are not increasing its necessary expenditures are increasing very rapidly with the steady increase of students and no sort of economy can stretch our means to meet the demands upon the treasury.

There will be, this year, a deficit of from $6,000 to $10,000, and it seems clearly unwise to seek to meet this by mere temporary expedients by asking our friends from year to year merely for the sum we happen then to lack. We ought, if possible,—and it ought certainly to be possible,—to obtain by subscription a sum which will, so to say, capitalize the deficit. The plan proposed for this purpose has been suggested to us by several men independently,—men who have themselves offered to become subscribers. They have suggested that we raise a subscription list of $100,000 a year for three years, which would enable us to spend $10,000 of the amount subscribed each year and at the end of the three years have enough invested ($270,000) to yield us an income of $10,000. This would tide us over the present period of financial depression and would set our treasury on a sound footing again.

The gentlemen named,—the list already includes some six names,—have agreed to give $5,000 apiece each year for three years, on the understanding, which would of course extend to all subscribers, that they shall be at liberty to withdraw, if they find it necessary, after any one of the three payments. Mr. Pyne, Mr. Cuyler, and I have taken up the scheme in earnest. It has been discussed in the Finance Committee of the Board and announced to the Board itself as our plan for the winter.

It has seemed best to obtain, if possible, chiefly $5,000 sub-scriptions, so as to make the number of subscribers as small as may be, and would avoid any general solicitation of money; but the needs of the University are too great and too pressing to make us choosers in such a matter, and we shall be glad to ac-cept subscriptions in any amount, even at the expense of a gen-eral advertisement of our deficit.

I know that you will not feel that I am taking an unwarranted liberty in laying this matter before you, and in asking that you give it your most serious consideration, because I know that I can depend upon you to receive it in the same spirit of frankness and of devotion to the interests of the University in which it is written. Princeton really needs the active assistance of her friends now as she has seldom needed it, in order to keep her from actually falling short of the pledges she has given the country of service and efficiency.

With warm regard

Cordially yours   Woodrow Wilson

Transcript of WWshLS (WP, DLC).
[1] Princeton 1887, he was associated with his father, Charles Lockhart, a pioneer in the oil industry and an early partner of John D. Rockefeller, in the management of his widespread business interests in the Pittsburgh area.
[2] James Hay Reed had given a reception for Wilson at the Duquesne Club in Pittsburgh when Wilson addressed the Carnegie Institute on November 5, 1903.
[3] About this affair, see the news reports printed at May 3, 1903, Vol. 14.

To John Heman Converse[1]

My dear Mr. Converse: [Princeton, N. J.]   14 Jan'y, '04

I am painfully conscious of the liberty I am taking in laying before you the financial needs of the University and asking you if you would be willing to aid us; but to do such things is, un-happily, one of the chief duties of a college president and must be performed with such hardihood as he can command. I know that you will not hear in what I write the tones of a mere beggar but will take it for granted that I am laying before you needs which cannot be postponed or neglected.

For the first time in a great many years we shall, at the end of the present academic year, be face to face with a deficit in the University budget,—not because the resources of the University have decreased but because the cost of maintenance and instruc-tion has greatly increased by reason of the growth in the num-ber of students and in the number of buildings to be maintained and an inevitable addition to our administrative force without any corresponding increase of endowment. This deficit will amount to between $6,000 and $10,000; and just because it is likely, with our present resources, to be not temporary but the measure of the permanent expenditures, we feel that it would not be wise to resort to mere makeshifts and ask for subscriptions to cover the mere sum of the deficiency itself. It seems the evident course of prudence to make a concerted effort to capitalize the deficit.

At the suggestion of several outside friends, who have themselves offered to subscribe, we have determined to seek a subscription list of $100,000 a year for three years; which would enable us to spend $10,000 of the amount subscribed each year and at the end of the three years have enough invested ($270,-000) to yield us an income of $10,000. This would tide us over the present period of financial depression,—which promises to last, I dare say, to a time well beyond the presidential election,— and would set our treasury on a sound footing again.

The friends of whom I have spoken,—the list already contains some six or eight names,—have agreed to give $5,000 apiece every year for three years, on an understanding, which would, of course, be extended to all subscribers, that they shall be at liberty, should they find it necessary, to withdraw after any one of the three payments. Mr. Pyne, Mr. Cuyler, and I, on behalf of the Finance Committee of the Board of Trustees, have taken up the scheme in earnest and are now trying to make the list of subscribers as long as possible.

Rather than make the number of the subscribers very large and resort to any general solicitation of money, we have hoped to obtain chiefly $5,000 subscriptions; but the needs of the University are too great and too pressing to make us choosers in such matters, and we shall, of course, be glad to accept subscriptions in any amount, even at the expense of a general advertisement of our deficit.

I know that I may bring this matter to your attention with the utmost frankness in the confidence that you will recognize my part in it as the performance of a clear public duty, and I am equally sure that whether you can help us or not you will act upon it as a matter of public concern. It seems the only prudent and businesslike method of making good the shortage in the resources of the University.

Pray remember me with the warmest regard to all the members of your household, and believe me,

Most respectfully and cordially yours

Woodrow Wilson.

Transcript of WWshLS (WP, DLC).

[1] Partner in Burnham, Williams & Co., locomotive manufacturers of Philadelphia, prominent Presbyterian layman, philanthropist, and long-time trustee of Princeton Theological Seminary and of his alma mater, the University of Vermont.

From Wilson's Diary for 1904

Thursday, January 14, 1904

Spent day in N.Y ,–forenoon doing errands. Lunched Café Savarin.

2.30 Meeting of Committee on Finance, wh. unanimously and cordially endorsed my action in the matter of Baldwin's salary. Cuyler mentioned several gratifying small gifts to the University.

Drank tea at 5 with Miss Cuyler[1]–where I was to spend the night.

Evening, delightful dinner at Isham's,[2]–nearly 40 men,–among the rest Botsford,[3] whom most of us had not seen since graduation; and "Buck" Blackwell,[4] now quite a swell among English electricians

[1] Eleanor De Graff Cuyler, who lived with her brother at 214 Madison Avenue.
[2] Another of the famous Isham dinners for members of the Class of 1879, about which see WW to EAW, May 6, 1886, n. 1, Vol. 5.
[3] Alfred Clark Botsford, cattle rancher in Colorado.
[4] Robert Winthrop Blackwell, an expert in electric railways and trolley lines, had taken up permanent residence in London in 1890 and was founder and president of the Robert W. Blackwell Co., manufacturers, engineers, and contractors.

Friday, January 15, 1904

Got back fr. New York a little after eleven, and plunged into business, from which I was not released till a quarter before 5.

At 5 went to the Hibbens' for a chat.

At 8.15 in the evening read my paper on Sir Henry Maine, ("A Lawyer with A Style")[1] to the "Graduate Club["], in Dodge Hall. Just before I started Dr Frissell, of Hampden [Hampton] Institute[2] came in to call on me. Sorry to miss a chat with him. His special errand in Princeton was to see Mr. Cleveland.

[1] It is printed at Feb. 25, 1898, Vol. 10.
[2] Hollis Burke Frissell, Principal of Hampton Institute in Virginia and a leader in the movement to improve education in the South for both Negroes and whites.

Henry Green Duffield to James Mark Baldwin

Dear Sir: Princeton, N. J., Jan. 15, 1904.

At a meeting of the Finance Committee of the Board of Trustees of Princeton University held on the 14th inst., the Chairman stated that he had received a communicaton from you in which you claimed that the resolution passed by the Board in October relative to the amount of salary to be paid you for your services for the half year had not been complied with by the Treasurer, and that there was a misunderstanding between yourself and the President as to the amount due.

The following motion was carried:

> "Moved that the Secretary inform Prof. Baldwin that the Finance Committee of the Board of Trustees of Princeton University at a meeting held Jan. 14th, 1904, after full discussion of all papers have unanimously decided that his claims cannot be admitted."

Very respectfully,   (signed) H. G. Duffield, Secretary.

TCL (WP, DLC).

To Henry Hughart Laughlin[1]

My dear Mr. Laughlin: [Princeton, N. J., c. Jan. 16, 1904]

I venture to write to you, I need hardly say with a great deal of hesitation, about a matter concerning your father which the Board of Trustees of the University were obliged, under their rules, to take cognizance of at their last meeting, on the 10th of December.

The by-laws of the Board provide that whenever any member of the Board is absent for four consecutive meetings his seat shall be regarded as vacant, and your father's case has fallen under this rule. Of course the Board did not act in the matter. They felt too deep a regard for your father and too sincere a consideration for you all; and their wish is to act in every way as Mrs. Laughlin would prefer. But they felt bound not to neglect the matter, especially in the case of an alumni trustee, and therefore requested me to write to you to ask what Mrs. Laughlin's wish, what the wish of the family, was in the circumstances. It seems to the Board particularly inadvisable to reduce by their own failure to act the all too small direct representation of the alumni.

I wish that I could convey to you some notion of the real feeling of sympathy and of loss on the part of the Board; and I hope that you will express to Mrs. Laughlin not only my own strong personal feeling in the matter but also the equally warm feeling of the entire governing body of the University.[2]

Sincerely and cordially yours,   Woodrow Wilson.

Transcript of WWshLS (WP, DLC).
[1] A.B., Princeton, 1900; E.E., 1902, and son of James Laughlin, Jr.
[2] See J. Laughlin, Jr., to WW, Feb. 15, 1904, for his letter of resignation.

To John Kissig Cowen

My dear Mr. Cowen: [Princeton, N. J.]   16 Jan'y, '04

The enclosed resolutions, passed by the Board of Trustees at its last meeting do not fully explain themselves. It was, I take it, because the full meaning of the Board could scarcely be expressed in the formal resolutions that I was directed to write to you in the matter.

I need hardly assure you of the cordial feeling towards you personally which was on all hands expressed in connection with the passage of the resolutions. It was evident that the Board as a whole felt for you the strongest sentiments of friendship and admiration and that those were the feelings which dictated a suspension of the by-law quoted. At the same time there was a general conviction that the rule repeated a just and necessary policy in the administration of the University, whose vitality and success are so intimately dependent upon the active and continuous exertion of the several members of its board of Trustees,—their likely [lively] interest, based upon a direct knowledge of its needs and opportunities,—and it was the unanimous opinion that we could not omit to call your attention to the question of your attendance and active cooperation in the business of the University.

I do not know how otherwise to approach the subject except with the utmost frankness; and I feel sure that that is the method which you will yourself most appreciate. I have thought that you would probably wish to determine in view of all the circumstances whether or not it is wisest for you to continue to try to carry this burden of business in connection with all the other engagements which press upon you. The Board would wish me to express in the warmest possible manner their appreciation of the service you have rendered the University in the midst of other cares, and also the feeling they attach to having so distinguished a name as yours upon the roll of the Board; but they would feel great and constant uneasiness at being obliged to harass you with arguments for your attendance upon their meetings.

I hope that you will understand that I am giving you the best evidence at my command of my confidence in your fond feeling for the University by thus laying a delicate matter before you without excuse or reservation.[1]

Believe me, with sincerest regard

Faithfully yours   Woodrow Wilson

Transcript of WWshLS (WP, DLC).

[1] Cowen's reply, if he ever wrote one, is missing. His membership on the Board of Trustees was terminated by his death on April 26, 1904.

From Wilson's Diary for 1904

Saturday, January 16, 1904

Principal interest of the day centred in the arrival of Prof. Frank Thilly, of the University of Missouri, of whom we have been thinking as Baldwin's successor, and who had generously consented to come here for a conference

Ellen went into N.Y. to take Jessie to see Dr. McCosh,[1] but came back,—on the same train, as it happened, with Prof. Thilly, tho. she was not aware of it,—at 4.25.

Ellen and I took dinner at the Hibbens' to meet Prof. Thilly, whom we found most ingenuous and interesting,—a man after our own hearts in simplicity and genuineness,—and withal of singular penetration and charm in his talk,—a highly trained native American of the Lincoln type, with his faculties released by education of unusual range and thoroughness. Other guest, Enno Littmann.

[1] Andrew James McCosh, M.D., Princeton 1877, eminent surgeon of New York and son of President McCosh.

Sunday, January 17, 1904

Henry van Dyke preached in chapel, with his usual charm and superficiality.

Prof. Thilly took dinner with us, and charmed Sister A. and Madge as he had charmed Ellen and me by his frank and open nature, his play of mind, his charm of directness and simplicity. After dinner had a talk of an hour and a half with him about Princeton, ourselves, himself, which ended only because of engagements. Quite made up my mind to call him.

At 4 Ellen and I went on our usual Sunday afternoon visit to the Hibbens'—Thilly, of course, the chief topic of conversation,— and at 5 went with them to see Miss Ricketts.

In the evening Jack had Fine, West, Ormond, and Warren[1] in at
tea to meet Prof. T.

[1] Howard Crosby Warren, Professor of Experimental Psychology at Princeton.

Monday, January 18, 1904

Lecture; and final talk (at Jack's) with Prof. Thilly[.] Asked his
permission to nominate him to the Board for the chair of Psychology. He promised to write after reaching home and consulting his wife, of whose charms we hear glowing accounts.
He left at 3.50. I lunched with him at the Hibbens'.
At 5 a chat with Jack and Mrs. Hibben about the whole thing,—
the two days of Thilly. Our joint impressions most favourable.
Evening: Committee on the Course of Study. Adopted Group in
History and Politics-Economics.

From John Lambert Cadwalader

My dear Mr. President,   New York, January 18, 1904
I have your letter in reference to funds. I shall try to do my
duty as an interested liberal minded alumnus—and should not be
content to let any such occasion pass without doing my fair
share.
I shall talk the matter over with you—perhaps on Saturday
when I shall be there.
Yours faithfully,
with good wishes,   John L. Cadwalader

ALS (WP, DLC).

From Wilson's Diary for 1904

Tuesday, January 19, 1904

Lecture at 10.30, concluding subject of Torts. Day of routine
tasks.
Afternoon, after office hours, called on Mr. Cleveland, whom I
found most admirable in his grief. Talked chiefly of the children and his desire to shield them from the terror and all the
last circumstance of Ruth's death. "It's not *time*," he thought,
"but other duties and care for others, that heals the wound,—
or, at least, lessens the pain of it,"—"by God's goodness," who
gives us other thoughts and directs us to other interests, in the
confidence that all is well with the one who is gone.

Evening: Ellen and I entertained at dinner, in honour of Professor and Mrs. Garfield. Other guests, Mr. and Mrs. Marquand, Henry van Dyke, Mr. and Mrs. Robbins, Dr. Elliott. Everything friendly and simple.

To Frank Thilly

My dear Prof. Thilly,   Princeton, 20 Jan'y, 1904

Ormond has just been in to say that he approves most cordially of my choice (your last conversation together convinced him entirely), and, though I have not the same *direct* assurance from Warren, I know indirectly that all is right in that quarter. There are *no* obstacles.

In haste, with warmest regard,

Cordially Yours,   Woodrow Wilson

ALS (Wilson-Thilly Corr., NIC).

From Wilson's Diary for 1904

Wednesday, January 20, 1904

Nothing but business.

Afternoon, interview with Ormond about his impressions of Mr. Thilly,—most satisfactory. Give him but time enough, and he will see all things in their right light. His last conversation with Thilly had evidently convinced him.

Academic Faculty at 5. Schedule of class hours for second term. Cameron disagreeable, as usual, because classes likely to be popular were put at the same hour with his.

Spent the evening in the sitting room,—sister A's last evening. Stockton came in and stayed about an hour.

To Theodore Marburg[1]

My dear Mr. Marburg: Princeton, N. J.   21 January, 1904

I am very much interested to learn that you are thinking of establishing disability pensions and insurance for the Faculty of Johns Hopkins.[2] I am sorry to say we have no system of the sort here, though the Trustees are very generous in taking care of men who have grown old in their service.

Very sincerely yours,   Woodrow Wilson

TLS (WP, DLC).

[1] Author, publicist, philanthropist, and trustee of The Johns Hopkins University.

[2] The letter to which this is a reply is missing.

From Wilson's Diary for 1904

Thursday, January 21, 1904

Sister off at 9.44 for Baltimore, her going made all the sadder
because this is the first anniversary of dear father's death
Spent an hour and a half, 5 to 6.30, with Mrs. Hibben, chatting.
Had three of the youngsters of the Faculty at dinner: Priest,
Critchlow,[1] Craig. Talked too much,—finally engrossing the
conversation

[1] Frank Linley Critchlow, Instructor in French.

Friday, January 22, 1904

Went to Montclair (by 1.21 train) to address "The Outlook Club"
on "Americanism." It was a beastly night, cold and pouring
rain, but the audience was quite good and most appreciative.
Stayed with Mr. Benj. Graham, C. C. Cuyler's partner, and was
most delightfully entertained,—with dignity and simplicity.

A News Report of an Address in Montclair, New Jersey

[Jan. 23, 1904]

Dr. Woodrow Wilson, President of Princeton University, addressed a highly interested audience at the Outlook Club meeting last night.

Dr. Wilson's subject was "Americanism," the spirit and power of America as she now emerges in the field of world politics. He pointed out that all the world had within our own generation become intensely conscious of the existence of America and America by consequence had got a new self-consciousness, which was not like the old self-consciousness of youth, but a self-consciousness of manhood. We have been aware of a new turn in the play of the world's affairs, a dramatic situation, in which we are forced to the centre of the stage with all the world for audience; and we are aware that that audience is not, on the whole, sympathetic, but hostile; and their very hostility has forced upon us an assessment of our own purposes and our own character. Foreign

statesmen have spoken of the American peril, of the Americanization of society and of industry. They fear the Americanization
of politics as well, and have a dread as vague as it is vivid of what
the consequences may be of the growing power of the United
States.

Certainly "Americanism" is a fact and invites analysis; and yet
the analysis is deeply difficult. It is always a matter of the utmost
difficulty to make a successful analysis of national character.
Certain of our broad traits as Americans are evident enough—
our alertness, inquisitiveness, unconventionality, readiness for
change, eagerness for the newest things and the most convenient.
The foreigner feels in us the defects of these qualities—a lack of
form, a lack of respect for things long established, a lack of form,
a lack of respect for things long established [sic], a lack of reserve, a certain crudeness and immaturity as of men who do their
thinking and their work on the run.

Undoubtedly our charactertistics have been born of our life
and our tasks. We have just concluded a century of beginnings,
and entered upon a centery [century] of finishings, in which we
must turn about and examine what we have done within the
country itself, perfect it, test it, amend it, complete it. A century
seems to be our dramatic unit. We had first a century of coloniza-
tion, then a century of war to oust the French and the Dutch and
the Spaniard and gain independence; then a century of nation-
making; now, and last, we have entered upon a century whose
purposes and whose tasks remain to be revealed. Let us hope that
it will be a century as satisfactory as the three that have preceded
it.

The century of nation-making has certainly bred in us the gift
and strength of initiative. It has made us builders, builders of
States as well as great industries—and has taught us to build
strong and yet with the elasticity to take the strain off. It has
consequently made us constitutional lawyers, habituated to drawing the documents necessary for the building of States and en-
genious [ingenious] also in their interpretation when drawn.

The process of natural growth has made us also fit for frontiers, the establishment and advancement of frontiers having
been our work until the continent was crossed, and its habitable
portions filled in. It has fitted us, therefore, for rough and un-
sensitive work; it has made every man ready to use his own
hands, and to be boss or laborer by turns, and has kept us close
to practical tasks, giving us the temper of men who act without

too nice a theory of action, and push forward without deliberate calculation. We have emerged from the century with ideals but without sentimentality; with principles but without bigotry; confident of the validity of liberty, but, since our contact with the complicated problems of the East and the administration of undeveloped colonial possessions, no longer confident of the necessary and final forms of liberty or of law. Above all, our adventures have made us ready for anything but the impossible–skeptical of the impossible.

It is time, as we look ourselves over and made [make] ready for our part in the broader field of international politics, that we should be more mindful of the past and of human nature, and less blindly sanguine of the future and of our immunity from misfortune. There is now an American past, as well as a European, which shows that there is no special American human nature; but that America's past teaches us the invariable lesson that is taught by the experience of other races–that wisdom and right are of old and do not alter with environment. Our past has not rid us of ignorance or of provincialism or of noxious error, both in the field of politics and of morals, and it has itself, it is to be feared, dulled and obscured some of our ideals. We should hold no duty more sacred and imperative than that of making ignorance inexcusable by every process of education, provincialism impossible by every means of intercourse and common action, and error a signal for campaign. In order that we may keep in us the ardent blood and the unfaltering faith of the men who have gone before us, and be able to play the good part in respect of human liberty on the field of the world that we have played on our own field at home.[1]

Printed in the *Montclair, N. J., Times*, Jan. 23, 1904.
[1] There is a second news report of this address printed at Jan. 28, 1904.

From Wilson's Diary for 1904

Saturday, January 23, 1904

Returned fr. Montclair to a day of quiet routine, at the close of which I went, for about an hour, to a musicale at Mrs. Fine's. The music, however, did not begin till after I had left, one of the musicians not arriving till 9.45, the train to wh. I had to go to meet Tom Hall,[1] coming to preach to-morrow.

[1] Thomas Cuming Hall, Wilson's classmate, Professor of Christian Ethics at Union Theological Seminary in New York.

Sunday, January 24, 1904

Tom Hall in chapel in the morning and in the First Church in the evening. The second sermon better than the first; neither quite satisfactory. Too much like his talk,—interesting, even striking, but not of wholly sound fibre and without any power but that of personality. A big, interesting, unfinished mind and body.

Our usual afternoon programme not carried out. Jack absorbed preparing to lead Senior prayer meeting in the evening, Mrs. Hibben kept at home by callers, who began coming in before Ellen and I left. Ellen's cold was so bad, as a result of spending yesterday in N.Y., that I persuaded her to return home, and I went alone to see Miss Ricketts.

Saw the Hibbens for a moment after service at the First Church this evening

Monday, January 25, 1904

Committee on Course of Study in the evening, 8-10.30 discussing Physics "Group." The Committee seems drifting away fr. the idea of general culture in the science groups and inclining too much in the direction of specialization. Next Tuesday an all-day session projected, to hasten progress.

At four Ellen had a meeting of her Committee on the Infirmary[1] which lasted till 5.30,—after which I saw Mrs. Hibben and Jack a little while

[1] A subcommittee of the Ladies Auxiliary. The latter group had been organized in June 1902 to raise money for ladies' rooms in the new gymnasium. Mrs. Wilson was chairman of the Subcommittee on the Infirmary, which in 1906 metamorphosed into the Ladies Auxiliary of the Isabella McCosh Infirmary.

Tuesday, January 26, 1904

Dined with E. P. and Mrs. Davis[1] in Phila.,—a really delightful evening. Ellen kept away by her cold. Moreau Barringer there and his wife, Miss Susan Erwin,[2] and a doctor, a friend of E. P.'s whose name I did not catch. Talk was easy and free and the Davises are truly charming hosts, natural, sincere, warm friends.

[1] Wilson's classmate, Edward Parker Davis, M.D., Professor of Obstetrics at the Jefferson Medical College, and Ellen-Duane Gillespie Davis.
[2] The Editors have been unable to identify her.

From Harlan Page Amen[1]

My dear Mr. Wilson: Exeter, N. H., January 26th, 1904.

Your very kind letter of the 25th inst. is just received. I am more grateful to you than I can tell you in words for your willingness to come to us this year. In accordance with the desire expressed in your letter, we shall consider the date for your lecture fixed for the evening of Wednesday, February 17th. I am very glad that you can come to us at this time.[2]

Professor Richardson's[3] letter came yesterday, expressing a preference for March 9th. as his date. You have both chosen dates which suit us perfectly, and we can now definitely arrange all the lectures of the course. The third lecturer was awaiting your decision and that of Professor Richardson before arranging a final date with us.

You should be able to reach us easily from Syracuse.[4] You should be in Boston, if possible, a few minutes before 4 o'clock. The last good train from Boston for Exeter leaves Boston at 4:15 in the afternoon. This is an express train and will bring you to Exeter in about one hour and twenty minutes. There is a later train at 5:14. This is the last train by means of which you can reach Exeter on any day of the week at this time in the year.

The subject which you have chosen will, I am sure, be very acceptable to your audience.

Again thanking you for your generous decision to come to us, I am   Very sincerely yours,   Harlan P. Amen.

TLS (WP, DLC).
[1] Principal of the Phillips Exeter Academy.
[2] A brief news report of Wilson's lecture is printed at Feb. 20, 1904.
[3] Professor Rufus Byam Richardson spoke at the Academy on March 9, 1904, on "The Excavation of Corinth." He had recently retired from the directorship of the American School of Classical Studies at Athens and was living in Woodstock, Conn.
[4] Wilson was to speak at the University Club of Syracuse, N. Y., on February 16, 1904. A news report of this address is printed at Feb. 17, 1904.

From Wilson's Diary for 1904

Wednesday, January 27, 1904

After leaving the Davises, at 10, I called on Mr. Thos. B. Wanamaker, about the University, did a little shopping, sat for Gutekunst,[1] and took the three o'clock train for home
School of Science Faculty at 5
In the evening presided at meeting of the Nassau Club at which

there was a preliminary discussion of the Club's new constitution. My first visit to the new club house.[2] Home by 10, to
write a note or two.

[1] Frederick Gutekunst, photographer, who had studios at 712 Arch St. and
1700 North Broad St., Philadelphia.
[2] The Nassau Club of Princeton, organized in 1889, was formally incorporated
on June 15, 1903. The incorporation required the appointment or election of five
trustees, and the club was in the process of adopting a new constitution. The
new club house was at 6 Mercer St. and is the one presently used by the Nassau
Club. Wilson, an incorporator, was president, 1903-1904.

Thursday, January 28, 1904

Ellen and I were to have gone to Washington today to dine with
the President and Mrs. Roosevelt,—the last state dinner of the
season,—to the Supreme Court, but E's cold still made it im-
prudent for her to travel and we had to send our regrets.[1]

[1] Wilson's letter to President and Mrs. Roosevelt is missing in the T. Roosevelt
Papers, DLC.

A News Report of an Address in Montclair, New Jersey

[Jan. 28, 1904]

OUR ELASTIC CONSTITUTION

Its Capacity for Stretching Is What Saves It
from Tearing.

Dr. Woodrow Wilson's recent address before the Outlook Club
of Montclair, N. J.,[1] breathes the spirit of a broad Americanism.
Among other things he said:

"Perhaps the makers of our old Constitution wouldn't recognize it now, yet I have no criticism to make of the process of
interpretation which has been going on.

"We have been in the position of a corporation lawyer with a
charter, and a lawyer can read anything into a charter that is
necessary. The old statesmen weren't trying to put a straitjacket
on us, they meant us to accommodate ourselves to circumstances.
The decisions of the Supreme Court of the United States form
as nice a series of constitutional evolution as can be found.

"True, the last becomes far different from the beginning, but
if you don't skip you won't find any gaps. The Constitution is like
a snug garment stretched to cover so great a giant as the nation
has become. If it wasn't stretchable it would tear. We have done
our interpreting with good consciences.

"Our frontier disappeared less than fourteen years ago and now a new one has been given us in the Philippines. Our troublesome men used to go West and this may have had a great deal to do with the sedateness of character here in the East. Now there are the Philippines where they can go and butt their heads against primeaval nature and find how much harder primeaval nature is than their heads. It is always well to have a frontier on which to turn loose the colts of the race.

"Because of our Americanism we had no patience with the anti-imperialist weepings and wailings that came out of Boston, not because we didn't think them entitled to their fair opinion, but because we knew that the crying time was over and that the time had come for men to look out of dry eyes and see the world as it is.

"There is no use crying over spilt milk; that isn't the American spirit. The only reformer who is worth his salt is the one who will do the thing he can do and not mope over things he can't accomplish.

"There is this useful quality to help the future. The American is sceptical of impossibility, he is ready for anything. He admits theoretical impossibilities, but has never found them actual. This is what gives foreign statesmen pause, we so confidently walk into complicated situations and do what occurs to us.

"We hear that a door is going to shut in Manchuria, and we slapped a wedge in it so it could not while everybody else among the nations waited to hear it slam.[2]

"We are a sort of pure air blowing in world politics, destroying illusions and cleaning places of morbid miasmatic gases. We do some things that are very remarkable. We have done some such in Panama that will bear looking into; but that is not a finished story and we won't discuss it.

"It seems as if we were doing the first thing that occurs to us and forgetting the last; but though I don't understand the plot I daresay it will work out in the end."

Printed in the Philadelphia *Press*, Jan. 28, 1904.

[1] On January 22. See the news report printed at Jan. 23, 1904.

[2] Wilson was referring to the commercial treaty between the United States and China, signed on October 8, 1903, and approved by the Senate on December 18. An important article provided for the opening of the Manchurian cities of Mukden and Antung to international residence and trade. The Japanese signed a parallel treaty with China on October 8. Together, the treaties were intended to encourage the Chinese to resist increasing Russian encroachment in Manchuria. The *New York Times*, Dec. 19, 1903, announcing the Senate's approval of the treaty, referred to senatorial opinion that it was "an entering wedge for American trade." The Chinese-American Treaty of 1903 is printed in John V. A. MacMurray, *Treaties and Agreements With and Concerning China, 1894-1919* (2 vols., New York, 1921), I, 423-52.

From James Henry Lockhart

My Dear Dr. Wilson: Pittsburgh, Pa., Jan. 28, 1904.

Your letter of January 14th was received and carefully noted, and I can assure you that it was received in the same spirit in which it was written. I have thought this matter over for several days pretty carefully, and have come to the conclusion that I can see my way clear to join the group which is forming to give $5000.00 apiece for three years, in order to raise a fund which will keep the University from incurring the yearly deficit, and the interest of which later on, will be sufficient to overcome a deficit such as is imminent now. My subscription would be conditioned that the whole sum of $100.000.00 a year for three years be subscribed for before my subscription becomes binding, and like the others, I shall have the liberty to withdraw, if I find it necessary, after any one of the payments.

I wish you and the Committee success in getting the whole amount pledged, and when such an amount has been secured, if you will notify me, I will make arrangements for taking care of the first year's payment in accordance with your wishes.

With kind remembrances to your self, and wishing you and Dear Old Princeton every success, I am,

Yours very truly,   James H. Lockhart

P.S. If you can so arrange it—please mark this subscription as from an "alumnus."   J. H. L.

TLS (WP, DLC).

From John Heman Converse

My dear Dr. Wilson: Philadelphia, January 28, 1904

I duly received your communication of the 14th inst, respecting additional endowment for Princeton University.

In considering this matter I should be more inclined to make a donation for a specific object such as a scholarship, than for a general endowment, having already some years ago made a donation for the latter object. If it were both wise and practicable to do so, I should be attracted by the plan of endowing one or more scholarships for young men taking a Course in the University preliminary to a Seminary Course and the Christian ministry.

May I ask what amount is necessary to endow a scholarship, and whether a plan of this kind would assist both the University and the incumbent of the scholarship?

Very truly yours,   John H. Converse

TLS (WP, DLC).

To Charles Henry Marshall[1]

My dear Mr. Marshall: Princeton, N. J.   29 January, 1904.

I have received your circular of January 28, notifying me of the nomination of the Hon. Elihu Root for membership in the Round Table Club,[2] and write to say that I should be very much pleased indeed to see Mr. Root elected.

With much regard,
                              Sincerely yours,   Woodrow Wilson

TLS (Papers of the Round Table Dining Club, NHi).
  [1] Chairman of the New York Board of the Liverpool & London & Globe Insurance Co., Ltd.
  [2] About which, see WW to C. H. Marshall, Dec. 26, 1902, n. 3, Vol. 14.

To Charles Richard Van Hise[1]

                                        Princeton, N. J.
My dear President Van Hise: 29 January, 1904.

I greatly appreciate your kind letter of January 23. I have kept it a day or two in the hope that I might see my way clear to accept the very cordial invitation which it conveys to attend the Jubilee of the University. Unhappily, however, it will not be possible. The week you have selected is the week preceding our own Commencement, and during that week I am necessarily engaged upon preparing some of the most important business of the year for the consideration of the Board of Trustees. I beg to assure you that in any other circumstances I should have made it convenient to come.

I shall confidently hope to have some representative present for the occasion.[2]

                    Very cordially yours,   Woodrow Wilson

TLS (University of Wisconsin Autographs, WHi).
  [1] President of the University of Wisconsin.
  [2] Princeton was not represented at the celebration, which took place in Madison on June 5-9, 1904.

A News Item

                                        [*Jan. 29, 1904*]
PRINCETON UNIVERSITY

Restrictions at Examinations Regarded as Reflection on Honor-System Results.

Princeton, N. J., January 29—Rules regarding examinations, promulgated by the faculty, prohibit a student from taking his question paper out of the examination room, except in case of illness. This restriction of the freedom hitherto enjoyed in examinations under the honor system looks like a reflection on the workings of that system. The rules were drafted without consultation with the student body, and how far they will affect the undergraduates' pride in the honor system remains to be seen. It had been supposed that that system was working satisfactorily.[1]

Printed in the New York *Evening Post*, Jan. 30, 1904.
[1] The author of this report was in error. Wilson had issued a circular for the guidance of those conducting examinations, reiterating the regulations agreed upon by the student committee and the faculty when the honor system was inaugurated. For his response, see the interview printed at Feb. 6, 1904, and his letter to the Editor of the *Daily Princetonian*, Feb. 10, 1904.

From Wilson's Diary for 1904

Friday, January 29, 1904

In to N.Y. at 1.21 to attend dinner of The Pilgrims,[1] given to Sir Henry Mortimer Durand, the new British ambassador.[2] Jack Hibben on the train w. Beth[3] as far as Elizabeth,—to leave Beth there and then go on to N.Y. to join Mrs. Hibben at John Larkin's,[4] where they are to be till Sunday morning,—theatre, opera, etc.

The dinner was most interesting. The London Pilgrims[5] were meeting at the same time. We assembled at 7 o'clock,—midnight in London. The transatlantic cable was at our disposal for an hour, and all sorts of messages were interchanged,— none of importance, all of interest. At the dinner, wh. followed about 8 o'clock, Bishop Potter[6] presided. There were four speakers, Sir Mortimer Durand, ex-Attorney General Griggs,[7] and Mr. Beck,[8] and myself; and I am sure that everyone present formed the most agreeable impression of the new British ambassador,—a man of ability and modesty.

I lodged at the University Club.

[1] An organization of Americans and British subjects dedicated to the "promotion of the sentiment of brotherhood among the nations, and especially the cultivation of good fellowship between citizens of the United States and its dependencies and subjects of the British Empire."
[2] A news report of this affair is printed at Jan. 30, 1904.
[3] Elizabeth Grier Hibben.
[4] John Larkin '82, Hibben's classmate and prominent New York lawyer, and Ida Rahm Larkin.
[5] The London counterpart of the American society.
[6] The Rt. Rev. Henry Codman Potter, Protestant Episcopal Bishop of New York.
[7] John William Griggs, Governor of New Jersey, 1896-98; Attorney General of the United States, 1898-1901; and at this time a member of the Permanent Court of Arbitration at The Hague.
[8] James Montgomery Beck, prominent New York attorney and member of the firm of Shearman and Sterling.

From Theodore Roosevelt

My dear President Wilson: [Washington]   January 29, 1904.

I am very sorry you could not come to the dinner, and still more sorry for the cause.

With regards to Mrs. Wilson, believe me,

Sincerely yours,   Theodore Roosevelt

TLS (Letterpress Books, T. Roosevelt Papers, DLC).

A News Report of an After-Dinner Speech in New York

[Jan. 30, 1904]

CABLE UNITES PILGRIMS HERE AND IN LONDON

The Pilgrims of the United States and the Pilgrims of England exchanged by cable last night expressions of friendship and goodwill. The occasion was the giving of two dinners—one in London and one in this city—to the respective Ambassadors of the two countries. In this city, at Delmonico's, Sir Henry Mortimer Durand was the guest of honor, while in London, where the dinner was given at the Carlton, Joseph H. Choate[1] was the chief guest.

Between the Carlton and a room just off the big dining hall at Delmonico's direct communication by wire had been established. Inot [Into] each gathering place had been laid a wire connecting with one of the cables of the Commercial Cable Company, and over this direct connection were flashed over thirty messages. At the table where the messages were being received in this city were Bishop Potter, a superintendent of the Cable Company, and several members of the society, while the others who attended the dinner were grouped around the room.

The dispatches as they were received were read to the assembled diners and then the replies were sent back to the assemblage in London which had been kept together until a late hour in order to hear the expressions of regard from their brothers on this side. Because of the difference in time between the two cities the diners on this side had not yet enjoyed their dinner while those on the other side of the Atlantic had about reached the conclusion of the festivities. . . .

President Woodrow Wilson of Princeton University was the next speaker. In the course of his speech he said:

"I am going to take the liberty of saying that I do not very much believe in the adage that blood is thicker than water. Some water—in Philadelphia, for example—is much thicker than blood, (Laughter.) and I do not think that the thing that binds these two nations together is either their blood on [or] their speech. For example, when our common speech is used in The Saturday Review, how much does that bind us together? (Laughter.) One of the painful things about knowing the English language is that one cannot understand The Saturday Review; one cannot understand the unmannered and ill-informed things it says about the United States. I am ready to admit that we can, with less difficulty, understand the sentiment of The Times.

"What binds us together as the only instrument of friendship is the instrument which enables us to think the same thoughts and to see the same shades of meaning at the same time. You know we very nearly got into trouble with France because President Jackson had at his elbow somebody who didn't understand the French language. I believe that the useful thing is that we read the same books at the same time, and we can cement friendships only when men can understand the meanings of each other. You must understand all their words and meanings. The things which binds [bind] us together are the feeling and the meaning which we put in our words. They are the vehicle for destroying us as they are for helping us. If we did not think the same thoughts, we never should draw together, simply because we spoke the same language.

"Recent historical study has done a great deal toward restoring cordial feeling and a right attitude of thought between America and England. Historians on both sides of the water, for example, are coming to take the same view of the American Revolution as due, not to the intrinsic badness of English legislation, but to economic, social, and political causes which lay deeper than statesmen knew. They are beginning to doubt whether the Stamp act and the legislation which went with it were in fact economically injurious to the colonies, whether even the famous Navigation acts did not bring more benefit than damage, and are beginning to see that this revolution, like every other, arose, not so much out of measures as out of a state of mind—a state of mind with which Chatham and Burke and Fox and every real liberal man in England had the most vivid sympathy.

"I remember a very pretty incident which was told me of President McKinley. An American who had been in England came back to this country and found himself in Washington. He thought it would please the President to know of the talk that went around among Englishmen every day concerning the

United States. It was at the time when we were debating a formal treaty of alliance with Great Britain. The man said:

" 'Why, Mr. President, the talk on this matter is of the most cordial character. The two nations seem to be drawing together in a bond of amity. The whole of England is in the air.'

"The President smiled and said:

" 'I don't know but what that is a good place for it to be.' (Laughter.)

"I regard that as a sagacious utterance.

"The understanding of these two nations is the real basis of their union. We have come out upon a new plane. We now have difficulties confronting us in international matters, and I take it that we are in a position to go to school to those who are more experienced than ourselves.

"And in the proper temper of men who know how to consult experts, we should forego our ancient Revolutionary attitude toward England and seek to know how she has managed her foreign affairs. We should consult such men as the guest of the evening. In this way we shall show our mature wisdom. We should be partners with the nation that stands for things for which we stand.

"When you consider what the different nations of the world stand for, keeping in mind the specific purpose of England and America, you will see that there is but one course to choose and that is to carry forward in honesty and unselfishness that service to the world which has now been carried too far for us to turn back. The Anglo-Saxon people have undertaken to reconstruct the affairs of the world, and it would be a shame upon them to withdraw their hand. (Applause.) We know, Sir, that our people stand for what you stand for."[2]

Printed in the *New York Times*, Jan. 30, 1904; several editorial headings omitted.
[1] American Ambassador to Great Britain, 1899-1905.
[2] There is a brief WWhw outline, dated Jan. 29, 1904, of these remarks in WP, DLC.

A News Report

[Jan. 30, 1904]

PILGRIMS CHEERED BY NEWS OF PEACE

Herald Bulletin, Read at Banquet at Delmonico's,
Elicits Thunders of Applause.

Sir Henry Mortimer Durand, British Ambassador to the United States, received his first intelligence of the likelihood of peace between Russia and Japan[1] from the HERALD.

The Ambassador was the chief guest at a dinner given by the Pilgrim Society at Delmonico's, and former Assistant Attorney General James M. Beck had just finished a speech in praise of international amity when the following bulletin was presented and read by Mr. George Wilson, secretary of the Chamber of Commerce and a member of the society:

"The NEW YORK HERALD presents its compliments to the Pilgrims and submits the following bulletin:

"The State Department at Washington has been informed by Mr. Griscom,[2] at Tokio, that the British Ambassador at St. Petersburg has notified the British Legation at Tokio that Russia's answer to Japan is satisfactory and that Great Britain will prevail upon Japan to accept it. This means that there will be no war."[3]

The applause that greeted this announcement was thunderous. The diners arose in a body, waved their napkins and cheered again and again, while expressions of satisfaction were heard on every side. It was a fitting climax to the function of the evening, which Bishop Potter then declared at an end. . . .

President Woodrow Wilson, of Princeton University, said: "The news was the ambrosia at the feast. All lovers of peace will feel as though the message read 'Paradise regained.'"

Printed in the *New York Herald*, Jan. 30, 1904.

[1] Relations between these two nations had been deteriorating steadily for months on account of conflicting interests in Manchuria and Korea. News of this increasing tension and of ominous movements of military forces had filled the newspapers for weeks.

[2] Lloyd Carpenter Griscom, United States Minister to Japan, 1902-1906.

[3] The language of the bulletin was, to say the least, overly optimistic. Another news story in the same issue of the *Herald* offered a more judicious interpretation of the dispatch: "A high official of the State Department to-night said that the cable from Mr. Griscom would seem to indicate that progress toward peace had been made, but that it would not bear the construction that any one outside of the Russian high circles knew possibly [positively] that peace was assured. It was stated to the *Herald* by this official that Mr. Griscom had merely cabled the opinion of diplomats of Great Britain and not any positive news that they had obtained as to the contents of Russia's reply."

The Russian reply had been formulated at a conference of Russian officials in St. Petersburg on January 28 held to consider Japanese proposals submitted earlier in the month and which were taken to represent Japan's final position on the key issues. While the British Ambassador at St. Petersburg, Sir Charles Hardinge, may not at this time have known the actual wording of the Russian response, it is clear that he had based his optimistic message to the British Legation in Tokyo on some knowledge of the decisions of the conference of January 28. Thus the *Herald* bulletin announcing Griscom's cablegram and read at the banquet was the first public news of the possible nature of the Russian counterproposals. As it turned out, the formal Russian reply, signed by the Czar on February 2, did not reach Tokyo before February 4 and possibly not until February 7. Japan broke diplomatic relations with Russia on February 5, and the Japanese fleet opened hostilities against Russian naval units off Port Arthur three days later, even though Japan did not formally declare war until February 10. See John Albert White, *The Diplomacy of the Russo-Japanese War* (Princeton, N. J., 1964), pp. 95-131.

From Wilson's Diary for 1904

Saturday, January 30, 1904

Late breakfast, a little shopping (chiefly furniture for the Infirmary), lunch at the Jersey City station, and the three o'clock train for home

In the evening dinner at the Inn with a number of class secretaries to discuss ways and means of controlling the serious evil of drinking at class reunions at Commencement. The speeches made seemed to indicate very clearly that some very active and influential men among the younger alumni have taken hold of the matter in earnest and mean to work up a body of sentiment in the matter wh., in addition to sensible measures proposed and likely to be taken ought very soon to bring the evil within bounds. Wilder presided, with his unfailing, sometimes very irritating, wit.[1]

[1] A news report of this meeting is printed at Feb. 6, 1904.

From Morris Patterson Ferris[1]

My dear Dr. Wilson: New York City   January 30th, 1904.

I desire to re-iterate my invitation conveyed to you informally last evening, to attend the Banquet of the Sons of the Revolution in the State of New York on February 22nd, 1905.

I trust you will keep the date in mind and find it within the possibilities for you to accept.

We have a high appreciation of you and of the College you represent and the importance of your College in Revolutionary times makes it doubly important and interesting to have it represented at our banquet.

May I incidentally congratulate you upon the very able and interesting speech you made last evening at the very enjoyable dinner given to Sir Henry Mortimer Durand, to celebrate the establishment of friendly relations between this and the Mother Country.

Yours very truly,   Morris P. Ferris   Secretary.

TLS (WP, DLC).
[1] A New York lawyer and Secretary of the Sons of the Revolution in the State of New York.

To Frank Thilly

My dear Prof. Thilly,   Princeton, 31 Jan'y, 1904

I feel, from your long silence, that a great debate is in progress in Columbia which involves Princeton's interests most deeply, but in which we have no part. If any new difficulties have arisen, or any new phases of old difficulties, to which we have not had a chance to speak, may we be admitted to the discussion? We feel that we *must* have you,—and I am always

Cordially Your Friend,   Woodrow Wilson

ALS (Wilson-Thilly Corr., NIC).

From Wilson's Diary for 1904

Sunday, January 31, 1904

Dr. Patton preached his usual sermon,—but more than usually witty,—may almost be said to have kept the chapel in a roar. "Ye believe in God; believe also in me." Subject, Belief in God.

Went alone to Miss Ricketts's in the afternoon,—Ellen still disabled by cold, the Hibbens in Elizabeth. Miss Ricketts expecting to join her brother[1] in Arizona possibly within a couple of weeks. Mr. and Mrs. McClenahan and Miss Juliana Conover came in while I was there.

[1] Louis Davidson Ricketts, Princeton 1881, at this time a consulting engineer for Phelps, Dodge and Co. in the Southwest.

To Frank Thilly

Princeton, N. J.
My dear Professor Thilly: 1 February, 1904.

Hibben has just been in to lay before me the question which you have put to him in your recent letter, namely the church question.[1]

He retailed to me the conversation which he had had with you on the subject, and I think that the best way I can express my own feeling in the matter is to say that I agree perfectly with the position which he took. I think that matching your conversation with him on that subject with your conversation with me on the relation which I conceive teaching philosophy here should bear to revealed religion, you will be able to see the whole field clearly —for you may regard your conversation with him as having been a conversation with me.

Probably this letter will tread close on the heels of my letter of last evening, but the two coming together will show you how sincerely anxious I am to remove all obstacles to your coming.

Mrs. Wilson joins me in warm regard, and I am,

Most sincerely yours,   Woodrow Wilson

TLS (Wilson-Thilly Corr., NIC).
[1] Unfortunately, Thilly's letter to Hibben is missing in the Hibben Papers. Thilly was not a member of any church. He undoubtedly had informed Hibben of this fact, and he may have added that he did not consider philosophy to be a branch of revealed religion.

To Morris Patterson Ferris

My dear Mr. Ferris: [Princeton, N. J.]   1 Feb[r]uary, 1904.

I am very much obliged to you for your kind letter of January 30, and can assure you that I greatly appreciate your desire to have me speak at the dinner of the Sons of the Revolution next year.

I feel that it would be indiscreet, in view of the possible preoccupations of my official duty, to promise so far ahead; but you may be sure that I will not give the 22 Feb[r]uary, 1905, to any other outside appointment, and I shall confidently hope that when we take the matter up again next autumn, I shall be able to meet your wishes.[1]

Most sincerely yours,   [Woodrow Wilson]

CCL (WP, DLC).
[1] Wilson spoke to the Sons of the Revolution of New York State on February 22, 1905. See the news report printed at Feb. 23, 1905, Vol. 16.

From Wilson's Diary for 1904

Monday, February 1, 1904

Called at the Hibbens' at five and arranged to go to the Kneisel Quartette[1] in the evening,—Ellen being still unfit to go out.

The night was as glorious a one as I ever saw,—a perfectly brilliant moonlight upon a world of snow and frost, the air intensely cold and biting like an icy bath. The first part of the music was modern and disturbing, but the concluding part, fr. Beethoven, gave the mind tone again and sent us home happy.[2] I walked home with the Hibbens and sat with them till nearly eleven.

[1] About this famous ensemble, see WW to EAW, Feb. 4, 1895, n. 1, Vol. 9.
[2] Wilson had just attended the third concert of the academic year by the Kneisel Quartette in the Trophy Room of the gymnasium. The program was

Tchaikovsky, Quartet No. 2 in F Major, Opus 22; Mendelssohn, *Canzonetta* and *Scherzo* for solo violoncello (with the quartet's cellist, Alwin Schroeder as soloist); and Beethoven, Quartet in B Flat Major, Opus 18, No. 6.

From Susan Eliza Hall[1]

My dear Dr. Wilson,   Wilmington, N. C.   Feb. 1, 1904.

If it were not for the fact that I am directed to write this letter, you would probably miss it altogether, because I think it is destined to perish without fruit.

The entertainment committee of our church[2] earnestly invites you to stop in Wilmington some time soon and give a short lecture for the pleasure of our own church people. You will feel, I am sure, how hearty will be their welcome, and, if by any possibility the thing can be done, how proud and grateful will be the committee who were bold enough to ask it.

Yours very truly,   Susan E. Hall.

ALS (WP, DLC).
    [1] A teacher in the Wilmington, N. C., High School. Her mother, Margaret Tannerhill Sprunt Hall, was a sister of Wilson's old friend, James Sprunt.
    [2] The First Presbyterian Church of Wilmington, N. C.

From Wilson's Diary for 1904

Tuesday, February 2, 1904

Six hours and a half of the Committee on the Course of Study, 9-1 in the forenoon, 2.30-5 in the afternoon. Adopted Groups in Physics, in English, and in modern languages.

At 5.15, going fr. the committee room, met Mrs. Hibben coming fr. the Woman's Employment Society, extremely tired after a day spent in all sorts of charitable work, beginning with the degraded poor on Johns St. Took tea w. her and sat a little till she seemed cheered up a bit.

After dinner two undergraduates in fr. the Committee on the Honor System to say that they had discovered that certain men in town had stolen papers for the examinations fr. the printing office and were selling them to Freshmen. The Committee sent one Freshman to them, as a decoy and obtained copies of two papers. The Freshman gave a cheque for them for $30. Fine and I took these copies over to the printing office and verified them,—remaining there in consultation w. the Robinson's[1] till nearly midnight.[2]

    [1] Charles S. and Harvey L. Robinson, printers, 30 Nassau St., Princeton.
    [2] Subsequent documents will reveal the outcome of this affair.

From John Heman Converse

Dear Sir: Philadelphia, Feb. 2nd, 1904.

Your favor of Jan. 29th is at hand.

I will endow two scholarships in Princeton University, the privileges of same to be extended by the Faculty, to students looking forward to a seminary course and the Christian ministry, the Presbyterian ministry preferred. I will pay the amount either in cash or in satisfactory interest-bearing securities, by July 1st, 1904.   Very truly yours,   John H. Converse

TLS (WP, DLC).

From Harper and Brothers

Dear Sir: New York City   February 2, 1904

Your letter of January 29 with reference to the subscription edition of "WILSON'S HISTORY" is at hand.

In reply to your inquiry we beg to call your attention to the fact that our offer of this edition is coupled with a year's subscription to either one of our periodicals. The custom is to deduct the subscription price from the total amount.

The price of the books is $22.00, not $25.00, and when we sell the set without a periodical, we sell it for $22.00. This is the same method of accounting that obtains in our settlements with all authors whose books are sold by similar methods.

       Very sincerely yours,   Harper & Brothers

TLS (WP, DLC).

From Wilson's Diary for 1904

         Wednesday, February 3, 1904

Four Freshmen and an irregular student convicted by the student Committee of purchasing examination papers, and in the afternoon, at the meeting of the University Faculty, "required to withdraw fr. college"

Evening: one of our "faculty" dinings: guests: Prof. and Mrs. Blau, Prof. and Mrs. Walter Harris, Professor and Mrs. Geo. Patton, Prof. and Mrs. Lewis, and Mr. Brank.[1] Ellen really not fit to entertain. I myself quite upset in my bowels. We both forced ourselves and were a good deal the worse for wear.

Thompson and Kinney,[2] the two crooks who had been trading in examination papers, arrested.

[1] Rockwell Smith Brank, student at Princeton Theological Seminary and a friend of Mrs. Wilson's sister, Margaret Randolph Axson.

[2] John N. Thompson of 32 Jackson St., Princeton, and Thomas Kinney of Witherspoon Lane, Princeton.

Thursday, February 4, 1904

Wrote to the judge and the County prosecutor in Trenton explaining the gravity of Thompson's and Kinney's offense fr. our point of view

Kept the house all day but forced myself to dine again,—very foolishly, no doubt, as Ellen also forced herself, at great risk, the night being very chill and sharp. The dinner was at the Woodhull's. We had promised long ago and knew how they had counted on us.

From Frank Thilly

Dear President Wilson: Columbia [Mo.]   February 4th, 1904

I thank you most sincerely for your cordial letters to me; each one of them is an additional motive to my going to Princeton. My delay in sending you an answer has been caused by many circumstances. In the first place, I did not reach home until a week after leaving you. Then a week was lost waiting for the President of our Executive Board[1] whom I had promised not to reach a decision until after a conference with him and President Jesse.[2] Finally the thought occurred to me that I may not have expressed myself fully on the church question and that my coming to Princeton might possibly prove an embarrassment to you. Your last letter removes all my doubts, and I am now ready to accept the position which you so generously offered to me. With respect to the financial problem I have no more light than I had when I left Princeton. But there certainly must be men in your Faculty who have no private fortunes and who live on their salaries, and what they can do I ought to be able to do. I know that I am making a financial sacrifice in leaving Columbia, a greater one than I supposed I would be called upon to make when I discussed the matter with you, but I am willing to make it.[3] I tell you all this not to enhance my value in your eyes, but to show you how eager I am to come, how great is my confidence in Princeton University, and how strong is my personal regard for you. It is not easy to break the ties I have formed here and to turn my back upon the institution in which I have labored so long,[4] but the thought of the Princeton welcome makes the task less difficult.

I shall inform the authorities here of my acceptance of the Princeton chair and submit my resignation as soon as you desire me to do so.

I have accepted an invitation to be one of the speakers in the Ethics section of the International Congress at St. Louis, which is to be held during the week of September 19th-25th. I find upon consulting the Princeton catalogue that the University opens September 21. If you desire it, I shall try to withdraw my acceptance of the invitation.

In conclusion let me thank you—and that most sincerely—for the frank and openhearted manner in which you have treated me in this whole matter. I have felt all along that I was dealing with human beings, with men of heart and soul, and not with dead things, and the introduction of the personal, human element, has made everything so delightfully pleasant and warm for me.

With heartiest regards to Mrs. Wilson and yourself, I am,

Most cordially yours,   Frank Thilly

ALS (WP, DLC).

[1] Walter Williams, chairman of the Executive Board of the Board of Curators of the University of Missouri.

[2] Richard Henry Jesse, President of the University of Missouri, 1891-1908.

[3] It is not known what salary Thilly was receiving at the University of Missouri, or what that university offered in an effort to keep him; however, he came to Princeton at a salary of $3,600.

[4] Thilly had been appointed to a new chair of philosophy at the University of Missouri in 1893. "For the next eleven years," according to one historian, "he was probably the most potent spirit in the life of the University, at least of the college. His warm humanity, his breadth of vision, his intellectual alertness and courage endeared him especially to the younger men of the faculty." Jonas Viles et al., *The University of Missouri, A Centennial History* (Columbia, Mo., 1939), p. 271.

From William Francis Magie

Dear Sir: Princeton, N. J.   February 4, 1904.

At the meeting of the University Faculty held February 3, 1904, the following action was taken: It was RESOLVED, That, in order to secure the prompt issue of schedules for the first term, the stated meeting of the Committee on the Course of Study be held on the Wednesday preceding the meeting of the University Faculty in March; that the Committee shall at this meeting pass upon the curriculum for the following year, and shall report it at the March meeting of the Faculty; that schedules embodying the curriculum adopted by the Faculty be presented at the April meeting; and that the Catalogue Committee be directed to issue the necessary information to the students by May 1st.

Yours truly,   W. F. Magie

TLS (WP, DLC).

To John Work Garrett

My dear Mr. Garrett: [Princeton, N. J.]   Feby 5 [1904]

I hope that it does not in your opinion seriously enhance the impudence of a begging letter that it should be sent all the way across the sea.[1] There have been so many ways in which you have generously made us feel your vivid interest in Princeton and we have so many occasions to thank you as one of our immediate constituents that you do not anywhere seem very far away.

Your brother tells me that he has already spoken to you concerning a fund which we are trying to raise for the University. He, indeed, was one of the first to suggest such a fund, to be raised by annual subscription, and it is substantially upon the plan proposed by him that we are now working. We are trying to get guarantees which will secure us, if possible, a fund amounting to as much as $100,000 a year for three years; and our initial efforts have been very successful indeed. Fifty thousand dollars is already secured. All subscribers, so far, have subscribed $5,000 apiece for three years,—upon the understanding, however, that any one of them may, if he finds it necessary to do so, withdraw after any one of the three annual payments.

I find that this year the University will have to face a deficit of between $6,000 and $10,000. It is our purpose to spend out of the funds we are raising not more than $10,000 a year and invest the rest. This would give us at the end of the three-year term $270,000 of invested funds,—enough to capitalize the income of $10,000.

I do not feel, after all your liberality to the University, that I can urge upon you a subscription to this fund; but I know that your interest in the University justifies me in calling your attention to the matter and in asking whether you will not add to our debt of gratitude to you by considering a possibility of your doing so. Begging is certainly the most onerous, in some senses the most mortifying, duty of a college president; I shrink from it more than I can say. It is the more burdensome because those who have already been most generous have constantly to be urged to give more. But, apparently, it is the only means of growth, whether the University be supported by private endowment or public taxation, and I accept the inevitable. I know that you will understand.

You are very often in my thoughts. I can say with all sincerity that, as I do not know any career entered upon with higher motive or more interesting possibility than yours, I know of no career in which I am more deeply interested. I am glad to hear from your brother that you are all well; and I wish you with all my heart, Godspeed.

Always

Cordially and faithfully yours   Woodrow Wilson

Transcript of WWshLS (WP, DLC).
[1] At this time Garrett was Secretary of the American Legation in The Hague.

From Wilson's Diary for 1904

Friday, February 5, 1904

Ellen, I fear, a good deal worse, swellings developing in her ears.
  I no *worse*, but very shaky. We both kept very close and quiet all day, excused to everyone. I slept most of the afternoon.
Was to have gone to a committee meeting in N.Y. to-day, and to have dined w. the Round Table Club tonight.

From Edgar Gardner Murphy[1]

My dear Dr. Wilson: New York City, February 5, 1904

I am sending you to-day under another cover, a copy of the Proceedings of the Sixth Conference for Education in the South.[2] If a copy has already been sent you, you will, of course, make any use you like of the duplicate.

I am writing this morning to tell you how earnestly we hope you will be able to attend the next Conference and make one of the addresses of the session. We have desired with every year to have you with us, and as this desire finds no abatement with the passing of time, I trust that you will allow us to count upon you for this year's meeting. The Conference will open in the City of Birmingham, Alabama, on the evening of April twentieth and will continue through the twenty-first and twenty-second. Mr. Ogden[3] will supplement this bfief [brief] note with a personal word of his own, and if you can be with us, I will be glad to assign your address for any hour of the session that you may prefer. I will suggest a subject if you wish me to do so, but the Conference will be glad to have you deal with any topic which may especially appeal to you.[4]

With kindest regards, I am,

Very sincerely, Edgar Gardner Murphy.

I once heard you deliver an address at Old Point Comfort on Americanism[5] (I forget just how the title was worded).[6] This— with such direct applications to education as you might care to add, would make a helpful and inspiring message.

E. G. M.

TLS (WP, DLC).
    [1] A former Episcopal clergyman and student and publicist of southern social problems, Murphy was at this time Executive Secretary of the Southern Education Board and Vice President of the Conference for Education in the South.
    [2] *Proceedings of the Conference for Education in the South: The Sixth Session* (New York, 1903).
    [3] Robert Curtis Ogden, manager of John Wanamaker's department store in New York and President of the Southern Education Board and of the Conference for Education in the South.
    [4] As subsequent documents will disclose, Wilson accepted Murphy's invitation and later had to cancel the engagement on account of illness in his family.
    [5] See the news report printed at Feb. 1, 1902, Vol. 12.
    [6] The title of the lecture was, actually, "What It Means to Be an American."

A Report of an Interview About the Honor System

[Feb. 6, 1904]

A propos of the mid-year examinations, still in progress, a circular recently sent out by President Wilson '79 to the examiners caused some comment in the newspapers, which was evidently based upon a misapprehension. This comment gave the impression that in some quarters there was dissatisfaction with the way in which the examination system at Princeton has been working. In an interview with a representative of The Weekly, the President expressed himself as very much distressed that the impression should have got abroad that the "rules" printed in the circular for the guidance of examiners should have been considered new regulations adopted by the faculty, without consultation with the student committee on the Honor System. He pointed out that they are simply the regulations agreed upon at the outset between the student committee and the faculty, when the Honor System was instituted, and that the object of his circular was simply to remind those who were conducting examinations that these rules had recently been a little too much neglected. He felt sure, he said, that the faculty were unanimous in the feeling that nothing whatever should be done in the way of regulating the examinations, which was not done by a consultation between the student committee and the authorities of the University; that there is nothing in Princeton of which the faculty is prouder than the Honor System and nothing which they would be more punctilious to guard from any sort of interference, even their own. We may add, by way of assurance to the alumni, that there was never a time when the Princeton Honor System was working more successfully than at present.

Printed in the *Princeton Alumni Weekly*, IV (Feb. 6, 1904), 287.

A News Report of a Meeting with Class Secretaries about Reunions

[Feb. 6, 1904]

At a meeting of the Class Secretaries Association, at Princeton Inn, on the evening of January 30th, twenty Princeton classes were represented either by their Secretary, their President, or some other member. William R. Wilder '79, the Chairman of the Executive Committee of the association, presided, and President Wilson led the discussion, on the problem[1] presented by alumni reunions as they are at present conducted. Nearly every delegate present contributed to the symposium of opinion on this important question. The suggestions offered during the course of the evening are to be taken up in detail by a committee of the association and will form the basis of a report to be made later to the Secretary of each class, which will no doubt pave the way to some changes in the manner of conducting Commencement reunions.

Printed in the *Princeton Alumni Weekly*, IV (Feb. 6, 1904), 288-89.
[1] Excessive drinking.

From Wilson's Diary for 1904

Saturday, February 6, 1904

The preacher for to-morrow arrived at about bed time—Willis H. Butler, '95, of Northampton, Mass.[1]

The day darkened by deep trouble and distress at the Infirmary, —young Whelan's[2] illness and death—at evening. Called for a few minutes at the Hibbens to see Mr. Whelan, the father.

[1] Pastor of the Edwards Congregational Church of Northampton.
[2] Charles Smith Whelen, Jr., a member of the junior class from Philadelphia, whose father was a stock broker.

From Frederick Pollock

Dear Sir   [London]   Feb. 6 1904

Some days ago I saw a report of some observations of yours on the London Saturday Review,[1] which, from my slight acquaintance with that journal in its present condition, I believe were fully justified.

It is desirable that American publicists should know that the present Saturday Review has no real continuity with the old and distinguished journal of 1854–? or 1856–to 1894, which my brother Walter Pollock edited for about ten years, and to which I was a contributor for more than twenty.

In 1894 the late Mr. Beresford Hope's sons sold the Sat. Rev. (in haste and at an undervalue, I believe) to one Lewis Edmunds, half lawyer and half journalist, who after a short time sold it to Frank Harris, who ran it into the gutter, and then, some years ago, sold it to a syndicate.

There have been isolated clever writers in it, but it has nothing like the weight and reputation of the old Sat. Rev. and indeed can hardly be said to count as a serious journal. It would be unfortunate if it were supposed in America to represent any considerable section of British opinion.

I am   Yours sincerely   F. Pollock

ALS (WP, DLC).
[1] Probably in the London *Times*, Feb. 1, 1904, which quoted Wilson's remarks about the London *Saturday Review* and the London *Times* in the first news report printed at Jan. 30, 1904.

From Wilson's Diary for 1904

Sunday, February 7, 1904

Butler's sermon not so good as the one he preached last Commencement before the Philadelphian Society.[1] Rather crude in method, tho. excellent in form and spirit.

Jack away. Had gone to Phila. with body of young Whelan, who died last night at the Infirmary of pneumonia. The Hibbens had had Mr. and Mrs. Whelan at their house, to be near the boy, and had worn themselves out giving them the noblest comfort and support. Ellen being still confined to the house, Mrs. Hibben and I went alone to Miss Ricketts',—Mrs. Hibben stopping by the way to see Mrs. Turner.[2]

[1] There is a brief mention of this earlier sermon in the *Daily Princetonian*, June 10, 1903.
[2] Grace M. Turner of 31 Nassau St., apparently a widow.

To Frank Thilly

Princeton, N. J.

My dear Professor Thilly: 8 February, 1904.

I need hardly tell you how sincerely and deeply gratified we are by the contents of your letter of February 4, announcing your decision to accept the place here made vacant by Professor Baldwin's resignation. We shall certainly do our best to make you happy here both in your work and in your associations, and shall look forward to your coming with the greatest interest and pleasure.

The next meeting of our Board of Trustees will occur on the 10 March, and it is not possible for me to authorize before that date anything which would commit the Board. I regard them as committed, but, of course, it is an imperative point of courtesy to do and say nothing which will make this matter public before they have taken formal action. In the meantime, however, of course you have conferred confidentially with the authorities at Columbia, and I should think they were quite justified in regarding themselves as in a position to go to work on what must be, I fear, for them a very difficult and unwelcome problem of finding your successor. I wish I could think of some way to be of service to them in that matter.

I wonder if their attention has ever been called to Professor Roger B. C. Johnson, of Miami University?[1] He is one of our graduates, and a man who has won golden opinions at Miami both for his character and his scholarship. I should think he would be thoroughly worth considering.

I am asking the Treasurer of the University to send you his cheque for the amount of your travelling expenses.

Mrs. Wilson joins me in warmest regards and in the most cordial expressions of her pleasure at the news of your coming. I know that the Hibbens and Ormond and every one who met you here would join in these greetings if they knew I was writing.

Cordially and contentedly yours,   Woodrow Wilson

TLS (Wilson-Thilly Corr., NIC).
[1] Roger Bruce Cash Johnson '87; Ph.D., 1900. Professor of Mental and Moral Science, Miami University, 1888-1905; Preceptor in Philosophy, Princeton University, 1905-10; Professor of Philosophy, 1910-33; McCosh Professor of Philosophy, 1933-35.

From Wilson's Diary for 1904

Monday, February 8, 1904

Long talk with Mrs. Hibben in the afternoon. Did not leave the house till nearly seven.

In the evening met Committee at Dodge Hall to choose qu. for the debate with Yale next month.[1]

[1] The question chosen was "Resolved, That the government of the United States was warranted in recognizing the independence of the Republic of Panama." For the outcome of the debate on March 25, 1904, see WW to EAW, March 28, 1904.

Tuesday, February 9, 1904

Spent the day in Committee on Course of Study—completing preliminary work on the Groups by adopting those in Art and Archaeology and Geology and (partially, that in) Biology. Referred coördination of Groups and suggestion of schedule of hours to a sub-committee: West, Magie, Thompson, Neher.

To the Editor of the *Daily Princetonian*

[Dear Sir:]   [Princeton, N. J.,   c. Feb. 10, 1904]

Having been distressed to learn that the real character of a circular which I issued with regard to the examinations has been misunderstood, I avail myself of this earliest opportunity to state its real intention.

Its object was merely to call the attention of those conducting examinations to certain rules which have obtained since the very beginning of the present system of examinations, and which constituted part of the original understanding at the time of the institution of the honor system, but which had fallen too much into neglect. I want to say very distinctly that neither I nor any other member of the Faculty would ever suggest or support the enforcement of rules with regard to the conduct of examinations which had not been agreed upon between the Faculty and the Student Committee. There is nothing in Princeton which we value more highly than the present system of examinations, and we should certainly never do anything to put even an embarrassment in the way of its perfect execution.

WOODROW WILSON.

Printed in the *Daily Princetonian*, Feb. 11, 1904.

From Wilson's Diary for 1904

Wednesday, February 10, 1904

Academic faculty meeting,—lasted only ten minutes.

Evening: reception at the [Junius Spencer] Morgans',—a play, songs (by Evert Wendell),[1] supper, and a dance. Got away at midnight.

[1] Evert Jansen Wendell, gentleman of leisure of New York, noted as an amateur actor and singer.

From Edgar Gardner Murphy

My dear Dr. Wilson: New York City.   February 10, 1904

I thank you sincerely for your encouraging letter, and we are looking forward with the keenest interest to your presence with us. You will touch, at Birmingham, one of the most important centers of industrial development at the South. You will also have before you the brains and the conscience of the educational forces of the State, not to speak of a somewhat broad constituency gathered from every section of the South. To such a gathering the address which I heard at Old Point Comfort will bring an informing and inspiring message. Any other topic upon which you may have prepared an address would, of course, be suitable in case you should prefer it, but having heard the address at Old Point my appreciation of that lecture, is naturally quite definite.

At your convenience kindly let me know the time when it would be most convenient for you to speak and also be good enough to give me the definite title of the address. As to the time of your speech you would, perhaps, have the largest audience on the evening of the twenty-first or of the twenty-second. I am delighted that you are to go to Alabama, because there are many noble and fruitful influences at work in the State, and they need just the quickening and the direction which your personality will bring to them.

Very cordially yours,   Edgar Gardner Murphy

TLS (WP, DLC).

From Wilson's Diary for 1904

Thursday, February 11, 1904

At 1.21 off to Brooklyn,—without Ellen, alas! who was to have been the chief figure of the little trip,—planned when Miss Cutting[1] was in Princeton. Met at Jersey City by Miss Cutting and her father,[2] with a carriage. Mr. C. a most pleasing little gentleman, short and solid and full of good humour and quiet intelligence. Crossed by Cortdlandt St. ferry, crossed the city to the bridge, dropping Mr. Cutting at his business, and thence to 247 President St., Brooklyn.

A most interesting dinner party: Mr. and Mrs. Cutting,[3] Miss Cutting, Mr. and Mrs. St. Clair McKelway, Mrs and Mr. Bellamy,[4] and Dr. and Mrs. Riggs (née Cutting)[5]

After dinner a reception at the Barnard Club, where the persons I met seemed most pleasant and interesting.

[1] Elizabeth Brown Cutting, who lived with her parents at 247 President St., Brooklyn. She was managing editor of *Harper's Bazaar*, 1908-10, and "editorial assistant" on the *North American Review*, 1910-1927.
[2] Churchill Hunter Cutting, wool merchant, whose office was located at 345 Broadway, New York.
[3] Mary Dutton Cutting.
[4] Blanche Wilder Bellamy, author and editor in the field of English literature, and her husband, Frederick Putnam Bellamy, a lawyer and brother of the utopian novelist, Edward Bellamy. They lived at 260 Henry St., Brooklyn.
[5] Herman Clarence Riggs, M.D., and Grace Cutting Riggs, of 111 Montague St., Brooklyn.

Friday, February 12, 1904

My kind hosts had invited in to meet me at breakfast a most charming Miss Margaret Dreier,[1] who spoke Eng., wit, and sense with a truly engaging turn of the tongue. Sat and talked till noon.

Lunched with Dr. and Mrs. French (née Helen Wilson, uncle John's daughter)[2] and met also Mrs. Shope, Mrs. F.'s sister.[3] Found them both cultivated, thoughtful women, whom I shall be happy to see more of.

Reached home at 5.30

[1] Of 6 Montague Terrace, Brooklyn.
[2] Thomas R. French, M.D., and Helen Wilson French of 150 Joralemon St., Brooklyn. Mrs. French was a daughter of John Wilson, born in Philadelphia in 1810.
[3] Bella Wilson (Mrs. William Krebs) Shope, whose address at this time is unknown.

From Frederick Morris Warren[1]

Dear Wilson: New Haven, Feb. 12, 1904.

Mrs. Warren joins with me in asking you to stay with us during the session of Universities which is to be held next week.[2] We set up our Penates in a new atrium—is that where they kept them?—last autumn, and now wish that our friends could be induced to bow the knee before them on every and all occasions. We live at 46 Mansfield St.,—as you may know the town, it lies back of Prospect St.,—and are reached from the station by the Winchester car line which runs every twelve minutes. If you knew what train you would come by I could meet you at the station and see that you were not led astray by designing confidence men. We did not have the opportunity of viewing you at close range during your last New Haven visit,[3] and hope that no other host has anticipated us in seeking the balm of your companionship. Remember us most kindly to Mrs. Wilson and bring her with you if you can induce her to leave the young maidens.

As always   Your   F. M. Warren

ALS (WP, DLC).
[1] Street Professor of Modern Languages at Yale University and Wilson's old friend from the Johns Hopkins days.
[2] The fifth annual conference of the Association of American Universities met at Yale, February 18-20, 1904. Wilson did not attend the meeting.
[3] On October 23, 1901, when Wilson received the LL.D. degree from Yale during its bicentennial ceremonies. See the news report printed at Oct. 26, 1901, Vol. 12.

From Wilson's Diary for 1904

Saturday, February 13, 1904

At lunch Prof. Henneman and his young brother-in-law, Hubard,[1] to whom I showed one of the club houses and some of the library rooms, and then accompanied to the 3.50 train.
Walked a little, between five and six, with Jack Hibben.
Dr. Charles Wood, to preach to-morrow, came in fr. Phila. about a quarter past ten and we talked till eleven[2]

[1] John Bell Henneman, Professor of English at the University of the South and editor of the Sewanee Review, and Robert Thruston Hubard III of Bolling, Va., A.B., Hampden-Sydney College 1897, who had studied law at the University of the South, 1901-1902.
[2] Wilson discontinued his entries in the diary at this point.

From James Laughlin, Jr.

My dear Sir,   New York, Feby. 15th, 1904.

Having been providentially prevented by illness from being present at the regular meetings of the Board of Trustees, in excess of my allowable time; as an Alumni Trustee; and in order that the Board may be free to take action for a full Alumni representation, I hereby tender to you my resignation, to take effect at once, so that the vacancy can be filled at the coming June election.[1] I wish to assure you, and the members of the Board, that my health is now almost completely restored: and my devotion to the interests—and future, of Princeton University, & her Alumni, is even greater than ever and the rest and study since my absence from active work, will better fit me for a service that I have long contemplated & which I trust the future will verify. With great respect I remain

                    Yours most sincerely,   James Laughlin Jr.

ALS (Trustees' Papers, UA, NjP).
    [1] He was succeeded by Nathaniel Ewing, Princeton 1869, corporation lawyer of Uniontown, Pa.

From Edgar Gardner Murphy

My dear Dr. Wilson: New York City, February 15th 1904.

Because of serious local complications at Birmingham we are having to change our dates to the 26, 27, 28th of April. I regret this change more deeply than I can well say.

As you are arranging, however, for a general Southern journey we earnestly hope you can so adjust your other appointments as to meet your engagement with us without serious inconvenience. If you can come to us for the evening of the 27th I would suggest that date for your address. You will then have our largest & most representative audience.

Hoping that the change will cause you no serious trouble and cordially appreciating your cooperation, I am

                    Very Truly Yours,   Edgar Gardner Murphy.

The address upon "Americanism" will fit perfectly into the Program as we are planning it.

ALS (WP, DLC).

A News Report of Two Speeches in Albany, New York

                                    [Feb. 16, 1904]
                    University and Church.

In the ballroom of the Ten Eyck hotel last evening, Prof. Woodrow Wilson, LL.D., of Princeton university, addressed the members of the Presbyterian Union[1] on the subject of "The University and the Church." During the course of his address Prof. Winslow [Wilson] said the university should have but one aim, that it should inculcate the truth, and in that aim should include the church, and if the church cannot stand the inquiry of just and placid minds it ought not to live.[2] President Wilson is a well known speaker and his address last evening was a scholarly effort of logical and convincing conclusions.

After President Wilson's address the banquet of the Princeton Alumni Association of Albany and vicinity was held at the Fort Orange Club. Dr. Richmond,[3] the president of the association, was at the head of the table and had on his right hand as the guest of honor President Wilson. Dr. Richmond welcomed the members of the association and their guests and introduced Dr. Wilson, who responded to the toast of "Princeton." "The Advantages of College Life and Education" was discussed by Judge John Clinton Gray of the Court of Appeals, and Luther H. Tucker toasted "Yale." Then followed many impromptu toasts by the old Princeton men.

Printed in the *Albany Evening Journal*, Feb. 16, 1904.
[1] The Presbyterian Unions were city-wide associations in various cities that usually met monthly for lectures, discussion, and fellowship.
[2] There is no evidence that Wilson was referring to any specific controversy in the Presbyterian Church in the U.S.A. What he had in mind was probably that denomination's increasingly rigid position on matters of theological orthodoxy following several notable trials in the 1890's. See Lefferts A. Loetscher, *The Broadening Church: A Study of Theological Issues in the Presbyterian Church since 1869* (Philadelphia, 1954), pp. 48-89.
[3] The Rev. Dr. Charles Alexander Richmond, Princeton 1883, pastor of the Madison Avenue Presbyterian Church in Albany.

A News Report of an Address in Syracuse, New York

[Feb. 17, 1904]

THIS IS TRUE PATRIOTISM

Woodrow Wilson Gives a New Exposition of It.

It was a vigorous and thoughtful address on "Patriotism" that Dr. Woodrow Wilson, president of Princeton university, delivered in the assembly hall of the University building last evening. Dr. Wilson talks as he writes, in a forceful, witty, clean-cut manner and his address last evening was heard with interest by an audience of invited guests which filled the hall.

Doctor Wilson was in Syracuse yesterday as the guest of the local Princeton alumni and the University club. The features of his entertainment were a dinner at the Century club at 6 o'clock tendered by the Princeton alumni and a reception at the University club rooms after the address.

When Dr. John Van Duyn[1] and President Wilson stepped upon the platform at 8:30 o'clock they were greeted with a ringing Princeton cheer from a contingent of loyal Tigers, which was gratefully acknowledged. Doctor Wilson said that patriotism was too big a subject to cover fully in a half hour's talk, and he only hoped to speak of it in a general way. His address was epigrammatic. Some of the salient points were as follows:

It would seem that the people as a whole have never realized the true meaning of patriotism. To me it seems, like liberty, almost a living thing. Most people look upon patriotism as a sentiment, but to regard it merely so is wrong. There is principle to it also. It is true men are controlled by sentiment. Then principles transmuted into sentiment are most effective. It is said we are controlled by mind, but you will find that our minds too often are constitutional monarchs and we are usually governed by a tumultuous House of Commons of passions.

◇

It has become the fashion for men to conceal the sentimental part of their natures. Men are oftentimes ashamed to be called sentimental. But sentimentality is not sentiment. Sentimentality is sentiment gone to seed.

◇

Patriotism is a principle of conduct. It is like friendship, only on a greater scale. It is friendship written large. . . .[2] Love does not proceed from reason. If it did some loves would appear very unreasonable. Will a man lay down his life for something that he does not love? If you truly love your fellow citizens you will find it easier to love your fellow men. Nobility is a word we instinctively reserve as a badge of distinction for one who does not exert his powers selfishly. Nobility and patriotism are energies of character operating outside the narrow circle of selfish interests. The man who goes out of the world without having shared with others the energies of his character goes out not deserving to be mourned.

◇

It is more difficult at some periods, in some years or dec-

---

[1] Professor of Medical History in the College of Medicine of Syracuse University.
[2] This and all following ellipses in the original text.

ades to be patriotic than in others. It is easy to be patriotic in time of war. But there are other times when patriotism is just as necessary. It manifests itself in different ways at different times. In pioneer days there was the sound of patriotism in the crack of the rifle, in the ring of the wood chopper's ax and in the snap of the teamster's whip. . . . Muscle is the easiest thing we have to exercise. This is not generally accepted, however. Some people think that mind is the easiest thing to exercise, but such have not discovered their minds. In the days when thoughtful energy is required patriotism is not so easy.

◇

I must go to the poets rather than to the systematic writers on political subjects when I look for a text from which to speak on patriotism. Men must see visions to be guided aright in days of complicated affairs. Tennyson shall supply me with my text, "A nation yet, the rulers and the ruled."[3] The poet says we need some sense of duty, some reverence for the laws, some civic manhood firm against the crowd. . . . The man who asks "What's the matter with Kansas?"[4] is thinking sectional thoughts. We have noticed the inconsistency of some Presidential candidates in adjusting their remarks on national issues to the section in which they happen to be. Patriotism in the country is not compatible with lack of sympathy between the different sections of it. Opinions do and should differ, but difference of opinion should not alter the character of the people or their love for the common country. I could not feel sorry for the United States coming out into the field of international politics. I am an imperialist if you wish, but I cannot help feeling sorry for the anti-imperialists. We assumed in their case that because they did not agree with us about the wisdom of territorial expansion, therefore, they did not love our country. That was wrong.

◇

What do all the salaams and genuflections to the flag in the public school mean? The flag doesn't stand for genuflections. It does not stand for opinion rammed down the throat. It does not stand for "our country, right or wrong."

[3] From "The Princess, Conclusion."
[4] A reference to William Allen White's scathing anti-Populist editorial, "What's the Matter with Kansas?", which first appeared in the *Emporia*, Kan., *Gazette*, Aug. 15, 1896.

But it does stand for the biggest kick on record. The American revolution was carried through by a minority, even by a minority in this country. No man properly honors the American flag who does not recognize the right to difference of opinion.

◇

In democracy a noteworthy thing is the inexorable character of an accomplished fact. What is done usually must stand. That is why the anti-imperialists should now bend all their efforts to make the government in our new possessions the best it can be.

◇

I don't believe that calling our President "Teddy" is compatible with the dignity of our democracy. Although our President is elected by us, he is our ruler, and we in a sense are his subjects. The sense of duty is the balance of every people. Our obedience to the laws is the sign of our allegiance to the accomplishments of the race. The great majority of the laws under which we live were made before we were born.

◇

I sometimes fear that in the time of the American revolution, had I lived then, I would have been a Tory. Patient changes appeal to me. The dogged pressure of opinion brings reform just as surely, although more slowly than revolution. Every opinion that gets current was started by a minority. There is no virtue in a crowd per se. There have been seasons in the world's history when the finest thing in it was a single man with sword drawn against the crowd, saying "You may kill my body, but you cannot coerce my spirit."

◇

There are not enough men in politics who are there without ambition for offices or personal aggrandizement. We need more disinterested men who are in all the secrets and do not want anything for themselves. Such men make the professional politicians uneasy, but with a few such our modern Sodoms would be saved.

◇

It is easy to be deceived by books. We must correct books by life. But again, we should not be duped by men. Validity of opinion and good character unfortunately are not synonymous. . . . Progress is made more by following than by leading. More follow than can lead. The enthusiasm of the masses that follow is the excuse for parties. We cannot go forward as a rabble, but as an army with enthusiasm and esprit de corps.

◇

With more generous energy and ardor of character, wishing to do something for others, let us overcome the difficulties, and having found the straight road of duty walk in it, cheering and helping all who walk with us.

Printed in the *Syracuse Herald*, Feb. 17, 1904; one editorial heading omitted.

From Allan Marquand

My dear President Wilson,   Naples, Feb. 18 '04

When in Rome a few days ago I purchased for $500 an Italian painting for the Art Museum.[1] I ordered it shipped to Care of Tice and Lynch, 45 William St. New York, who in due time will notify you of its arrival. As this is to be paid for ultimately from the Museum Fund, you will have no difficulty in signing the document to the effect that it was ordered by the College & for the College.

I am expecting David Magie[2] this evening and tomorrow we shall probably start for Sicily and Greece. I have already been to Pompeii & to Paestum, in the rain.

Very sincerely yrs   Allan Marquand
care of the Ionian Bank   Athens, Greece.

P.S. The picture has been paid for by me—the bill for carrying charges will be met by Mrs. Marquand.

ALS (WP, DLC).

[1] A Tuscan altarpiece, Madonna della Cintola, 1484, of the School of Bontifigli. It is now part of the extensive collection of Italian paintings in the Art Museum of Princeton University.

[2] David Magie, Jr. '97, Instructor in Latin at Princeton. At this time he was studying in Europe for the Ph.D. in Classics, which he received from the University of Halle in 1904.

To Daniel Moreau Barringer

My dear Moreau: Princeton, N. J.   19 February, 1904.

No definite decision has yet been made with regard to the allotment of rooms in the new dormitory, but it has been tacitly understood that '79 men were to have the privilege of determining the allotment in the first instance.

If you will be kind enough to drop C. C. Cuyler a line on the subject, he can bring it to the attention of his Committee, the Committee on Grounds and Buildings, and prepare the necessary resolution for the Board of Trustees.[1] In the meantime I think it practically certain that you can secure a room for young Churchman.[2]

It is always a pleasure to hear from you, and you may be sure that I shall come to "Poplar Grove," if I can tear myself away from exacting routine.

With warmest regards,

Always,   Cordially yours,   Woodrow Wilson

TLS (WC, NjP).

[1] This matter was never brought before the Board of Trustees.

[2] Probably Philip Hudson Churchman '96, Instructor in French at Princeton, 1900-1904, who was on leave studying in Paris during the academic year 1903-1904.

Notes for a Talk to the School Children of Princeton[1]

2/19/'04   12 M.

Princeton Public School 19 Feb'y, 1904, 2.30 P.M.

Washington.

We affect to be *tired* of Washington and use a silly invention to make him *common*

But only the *real* Washington dominates our imagination and rules our spirits

Sh. be as real to us as John Witherspoon: for he walked these sts. as Witherspoon did.

The man: 1. A stern man who loved children

2. An imperious man who never served himself

3. An impatient man who knew how to do labourious, patient work.

5. A man who spent himself outside his own interest

4. A hot tempered man who had himself always in hand.

WWhw MS. (WP, DLC).

[1] The *Princeton Press*, Feb. 27, 1904, reported only that Wilson spoke on Washington at the Public School on February 19, 1904, under the auspices of the Junior Aid Committee of the Village Improvement Society (described in n. 1 to the news report printed at May 20, 1902, Vol. 12), and that his address was "enthusiastically received and appreciated."

A News Report of a Lecture at the Phillips Exeter Academy

[Feb. 20, 1904]

LECTURE.

All those who were fortunate enough to attend the lecture last Wednesday evening enjoyed to the utmost the instructive and entertaining talk of President Wilson, of Princeton University. Mr. Wilson pointed out in his inimitable and easy manner the vast benefits to be derived from a college course in a university of to-day. He drew pleasing similes of the preparatory school as a work shop, in which the use of the tools of life was taught, and showed that the university was the place where these tools were given, and that the accomplishment of the tasks in college was the result of a knowledge of their use.

During his remarks Mr. Wilson kept the audience in the best of humor by his clever stories and anecdotes.

Printed in the Exeter, N. H., *Exonian*, Feb. 20, 1904.

To Edward Warren Ordway[1]

My dear Sir: Princeton, N. J.   20 Feb[r]uary, 1904.

In reply to your circular letter of Feb[r]uary 18, I am sorry to be obliged to say that I do not think the movement in favor of Philippine independence either wise or opportune and that I cannot, therefore, of course consent to have my name used in connection with the agitation looking in that direction.

Very truly yours,   Woodrow Wilson

TLS (E. W. Ordway Papers, NN).
[1] New York lawyer and Secretary of the New York Anti-Imperialist League.

To Simon Gratz[1]

My dear Mr. Gratz,   Princeton, 20 Feb'y, 1904

I have learned through Mr. Bayard Henry of your thoughtful kindness in putting us in the way of acquiring a valuable collection of autographs,[2] and I wish to give myself the pleasure of expressing to you directly my warm appreciation. It is most gratifying to have friends of that sort.

Sincerely and Cordially Yours,   Woodrow Wilson

ALS (Gratz Collection, American Historians, PHi).
[1] Lawyer, civic leader, and noted autograph collector of Philadelphia. His principal collection of some 175,000 manuscripts is now in the Historical Society of Pennsylvania.
[2] There is no evidence that Princeton ever acquired this collection.

From Alfred James Pollock McClure

Philadelphia, Penna.
My dear Woodrow: February 22, 1904.

It is very dreadful, and I am down among the abjects in spirit, but what will a man not do to keep the faith and finish the course of his sons at Princeton? The boys are at the end of their second year and I have nothing to pay—alas this is no figure of speech. I have put off the evil day when it might be necessary to write you again,[1] indeed I had hoped to earn and have the boys earn and economize and so avoid such a crisis, but how could I foresee that a second operation more serious than the first, would need to be performed this time upon Mrs. McClure's brain,[2] after I was struggling with the expense of the first.

But why should I weary you and humiliate myself with a recital of private straits and "frustrations." I could write to no other college president in this way. The sum of the matter is I owe Princeton University, beyond what I can pay, on bills just received, (all back bills are paid thank the Lord) two hundred and eighty seven dollars. As I wrote you about this time last year,[3] it is up to me either to withdraw the boys or to get from you, as you so blessedly wrote, "the needed additional sum in such a way that it would come through me solus"; and as I continued in my letter to you, and now repeat, because it expresses what I feel now as then—If this is an impersonal resource, and if I can justify the acceptance of it, as I do a scholarship, and by reason of the fact as you have written that "the cause of education after all stands on a somewhat exceptional basis," then, my dear Woodrow, I beg to send you a copy of the letter you wrote three months later. I did not remind you you [sic] of the additional sum promised in the Autumn, because I thought up to date that the boys and I could manage the business. But I can't. I am distressed more than I can tell you by the necessity of writing you, and by adding one straw to your abundant cares and responsibilities. Forgive me.

If there are "resources" won't you let me know, so that I can arrange with Treasurer Duffield, who is sharp on the trigger, as of course he ought to be.[4]

With cordial regard, I am,

Very sincerely yours,   Alfred J. P. McClure.

TLS (WP, DLC).
[1] See A. J. P. McClure to WW, June 10, 1902, Vol. 12, and WW to A. J. P. Mc-Clure, June 1, 1903, Vol. 14. McClure's sons were Jay Cooke McClure and Alfred James McClure, both of the Class of 1906.
[2] Louise Foster Cutter McClure survived with her husband to celebrate their Golden Wedding anniversary on January 1, 1930.
[3] This letter is missing, as are those mentioned subsequently.
[4] Although Wilson's reply is missing, he did find the funds to aid the McClure boys.

Notes for a Religious Address

23 Feb'y, 1904[1]

Pennsylvania Sunday School Association

Pittsburgh, 13 Oct., '04[2]   Philadelphia, 26 Feb'y, 1904[3]

The Young People and the Church.

I. Our object, to *win, mould, instruct.*
   Each generation must indoctrinate and stamp itself upon the next.

II. *Our means: Life*
                 Organization,—as a means of expressing Life, widening it, extending it. E.g. the Sunday Sch.

III. *The Home*: the lives of their elders ⎫
     The Church: the place of witness   ⎪ The moral power of
     The School: the place of instruction ⎬ the pastor.
     Society, the school of observation ⎪
        and experience   ⎭

IV. *What chiefly commands* the Young?
     1) *Authority*
     2) *Conviction*
     3) *Sober, earnest force*, as if of business—something essential to life.
     4) *Dignity*, simplicity, impressiveness
Religion is a personal relationship and a way of love and service, and progresses by life,—by system only as a vehicle of life.

"Pure religion and undefiled before God and the Father is this, To visit the fatherless and widows in their affliction, and to keep himself unspotted from the world." James I., 27.

WWhw MS. (WP, DLC).
 [1] Wilson's composition date.
 [2] The text of Wilson's address in Pittsburgh is printed at Oct. 13, 1904, a news report of it at Oct. 14, 1904.
 [3] A news report of the Philadelphia address is printed at Feb. 27, 1904.

To Charles Freeman Williams McClure

My dear McClure: Princeton, N. J. 24 Feb[r]uary, 1904.

I think that I am likely to have leisure to give the biological group my real attention tomorrow, Thursday, afternoon and [at] a quarter past two. I am particularly desirous of talking over some phases of the matter with you.
 Always,
       Cordially yours, Woodrow Wilson

TLS (McClure Zoological Autograph Coll., NjP).

From Susan Eliza Hall

My dear Dr. Wilson, Wilmington, N. C. Feb. 25, 1904.

Mother wishes me to say it is not she who takes so long a time to answer your letter. But my delay is not from neglect or forgetfulness. Your letter brought quite too much pleasure for that.

We are all delighted—all of us who share the secret—at the prospect of a visit from you. When you have your plans completed, the committee will be glad to consult with you about any arrangements necessary to be made.

I hope your household are all quite well, and your large adopted family prospering. I have charge this winter over the studies of a future Princetonian whom I am sure you will approve. I mean Uncle James Sprunt's only son, Laurence.[1]

I send you my sincere thanks for the delightful surprise, and with cordial wishes I am
     Yours very truly, (Miss) Susan E. Hall.

ALS (WP, DLC).
 [1] James Laurence Sprunt entered Princeton in 1906 and was graduated with the Class of 1910.

A News Item

[Feb. 26, 1904]

FIRST TRASK LECTURE[1]

Mr. William Travers Jerome, District Attorney of New York City, delivered the first Trask lecture of the season, last evening, in Alexander Hall, taking as his subject, "The College Man in Politics." President Wilson introduced Mr. Jerome. . . .

Printed in the *Daily Princetonian*, Feb. 26, 1904; one editorial heading omitted.
    [1] About this series, see n. 1 to the extract from the Minutes of the Princeton Faculty printed at Dec. 2, 1896, Vol. 10.

A News Report of an Address on Young People and the Church

[Feb. 27, 1904]

SABBATH WORK LEADERS CHOSEN

The annual election of officers of the Philadelphia County Sabbath School Association was held at the afternoon session at the Grace Baptist Temple yesterday afternoon. . . .

Sermons for doubting pulpits and musical services that predominate over the religious element were subjects of attack by Dr. Woodrow Wilson, president of Princeton University, at the evening session. His subject was: "The Young People and the Church." Regarding sermons of lukewarm preachers, he said:

"Much of the prevailing unbelief of the young people of today, I am firmly convinced, is due to the analytic and doubting preachers of our pulpits, men who as much as tell their hearers 'I don't know whether I believe what I am saying or not.'

"Such a method of teaching cools the process of belief and kills the power of acceptance. Will you believe a man who does not believe what he is saying himself? Are you going to believe a doctrine which has a great question mark around it? If you rob your teaching of authority you cannot hand your doctrines on from one generation to another. Youth respects authority. If you doubt what you say, those who listen to you will doubt, and if you disbelieve, those who listen to you will disbelieve.

"I would not say that music does not go with dignity, but when you substitute music for the administration of the word of God you are admitting that the word of God is not effective. You do not impress young people by making pleasing services. Or if you do, they don't get what you want them to when they come to church."

Printed in the *Philadelphia Inquirer*, Feb. 27, 1904; one editorial heading omitted.

To Charles Williston McAlpin

Princeton, N. J.

My dear Mr. McAlpin: 29 Feb[r]uary, 1904.

Mr. David Metcalfe, 10 South Reunion, a member of the senior class of the School of Science, finds himself unable to pay all of his second term bill, and wishes to make some arrangement by which he can have some extension of time without losing his degree. Mr. Duffield informs me that there is enough money in the loan fund in his hands to justify a loan to Mr. Metcalfe of $50, which would make it possible for him to meet his bill. I have reason to think that Mr. Metcalfe is a thoroughly worthy man, and write therefore to say that if you approve of it, I think it would be just to him to authorize a loan of $50 to him by the Treasurer.

As you know, I wish to concentrate all these matters in your hands and not myself to intervene, so that this is a suggestion, and if accepted the Treasurer must get his authorization from you.

Very cordially yours,   Woodrow Wilson

TLS (McAlpin File, UA, NjP).

To Austin Scott

Princeton, N. J.

My dear President Scott: 29 Feb[r]uary, 1904.

All the information, so far as I know, which has reached this country with regard to the awarding of the Rhodes scholarships is contained in the convenient Bulletin of the University of Mississippi,[1] which I take pleasure in sending you under another cover. I have been expecting to learn from Dr. Parkin, the agent of the Trustees of the Rhodes Fund, what arrangements they wished made with regard to the time and manner of holding the examinations, but I have heard nothing. I will, of course, communicate with you the moment I have any information, and we can then act as a Committee in the matter.

Cordially yours,   Woodrow Wilson

TLS (A. Scott Papers, NjR).
[1] "The Cecil Rhodes Scholarships," *Bulletin of the University of Mississippi*, Series II, Supplement (Aug. 1903).

From Franklin Blake Morse[1]

My dear President Wilson: New York, Feb. 29th. 1904.

Among the things left by my father[2] who recently died, is a collection of Japanese Netsukes (ivory carvings) which he gathered together during his residence in Japan covering a period from 1859 to 1884.

There are between 450 and 500 Netsukes in the collection varying in size from the dimensions of a walnut, to carvings three or four inches in diameter and as many inches in height. These carvings are all old ones and are but rarely to be picked up nowadays in Japan. Their value like all old works of art is difficult to fix, but were held by my father at a valuation of ($10,000.00) Ten Thousand dollars.

He had often spoken of loaning this collection to the New York Metropolitan Museum of Art, but for one reason or another he never took action in the matter.

Since his death however, my brother William O[tis]. Morse of the class of 1902, and myself, have consulted with my mother and sister in regard to presenting Princeton University with the collection as a memorial to father should it be acceptable.

The only stipulations we would make in presenting it are:

1. It shall be known as "THE WILLIAM HORACE MORSE COLLECTION."

2. It shall be properly enclosed and set up in *a show case* in the University Library or Art Museum as may be deemed the more appropriate, and to be *cared for* and *held by* the University in perpetuity.[3]

In order that you may better know what the collection is, the space it will occupy (which will be quite little) necessary to properly exhibit it, and various other details you may require which may be necessary prior to any decision from the University in regard to the acceptance of the gift, I would say that the collection is at our home, 24 West 96th. St. where we would be glad to show it to your proper representative.

Yours very truly,   Franklin B. Morse.   *Class of '95.*

TLS (Trustees' Papers, UA, NjP).

[1] A member of the Class of 1895 who was not graduated, Morse was employed at this time in his father's firm of Smith, Baker & Co., importers, of New York and Kobe, Japan.

[2] William Horace Morse.

[3] This collection is now in the Art Museum of Princeton University.

An Announcement

[March 5, 1904]

The Baccalaureate Address at this year's Commencement is to be delivered by President Wilson '79, at the special request of the Senior Class Day Committee.[1]

Printed in the *Princeton Alumni Weekly*, IV (March 5, 1904), 355.
[1] It is printed at June 12, 1904.

To Victor Rosewater[1]

My dear Mr. Rosewater: Princeton, N. J.   7 March, 1904.

I esteem it a very great compliment that I should be asked to consider an invitation to deliver the oration at the approaching celebration of the Semi-Centennial of the Anniversary of the Territorial Organization of Nebraska, and can assure you that it would give me the greatest pleasure to accept such an invitation if it were possible for me to do so; but my engagements are already too many. It would be literally impossible for me to prepare an oration within the time now remaining, even if I could at the date named conscientiously absent myself from Princeton. It is a date so nearly on the eve of our Commencement that, I fear, I should in any case be obliged to decline an invitation which would involve my going to a distant place at that time.

Pray accept my warmest thanks for your kind letter and convey to the Committee in charge of the Celebration my heartiest expressions of obligation and regret.

                    Very sincerely yours,   Woodrow Wilson

TLS (WC, NjP).
[1] Managing Editor of the Omaha *Bee*.

From George Petrie[1]

My dear Doctor Wilson,   Auburn, Alabama.   March 7, 1904.

We have been hoping and planning for some time to have you lecture here and at other points in Alabama. Last Fall Mr. A. C. Harte, the Y.M.C.A. Secretary of Mobile, Professor H. O. Murfee of Marion, Alabama, and I had a conference in regard to the matter. Murfee now writes me that he has had some correspondence with you about it. I infer from his letter that it is possible you may come a little later in the Spring. Mr. Neal Anderson[2] of Montgomery also writes me that you may come down to the Educational Conference at Birmingham in April, and give several addresses on that trip. I do hope that we may see you in Alabama either then or at some other time in the near future.

Murfee is authorized to speak for us as well as himself, and to avoid confusion, I have left all arrangements in his hands; but personally I wish to express our earnest desire to have you in Auburn. In saying this I speak not only for myself, but for the entire faculty and the students. We have a wide-awake, growing college,—the most vigorous in the state. In many respects it has been the pioneer in technical education in the South. Therefore I believe we are a fine field for one who has an educational message. We need it, and are not too set in our ways to heed it. We are, moreover, anxious to cultivate closer relations with the large universities. Our men are earnest and aggressive, and frequently after graduating here go elsewhere for more advanced work.

I earnestly hope that you can arrange to visit us. If you can, I would suggest that you write either to Murfee at Marion, or to me, stating when you can come and on what terms.

With kind regards, I remain

Yours very truly,   George Petrie

TLS (WP, DLC).
[1] Professor of History and Latin at Alabama Polytechnic Institute.
[2] The Rev. Neal Larkin Anderson, pastor of the Central Presbyterian Church of Montgomery, Ala.

To the Board of Trustees of Princeton University

Princeton, N. J.
To the Trustees of Princeton University: 9 March, 1904.

The Committee on the Curriculum would respectfully report the following recommendations:

1. That Frank Thilly, A.M., Ph.D., be elected Stuart Professor of Psychology.

2. That Professor Jesse Benedict Carter be given leave of absence for two years, with such allowance of salary as the Committee on Finance may sanction.

3. That Professor Arthur L. Frothingham be granted a half year's leave of absence on full salary.

4. That Assistant Professor W. U. Vreeland be promoted to the rank of Professor of Romance Languages.

5. That the following recommendations of the University Faculty with regard to the arrangement of the calendar for the University year be adopted (See File A.)[1]

6. That the following recommendations of the University Faculty with regard to examination and matriculation fees be adopted (See file B.)[2]

7. That Professor H. A. Garfield be authorized to give an elec-

tive course on The Government of Dependencies to the Seniors.

8. That the courses in Music be discontinued after the present academic year.

9. That the requirement of graduation theses from candidates for the degree of Bachelor of Science be abolished.

10. That the Faculty be authorized to admit students of the Princeton Theological Seminary, in exceptional circumstances to special restricted undergraduate courses upon the payment of five dollars per schedule hour per term for the courses taken.

11. That the "Class of 1860 Fellowship" in experimental science be restricted to the departments of Physics and Chemistry, be made a "University Fellowship," and be granted upon such an allotment of the funds to one or more fellows as the University Faculty may direct,—provided the consent of the donors or of the legal representatives be first obtained to such of these changes as may appear to be inconsistent with the deed of gift.

12. That the degree of Bachelor of Arts be conferred upon Mr. John Adams Wilson as of the class of 1873.[3]

Woodrow Wilson   Acting Chairman[4]

WWhwRS with TS addenda (Trustees' Papers, UA, NjP).
    [1] Not printed.
    [2] Not printed.
    [3] Wilson's first cousin, identified in J. A. Wilson to WW, Jan. 17, 1894, n. 1, Vol. 8.
    [4] All these recommendations were approved by the Board of Trustees on March 10, 1904.

From Andrew Fleming West

Princeton

Dear Wilson—   Wednesday afternoon   March 9 [1904]

The accompanying letter and telegram[1] announce that Mr. Cadwalader and Col. McCook cannot be at the committee[2] meeting tonight. The other members of the committee are yourself, Mr. Cleveland, Mr. Jones, Mr. Pyne, Mr. J W Alexander the chairman (Dr McPherson) and myself.

The subscriptions for equipping and running the residence on the Bayles Farm[3] for three years are as follows:

M. Taylor Pyne $250 annually	=	$750
Junius S. Morgan $200 "	=	600
Charles Scribner $250 "	=	750
Arthur H. Scribner $250 "	=	750
		$2850

In addition to these Colonel McCook has told me he would subscribe, but thus far I have not had an opportunity to see him
and get the amount fixed. But his subscription may be counted
as certain. The total amount necessary is $6250,—as follows:

Furnishing the house (at least) $1000
3 years rent, at $750 annually   2250
Guarantee for expenses, $1000
      annually   3000
                                    ——————
                                      $6250

If this project is to go into effect the money ought to be secured
by the first of May, because some time must be left to make the
arrangements known to the graduates before they leave.

Ever yours   Andrew F. West

ALS (WP, DLC).
  [1] They are missing.
  [2] That is, the Trustees' Committee on the Graduate School.
  [3] This plan to use the house on this estate adjacent to the eastern side of
the campus as a residence for graduate students was soon abandoned because
West was unable to raise the necessary funds in time.

A Resolution

[March 10, 1904]

Resolved That, in view of the splendid gift of a dormitory
about to be presented to the University by the class of 1879, the
President of the University be requested to convey to the official
representatives of the class an intimation of the wish and policy
of the Board that each dormitory should bear a personal name,
either the name of the donor or some name selected by those
who make the gift, or by the authorities of the University,—pref-
erably the name of some distinguished man connected with the
history of the University itself.[1]

That the President be requested, in making this intimation to
express to the representatives of the class once more the Board's
warm appreciation and admiration of the unexampled loyalty
and generosity of the class in making so noble a gift to the University, and its strong desire that the source of this gift should not
be lost under the name given the building, but marked and distinguished by some conspicuous, permanent, and unmistakable
inscription upon the building itself.[2]

WWhw MS. (Trustees' Papers, UA, NjP).
  [1] As will become clear from following documents, Wilson very strongly favored
naming the dormitory for President McCosh, while a majority of the class insisted upon naming it Seventy-Nine Hall. Considerable controversy ensued, but
the majority had its way.

2 This resolution was approved and spread on the Minutes of the Board of Trustees, March 10, 1904.

Henry Burchard Fine to the Board of Trustees' Committee on Morals and Discipline

Gentlemen: PRINCETON UNIVERSITY, MARCH 10, 1904.

I have the honor to present the following report for the three months which have elapsed since the last meeting of the Board of Trustees.

I DISORDERLY CONDUCT

So far as I have been able to learn there has been but little drinking or other serious disorder during the three months covered by this report.

Six students have been reported for drunkenness, three for the first time and three for the second time. Those reported for the first time were admonished and warned, and those reported for the second time were suspended for a period of six weeks.

Two freshmen were guilty of the offense of visiting one of the lodging houses on University Place and of disturbing its inmates and damaging property. They were given an eight weeks suspension. Still another student just after Christmas was suspended for the remainder of the year because of extreme irregularity in attendance and for paying certain of his bills with worthless cheques.

Happily there has been no revival this February of the practice of daubing property with paint, which until last year had been so serious a nuisance to the community.

II DISHONESTY IN THE LAST EXAMINATIONS

In the recent mid-year examinations several of the Freshmen were guilty of dishonesty. A low person named Thompson, resident in the town, had succeeded in getting possession of certain of the examination papers through his son, an employee in the office where they were printed. A confederate of his named Kinney, a waiter in one of the Freshmen clubs, approached certain of the Freshmen, whom he knew to be apprehensive of the results of the examination, with an offer for suitable compensation to get from Thompson the papers which they needed. Six Freshmen and one Special Student yielded to this temptation and purchased one or more of the papers. Fortunately some of the men approached by Kinney had a higher sense of honor and one of them had the courage to inform the Student Committee on the Honor System of the traffic which was going on. The Committee at once met and undertook an investigation which was marked by extraordinary thoroughness and cleverness, and which resulted in the discovery of the students who had purchased the papers. The Committee succeeded in getting confessions from all these men and recommended to the Faculty that they be finally dismissed from college. They also recommended that another Freshman who confessed to having arranged for the purchase of a paper, but was able to prove by witnesses that he had destroyed it without looking at it, be suspended until May 1st. The Faculty voted unanimously to adopt all these recommendations of the Committee.

Thompson and Kinney were arrested on complaint of Mr. Robinson, the University printer, and were lodged in the Trenton jail. Thompson who has plead guilty is now awaiting sentence[1] and Kinney is to stand trial next week or the week following.

This unhappy incident shows the need of greater precaution in the guarding of our examination papers, but fortunately for us the incident has resulted in the discovery and punishment of two dangerous characters, and it has demonstrated in a most convincing way the genuineness of the devotion of the body of our students to the Honor System. The impartiality and unsparing thoroughness of the Student Committee are above all praise.

III RESULTS OF THE MID-YEAR EXAMINATIONS

Seventy-five students have been "dropped" because of failure in more than half of the work of a term as shown in class room and by the recent mid-year examinations. These students are distributed among the several classes as follows:

Academic Department

Juniors	3	Freshmen	7
Sophomores	2	Specials	3
	Total	15	

School of Science

B.S. Juniors	6	Freshmen	15
Sophomores	10	Specials	10
C.E. Seniors	2	Sophomores	4
Juniors	1	Freshmen	12
	Total	60	

The most striking fact revealed by these statistics is this: Four times as many students were dropped from the School of Science as from the Academic Department, although the enrolment in the latter department is the larger. No doubt one reason for this extraordinary difference is that because of its lower entrance requirements a greater proportion of students of inferior ability and attainment gain access to the School of Science than to the Academic Department. But in the opinion of the Faculty the principal reason is that while the Academic students had learned by the actual experience of a year to expect a rigorous enforcement of the rules of standing, the students of the School of Science, though frequently warned that this year the rules were to be enforced with equal rigor in both departments of the University, could not be made to take the warning seriously, and neither during the term nor at the time of the examinations worked with the regularity and energy shown by the Academic students.

In the Academic Department a year ago twenty-seven men were dropped, this year only fifteen. And I am convinced that after this demonstration that the rules are to be strictly enforced, there will be such a toning up of scholarship in the School of Science that next June not half so many students of that Department will come under the rules for dropping as now.

I may add that the students dropped at this time have been required to leave college for the remainder of the year. In all but two or three cases they will be allowed to re-enter college at the opening of the next academic year either as members of the next lower class, or as Special Students with schedules which will enable them, if industrious, to meet our requirements for the degree by the February after the classes to which they have hitherto belonged have graduated. A large proportion of the dropped students have already indicated their intention of returning next September.

Respectfully submitted,

H. B. Fine   Dean of the Faculty.

TRS (Trustees' Papers, UA, NjP).
1 He was sentenced to a one-year term in the state penitentiary.

To Frank Thilly

Princeton, N. J.

My dear Professor Thilly: 11 March, 1904.

My telegram of yesterday informed you of your election by our Board, but I wish to follow it up with a few lines in order to express the universal gratification which is felt at the prospect of your coming. I feel confident that it will not take you three months to feel perfectly at home and to find how easily the most delightful comradeships can be made here.

The Board voted the salary of $3600, and also authorized the Treasurer to pay the cost of your removal from Columbia to Princeton.

President Jesse was in town the other day and I had a very pleasant call from him. I hope he carried away pleasant impressions of the place.

With warmest regards in which I hope I may include Mrs. Thilly and the children,

Cordially yours,   Woodrow Wilson

TLS (Wilson-Thilly Corr., NIC).

To Williamson Updike Vreeland

Princeton, N. J.

My dear Professor Vreeland: 11 March, 1904.

I took pleasure in recommending to the Board at its meeting yesterday that you be promoted from the rank of assistant professor to the rank of professor. I wish very heartily that an increase of salary went with this change of rank.[1] Though the present financial condition of the University forbids that, I most sincerely hope that an increase can be managed so soon as our prospects look up a little.

With much regard,

Cordially yours,   Woodrow Wilson

TLS (WC, NjP).
[1] Vreeland's salary at this time was $1,500 a year.

From John Young Graham[1]

Dear Sir: University, Ala.   March 11, 1904.

It has been a source of great satisfaction to me to learn that there is a prospect that this institution may have a visit from you during your Southern trip. Mrs. Graham joins me in the earnest wish that you will honor us by being our guest at that time. I urged upon President Abercrombie that this should be my privilege as a Princeton Alumnus.

May we then hope that you will make our house your home?

Yours most sincerely,   John Y. Graham.

ALS (WP, DLC).
[1] B.S., Princeton 1892; Ph.D., University of Munich 1897, and Professor of Biology at the University of Alabama since 1897.

From Franklin Potts Glass

My dear Mr. Wilson: Montgomery, Ala.   3-14-1904.

Yours of the 9th inst. came to hand Saturday. I beg your pardon for not having attended to your request in reference to the railway schedules more promptly. I have been in a great rush ever since my return home and had overlooked the matter.

I have looked into the matter very carefully, and there is not very much choice as to routes in covering the ground you desire. I believe, however, that this is about the best that can be done:

Leave Atlanta at 6 a.m. and arrive at Montgomery at 10:55 a.m.

Leave Montgomery any day at 11:15 a.m. and arrive at Mobile at 4:19 p.m.

Leave Mobile at 5:55 a.m. and reach Selma at 11:59, noon. Stop over in Selma until 4:35 p.m., and reach Marion at 5:46 p.m.

Leave Marion at 10:52 a.m. and lay over in Selma from 11:59 a.m. to 5:45 p.m., and reaching Birmingham at 10:05 p.m.

Or, leave Marion at 7:40 a.m. for Birmingham, via Akron, reaching Akron at 11:55 a.m. and staying over there to 4:32 p.m., and reaching Birmingham at 6:45 p.m.

Marion is on a sideline railroad with only one train a day each way, and you are bound to lose time at Selma either going or coming, or both ways.

I believe this general outline will be the most comfortable way you can arrange, especially if time is not too much of an object to you so that you can stop over in Montgomery more than one day, and in Mobile more than one day. On most of the roads over which you will travel there are two trains a day. For instance, you can leave Atlanta at 4:30 p.m. and reach here at 9:20 p.m., and get a fair night's rest and all next day, before undertaking anything. There are also several trains a day from here to Mobile—one going at 9:30 at night, but this would throw you into Mobile at 3 a.m., which would be very unsatisfactory. Take it all in all, I am inclined to think that the above arrangement is probably the best that can be fixed to comply with your requirements.

We have not yet arranged in Montgomery just what we expect to do for your purposes. A committee of us will meet in the next few days and try to outline a program for you. As soon as this is done, I will try to let you know what we expect of you here.

Frank writes me that he is getting along splendidly and weighs more than before he was sick. He has been putting on so much flesh that he has gone into the gymnasium to work some of it off. I think his nervous system is now in good shape, and that he will be able to get down to good hard work on some of his deficiences.

With my kindest regards to Mrs. Wilson, and with best wishes for your welfare in every respect, I am,

Sincerely yours,   Frank P. Glass

TLS (WP, DLC).

From David Benton Jones

My dear Sir: Chicago   March, 15th., 1904.

I was sorry not to have a fuller talk with you before I left Princeton.

So much has been done in the few months since you have taken charge that it is now seemingly more important than ever that the few remaining things should be carefully considered, in order to complete the work of regeneration, as this is what it really means for Princeton.

The quickening of the intellectual life of the place, following the change of administration, is of course, the fundamental thing. This is fully under way and I have no doubt will be still more thoroughly done as time goes on.

Nothing has given me more encouragement, hardly as much encouragement, as what I learned of your practical determination to do something in the way of regenerating the Board. You are justified in taking this position on the ground, that as it stands, it virtually makes further progress on your part extremely difficult, if not impossible. In the minds of those who consider Princeton's interests, there can be but one opinion. Some will consult their social and personal comfort and hold back, but progress at Princeton requires submission on the part of these unwilling ones.

In the nature of things, there will be other vacancies created during the next year, and it is on this point especially that I want to tell you how I feel. It is a positive detriment to elect a member of the Board simply because he is a very rich man. The possession of wealth should not disqualify a man for membership, but it should not in any case be the sole qualification. We have on the Board now two or three very rich men and the feeling outside is, that it is more or less of an impertinence to ask support for the development of Princeton while these men are doing little or nothing. If we should elect two or three more very rich men simply because they are rich men, your task will be almost hopeless. The type of men we should have is well illustrated by Mr. Converse, President of the Grant Locomotive Works, Philadelphia. I understand he is prominent in Presbyterian matters, a very successful man of business who would command the confidence of men of means, but himself not a very rich man.[1] Mr. Robert Garrett would also, I think, be a good man, by reason of his interest in Princeton and his work in connection with it;[2] Dr. Starr[3] of New York and possibly Cleve Dodge.[4] I mention these men, not as indicating my specific choice, but as illustrating what I have in mind as Princeton's greatest need. If a man intending to take an interest in Princeton were to attend one of its Board meetings, or if with a fair acquaintance with the members, he should go over the list of trustees as it now stands, it would, I am satisfied, neutralize any appeal you might make. This is my reason for saying that nothing has encouraged me as much as to know that you look upon the regeneration of the Board as the next most important step. I did not think it was possible that so much could be done in so short a time.

As to the Emergency Fund, it is unfortunate that the notice has gone out—at least to some of the subscribers, calling in subscriptions immediately and before the sum announced to be raised has been subscribed. This notice follows closely upon the irritation caused by the muddling of the gymnasium subscriptions, or rather the interests of the so-called guarantors. I mention these matters to you simply by way of explanation of my position. It would, I think, have been wiser to have allowed some time to elapse, certainly to have waited until the gymnasium matter was closed up and out of the way before actually calling in the subscriptions to the Emergency Fund. Many of the subscribers to the Gymnasium Guarantee Fund sent their notes for their pro-rata amount, to the Farmers' Loan & Trust Co., being assured in writing that not only would the interest on the notes be paid by the Committee, but that subscriptions which were expected would be applied in part liquidation of the notes. They are now called upon, not only to pay the principal in full, but to pay the interest on the notes as well.

In the second place, I certainly understood—and others also

have understood, that they were asked to subscribe to the Emergency Fund on condition that $100,000.00 annually should be raised. To call in subscriptions when only about half the amount has been subscribed, is a blunder. This fund can be raised, but in my opinion it can only be raised by considerable co-operation, or by some extremely well considered plan of proceedure.

I am prepared to subscribe to anything any one may say in regard to Mr. Cuyler's zeal and loyalty to Princeton and to his friends, and it seems ungenerous and almost unjust to criticise anything he does, but after all, it is Princeton that we must keep in mind and I am sorry to say I do not regard him as a safe adviser, or as having sound judgment in regard to such matters. I am speaking with great plainness and with full knowledge of his friendship for you and the thorough going way in which you reciprocate it. I do not wish in the least to even throw a shadow over that, but in matters of business if you could confer with Mr. Cadwalader, there is no one on the Board as likely to make safe and sound suggestions as he.

There is nothing in this letter calling for a reply or acknowledgement, and I have written so frankly that I am sure you will agree with me in thinking that it is wiser it should not find its way into your files, but rather into the waste-paper basket. To give you my point of view is my sole object, and to serve Princeton, my sole desire.

Very sincerely yours.   David B. Jones.

I hope you will pardon this long disquisition. I had no time to make it short & so encroach upon yours, and I mean it when I say no reply is called for & this also is the part of wisdom.

D B J.

TLS (WP, DLC).
  [1] Converse was elected to life membership on the Board on June 13, 1904, but declined the election. As has already been noted, he was at this time a partner in Burnham, Williams & Co., locomotive manufacturers of Philadelphia.
  [2] Robert Garrett was elected a Life Trustee on June 12, 1905.
  [3] Moses Allen Starr '76, a prominent New York physician. He was never elected to the Board of Trustees.
  [4] Cleveland H. Dodge was elected a Life Trustee on June 13, 1904.

From St. Clair McKelway

Brooklyn, New York.

Dear Mr President   [c. March 15, 1904]

The gratifying surprise of the honor the Trustees have conferred on me reached me in official form to-day[1]

I will report according to instruction on June 15.

I am convinced that I owe the distinction in main part to your kind and unmerited consideration, and I am very grateful to you.

Nothing in the name of education has come to me which is so rewarding and yet so humbling, considering my small measure of service, as this honor is.

Sincerely St Clair McKelway

ALS (WP, DLC).

[1] The Board of Trustees, at its meeting on March 10, had voted to confer the LL.D. degree on McKelway.

From Alvey Augustus Adee[1]

Sir: Washington.   March 15, 1904.

I have the pleasure to inform you that by a Royal Order of the 12th ultimo, a copy of which has been furnished to this Department by the United States Minister at the Hague, it is decreed that the certificate of Bachelor of Arts granted by the Princeton University will be recognized as admitting the holders thereof to study in the universities of the Netherlands.

If you desire a copy of the order, the Minister will doubtless be pleased to obtain it for you on your application to him.

I am, Sir,

Your obedient servant Alvey A. Adee
Second Assistant Secretary.

TLS (WP, DLC).

[1] Second Assistant Secretary of State.

From Henry Fairfield Osborn

My dear President Wilson: New York, 15 March, 1904.

I enclose a table from the Columbia *Quarterly* which may give you some useful information for our Trustees.[1]

I am glad to hear on all sides of the substantial internal progress of the college. My son Perry[2] has greatly enjoyed this year's work.

Not from him but from others I have learned that there is some feeling in the college that the discipline is rather that of a school than a university. This criticism, however, may be entirely unwarranted.

Hoping soon to see you, I am,

Always sincerely yours, Henry F. Osborn

TLS (WP, DLC).

[1] The enclosure is missing. The table, from the *Columbia University Quarterly*,

vi (March 1904), 220, listed the enrollments in the undergraduate, graduate, and professional schools in each of twenty major American universities, including Princeton.

2 Alexander Perry Osborn '05.

A News Report of an Address in Jersey City

[March 16, 1904]

UNIVERSITY CLUB'S ANNUAL BANQUET

College men of greater and lesser degrees, from the "don" with LL.D. after his name to the lively "grad" with only A.B. behind him, ate, drank and were merry last night at the annual banquet of the University Club of Hudson County. . . .

Grace was said by Rev. Dr. Brett,[1] and for the next hour there was the usual clatter and "klink," enlivened at intervals with part songs from the Glee Club table in the centre, and throughout their staging was excellent. As the men began to blow rings from their cigars and cigarettes President Wilson began his address of welcome.

Annual dinners, he said were object lessons. He had asked a Board of Trade man why, and the reply was that if folks forgot to eat it would hurt trade. A doctor's reply to the query was that there was a distinct relationship between "esculent and Esculapius" (laughter). The question put to a lawyer, he said, elicited the answer that Justinian, the codifier of laws, had written a monumental "Digest," and their dinner was in memory of that achievement. (Laughter.)

A University Club man, in reply to the query, said the dinner was so the members could eat, which, said Mr. Wilson, proved that a college education was at least conducive to truthfulness.

Mr. Wilson spoke of the formation of the club[2] and evoked roars of laughter when he said:

"Our purposes were threefold: to free Cuba, bore the North River tunnel[3] and force down the price of steel;[4] and I am glad to say that since the club was organized all these things have come to pass."

Scarcely had President Woodrow Wilson risen to speak when from all the diners, led by the glee club, came the strains of that classic air of "Mr. Dooley" to these words:

> "For Woodrow Wilson, oh, Woodrow Wilson.
> He's one of us, a son of Nassau Hall.
> It's Woodrow Wilson, it's Woodrow Wilson,
> It's Wilson, Wilson, Wilson, that is all!"

Princeton's president smiled, and when he had a chance to speak said that he realized he was trying to play a difficult role as college president, and he was fearful at times that his disguise was not sufficiently ample. It reminded him of a woman who went to a circus and in one of the side shows saw a man apparently read a newspaper through a two-inch board. She rushed away, exclaiming, "My, this is no place for me with these thin things on." (Roars of laughter).

Coming to his topic of "University Men and the Country," Dr. Wilson said that a university man goes through a process of translation better than the translation the student himself often made (merriment), and the result should be a better all around man. The college courses offered an opportunity for betterment for which every college man would be held to account. It was an opportunity not to be neglected, though college men themselves had to admit that some men got along very well without it, the explanation of which, he said, reminded him of a bishop who was examining a curate whom he had sent out to preach for the first time. The embryo bishop had selected as his text "How Can We Escape, if We Neglect So Great a Salvation?" and being asked how he divided his subject replied that in the first half of his sermon he spoke of the excellence of salvation, the absolute necessity of it and the great danger of neglecting it, and in the latter half of the sermon tried to point out some of the ways of escape, if they did neglect it. (Laughter.)

"Speaking of salvation," continued President Wilson, "reminds me of a question once put to a bishop: 'Could a man who smoked go to heaven?' and the bishop, who was a smoker, asked if his querist had found any scriptural authority forbidding it and being answered in the negative, replied: 'Then be careful, young man, how you put your private interpretation upon the scriptures or you'll smoke yourself.'" (Laughter.)

In a serious vein Dr. Wilson spoke of University life. A college man, he said, should possess a vision to see things beyond mere material success. Four years of college life should detach him from personal interests long enough to place him on a coign of vantage so that he could look on the map of life and see ahead of the mere strife of to-day. College education, while it doesn't attempt to complete a man's education, for the experience of life alone can do that, at least gives a man the key of life. A greater responsibility, said the speaker, is laid on the college man than on others, and in conclusion President Wilson emphasized the fact that college bred men were being put more and more on their mettle.

Prolonged cheers greeted Dr. Wilson at the close of his address.

Printed in the Jersey City *Evening Journal*, March 16, 1904; two editorial headings omitted.

[1] The Rev. Dr. Cornelius Brett, pastor of the Bergen Reformed Church in Jersey City.

[2] In 1897.

[3] Wilson referred to the completion of the boring of the first railroad tunnel under the Hudson River connecting Jersey City with Manhattan Island on March 11, 1904.

[4] The prices of pig iron and basic steel had undergone a substantial reduction as a result of the business recession beginning in the second half of 1903. For example, the price per ton of steel billets quoted at the mill in Pittsburgh fell from $30.25 in May 1903 to $23.00 in March 1904.

From Frank Thilly

[Columbia, Mo.]

My dear President Wilson: March 16th, 1904

I thank you very much for the telegram and letter announcing my election to the Stuart professorship of psychology. I am looking forward with great pleasure to being associated with you, and I hope that my work will always be of such a character as to make you satisfied with your choice. The feeling is strong in me that I already have a number of warm friends in Princeton who will help me to get my bearings in the beginning, and I am sure that I can always count on you for advice and support.

With heartiest regards, I am,

Cordially yours,   Frank Thilly.

ALS (WP, DLC).

A News Report of a Religious Talk

[March 18, 1904]

OFFICERS ELECTED.

For Ensuing Fiscal Year of the Philadelphian Society.
Address by President Wilson.

The annual election of officers of the Philadelphian Society was held last evening in Murray Hall after the regular weekly address. . . .

The regular weekly meeting was addressed by President Woodrow Wilson, who took as his subject, "Public Life." Not every man must go into law, medicine and the other professions, he stated, but each one must go into public life in some degree if

he has a sound conscience. It is well to distinguish between public life as a career and as a duty. The arrangement of our politics
is such that few men can enter public life as a career, for under
the present organization there is no assurance that one who has
served faithfully will receive any reward. We must admit that
unless a man is of independent means his political services are
apt to put an uncommon strain upon his conscience. The best
public service has been rendered by men who have not made a
living out of it.

Public life is a duty to all because we should let our light so
shine that our fellow-citizens will glorify God for the good works
that they see in us. There are two things with which the college
man should supply the country, first, a sense of identity of past
events with present, and secondly, criticism. The trouble with
the uneducated man is that he does not know the history of his
own country. It is the business of the instructed man to maintain for a long time a bright recollection of what has happened,
and thus keep others in possession of a knowledge of the experiences through which the country has passed. After the people
come to know what has been they will have a better knowledge
of what to wish for in the future. When we criticize others we
should see their point of view. The knowledge of the fact that
the process of right thinking is accomplished by means of a slow
elimination of error ought to convince us that no thought can
be entirely free from error. It is the duty of every college man
to carry throughout the world the knowledge and the light of
the revealed love of God.

Printed in the *Daily Princetonian*, March 18, 1904.

From Frank Thilly

Dear President Wilson: Columbia, Mo., March 18th [1904]

I send you to-day a copy of a local paper containing some resolutions about my going-away.[1] I hope you will forgive me for
feeling proud of the action of our student-body and for wanting
you to know of it. You will be glad, I am sure, that you are not
getting some one whom they are anxious to get rid of here.

I also wish to call your attention to the fact that the statements
at the end of the paper article purporting to be mine are per-
verted. I told the students that it had not been easy for me to
decide to leave Columbia, which was true. I also told them that
I did not see how I could do better work for Princeton than I had

tried to do here. I did not say, of course, that President Wilson kept urging me to come and that I had finally made up my mind with great reluctance to go. One would think from the statements attributed to me by the reporter (who by the way was not present at this gathering of the students) that I had been overpersuaded by you "to leave my happy home" and that I now regretted my decision when it was too late. It is a mystery to me how any one could have received such an impression from what I said, but you know the reporter's mind is fearfully and wonderfully made.

With warmest regards, I am,

Cordially Yours,   Frank Thilly

I thank you for the copy of the Princetonian which I was glad to read.[2]   T.

ALS (WP, DLC).
   [1] It is missing, but he referred to a news story in the Columbia *Missouri Herald*, March 18, 1904, which described a mass meeting of students called after the announcement that Thilly had accepted a professorship at Princeton. At this meeting, resolutions were adopted expressing high regard for Thilly, urging him to reconsider, and calling upon the University's Board of Curators to make "all possible efforts" to induce him to remain. A number of students gathered afterward at Thilly's home, and he was reported to have said to them that "he would have to go as he had given his word to President Wilson, of the University, and that he had not made his final decision until urged by the Princeton president and then with the utmost reluctance."
   [2] Probably the issue of March 12, 1904, which contained a brief story on Thilly's appointment and a sketch of his career.

A News Report of the Annual Dinner of the
Daily Princetonian

[March 19, 1904]

At the annual dinner of The Daily Princetonian on Wednesday night, the sophomore club system came in for some rather severe criticism. . . . The new Editor-in-Chief of the Daily, Edward H. Hilliard '05, likened sophomore club politics to the unsavory methods of city politics, and called the clubs down for combining to "buck" the lately established freshman commons,— an institution which all well-wishers of Princeton ought to recognize as a laudable attempt to improve the freshman boarding facilities and, in general, the spirit of our freshman eating clubs. Mr. Hilliard declared that unless there should come a gradual improvement upon the present sophomore club situation, there will be trouble. President Wilson approved of these sentiments. We trust that the members of the sophomore clubs will take them to heart.

This was the sixth annual banquet given by our esteemed Daily. It was the largest yet, about seventy editors and guests being present,—which speaks well for the prosperity of the paper. And it was a most successful dinner. Joseph R. Truesdale '04, the able business manager of the retiring board, presided as toast-master, with dignity and grace. Francis W. Dinsmore '04, the late Editor-in-Chief, responded for The Retiring Board, and Edward H. Hilliard '05, the present Editor-in-Chief, for The Incoming Board. Mr. W. K. Van Reypen, Jr., brought the felicitations of the Yale Daily News, and Mr. W. R. Bowie, representing the Harvard Crimson, made a very agreeable impression. For the faculty, Professors Garfield, Carter '93 and McElroy '96 responded, with well deserved praise for the Daily, and President Wilson '79, in responding to the toast Princeton University, made an eloquent address, which stimulated the Princeton loyalty of those who heard him, and impressed them with the dignity of true scholarship. A quartette from the glee club led the singing, which was excellent. Also, several of the speakers referred with pride to the late vindication of the Honor System.[1]

Printed in the *Princeton Alumni Weekly*, IV (March 19, 1904), 386-87.
[1] That is, in the recent case of the theft of the examination papers.

To David Benton Jones

My dear Mr. Jones,   Princeton, N. J.   20 March, 1904.

I know, of course, what you mean when you say that your letter of the 15th needs no answer. You must have known that what you said would jump at every point with my own feeling and judgment: you need no assurance of that. But I *may* indulge myself in a line or two to thank you for your straightforward candour. I know of no other way half so good by which to clarify and advance business.

What you say is true, even if painfully true. We are not engaged in pleasure but in the performance of serious and pressing duty in administering the affairs of the University; and we must speak of all things as they are. I shall try to act in the spirit of your counsel.

With warmest regard,

Most appreciatively and faithfully Yours,

Woodrow Wilson

ALS (Mineral Point, Wisc., Public Library).

To Ellen Axson Wilson

Princeton, N. J.

My Eileen, my own darling, 21 March, 1904

There's nae luck aboot the house noo ye are awa!¹ And to think that as I sit here and write in this quiet room, at the old desk, my sweet one is out, hundreds of miles, upon the broad seas! Ah, weel, it's ma ain do'in; and I'm no repinin'. I'm but lettin' ma heart gae its ain gait the moment!

The address to the schoolmasters, and mistresses, was a grand affair.² Standing on my little platform there in the tenth story of the building of the University of the City of New York, on Washington Square, I looked straight out on the stream of the river itself, and expected to see the nose of the white steamer thrust itself into sight any moment. And what poetical, impossible counsels of perfection I did give those poor wondering souls who sat puzzled and gaping before me, not knowing what stirred the fancy within me. I showed them an idyl of how American history should be taught and filled them with a glow that could not possibly help them to do anything I can think of, except make love! Oratory is surely an imaginative art, but who shall explore its sources?

I rushed away to go to Nell and Madge at Purcell's, where we all, Mr. Brank included, took lunch; and then we went our several ways: Madge and Mr. Brank to hear [Richard] Mansfield in Beau Brummel, Nell and I to the circus.³ We found Mrs. Hibben and Beth without any trouble; and the extraordinary show,—*truly* extraordinary and full of wonder,—proved the best tonic I could have taken. It took me quite out of myself and for the time being made children of us all. It was over by 4.30 and, by rushing, we caught the 5 o'clock train, and were at home for dinner.

Yesterday, Father Huntington⁴ and the painful struggle of conducting the service for him!⁵ But the chapel was crowded and there was the reward of seeing the man take hold on the boys and sway them towards the good. I walked over to the Armour's⁶ to fetch him, the morning bright and mild and full of genial promise of the Spring. In the afternoon, and in the evening again, the dear Hibbens, who came in to tea, to keep us from seeing too suddenly the smallness of our tiny circle. (Do three make a circle?)

To-day lecturing, letters, and the routine of office hours have brought me to the steady, and steadying, round of familiar duties again,—and so we are off for the voyage, my heart and you. Fortunately *it* need not stay at home!

How brave and sweet and fine my darling was, those last hours and those last moments of parting! Shall I ever forget the tender light in her eyes, and that parting touch of her lips! Ah me, I am blessed beyond all thought in her; and my happiness in her pilgrimage to the sights she has looked forward to since her sweet girlhood knows no bounds and no alloy even amidst the exquisite pain of being separated from her!

We are all perfectly well. Nell went to school this morning and played a game of basket ball this afternoon. We all love you and all send love without measure to Jess and the dear Smiths. But no one loves you like

Your own   Woodrow

ALS (WC, NjP).
  1 Mrs. Wilson and Jessie Wilson, together with Mary Smith and Lucy Smith of New Orleans, had sailed on March 19 on the North German Lloyd's *Hohenzollern* for a two-month tour of Italy.
  2 As Wilson's desk diary described at Jan. 1, 1904, discloses, he spoke on "The Teaching of United States History in Grammar & High Schools" to the New York Educational Council, an organization of principals of high schools and grammar schools in the New York area. No newspaper report of his address has been found, but for a retrospective summary by one listener, see Marion P. Hilliard to WW, March 25, 1905, Vol. 16.
  3 The Barnum and Bailey Circus had opened at Madison Square Garden on March 19.
  4 The Rev. James Otis Sargent Huntington, Superior of the Order of the Holy Cross of West Park, N. Y.
  5 Apparently it went against his grain to conduct the service for an Anglo-Catholic priest. About Wilson's role in the Sunday morning services in Marquand Chapel, see WW to D. M. Barringer, Sept. 16, 1902, Vol. 14.
  6 George Allison Armour and Harriette Foote Armour of 83 Stockton St.

To Frank Thilly

My dear Professor Thilly: Princeton, N. J.   21 March, 1904.

I don't wonder that you feel proud of the action of the students at Columbia with regard to your leaving. I knew perfectly well that they would feel in that way, and I have really felt badly to think that I was depriving them of inspiration for our own sake.

It is very delightful to read of these things, and I should have been very much disappointed if you had not sent me the paper containing them. You need not have given yourself any uneasiness about the impression that would be made upon my mind by waht [what] you were reported to have said. I have suffered so many unspeakable things from the reporters myself, that I am not likely to take their word too seriously with regard to others.

Every one here looks forward with the liveliest expectations of pleasure to your coming, and Hibben and I are doing all we can to find you a comfortable house.

With warmest regard,

Cordially and faithfully yours, Woodrow Wilson

TLS (Wilson-Thilly Corr., NIC)

To Edward Ingle

My dear Ingle: Princeton, N. J.   22 March, 1904.

I have read with a great deal of interest your letter of March 21.[1] I heartily agree with you that we must go on dreaming our dreams, and talking about them, and believing in them, until we make them the fashion, whether in our own day or in the day that comes after it, and you may be sure that I shall not stop doing my part of the proclaiming.

Always,   Cordially yours, Woodrow Wilson

TLS (E. Ingle Papers, MdHi).
[1] It is missing.

From Abram Woodruff Halsey

My dear Wilson: New York   March 22, 1904.

Your kind letter of March 5th, together with the resolution[1] passed by the Board of Trustees at its meeting March 10th, 1904, received. I will refer the letter to the Class Committee at its next meeting, April 29th. I am sure the Committee, as well as the Class, will be only too happy to follow the wishes of the Trustees in this as in all other matters affecting the University.

We are struggling with the money question for the Dormitory, but are now on the last lap, and I think we can carry out our original intention which was to go to Princeton with every dollar paid. I hope to be in Princeton in the course of the next ten days, as I wish to talk over with you some matters connected with the Class Reunion.

Always yours,   A. W. Halsey

TLS (WP, DLC).
[1] Printed at March 10, 1904.

An Announcement

[March 23, 1904]

RHODES SCHOLARSHIPS.

Conditions Announced. President Wilson
Chairman of Committee for New Jersey.

The Rhodes Scholarship Committee has issued a memorandum for the benefit of those intending to compete for the scholarship this year. The more important parts of the circular are as follows:

A written examination will be held, beginning on April 13, at a place fixed by the Committee of Selection for each State. President Woodrow Wilson, Chairman, Dean H. B. Fine, and President Austin Scott, of Rutgers, compose the Committee of Selection for New Jersey. This Committee will appoint a suitable person to supervise the examination, and will arrange for its impartial conduct. It should be clearly understood that this examination is not competitive, but simply qualifying, and is intended to give assurance that no elected scholar will be unable to pass the Responsions, which are the first examinations that Oxford University demands of all candidates for the B.A. degree. The University of Oxford has agreed to accept in lieu of Responsions the certificate of its examiners that students have passed this examination, so that all scholars elected will be excused from that test when they come into residence at Oxford.

As soon as the report of the examiners has been received, the Chairman of the Committee on Selection will be furnished with a list of the candidates who have passed, and are therefore eligible for election. The Committee of Selection will then proceed to choose the scholar for the year. In accordance with the wish of Mr. Rhodes, the Trustees desire that "in the election of a student to a scholarship, regard shall be had to (1) his literary and scholastic attainments, (2) his fondness for and success in manly out-door sports, such as cricket, football, and the like, (3) his qualities of manhood, truth, courage, devotion to duty, sympathy for, and protection of the weak, kindliness, unselfishness and fellowship, and (4) his exhibition during school days of moral force of character, and of instincts to lead and to take an interest in his schoolmates." Mr. Rhodes suggested that the second and third of these qualifications should be decided in any school or college by the votes of an applicant's fellow-students, and the fourth by the head of the school or college.

To aid in making a choice, each candidate will be required to furnish to the Chairman of the Committee of Selection: (a) A certificate of age, (b) A certificate from his school or college that he has been selected by that school or college as the candidate who best fulfills the ideas of Mr. Rhodes' bequest, and (c) A statement from his school or college of the grounds upon which he was chosen, including his educational qualifications, his record in athletics and testimonials in reference to the qualities indicated by Mr. Rhodes, as seen best adapted to guide the judgment of the Committee of Selection. Should it seem advisable, the Committee of Selection is free to apply to the candidates, or to any selected number of them, such further intellectual or other tests as they may consider necessary.

In the qualifying examination six papers will be given for each of which two hours are allowed. The place at which the examination is to be held will be announced later.

Printed in the *Daily Princetonian*, March 23, 1904.

From Philip Hudson Churchman

My dear Dr. Wilson   Paris, March 23, 1904

Prof. Vreeland's letter announcing the good news that my leave has been extended for another year, has arrived, and I desire to assure you of my most hearty thanks for the privilege you thus grant me. Handicapped as I am by poor health, I do not profit by my opportunities as I should like; but I am constantly improving and always endeavor to put my limited time to the best use possible.

Honesty compels me to correct an erroneous impression concerning my agreement with Dr. Patton. He did *not* promise without qualification to hold a position open for me: his statement of his policy was similar to yours, possibly a *little* more binding, but not much. Judging from the experience of other men, and from Dr Patton's general tone, I took the qualifications to be rather nominal than real, but at any rate the fact stands that a binding promise was not given to me—(though it seemed to be taken for granted that the man who took my place would be considered a temporary substitute).

The question of a degree as a necessary part of my work did not enter into my conversation with Dr. Patton, and I am sorry that it is to be considered essential to a satisfactory conclusion of my work abroad; for I shall not disguise the fact that I feel by no means sure of getting it next year. The reasons for this are simple: *First*, I have aimed very high as my "chief" is the very first Spanish scholar in France and reputed to be a very exacting man. *Secondly*, my working strength is sadly limited. I do not accomplish in two days what most men would do in one, and a sleepless night or a wretched headache far too often incapacitate me for good work. I must frankly tell you that *cost what it may to my future*, I cannot allow myself to set the pace that has shattered the health of stronger men than me, and has twice already brought me into a state of nervous torment for which no sort of promotion could compensate. Still I shall do what I can, and not look too far ahead. Possibly if the outlook is bad next year I can run off to some easier man and get my title—but I should not be proud of such a move. At any rate, for the present I am happy and interested and deep[ly] grateful for the chance to continue my work.[1]

I trust that it will not be considered presumptuous for me to express the pleasure it gives me to read of the severity that has been displayed in dealing with delinquent students. We younger men from our undergraduate recollections and from our close contact with the students have a pretty keen appreciation of the harm done in the past.

Sincerely yours,   Philip H. Churchman

ALS (WP, DLC).
[1] Actually, Churchman resigned at the end of the academic year; taught at the United States Naval Academy, 1904-1905, and at Harvard, 1906-1908; received the Ph.D. from Harvard in 1908; and afterward taught at Clark University.

A News Item

[March 24, 1904]

FORTNIGHTLY CLUB ADDRESS.

President Wilson addressed a meeting of the Fortnightly Club[1] last night, on the subject "Leaders of Men."[2] His main theme was that the practical men who have personality and insight to appeal to the masses, and not the men of letters or theory who seek to influence the individual rather than the multitude, are the successful leaders of men. He showed how a leader must be guided by sympathy and love for the masses, and a masterly analysis of the characters of men.

Printed in the *Daily Princetonian*, March 24, 1904.
[1] A small undergraduate literary club organized during the academic year 1900-1901.
[2] It is printed at June 17, 1890, Vol. 6.

To Ellen Axson Wilson

My own darling,   Princeton, N. J.   24 March, 1904

I dare say this long, long voyage is seeming even longer to us than to you. To sit still at home, without the novel incidents of travel to divert us, and wait twelve days to hear of the end of the journey by telegraph, twenty-four days by mail, is a thing to test the nerves and the steadfastness of the will. My darling has twice gone through the experience, God bless her! and does not need to be told what it is like. Neither, I am sure, does she need to be told of the sweet pleasure of dreaming of the delights it all means for the dear one who is on the journey (I prayed in chapel last Sunday for all who were on journeys, and my voice nearly betrayed me: a sudden convulsion gripped my throat,—I ought not to have risked it!). And the gladness overcrows the grief, and makes the struggle easy!

Nothing happens to us. The days go by in the quiet way that is so familiar. I've not seen quite as much as usual of the Hibbens. Jack's aunt, his father's sister, whom he dearly loves, Mrs. Dill,[1] is here, and they are very much absorbed in her; and I have been equally absorbed in my own affairs,—going into New York as I did yesterday, for example, to consult Mr. Cadwalader, (for he seems to me worth consulting) about Guyot Cameron (he says 'Go, ahead; a little row wont hurt when you are in the right and the matter can be explained to everyone whose opinion is worth being concerned about.' But, of course, I shall remember my promise to my darling and not do *any*thing till she returns). This evening, though, we had them in at dinner, to show Mrs. Dill the attention as well as to enjoy the Hibbens; and to-day at noon Jack and I went to see Mrs. Fielder's house,[2] for Thilly. I think it will answer very well indeed, and the price is just what he wants to pay.[3]

To-morrow evening (Friday) comes the Yale debate, and I shall have to go. Beforehand I am to take dinner with the Richardsons[4] (how is that for Mrs. R!) to meet Mr. Edward M. Shepard, the noted Democratic statesman (?),[5] who is to be one of the judges, and Dr. Richardson's guest. None of this is very exciting, but it serves to keep me amused. And all the while love sings at my heart, 'My sweetheart is off to the land of beauty where she belongs,—long enough to *realize* it and bring it away in her heart!' It *is* lonely, dear, *very* lonely without you, and the nights and mornings are desperately hard to bear; but, ah, there are deep compensations, and the love that is unselfish is a love full of

the deepest, most satisfying delights! My thoughts of you would
make you very happy, could you read them (you can, can't you
dear?), and they make me as happy as you could wish me to be.
It is sweet to love you as I do now. It will deepen and broaden
the stream of my love for ever. It reveals you to me more perfectly than ever, and my own feeling for you, as the centre and
object of my life. And, ah, what a lovely image it is of my beloved
darling that I dream of all the time. Every time of our life brings
us closer, in a more intimate embrace of love, and I am more
profoundly

                                        Your own   Woodrow

All well and all send full hearts of love to all.

ALS (WC, NjP).
  [1] Mrs. James Livinia (H. Hibben) Dill.
  [2] The home of Phoebe Warren Fielder of 67 Prospect Ave., widow of John
Wesley Fielder, Jr., insurance and real estate broker, who had died on September 15, 1903.
  [3] Thilly bought the Fielder house.
  [4] Ernest Cushing Richardson and Grace Ely Richardson of 220 Mercer St.
Richardson was Librarian of Princeton University.
  [5] Edward Morse Shepard, New York lawyer and Democratic politician, Tam-
many's unsuccessful candidate for Mayor of New York in 1901.

From Ellen Axson Wilson

My own darling,   "Hohenzollern," March 26 [1904]
    A week today since we sailed and all well!—the sea deeply,
darkly, beautifully blue, as well as very smooth, the sun bright
& everybody well & happy! "It was *not* ever thus"! It was very
rough for some three days after the first; poor Lucy was *very* sick
& Mary a close second. Jessie & I have been *quite* well except
for a very few qualms Sunday morning. After that we had our
breakfast in bed while the rough weather lasted and kept perfectly well,—rather to our own delighted surprise, for most people
were ill. The captain said it was a touch of the equinoxial; and
the ship is really far from steady. All declared that they waked
in the morning sore from the labour of keeping in bed. One man
put his mattress on the floor declaring he "had as well be there
first as last." There were four fences down the table to keep the
crockery on, and in spite of them all one day the table was
cleared,—the dishes taking the fences gallantly!
    Poor Lucy went to bed one night in her shoes & hat,—positively
refusing to be touched, and kept them on all night! They had to
stay *out* on deck constantly because of the sickness, & I had to

stay *in* because of the cold, which was severe. I sat in the corner of my divan with a hot water bag and a book & was perfectly comfortable. Jessie made friends with some Princeton people, Howells '83, with his wife & 14 year old boy.[1] So they played games together & were very jolly. Mr. Howells is a huge good-natured creature, a perfect bruiser in appearance, the wife & boy very nice & good looking.

For the last four days the weather has been glorious, and all the little ship's company of 70 have been making friends; there are some extremely nice people among them. We are rather un-lucky in being at the top of the captain's table among a lot of foreign men who don't please us altogether. On one side of the captain is an Italian, then a Russian, then an old American army officer & another Italian. On the other side is a Frenchman then ourselves. Neither of the Italians can speak a word of anything but Italian. One is a surgeon in the navy sent over to see how the steerage passengers are treated by the steamship company; the Captain is extremely polite to *him*! We like him best of the crowd,—possibly because he can't talk! He is a middle-aged man with a beautiful face and a charming manner. The Frenchman is Harry de Windt who lectured in Princeton a few weeks ago on "An overland journey from Paris to New York."[2] He is a war cor-respondent & is going to Manchuria;—has seen a great deal of the world & is a rather good talker. The captain is a young wid-ower beginning to "take notice,"—excessively attentive to all the women; a German with a French manner, very good looking but rather underbred. This is his first ship and he has had it only since Xmas. They changed our berths, by the way, and gave us all perfectly splendid ones! You never saw any so large,—larger than most "hall bed-rooms." Besides the two berths, the large divan, and the two wash stands, they contain a chest of drawers, a large table & a chair. The Smiths have one exactly like ours. *Such* a comfort as it is—, especially on such a long voyage!

Yesterday morning we passed the Azores & spent the forenoon studying them through glasses, &c. They are *beautiful*! How we

[1] George Coes Howell, Princeton 1883; his wife, Mary Alice Streit Howell; and their son, George Samuel Howell of Newark. Howell was in the wine im-porting business in New York.

[2] A free-lance journalist who wrote travel and adventure stories based upon his personal experiences for various London newspapers and magazines. Al-though born in Paris, he was educated at Magdalene College, Cambridge, and was a brother-in-law of Rajah Brooke of Sarawak; at this time he maintained residences both in Northumberland, England, and in Paris. His illustrated lecture in Princeton, delivered on January 21, 1904, was an account of his journey from Paris to New York via Siberia, Bering Strait, and Alaska, between Decem-ber 1901 and August 1902. See the *Daily Princetonian*, Jan. 21 and 22, 1904.

did want to land. They are really very large with a great variety of scenery, bold cliffs, mountains with *lovely* sky lines, and orange groves & vineyards in profusion. They are very highly cultivated & are said to produce the finest oranges in the world. Sea & sky were both so blue & the air so clear that it is a sight to remember always,—something like our approach to the Irish coast but more beautiful because of the exquisite sky-line.

There will not be anything else so exciting of course until we reach Gibraltar. We get there at six o'clock Monday morning and will have until noon to go about & see the place. Ah! if you could only see it with us! I shall of course add to this after that; the captain tells us that letters reach America sooner from Naples than from Gibraltar. I had expected to mail one there.

I hope you will pardon my writing in pencil. The writing facilities are very bad on the ship & if I went to the only desk I should feel hurried & be brief. It is the only respect in which things are not entirely satisfactory.

The fare is excellent and there could not be a more *comfortable* boat. The bath rooms are white as the driven snow & we have the most delicious baths of warm salt water up to our necks. Then there is a charming little *roof deck* where we lie about on the softest cushions & read to each other or dream. I think constantly how much you who are so fond of the sea, would enjoy this long voyage under such pleasant conditions. My own *darling*! It is hard to be reconciled to being here without you; in fact it is impossible. Perhaps it will be easier when I am doing something which I know you would not care for as much as this;—doing museums &c. But I know how you love the sea, & you confessed to a longing to see Gibraltar! Oh dear! it is not well to dwell on these things.

How I should like to know how the lecture came off last Saturday, and the circus trip,—and in fact everything great & small that has happened from that moment to this! I suppose dear Margaret is reaching home today,[3] and dear little Nell will have a chum for a while. I am so glad.

Tuesday, March 29. We have now been to Gibraltar & are again on our way, & you I hope have our cablegram from there.[4] I also hope you could read it! I find the code very unsatisfactory,— none of the words mean what I wish to say; am so sorry we did not arrange a code for ourselves before I left. Two weeks after landing I shall (on the theory that you have received this letter,)

[3] For her Easter vacation.
[4] It is missing.

begin to cable the word "Charcos" to mean, "All quite well, lodgings satisfactory, and everything going smoothly and happily."

You may send me the same word to mean the same things. I should like two cables, one just after you get our Rome address* & one just before I sail, sent to the steamer at Genoa. If I write "Charcose" it will mean all well except me & I have only a trifling indisposition. "Charcosj" will convey the same idea about Jessie, while adding L. M. or H. will simply mean that one of the Smiths or Mary Hoyt[5] is a little out of sorts. It is hardly worth while to cable such unimportant facts, but perhaps it is just as well to be truthful!

Yesterday was a *wonderful* day from dawn to sunset! We were up long before sunrise watching the approach to the rock, for it is most imposing at that hour. At eight we went over in a little steam tender to Gibraltar, where we had three hours of sightseeing. We could scarcely make ourselves believe that it was not all a dream; everything seeming so stupendous, so enchantingly beautiful, so strange and so picturesque. The town itself is exactly like the pictures of Algiers, & there were magnificent looking Moors strolling about alongside of smart English officers and I think every other possible variety of human being. We took a carriage & drove for two hours, seeing the fortifications[,] the "Alemeda" a magnificent English pleasure ground, &c. &c. The Alemeda is like an English park & an Italian garden combined & both set up on end as it were. It was a perfect wilderness of semitropical bloom,—and oh! the *views* from it,—the blue, blue Spanish hills & the bluer sea, seen down long vistas of pine or ilex! We also drove across the "Neutral ground" (with the English & Spanish sentries pacing back and forth within three hundred yards of each other,) to the gate of the Spanish town, leaving our cab there and walking through it. So we have been to Spain! Then we came back & had another hour to stroll about the streets & markets of Gibraltar. The Moorish market was *fascinating*,— especially the Moors themselves. One superb fellow was commending his wares to us while we stood solemnly around gazing fixedly at *him*,—utterly oblivious of his baskets! At last he broke into the merriest laugh—perceiving plainly enough how the case stood.

We came back to the ship, ate a hasty lunch, and then spent four hours watching from the upper deck the snow-clad Spanish mountains. It was an incomparably gorgeous panorama. Such colour effects I have never seen before, beginning with deepest

[5] Her first cousin, who was to join the party in Rome.

blue in the sea and bold strong outlines and purple shadows in the mountains, and fading softly until, just before sunset, sea & sky and mountains were all one glory and mystery of rose and violet, silver & gold—opalecent tints blending & changing so subtly and wonderfully that it was almost more than one could bear. There was a real "Alpen glow" on the snow-covered peaks. The pageant finally ended with a *magnificent* sun-set spread over the *whole* circumference of the heavens. I really went to bed completely exhausted,—as if I were a musician and had been listening to Wagner operas for fifteen hours! Oh if my darling were only with me! I longed for you so at Gibraltar that it was a positive pain. I would feel over and over a catch in my throat that was almost a sob,—I wanted you so.

I have not changed my "time" from that of Princeton yet,—(on my watch I mean), and I find a great pleasure in looking at it and imagining what you are all about. It is one o'clock at home now and nearly six here. I can almost see you sitting in the study,—though perhaps you are not even in Princeton. But I can't dwell on the subject,—it makes me choke!

We are all perfectly well, and the weather is still ideal. Tomorrow is our last day at sea so I must close this now. We reach Naples about sunrise on Thursday, but of course do not land for some hours.

My dear *dear* love to all, kisses too to my *darling* little girls, and for you sweetheart all the love that you want. I cannot tell you how devotedly absorbingly, passionately I love you, my darling, my Woodrow my own love. Always and altogether,

Your own   Eileen.

[*] We will be in Rome until the 26 of April.

ALS (WC, NjP).

From Franklin Blake Morse to Charles Williston McAlpin

My dear Mr. McAlpin: New York, March 26th. 1904.

I thank you for your favor of the 24th. inst. and hasten to reply and ask that you correct an impression in regard to my father's collection of Netsukes viz. that my brother and myself are the only donors. This is quite wrong, for the collection is given by my mother, Sarah Virginia Morse, as a memorial as from the family which includes my sister Virginia Center Morse, Will and myself. I would therefor specially ask that when formal acceptance of the gift is made that the above be understood.

Mother is now away to be gone for about two weeks and I know she would not want to have the collection removed until her return, but I would be glad to show it and make any necessary arrangements at any time during the interval. The collection could readily be packed in the space of two dress suit cases and it might perhaps be best to take them by hand in this way to Princeton when they are transferred.

Very truly yours,   Franklin B. Morse

TLS (Trustees' Papers, UA, NjP).

From Hopson Owen Murfee

Dear Sir: Marion, Alabama.   26 March 1904

We rejoice to learn through your letter of the 24 that you are making definite plans for a Southern trip, and that you will honor the Institute with a visit on Saturday, the 23 April.

May I request that you bring our boys some words of counsel for the work of self-government which they have undertaken? Dr. Lovett will be able to tell you something of it.

Some words of yours at the University of Virginia have been of lasting influence in my life, and I rejoice to know that our boys will have the privilege of hearing you.

We hope that it will be possible for you to be our guest for more than a day. Marion is a good place to spend the Sabbath.

Very sincerely yours   H. O. Murfee

TLS (WP, DLC).

From Olivia Goldthwaite Arrington[1]

My dear Sir   [Montgomery, Ala.], March 27th [1904]

Absence from home has delayed this letter acknowledging the receipt of the book[2] that you so kindly presented to the No Name Club.[3] The celebration of Washington's Birthday passed off most delightfully. Your beautiful book was presented to the winner by Mr Thomas Owen who is in charge of the historic archives of Alabama.[4] Your friend Miss Nellie Jackson[5] was present[.] She will tell you and Mrs. Wilson "about the party."

Houdons bust of Washington draped in a voluminous American flag was the center of attraction. A Copley portrait of great-great grandfather Col Thomas Goldthwaite who commanded Boston Bay just before the Revolution, and who threatened to disinherit any of the family who bore arms against the king was "among those present."⁶ Hoping that I shall have the pleasure of seeing you when you come to Montgomery, believe me

Very truly yours   Olivia Goldthwaite Arrington

ALS (WP, DLC).
[1] Daughter of the late Judge Thomas Mann Arrington of Montgomery.
[2] Wilson's *George Washington.*
[3] The No Name Club of Montgomery was a women's literary and philanthropic organization founded in 1893.
[4] Thomas McAdory Owen, Director of the Department of Archives and History of the State of Alabama.
[5] She is unknown to the Editors.
[6] This portrait by Robert Feke is now in the Boston Museum of Fine Arts.

To Ellen Axson Wilson

My own darling,   Princeton, N. J.   28 March 1904.

Your cablegram from Gibraltar came this morning and gave me the deepest thrill of pleasure I have had for many a long day. Ever since the Hohenzollern sailed nine days ago I have had the dismal sense of not knowing *where* my darling was,—as if she were somehow *lost*; and now she seems *found* again. The cable could carry my words to her, if there were need, as it has brought her words to me. Presently she will be writing to me and I shall see her dear handwriting again, and read once more the sweet words of love and endearment for which my heart is longing! Was ever mortal man so dependent upon love,—upon the dear *wife* love which you, my darling, give in such infinite perfection. You seem somehow to carry the pulses of my life about with you,— in that dear heart which you have, of sheer generosity, dedicated to me. Ah, my pet, I could almost believe this cablegram a physical part of yourself,—or at the least something direct from your hand,—a handkerchief or a flower,—so strong, and for a little overpowering, is the flood of warmth it has brought into the chill and empty room of my heart! I *love* it as if you had tossed it to me oversea with a kiss and a smile. May God bless you and keep you!

Dr. McEwan¹ came on Friday, instead of Saturday, to have a nice, long visit with you; and was mightily crestfallen when he found that you were well on your way to the Mediterranean! He amused himself visiting old friends and was not hard to take care of; and on Sunday preached an admirable sermon,—much better than the one he preached last time. Margaret (for the dear child came herself on Friday, you know) asked immediately "Are you going to invite him again," and clapped her hands in delight when I said 'Yes.' So I will allow you to see him again next winter!

The enclosed paragraph will amuse you.[2] It is substantially correct. There are many funny things told about the affair, which seems to have been most cleverly managed. Two boys fainted. The whole story reminds one of Bobby Inch's[3] narrative of the shooting.[4]

The Yale debate came off on Friday evening,—and we lost! I sat it through, and it sadly affected my nerves; but it was so evenly balanced that I had no criticism of the judges' decision to offer, deep as was my disappointment.

The days go very smoothly—a little monotonously. I have no out-of-town engagements: they closed for the time being with that memorable address to the school teachers on the day you sailed. I see a good deal of the Hibbens, and they are extremely sweet to me, knowing how lonely I am, but not more often than when you are here. The days go just as usual,—though with such a difference, without any kiss from you,—without those constant little calls upon you and those nights and mornings with wh. I keep my strength. But we are all well, and my spirits are as steady as my thoughts of you. I am glad to the bottom of my heart that my darling is where she is, and that I can be in *this* wise

Her own   Woodrow

Love fr. us all to the dear Smiths and love unspeakable to darling Jessie

ALS (WC, NjP).
 [1] The Rev. Dr. William Leonard McEwan, pastor of the Third Presbyterian Church of Pittsburgh.
 [2] The clipping is missing, but it was probably from the *New York Times*, March 28, 1904, reporting on an undergraduate prank on March 27. Some students dressed up a dummy to make it appear that it was a man whose throat had been cut and put it in a bed in one of the dormitories. The student discovering the dummy became greatly excited and called a proctor who in turn summoned a doctor. The doctor did not give away the joke, and more than a thousand students had gathered at the scene before the hoax was exposed. There is a detailed account of this incident in *The Nassau Herald of the Class of 1906, Princeton University* (Baltimore, 1906), pp. 52-53, and a brief report in the *Princeton Press*, April 2, 1904.
 [3] Robert Alexander Inch '95.
 [4] This episode, famous in Princeton annals, occurred on June 8, 1895. Two undergraduates, Frederick Ohl '98 and Garrett Cochran '98, were shot after an altercation in front of Anderson's Saloon on Nassau Street by a townsman, John Collins, in company with Steven Downes. Three physicians were rushed by special train from New York for emergency operations in the Infirmary. Cochran recovered, but Ohl died on June 12. Meanwhile, immediately after the shootings, a large crowd of students had gathered at the town jail, and there was talk of lynching. However, the police had removed Collins and Downes to the safety of the Mercer County jail in Trenton.

From Franklin Potts Glass

My dear Wilson: Montgomery, Ala. 3-28-1904.

Yours of the 24th inst. is at hand. I am very glad that the information I gave you in my last letter was of some service to you. It will be entirely agreeable to me for you to be in Montgomery on Tuesday, April 19th, and to remain here as many days thereafter as suits your convenience. I will take pleasure in doing everything in my power to make your stay here pleasant. I am getting together a committee of all the Princeton men there are in Montgomery for a meeting in the next day or two, and as soon as we can mature our plans, I will write you fully.

I sincerely hope your visit to Alabama will be agreeable and profitable in every respect.

Sincerely yours,   Frank P. Glass

TLS (WP, DLC).

Two Letters from Samuel Russell Bridges[1]

Dear Sir: Atlanta, Ga.   Mch. 28, 1904

Your letter to Mr. Paxon[2] in regard to your lecturing in Atlanta on April 18th has been referred to me for reply.

The people of Atlanta have been very anxious to have you lecture here for the past two seasons but we had about given up hopes of your coming, so when your letter was received we at once saw the manager of the Opera House where our attractions appear and we find that April 18th and 19th are booked, but we can have either April 20th or 21st.

We have decided, according to our telegram to you, that although our course has been made up for this season we would arrange for you to lecture for us as an extra number provided you will come at the fee of $100 as this is all that we will be able to pay for an extra number, and if you can give us either April 20th or 21st, preferably the 21st, as we have Mr. Hamilton W. Mabie[3] April 15th and would like to get this date about a week from his. This is the only chance it seems to have you lecture under the auspices of the Atlanta Lecture Association.

Please wire us upon receipt of this, if you have not already done so, if you can give us either of these dates, or we could use April 29th if you will be in this section then.

Hoping to hear from you favorably, I beg to remain,

Yours very truly,   S Russell Bridges   Mgr.

1 Secretary and Manager of the Atlanta Lecture Association.
2 Frederic John Paxon, president of the Davison-Paxon Co., a department store in Atlanta.
3 Hamilton Wright Mabie, Associate Editor of the New York *Outlook*.

Dear Sir: Atlanta, Ga., Mch. 28, 1904

It has occurred to me since writing the other letter that possibly April 18th is the only date you can be in Atlanta and that you would like to spend that day here. We could possibly arrange for you to lecture here on that night at the big Tabernacle, but could not make any fixed price. We would advertise the date, however, furnish the Tabernacle and give you half the receipts, if you cannot be here at any other time so we can have you speak for the Atlanta Lecture Association. Let us know about this, and oblige, if you cannot arrange the other date.[1]

Yours very truly,   S. Russell Bridges

TLS (WP, DLC).
1 See n. 1 to the announcement printed at April 2, 1904.

From Peter Joseph Hamilton

My dear Wilson,   Montgomery, Ala., Mch 28, 1904

I am here on a law case and write now only to say I received your letter and we shall be glad to have you April 21st—or any other time you may come. Harte has gone to Palestine for the Summer but our public school teachers & others want to hear you and I want you to meet some college men at a little dinner at my home. So don't fail us at Mobile.

Let me know if you will be alone or not, so I can arrange accordingly.

Very sincerely   P. J. Hamilton '79

ALS (WP, DLC).

From James Harmon Chadbourn[1]

                                             Wilmington, N. C.
My dear Dr. Wilson: March 29th., 1904.

Your welcome letter of the 24th. inst. addressed to Miss Susan E. Hall, in which you say that you can be in Wilmington on the evening of Friday, the 15th. of April, and asking if it will be possible and convenient for her to arrange for your speaking here at that time, has been handed me for reply.

In the working of our Church "Committee of Entertainment," of which Miss Hall is chairman, matters of pleasure, entertainment and education are planned and worked out to a certain point; when, for a moment, they are turned over to me, their "financial agent," as they are kind enough to call me, for further action.

Now, my dear Doctor, representing this Committee, I ask, in a plain business way, what will your trip to Wilmington and address here cost us?

In answering this, I ask that you do not consider our former ties with you and your beloved Father, but that you treat Wilmington the same as other places visited by you.

According to present plans of the Committee, your address will be delivered in our Church Hall (Abbie E. Chadbourn Memorial Hall), mainly before our own congregation, and while the time named by you, 15th. of April, will suit most of us, a few of our members will be disappointed as they are engaged on that evening in an entertainment given by local talent in our Opera House. In view of this could you not make your time the 14th. or the 16th., but of course if you cannot change, we shall be delighted to have you on the 15th.

In conversation with our mutual friend Mr. James Sprunt this morning, he requested me to write asking you to stay with him during your visit here, and to say that Mrs. Sprunt and he would be delighted to have you spend the Sabbath with them.

With warmest regards, in which Mrs. Chadbourn[2] joins me, I am,

Sincerely yours,   James H. Chadbourn.

TLS (WP, DLC).
[1] President of the Chadbourn Lumber Co. of Wilmington, N. C., who lived at 323 South Front St., Wilmington.
[2] Blanche King Chadbourn.

From John William Abercrombie

My dear Sir: University, Ala., Mar. 29, 1904.

I am pleased to learn through our Professor Graham that you will visit the University during the month of April. Our faculty and students look forward to your coming with much pleasure.

On account of local conditions, it will be necessary for us to set your address for the forenoon of April 26th, unless you can be with us on the night of the 25th. You could be given an hour during the forenoon of the 27th and still reach Birmingham in time for your address on the evening of that day. Please let me know as soon as possible what day and hour you prefer.

Yours very truly,   John W. Abercrombie.

TLS (WP, DLC).

To Edward Wright Sheldon

My dear Ed: [Princeton, N. J., c. March 30, 1904]

I could be very happy in administering the affairs of the University if only I did not have to beg for money. The necessity to do that lies, I must say, like a burden on my spirits. But I knew when I took the office that I should have to do it and I try not to wince too much. I wince most, I believe, when I have to come to a man like yourself whom I know to be generous to a point of self-denial and who, when asked for money do not think of themselves.

I dare say Mr. Stewart or C. C. has spoken to you of our effort to meet in a businesslike way the deficit which this year's budget discloses. It promises to amount to from $6,000 to $10,000 and is evidently no temporary thing. It is not due to loss of funds or to any sort of mismanagement; and it is not due to an increase of expenses to be met only this year. It is due to an increase in cost of maintenance and administration which is quite normal and quite certain to be permanent.

It seems unwise, therefore, to seek to meet it by subscriptions (which would be easy enough to obtain) intended merely to cover it and not a proposition for taking care of it in the future. The plan we have hit upon, therefore, is to seek subscriptions which will aggregate $100,000 a year for three years in order that we may spend $10,000 a year and have $270,000 by the end of the three years for investment,—a sum sufficient at 4% so to say to endow the deficit.

We have met with a good deal of success, though we have been only a short time at work on the scheme. Twelve men have already pledged themselves to subscribe $5,000 a year each for three years,—on the understanding that after any one of the three payments they may, if they find it necessary to do so, withdraw from the arrangement. Five thousand dollars is not, of course the fixed or necessary figure of the individual subscriptions. We shall be glad to receive subscriptions for any sum from $500 up. We hope, having that, we shall not be obliged to make the subscription list so large as to go beyond the circle of our immediate confidential friends in soliciting contributions to the fund.

I know how extraordinarily generous you have been in contributing to the fund for the class dormitory, and I feel that in the circumstances I am perhaps overstepping the bounds of considerate friendship; but I am counting, my dear fellow, on your knowledge of me and of my motives to explain and to excuse what I am doing and on your frankness to meet it in the spirit in which it is sent.

It was a great pleasure to see you the other day in Mr. Stewart's office, and almost as great a pleasure to hear the warm terms of confidence, admiration, and affection in which Mr. Stewart spoke of you after you had left the room.

Always
Sincerely and faithfully yours   Woodrow Wilson

Transcript of WWshLS (WP, DLC).

To Benjamin Franklin Jones, Jr.[1]

My dear Mr. Jones: [Princeton, N. J., March 30, 1904]

You will, no doubt, remember a conversation I had with you last winter concerning the endowment of the University. I received assurances at that time which led us confidently to expect that several large gifts would be made to the University; but the blight which immediately fell on the money market has necessarily resulted in postponement of the time when large promises can be fulfilled. Meanwhile the University grows, whether we get endowments to support its growth and maintain its efficiency or not. Every increase in the number of students means a necessary increase in the number of instructors for which the fees of the students do not sufficiently provide. Every addition of any endowed building, like the gymnasium, means an additional tax on the general fund with no new source to draw upon. Every increase of equipment means an increase in the cost of maintenance. The result is that, without any loss of income as compared with previous years and without any mismanagement, we find ourselves certain to be face-to-face, at the close of our present fiscal year, with a deficit of between $6,000 and $10,000.

It would be easy to raise that amount, if it were prudent to meet the situation in that way. But another year will probably find us with a similar deficiency and the Finance Committee of the Board of Trustees has deemed the only wise course to be a capitalization of the amount. To that end, we are seeking subscriptions to aggregate $100,000 a year for three years. Twelve gentlemen have already pledged themselves for $5000 a year for three years, and two have promised $1000 a year. Our plan is to spend $10,000 a year and invest $90,000; so that at the end of the three-year term, we may have $270,000 invested and an annual income equal to the present deficit secured. Subscriptions have been taken upon the understanding that any subscriber may, if he should find it necessary to do so, withdraw his name after any one of the three annual payments.

I write to ask if you will not become one of the subscribers. Nothing goes harder with me than this particular duty of my new office as President of the University. To ask for money is unpalatable to any man's spirit, even though he ask, not for himself, but for the best cause in the world. But the need of the University leaves me no choice in the matter. The money must be obtained; and I cannot urge too strongly or too gravely upon you our desire to secure your assistance.

I will offer no apologies: I know that you will prefer to be dealt with in this direct, straightforward manner; and I feel confident that we can count upon your support if you are able to give it.

With much regard,

Sincerely yours,   Woodrow Wilson.

Transcript of WWshLS (WP, DLC).
1 Princeton 1891, President of the Jones and Laughlin Steel Co. of Pittsburgh.

To Ellen Axson Wilson

Princeton, N. J.

My precious, precious darling   31 March, 1904

I am hoping that before I close and mail this letter your cablegram from Naples will come. The one from Gibraltar came on Monday, twenty-four hours before I expected it, and this is Thursday, twenty four hours before I expected to hear of your arrival at Naples. Of course, though, I shall not be nervous or anxious now that you are within the pillars of Hercules; and everyone who has taken the trip goes into such ecstacies over the sights, the exquisite coasts, to be seen between Gibraltar and Naples,—Spain, untouched since the Middle Ages, Sardinia, and all the rest,— that I could almost wish that you might linger on that part of the voyage and have your fill of the beauty it affords. It is so delightful to think of my darling in association with things which seem her proper frame and environment,—exquisite bits of natural scenery touched with romance, and with the soft light upon them from which the light in her own eyes must have come, and ancient places where the old masters had their birth and their home. You are somehow in my mind yourself an image of the things of the imagination which have centered in the Mediterranean. Not that you yourself are *of* them, but the beauties and perfections that are in you are so like the beauties and perfections that are in them, and you seem to be kin to that time of beauty and poetic fervour which has made Greece and Italy forever the places to dream in and remember. Ah, my sweet love, you are picture and poem in one sweet epitome for me. Every beautiful thing in Nature or Art seems to me somehow subtly to express you, and you it. I should not wonder if you never came back to me, but were lost and caught up in the things you have dreamed of and loved ever since long before you loved me!

The cablegram has come,[1] and you are not lost *yet*, bless you! I conclude from the "everything satisfactory" that the nuns at the convent[2] were expecting you and had your rooms ready for you, —I hope they did, though it gives a fellow a queer turn to learn that his wife has entered a nunnery! Ah, my sweet one, this telegram has made my heart light again. The voyage is over and my darling, whose pleasure and happiness are the very breath of my life, is where I have so long dreamed she should be[.] I can't drive the loneliness off or the sense of separation by any trick of thought, but I *can* be happy—with the best sort of happiness, the sort that has no thought of myself in it. It is a novel exercise which may make a man of me!

Dear little Nellie has had a cold, with some trouble in her ear the last three days,—since my last letter,—and we have kept her in bed two days; but she grows constantly better and this morning seems nearly all right again. Bed is for caution, not from necessity, and there is not the slightest ground for anxiety. Even Dr. Wikoff makes light of it, and drops no foreboding hints. The rest of us are all well. Dear Margaret is with Nellie most of the time and just as sweet to her as possible. We all send unbounded love to you both,—love to you all,—but none so much as

Your own   Woodrow

ALS (WC, NjP).

  [1] It is missing.

  [2] For a description of the convent and Mrs. Wilson's stay there, see EAW to WW, April 3, 1904.

To Robert Bridges

My dear Bobby: Princeton, N. J.   31 March, 1904.

I am very much obliged to the editors of the Lamp[1] for wishing to put a portrait of myself in as a frontispiece, but I am a good deal puzzled to see how I can find time to give the artist the sittings he needs.[2] I am expecting to be in New York early next week, probably on Tuesday, and will drop in to see you about the matter.

Yes, all the stone and brick work on the building[3] is completed, except the groining which is to sustain and constitute the roof under the passageway in the arches. That is a complicated part of the job and will probably go slowly, but it will not so far as we can see delay any other part of the construction, and I think that Sutton[4] is justified in his confidence that nothing that we can now foresee can prevent the completion of the whole thing by the first of June. This is going to be a most satisfactory piece of work.

Always,

Faithfully and affectionately yours,   Woodrow Wilson

TLS (WC, NjP).

[1] The Lamp: A Review and Record of Current Literature, published monthly by Charles Scribner's Sons.

[2] George Timothy Tobin executed a series of colored drawings for the frontispieces in The Lamp of, among others, Emerson (March 1904), C. W. Eliot (April 1904), Ruskin (May 1904), A. T. Hadley (June 1904), and Edwin Markham (July 1904). The portrait of Wilson appeared in the October 1904 issue. It is reproduced in the photographic section of this volume.

[3] That is, Seventy-Nine Hall.

[4] Obviously the supervisor of construction work on Seventy-Nine Hall, whom the Editors have been unable further to identify.

To Uzal Haggerty McCarter[1]

My dear Mr. McCarter: [Princeton, N. J.]   31 March, '04

I take the liberty of writing to lay before you the more immediate financial needs of the University. I need not tell you with what reluctance I perform my official duty as the beggar of money. I never had anything quite so unpalatable to do before in all my life. But neither need I tell you how imperative and constantly necessary the performance of that duty is. I must, therefore, throw myself upon your indulgence.

At the outset of my administration, before the present blight fell on the money market, we saw ourselves in a fair way to receive several large gifts. My first begging had evidently made a considerable impression. But since the changes came which produced the existing situation the fulfillment of such expectations has had to be postponed. The growth of the University, however, does not halt or wait. With the increase in the number of students increases must be made in the number of instructors for which the fees of the students do not suffice to pay. Every addition of an unendowed building like the gymnasium adds to the cost of maintenance and administration, as does also every extension of the campus and every increase of equipment.

The consequence is that we shall certainly have a deficit to meet at the end of our present fiscal year (1 August) which will amount to between $6,000 and $10,000. The Finance Committee of the Board thinks, and I believe is right in thinking, that it would be shortsighted to seek merely to cover the actual deficit by subscriptions which would certainly have to be solicited again at the end of another year; for the deficit, being the result of growth and not of loss of income or any mismanagement, is certain to recur until new endowment covers it. We are, therefore, seeking subscriptions to aggregate $100,000 a year for three years,—so that we may spend $10,000 additional each year and invest $90,000. This would give us $270,000 invested at the end of the three years,—enough to yield the $10,000 income with a little balance for premiums in buying desirable securities.

Twelve gentlemen have already subscribed $5,000 a year each, for three years, and two have subscribed $1,000 apiece; with the understanding in each case, that the subscriber may, if he finds it necessary to do so, withdraw after any one of the three annual payments. Subscriptions are being made, moreover, contingent upon the securing of the entire sum.

Will you not consider adding your name to the list? I feel justified in urging it upon you as a really essential and critical matter for the University. We have made so much progress already that we are very much encouraged, but we feel that success is absolutely necessary. We cannot afford to fail. Success, moreover, will probably put us beyond the period of the present financial strain and depression and bring us to the time when we can at last get the large endowments we need. I know that you will give the matter the serious consideration it deserves and that I can count upon you to do what you can.

With warm regard,

Sincerely yours   Woodrow Wilson

Transcript of WWshLS (WP, DLC).
[1] Princeton 1882, Executive Manager of the Fidelity Trust Co. of Newark.

To Thomas Nesbitt McCarter, Jr.[1]

My dear Mr. McCarter: [Princeton, N. J.]   31 Mar. '04.

I know that you are engrossed in business of the first consequence, which affects the convenience and welfare of the whole state, and I fear that it is an almost inexcusable liberty I am taking in thrusting the affairs of the University also upon your attention. I can plead only my duty to be its guardian in season and out of season and my knowledge of your serious interest in its success. We have come upon a matter which seems to us rather critical and action upon which I cannot postpone.

The rapid growth of the University without any considerable increase of income yielding funds has become an actual embarrassment. The present state of the money market has made it necessary for us to forget for the time being the active solicitation of large endowments and also to postpone our supplication of large gifts which, before the blight came, were virtually promised to us. At the same time the increase in the number of students, the addition of unendowed buildings like the gymnasium, which must be lighted, heated and administered, and an enlargement of the campus and of indispensable equipment in the laboratories and elsewhere have gradually increased the cost of instruction and of maintenance. We are, therefore, face to face with a deficit of between $6,000 and $10,000,—a deficit which marks no loss of income and no mismanagement and which promises, unless taken care of, to recur from year to year.

We are seeking, therefore, in mere prudence, to capitalize it. Twelve gentlemen have promised $5,000 a year each for three years; and two have promised $1,000 a year for the same period (a total of $62,000 a year); and we are trying to raise the total to $100,000 a year, in order that we may each year have $10,000 to spend and $90,000 to invest, and at the end of the three-year period enough invested ($270,000) to yield an income of at least $10,000 a year.

This is the matter I am making bold to bring to your attention, with the very earnest request, which I make with real diffidence and with a strong inclination to apologize even for what I know to be my duty, that you allow us to add your name to the list of subscribers. The understanding going with each subscription is that the subscriber may, if he finds it necessary to do so, withdraw after any one of the three annual payments, and that we will try then to replace his name on the list for the remainder of the three-year term.

I know how warmly everyone concerned will appreciate it, if you can see your way to do this, and beg you to accept the warmest assurances of my regard and confidence.

Most sincerely yours,   Woodrow Wilson.

Transcript of WWshLS (WP, DLC).
[1] Princeton 1888, President of the Public Service Corporation of New Jersey. McCarter was the principal organizer of this company, formed in 1903, which was a consolidation of most of the gas, electric, and transportation utilities of New Jersey.

Two Letters from Hopson Owen Murfee

Dear Sir: Marion, Alabama.   31 March 1904

We have just received letters from friends in Mobile and in Selma asking if you would not consent to speak in these places. I hope that it will be possible for you to do so, especially in Mobile. Your words in such centers of influence would be of inestimable service to the cause of education in Alabama. The need of the state is a proper public opinion, and such public opinion can be best established by the living words of those who speak from a large experience and with the voice of authority.

Last summer Mr. A. C. Harte, of Mobile, Mr. George Petrie, of Auburn, Mr. Neal L. Anderson, of Montgomery, Dr. J. H. Phillips, of Birmingham,[1] Mr. D. I. White, of Huntsville,[2] and Mr. E. H. Hobbs, of Selma,[3] expressed to me their earnest desire to have you speak in these cities, and to make arrangements for your coming. You have doubtless planned the details of your trip already; but if you find it possible to speak in any of these cities in which you have not already made engagements, I should be glad to serve you in any way within my power.

We should appreciate your kindness in furnishing us a copy of your address for publication in the quarterly bulletins of the Institute. We wish to increase its influence and usefulness by sending it to several thousand homes of the lower South.

Very sincerely yours   H. O. Murfee

[1] John Herbert Phillips, superintendent of public schools in Birmingham.
[2] David Irvine White, lawyer of Huntsville.
[3] Edward Henry Hobbs, jeweler.

Dear Sir: Marion, Alabama.   1 April 1904

We are glad to know through your letter of the 29 of March that we may have you in our home Sunday also.

Mrs. Murfee reminds me that we are indebted to Mrs. Wilson for THE STATE and for much else, Mrs. Murfee maintains, which we admire, and I wish to join her in the request that you bring Mrs. Wilson with you.

Very sincerely yours   H. O. Murfee

TLS (WP, DLC).

An Announcement of Wilson's Southern Itinerary

[April 2, 1904]

President Wilson '79 will deliver a number of addresses in the South, in the latter part of April, speaking at Wilmington, N. C., on April 15th; Montgomery, Ala., on April 19th; Mobile, Ala., on April 21st; the Military Institute at Marion, Ala., on April 23rd; the University of Alabama, on April 26th; and before the Southern Educational Council at Birmingham, Ala., on April 27th.[1]

Printed in the *Princeton Alumni Weekly*, IV (April 2, 1904), 418.

[1] An undated WWhw itinerary in WP, DLC, indicates that Wilson also planned to speak in Auburn, Ala., on April 18, and that he had not found it possible to speak in Atlanta. About the Auburn engagement, see also G. Petrie to WW, April 7, 1904.

From James Sprunt

My dear Doctor: Wilmington, N. C.   April 2nd. 1904

I have just received your esteemed lines of the 31st. of March promising us the pleasure of entertaining you at our house on the occasion of your intended visit to Wilmington on the morning of the 15th. of April. We look forward to this with much satisfaction and have no doubt your many friends here will be delighted to see you again. I will rely upon definite information from you as to the time of your arrival so that I may meet you at the train.

With kindest wishes,

Yours faithfully,   James Sprunt

TLS (WP, DLC).

From Ellen Axson Wilson

My own darling,   Naples   April 3 1904

I have just come in from church to find my love's *dear* letter awaiting me—so you may conceive how happy I am. It is a piece of good fortune greater than I had dared hope for to get it so soon;—in fact as we are leaving for five days tomorrow I had feared that a letter was out of the question until Friday night. It was such a sweet satisfactory letter too, and gives me so happy a feeling that all is well at home. Am so glad that Saturday was such a success;—and how I should have *loved* to hear that speech!

The same mail brought me a letter from Madame Rinaldi, Mr. [David] Magie's landlady at Rome saying that she can give us the rooms—sunny ones. So that will probably be our address for two weeks & four days beginning with next Sunday—the 10th. We have got another good address & if the "hundred steps" prove *too* dreadful we *may* change. We have 87 steps here & it is pretty bad for the Smiths as well as for me. But a party of American globe-trotters here tells us that Rinaldi's is the best pension in Rome, so we don't like to give it up. The other addresses we have are from them, one on a second floor and one with an elevator. I have heard from Mary Hoyt. She is still at Nice; so we are making our own arrangements for Rome including her. We pay $1.20 apiece here & at Madame R's $1.30 a day. We are perfectly charmed with the convent, everything is so quaint and interesting, and the sisters are simply lovely. They are as pretty as pictures to begin with, and they have the most extraordinary sweetness and charm of manner. Then they are kindness itself,—pet us & call us "cherie,"—almost tuck us in bed,—besides helping us to plan all our out-goings, bargaining with the cabbies &c. &c.

So far everything has been ideal, and we have had no trouble whatever,—even at the custom-house. They did not even unlock our trunks,—simply asked if we had "whiskey or cigars" and then put on the stamps. There are Cook's interpreters at every wharf and station over here dressed in uniform. We engaged one as soon as we stepped on shore, who managed everything for us until we reached the sisters,—and refused to take a penny for it!

We have bought our tickets from Cook for the usual "round," on which we start tomorrow morning at 10 o'clock, getting back Friday afternoon. We have, you see, an extra 24 hours which we will spend either at Amalfi or Sorrento. I enclose the circular that you may see what we are about.[1] It is said to be one one [sic] of the most enchanting trips in the world. We have a special courier (Cook's) "in plain clothes" (!) paying only $2.00 a piece more for him; without him we would, in this country, have been cheated out of a good deal more than that. With him

[1] She enclosed a copy of *Cook's Excursion to Pompeii,* a printed program of a tour to Naples, Pompeii, La Cava, Paestum, Sorrento, and Capri.

we won't have a care in the world & will have our minds perfectly free to enjoy ourselves. In one of the large Cook parties the price was $24.00; by ourselves $26.00 including every*thing*, & staying at the best hotels. That is of course the most expensive part of our trip, yet that isn't so *very* bad!

We have found Naples charming, in spite of the dirt. We reached the convent about ten Thursday morning, lunched at twelve, then went to the banker's, the Lloyd office & Cook's, after which we took the most enchanting drive up the "Posilipo." The road wound up and up along the very edge of the bay with charming villas all the way clinging to the cliff above us and the bluff below, each in its own terraced garden filled with orange & lemon, peach & fig trees all in full bloom. There was a wilderness of flowers of every kind, the wisteria being especially beautiful. The orange and lemon trees were laden with ripe fruit as well as blossoms, after their singular habit of growth. Of course words fail me to tell how almost impossibly picturesque it all was, or how glorious the distant view of Vesuvius, Capri, the city and the bay.

The next afternoon we took an equally beautiful drive to "Capodimonte," a high mountain on top of which is an old royal palace with beautiful pleasure grounds, the road as before winding up between villas & gardens and commanding magnificent views of whole ranges of mountains, &c. &c. And *think*! we only paid each day 30 cts. apiece for the carriage for 2 hours. Yesterday afternoon we also drove, going to Virgil's tomb, the Aquarium, the Cathedral, &c. We spent Friday morning, and afternoon to four o'clock, and yesterday morning at the Museum. There are a few pictures, especially certain Titians, worth coming to Italy to see; but the collection of paintings is as a whole second-rate. But the antiques!—well, it is useless trying to say how beautiful some of them are or how I enjoyed them. There are no catalogues and the things are not labelled so we thought it would be a good idea to have a guide for an hour to help us get our bearings. The result was comical for he turned out to know neither English nor art. We went into a room full of the *early Tuscan* school and he began by pointing out the biggest one as a "Van dyke," and of course I contradicted him flatly. Then he told us a great picture of the Venetian school was a "Botticelli." It was really a "Cesare da Sesto." That is a specimen! At last I tried him with three I knew, and he said they were all "Ghirlandaios," so I told him one was a "Lorenzo di Credi," one a "Lippo Lippi," and the third a "Botticelli," and that we had no further use for his services! We paid him for the half hour and then struggled with him almost as long before we could shake him off!

I must not forget to tell you about "Miss Baylor." When we entered the parlour at the convent & were waiting to go to our rooms she was sitting there and opened upon us immediately a flood-gate of conversation. When she paused for breath I smiled & said "You are from the south, aren't you?" "Yes," she was from Albamarle Co. Va.;—and then she went on with her narrative in the course of which it came out that she is the *very one* with whom Mary Hoyt travelled last fall in the Tyrol &c. &c.! They were two months together. Isn't that a curious coincidence? Of course the Smiths and she have thousands of acquaintances in common. We have a very pleasant crowd here. One is from Alabama, one from South Carolina, one from Va. one from Washington, D. C. (Very southern though.) Ourselves from Geo. & La., two or three from Mass. & New York, a young Scotch woman, two Australians, & four or five Italians, two being old Countesses who live here all the time. This is a "nursing order" of nuns and it is a very pleasant refuge for old dowagers in their last days. Lucy was much entertained at their comments in French between themselves upon us, which we were supposed not to understand. They were very kindly; Jessie was pronounced a "charming jeune fille bien elevée," and Lucy was "bon enfant"; &c.

We are just as well as possible; the weather is perfect, neither hot nor cold; of course we are enjoying every minute of it,—yet all the same I am counting the days that lie between my love & me. There are nine weeks & three days. I had a beautiful dream about you last night; I stood on that Posilipo road and saw you distinctly a few hundred yards below me holding out your arms to me. I ran breathlessly down and flung myself into them,—and then alas! I waked. But ah! it was sweet while it lasted. Jessie is writing to dear Nell & "as they say" "there will be nothing left for me to tell about," so give her & dearest Margaret my devoted love & many kisses. Best love to Madge & Stockton too;—how anxious I am to know how he is.

Have you the Rome address "Madame E. A. Rinaldi, 45 Via Rasella."

If you get this in time send a cablegram there please! Everything is arranged about my return passage & I have a first-rate state-room. I shall send my trunks to Genoa from Florence,—so moving them only twice.

Goodbye, my darling, my love, my life! My heart is filled almost

to breaking with love & longing for you, dearest, in spite of the
delight of it all. I am *yours*, always & altogether,

Your own   Eileen.

ALS (WP, DLC).

To Ellen Axson Wilson

My precious darling,   Princeton, N. J.   4 April 1904

Nellie has the measles! How is that for a misadventure? She
caught it, undoubtedly, at the circus. The period of incubation
figures that out exactly. She is as comfortable as possible, there
is nothing in the least disquieting or abnormal about the case;
and I have secured Miss Andrews,[1] the sweet young Princeton
woman who was once with you, you remember, and whom Nellie
likes, to come and take charge. She came Saturday, and is in-
stalled. Nellie is in your room, Miss Andrews in mine; and I am
in the blue room. Nellie was getting well from her "cold," apparently, as I wrote you, and the doctor (Wikoff) told her she might
get up and dress; and it was in the process of dressing that she
observed the "rash" on her chest which disclosed the mischief.
She is now very much broken out, but feels singularly little dis-
comfort, and the doctor makes light of the whole matter,—quite
contrary, as you know, to his usual habit. The disease will have
disclosed itself a full week when this letter sets sail for Italy;
the course of it is but two weeks; before the letter reaches you,
therefore, it will all be over,—unless Margaret has caught it,
which is most unlikely, we think. She gets a week more holiday,
to make sure! How glad I am that you and dear Jessie are away,
and will not know anything about it until it is all over! We do
not need you at all, thank you! And you need not feel the least
uneasiness, you know, about consequences. Measles has no "se-
qualia" like scarlet fever. The only thing to be careful about is
the eyes; and of course we will be *very* careful to see that she
does not use them too soon or too much. How bored I am to be
obliged to tell you all about this passing flurry,—but how interesting a circumstance it is that this should all have come from the
circus, to which I took her to console her for your departure, or,
rather, to divert her thoughts from it! *Now* I have to divert your
thoughts from the good time you are having by narrating the consequences! It's a queer world, my masters!

But it's a sweet world, too; for it is delightful to discover, even
by these means, the sort of love I have for my darling over sea,—

how distinctly I enjoy having this experience in her stead, being
her proxy in this minor misfortune! I too often feel that my love
is wholly selfish, that I love my darling only because she has the
gifts and graces and the charm that give me pleasure and deepest
satisfaction, *only because she is lovely and is mine*, to have and
to enjoy. These days give me welcome proof of something more
ideal, more profound, and I know that I love *her* as well as
myself!

The rest of us are all perfectly well, and all things go as usual
with us. Yesterday—Easter Sunday—was unlike other Sundays,
of course. There was no chapel service; I helped to administer
communion in the Second Church, where I felt quite like a
stranger; and the Hibbens were in Elizabeth. I made an afternoon call at the Pynes'. They were here for the day,—and before
that I got an hour's nap. My heart is all the time with precious
little Nen., but I cannot sit with her, though I do frequently look
in.

I suppose that you saw a regular Roman Catholic Easter. It
must have seemed very real and very close to you in the Convent.
I try to fill my imagination with what my darling is doing, but
Italy,—the Italy of Naples and the cities, is a very vague, picture
country to me and I can make little of it. I only know that your
eye and mind are full of it, and I *can* picture you, my beautiful
darling, with your eyes full of wonder and enjoyment.

Stockton looks in on us frequently, to see how we fare without
our sweet mistress, and seems quite well and steady, very bright
and full of talk upon general matters, quite like his normal self,—
if, indeed, he can be said to have a perfectly normal self. He
drops in and smokes while we finish dinner, and last night sat
till half after nine as if he were without nerves and were entirely
enjoying the loaf. It is pleasant and restful to see him in such
natural, unconscious moods.

The other day Mr. Joseph Gilder (Mr. Richard Watson Gilder's
brother, whom you may remember) came in to say that he was
setting up to be a literary agent, middleman and common friend
to author and publisher, the writer and his market. I explained
to him, as usual, that I was, for the time being, at any rate, not a
literary man, but a man of business, executive work having
supplanted writing. Whereupon he went off and, after reflection,
wrote to me proposing an essay on "The Tragedy (or Pathos) of
Success." What do you think of that for mere gall? Mr. Cleveland,
he tells me, has become his client! Mr. C. will end, as Dr. Weir
Mitchell has ended, by becoming a mere man of letters if he is

not careful. How easy, how wide open to everybody is the art of the writer in this democratic day of ours!

Ah, my love, how my heart longs for a letter! *There's* the rub! It may be several days yet before I see the dear handwriting I am fainting to see. How deeply these days make me *know* my love for my precious little wife. And how fine it is to sit and think of her and all she has bestowed on me: the charm with which she has filled and surrounded my life; the inspiration she is to me, the daily incentive to be my best, to *be* what she deems me. *Every-*one here speaks of you with love,—this household with adoration; but who can know your full charm and beauty except

Your own   Woodrow

Love from all to dearest Jess. and to the Smiths and Cousin M.

ALS (WC, NjP).
¹ Edith R. Andrews, a trained nurse of 42 Wiggins St.

From Winthrop More Daniels

My dear Wilson: Princeton, N. J.   Apr. 4, 1904.

The Department of Politics and History met today, and voted after discussion not to ask for a reversal of the decision already rendered by the Com. on Entrance Exams. with reference to History. The Com. on Entrance Exams. had declined the request presented by Penn Charter School and by Lawrenceville that applicants for entrance to Princeton be allowed to stand the Exam. in Greek History at one time, and the exam. in Roman History at a later time.

The reason why the Department voted against the dividing of the examination seemed to be that the schools already give but scanty attention to the subject of History, and that to lighten the requirements by dividing the examination would be equivalent to discouraging more thorough work in History in the schools.

Prof. Paul van Dyke was designated to convey the decision to Dr. McPherson of Lawrenceville. The motion declining Dr. McPherson's request was put, not in the shape of a direct refusal, but as a determination not to attempt a reversal of the action of the Com. on Entrance Exams. by whose action the request had been previously declined.

Dr. McPherson submitted a written statement, showing that his request was likely to prevail with other colleges, notably Yale. This statement is enclosed herewith. If for any reason the action of the Department should, in your judgment, need reconsideration, will you kindly notify Prof. van Dyke to defer making a reply to Dr. McPherson until such reconsideration can be had.

Yours very Sincerely   W. M Daniels.

ALS (WP, DLC). Enc.: "Requirements in History for admission to Amherst, Brown, Chicago, Columbia, Harvard, Pennsylvania, Williams and Yale," T memorandum (WP, DLC).

From John William Abercrombie

My dear Sir: University, Ala., Apr. 4, 1904.

I beg to acknowledge receipt of your letter of the 1st inst. In reply let me say that you can get a train at Birmingham for Tuscaloosa at 4:30 P.M., at 10:00 P.M., at 5:45 A.M., or at 10:00 A.M. The trains leaving Birmingham at 4:30 P.M. and 5:45 A.M. are locals and reach Tuscaloosa in about two hours. The other trains are through trains and make the distance in about one and a half hours.

If you should reach Birmingham on the 25th in time to leave on the 4:30 P.M. train, it would be possible for you to deliver your address that evening. Not knowing what hour you will arrive in Birmingham, I hardly know what to suggest. Please let me know as soon as you learn definitely the hour of your arrival there.   Yours very truly,   John W. Abercrombie.

TLS (WP, DLC).

To Robert Randolph Henderson

My dear Bob: Princeton, N. J.   6 April, 1904.

I am sincerely sorry that I am going to be in Tennessee on April 29,[1] and must again deny myself the pleasure of being the guest of the Maryland Bar Association. I have never been to Annapolis and the fact that the Association is to meet there would add a great deal to the interest of my visit could I be there, but I am booked for a Southern trip which will keep me away until the first of May.

I am sincerely obliged to you. As far as I am concerned the Association consists of yourself, and I shall count upon my disappointment in not seeing you this month being made up by seeing you at Commencement.

Affectionately yours,   Woodrow Wilson

TLS (WC, NjP).

[1] He intended to visit his brother, Joseph R. Wilson, Jr., and his family in Clarksville, Tenn., on his way home from Alabama.

From Benjamin Franklin Jones, Jr.

My dear Mr. Wilson: Pittsburgh, April 6th, 1904.

An earlier answer to your letter of the 30th ult., has been impossible, as, through some mistake, your letter was delivered to my Mother's house during her absence from town, and I only received it yesterday.

I thoroughly appreciate the necessity for an increase in the income of the University, and would take great pleasure in making a substantial donation, but I do not feel that I can do this at the present time. However, I will do what I can in a small way and will agree to donate, under the terms of your letter, $500.00 a year for the next three years. If you wish a formal guarantee to cover this donation if you will kindly have one drawn up I shall be pleased to sign it.   Yours truly,   B. F. Jones Jr.

TLS (WP, DLC).

From Ellen Axson Wilson

My own darling,   Sorrento—April 7 [1904]

I am writing,—with an impossible pen,—in a window looking out upon the bay of Naples,—Vesuvius, and Naples itself across the water,—a wonderful prospect indeed, though robbed of a part of its glory by an overcast sky. We left Amalfi at 8.30 and had a wonderful four hour drive through the wildest and most picturesque scenery. The air was so deliciously fresh & cool that it partly atoned for the absence of yesterday's intense colour. Yesterday was the most glorious day we have had. It was a perfect riot of colour,—a debauch of beauty from early morning until night. We went to bed feeling positively drunken. But to return for a moment to the beginning. We left Naples,—on a train that went about a mile an hour—reached Pompeii at lunch time & spent the afternoon in the ruins. It was intensely interesting even more so than I expected;—very hard walking however for several hours; we reached La Cava at dinner time rather used up. After a very comfortable dinner & bed we started bright & early for Paestum. It threatened rain but held up for a time and we had a beautiful little railway journey & then a pleasant walk to the temples,—which are all my fancy painted;—no picture can give the impression of their majesty and nobility. While we were still at the temples the rain began in good earnest; but we were prepared for it and got no harm. Indeed the dark skies rather suited the melancholy beauty of the place.

The carriage was waiting with our luggage at Salerno to take us to Amalfi,—that glorious drive of 3½ hours around the cliffs and through some dozen fascinating little villages. We were of course disappointed at the prospect of visiting it in the rain, but there was no help for it. I got a drink of brandy for Jessie & myself, & had my water-bag filled at the station, then we bundled up in our steamer rugs & started,—and to our surprise & delight we had for 4/5ths of the way the most superb effect of light & shade & colour on sea & mountain & cliff that I have ever imagined. I wouldn't have missed it for *anything*! The last two or three miles the rain and mist closed in upon us, & we saw practically nothing. So, the next morning turning out a *glorious* day, we drove back for several miles so as to see for once the true intense southern blue of sea & sky. It was *wonderful*; and the little villages, Minora, Majora, &c. &c. were enchanting,—the people all modles [models] for artists;—and then the flowers, and the groves of orange & lemon, and the cherry & peach blossoms! Just after lunch we started again on the famous excursion up the mountain to Ravello;—& there we simply reached the *limit*! There are no words for such loveliness as that! It is a large village of which the architecture is chiefly Moorish, with a wonderful old Byzantine church filled with antique mosaic work. But the chief thing is the old Saracen palace with its *wonderful* gardens and its view between columns & trellises of the mountains and the sea. We returned—as I said, in a state of intoxication,—stopping to see Amalfi itself, and the beautiful mosaics in *its* Byzantine church. Amalfi is a famous old fishing town, & its patron saint is Andrew the apostle. His body was brought here from Constantinople in the 12th Cen. so this cathedral is one of the most sacred spots in Italy, and there is a splendid great bronze statue of the Saint, by one of the masters of the great time.

I haven't time to tell you of our enchanting hotel at Amalfi,— the old Capuchin monastery—for we have only the afternoon here & the girls want to go out.

The queen of Holland[1] & her suite are in this hotel with us! I hope we may see her.

We are all just as well as possible, and I love you, my own dearest one, beyond all words,—I think of you *constantly*. You seem to doubt the possibility of that but I swear it is the *simple truth*. With devoted love to all, I am

Yours always & altogether,   Eileen.

Since I began to write the sky has cleared & the sea is a deep burning blue—gorgeous!

ALS (WP, DLC).
¹ Queen Wilhelmina.

From George Petrie

My dear Doctor Wilson,   Auburn, Alabama.   April 7, 1904.

We are delighted to hear by your letter of April 4 that you will certainly come to Auburn. We shall count on you for the date you suggest, April 18, Monday.

You can, as you say, get a train from Atlanta at about six o'clock that morning, and reach here at nine. We shall be delighted to have you come at that hour and spend the day, resting, meeting our faculty, looking over the college, or doing just exactly what you happen to feel like doing. But if you prefer to avoid the early morning trip, there is another train from Atlanta that reaches her [here] at half past four in the afternoon. It leaves Atlanta about one o'clock. We shall be glad to have you come early as you can and stay as long as possible. I enclose schedule of our railroad.

Our president will, of course, wish part of your time, but we shall expect you to make our home your headquarters while you are in Auburn. I am mighty sorry to hear that Axson can not come with you. When your plans are complete, please write or wire me on what train to expect you.

Yours very truly,   George Petrie

TLS (WP, DLC). Enc.: printed schedule of the Western Railway of Alabama, effective March 26, 1904.

To Ellen Axson Wilson

University Club [New York]

My own darling,   Friday, 8 April, 1904

I am in New York for two dinners (by which you may infer Nellie's improvement), one last night at Mr. James W. Alexander's,—a man's dinner, with lots of distinguished persons present, Mr. Root, ex-Gov. Levi P. Morton, and the like,—another to-night, the Round Table Club. I enjoy this, so to say, miscellaneous hobnobbing more than I used to. Some of the men a[re] quite interesting and companionable.

Dear little Nen. was very bright indeed when I left home yesterday afternoon. It was a week on Tuesday since the disease developed and it lasts only about two weeks so that four more days ought now to bring her out of it. The irruption is fading rapidly, and her temperature has been normal for several days. She has excellent nights now that the fever has passed away, and has not at any stage suffered at all. She has even been free from headaches. She and Miss Andrews have fine times together,— either reading stories aloud (for of course Nell does not read herself) or playing games. I feel that we have been peculiarly fortunate in securing Miss Andrews. She is *very* sweet and satisfactory. In the afternoons I go into the room and read to Nen. while Miss A. takes the air for an hour or so. Isn't it hard luck that Nell. must miss the Ben. Greet Company? They give two performances,—The Merchant of Venice and Twelfth Night,— afternoon and evening, to-morrow.[1] At any rate Margaret will see them. She does not go back till Monday.

To-day one of Scribner's artists, a man named Tobin, is to draw my portrait,—at least I am to give him the first of two sittings,— or, it may be, *standings*, for he wishes, he says, to draw me "in a speaking position." The portrait is to appear as a frontispiece to (I think) the June number of the *Lamp*, Scribner's critical publication which used to be called Book Notes, or something to that effect. Mr. Tobin does his work in colour and it is reproduced in colour,—monochrome, very nearly flesh tint,—and some of the things he has done, notably a likeness of the Marquis of Salisbury, are quite stunning. In a few years I may make my way up (down) to Sargent.[2] The rest of the persons whom you love and who love you keep perfectly well, and, now that Spring seems at last actually to be coming, ought to continue to keep so. It was exceeding hard to leave home yesterday on the very day on which we had reasonable hope of getting a letter from our dear travelers from Gibraltar. If I had realized beforehand what my acceptance of Mr. Alexander's invitation meant in *that* regard, I would have declined instead of accepting. Ah, how the days will change when the dear letters begin to come! My love, my love! My passion for you grows with a terrible, a delightful ardour. Your lover is more your lover every day of his life,—and would yet give his life, which you make delightful, for you!

Your own   Woodrow

Love fr. all to all

ALS (WC, NjP).

[1] Phillip Barling Ben Greet, theatrical manager and producer, had led touring repertory companies through the United Kingdom and the United States since the 1880's. At this time, his company was under the sponsorship of the Elizabethan Stage Society of England and was presenting both open-air and theater performances of Shakespeare's plays. Greet's company later became the nucleus of the Old Vic Company of London. The two plays mentioned by Wilson were presented in Alexander Hall.

[2] Wilson did in fact sit in 1917 for a portrait by John Singer Sargent. It was commissioned by the National Gallery of Ireland in Dublin, where it now hangs.

From Susan Eliza Hall

My dear Dr. Wilson,　　　　　Wilmington, N. C.　Apr. 8, 1904.

Although our correspondence may be said to have gone into the hands of a receiver, it has been closed at least to the great satisfaction of the debtors. But the thanks of the committee are still due you from me. We are all looking forward to your coming with a very great pleasure. And the committee is taking great care, so as to have as many people as possible hear you, in spite of our limited accommodations. Please accept, through me, the cordial good wishes of the committee and of the church.

Yours sincerely,　Susan E. Hall.

ALS (WP, DLC).

From Peter Joseph Hamilton

My dear Wilson:　　　　　　Mobile, Ala.　April 9th, 1904.

I wrote you some days ago to ascertain exactly what time you expected to be here and how long you could stay, so that I could make the necessary arrangements. Glass told me at Montgomery the other day that you expected to leave there in the fore-noon of April 21, and if so that would bring you here about four o'clock that afternoon. I see you speak at Marion on [t]he 23rd, and I presume you will stay here until that morning, or at all events until a late hour the night before. What I am driving at is for you to get in two evenings at Mobile. I would like to have you meet a few friends say the first evening, and the next day show you around, particularly down the shell road. Friday evening would then be available for a talk to teachers or other public matter, if agreeable to you. As it takes a few days to arrange these things, I would be glad to hear from you as soon as practicable.

With kind regards, I am,

Yours very truly,　P. J. Hamilton

TLS (WP, DLC).

From Ellen Axson Wilson

My own darling,   Rome, April 10 1904.

I hope the cablegram which I sent yesterday[1] added to your comfort in that you will now know us to be comfortably settled for more than two weeks,—no more hurried moving from place to place at all, except for the two or three days at Perugia & Assissi on our way to Florence. I found your second dear, *dear* letter awaiting me one [on] our return to the convent Friday night, and I was overjoyed to get it! I hope mine will reach you as promptly & regularly. I shall number them so that you may know if they "go straight." The rest of our little tour went off quite smoothly and satisfactorily. After I wrote you at Sorrento we walked about the charming place; and at night had at the hotel "the Tarentella"—national dances, character songs &c, very pretty, and amusing. We hoped it would "draw out" the little queen, but she kept herself close. She is said to be unwell; some others who saw her walking said she had a very "discontented expression."

The next morning we set off early to Capri in an open boat for a time,—which was charming—and then in a steamer. The visit to "the blue grotto" was a perfect success; the colour was all our fancy had painted; the only draw-back is that too many boats go in at once & there is too much shouting & confusion. Capri is very much like Amalfi, but we found the latter more beautiful, chiefly because there we had bluer skies & water. We drove up to Anacapri, a town of villas & gardens at an enormous elevation, and where we had superb views; then we took the boat for Naples arriving at six. It was very amusing to see the English making "afternoon tea" on deck, lighting stoves, boiling water &c. &c; actually on their knees,—prostrating themselves as it were before their national altar! I believe that if instead of the Bay of Naples, heaven opened before them,—or even the other place,—they would go on calmly drinking tea!

Yesterday we had our first serious struggle with luggage and were somewhat worsted. Our train was to leave at 8.20 and we were at the station three quarters of an hour before,—yet we did not succeed in getting our luggage weighed and on in time,— even with the help of a "Cook's man." We had secured good seats & put Lucy & Jessie to defend them & our "small baggage," so when our prospects grew dark I ran back so as not to be separated from Jessie & Lucy came to Mary, as they too preferred to die in each other arms! We were to hold the fort & they were to gain it if possible! As I said, they failed & came on later, reaching Rome at three. We arrived at one & were met by Mary Hoyt, came here & had a good lunch; & then she very kindly went to meet the others. It is only a short way on the train. The trunks were brought up in a queer little hand-wagon & carried up the hundred steps for 20 cts each! It was a dollar each to bring them to Rome, —less than I expected. The girls had, as usual, made friends and much to my relief had been given luncheon on the way.

This place is shabby in appearance but very comfortable & the food is most tempting. Madame [Rinaldi] is kindess itself. It is a very shabby little street but well located; the Ba[r]barini Palace for instance is just around the corner. It is a small place & quite full, so that, much to my regret, Marguerite & her mother,[2] whom we left at the convent, can not get in.

Of course we have not yet "seen Rome" & have "nothing to communicate" on that subject! We slept late and then went to the Presbyterian church where we heard a *splendid* sermon by Dr. [Henry] Cowan, Prof. of church history at the University of Aberdeen. I enjoyed it exceedingly; it seemed especially good to hear such a fine strong, bracing, intellectual address after our ten days of rioting in sensuous beauty; it had a sort of tonic effect. Then we took a short walk at random seeing nothing in particular; and since lunch Mary Hoyt and I have been hard at work with our Baedekers trying to work out a programme for our Roman campaign. The number of things we "ought to see" is certainly appalling. She has turned continental,—went to early mass and then sight-seeing today. She is looking very well and is perfectly happy.

Tomorrow there is to be a great celebration at St Peters in honour of the 13th centenary of Pope Gregory the Great,—tremendous papal function, high mass of course by the pope & singing by a thousand trained voices. Mary Hoyt managed to get tickets and they go at seven and will have to stand until eleven or twelve. Of course I declined to go,—couldnt possibly stand the fatigue. But now somewhat to my dismay Madame has got a *seat* for me & I shall have to go I suppose. It was very good in her, but I dread the crowd. I must go in a black dress & veil,—no hat. The others will probably leave before it is over.

But I have been much interrupted since writing this & must now stop & get to bed—since we rise so early in the morning. Besides I have still to write Marguerite. Just think it is now only six weeks & three days before I start for home,—eight weeks & two days before I reach home! The time is slipping by and how I do enjoy scoring off the days! We will be in Florence on Sat. the 30th of April, & we have already secured rooms at the "Pension Jennings-Riccioli, 37 Corso dei Tintori."

Goodnight, my dear, *dear* love! How I wish I could tell you how I love you, or with what emotions I read these dear letters of yours. But you know do you not? *darling*!

Your own   Eileen.

We are all perfectly well & the weather is ideal,—neither hot nor cold.

ALS (WC, NjP).
 [1] It is missing.
 [2] As Mrs. Wilson soon discloses, their last name was Walbridge. They were obviously old friends of the Wilsons and probably from Atlanta. Marguerite Walbridge wrote to Wilson from 172 Capitol Ave., Atlanta, in 1910, but neither she nor her mother appears in the Atlanta city directories from the mid-1890's to 1920.

To Daniel Moreau Barringer

My dear Moreau: Princeton, N. J.   11 April, 1904.

Thank you most sincerely for your letter from Phoenix[1] and for the cheque which it enclosed. I think that the contribution is very generous indeed, and I appreciate it most warmly. It was like you to respond so generously and so willingly. These are hard cases to handle, and I think that this minor sort of begging particularly trying to manage.[2]

I am expecting to be off this week for a trip through the South, principally in Alabama, from which I shall not be back until the beginning of May. I do not know what May has in store for me, but it would be delightful if I could come if only for a single night to see you at Poplar Grove.

Always,   Affectionately yours,   Woodrow Wilson

TLS (D. M. Barringer Papers, NjP).
 [1] It is missing.
 [2] Wilson had probably asked Barringer for money to help some needy student.

From Charles Williston McAlpin

My dear Dr. Wilson: [Princeton, N. J.]   April 11, 1904.

The addresses that you asked me to send you are as follows:

The Right Hon. John Morley,[1]
Flowermead, Wimbledon Park,
London, S.W.

Sir William Mather,
Wood Hill,
Prestwich, Manchester.

I have omitted the M.P. from Sir William's name as I read in the papers recently that he had resigned his seat in Parliament.

I remain,

Sincerely yours,   [C. W. McAlpin]   Secretary.

CCL (McAlpin File, UA, NjP).

[1] The Princeton Board of Trustees had voted on March 10, 1904, to confer the LL.D. degree upon John Morley and Sir William Mather, British industrialist and M.P., 1885-86, 1889-95, and 1900-1904. When they were unable to attend the June 1904 commencement, Wilson invited them to receive their degrees at the university's annual Commemoration Day on October 22, 1904. The entire celebration of Commemoration Day had to be canceled because neither Morley, Mather, nor other persons subsequently invited could be present. Morley never did receive an honorary degree from Princeton. Mather received his in June 1905.

To Ellen Axson Wilson

My own darling,   Princeton, N. J.   12 April, 1904

The plot thickens! Margaret has the measles, on schedule time! Fortunately, provoking as it is, it is not serious. Nellie is so nearly well that the doctor will probably let her sit up to-day. In a very few days more she will be out, and, if her eyes show no signs of weakness, at school again. The only really distressing thing about Margaret's getting it is the amount of time she will lose from her college work. But we are taking it all very philosophically, I can assure you,—and shall be sorely disappointed if you do not. Margaret will be well when this reaches you,—so that you will not even have the opportunity to think of her as ill. That's a most satisfactory circumstance,—to us. We can know at least that you *must* think of these things in the past tense, and *cannot* worry about them as actual distresses. Miss Andrews is *most* satisfactory, and will, of course, assume charge of the new case. We will put Margaret in your room with Nellie, so that Miss A. may be at hand at night. Isn't it a rum go! And yet I must say that the amusing side of it appeals to me most strongly. Happily, measles is a disease which one *cannot* take tragically. And in one way it brings me real relief. I shall of course give up my southern trip. I had allowed myself to be persuaded to crowd so many engagements into it, and the southern places are separated by such unconscionable distances and such hard travelling that I found myself looking forward to those two weeks with real dread and almost an expectation of returning ill. It is already quite certainly warm in the South and debilitating, and constant travel goes hard with me at best. I am decidedly easier in my mind to have got clear of the risks. I was wondering, for one thing, how I should manage to get my letters to my darling off regularly and at intervals properly caculated [calculated] for the sailing time of the steamers, twice a week. Moreover it seemed likely that your first letter, due this week, might come the very day I left, and too late! That would have been heart-breaking. And how could I manage to have the dear letters that followed find me? I could not go without them when they were in the country. I have hardly been able to wait for them to begin coming. How I shall pounce upon and devour the first one,—and all that come after, as if they were pieces of my dear one's self sent back to me over sea! Your third cable, from Rome, came on Saturday. The Italian operators, apparently, find your writing a little difficult, at least this time. The first two cablegrams were all right, but in this third one the two words were transmitted wrong. The first was easy enough to identify, but the second was very much mutilated. We think we have made it out, however, and we are at least certain that our precious ones are all right. Perhaps you had better *print* these singular code words, as a child would, letter by letter.

My darling, my darling, how I hope that these letters of mine, in spite of the news of measles, give you some direct impression of how happy I am in your trip and how profound and joyous, though yearning and full of longing for you, my love for you is. When I get you again I shall not be able to understand how I ever did without you. I am wholly and in all things

Your own   Woodrow

Love fr. all to Jessie and all.

ALS (WC, NjP).

To Sarah Baxter Bird

My dear Mrs. Bird: Princeton, N. J.   13 April, 1904.

Will you not forgive a busy man a type-written letter? I am writing in the midst of my morning business to tell you that our dear Margaret is here at home in bed with the measles.

She came home to spend her brief Easter vacation and while she was here Nellie broke out with the measles, so that we had to keep Margaret ten days under observation. Very promptly at the end of these ten days she went to bed with the disease. She begged me to write you this in view of the fact that she had expected to have the pleasure of being at the little Euchre party you are planning for Friday evening.

Ellen you know is in Italy. She sailed on the 19 of March, and has now been in Italy something over two weeks. There has not yet been time to hear from her by letter, but I have had three cablegrams from her which assure me of her safety and welfare. You see, therefore, that I am both mother and father to the sick girls. Ellen will be horrified when she hears of the situation.

I hope that you are all well and happy. With warmest messages of regard from all,

Affectionately yours,   Woodrow Wilson

TLS (Berg Coll., NN).

To Frank Thilly

My dear Professor Thilly: Princeton, N. J.   13 April, 1904.

Allow me to thank you for your letter of April 10.[1] I am sincerely sorry that it should be necessary for you to go to Europe on account of your health, but I am very glad indeed that you are going and I most sincerely hope that the doctor's predictions will be entirely fulfilled in respect to your complete restoration to strength.

I found out for myself some eight years ago the certain consequences of working for years together without a vacation, and I am glad to infer from what you tell me that you have discovered them as I did at the beginning instead of at the end of their effects.

I do not feel that I deserve any thanks for the very small part I played in helping to look up a house for you. Such little as I did, I undertook merely from inclination and because I am sincerely interested in your comfort. We shall look forward with the greatest interest to your coming in the fall and with the greatest pleasure to the prospect of meeting Mrs. Thilly and including her in the circle of our friends.

Wishing you the best and most profitable of vacations,
Most cordially yours,   Woodrow Wilson

P.S. Hibben said something about your coming here in August; I feel that we ought to warn you that August is our most depressing and most uncomfortable month.

TLS (Wilson-Thilly Corr., NIC).
 [1] It is missing.

To Herbert Stearns Squier Smith[1]

My dear Smith: Princeton, N. J. 13 April, 1904.

The Finance Committee of the Board of Trustees has found it necessary, in view of the rapid growth of the University without any corresponding increase in its endowment, to raise an emergency fund which will cover the years of financial depression, not because any of our funds have depreciated or there has been any mismanagement, but simply because the expenses have outrun the endowment.

I take the liberty, therefore, of writing to you as Secretary of your class to ask if you could give me a list of the men in your class who would be likely to be able to subscribe from $1000 to $5000 a year for three years to such a fund? If you will do this, you will be rendering a service to the University.

Very sincerely yours, Woodrow Wilson

TLS (WC, NjP).
1 C.E., Princeton 1878; Professor of Applied Mechanics at Princeton University.

To Ellen Axson Wilson

Princeton, N. J.

My own darling, 14 April, 1904 (Thursday)

Your third cable, from Rome, was a great comfort, but I find that cables do not wholly agree with me as an exclusive diet, and that I am growing inordinately hungry for a letter, a letter, a letter! It is two weeks to-day since the cable came which announced your safe arrival in Naples and I have seized every mail, both yesterday and to-day, and sorted it in eager haste to find the handwriting I love and long to see. But not yet! I wonder how often I shall read the dear missive when it comes, and kiss each page of it because it comes from you. Separation could not make me value your sweet presence [more] than I do when I have it,—I think you will bear me out in that,—but it certainly gives poignant keenness to my sense of all that that dear presence and precious companionship mean to me. The sense of vacancy and loneliness is emphasized almost beyond what I can bear. It is then, my incomparable darling, that there is defined in my consciousness so vividly that it seems part of my thought waking or sleeping, with the friends I love or away from them, at business with committees or alone, the essential difference there must forever be between my feeling for you and my feeling for the friend I most love and depend upon. I wish I could define it in words as vividly as it is defined in my consciousness,—the total inadequacy of *any* substitute companionship! I now know that in ordinary days, those *real* days when you are by, when the house is full of you and there is for me no one else 'at home,' my *life*, my impulse, my sustenance are in you, only my vacation pleasure, the satisfaction of my moments of excursion and adventure, the delight of intimate and affectionate friendship are elsewhere; and when you are away the days, the working, living days are empty, sweet and tender as my friends are. You are *part of me*[;] they are outside of me.

Even hard and successful work does not take the loneliness off. To-day our Committee on the Course of Study completed its labours, and next week our report,[1] with which we are all really delighted (the scheme has worked out wonderfully well, and all doubts have been removed from the minds of the members of the Committee), will be laid before the Faculty in a series of meetings next week. Fine will take the chair of the Faculty, and I, as chairman of the Committee, will take charge of the measure on the floor in debate. It is all most interesting, a bit exciting, and most encouraging; but not for a moment do I forget that my darling is not here! I am not complaining[.] I would not have you think me unhappy. I am not. I am simply wholesomely lonely, deeply, blessedly aware of my utter dependence on you, my utter love for the wife of my heart. It makes me happy, but not gay; for shall I not have her again, with all the joy my heart can contain?

The patients are doing finely. Nell is practically well; Margaret is already over the worst. We are in need of no sympathy and send you all every cheerful message of love.

Your own   Woodrow

ALS (WC, NjP).
  ¹ It is printed at April 16, 1904.

From Herbert Stearns Squier Smith

My dear Wilson: Princeton, N. J.   April 14, 1904.

'78 has but few wealthy members and perhaps I am overestimating the ability of some in the following list: but I have tried to name those who either have the ability or would like to be asked.

Alexander Brown, 135 East Baltimore St., Baltimore
C. C. Clarke, 97 Chambers St. New York.

Wm. Dulles, Jr., 277 Broadway, New York. I know his willingness but question his ability.

Rev. Franklin B. Dwight, Convent Station, N. J. The real donor would be Mrs. Dwight who was a Maitland. Mrs. McCosh might help.

David Fleming, 325 North Front St. Harrisburg, Pa.

George A. Howe, Colonial Steel Co, Keystone Bank Bdg., Pittsburg, Pa.

W. W. Lawrence, 100 William St. New York.

Percy R. Pyne, 52 Wall St. New York.

W. D. Van Dyke, 916 Wells Bdg. Harrisburg, Pa.

I sincerely hope that you may have great success in your difficult task and that this list will be of some service to you.

Yours very faithfully   H. S. S. Smith[1]

ALS (WP, DLC).

[1] More or less similar replies from other class secretaries were J. H. Dulles '73 to WW, April 14, 1904, TLS (WP, DLC); E. S. Simons '82 to WW, April 14, 1904, ALS (WP, DLC); F. Evans '86 to WW, April 14, 1904, TLS (WP, DLC); T. W. Harvey '75 to WW, April 16, 1904, ALS (WP, DLC); W. M. Daniels '88 to WW, April 16, 1904, ALS (WP, DLC); W. S. Arbuthnot '87 to WW, April 18, 1904, TLS (WP, DLC); A. G. Todd '84 to WW, April 30, 1904, TLS (WP, DLC); and E. H. Rudd '83 to WW, c. May 1, 1904, ALS (WP, DLC).

From Uzal Haggerty McCarter

My dear Mr. Wilson: Newark, N. J.   Apl. 14th, 1904.

I have given the matter referred to in your previous letter, considerable thought, and while at the moment, a contribution to any purpose for any amount is inconvenient for me; at the same time, feeling the exigencies of the occasion and realizing my liability as an Alumnus of the University, and with the further desire to see your administration as successful as possible, I will subscribe this year and will pay when called upon by you, $5,000. for the purpose for which you wrote. I desire this to be a contribution for this year, and not a subscription for three years. I may do so again at that time, but am unwilling to bind myself at the moment beyond the above amount. Trusting that this will assist you somewhat in the magnificent effort in which you are engaged, I remain,

Very truly yours,   Uzal H McCarter

TLS (WP, DLC).

From Harold Griffith Murray[1]

Dear Dr. Wilson: New York, April 14, 1904.

You have from time to time received communications relative to the 1892-1901 Alumni Dormitory Committee,[2] so that I do not think it will be necessary for me to enter into a lengthy explanation of the purpose of this Committee or the object for which it was formed, further than to tell you that last Saturday night a permanent organization was effected with myself as permanent Chairman, and Mr. Andrew C. Imbrie, '95, as Secretary. The amount of cash that has been collected, and is now deposited in various banks and trust companies, aggregates $40,000; pledges in subscriptions not yet due, and overdue, aggregate $45,000, making a total of $85,000 in subscriptions and cash on hand.

When it is taken into consideration that it is not until a class has been graduated for seven or eight years that Memorial Fund assumes any proportion, it is a fair assumption, I think, that we will have no difficulty in raising $125,000 with which to erect the Alumni Dormitory. That enthusiasm may be kindled in the breasts of various delinquent subscribers, the Committee in charge desire to put forth as much information as possible about your ideas relative to the development of Princeton's campus, and the part that the Alumni Dormitory will play in this general scheme. You have very kindly supplied various members of the Committee from time to time with information, but I am going to ask you to be kind enough to let me have at your convenience as full and complete an expression of your ideas on the subject as you are willing to give, that it may be sent to each and every member of the subscribing classes. The members of the subscribing classes seem to be particularly desirous of knowing where the Dormitory is to be erected on the campus, a question that I do not know whether you could answer now or not, but any information which you can give me as to your attitude toward the scheme, and general information which I have asked for, I will very fully appreciate.

Will you kindly address me care of the Board of Health, 55th street and Sixth avenue, New York City.

          Yours very sincerely,   H. G. Murray '93

TLS (WP, DLC).

[1] Princeton 1893; Secretary to the Commissioner of Health, New York City.
[2] They are missing, but see the news report printed at April 16, 1904.

From Ellen Axson Wilson

My own darling,   Rome, April 15, 1904

I am distressed to be so late in the week getting off my second letter; but still it is only Thursday, 2 P. M., so I trust it will go on a Saturday steamer. I tried to write both last night & the night before but was too tired,—couldn't even hold my hand steady! In our first enthusiasm we naturally worked pretty hard for a few days; now we have called a halt and are going to take things easier; we will stay in and rest until four and then simply drive to the "Protestant Cemetery" seeing two churches on our way, which have fine mosaics, &c. We are all perfectly well and have splendid appetites. I don't know when I have been so hungry, and Jessie is ravenous,—eats everything that is offered her,—no matter how queer and foreign it is.

We have had a truly *wonderful* week! Every day has been an epoch in my life! It is impossible to say how I have enjoyed the Michael Angelo's and the Raphaels,—what revelations they have been of glorious beauty & majesty. Of course the photographs give a fairly good idea of the separate figures in the Sistine Chapel; but I really don't think they prepare on [one] at all for Raphael's great compositions because the "composition" has everything to do with it. It is the largeness of the whole conception, the harmony of line and mass, the sense of air and space, the wonderful grouping of all those glorious, majestic, serenely god-like figures who are holding high converse together. "Such harmony is in immortal souls." It is hard to keep away from them & do one's duty to all the lesser lights. And yet the rest are so enchanting too!—I wouldn't miss them for the world. I saw for instance this morning at the Corsini gallery a "Fra Angelico" that was perfectly adorable, and some six other masterpieces that I will never forget, mixed up with an acre or two of trash. I should think people who did not know what they were looking for would have a dismal time in the private galleries here. We were in two of them this morning & in two churches. One of the latter was *most* beautiful; both in general effect and in the *glorious* early mosaic work all over the apse. It was like jewels,—and quite made up in this instance for the want of the stained glass of the Gothic cathedrals.

But to return for a moment to the first of the week, which we began by going to the great papal function. I had a splendid seat next to the barrier so that there was no one between me & the procession. The pope[1] was stopped for some time just beside me so that I had an opportunity to study his face—a very beautiful & noble one. I can't say as much for the cardinals & bishops. The latter almost without exception looked like imbeciles and *pigs*! Some of the cardinals had rather interesting, keen, worldly-wise faces, and a stately bearing, reminding one of old Italian portraits,—and some of the young monks & priest[s] had really ideal heads. The music,—Gregorian chants &c., was magnificent. The rest of the party had to stand & almost had the breath crushed out of them; yet they declared that they enjoyed it greatly! I felt ashamed to be faring so much better than the rest.

That afternoon we took a general drive to get our first impression of the city. The next morning we spent with the Raphaels and in the afternoon we drove on the Appian Way, and went down into the catacomb of St. Calixtus. The drive was delightful and you can imagine how interesting. My taste in catacombs is very undeveloped—but it was *fine* to come out!

Yesterday we spent the morning in the Sistine Chapel, and in the afternoon saw the Borghese collections and then drove about the Borghese park which is *beautiful,* and on the Pincian Hill, stopping at another famous church on our way home.

But I had best leave the diary style to Jessie who does it so much better. I read her last Sunday's letter & was charmed! Do don't [*sic*] let the children lose them.

I have had no more letters as yet,—I suppose they have gone to Paris. Two weeks now since we landed, so I hope my darling has got a letter. It is *good* to think that I will be sailing in six weeks now. Give my devoted love to all, and remember, dear love, that I am now and always yours in every heart throb.

Your own   Eileen.

ALS (WP, DLC).
[1] Pope Pius X.

A News Report About the Alumni Dormitory

[April 16, 1904]

Another dormitory on the campus, the "Globe-Wernicke" building[1] to be erected by the ten classes from '92 to '01, inclusive, seems fairly assured. A meeting of the representatives of the classes pledged to this interesting scheme was held at the Princeton Club of New York on April 9th, and a permanent committee was organized with Harold G. Murray '93 as Chairman, Andrew C. Imbrie '95 as Secretary, and Professor W. K. Prentice '92, W. F.

Meredith '94, C. B. Bostwick '96, J. H. Keener '97, N. S. Schroeder '98, J. H. Harrison '99, F. P. King '00, and W. E. Hope '01 as the other members, formally appointed to represent their classes. An inventory of the several memorial funds of the ten classes showed the total cash already collected to be $38,066.39, with additional subscriptions pledged but not yet collected, amounting to $46,941.85. This makes $85,008.24 already pledged to the class memorial dormitory scheme. It is expected that from $10,000 to $12,000 will be required for each of the ten entries of the building (each class paying for an entry), making a maximum figure of $120,000 to be raised. With more than two-thirds of this maximum sum now in sight, we may expect that some satisfactory plan of financing the enterprise will be devised in the near future, without waiting till the entire fund is actually in hand.

Printed in the *Princeton Alumni Weekly*, IV (April 16, 1904), 449-50.
1 The Globe-Wernicke Co. of Cincinnati manufactured, among other things, office and library furniture. The phrase in quotation marks first appeared in the *Princeton Alumni Weekly*, III (Jan 17, 1903), 244, where the projected dormitory was first described as follows:
"There is a movement on foot among the classes from '92 to '97 to institute a new and useful scheme of class memorial instead of each doing something different, without reference to the plans of the others. It is proposed to combine and build a great and beautiful Gothic dormitory, each class paying for a single entry distinctly and appropriately marked. The beauty of this plan, besides the architectural beauty, is that it need not stop with these classes but can go on indefinitely—like a Globe-Wernicke bookcase, it is said."

A Report to the Princeton University Faculty

PRINCETON UNIVERSITY,
To the University Faculty: *April 16, 1904.*

The Committee on the Course of Study beg leave to report as follows:
The present curriculum leading to the degrees of A.B. and B.S. has been considered, and a plan for its revision has been formulated and is here presented. The curriculum leading to the degree of C.E. has not yet been considered.

THE COMMITTEE MAKE THE FOLLOWING RECOMMENDATIONS:

Recommendation I.
   That the entrance requirements for each course of study leading to a Bachelor's degree be made equivalent in amount.

Recommendation II.
   That in addition to the existing degrees of Bachelor of Arts and Bachelor of Science, the degree of Bachelor of Letters (Litt.B.) be constituted, to be open only[1] to those who enter without Greek and subsequently

1 At some point in the faculty discussion about this report, this word was deleted by common consent.

concentrate in one of the Departments in philosophical, political, literary, or other humanistic studies,—and that hereafter the degree of Bachelor of Science be open only[2] to those who enter without Greek and subsequently concentrate in one of the mathematical or scientific Departments.

Recommendation III.

That in constituting the entrance requirements, Trigonometry and Solid Geometry be taken as equivalent in amount to part of the Greek, when Greek is not offered, and that the other part of the Greek be replaced by a second Modern Language, or by Physics and an additional amount of the first Modern Language already required. The requirements to be as follows:

Entrance Requirements

A.B.		B.S. and *Litt.B.*
English	=	English
Latin	=	Latin
Mathematics	=	Mathematics
Greek / French A or German A } equivalent in amount		{ Advanced Mathematics / French A and German A } or { Physics with / French B or German B }

Recommendation IV.

That the course of the Freshman Year consist entirely of required studies, and be as follows:

Freshman Year

A.B.	Hours per week	B.S. and *Litt.B.*	Hours per week
English	2	English	2
Latin	4	Latin	4
Mathematics	4	Mathematics	4
French or German of entrance 2 } / Greek 4 } 6		{ Physics (3) with / French (3) / or / German (3) } or { French (3) and German (3) } 6	
	16		16

Recommendation V.

That all undergraduate courses after Freshman Year be put on a three-hour basis.

Recommendation VI.

That the schedule of every Sophomore, Junior, and Senior consist of five courses, subject only to such exemptions as may be established for candidates for Special Honors.

Recommendation VII.

That the Sophomore courses, required and elective, be so arranged as to include elementary courses prerequisite to the subsequent studies of the various Departments according to the following plan, and that the *Sophomore Elective Courses, Prerequisite or Advised for the Departments in the Junior Year,* be as given below:

[2] This "only" was also deleted by common consent.

Sophomore Year

[All courses three hours a week. Two elective courses to be taken]

A.B.	B.S. and *Litt.B.*
Required	*Required*

Required (A.B.)

Physics
Logic (1st term), Psychology
  (2nd term)
Greek (1st term), Latin (2nd term)

Required (B.S. and Litt.B.)

Physics
Logic (1st term), Psychology
  (2nd term)
Mathematics or Latin

Elective (A.B.)

{ Latin (1st term), Greek (2nd
  term) or Chemistry }

Mathematics

History (1st term), English (2nd
  term)
French
German

Elective (B.S. and Litt.B.)

{ Latin, if not taken required
  or Chemistry }

{ Mathematics, if not taken required, or Graphics, if Math.
  is taken required }

History (1st term), English
  (2nd term)
French
German

NOTE.—Beginner's courses to be open in French and German.

Sophomore Prerequisite and Advised Elective Courses.

(PREREQUISITE Sophomore Elective Courses in small capitals.)
(*Advised* Sophomore Elective Courses in italics.)

	Department	Prerequisite and Advised Courses	For Degree of
I.	*Philosophy*	*A foreign Language*	A.B. & Litt.B.
II.	*History, Politics, and*	HISTORY	} A.B. & Litt.B.
	Economics	*A foreign Language*	
III.	*Art and Archæology*	CLASSICS	A.B.
		LATIN	} Litt.B.
		A modern Language	
IV.	*Classics*	CLASSICS	A.B.
V.	*English*	ENGLISH	} A.B.
		A foreign Language	
		ENGLISH	
		LATIN	} Litt.B.
		A modern Language	
VIa.	*Modern Languages*	} GERMAN	A.B. & Litt.B.
	Germanic Section		
VIb.	*Modern Languages*	FRENCH	} A.B.
	Romanic Section	*Classics*	
		FRENCH	} Litt.B.
		LATIN	
VII.	*Mathematics*	MATHEMATICS	A.B. & B.S.
VIII.	*Physics*	MATHEMATICS	} A.B. & B.S.
		Chemistry	
IX.	*Chemistry*	CHEMISTRY	} A.B. & B.S.
		Mathematics (must be taken here or in Junior Year.)	
X.	*Geology*	CHEMISTRY	} A.B. & B.S.
		A modern Language	
XI.	*Biology*	CHEMISTRY	} A.B. & B.S.
		A modern Language	

[The student's choice of a Department for Junior and Senior Years is largely conditioned by his selection of the electives in the Sophomore Year.]

Recommendation VIII.

That instead of the present required courses of Junior Year, each Junior shall choose a Department in which to concentrate his studies, and shall take all the Junior Year courses of that Department, as indicated in the list of Junior courses, as well as the courses which are there stated to be cognate to that Department. Three of his five courses shall, in all cases, be in the Division in which the Department chosen lies, and one course shall be outside of the Division in which this Department lies. Courses scheduled at the same hour are mutually exclusive.

LIST OF COURSES OF JUNIOR YEAR.

[All courses three hours a week. Five courses to be taken.]

A. DIVISION OF PHILOSOPHY.

   I. *Department of Philosophy.*
      31, 32. History of Philosophy.
      33. Advanced Psychology. 34. Advanced Logic.
      (*Advised elective:* Politics.)

   II. *Department of History, Politics, and Economics.*
      31, 32. History.
      31, 32. Politics.
      31, 32. Economics.
      (*Advised elective:* History of Philosophy.)

B. DIVISION OF ART AND ARCHÆOLOGY.

   III. *Department of Art and Archæology.*
      31, 32. Art and Archæology.
      (*Requisite cognate courses:* One course in Classics.
                             One modern language.)
      (*Advised elective:* History of Philosophy.)

C. DIVISION OF LANGUAGE AND LITERATURE.

   IV. *Department of Classics.*
      31, 32. Greek.
      31, 32. Latin.
      (*Advised elective:* History of Philosophy.)

   V. *Department of English*
      31, 32. English Literature.
      33, 34. English Philology.

   VIa. *Department of Modern Languages.* *Germanic Section.*
      31, 32. German.
      (*Requisite cognate course:* 33, 34. English Philology.)

   VIb. *Department of Modern Languages.* *Romanic Section.*
      31, 32. French.
      31, 32. Italian, or 31, 32. Spanish.
      (*Requisite cognate course:* Latin.)

D. DIVISION OF MATHEMATICS AND SCIENCE.

   VII. *Department of Mathematics.*
      31, 32. Mathematics.
      33. Mathematics, and 34. Analytical Mechanics.

   VIII. *Department of Physics.*
      31, 32. Laboratory Physics.
      34. Analytical Mechanics.
      (*Requisite cognate course:* 33. Mathematics.)
      (*Advised elective:* 31, 32. Mathematics.)

IX. *Department of Chemistry.*
    31, 32.   Chemistry.
    33, 34.   Chemistry.
    (*Requisite cognate course:*   Laboratory Physics.)
      (The free elective must be the Sophomore Mathematics unless that course has been taken during the Sophomore year.)

X. *Department of Geology.*
    31.   Mineralogy, and 32.   Geology.
    34.   Physical Geography.
    (*Requisite cognate courses:*   31.   Astronomy.
                                 Chemistry or Biology.)

XI. *Department of Biology.*
    31, 32.   Biology.
    33, 34.   Biology.
    (*Requisite cognate course:*   Practical Chemistry.)

Junior courses falling under Division D, but which are not in any one of the Departments of that Division:
    31.   Astronomy.
    31.   Graphics.
    32.   Geodesy.

Recommendation IX.

That each Senior shall continue his studies in a Department in which he has satisfied the requirements of the Junior year, and shall take three courses in that Department as indicated in the list of Senior courses. Or in case three courses are not thus indicated, three of his courses shall, in all cases, be in the Division in which his Department lies.

LIST OF COURSES OF SENIOR YEAR.

[All courses three hours a week. Five courses to be taken.]

A. DIVISION OF PHILOSOPHY.
    I. *Department of Philosophy.*
        41, 42.   Philosophy.
        43, 44.   Philosophy.
        45, 46.   Ethics.

    II. *Department of History, Politics, and Economics.*
        41, 42.   History.
        43, 44.   History.
        41, 42.   Politics.
        43, 44.   Politics.
        41, 42.   Economics.

B. DIVISION OF ART AND ARCHÆOLOGY.
    III. *Department of Art and Archæology.*
        41, 42.   Art and Archæology.
        43, 44.   Art and Archæology.
        (*Requisite cognate course:*   Classics or Italian.)

C. DIVISION OF LANGUAGE AND LITERATURE.
    IV. *Department of Classics.*
        41, 42.   Greek.
        43, 44.   Greek.
        41, 42.   Latin.
        43, 44.   Latin.

V. *Department of English.*
   41, 42. English.
   43, 44. English.

VIa. *Department of Modern Languages. Germanic Section.*
   41, 42. German.
   43, 44. German.

VIb. *Department of Modern Languages. Romanic Section.*
   43, 44. Romanic Philology.
   ⎰ Two of the three languages: ⎱
   ⎱ 41, 42. French, 41, 42. Italian, 41, 42. Spanish. ⎰

D. DIVISION OF MATHEMATICS AND SCIENCE.

VII. *Department of Mathematics.*
   41, 42. Mathematics.
   43, 44. Mathematics.

VIII. *Department of Physics.*
   41, 42. Physics.
   43, 44. Physics.

IX. *Department of Chemistry.*
   41, 42. Chemistry.
   43, 44. Chemistry.
   45, 46. Chemistry.

X. *Department of Geology.*
   41, 42. Geology.
   41, 42. Mineralogy.
   43, 44. Palæontology.
   45. Physical Geology, and 46. Physical Geography.

XI. *Department of Biology.*
   41, 42. Biology.
   43, 44. Biology.
   (*Requisite cognate course:* 43, 44. Palæontology.[)]

Senior courses which are not in any one of the eleven Departments above:
   42. History of Natural Philosophy (*falls in Divisions A and D.*)
   45, 46. Roman Law (*falls in Division A.*)
   41, 42. Sanskrit (*falls in Division C.*)
   41, 42. Semitics (*falls in Division C.*)
   41, 42. Practical Astronomy (*falls in Division D.*)

Recommendation X.

   That the various courses of study offered be open only to students of that
   year to which the courses belong, except in cases where students are
   allowed or required to take a course belonging to a preceding year.

Recommendation XI.

   That provision be made for General Honors as at present, except that
   no Senior who has not taken the Junior year shall receive General
   Honors.

Recommendation XII.

   That provision be made for Special Honors as follows:
      Freshmen and Sophomores who stand in the first or second group
   in any subject are to receive Special Honors in that subject. (Names
   and groups are to be printed in the catalogue.)

Final Special Honors to be based on the work of the Junior and Senior years, as follows: A Junior who maintains a standing for the year not below the second group in each of the courses of his Department and a general standing not below the third general group is entitled to be a candidate for Final Special Honors, and as such may substitute for one of the elective courses in his Senior Year the Proseminary of his Department.

These Final Special Honors are to be of three grades: Highest Honors, High Honors, and Honors.

Highest Honors shall be awarded to the Senior who in Junior and Senior years maintains a first group standing in each of the courses of his Department and a general standing not below the second general group.

High Honors shall be awarded to the Senior who in Junior and Senior years maintains a first group standing in at least half of the courses of his Department, with a standing not below the second group in any of these courses, and also a general standing not below the second general group.

Honors shall be awarded to the Senior who in Junior and Senior years maintains a standing not below the second group in each of the courses of his Department and a general standing not below the third general group.

(Special Honors may be awarded to a Senior who has not taken the Junior year in Princeton.)

Recommendation XIII.

That a Proseminary be established in every Department for Seniors who are candidates for Final Special Honors. That each Proseminary be in charge of one instructor, who shall conduct a session of the Proseminary at least one hour each week during the term or year.

That the sessions of each Proseminary be devoted to the presentation and discussion of work prepared by the individual members of the Proseminary.

The Committee further RECOMMEND:

1. That the revised curriculum go into full effect with the opening of the Academic year 1905-1906.
2. That the Committee on the Course of Study prepare a transitional curriculum for the year 1904-1905.
3. That the Committee on the Course of Study prepare and issue the necessary weekly schedules and all other needed information regarding the revised course of study.

Respectfully submitted,

WOODROW WILSON, *Chairman.*
A. F. WEST, *Secretary.*

TABLES SHOWING THE DEPARTMENTS IN DETAIL

I. DEPARTMENT OF PHILOSOPHY

Open to candidates for the degrees of A.B. and Litt.B.

Advised Sophomore Elective

A foreign language

Junior Courses

31, 32. History of Philosophy (H)
33. Advanced Psychology (H), and 34. Advanced Logic (H)
A course from Div. A (Politics *advised.*)

A course not in Div. A
An elective

Senior Courses

41, 42. Philosophy
43, 44. Philosophy
45, 46. Ethics
An elective
An elective

II. DEPARTMENT OF HISTORY, POLITICS, AND ECONOMICS
Open to candidates for the degrees of A.B. and Litt.B.

Prerequisite Sophomore Course

History

Advised Sophomore Elective

A foreign language

Junior Courses

31, 32. History (H)
31, 32. Economics (H)
31, 32. Politics (H)
A course not in Div. A
An elective (History of Philosophy *advised*)

Senior Courses

{ Three courses in
  History, Politics,
  and Economics
An elective
An elective

III. DEPARTMENT OF ART AND ARCHÆOLOGY
Open to candidates for the degrees of A.B. and Litt.B.

Prerequisite Sophomore Courses

Elective Classics for A.B.
Latin for Litt.B.

Advised Sophomore Elective

A modern language for Litt.B.

Junior Courses

31, 32. Art and Archæology (H)
A course in Classics (H)
A modern language
A course not in Div. B (Hist. of Phil. *Advised*)
An elective

Senior Courses

41, 42. Art and Archæology
43, 44. Art and Archæology
Classics or Italian
An elective
An elective

IV. DEPARTMENT OF CLASSICS
Open to candidates for the degree of A.B.

Prerequisite Sophomore Course

Elective Classics

Junior Courses

31, 32.   Greek (H)
31, 32.   Latin (H)
A course from Div. C
A course not in Div. C (Hist. of Phil.   *Advised*)
An elective

Senior Courses

⎧ Three courses
⎨ in Latin
⎩ and Greek
An elective
An elective

V.   DEPARTMENT OF ENGLISH

Open to candidates for the degrees of A.B. and Litt.B.

Prerequisite Sophomore Courses

English for A.B.
Latin and ⎫
English   ⎬ for Litt.B.
              ⎭

Advised Sophomore Electives

A foreign language for A.B.
A modern language for Litt.B.

Junior Courses

31, 32.   English Literature (H)
33, 34.   English Philology (H)
A course from Div. C
A course not in Div. C
An elective

Senior Courses

41, 42.   English
43, 44.   English
A course from Div. C
An elective
An elective

VIa.   DEPARTMENT OF MODERN LANGUAGES—GERMANIC SECTION

Open to candidates for the degrees of A.B. and Litt.B.

Prerequisite Sophomore Course

German

Junior Courses

31, 32.   German (H)
33, 34.   English Philology (H)
A course from Div. C.
A course not in Div. C
An elective

Senior Courses

41, 42.   German
43, 44.   German
A course from Div. C
An elective
An elective

VIb. DEPARTMENT OF MODERN LANGUAGES—ROMANIC SECTION

Open to candidates for the degrees of A.B. and Litt.B.

Prerequisite Sophomore Courses

French for A.B. and Litt.B.
Latin for Litt.B.

Advised Sophomore Elective

Elective Classics for A.B.

Junior Courses

31, 32.   French (H)
31, 32.   Italian (H), or 31, 32.   Spanish (H)
Latin
A course not in Div. C
An elective

Senior Courses

Romanic Philology
⎰ Two of the three languages:
⎱ 41, 42.   French, 41, 42.   Italian, 41, 42.   Spanish
An elective
An elective

VII. DEPARTMENT OF MATHEMATICS

Open to candidates for the degrees of A.B. and B.S.

Prerequisite Sophomore Course

Mathematics

Junior Courses

31, 32.   Mathematics (H)
33.   Mathmatics (H), and 34.   Analytical Mechanics (H)
A course from Div. D
A course not in Div. D
An elective

Senior Courses

41, 42.   Mathematics
43, 44.   Mathematics
A course from Div. D
An elective
An elective

VIII. DEPARTMENT OF PHYSICS

Open to candidates for the degrees of A.B. and B.S.

Prerequisite Sophomore Course

Mathematics

Advised Sophomore Elective

Chemistry

Junior Courses

31, 32.   Laboratory Physics (H)
33.   Mathematics, and 34.   Analytical Mechanics (H)
A course from Div. D (31, 32.   Mathematics *advised*)
A course not in Div. D
An elective

Senior Courses

41, 42. Physics
43, 44. Physics
A course from Div. D
An elective
An elective

IX. DEPARTMENT OF CHEMISTRY

Open to candidates for the degrees of A.B. and B.S.

Prerequisite Sophomore Courses

Chemistry
Mathematics (may be taken in Junior Year)

Junior Courses

31, 32. Chemistry (H)
33, 34. Chemistry (H)
31, 32. Laboratory Physics
A course not in Div. D
An elective (must be 21, 22. Mathematics, unless taken in Sophomore
    Year.)

Senior Courses

41, 42. Chemistry
43, 44. Chemistry
45, 46. Chemistry
An elective
An elective

X. DEPARTMENT OF GEOLOGY

Open to candidates for the degrees of A.B. and B.S.

Prerequisite Sophomore Course

Chemistry

Advised Sophomore Elective

A modern language

Junior Courses

31. Mineralogy (H), and 32, Geology (H)
31. Astronomy, and 34. Physical Geography (H)
Chemistry (H) or Biology (H)
A course not in Div. D
An elective

Senior Courses

{ Three of the following four courses: 41, 42. Geology,
{ 41, 42. Mineralogy, 43, 44. Palæontology,
{ 45. Physical Geology, and 46. Physical Geography
An elective
An elective

XI. DEPARTMENT OF BIOLOGY

Open to candidates for the degrees of A.B. and B.S.

Prerequisite Sophomore Course

Chemistry

Advised Sophomore Elective

A modern language

Junior Courses

31, 32. Biology (H)
33, 34. Biology (H)
Practical Chemistry
A course not in Div. D
An elective

Senior Courses

41, 42. Biology
43, 44. Biology
43, 44. Palæontology
An elective
An elective

In the above statements of the Departments the courses in the Junior year which are marked with (II) are the courses central to the Department in which a Junior must maintain a standing not below the Second Group in order to be a candidate for Final Special Honors, according to the 12th recommendation.

The word Philology, as employed in the statements for the English and the Modern Language Departments, is to be so interpreted as to include courses in linguistic science or courses in mediæval literature.

Printed document (WWP, UA, NjP) with WWhw inscription: "Copy used in Faculty   Adopted April 26, 1904."

To Ellen Axson Wilson

My own precious darling,   Princeton, N. J.   17 April, 1904

My spirits have mounted skyward: my darling's letters have begun to come, and, ah, how sweet, how delightful, how perfect they are! How much of herself my dear pet, with her unconscious literary gift, crowds into the unstudied, spontaneous lines of these *real* letters! I admire them as much as I treasure them. They began to arrive on Friday evening (the 15th). The one written on the 3rd., the Sunday after your landing, came first, that evening, and the one written on the steamer the next morning,—by another, slower boat, perhaps. And how many times I have read them, to myself and aloud, to Madge, to the children, to Stock. I have quaffed them as a man perishing with thirst would quaff water from a life-giving spring and then more slowly, more deliciously, as a connoisuer would quaff honest wine. They are singularly vivid letters, my Eileen. I seem to know just how the voyage went and just what the first taste of Italy has meant to you,—and to share in some subtle way the joy to which I had been looking forward with such longing,—*your* joy, the delights of sense and sight which have come to my darling. And the passages that were only for my own eye,—the longings that answer so passionately to mine, the love that sings and calls to mine—

how shall I ever speak the deep joy that these bring me! Oh, it is sweet to long for such a perfect little lover even when you cannot have her—the exquisite knowledge that she equally longs for you cures the wound your own longing makes. May God bless and keep you, my incomparable little wife! May all your letters tell thus of your welfare and happiness and love for him whose life stands still till you come home!

I have none but the most cheerful news of ourselves. My cable of yesterday[1] tells the whole truth in brief epitome: "Everything prosperous." Margaret gets well apace; Nell ought in a day or two to be let out of the room as free as ever. The two are as gay and happy as possible together. The most cheerful sounds come from the room every time the door is opened. They have revelled in the letters, yours and Jessie's. How full and interesting dear Jessie's "diary" from the ship was! It has been devoured by all of us with the keenest relish. With yours, it seems to tell us everything. How happy a voyage,—and how happy it makes us to hear of it!

I have the best news, too, about Stockton. He is in *excellent* shape. Indeed he has been these three weeks. It has been *very* stupid of me not to tell you so before; but I forgot how far from well he was when you sailed. He is well and in capital, equable spirits,—more so, I think, than he has been this college year. He looks, speaks, acts like a normal, healthy citizen of a hopeful country. All our clouds are thus, you see, breaking away,—and real Spring coming, too, at last. With your letters coming, I see only peace and quiet work ahead,—if *you* only keep well, which God send!

The work is: to write my baccalaureate address and get the new system of studies through the Faculty. The latter task begins on Tuesday evening next, the 19th, as I think I told you in my last letter. Harry Fine is to preside: I am to take charge of the measure on the floor, as chairman of the Committee; and we are to have nightly meetings of the University Faculty until the legislation is complete. We do not look for any serious opposition. A week or two ought to settle the business. I hope that the same thing will take place in the Faculty that took place in the Committee. There we began a group of individuals and ended a *body* agreed in common counsel,—except for a final, purely temperamental "kick" by Wick Scott,[2] who will quietly get over it.

18 April—This morning came your second cable from Rome,— the word "Charcos," so full of comfort.[3] How these telegraphic messages do restore my tone. A week from to-day I could answer

with the same word, no doubt. I could to-day except for the *formal* sickness, so to say, which comes after the real *attack* of the measles is over. The doctor passed us over to-day and did not come at all, even to look at the children. The "children," and Margaret eighteen! Saturday, the 16th, was her birthday, of course, and, though her friends could not come to see her, they filled the table by her bed with flowers,—violets, heliotrope, daffodils, & the like, and she was very bright and happy. To-day dear Jessie's second letter to Nell and her letter to Baltimore to Margaret turned up and the dear patients had a perfect feast. To think, my Eileen, that we have a daughter eighteen years old! How short these eighteen years have been, because full of love and happiness. May all blessings rest upon your dear head for all you have been to me! If I have given you as much joy and as constant pleasure as you have given me, how wonderful it has all been!

I shall not venture to address this letter to Madame Rinaldi's. It takes two full weeks for a letter to pass from one of us to the other, and you will be gone from Rome before this could get there. I had forgotten the name Magie gave you, and so stupidly did not understand the "Rinaldi" in your first cable from Rome.

To-morrow Mrs. Hibben's sister is to be married,[4] and "the Hibbens" are of course in Elizabeth. Jack and Beth. went up last night; Mrs. Hibben has been there for nearly a week. The whole of the Elizabeth household seems "in a state of mind."

Good night, my sweet, sweet love. I dare not tell you how my heart yearns for you: I can tell you only the part that fills me with gladness, my love for you, that passes all words and is the *life* of

Your own   Woodrow

All unite in love without measure to darling Jessie. Love to the dear Smiths and to Cousin M.

ALS (WC, NjP).
  [1] It is missing.
  [2] William Berryman Scott.
  [3] This cablegram is also missing.
  [4] Daisy Davidson; she was married to Leonard Everett Ware, Harvard 1899.

Two Letters from Ellen Axson Wilson

My own darling,   Rome, April 17 1904

At last the longed-for letters from Paris have come,—three of them,—this morning. I am glad I read them in the order in which they were written, for the first two made me *so delightfully* happy, and I had that joy before I learned from the last about Nellie's measles! Of course I am trying to be sensible about it, & I am *not* going to borrow trouble but I am inevitably a good deal disturbed. How I wish I knew whether Margaret took it! The cablegram came this morning before the letters and is in a way reassuring; but I noticed with a little misgiving when it came that you did not say all were "well," but only "everything prosperous"; that struck me then as very vague; & now that I know about the measles it seems even more so. One can have typhoid fever "prosperously"! But I will *not* worry! Surely with a good trained nurse and strong healthy children there can't be any danger. I am *so* sorry my darling should have the extra care and mental burden of it all. Something always happens when I leave home! I'll never do it again. My conscience has hurt me from the first about this journey & now of course more than ever.

Jessie had a little sick turn night before last; doubtless one of the queer dishes disagreed with her; but she got entirely rid of it whatever it was. We kept her perfectly quiet yesterday, and she is *perfectly* well again today, though just as a precaution I did not let her go out to church in the hot sun. She was dreadfully disappointed at getting no letters from the children; there were tears in her eyes, poor child! Was Margaret forbidden to write her because of possible infection? At best they have treated her rather badly, for I had four letters from you written before the measles began & she has not had a word from anybody! Yesterday was dear Margaret's birthday, and we all gave Jessie little presents in celebration of it! So we are faithful to old customs even in foreign lands.

I am perfectly well, the weather continues beautiful, and all goes smoothly and delightfully; Jessie's little turn was nothing to worry about & I think she was rather glad of a quiet day at home. We spent the morning among the antiques at the Vatican, & in the afternoon staid in until late, when we saw one church & bought a few photographs,—they are wonderfully cheap & good here,—much cheaper than in Paris. You should see us starting out on our rounds with our Baedaker & handbooks, our opera-glasses & *mirror*!—a very important adjunct. We take the hand mirrors everywhere in our bags, but for the great Sistine ceiling we were not content with that but took the large mirror from a bureau. It was a grand success; we could see the whole ceiling at once in it and study it in perfect ease & comfort. We were the envy of the whole crowd in the chaple [chapel], & generously gave all the other women present a look! An opera-glass of course is an abso-

lute necessity in Rome, and we were all foolish enough to come
without them; Mary even had left hers in Paris. So to my great
disgust I had to buy one. But I can hardly regret it now for somehow I could never see anything much through those at home &
these are *splendid* because the glasses are extra large in diameter
—the largest made. We can see the expression of every face perfectly. I paid $10.00 for them(!) and I am trembling over the
duty.

We have a handsome American girl here from Philadelphia
a Miss Peters who seems to be an habitué of Princeton and a tremendous admirer of *yours*. She has met you somewhere. She
looked really awe-struck when she heard I had the honour of
being your wife. She spends most of her time in anti-chambers
trying to get audiences with the Pope & the two queens, while her
mother and her artistic sister, who studies art in Paris, do the
galleries. Do you remember them? The artist is Edith, the beauty
Ethel.[1]

There is just *one* man in this house, Mr. Rinaldi himself,—son
of the Madame. There were really more at the nunnery, for it
was infested with priests. Mr. Rinaldi is, he says, a "military
artist," is quite good-looking & is thought by his mother to be a
Prince Charming; so he is put exactly in the middle of the long
table to entertain the crowd. He is really a very clever man and
interesting talker, but is inclined to make a fool of himself with
his grimaces & contortions. His mother calls him "Ninni" & their
behaviour to each other is as good as a comic play. It seems they
are cadets of a noble house & he has a very fine dignified English
wife. He has taken it into his head to admire me; told me to my
face that I ought to be painted—& that my mouth was the most
exquisite imaginable; and amuses me extremely with his con-
templative stare at table;—but he really does not mean it for
impudence, it is only a manifestation of "the artistic temperament." I do it myself often; the other day I stared at a young man
so long that he began to smirk at me—and completely spoiled the
picture!

It is only five weeks & four days now before we sail;—it is harder
than ever today to restrain my impatience with these three dear
letters before me. Oh my dear, my dear! how I love you how I
want you! *Nothing* can make up for separation in such a world
of change & danger as this is! I do not see how I can wait seven
more weeks to see my treasures! But I *will* not write thus. Thank
you for the good news of Stockton. I have been longing for news
of him, for I have been troubled with bad dreams about him, &

a good many anxious thoughts. With a heart full of love & sympathy for my baby, & for all the rest, believe me darling in every heart-throb, Your own, Eileen.

1 Edith and Ethel were the daughters of Richard Peters and Harriet Felton Peters of 1101 Spruce St., Philadelphia. Peters seems to have been a man of leisure, although the Philadelphia city directory for 1903 indicates that he was in the "iron business."

My own darling, Rome, April 20 1904

Your letter from New York has just arrived and it is a great comfort to hear again from the *measles*,—to know that Nellie was almost convalescent and that Margaret had not taken it. I am more sorry than I can say that dear little Nell had to miss the Ben Greet Co. I know it was a great disappointment, for the children were looking forward to that all winter. I was glad to hear of you, dearest, away from home; I am sure the change and the dinner were refreshing, after the sickness and responsibility at home. But I am deeply concerned to find that you were looking for a letter at least five days before it was possible! You don't know how it hurts me, darling, to think of your disappointment; and also that you may think it my fault. Of course we *meant* to mail a letter at Gibraltar but the Captain advised us not to, saying it would be slower in reaching you than if we sent it from Naples. We consulted the steward about it too and he was quite sure that such was the fact,—said the mail service from Naples was especially fast & good, and from Gibraltar wretchedly slow & uncertain. It was quite a disappointment to me *not* to send it from there, for I was counting on saving several days in that way.

We are having a very pleasant & successful week;—have now finished up all the churches and smaller museums & galleries which have, each of them, from one to six or eight masterpieces, and now we have all the rest of our mornings for re-visiting the Vatican, the afternoons for the Forum &c. and "villas"—that is for the gardens of the villas.

We have been to 17 churches & ten galleries not counting our four mornings at the Vatican. It is the extraordinary way in which the art treasures of Rome are scattered broadcast which makes the place so extremely difficult to see in a short time,—indeed *impossible* to see without an almost reckless expenditure in the matter of cabs. Fortunately they are rather cheap, there are several of us to share the expense and Mary Hoyt is a wonderful hand at at [sic] making bargains with them! She is perfectly splendid, better than a courier,—insists on doing all the disagreeable work in the most masterly manner, and leaves me without a care in the world.

Was called away here,—and have since spent the afternoon at the Forum. Of course we saw it superficially before but now we have worked it all out. And who do you suppose acted as our very efficient guide? *Jessie*! She had studied it so thoroughly that she knew it all by heart and could lead us straight to everything and tell us all about it. The rest of us including Mrs. Walbridge & Marguerite followed her about like school-children. She was perfectly charming—so eager and enthusiastic, so intelligent and, as always, so entirely without self-consciousness.

But it is impossible to write coherently with four people talking & laughing about me & besides the afternoon has left me very tired so I will say "good-night," dear heart.

We both send devoted love to dear little Nellie and to all the rest. We are *perfectly* well & the weather is even better than before—cooler. Only about 5 weeks now before I sail! With love, *love, love* unspeakable.

Your devoted little wife,   Eileen.

ALS (WP, DLC).

To Ellen Axson Wilson

My own darling,   Princeton, N. J.   21 April, 1904

"It's a long time between drinks": the mails are painfully slow about repeating the treat of last Friday and Saturday. But I can afford to wait a week for such satisfying feasts of love and vivid narrative as my darling's letters bring! How deeply, how intensely I delight in all that you write. It rings so true to yourself in taste and feeling and judgment, and I dote upon your*self*, your *whole* self! Nothing else in the world satisfies me. *I want* you! How do I ever manage to part with you for so much as an hour of real separation? Ah well, you'll be back, richer, happier, younger, sweeter than ever, and what we have lost will be recovered with usury! May God keep you!

We are prospering here famously. Dear Nen. is out of quarantine, fat and happy. She is not allowed to read yet, of course, and we are having a still further postponement of Spring (the thermometer registered only 24° yesterday morning at seven) and it will be some days before she gets out of doors, so that she is a good deal at a loss what to do with herself; but she is as happy as a lark, nevertheless, the dear, bright, charming little thing.

It is such a pleasure to have her about again, and at the table. Madge and I have been having rather lonely tête-à-têtes at meals, though Stock. drops in for lunch or dinner not infrequently. Margaret fares famously. The irruption came sooner and is fading more rapidly with her than with Nellie, and we think that in a couple of days she will be sitting up. Miss Andrews and our servants are such trumps that everything goes as smoothly as possible. We have really had not a moment of real anxiety. I only wish I had not been obliged in conscience to tell you anything about the trifling trouble!

The first meeting of the University Faculty to consider the report of the Committee on the Course of Study was held Tuesday evening, and passed off very quietly. It was only explanatory, preliminary. I spoke for about an hour in exposition of the report, a few questions were asked and answered, and we adjourned. To-night we meet again, and expect the real debates to begin. We may see then just where we stand.

The Hibbens are back at last, full of the most interesting news and talk about the wedding. Mrs. Hibben, who was evidently the king pin of the household throughout the critical stages of the whole affair, has come back very tired and jaded, but very cheerful, none the less, because of all the interesting things there are to tell and remember. It is great fun to hear about it all without having to go through it.

I can end this epistle in quite another tone than that in which I began it: two more letters have just come in, the second one from Naples (or, rather, from Sorrento) and the first one from Rome, and my heart bounds with the delight they have given me,—the delight in my darling's series of keen pleasures and the delight, thereby enhanced, in her impatient desire to get back to me. How can I ever repay you, my sweet one, for the incomparable love you give me; and, ah, what love is yours in return! I live and am happy because you love me and I am, by your love,

Your own   Woodrow

ALS (WP, DLC).

From William Royal Wilder

My dear Wilson,   New York, April 21st. 1904.

Pray excuse delay in responding to your favor of the 15th inst. enclosing copy of Resolution passed by the Board of Trustees on the 10th of March, 1904. I understand that a similar letter, together with a copy of the Resolution, has been received by Halsey, and both your notes and the Resolution will be called to the attention of the Class Committee at a meeting which will be held on the 29th of April upon the return of Cuyler from Mexico.

Personally, I am gratified at the interest shown by the Trustees in what they truly characterize as a "splendid gift." Such inquiry as I have been able to make among the Faculty and Trustees, has resulted in my reaching the conclusion that the policy of the Trustees was to name after famous Presidents the Buildings erected by them as a body, as for example,—Witherspoon, Edwards, etc; and that individual donors were at liberty to name Dormitories after themselves, as for example,—Blair, Little, Dod and Brown.

Personally, I really fail to see why the Trustees should have gone out of their way to 'intimate as the wish and policy of the Board that each dormitory should bear a personal name, either the name of the donor or some name selected by those who make the gift.' The Class at the present time is proceeding on this very theory, and nearly sixty men have already registered their votes, some in favor of naming the Dormitory after the 'donor,' to wit,— "Seventy-nine," and others after a 'distinguished man connected with the University itself,' to wit,—old 'Jimmy' McCosh.

You will be pleased to learn that the name of 'Wilson Hall' has been voted for.

In view of the Resolution of the Board, I do not see but what the majority vote of the Class, whichever way it goes, is bound to be acceptable not only to the Class, (*whose wish ought to control*), but also to the Board of Trustees which is exhibiting so lively and cordial an interest in its title.

Very cordially yours,   Wm. R. Wilder

TLS (WP, DLC).

From Norman Bruce Ream[1]

My dear Doctor: New York   April 23, 1904.

I am in receipt of your letter of the 20th. instant and note your statement of deficit of $6,000 to $10,000 per annum in the operation of your University; also note your plan for raising $100,000 per year for three years and further, that you have already received subscriptions for that fund to the extent of $67,000.

I authorize you to enter my name on such list for $2,000 toward the fund of $100,000 for the first year. In making this donation I do not care to incur future obligations but prefer to meet each year on its merits as it comes along. You state in your letter that subscriptions will not be called until the $100,000 fund is made up complete; hence when it is completed, if you will kindly advise me it will give me pleasure to send you a check for $2,000.

With every wish for the success of the institution and for you personally, I remain,

Yours sincerely,   Norman B Ream

TLS (WP, DLC).
[1] A capitalist who had made his fortune and reputation in Chicago, but who had lived in New York since 1895 and been involved in many major railroad and industrial consolidations since that date. He was the father of Edward King Ream '05.

A News Item

[April 23, 1904]

On account of illness in his family, President Wilson '79 was obliged to abandon his trip to the South, for which he had accepted invitations to deliver a number of lectures. On May 12th the President is to address the members of the New York Institute of Bank Clerks, at their annual dinner.[1]

Printed in the *Princeton Alumni Weekly*, IV (April 23, 1904), 466.
[1] A news report of this affair is printed at May 13, 1904.

An Anecdote About a Classroom Incident

[April 23, 1904]

Personal anecdotes about distinguished men are among the penalties of eminence. "If Lincoln told all the stories attributed to him," etc. . . . But Princeton graduates can readily believe this, from the Philadelphia Press: Up at the Princeton Club a night or two ago, President Woodrow Wilson was the topic of conversation, and a graduate of the early '90's told this story in evidence of the statement that Prof. Wilson is distinctly a disciple of the strenuous life. "Back in those days a custom was in vogue among the underclassmen to find out just how 'easy' each 'new prof.' was. One morning as Wilson was about to open his lecture, he was [saw] a drunken man rise from one of the front seats and begin to perform a few well-selected antics. 'Who asked you to come in here, sir?' was the quiet but hard-toned question that came from the platform. 'The students invited me in,' was the prompt and somewhat tremulous reply. 'Well I'll invite you out again,' said Prof. Wilson. And taking the intruder by the coat collar he hustled him down stairs three steps at a time. That was one of the little things which helped to make this particular 'new prof.' one of the most popular men who ever taught at Old Nassau."

Printed in the *Princeton Alumni Weekly*, iv (April 23, 1904), 466-67.

A News Report About Examinations for a Rhodes Scholarship

[April 23, 1904]

Six candidates for the Rhodes Scholarship at Oxford to be filled this year from New Jersey, appeared at the examinations last week at the Public Library in Trenton. Two of them are Princeton seniors, three are students at Rutgers College, one is a University of Pennsylvania student whose residence is in New Jersey. The examinations, which are equivalent to the Oxford responsions, were conducted by Professor W. F. Magie '79, who was appointed for this purpose by the New Jersey committee on the Rhodes Scholarships,—President Wilson '79, Chairman; Dean Fine '80, and President Scott of Rutgers. The examination papers have been forwarded to Oxford, and when the committee shall have received a report upon them, they will appoint the first Rhodes Scholar from New Jersey, in accordance with the requirements laid down in the founder's will. It will take a pretty good all-'round man to approximate the qualities enumerated by Mr. Rhodes.

Printed in the *Princeton Alumni Weekly*, iv (April 23, 1904), 468.

From Ellen Axson Wilson

My own darling,   Rome, April 24, 1904.

Our last Sunday, almost our last day in Rome, for we leave Tuesday morning. I almost wish we had planned to go yesterday; the crowds and confusion incidental to Loubet's visit[1] are already becoming so great that I should like to be out of it all. But of course it is not troubling us today, which we are spending at church and in the house as usual. We had another Aberdeen man, "Principal something,"[2]—not so good a preacher as the other. Last

[1] Émile François Loubet, President of the French Republic, was on a state visit to King Vittorio Emanuele III of Italy.
[2] The Rev. Dr. John Marshall Lang, Principal of the University of Aberdeen.

week we had the pastor, Dr Grey,[3] a learned man but a dry
preacher. He called on me, this week, I don't know why. We had
written, by request, our names in the visitors book at the church
but did not give our Rome address. Of course we missed him.
After arriving and looking over the ground we promptly decided
that we could not spare an *hour* for social engagements & that
we would send *no* cards of introduction either to the Princess
Ruspoli[4] or to Miss West's[5] friends. She had sent us some cards
to the steamer in New York. It was a wise decision. We have had
a *most* delightful & successful two weeks here, and have seen the
place remarkably well considering the shortness of the time. Our
only partial failure was the trip to Tivoli and Hadrian's Villa
which we undertook because Mary Hoyt had so set her heart upon
it. It is a beautiful three & a half hours drive to the Villa. We enjoyed that very much, but it began to rain heavily soon after we
reached it so that we could not explore it thoroughly. We spent
some two hours under the shelter of a covered passage-way, the
only part of the palace that still has a roof. Then we gave up and
drove home in the rain without even getting to Tivoli. But Mary
says she would rather have seen the Villa *so* than not at all, and
it was certainly all very beautiful. The great avenues of cypresses
that looked as if they might be a thousand years old and the great
groves of equally old olive trees were the chief beauty,—that and
the vistas between broken arches, &c. of the campagna, and the
Alban Mountains.

Yesterday it also poured rain all the morning so that the light
was too bad for me to see the Michael Angelos again as I had
planned; but Jessie and I drove to the Vatican & spent the morning among the Antiques instead. I still have one last morning for
the Sistine, and I am tempted to fill my shopping bag with bis-
cuits and stay until it closes at three! Dr. Grey, to whom I spoke
this morning because of his call, took me aback by proposing "if
he can get off," to take me to the Palatine Hill and "do" it with
me! He is an archaeologist of some distinction it seems—but *I* am
not and I cannot possibly sacrifice my last precious morning at
the Vatican to those heaps of shapeless ruin. I am praying that
he cannot get off, for alas! I had not presence of mind at the time

3 The Rev. Dr. James Gordon Gray, pastor of the United Free Church of
Scotland in Rome.
4 Giuseppina Ruspoli, Principessa di Poggio Suasa. Her late husband, Emanuele Ruspoli, Principe di Poggio Suasa, had been a deputy and senator in the
Italian parliament and, most recently, Mayor of Rome.
5 Clara Lindforth West, who lived with her brother, Andrew F. West, in
Princeton.

to plead "another engagement" but only to protest that I could not think of troubling him.

We have our tickets now for all the rest of our tour,—Cooks tickets. Perhaps it would interest you to know our route in detail so that you can "place" us constantly. Tuesday at 12 we start for Assissi getting there in time to see the same afternoon, "fairly well," the Giottos in the old Church of St Francis. We spend the night there and early the next morning *drive* over to Perugia, which is said to be a charming experience in good weather! We have 1 day there, far too little of course, but tis the best we can do, starting for Sienna Thursday. It is a seven hours journey and we spend two nights there, reaching Florence Sat. afternoon the 30th of April. We will be there two weeks and a day, leaving for Parma via Bologna on Monday the 16th. Wednesday morning we leave Parma for Venice arriving at mid-day. After five and ½ days at Venice we go, on Tuesday morning to Milan, spending that afternoon & the next morning there and reaching Genoa before dark. On Thursday at ten, four weeks and four days from the present we sail for *home*! Oh how my heart leaps at the thought, how I long to sweep away the days between us, full as I expect them to be of delights! And never, never, never will I be separated from you again of my own free will.

We are perfectly well and the weather is beautiful again; all has gone quite smoothly in every respect. Our tickets for the rest of our stay were about $52.00 for Jessie & me, which seems fairly reasonable. We shall be rather glad to leave this house because all the nice people who were here when we came have gone and it has filled up with a most impossible crowd of American & Eng. women. This is certainly the woman's century! They have taken possession of the *earth*! Everywhere one goes there are at least nine women to one men,—women travelling alone,—women of *all* nationalities from Swedes & Russians down to the Indies,— all, all equally emancipated! As for the German women whom we were taught to believe were mere beasts of burden, there are more of them than of the Americans even; they swarm like locusts and are as disagreeable,—*and* of an ugliness! There *is* one in the house though who is quite young and pretty. She has recently been to Greece and up the Nile quite alone. Indeed she spends her whole life travelling quite alone,—has been all over the world. We have four from California, all quite young, unchaperoned, & perfectly dreadful! The day after their arrival one of them and the irrepressible "Ninni" (Mr. Rinaldi) spent their time at the dinner table experimenting to see which was the most ticklish! And their accent is as bad as their manners. One of them, a striking blonde, drove up from the wharf at Naples on the seat with the driver but with her back to the horses and her feet in her sisters lap! So when they had been there 1½ days they had a call from an American married to an Italian, who wished to engage as their chaperone, saying that she moved in the first circles & could supply them all with the most eligible husbands. They were very indignant; for the poor things are perfectly respectable,—merely wild colts.

But Marguerite has been making a long visit & now it grows late. I will leave it to Jessie to tell what galleries & churches we have seen this week. The "Sophocles," "the Marble Faun," & the "Moses," are the three greatest things we have seen this week. How *you* would have liked them all! The Sophocles is indescribably noble in its calm, lofty beauty;—suggesting Tennyson's line, "self-reverence, self-knowledge, self-control." Raphael's men in the Stanzas are all of the same blood, the same spirit, and they all breathe "an ampler ether, a diviner air." They are just as grand as Michael Angelo's, only one has the serene glory of the sun and the other the darker majesty of the storm.

We have also seen one entirely beautiful church this week, the Santa Maria Maggiore, and that was a great comfort for most of them are very ugly. One visits them only for some particular great thing they contain, a fine mosaic[,] a ceiling by Raphael or Perugino, or a statue by Michael Angelo. Several of them have the most *exquisite* cloisters, however, with the gardens all a riot of climbing roses.

I have had no more letters of course since I wrote last;—can only hope & trust that all is well with my darlings—& dear little Nell back at school again. You perhaps are away down South. I hope you will enjoy the trip, dearest, and find it a rest from the routine of Princeton,—and its occasional hard problems,—like that wretched Cameron case. This is a passage about a *cardinal* (!) in a Catholic book I was looking through yesterday, and it made [me] think of you (as what does *not* bring thoughts of you, dear!) "Such a load of serious thought lay upon his soul that it would have been too much but that sometimes he felt the arm and shoulder of Christ slip under the burden and lift its weight with him, and lift him with it, and bear him along in some miraculous hour of heavenly comfort."

But now I *must* stop for it grows dark. Dearest love to all the loved ones and all friends. What news from the Ricketts? Poor Jessie has still had no letters from anyone.

God bless you, my own love, and keep you safe and well and happy, and speed the days until I am in your arms again! Ah how I long to be there! How I love you!

Your little wife   Eileen.

Send Mary's $100.00 to American Express Co., No. 3 Waterloo Place London.

ALS (WP, DLC).

EDITORIAL NOTE

THE NEW PRINCETON COURSE OF STUDY

The adoption with minor amendments of the report of the Committee on the Course of Study on April 25, 1904, achieved the first thoroughgoing reorganization of the curriculum of Princeton University in its history. The reader can perhaps best perceive the scope of the changes wrought by a comparison of the essential points of the new plan with the corresponding features of the Princeton educational program as it existed at the time the report was adopted.

One major objective of the revision of the curriculum was the thorough integration of the work of the School of Science with that of the Academic Department. Wilson stated the case in his article, "Princeton's New Plan of Study," printed at August 29, 1904: "Hitherto, at Princeton as at many other universities, the two sections of the University, the School of Science and the Academic Department, have been somewhat sharply separated and contrasted,—a reminiscence of the day when scientific studies were added to the old group of classical, literary, and philosophical studies, but were set apart as courses to be separately administered; not received into the ancient, exclusive circle of accepted subjects but put upon trial by themselves. The new plan at Princeton will have the effect of doing away with this difference and unifying the curriculum of the University on the theory that the new humanities which centre in the laboratories are to be embraced in schemes of study on the same footing as the old."

Hence, the Committee on the Course of Study, among other things, recommended that the entrance requirements for each course of study leading to an undergraduate degree "be made equivalent in amount." Heretofore, all applicants for admission both to the program leading to the Bachelor of Arts degree and to that for the degree of Bachelor of Science had been required to show proficiency in English, Latin, mathematics, and either French or German, the exact level of competence required in these subjects being set forth in detail in the annual university catalogue. Candidates for admission to the A.B. program had to demonstrate a considerable proficiency in Greek and also some knowledge of ancient history. However, Greek was not demanded of B.S. candidates, who could offer a variety of so-called "elective subjects" for entrance, ranging from the Spanish language or American history and civil government to solid geometry and chemistry. These in turn might be combined in a bewildering variety of groupings as set forth in the School of Science section of the university catalogue.

Under the new program, all applicants were required as before to show proficiency in Latin, English, and mathematics through plane geometry. Moreover, everyone had to offer either French or German.[1] A.B. candidates were still required to show competence in Greek. Candidates for the B.S. or a new Litt.B. degree had to offer solid geometry and plane trigonometry and either a second modern language (French or German) or a combination of physics (chemistry was soon made an alternative to physics)[2] and an additional amount of the first modern language already required. These last requirements for the B.S. and Litt.B. were considered, under the new plan, to be the "equivalent" of the Greek requirement for the A.B. The principal effect of these changes was to bring the entrance requirements of the B.S. and Litt.B. degrees much closer to those for the A.B. In practice, also, it had the effect of tightening up the hitherto notoriously lax entrance standards of the School of Science.

The second major change of the new plan of study was the creation, novel to Princeton, of the degree of Bachelor of Letters, which was to be open to those who entered without Greek and subsequently concentrated in one of the departments in philosophical, political, literary, or other humanistic studies. Furthermore, the new plan provided that hereafter the Bachelor of Science program was to be open to those who entered without Greek and subsequently concentrated in one of the mathematical or scientific departments. Wilson himself provided the best explanation of these changes in his speech at the annual alumni luncheon in Princeton on June 14, 1904.[3] "We have for some years past," he said, "been introducing the more modern schemes of study in a way which has come to us to seem not entirely frank. For example, we have permitted men without any restraint whatever to enter as candidates for the degree of Bachelor of Science and yet pursue purely humanistic studies. . . . And it also came about and is still true that the candidate for the B.S. could get practically as much of the A.B. studies as he wanted, with the single exception of Greek. Therefore a large majority of the men who are candidates for the degree of Bachelor of Science are really pursuing academic studies. Now that, I say, is not frank to the public. If we are to give men a humanistic training of this type, without Greek, we must give them the right label. They are not Bachelors of Science. One of our propositions, therefore, is to institute a third degree, namely, that of Bachelor of Letters; for the purpose, the perfectly valid purpose, of preserving the historical significance of the Bachelor of Arts." Wilson defined the Litt.B. as "a label for those men who want a humanistic training with-

---

[1] Later, at the insistence of Simon J. McPherson, Headmaster of the Lawrenceville School and a Princeton trustee, applicants were also required to offer either American history and government, English history, or ancient history. See S. J. McPherson to WW, May 20, 1904, n. 3.

[2] Again at McPherson's insistence.

[3] It is printed at that date in this volume.

out Greek" and pointed out that it was already widely used in other colleges and universities.[4]

The decisions to retain Greek as a prerequisite for the A.B. degree and to create a new degree in humanistic studies not requiring Greek reflected the bitter controversy over the necessity of Greek as a requirement for the traditional Bachelor of Arts degree which convulsed the American academic world in the late nineteenth and early twentieth centuries. Wilson and his colleagues in the Princeton faculty were too conservative to abandon Greek and the traditional A.B. degree. As Wilson put it in his speech of June 14, 1904, "You understand, gentlemen, that we are for liberal culture, and that we also stand by preference for classical culture. We believe that the old methods are excellent methods; but we do not believe that the more modern methods are not also excellent." The result was the rather awkward compromise of two liberal arts degrees, one with and one without a Greek requirement. This anomaly remained in effect until March 17, 1919, when the Princeton faculty, in the course of the next major revision of the undergraduate curriculum, voted to drop Greek as a requirement for the A.B. degree and to abolish the Litt.B. degree. A total of 1206 students were awarded the Litt.B. at Princeton.

Under the new program in 1904, the entire course of the freshman year consisted of required studies. The program for A.B. candidates was much the same as previously: Latin, mathematics, and Greek, each four hours a week, and English for two hours a week. The only change in the A.B. program was that freshmen were now required to continue the modern foreign language (French or German) which they had offered at entrance, whereas before they could elect to begin or continue either language. The old B.S. freshman program had been more flexible. Students in that program had been required to take three hours of English composition, four hours of basic mathematics, and either general chemistry or elementary physics, each for three hours. They were also to elect two three-hour courses from a choice of Latin, German, and French. However, the most important difference between A.B. and B.S. freshman programs under the old system was that the content of the courses open to B.S. freshmen was often on a more elementary level and was frequently (though not always) taught by inexperienced, if not inferior, instructors.

The new program eliminated this system of second-class students at one stroke by bringing B.S. and Litt.B. freshmen into the same courses taken by A.B. candidates. All freshmen took the same required courses in English, Latin, and mathematics. In addition, the B.S. and Litt.B. men took three hours a week of the modern language (French or German) offered for entrance and three hours either of the other modern language or of physics, depending upon whether they had offered physics for entrance. In any given freshman course, all students for whatever degree were taught by the same faculty member or members. It appears also from the catalogues of 1904-1905 and later that many teachers took this opportunity to upgrade the level of instruction in freshman as well as in upperclass courses.

[4] See also Wilson's elaboration of this whole matter in his "Princeton's New Plan of Study," printed at Aug. 29, 1904.

Wilson's comment at the alumni luncheon of 1904 on the program of required studies for the freshman year is illuminating: "The discipline of the University is different from the discipline of the schools. Moreover, the men . . . come to us from all over the country, from schools of every kind, with preparation of every sort, and they have to be licked into shape, into the same shape. They have all of them to be put into the mill that enables them to do the things that have to be done after freshman year."

One of the less conspicuous innovations of the new course program was that all undergraduate courses after freshman year were to be put on a basis of three class hours per week. This change assumes considerable significance when it is realized that heretofore the great majority of upperclass courses (including, for example, those given by Wilson) were on a two-hour basis, though many courses, especially in the sciences, had required three or four hours per week, including laboratory work. Under the new system, upperclassmen were to take five courses per term, rather than seven as previously. Obviously, this revision in itself would lead in time to a vast alteration in both the content and scope of the curriculum.

In the sophomore year, A.B. candidates under the old system had been required to take two hours a week each of Latin and Greek throughout the year. In addition, they had to take one-term courses of two hours each in general history, English literature, elementary physics, general chemistry, and logic, as well as a one-term, three-hour course in intermediate mathematics. Beyond this, they might choose two two-hour elective courses each term from additional courses open to sophomores in Latin, Greek, mathematics, French, and German. Here again, the old program for B.S. candidates had been more flexible. They had been required to take one-term three-hour courses in mathematics and English literature, and the two-hour course in logic, along with the two-term, three-hour course in elementary physics unless already taken in the freshman year. Under the old program, the B.S. sophomores also had to take a full-year, three-hour advanced language course continuing their previous work in Latin, French, or German. Beyond this, they could choose either three or five one-term courses (depending upon whether or not they still had to take physics) from among courses of three or four hours each in ten subjects in both scientific and non-scientific fields.

The new sophomore program was arranged both to satisfy certain basic requirements and to prepare the student for a field of concentration in his junior year. All students were required to take one-term courses both in logic and psychology (psychology had formerly been required in the junior year). Both A.B. candidates and B.S. and Litt.B. candidates were required to take a full year of general physics. However, here there were two separate courses of somewhat varying content for the two groups, since A.B. men would have had no physics, unless in secondary school, while B.S. and Litt.B. students would have either offered it for entrance or taken a one-term course during freshman year. In addition, A.B. candidates were required to take one-term courses in Greek and Latin while B.S. and Litt.B. candidates had to take a full year either of mathematics or of Latin.

As the new plan of study stipulates, the elective courses open to sophomores were so arranged as to include elementary courses prerequisite to the subsequent studies of the various departments in which the student might concentrate in his junior and senior years. The reader, by examining carefully the list of sophomore electives and the chart describing the prerequisite and advised sophomore electives for each department included in the plan of study printed at April 16, 1904, can readily perceive how the new system worked. It should perhaps be noted that while, as the new plan of study states, "the student's choice of a Department for Junior and Senior years is largely conditioned by his selection of the electives in the Sophomore year," it was also true that any given elective or a well-chosen combination of them would allow a student to major in any one of several departments if he changed his mind before the beginning of his junior year.

The reader will recall that Wilson had instituted a new departmental structure in November and December 1903.[5] Since that time, as the plan of study printed at April 16, 1904, indicates, the eleven new departments had been further loosely reorganized into four large "Divisions." This was done, apparently, to clarify both the relationships between departments and the cognate courses required of or advised for students concentrating in a particular department. Moreover, as Wilson stated in his address to the alumni on June 14, 1904, the largest of the divisions, that of Mathematics and Science, was henceforth to "constitute our School of Science."

The old program for the junior year had included some required courses for both A.B. and B.S. candidates. A.B. students had been required to take one-term two-hour courses in psychology, ethics, and political economy and a one-term three-hour course in physics. B.S. students took similar courses in psychology, ethics, and political economy as well as a one-term, two-hour course in geology and a full-year, four-hour course in physics. In addition, B.S. candidates specializing in chemistry had been required to take three one-term courses in applied chemistry totaling ten hours a week. All other courses of the junior year were elective: for A.B. men, this meant five two-hour electives each term; for the B.S. "General Science" men, three electives each term; and for B.S. chemistry men one elective each term. Under the new program, the old required courses in physics and psychology were moved to the sophomore year, while those in ethics and political economy were dropped.

The central change of the new course of study was the requirement that juniors choose one of the eleven departments for concentration and take all of its junior year offerings. Here again, the reader can readily grasp the operation of the system by examining carefully the statement of Recommendation VIII of the report printed at April 16, 1904, and the list of courses of junior year appended thereto. It should be noted that the list includes *all* courses open to juniors: the student had to select his electives from this same list. It might be mentioned also that in general the content of junior year courses was at a basic or intermediate level of the discipline concerned. Wilson, in his speech

[5] See the memorandum and notes thereto printed at Nov. 20, 1903.

to the alumni on June 14, 1904, stressed that it was possible for a student to change his department of concentration at the end of his junior year, provided only that he had chosen his required and elective courses of junior year with some care.

Under the old system of study, the senior year represented Princeton University's nearest approach to a completely free-elective system. Indeed, A.B. candidates and B.S. candidates in the "General Science" program were free to elect any seven courses open to seniors each term. Some small amount of coherence was induced by the fact that many advanced courses had basic courses as prerequisites but, aside from that, the student could elect almost anything he wanted among the courses offered for seniors. Only B.S. students specializing in chemistry had the bulk of their course program prescribed for them, with five required courses in applied chemistry and two in mineralogy. Recommendation IX of the report of the Committee on the Course of Study sets forth clearly the requirements and courses open to seniors. The courses on the senior level were, for the most part, advanced and somewhat specialized.

The awarding of honors at Princeton both before and during Wilson's presidency is a subject almost unavoidably confusing to the modern reader. Moreover, it cannot be said that the recommendations of the Committee on the Course of Study did much to clarify or improve the situation as it had existed prior to the spring of 1904. The root of the difficulty lay in the rather muddled system of determining an individual's standing in particular courses, in his class at the end of each year, and in his class for the entire four years of college. This was done by what was called the "group system." In every course in the university, the instructor combined the grades on recitations and examinations to arrive at a "mark" between zero and one hundred: one hundred was the highest mark possible; fifty was the minimum passing mark. Then the instructor was to divide his class into five groups "in the order of merit." According to the university catalogue for 1903-1904, the groups were as follows:

"The first group indicates very high standing and contains not more than ten per cent. of the entire class.

"The second group indicates high standing and contains not more than twenty per cent. of the entire class.

"The third group indicates medium standing and contains not more than thirty-five per cent. of the entire class.

"The fourth group indicates low standing and contains not more than twenty-five per cent. of the entire class.

"The fifth group indicates very low standing and contains not more than twenty-five per cent. of the entire class."

Apparently it was entirely left up to the individual instructor not only to determine a student's grade but also to decide what percentage of the class fell into each of the groups. On this shaky basis, the standing of the student for both the year and the entire college course was arrived at: "The general rank of a student is determined by combining his group numbers in the several courses in proportion to the allotted schedule time of each. The student whose averages are highest, and above an established limit, are assigned to the first general group; those next highest to the second general group, and so on through the general groups." If all this were not confusing enough, it was further stated that "essays count as one hour per week throughout each of the four years," and that account was taken of "attendance and conduct as well as scholarship."

This method of determining standing remained exactly as before under the new program of study except that the fifth and lowest group was now defined to include "the remainder of the class" rather than any specific percentage. Upon this method depended the awarding of all honors.

General honors were awarded "for general excellence in studies" at the close of freshman, sophomore, and junior years: "High General Honors" to those whose average rank for the year was in the first group, and "General Honors" to those in the second group. At graduation, "High General Honors" were awarded to those whose final average rank for the entire four years was in the first group, "General Honors," to those in the second group. The same regulations governing standing and honors applied to all students in both humanistic and scientific programs. The names of all honors men were printed in the university catalogue of the following year.

Under the old program, "Special Honors" were awarded "for excellence in single leading departments" at the close of sophomore year. The "leading departments" in 1904 consisted of Latin, Greek, and mathematics. "High Honors" were given to those who ranked in the first group in the freshman and sophomore courses belonging to these subjects and "Honors" to those in the second group, provided that the general standing of these men for the sophomore year was not below the third group. The new program extended the privilege of "Special Honors" to freshmen and applied to courses falling in any of the eleven departments.

The awarding of "Final Special Honors" remained much the same under both the old and the new programs. Indeed, the university catalogue for 1903-1904 even used the word "departments" in describing the nine subject areas in which "Final Special Honors" were awarded: philosophy; history, jurisprudence, and politics; archaeology and art; classics; modern languages; English; mathematics; physical science; and natural science. The only real change effected by the new curriculum was the addition of "Highest Honors" to the previously existing "High Honors" and "Honors."

The establishment of a proseminary in every department for seniors who were candidates for "Final Special Honors" seems to have been intended largely as a further inducement to talented students to encourage them to work for honors. Though modeled on the graduate seminar, they did not necessarily entail the preparation of a major research paper, nor did the proseminary count any more in the determination of standing and honors than any other single course. The format of each proseminary was left largely to the determination of the department and professors involved. Wilson's comment on the proseminary in his speech to the alumni of June 14, 1904, suggests that it was regarded as honorific in itself: "Among his chief privileges, the honor man can graduate into manhood, and take a course which is modeled in character after graduate courses, a course in which he is set at work of his own with a free hand, under the guidance of an experienced teacher."

Wilson's general comments to the alumni on the honors program indicate plainly the problem faced by the Committee on the Course of Study: "We have been trying to think of other privileges and tempting distinctions which we could confer upon the men who are candidates for honors, because after all they are the men who ought to wear the University P; they are the best players on our scholarship team. . . . What we are trying to do is not to discredit the athletic team, but, to put it plainly, to give the scholar as good a standing as the athlete." This was a problem which was not to be resolved for many years.

In summary, the report of the Committee on the Curriculum accomplished several major objectives. The most important and obvious was the introduction of coherence into the program, particularly of the upperclass years, by requiring a student to concentrate in a single department. This had the important, if incidental, effect of putting an end to the completely free elective system of senior year and restricting even more the electives of earlier years. Another major change was the complete integration of the School of Science with the Academic Department to create a unified undergraduate curriculum. This, together with the general revision of the hours and content of the courses, had the effect of upgrading considerably the quality of courses open to all students. Last, and probably least important in the long run, the new degree of Litt.B. was created for those students who wanted a humanistic education but were unwilling or unable to meet the Greek requirement for the A.B.

The revision of the curriculum effected by the Committee on the Course of Study was the culmination of lengthy discussion and debate since the inauguration of President James McCosh in 1868. It was only late in the administration of President John Maclean (1854-1868) that the fixed liberal arts curriculum dating from the colonial period had begun to be modified by the addition of courses in newer areas of study such as the social and natural sciences. However, the new courses were all required, which resulted not only in a broader course of study but in less time being available for individual subjects. In his inaugural address, McCosh called for a basic core of required courses to which might be added electives in special fields. As it turned out in practice during his regime, there were no electives for freshmen and sophomores, and only a limited number were offered to juniors and seniors. None the less, McCosh had begun a revolution, even though he later strongly criticized Charles W. Eliot's free elective system at Harvard. In the early years of the administration of President Francis L. Patton, the number of elective courses gradually proliferated, thus creating a considerable degree of confusion in the curriculum. The School of Science, founded in 1872, also grew apace, to a considerable degree owing to the fact that Greek was not required of its students.[6]

6 See Thomas J. Wertenbaker, *Princeton, 1746-1896* (Princeton, N. J., 1946), pp. 287-88, 293, 304-309, 385-86.

As a consequence of the Sesquicentennial celebration and the re-naming of the College of New Jersey as Princeton University in the autumn of 1896, a Special Committee on the Affairs of the University, consisting of seven members of the Board of Trustees, was appointed on December 10, 1896. This committee was instructed to "inquire into the affairs of this University, to consider what changes if any are desirable in its policy, methods of administration, curriculum, or corps of instructors."[7] The committee's preliminary report on June 14, 1897, had little to say on the curriculum except for the significant comment that "studies should be better co-ordinated."[8] Its final report, submitted a year later, began with a favorable judgment: "It appears that our curriculum embraces a wide range of subjects; classified into several great departments, and with few exceptions properly arranged and co-ordinated." However, the comments in the section of the report dealing in greater detail with the curriculum were more critical. There had been "various criticisms" of the School of Science, it pointed out, but it was hoped that the revision of the B.S. curriculum then under way would solve the more serious problems. Moreover, the committee recommended that at least some elective courses be combined and offered three hours a week instead of two.

The bulk of the section of the committee's report on the curriculum dealt rather inconclusively with the problem of forcing students, especially upperclassmen, to work harder at their studies. "The University needs a decided intellectual quickening," the report said, "without this, improvements in the curriculum, no matter how admirable they may be, will have but little effect." Perhaps the poorer students should be required to follow a prescribed curriculum throughout their four years; this, the committee stressed, was only a tentative suggestion. The committee did have one positive proposal—creation of seven "Honor Schools" in philosophy; jurisprudence, politics, and political economy; history, art, and archaeology; ancient languages; modern languages; mathematics and physical science; and natural science. The details of the organization and operation of these "schools" were left quite vague, but the proposal was significant as a foreshadowing of the system of proseminaries created in 1904. The committee recommended that President Patton elaborate the scheme for early presentation to the full Board of Trustees, but Patton characteristically did nothing to implement the suggestion.[9]

The next serious effort to revise the Princeton curriculum began on November 21, 1900, when the Academic Faculty resolved "that a Committee be appointed to consider the question of the scholarship of the Academic Department, and to propose such measures as seem suited to promote a high standard thereof, including any changes which seem advisable in the regulations concerning conditions." A nine-member committee, with William F. Magie as chairman, was

[7] See the Minutes of the Trustees of Princeton University printed at Dec. 10, 1896, Vol. 10.
[8] See the Minutes of the Trustees of Princeton University printed at June 14, 1897, *ibid.*
[9] See the Minutes of the Trustees of Princeton University printed at June 13, 1898, *ibid.*

appointed at the same meeting. Although Patton was unenthusiastic about the committee, he did indicate the thinking among faculty members which led to its appointment: "There is a feeling in the Faculty that the Elective System which controls the third and fourth years of the University curriculum is working badly in regard to the students who constitute the lower half of the class in those years. Far too little work is done, and there is a very general disposition among students to defer study in the departments where instruction is given by lecture, and cram for examinations toward the end of the term."[10]

Patton seems to have succeeded in preventing any action by the Academic Faculty's scholarship committee for at least a year. However, in October 1901, the faculty of the School of Science requested the President to appoint a committee of its members to act with the committee of the Academic Faculty. Patton did so in December 1901, and a joint University Committee on Scholarship went to work on a report which was presented to the University Faculty on March 26, 1902. The report was discussed at several meetings and was then finally recommitted to the committee on April 16, 1902.[11]

The report of the University Committee on Scholarship constituted the sharpest attack yet made on the then existing course of study. "Your Committee is convinced" the report began, "that the condition of scholarship among our students at the present time is one of demoralization, especially in the two upper years. In our judgment the present plan of studies is not and cannot be applied effectively and beneficially. The most obvious fault of the system now in operation is the abundant opportunity it offers for taking courses in which study is not exacted, and cannot be exacted so long as these courses have to be conducted almost entirely by lectures. The majority of Juniors and Seniors make up their elective lists mainly from these courses, some of which are common to both classes, thus increasing the difficulty. We also think that the number of studies which must now be taken simultaneously by a student is too large, and that the time allotted to each study separately is too small. This scatters the student's interest and dissipates his energies instead of combining them upon a few studies each of which has enough time assigned to it to make it really substantial and valuable. Moreover, as the choice of electives is often determined by the convenience of the hours at which the exercises are held, as well as by a preference for the easier courses, the result is frequently an entire abandonment of a serious or even coherent plan of study."

Some of the committee's recommendations were aimed at encouraging undergraduates to study harder. All freshmen and sophomore instruction, it suggested, should be in recitation courses "in which the classes recite orally in small divisions." Even in junior and senior courses, a considerable portion of the student's time should be devoted to oral and written recitations. These recommendations to some extent anticipated the preceptorial system inaugurated in 1905.

Most of the committee's recommendations, however, concerned the

10 See n. 2 to the notes for a talk to the St. Louis alumni printed at Nov. 21, 1901, Vol. 12.
11 *ibid.*

curriculum, both of the Academic Department and the School of Science. The committee recommended first that required and elective courses be so coordinated as to "provide a curriculum of liberal education of the purely collegiate type throughout the first three years." Though rather vague, this obviously pointed to a drastic reduction of electives in the junior year. The studies of the freshman year were to remain largely as they were. Some electives might be allowed in sophomore year if they were conducted by the recitation system. All junior and senior courses were to run for three hours per week. All courses open to juniors were to be of a general, and not of a specialized character, and their number was to be limited so as to include only "leading subjects of importance in a liberal education." Every junior was to be required to take throughout the year one course each in philosophy and science; his other three courses would be elective. Courses open to both juniors and seniors were, with few exceptions, to be abolished. General Honors were to be continued, but "more efficient provision should be made for Special Honors as an inducement both to coherency and to serious purpose in the choice of electives." A committee of the University Faculty was to be appointed to exercise supervision of the choice of electives and the awarding of honors; obviously, this too was intended to promote a coherent program of study for each student.

This report then went on to outline the program of the four-year course for academic and scientific students in considerable detail. The most significant feature of the plan was that the five courses per term of senior year were to remain freely elective for all students. In addition, a division of subject fields was outlined which closely resembled Wilson's later division of the faculty into departments in 1903.[12]

Obviously, the report of the University Committee on Scholarship of 1902 foreshadowed in many respects the reorganization of the curriculum in 1904. The major defect of the earlier report was that it failed to require upperclass students to concentrate their work in a coherent area, such as a single subject or an area of related subjects, for seniors would still have had a free elective program. Moreover, while the committee obviously hoped to make the work of the School of Science parallel in quality and quantity to that of the Academic Department, it made no real effort to integrate the two schools into one efficient operating unit. In any event, the work of the committee had no immediate effect, for not only was its report returned to it for further consideration on April 16, 1902, but on November 12, 1902, shortly after Wilson's inauguration as President of Princeton University, the committee reported to the faculty that it felt unable to take effective action because of its limited mandate and asked to be discharged. The request was granted.

If Wilson had much to say about the Princeton curriculum prior to his presidency, the documentary record does not disclose it. His Sesquicentennial address, "Princeton in the Nation's Service,"[13] revealed him as a conservative advocate of the traditional liberal arts.

[12] See the report of the University Committee on Scholarship printed with the University Faculty Minutes at April 16, 1902, Vol. 12.
[13] Printed at Oct. 21, 1896, Vol. 10.

In particular, he argued in favor of "holding every man we can to the intimate study of the ancient classics"; Latin and Greek should be retained, not simply for their value as disciplines of the mind, but as indispensable keys to the study of the literary classics of antiquity.

In the spring of 1897, the Special Committee on the Affairs of the University sent a questionnaire to faculty members requesting information about their work and their views both of their own fields and of the work of the university in general. Wilson's reply betrayed his dissatisfaction with the underdeveloped state of his own field of politics and that of history. In answer to the general questions, "Should required studies be increased? Should the number of electives be increased or reduced?", Wilson replied: "With regard to required studies, I do not favour an increase of their number. . . . I think that electives should be added in the Junior year only in accordance with a carefully devised plan of co-ordination. Electives might well be added very freely to the list of Senior Studies."[14] Obviously, he was not yet concerned about the problem of electives in senior year, but he did perceive a need for greater coherence in the studies through the junior year.

It is curious and perhaps also significant that Wilson seems to have taken almost no part in the work of the University Committee on Scholarship of 1901-1902. The minutes of the faculty debates on the committee report in March and April 1902 do not record his participation in the discussion until the final meeting on April 16, 1902, when he spoke apparently on the resolution to recommit the report to the committee.

Two explanations have been advanced for Wilson's silence during the faculty debates. Some persons have suggested that he knew that he was in line for the presidency of the university and did not wish to offend Dr. Patton, who was still unenthusiastic about curricular reform.[15] Actually, the matter cannot be stated so baldly. At this very time, Wilson, as the documents in Volume 12 have disclosed, was deeply involved in high-level maneuvers by a group of trustees and faculty members looking toward establishment of an executive committee to take control of the university from Patton's hands. Perhaps he wanted to do nothing to cause Patton to suspect that he was involved in this cabal. Wilson also well knew that the result of the discussions and negotiations then under way might be Patton's resignation; perhaps he did not want to jeopardize his own chances of election to the presidency by openly aligning himself with the anti-Patton leaders in the faculty who were supporting the report of the University Committee on Scholarship.

Stockton Axson in later years offered the second explanation: Wilson kept quiet because he thought that the reforms proposed by the committee were mere patchwork.[16] There is some evidence that this may have been true. Wilson referred to the work of the University Committee on Scholarship in several speeches during the spring

[14] See WW to C. E. Green, June 17, 1897, Vol. 10.
[15] Henry W. Bragdon, *Woodrow Wilson: The Academic Years* (Cambridge, Mass., 1967), 275, 459n16.
[16] *ibid.*

of 1902. Most revealing of his own conception of an ideal undergraduate curriculum is the following portion of his notes for an address to the University of Virginia alumni in New York on April 12: "Election, but of substantial *subjects*, not innumerable *courses*,—and the whole cycle required for a degree."[17] This would seem to indicate that Wilson believed that the committee's plan was inadequate because it failed to require upperclassmen to concentrate in coherent subject fields. Wilson's memorandum printed at June 1, 1902, Volume 12, also put heavy emphasis upon the co-ordination and integration of undergraduate studies.

Whatever reluctance Wilson may have had to becoming involved in the details of reform of the Princeton curriculum vanished after his election to the presidency. His memorandum to serve as a guide to his first report to the Board of Trustees, drafted on August 31, 1902, contained the significant question, "What is necessary (besides reorganization of studies)?"[18] And in his first report to the trustees, on October 21, 1902, he pointed to the pressing need for curricular reform. "I believe," he said, "that some part of the strain of routine work we are now under can be removed by a thorough-going readjustment. The University has had a remarkable growth in the last thirty years, but it has been a growth which has resulted, I dare say, from the necessity of the case, in a miscellaneous enlargement rather than in a systematic development. It has consisted in a multiplication of courses which have in large part remained uncoördinated. The order of studies, their sequence, their relation to one another, their grouping, their respective values: all these things need immediate reconsideration. The Faculty is inclined to take these questions up with zeal and in the best spirit, and I believe that before the end of the year we shall have thrown the whole schedule of studies into the new and better scheme, which may be expected to effect a real economy both of time and of effort."[19] To achieve these objectives, he appointed the new standing faculty Committee on the Course of Study, with himself as chairman, on January 7, 1903.

The best general view of Wilson's ideas at this time about the right kind of undergraduate curriculum is to be found in his inaugural address, "Princeton for the Nation's Service," delivered on October 25, 1902. His central argument was that the proper task of the college was to produce men with trained minds and breadth of vision, not subject specialists. He recognized that this objective could not be achieved solely by the traditional disciplines of Greek, Latin, mathematics, and English. The "circle of liberal studies" had enlarged too much for that. Science had opened "a new world of learning as great as the old" and had transformed even many of the older fields of study. However, it was impossible to teach everything. His solution was to "seek in our general education, not universal knowledge, but the opening up of the mind to a catholic appreciation of the best achievements of men and the best processes of thought since days of thought set in." In order to achieve this, the undergraduate curricu-

[17] Notes for a talk printed at April 12, 1902, Vol. 12.
[18] See the memorandum printed at Aug. 31, 1902, Vol. 14.
[19] See Wilson's report to the Board of Trustees printed at Oct. 21, 1902, Vol. 14.

lum should include those disciplines which were distinguished for their "definiteness and their established method." It was, he said, "their age and completeness that render them so serviceable and so suitable for the first processes of education." For this reason he would include Greek, Latin, mathematics, and English in his basic curriculum.

However, the newer fields of science also had to be included; the problem was which to include. Here Wilson made the argument most objectionable to scientists: "Special developments of science, the parts which lie in controversy, the parts which are yet but half built up by experiment and hypothesis, do not constitute the proper subject matter of general education. For that you need, in the field of science as in every other field, the bodies of knowledge which are most definitively determined and which are most fundamental." The truly fundamental sciences, he declared, were physics, chemistry, and biology. To these, he added geology and astronomy, because they gave the mind "the stimulation which comes from being brought into the presence and in some sort into the comprehension of stupendous, systematized physical fact."

In addition, Wilson added philosophy, history, politics, economics, and the modern languages to his list of basic studies. However, he asked, "How are we to marshal this host of studies within a common plan which shall not put the pupil out of breath?" His answer contained the germ of the system of concentration of studies which was to be the heart of the reorganization of 1904, as well as his own most sweeping attack on the free elective system:[20] "No doubt we must make choice among them, and suffer the pupil himself to make choice. But the choice that we make must be the chief choice, the choice the pupil makes the subordinate choice. Since he cannot in the time at his disposal go the grand tour of accepted modern knowledge, we who have studied the geography of learning and who have observed several generations of men attempt the journey, must instruct him how in a brief space he may see the most of the world, and he must choose only which one of several tours that we may map out he will take. Else there is no difference between young men and old, between the novice and the man of experience, in fundamental matters of choice. We must supply the synthesis and must see to it that, whatever group of studies the student selects, it shall at least represent the round whole, contain all the elements of modern knowledge, and be itself a complete circle of general subjects."[21]

That Wilson devoted further thought to the revision of the curriculum in the autumn of 1902 is revealed by his memorandum, dated November 20, 1902, sketching out proposed courses to be included in several fields of concentration,[22] and by the long letter of November 24, 1902, from Fred Neher, then Assistant Professor of Chemistry, who at Wilson's request submitted his suggestions for the "consolidation and co-ordination of the courses in Chemistry" offered at Prince-

[20] However, see also Wilson's strong attack on the free elective system in his address, "The College Course and Methods of Instruction," printed at Dec. 12, 1903.

[21] "Princeton for the Nation's Service," printed at Oct. 25, 1902, Vol. 14.

[22] See the memorandum printed at Nov. 20, 1902, Vol. 14.

ton.[23] However, as it turned out, the real work on the reorganization of the curriculum did not begin until the autumn of 1903. The letter to Wilson from John H. Westcott of October 19, 1903, enclosing a proposed curriculum in classics, indicates that the process was by then under way. Another letter, from Winthrop M. Daniels to Wilson, of December 4, 1903, reveals that the Committee on the Course of Study had begun to meet to plan the new curriculum. Wilson reported to the Board of Trustees on December 10, 1903, that the committee was now holding weekly meetings. In a letter to his wife on April 26, 1904, Wilson observed that the report, as finally adopted, was "not . . . exactly the scheme I at the outset proposed but it is much better." Hence, it seems clear that in the early stages of the process Wilson submitted a plan which then formed the basis of discussion. This "scheme" does not seem to have survived, if, indeed, he ever set it down on paper. As his letters to his wife and the extracts from the University Faculty minutes printed herein reveal, Wilson presented the report of the Committee on the Course of Study to the faculty in an hour-long speech and served as the committee's floor manager during the debates which ensued. Obviously Wilson, at least from the autumn of 1903 onward, was the prime catalyst and organizing and driving force in the successful movement for the new curriculum.[24]

It is extremely difficult to assess with any confidence the impact of Princeton's curricular reform upon American higher education. The new Princeton plan was widely publicized both when it was adopted and later.[25] Clearly, the elective system had passed its zenith by around 1900, and something of a reaction had already set in at least among some academic leaders by 1904. There were a large number of institutions of higher learning in the United States at this time, and they varied in size and character. While it is certainly true that almost every institution had to reconsider its own course of study in the light of the revolution brought about by the free elective system, the extent to which it was adopted or rejected varied tremendously. As more than one commentator has pointed out, the acceptance or rejection of the elective system, especially in the smaller institutions, might be as much a matter of economics as of ideology.[26]

Moreover, many institutions had already worked out or were working out some sort of compromise between a rigidly prescribed curriculum and free electives. One scholar has found at least five major divisions in the types of curricula in American institutions of higher learning about 1910. Many smaller institutions, especially in New England, the South, and those with strong religious affiliations, still adhered to a curriculum that was largely prescribed. At the opposite extreme, a few wealthy institutions such as Harvard, Cornell, and Stanford had a system of virtually complete free election. Perhaps

<hr>

[23] F. Neher to WW, Nov. 24, 1902, Vol. 14.

[24] All of the documents referred to in the above paragraph are printed in this volume under the dates cited.

[25] See, for example, editorials in the New York *Evening Post*, Sept. 20, 1904, and the *New York Times*, Oct. 23, 1904.

[26] See, for example, Frederick Rudolph, *The American College and University: A History* (New York, 1962), pp. 300-305.

the most common type was that in which the studies of the first two years were prescribed, while those of the junior and senior year were largely or completely elective. In addition, there was the so-called "major-minor" system, in which a student in his upperclass years was obliged to take a certain number of courses in a major field and also in one or more minor fields. Finally, there was the "group" system, in which studies were classified into a few large areas such as "science," "language," "history," and "philosophy," with the student being required to take a certain number of courses in each group.[27]

The new system at Princeton obviously resembled to some degree each of the last three "compromise" systems described above. It is very difficult to determine who influenced whom in this matter. However, Princeton clearly was one of the first major institutions not only to call in question the free elective system but also to formulate a new course of studies designed to remedy its abuses. As the reaction against the excesses of the elective system gathered momentum, Princeton certainly served as a kind of symbolic leader. This was clearly true in the revolt against the free elective system in its citadel, Harvard University. In 1902-1903, a committee of the Harvard faculty dominated by Abbott Lawrence Lowell and LeBaron Russell Briggs investigated the quality of instruction in Harvard College and attributed many of the defects they found to the elective system. Although the report itself dealt largely with methods of instruction, one of its outgrowths was the adoption in 1908 of an honors program which required, among other things, that a student pass with distinction eight courses in a department of concentration. Soon after Lowell's election to the presidency of Harvard in 1909, new rules were promulgated which required every undergraduate to "concentrate" at least six of his courses in a recognized field of study and to "distribute" six other courses among major areas outside his field of concentration. Throughout this period, Lowell and the like-minded group around him looked to Wilson and Princeton as an example. Shortly after his selection as President of Harvard, Lowell invited Wilson to give the Phi Beta Kappa address in June 1909. Wilson's oration, "The Spirit of Learning," consisted largely of a covert attack on the free elective system. Lowell, Charles Francis Adams, and others praised Wilson's speech and openly supported his ideas.[28] Thus, in at least one important instance, Princeton played an effective role in the modification of the elective system. Probably there were others as well.[29]

[27] See R. Freeman Butts, *The College Charts Its Course: Historical Conceptions and Current Proposals* (New York and London, 1939), pp. 243-46.

[28] See Samuel Eliot Morison (ed.), *The Development of Harvard University. . . . 1869-1929* (Cambridge, Mass., 1930), pp. xlv-xlviii, and Laurence R. Veysey, *The Emergence of the American University* (Chicago, 1965), pp. 248-51.

[29] The only thorough study to date of curricular reform at a major college in the late nineteenth and early twentieth centuries is George Wilson Pierson, *Yale College: An Educational History, 1871-1921* (New Haven, Conn., 1952), especially pp. 167-266, 304-45. This provides an interesting comparison with the Princeton reforms, since almost all of the same issues and ideas appeared at Yale between 1899 and 1910, though the solutions adopted were often very different.

Drawing of Wilson in 1904, by George Timothy Tobin

James Mark Baldwin

Arnold Guyot Cameron

Harry Augustus Garfield

Frank Thilly

Monday, February 1, 1904

Called at the Hibben's at five and arranged to go to the Kneisel Quartette in the evening, — Ellen being still unfit to go out.

The night was as glorious a one as I ever saw, — a perfectly brilliant moonlight upon a world of snow and frost, the air intensely cold and biting like an icy bath. The first part of the music was modern and disturbing, but the concluding part, fr. Beethoven, gave the mind tone again and sent us home happy. I walked home with the Hibbens and sat with them till nearly eleven.

Facsimile of a page of Wilson's diary for 1904

PRINCETON UNIVERSITY
PRINCETON N. J.

PRESIDENT'S ROOM

21 March, 1904

My Eileen, my own darling,

There's nae luck aboot the house noo ye are awa! And to think that as I sit here and write in this quiet room, at the old desk, my sweet ane is out, hundreds of miles, upon the broad seas! Ah, weel, it's ma ain do'in; and I'm no repinin'. I'm but lettin' ma heart gae its ain gait the moment! — The address to the schoolmasters, and mistresses, was a grand affair. Standing on my little platform there in the tenth story of the building of the University of the City of New York, on Washington Square, I looked straight out on the stream of the river itself, and expected to see the nose of the white steamer thrust itself into sight any moment. And what poetical, in-

Facsimile of Wilson's letter
to Ellen Axson Wilson, March 21, 1904

Charles Williston McAlpin

Jenny Davidson Hibben

John Grier Hibben

Ellen Axson Wilson

From the Minutes of the Princeton University Faculty

8 p.m.   April 19, 1904.

Special meeting called to consider the report of the Committee on the Course of Study on the revision of the Course of Study.

The Faculty met, the President presiding. The Dean was called to the chair and the President, as Chairman of the Committee, presented the report. It was

Resolved that in the consideration of the report of the Committee on the Course of Study all amendments suggested shall be submitted in writing; and that no amendment be debated or acted on until referred to and reported upon by the Committee on the Course of Study for the purpose of determining its relation to the leading principles and general scheme of the report.

It was moved that the report be adopted.

After a general debate, it was

Resolved, that the Faculty adjourn to meet in No. 8, Dickinson Hall on Thursday evening at 8 p.m., and that it shall meet thereafter every weekday evening except Saturday next until the report is disposed of. The Faculty then adjourned.

Approved April 21, 1904   W. F. Magie   Clerk

◇

8 p.m.   April 21, 1904.

Special Meeting. The Faculty met, the Dean presiding. The minutes of the meeting of April 19 were read and approved.

The report of the Committee on the Revision of the Course of Study was taken up seriatim.

Recommendations I, II, III, with an amendment to Recommendation III, offered by Professor Hoskins,[1] were adopted.

Recommendations IV, V, VI, were adopted.

Recommendation VII was moved.

Amendments were offered by Professors Parrott, Cornwall and Frothingham.[2]

The Faculty then adjourned.

Approved April 22, 1904   W. F. Magie   Clerk.

[1] This amendment added the word "Plane" before "Trigonometry" in Recommendation III.

[2] Only the Frothingham amendment was adopted. See the Princeton University Faculty Minutes printed at April 22, 1904, n. 2.

◇

8 p.m.   April 22, 1904

Special Meeting. The Faculty met, the Dean presiding. Professor J. B. Carter was appointed Clerk *pro tem.* The minutes of April 21 were read and approved.

The Committee on the Course of Study reported on the amendments offered at the last meeting.

Recommendation III was adopted without amendment.[1]

Recommendation VII was amended by the adoption of the amendment presented by Professor Frothingham[2] and was then adopted.

Recommendation VIII was adopted with amendments pending offered by Professors Cameron, Lewis, Frothingham and McMillan.[3]

Recommendation IX was adopted with amendments pending offered by Professors McClure and Frothingham.[4]

Recommendations X, XI, XII, XIII, were adopted.

Resolved (1) that the revised curriculum go into full effect with the opening of the Academic year 1905-1906.

(2) that the Committee on the Course of Study prepare a transitional curriculum for the year 1904-1905.

(3) that the Committee on the Course of Study prepare and issue the necessary weekly schedules and all other needed information regarding the revised course of study.

The Faculty then adjourned.

Approved April 25, 1904

Jesse Benedict Carter   Clerk pro tem.

W. F. Magie   Clerk.

---

[1] That is, without further amendment, the Hoskins amendment having been adopted on April 21.

[2] This amendment provided for clarifying textual changes to make "Latin [etc.], if not taken required" read "Latin [etc.] if not taken as a required subject."

[3] For action on these amendments, see the Princeton University Faculty Minutes printed at April 25, 1904, n. 1.

[4] For action on these amendments, see the Princeton University Faculty Minutes printed at April 25, 1904, n. 2.

◊

8 p.m.   April 25, 1904

Special Meeting. The Faculty met, the Dean presiding. The minutes of the meetings of April 6 and April 22 were read and approved.

Recommendation VIII was amended by changing Section VIb to conform to an amendment offered by Professor Lewis, and by the adoption of an amendment offered by Professor McMillan and was then adopted.[1]

Recommendation IX was amended by adopting the amendment to section XI offered by Professor McClure and was then adopted.[2]

By unanimous consent Recommendation VII was altered by striking out the brackets connecting Latin and Chemistry under "Sophomore Year; Elective."[3]

Recommendation IX was reconsidered and an amendment to that section was offered by Professor Paul van Dyke.

The President reported from the Committee on the Course of Study the following resolution, which was adopted

Resolved, that hereafter the weekly schedule be constructed on a basis of six days of six consecutive hours, ending at two o'clock.

A recess was taken until 9:30 p.m.

After the recess the Committee on the Course of Study reported on the amendment of Professor Paul van Dyke.

Recommendation IX was adopted without amendment.

It was then

Resolved, that the report of the Committee on the Course of Study be adopted.

The Faculty then adjourned. . . .

W. F. Magie   Clerk.[4]

[1] These amendments to Recommendation VIII added the specific course numbers 31 and 32 before all advised electives and "Laboratory Physics" in "IX. *Department of Chemistry*"; substituted Latin 31 and 32 in VIb as an advised elective for an unnumbered Latin course as a required cognate course; and added "32. Graphical Statics" to the junior courses "falling under Division D, but which are not in any one of the Departments of that Division."

[2] This amendment eliminated the required cognate course, Palaeontology 43 and 44, for seniors majoring in biology and added the Theory of Prime Motors 41 and 42 to the senior courses not listed in the eleven departments.

[3] The effect of this amendment was to establish chemistry as an independent elective for all degree candidates during their sophomore year.

[4] Following this entry, the amended report of the Committee on the Course of Study, without the tables showing the departments in detail, was spread upon the minutes.

To Ellen Axson Wilson

My precious darling,   Princeton, N. J.   26 April, 1904

Nothing but good news this morning. The dear patients are both *perfectly well*; Miss Andrews left day before yesterday; Margaret will probably go back to college the first of next week. Both she and Nellie look singu[la]rly well and strong. Their eyes are the only things to look out for, and you may be sure we are taking every precaution. Margaret will spare her eyes a great deal even after she returns to Baltimore; but she can attend all her classes and save a good deal of loss in that way. Nell will go back to school, too, almost at once. In brief, everything is straightened out.

The other piece of good news,—and it is *very* good,—is that the new course of study was last night finally, and unanimously, adopted by the University Faculty. It took only four meetings to put it through all its stages. A few amendments of detail were proposed, but none adopted except such as the Committee was willing to accept. There was singularly little debate,—practically none at all, only informal canvassing of details;—everyone seemed to accept the *principle* of the report and all the main features of the scheme at once and without cavil; and the final adoption was characterized by real cordiality. All of which makes me very happy. It is not, as it stands now, exactly the scheme I at the outset proposed, but it is much better.

We have just enjoyed a great intellectual treat. Professor Butcher[1] (the translator of the Odyssey) lectured here Saturday evening on "Greece and Phoenicia: two Contrasted Civilizations," with a delicacy and beauty of style and a luminous power of interpretation which quite carried me away. We did not attempt Alexander Hall, but put him in Murray Hall; and there only those who appreciated him assembled. I think everybody of discrimination and taste was delighted.[2] He stayed with Henry Van Dyke. His personality is charming, showing that combination of simplicity, spontaneity, and intellectual eagerness and companionableness which makes the finest type of cultivated Englishman so admirable and enjoyable. He is an Irishman, by the way, born in Dublin, son of the Bishop of Meath. He married a daughter of Archbishop Trench.[3] How I wish you might have met him!

Another cable (another "Charcos") has come this morning[4] to make my heart sing. And your letters, my darling, what perfectly delightful reading they are,—for all of us, but particularly for the one who loves you best,—to whom your happiness and enjoyment are an unspeakable delight! How they do glow with colour and pulsate with the keen ardour I knew would come to my precious one in her real native land! How sweet it is to *know* by these charming letters that just the joy has come to you that I planned and expected! I dream all day of that dear look of deep wonder and delight that must be almost always in your eyes now, —the look I have seen in them in the Louvre and in the English lakes,—and sometimes when you have looked at me, when my heart leaped within me,—the most wonderful[,] the most beautiful depth of exquisite, pure feeling, mixed of mind and emotion, that ever was seen in mortal eyes,—the look by which I know the incomparable beauty of thought and feeling that is in the dear little lady who has blessed me with her love. No dreams could make me happier, with the exquisite satisfaction of an unselfish happiness. All,—every one I meet,—send you both love and God speed; and there is a little household here who love you both altogether. Love to M. H. and the Smiths.

Your own   Woodrow

ALS (WC, NjP).
  1 Samuel Henry Butcher, formerly Professor of Greek at the University of Edinburgh, at this time living in London. Butcher was in the United States primarily to deliver a series of lectures at Harvard University.
  2 A report of Butcher's Trask lecture appeared in the *Daily Princetonian*, April 25, 1904.
  3 Rose Julia Trench Butcher, who had died in 1902.
  4 It is missing.

From Ellen Axson Wilson

My own darling,   Rome   April 26 1903 [1904]

This is our last day in Rome, the trunks went to Florence yesterday, our packing is all done and we leave in about an hour, our train starting at 12. This is the day for the great military parade in honour of Loubet, troops are marching and bands playing all over the city. The others all went out early to see what they could see. Mary Smith has just returned reporting that they saw the king, the queen,[1] Loubet & the court! I am very glad we're in such luck! My dislike for a crowd is such, that I wouldn't stand in a crush for all the kings in Europe! They have also gone now to drink of the fountain of Trevi and throw in their coin,—which you know ensures their return to Rome some time.

It seems this visit of Loubet is considered of great political importance, and of most happy omen, so the preparations have been most elaborate. The street decorations were interesting because they were exactly like those of imperial Rome, as one sees them in pictures and bas-reliefs of triumphal processions; *entirely* unlike what one sees elsewhere. We are just around the corner, so to speak, from the palace, and yet we ourselves are in the slums, on a miserable, narrow, dirty street, of small shops. How curious these old cities are in that respect! There is no "East" & "West End." The poor they have always with them, and perhaps it is just as well,—"lest we forget." Still I rather hope we may be in better surroundings in Florence. Our street in Naples was *vile*,—though when one got behind those high convent walls all was changed,—sweet & clean and fragrant. I am rather glad to be leaving Rome, for there is doubtless less danger of illness in Florence than in either Rome or Naples, & I have, of course, had all the time more or less dread of Jessie's getting ill, for she has never before been exposed to a malarial climate; all the rest of us grew up in it and are more or less "proof." It is a good thing that I have her on my mind for it makes me the very *soul* of prudence while the others are quite reckless—sleeping with their windows open, staying out at sunset, and all the rest of it!

I suppose I will not have another moment to write until we reach Florence; and I am very eager to get there for the sake of my own letters; as I have not heard for a week. We are *perfectly* well; Jessie is the very picture of health; and I am scarcely ever tired even. Nothing much has happened since I wrote you last. I spent yesterday morning of course, at the Vatican;—it was pretty hard to turn my back on it forever! I could scarcely keep from crying,—it is the only place I have had any such feeling about. But I was so fortunate in one respect; one corner of the Sistine Chapel was covered by scaffolding, hiding the Delphian Sibyl,—*much* the most beautiful of all,—so that I had given up all hope of seeing her. But yesterday, the scaffolding, which is on great rollers, had been moved along a little and she stood revealed!—and she is one of the two most beautiful creatures in the world!—the Venus of Milo of course being the other. The pictures, lovely as they are, do her no justice at all. There is no other face so truly inspired. Beyond any doubt she sees in a vision "all the glory that shall be." The others had all gone to the Palatine for the morning; but when I told them the news they rushed away from the lunch table, and so managed to get ½ hour at the Vatican before it closed at three.

But I must stop at once. With love unspeakable.

Your devoted little wife,   Eileen.

Dearest love to all.

ALS (WC, NjP).
¹ Queen Elena of Italy.

From William Church Osborn

My dear President Wilson: New York. April 26, 1904.

I do not know what you were able to do with the $1,500. which I sent you last fall for use in the English Department,¹ but it occurs to me that if you were successful in getting good men and desire to retain them over the next year, you will be thinking about ways and means, about this season. When you have time, will you not write me what you were able to do this winter and what your plans are for the ensuing year? I would like to consider renewing my gift next fall if the experience of this year seems to make it desirable.

With kind regards, believe me,

Cordially yours,   Wm Church Osborn

TLS (WP, DLC).

[1] See W. C. Osborn to WW, Sept. 18, 1903, n. 2.

From Ellen Woodrow Erwin

Dear Mr. Wilson   Salem, [N. C.] Apr. 26, 1904

Will you please send me ten dollars for my ticket home and some little things I am compelled to have[.][1] I would'nt ask you for it but Papa[2] cant send it to me. Ask Aunt Ellie to take that much off what she sends me in June[.] I will be very much obliged to you if you will please send it as soon as you can. Give my love to the girls.

Sincerely   Ellie Erwin

ALS (WP, DLC).

[1] See EAW to WW, Aug. 26, 1902, and WW to EAW, Aug. 29, 1902, n. 2, both in Vol. 14.

[2] Hamilton Erwin of Morganton, N. C.

From Edward Field Goltra[1]

My dear Dr. Wilson: St. Louis, Mo.   April 27, 1904.

I find your favor of the 20th inst. awaiting me upon my return from the North.

It gives me pleasure to say to you that I will subscribe $1,000 for the first year, and will probably continue the same amount for the other two consecutive years, and you may enter my name on the subscription list accordingly. I trust I may always be able to say "present" when Princeton calls.

Your plan of financing the deficit strikes me as very good, and should be successful.

Thanking you for bringing the matter to my attention, believe me, with much regard,

Sincerely yours,   Edward F. Goltra

TLS (WP, DLC).

[1] Princeton 1887, organizer and first president of the American Steel Foundry Co. of Granite City, Ill., a suburb of St. Louis.

To Ellen Axson Wilson

My precious darling,   Princeton, N. J.   28 April, 1904

The sweet letter came to-day which was written the day the first news of the measles reached you. How I did *long* to let you know *at once* that we are all *perfectly well* again! But, alas! I cabled that reassuring news three days ago and got this message back: "Yours Wilson Rinaldi Rome undelivered. Addresse left." Where had my sweet one gone? I did not know how to send a message wh. would trace and follow her to other lodgings. And why were they so stupid at Madame Rinaldi's as not to *know* where you had gone? I could only conjecture and stand helpless. A cable will go to you on Monday to try the Florence address while it is young. Did Mr. Rinaldi, "the military artist," drive you from the Via Rasella by his attentions? Ah, my pet, how my thoughts hover about you with every possible conjecture and every guardian thought! He was right about your mouth! It *is* "the most exquisite imaginable," and I feel to-night as if I would give my life to have my lips upon it, my little wife in my arms.

Nellie says she wrote to you to-day and said that Maggie,[1] as well as Margaret and she herself was well. Was I naughty to think that my promise to you did not extend beyond the loved ones, and not to tell you that Maggie, too, had taken the measles? She took them and got over them exactly when Margaret did. Her sister came in to help; the other servants were splendid, as usual; and we really suffered no inconvenience. Now that it is *all* over, it *all* (thanks to Miss Andrews) seems like a trifle. We are all *perfectly* well and serene.

Two of the Trustees have died within the week, Mr. Stafford Little and Mr. Cowan. I went to Matawan yesterday to attend Mr. Little's funeral; Mr Cowan is to be buried in his native place, Millersburg, Ohio, to-morrow morning. I dare say Mr. Cadwalader will be transferred from the alumni to the life list, to fill Mr. Little's chair, and that Bob. Garrett will be put into Mr. Cowan's place.[2] If Dr. Craven should die before the Commencement meeting I shall be sorely put to it to determine what *minister* to favour for the vacancy![3]

The Emergency Fund has grown to $72,500. Slow work!

Mrs. Hibben has told you, I believe, that she and Jack and Beth are to sail June 7th, the very day before your ship is expected! Jack, you remember, has to go to Scotland and England to get men to write several of the volumes of the "Epochs of Philosophy" he is to edit for the Scribners[4] (the Scribner's contributing $500 towards his expenses) and Mrs. Hibben and Beth, it has been decided, are to go too, settling down in some quiet place in the south of England while Jack goes to and fro on his errands. They are quite excited and full of their plan, as you may imagine. They are a great comfort to me!

I dined last night, after getting back from Matawan, at the Garfield's,—an odd mixture of people: Mrs. Marquand (who sails on Saturday,—the day this letter sails,—to join her husband on *your* side of the water), the guest of honour, Mr. and Mrs. Armour, Mr. and Mrs. Robbins, and Professor Thompson. The Garfields have the art of getting up a dinner of delightful dishes not one of which I ought to eat! I got home pretty tired, but in excellent shape, considering the fatigues of the day. I am a robust customer, after all!

My pet, my pet,—what a privilege it is merely to be allowed to *think* of you as my own and write these little nothings of my quiet days, with the knowledge that you will be interested in any trifle that concerns me! Your love seems to fill my heart, as the all-sufficing thing that makes life worth living. When I think of all that you are, of all that you have given me of stimulation, inspiration, insight into all things beautiful and pure and full of refreshment,—a veritable education in the things that make for happiness, my heart fairly melts within me,—and in the midst of my very longings for you,—longings which my heart can hardly endure—I rejoice at the feast of beauty and pure enjoyment my sweet little lover and benefactor is having,—*some* recompense for what she has given besides the absolute love and devotion of

Her own   Woodrow

Love without measure to precious Jessie from us all, as well as warmest love to the dear "cousins," real and adopted.[5]

ALS (WC, NjP).

[1] Maggie Foley, who had been a servant of the Wilsons for many years.

[2] As it turned out, John Lambert Cadwalader was re-elected to a five-year term as Alumni Trustee in June 1904, and the trustees chose Cleveland Hoadley Dodge and John Heman Converse to fill the vacancies created by the deaths of Henry Stafford Little and John Kissig Cowen, respectively. Converse declined to serve, and the trustees, in December 1904, elected in his stead Archibald Douglas Russell, brother-in-law of Moses Taylor Pyne and wealthy New York lawyer who lived in Princeton. Robert Garrett was elected a Life Trustee in June 1905. See also D. B. Jones to WW, March 15, 1904.

[3] Dr. Craven, who was in very poor health at this time, survived until 1908.

[4] Hibben's activities as editor of this series will be revealed in the correspondence between Wilson and Professor and Mrs. Hibben during the summer of 1904. Only two volumes in the series were ever published—Hibben's own *The Philosophy of the Enlightenment* (New York and London, 1910) and Robert Drew Hicks, *Stoic and Epicurean* (New York and London, 1910).

[5] The adopted cousins were the Smith sisters.

From William Church Osborn

My dear President Wilson: New York. April 28, 1904.

I am very glad to learn by your letter of the 27th, that you were able to obtain the services of two efficient assistants in the English Department out of the $1,500 which I sent to you last year. If, as I gather from your letter, you feel that the money would be well spent, I shall take great pleasure in sending you $1,500 next autumn for the same purpose.

Allow me to add that I am delighted with your course in holding the students up to a higher standard of scholarship this winter. We can well afford to lose a lot of men for defective scholarship as it must inevitably result, to my mind, in attracting to us the ambitious men who desire to be educated where the standard is severe.

With kind regards, believe, me,

Cordially yours   Wm Church Osborn

TLS (WP, DLC).

From Ellen Axson Wilson

My own darling,   Hotel Leone, Assisi, May 1 [1904]

I will begin this letter as you did yours on a certain memorable occasion by telling you that I have some good news for you![1] Of course it wont strike you so at first, but if you were here you would be quick to agree with us that we have the profoundest cause for gratitude. Jessie has had dipththeria, but her throat is already perfectly clear and has been since yesterday morning. It was a short sharp attack,—extraordinarily short. Of course she is not to raise her head from the pillow for a week more, to guard against heart trouble, and every possible precaution is being taken just as it would be at home, but the disease itself is already conquered. She had antitoxine twice,—given once by the Italian doctor here,[2] and then by the doctor,[3] whom I telegraphed for, from Rome.

The rest of us are perfectly well and I have a splendid trained nurse from Rome, an English nun, sent me by Dr. Bull[4] himself. You can't imagine how kind & good everyone is to us. The hotel keeper & his wife are really wonderful,—so sympathetic & kind, and not in the least afraid. She is a pretty young *Englishwoman*, and that last fact saved my reason, I think, when the blow first fell, for the doctor could not speak a word of anything but Italian, and she was apparently the only person in Assisi who could act as interpreter. She has two pretty little boys of her own and you may imagine how I feel to have her exposed, but she simply says "it is all as God wills,"—half saint & half mad woman one would think. But of course after the nurse came she was no longer exposed. The doctor from Rome says it is not nearly so contagious here as in more northern countries and much milder in every way, "more bland" as he expressed it. It seemed a great disaster that we had got away from Rome to this primitive place before the disease developed, but that too turns out for the best, for Dr. Bull says she will make more progress toward complete recovery in two weeks here than in four weeks in Rome, the air here being so singularly fine and pure.

We left Rome Monday [Tuesday] at twelve, you know; I wrote & cabled[5] you both, that morning, that we were all quite well. Jessie was looking splendidly. (She *had* said early in the morning that she felt a "very slight roughness in her throat[.]" I gave her rhinitis & told her to use my listerine and it seemed to pass away. But about five as we were driving up from the station to Assisi, which is on a mountain top, she put her hand to her throat & said it was beginning to hurt "a good deal." As soon as we reached the Inn I looked at it & to my horror saw a huge solid white patch larger than a silver dollar. I sent at once for the doctor (a very kind, intelligent man; and Dr Bull pronounced him an excellent doctor.) He is of German ancestry & looks like *Bro. George*,[6] especially in his *expression*;—Jessie & I confessed to each other that our confidence in him was greatly increased by the fact that he didn't *look* Italian! He thought it was dipththeria,—and was *sure* the next morning when it had spread all over the throat, though she was treated through the night every hour. So early in the morning I telegraphed to Dr. Bull, "physician to the American embassy," and the only doctor in Rome whom I ever heard of, saying (and I am sure you won't blame me this once for working your position for all it was worth!). ["]The young daughter of Pres. Wilson of P. U. is seriously ill with dipththeria at-&c. I implore you to come at once prepared to give antitoxine." It did not reach him,—as he was out—in time for the morning train & there are but two in the day. A telegram at five said, "My first, best assistant will leave for Assisi at 10 P. M." In the meantime Dr. Alari had sent to Perugia for the "serum" & gave it Wed. night. The assistant—Dr Wild, a Swiss,—came early Thursday morning and again injected serum of a very superior quality. He staid until the next morning & as he was at the hotel he saw her every two hours & himself gave all the treatment. The nurse came Thursday afternoon bringing various necessaries,—you can get *nothing* here—not even toilet paper. Then to my surprise Dr. Bull telegraphed that he would come himself & he arrived Friday afternoon. The throat was already improving wonderfully & Saturday morning when Dr Bull left it was perfectly clear of the white, and the doctor pronounced us "out of the wood." She has scarcely suffered at all and looks as bright and well as can be, and is a perfect little *angel*[.] I never saw such a child. Of course Mary Hoyt and the Smiths are as good as gold. Mary & I nurse her during the day while the nurse sleeps. The Smiths, of course, I have not allowed to be exposed to it since she was put to bed, and they will leave for Florence tomorrow. Dr. Bull was so kind as to volunteer to take our "circular tickets," for which of course we have no use now, back to "Cooks" & get them to refund the money. He is quite sure that we will be able to sail as we expected on the 26th[.] Ask Mr. Westcott to tell you about Dr. Bull,—it will make you feel better about us! One *very* seldom sees a man who impresses one so instantly and so profoundly with a sense of his power & efficiency. It is a very strongly marked individuality,—a good deal of brusqueness in manner, but *such* kindliness with it all. He is an old man & not well,—says he would'nt have come if we had not been Americans. I suppose the bill for such a great man will be something frightful, but I am sure you will understand that there was no help for it. You can imagine what a blackness of desolation it was that first night and day. I am so inexpressibly grateful to God for so tempering the wind.

Of course to be perfectly frank I am still miserable on the subject of heart failure, but the doctors are most reassuring, and Dr. Alari seems to understand as well as Dr Bull that it is the point to be guarded against. She is doing well in that respect as in all others; the nurse has stricknine to inject in case of need, she has stimulants constantly &c. &c. Dr Bull wishes us, if all goes well, to go in about two weeks to a "convalescent convent home" at Fiesole near Florence so as to break the journey to Genoa, and he says I must of course, keep the nurse until we sail, as she must for a month be treated & watched scientifically. He says Mary & I are all right & in no danger and he gave us a gargle to use. Mary begs you not to let Margaret Wilson tell Florence Hoyt that anything has gone wrong. Ah me! that my darling must know is very grievous to me! I swear, my dear one, that I am keeping absolutely nothing from you,—that at this moment all is well, and will, we

(0) 353 ✓ Hotel Leone, Assisi, May 1

My own darling: I will begin this letter
as you did yours on a certain memora
ble occasion, by telling you that I have
some good news for you! Of course it
wont strike you so at first. But if you
were here you would be quick to agree
with us that we have the profoundest
cause for gratitude. Jessie has had
diphtheria, but her throat is already
perfectly clear and has been since
yesterday morning. It was a short
sharp attack, — extraordinarily short.
Of course she is not to raise her
head from the pillow for a week
more. So guard against heart trouble
and every possible precaution is
being taken just as it would be
at home, but the disease itself is
already conquered. She had antitoxin
twice, — given once by the Italian
doctor here, and then by the doctor

The first page of Mrs. Wilson's letter of May 1, 1904 to her husband.

have every reason to trust, remain so. I love you inexpressibly, too much to talk about it today.

Your devoted little wife,   Eileen.

I have taken precautions as regards this letter, as Dr Bull directed. Still don't let anyone touch it but yourself & disinfect your hands after.

ALS (WC, NjP).
   [1] When Mrs. Wilson was visiting the Smith sisters in New Orleans and Wilson, in WW to EAW, Feb. 8, 1900, Vol. 11, had written: "I have a great piece of good news for you, which I know will rejoice you when you are over the surprise. Stock. was successfully operated on to-day for appendicitis. . . ."
   [2] Later in this letter, she identifies him as "Dr. Alari," although in her letter to Wilson of May 4, 1904, she refers to him as "Dr. Armanni."
   [3] Probably Giorgio Wild, Medico Chirurgo, Via Borgognona 12, Rome.
   [4] William Bull, Medico Chirurgo, Piazza di Spagna 20, Rome.
   [5] Her cablegram is missing.
   [6] Wilson's late brother-in-law, George Howe, Jr., M.D.

To Ellen Axson Wilson

My precious darling,   Princeton, N. J.   3 May, 1904
   Your cable from Assisi came to-day,[1] with its distressing news of dear Jessie's illness,—just after we had read the letter from Rome which gave the delightful picture of Jessie as guide in the Forum. The terms of the dispatch are as reassuring as possible in the circumstances, but I cannot help being a little upset. May God bless and keep my dear ones, and bring them safe home again, is the constant prayer of my heart! I sent *you* a cable to-day,[2] thinking that you were by this time in Florence,—my second attempt to get the news to you that our troubles are all over and everybody perfectly well again. I hope that they will have sense enough at the Jennings-Riccioli pension to keep it until you get there. Dear Margaret went back to Baltimore yesterday, well and in her usual sweet spirits. Dr. Jones[3] went on the same train. He preached for us two splendid sermons, in his best vein—in the morning in the chapel and in the evening in the First Church,— and he proved a most delightful guest. How I wished that you might share the various sorts of enjoyment he gave us!
   Last night came *the* lecture event of the season, Mr. Cleveland's address on the Chicago riots, and the federal intervention of 1894.[4] It was most successfully done and exceedingly impressive. Alexander Hall was filled, crowded, up-stairs and down.
   John Westcott, on his way to the lecture on his wheel, ran into an obstruction on the hill near his house and was badly thrown. Very alarming rumours of the accident came to me this morning,

but when I went out to see him this afternoon I found that he was only very stiff and full of bruizes. That's all the news, I believe, my sweet one. Just think, I can get only *three* more letters to you before you sail, on the 26th! How my heart bounds and throbs within me when I think of it,—of the unspeakably sweet reunion that, please God, will come to us on that blessed eighth of June that is expected to bring the *Prinzess Irene* into port! We will not care *what* the customs man does or says, will we dear? so we may stand side by side and look into each other's eyes again,—or how long he keeps us waiting! And when home *is* home once more,—when *you* are in it, not all the fatigues and distractions of Commencement can drive the serene content out of my heart. Commencement will last only five days, and then, with peace in the dear old sleepy place, we may spend our days like lovers and be happy as the days are long. It keeps me alive to think of it all. *Then*, my sweet one, what delicious memories of Italy will come to you, and what refreshing delight it will be to me to hear you talk! No one talks as you do when your mind and heart are *both* full, and your imagination kindled; and, sitting or lounging close beside you, your sweetness and charm will be to me more than Italy, or anything but love and *you*, could be. Enjoy every minute, my queen, and come back to me just so much younger and fresher and more joyous. That's what *I* am counting upon getting out of this trip.

*Every*body here seems deeply interested by everything I have to tell of your travels and your welfare, and you may be sure I love to tell everything, if only for the pleasure of talking about you!

Stock. continues unusually well and bright,—looks quite like his old self, indeed. All of us,—and the Hibbens,—unite in unbounded love to all the dear party,—and my heart calls to you night and day!   Your own   Woodrow

ALS (WC, NjP).
  ¹ It is missing.
  ² This cablegram is also missing.
  ³ The Rev. Dr. John Sparhawk Jones, pastor of Calvary Presbyterian Church in Philadelphia.
  ⁴ See the news item printed at May 7, 1904. Cleveland's lecture was printed in *McClure's Magazine*, XXIII (July 1904), 227-40, and in Cleveland's *Presidential Problems* (New York and London, 1904).

From Ellen Axson Wilson

My own darling,   Hotel Leone, Assisi, May 4 [1904]

At last I have letters from my darling again,—three of them, those of the 12th, the 19th, & the 22nd of April! And the cablegram announcing Margarets return to Balt. also came today, forwarded by the Smiths from Florence. So, as you say, it is too late for anxiety about dear Margaret,—except indeed a little about her *eyes*! They are her weak point you know, and I am so afraid she will overtax them in her efforts to "catch up." She is very much inclined to get up and study very early in the morning before she has had anything to eat, and the oculists say there is nothing in the world so bad for the eyes. Will you please warn her —indeed *command* her on that point? It is well known how badly measles affect the eyes. Since her illness has kept you from taking the Southern trip, it almost resigns me to it, for I dreaded it for you exceedingly, and for myself too; for it seemed to make the separation more absolute. It has taken a great load off my mind to know that it is not to be,—or rather has not been!

But that Margaret too has been ill certainly makes the situation complete! That they should *all* be ill, and that one or another of them should be ill during practically the whole time of my absence from home is strange indeed. I am certainly being bitterly punished for my selfishness in leaving home. And last year when I went Jessie was paralysed,[1] and when I went south Stockton had appendicitis![2] Well, I hope I have my lesson by heart at last!

The doctor says Jessie is doing splendidly; her throat is *well*; she is very bright, says she does'nt feel weak, and is "hungry all the time." She has been living on milk with egg & whiskey in it but now, after provoking delays of three or four days, we have a lot of fine chicken jelly from Rome, also some delicious zwieback to make milk toast with, and I think she is already better for it. In spite of the many good symptoms,—kidneys also in perfect condition,—I have been miserable because her pulse was so slow and I am inevitably, after the Cleveland and Finley cases, haunted with the dread of heart failure.[3] The pulse varied from 58 to 64, 80 you know being normal, but today it has got up to

---

[1] That is, when they were in Europe during the summer of 1903. The letters from Wilson's sister, Annie Wilson Howe, while she took care of the Wilson girls are missing, and nothing is known about Jessie's illness.

[2] See the extensive correspondence about this episode in Vol. 11.

[3] Ruth Cleveland, daughter of the former President, died of diphtheria on January 7, 1904, at the age of twelve. John Huston Finley's daughter, Margaret Boyden Finley, died of the same disease on May 18, 1901, at the age of four.

74, so I am much more cheerful. It seems to vary with people anyhow, mine is 80 but Mary Hoyts is only 72 and the nurses 68. Jessie's is perfectly regular & not weak, & the doctor assures me I have nothing to fear. He says he was anxious about it at first but she is doing so *very* well, that he is now sure she must have naturally a slow pulse. She is given a little stimulant every two hours. I have written to Dr. Bull to consult him about the pulse. Her heart is examined every day with a stesthoscope [stethoscope] and is declared all right. Dr. Armanni seems very capable & intelligent; and you cannot imagine anyone more kind and sympathetic. We all simply *love* him. He brings Jessie flowers every day or sends them by his beautiful little girl. They are the most reckless people here about contagion you ever imagined; doctor, landlady & all insisted that Mary and I should go down to our meals; and to protect those poor unsuspicious tourists *I* had to *beg* Dr Bull to forbid my doing so. Even he said that "if the landlady was willing it was all right." Can you wonder that Jessie caught it in such a country. I of course am uneasy about spreading the contagion by means of the drives which Mary & I are ordered to take every afternoon. We go from 5 to 6, & they certainly do me a world of good in resting & cheering and generally toning me up. The country and the weather are both *exquisitely* beautiful; spring is at its most perfect moment, and there is an indescribable wea[l]th of wild-flowers. We bring Jessie several new sorts every day and her room is a perfect bower. How lovely it will be when she can take the drives too! There is surely healing in this delicious air. There is absolutely no element of beauty lacking in the landscape. The humblest peasant's cot is a thing of beauty and the old grey town is truly noble with its great beautiful old churches and campaniles and its weather-beaten but stately palazzos that seem an original part of the everlasting hills. Most of them date from the 13th Century,—St Francis time,—when Assisi was a gay & wealthy city;—but now its only importance is ecclesiastical. There is a bishop, and the Franciscan monks, of course, swarm in it with their schools, asylums, &c.

Our throats continue perfectly well, so we have almost certainly escaped the dipththeria. Mary Hoyt is a perfect angel,— such an *unspeakable* help & comfort! I tried *hard* to get her to go on with the Smiths, or at least to go the first of next week, but she insists she will not leave us until we are on the steamer at Genoa. *Isn't* it good in her to give up so much of her precious time in Europe?—and I actually had a battle to get the proud thing to let me pay her board here. As if it would not be perfectly disgraceful if I didn't, when she is giving up so much for us and nursing Jessie too.

Dr. Bull's bill has come and for him and the assistant it is $160.00! Terrible! isnt it? And I had to pay their board here, carriage hire, &c besides. I am now paying board for four people all the time, & there still is the Assisi doctor, the trained nurse for a month, &c. &c. My Rome druggists bill is also $20.00. I begin to be afraid that even my big thousand dollar, letter of credit will not take me safely home! I have spent $300.00 including bills here at hotel up to date. Dr Bull & the drugs would make it nearly $500.00. If it turns out at the last that I really need more Mary can let me have a hundred dollars, and will you please, in that case, send to her at the American Express Co. in *London* $100.00 worth of American Express Co. checks. I will enclose the address on a separate piece of paper. She has these "checks" instead of a letter of credit. Alas, my poor dear! I am sorry this ill-fated visit must be so expensive too!

We are having the most amusing time for want of our trunks! They were sent from Rome to Florence ten days ago. We telegraphed for them to be returned here, & had a note from the company on *Saturday* that they would be forwarded "as soon as they reached Florence." The Smiths found them calmly reposing at the Pension, and now by my orders will unpack them & send me just what I need, so that the rest need not be exposed to infection. Perhaps by Sat. next we may have a change of clothing. Jessie & I have each *one* nightgown; Mary, the nabob has *two*, & has given of her superfluity to Jessie. My one gown is also gracefully draped about my waist all day to protect my one skirt from dirt & germs.

> A gown designed a double debt to pay,
> A gown by night, a pinafore by day![4]

It is astonishing how much one can do without when one must, —with perfect equanimity too!

This is a comically primitive place. The medecine is sent from the chemist in an old chianti (wine) bottle with the woven straw about it; the disinfectant in another larger one with no lable &

---

[4] Mrs. Wilson was paraphrasing and combining lines from Goldsmith's "The Deserted Village":

> "The chest contrived a double debt to pay,—
> "A bed by night, a chest of drawers by day"

and from his "Description of an Author's Bed-Chamber":

> "A night-cap deck'd his brows instead of bay,
> "A cap by night, a stocking all the day."

not even a cork! Yet the doctor is so intelligent & more "antiseptic" in his methods than Dr Wykoff.[5]

But it is time for me to stop & go back to my little one. You must not think of us, dear heart, as unhappy. I am, on the contrary, unspeakably thankful & relieved and my anxiety grows less every day. Now that the pulse is going up I expect that by Saturday I will not be anxious *at all* but will be enjoying deeply this *beautiful* place & even, next week, going to see the great "Giottos" that we came here for! I do not dare to say how unspeakably I love you, darling, or how my heart bleeds to think of the anxiety we must cause *you!* But to think how happy we will be when we are in each others arms again. Dear love from us both to *all*,—am *so* relieved to hear of Stocktons well-being.

Yours in every heart-throb   Eileen

I did not mention "dipththeria" in my cablegram for fear you would worry about my throat.

ALS (WC, NjP).
[5] Their Princeton physician, Dr. James Holmes Wikoff.

To Ellen Axson Wilson

My precious darling,   Princeton, N. J.   6 May, 1904

Comparing the dates in your letter of April 24 with regard to your plans for Assisi, Perugia, Sienna, etc., with the date of your cablegram from Assisi, it seems that you were in Assisi a week later than you expected to be. You planned to be there on Apr. 26, and your cable is dated May 3. Dear Jessie's illness must have kept you there a whole week, alas! a week of deep anxiety and a week taken from the full and happy days you were to have spent in Florence! My heart grows very heavy at these thoughts; but I am not going to weight this letter with them, which will not reach you till it is all over and the whole scene changed! I can only pray that God in his mercy will keep and guard my precious ones,—oh, so unspeakably, so *terribly* precious! You have been overexerting yourselves, that is plain. I catch that once and again from the note of fatigue in your dear letters. *How* dear they are. The infinitely sweet impression they convey of your*self* in every line, penetrates me like pain. There *is* pain,—is there not?—sweetheart, in love such as ours in time of separation. It seems more than one can bear to love you as I do and yet not have you all the day and all the dear night at my side, in my arms, in close comradeship always, when that bliss has been mine for nineteen years. To have had it makes it almost intolerable to lose it even for a little while. But think of the summer that is ahead of us, dear, the long, sweet, quiet days which will be wholly ours, and when every obstacle to our *constant* enjoyment of each other will be taken away! Isn't *that* something to make good all that this separation has cost us. And when this letter reaches you you will be within a week of your sailing. I can live, despite the present anxiety, on the joy of what will come when you are in my arms again. A moment of your presence and your caresses, two of your kisses, will blot out the two months of your absence, and leave only the joy of the exquisite store of beauty that will be laid up in your mind and heart by reason of your days with the perfect things to which you are kin. I love you,—I love you—it is all I can do to keep from crying out with it, as if my voice could reach you!

We are all perfectly well. Dear little Nell is so happy to be back with her chums again. Susie Fine,[1] too, had the measles,—taking them, no doubt, from Nell; but she is all right again,—though looking a little "peaked." Nell seems *perfectly* well and strong. Her eyes have given her no trouble at all. Neither have Margaret's shown any signs of weakness, so far as we have yet heard. Nell and Beth[2] are more together than ever and seem very truly devoted to one another. Nothing happens to us; but the days are full of business for me. We are hard at work making plans in each Department to carry out the new scheme of studies and put it, so far as possible, into operation next year, so as to waste no more time in the present chaos. Dr. Patton, by the way, professes to admire the new plans very much indeed,—though of course he has *some* cynical remarks to make upon them. Perhaps he does not foresee that they will involve a good deal more work for George.

Everyone asks after the two dear travellers in the most affectionate manner, and takes every opportunity to send messages of love and all good wishes. Our friends are all well; excellent news comes from the Ricketts (though "Palmer"[3] has half broken down again and is to go to Europe at once). All of us send love to all, and I am, with unspeakable longing and devotion,

Your own   Woodrow

ALS (WC, NjP).
[1] Dean Fine's daughter, Susan Breese Packard Fine.
[2] That is, Elizabeth Grier Hibben.
[3] Palmer Chamberlaine Ricketts, Jr., President of Rensselaer Polytechnic Institute.

A News Item About an Introduction of
President Cleveland

[May 7, 1904]

Alexander Hall was crowded to the roof on the evening of May
2nd, when the Hon. Grover Cleveland delivered his notable Stafford Little Lecture on the Government in the Chicago Strike. The
Ex-President received an ovation when he appeared on the platform, and again when President Wilson '79 said: "I am not here
to introduce the foremost citizen of the United States,"—with
emphasis on the "introduce." . . .

Printed in the *Princeton Alumni Weekly*, IV (May 7, 1904), 498.

From Ellen Axson Wilson, with Enclosure

My own darling,   Hotel Leone, Assisi, May 7 [1904].

Jessie is doing splendidly in *every* respect, and I am just as
happy as I can be. Her pulse even is rising and in every other
respect she is *well*. She sat up an hour and a half today without
feeling tired at all she said, and she certainly did not *look* so. She
has a good colour, tongue perfectly clean, kidneys all right, &c
&c. It is really *wonderful* how fast she is recovering. Oh I am *so*
thankful & happy! I wrote to Dr Bull about the pulse & received
the enclosed reply which of course relieved my fears. My only
anxiety now is that she should not overexert herself in any respect. The journey to Fiesole seems very formidable, and I long to
stay here until it is time to sail, only breaking the journey long
enough to rest her. But she gets perfectly *frantic* at the mere suggestion, sobbing herself almost into a fever, so that both nurse &
doctor say she *must* be humoured—and I must make every effort
to satisfy her. She certainly is a *wonderful* child; to all appearances she hasn't given her own disappointments a thought, but
is breaking her heart at the interruption to my plans & Mary's;
we had a dreadful scene with her about it all at first, she crying
that it would be "very, *very bad*" for her if I failed to "see the pictures"; and trying to persuade me to leave her here with the sister
after her throat cleared. I never in my life exercised more inge-
nuity than in trying to satisfy her, but I succeeded at last,—only
she has a relapse into tears & excitement at any hint of postpon-
ing our leaving. She is a perfect *angel* of unselfishness;—but it is
adding to my difficulties and anxieties all the same. I have promised her to leave her in the mornings with the sister in Fiesole

and to "see as much in ten days as I would have done in two weeks"; & I have persuaded her that I did not care for Sienna,—was only going there to please Cousin Mary. Venice & Milan it was *much* harder to dispose of; it seemed as if she would have a fever about my missing Venice in spite of all I could do. But I told her they were so far north that "one could easily run down to them from Switzerland some summer." Then I must "solemnly promise" that I would do so; when I hesitated the nurse hastily motioned to me to humour her & I did so; then at last she drew a long sigh of relief & began to smile through the tears,—poor darling! It was the most touchingly unselfish thing I ever saw.

Then I had a struggle trying to persuade Mary Hoyt to leave us. But I have ceased worrying about that now for I cannot help seeing that she really does enjoy, more than any picture gallery, watching Spring reveal herself in old grey Assisi and among the beautiful, "olive-girdled" Umbriam [Umbrian] hills. *I* too am enjoying it intensely, now that my anxieties are, for the time being, over; when Jessie can go out to drive with us it will be *heavenly*; —indeed I foresee that we will leave it almost in tears in spite of our tragical beginning,—(It poured rain & was miserably cold the first three days we were here;—just to illustrate "the pathetic fallacy" of nature's sympathy with man!) As for the doctor I don't see how we are to leave him *at all*! he is "perfectly lovely,"— a beautiful bald-headed angel. I have lost my heart to him entirely,—and I more than suspect that the feeling is mutual! It is really piquant, is it not?—for two persons who cannot speak to each other to indulge in such tender sentiments! Seriously it is pleasant to find that there is an international language in which to express kindness of heart, sympathy, gratitude, reassurance, courtesy and many other kindly, gentle feelings. The doctor's family are as nice as himself. His two handsome young daughters, one twenty one twelve, have an unaffected charm of manner that is enchanting. How I wish that exquisite flower of courtesy could be transplanted to American soil! It is simplicity itself, yet it has about it a delicate grace that suggests "old, forgotten, far-off days." And they are as clever and ambitious as American girls too; even Gabrielle, the little one, is already proficient in Latin, French & German, and a very hard student. Mary takes conversation lessons in Italian from the elder, and the younger is sent here almost every day with flowers & aspic jelly for Jessie;—regardless of the danger of contagion! We cannot get over our amazement at their recklessness in that respect. Fortunately *we* know what ought to be done before we leave & are insisting upon it rigidly. Our landlady actually sends up her children's toys,—puzzle blocks, &c.—for Jessie to play with; and when we expostulate shrugs her shoulders and says "oh its nothink!"

That reminds me of Dr. Bull & his letter again; I meant to say that though he has such a very English name he is really a Dane, which explains the peculiarities of his style. I suppose the final compliment to me is intended to make me more cheerful about the size of his bill! Cook is ugly about returning our money, & Dr. Bull has taken the matter to the American Consul. They say we will get the money back in "some months." So for present purposes I am out some $45.00 more! Moreover I can't get into the convent at Fiesole & am ordered to the hotel there,—an expensive place. It seems impossible to calculate how much I shall need to get home, but with Dr Bull's $160.00, the nurse, &c. I know I shall run pretty close, & I don't want to depend on Mary's hundred, because it has not *arrived* yet. The only thing to do to feel safe is to telegraph to you for more! How I *hate* to do it! How I wish I were like that classical person who had "nothing on his mind but his hair"! If I could stay quietly here for a month I would feel free from care. It is having Jessie travel so soon that keeps me tremulous; I will heave a *long* sigh of relief when we are finally on the steamer! But all these ups & downs will be over, darling, long before this reaches you, and I ought not to trouble you with them. Somehow it is a comfort to pour it all out to you, just as if the dear eyes were going to see it tomorrow at the latest. You will know, God willing, even while you read, that all the trouble is over,—our darling really *well* & at least fairly strong, so you will not be troubled by my tremours. But it is time for me to relieve dear Mary. We are *perfectly* well & now out of danger, for Jessies throat has been quite clear for a week. To all my dear ones love, & to my dearest one love unspeakable, from

His little wife   Eileen.

ALS (WC, NjP).

E N C L O S U R E

William Bull to Ellen Axson Wilson

Dear Mrs. Wilson   Rome, 5.5.04

Two lines immediately to answer on your kind note received this morning. You must be in *no anxiety* about your little girl's pulse; it happens often after diphteria that the pulsation gets down to 50 à 60 & it can remain on that point long time & the patient feeling and being in good state of health. The poison of difteria being still in the blood explains that fact. The important thing is that the pulse is regular. It may be that your daughter has always had a slower pulse than children of her age. She has to take a little cognac or whiskey in *hot* milk several times daily & during the night & no strychnin injection if not quite quite [sic] necessary. Glad to see that the urine in perfect condition. The patient must drive out 2 or 3 times before she undertake the travelling to Fiosole.

I am sure that you must be happy knowing that *you* have saved your childs life in acting immediately in right time and on the right way.

With my love to the little patient

Yrs very sincerely,   Prof. W. Bull, M.D.

ALS (WP, DLC).

To Edward Warren Ordway

My dear Sir: Princeton, N. J.   7 May 1904.

In reply to your circular letter of May 7, I would say that I cannot sign the petition which you enclose.[1] It seems to me inopportune and unwise.

Very truly yours,   Woodrow Wilson

TLS (NN).
 [1] Both the circular letter and petition are missing, but see WW to E. W. Ordway, Feb. 20, 1904, for an indication of their probable subject matter.

Notes for an Address on Community Cooperation[1]

8 May, 1904[2]

Village Improvement Society 10 May, 1904

The Spirit and Object of the Work:

Difficulties in the way of entire sympathy with schemes of "social betterment,"—doctrinnaire, patronizing.

In a small place the problem greatly simplified.

The Object of the Work:

(a) Actual betterment (*relative* standard)

(b) New standards to be made common: new tastes, new desires: a new community of feeling and object.

(c) Communion of classes.

The Spirit of the Work
(1) *Not* tolerance, but catholic comprehension, political as
    well as social: to understand those politically responsible
    and their peculiar problems, and assist them.
(2) Human, *unclassed* sympathy, with no "above" or "below"
    in its motive,—upon a footing where the only conscious
    differences between classes is a difference, not of intrinsic
    excellence, but of opportunity.

WWhw MS. (WP, DLC).
    [1] A news report of this address is printed at May 14, 1904.
    [2] Wilson's composition date.

To Ellen Axson Wilson

My own precious darling,   Princeton, N. J.   9 May, 1904.

At last we are having, not Spring, but Summer, and the garden
has come out with a sudden burst,—its first dainty crop, the daffodils and tulips,—long lines of tulips, white, yellow, pink, standing up stiff and yet beautiful, as if (to quote Mrs. Hibben) taken
out of a picture by Botticelli. How I do wish that you could see
this delightful display of your own inerrant taste! The garden is
transformed, and is become one of the most beautiful in Princeton. No doubt, as the successive rows of plants bud and bloom it
will grow more and more charming. The roses have evidently
suffered a good deal from the unprecedented and long continued
frosts, but most of them have survived, and I hope that they will
be blooming in all their glory to greet my darling at her home-
coming!

Evidences of the closing of the university year begin to abound,
and with the end of the year will come the end also of these dreary,
these terrible days of separation. How happy even the tiresome
days of Commencement will be with *you* to look at, you to turn to
after each dull incident is over,—light enough in your eyes when
they meet mine to drive all shadows away and put sunshine into
my heart! I deliver my last lecture of the year to-morrow morning.
Things will culminate fast after that: there will be barely time
enough in which to do the tasks with which the year closes. And
yet, how even the fullest days will drag until my sweet one comes
home again. *Nothing* has zest in it when she is not here.

Never mind! this is the next to the last letter that I can get to
her before she sails. *That's* a fact that makes her home-coming
seem actual, real,—not remote, shadowy, unreal, as it has till now

seemed,—a thing to be longed for, dreamed of, but *not* expected. I wish, my precious one, that I could receive some special gift of lover's speech for these last letters, so that I might show you in very truth what your return means to me! This separation has spoken volumes to my heart. Never before have I known what it was to be the one left in the empty home and the sea between us, the terrible spaces of ocean *and time*! It's the *time* that tells on the imagination and the heart. But, if to have a lover whose life is wrapped up in you, whom twenty years of loving intercourse, nineteen of the blessed intimacy of marriage, has made your lover forever, the motive of whose existence seems somehow inseparable from you, is a source of happiness to you, you ought to have some very sweet thoughts to dwell upon as the *Prinzess Irene* bears you homeward. You will come with a mind and imagination more richly furnished than ever, will you not, my pet? Are you sure you will not find me dull and *perceive* the contrast, now more emphasized than ever, between your mind of poetry and my mind of prose? What a joy it will be to *hear* what you will have to tell and describe. Your dear eloquent tongue will have delightful occupation for months to come, and I shall be the happiest listener in the world! We are all well and all send uncounted messages to [of] love to precious Jess. and all,—and love unutterable goes to you from   Your own   Woodrow

ALS (WP, DLC).

From Joseph R. Wilson, Jr.

My dearest Brother: Clarksville, Tenn.   May 9, 1904.

I wrote you some days ago of my earnest desire to change my location and my determination of securing at the earliest date possible a position in a wider field where there is some future for a young man of determination and ambition.[1] I have received provisional offers from two of the papers in St Louis, the Republic, a democratic morning paper who state that they are expecting to enlarge their force soon; and the Star a republican afternoon daily the editor of which states that they are always on the look-out for good men and says, in substance, that should I go to St Louis and we were pleased with each other, could agree upon terms &c., he could give me employment. This is a bad time to go to St Louis owing to the high cost of living incident to the World's Fair, but if I can get suitable work there, I feel that I should not miss the chance.

I told you in my last letter than [that] I did not want you to be responsible for the work that I might do should I get an appointment on one of the larger papers, but I did want you to assist me in securing such an appointment with the understanding that I was to stand on my own merits after securing the place. I am sure that letters from you would have great weight owing to the position you hold and the name you have won for yourself all over the country. You, too, are intimately acquainted with Mr. Cleveland, whom, I am sure, would write a letter if [of] introduction for me, at least, upon your request. With these backings, I feel that I could win in the end. I have often been asked why I do not go to you for help along this line, my friends realizing as I do that it is some such influence as this that secures the best positions these days, but I have refrained from saying much to you on the subject feeling that you might not be entirely willing to commit yourself. All I ask now is some help to get the start in a wider field I so much desire, and I will undertake to hold my own when the time comes. Do not understand from this that I am blaming you in the least, far from it, but I know that you feel a delicacy in using your position towards such ends as I suggest, and for this reason it is only at the start that I ask for aid being willing to stand alone on my own merits for the rest.

I may work myself gray-headed in Clarksville and can never accomplish more than I have already done, for the opportunity for advancement is not to be had here. Unless I make a move soon it will be harder than ever to do so and I cannot be content to stand still until the end of my best days. I am ambitious to reach the top in my profession and believe that I can do so if I can get the opportunity. In order the more quickly to get the opportunity, I ask for some assistance as indicated.

I hope the sick ones are greatly improved by this time. Kate and Alice[2] have just returned from a visit to relatives in Illinois and Kate seems to be much improved in health.

Please let me hear from you at once.

With love,   Your aff. brother,   Joseph.

TLS (WP, DLC).
  [1] This letter is missing.
  [2] His wife and daughter, respectively. His second daughter, Jessie Woodrow Wilson, had died in 1901.

From Ellen Axson Wilson

My own darling,   Hotel Leone   Assisi   May 11 [1904]

We are a very happy crowd here today; we are out of quarantine; Jessie has been this morning on the balcony, and this afternoon she takes her first drive. She is to be lifted up & down the stairs, much to her disgust, for she says she does'nt feel weak at all;—and indeed it is *wonderful* how well she looks. Yet I have weakened as regards the journey, and have decided to stay on here indefinitely, until there will be *no* risk to her heart in travelling. It seems to me *madness* to take a complicated journey with a child just up from dipththeria, and the nearer the time came the more miserable I grew about it. Of course the doctor had authorized it, but I fear Jessie's eagerness to get away had influenced him;—and even he said she must have three drives first,—and that she could take neither the drives nor the journey unless the weather were absolutely right—neither too hot nor too cold,— no wind & no damp! We were allowing *no* margin for bad weather —and the weather turned *very* bad,—two days of pouring rain & chill. Jessie's spirits sank to zero at the delay about the drives, &c.; so the bad weather, & the fact that her pulse dropped very low one night finally determined me. I don't know what caused it but it dropped to 48 one night, & was irregular too, for the first time. It was the *only* time; it is normal now all day, & varies from 70 to 76 at night, so with prudence we trust that trouble is over. I have explained in former letters Jessie's state of mind about Florence; if she were a small child everything would have been simple, for I could stay here ten days longer & still make my steamer. But the suggestion of my missing Florence throws her into a condition that can only be described by the word "*frantic*." The doctor & nurse say she simply *must* be yielded to in the matter or she will be ill again. And so the conclusion of it all is that I have been obliged to postpone our sailing two weeks! Now at last everything is serene, Jessie is as happy as a lark and that nightmare journey is off my mind. But oh, *how* I hated to do it, and how *desperately* homesick it made me to think of the two weeks longer away from my darling! It seems sometimes as though I really *can't* bear it! And to leave you in the lurch during commencement and the '79 reunion and all! It is almost *too* hard. And now a letter has come from Mrs. Hibben saying that she too will be gone; that adds immensely to my distress over the situation, for of course she would have been a tower of strength to you during commencement week. Can't they postpone sailing *one* week? At any rate it is good that Madge is there & that she has so much self-posession & charm of manner and "savoir faire." I know she will do the honours beautifully as hostess. Tell her that, in the absence of Mrs. Hibben, I think her friend Mrs. Robbins would be a good one to consult in any little difficulty. She has a great deal of tact and knowledge of the world & Madge knows her well enough to do it.

It is also awkward that I should be away when that committee of women meets.[1] You know Mr. Duffield was to provide me with all the figures as to the expenses of the Infirmary, and the women were to be asked to decide whether they would try to support a young doctor at $1000 a year, or go on as they have done paying for nurses & maids. You will have to send Mr. Duffield's figures, together with your (or say *our*) opinion on the whole situation to Mrs. Junius Morgan. I think that in view of everything it would be wiser to let things remain in statu quo one more year, so as to give ourselves ample time to decide what is best to do about a college physician and who would be the best physician to have. In that case it would be better not to mention the subject of a physician at all to the *general* committee this commencement. But we had more money than we needed for the *extra service* last year, and yet we needed money for other things sadly. So I think Mrs. Morgan should be advised to ask the women to vote that whatever money is left after the "service" is provided for can be appropriated for other Infirmary purposes at the discretion of the executive committee; for instance that it can be used for necessary improvements or furnishing at the Infirmary or for helping poor boys pay their doctor's bills &c. &c. There is a surplus now part of which should be voted to pay for all that linen & the general supplies which I paid for out of *my fund*,—(though it was not given for such things.) and then Mr. [James MacNaughton] Thompson "went and" eucred me out of *my* surplus! You know I left just at that crisis, and am very anxious to know how bad the situation was when Mr. Krespach's[2] bill, & all, came in. Do let me know the *worst*! I owe Mr. Thompson a grudge for getting me into such a scrape. It was inexcusable in him.

We have come back from the first drive, and Jessie says she feels "perfectly well." Oh what a blessed relief it is to have it practically all over! How unspeakably thankful I am;—in spite of all minor difficulties,—in spite even of the $550.00 which it seems probable this attack of illness is going to cost us,—count-

---

[1] That is, the subcommittee on the Infirmary of the Ladies Auxiliary.
[2] Frank L. Krespach, upholstering and furniture repairing, 7 and 9 Nassau St.

ing extra board, railroad tickets for the nurse, & everything. And of course I must travel first-class now. I was getting on so well too in the matter of expense,—expected to start from Genoa having spent but $500.00. It is a *great blow* to have had to cable today for more.[3] We went, Mary & I, to Perugia yesterday to get money from the bank there—could'nt be had here, & I have today sent off $200 to Drs. Bull & Wild & the Rome druggist. Now that we are out of our troubles Mary is to go on to Florence, Friday or Sat. I have almost to turn her out of the house, she hates so to leave me,—dear girl. Indeed I should never succeed at all but that she too is burdened with a "Cook's ticket" for the Italian lake district which must be used early in June.

We had a beautiful day at Perugia yesterday; we drove over of course,—2 hours—and it was an enchanting drive. It is "perhaps the most wildly picturesque town in Italy," and it has a few really great works of art. It was as of course you know, the centre of the Umbrian school of art and the only place where one can see Perugino and his pupils at their best. And Perugino's "best" was indeed a revelation to me; I always thought him very sweet and tender & charming both in colour, line & expression, yet over-sentimental and often weak. But his frescoes at the Cambio are *superb*,—great and noble in their *every* quality,—worthy of Raphael,—whom of course they constantly suggest. (You know Perugino was Raphael's master.) I came away with almost the same feelings with which I leave the Vatican,—with a sort of *uplifting* of the whole nature, moral, intellectual and aesthetic. They are a series of elaborate compositions illustrating the cardinal virtues and the Christian graces, and the result is a noble company of the great ones of the ages, the heroes & sages of Greece and Rome, prophets sybils and saints. And ones sense of beauty is completely satisfied by the fact that these beautiful pictures form the wall decoration of the most beautiful little room I have ever seen. The ceiling is also by Perugino, treated decoratively in rich soft colouring, yet full of interesting symbolism too, —an exquisite piece of work. All the wood-work of the room,— doors, panels, desks, chairs,—is of dark walnut and every inch of it carved and inlaid with the most wonderful, delicate 15th century work. The richness and harmony of the whole effect is indescribable,—and all this glory merely to adorn a little council-chamber in a guild-hall! The other two superlatively fine things in Perugia are the glorious 13th Cen fountain by the two Pisano's

[3] This cable is missing.

and the *perfectly* lovely facade of the Oratorio of San Bernardino by Duccio. Both fountain & facade are largely covered with panels in bas-relief, the latter having also large figures in niches. The colour of the facade is a *dream*, the carvings of old ivory with backgrounds of robins-egg blue combined in the subtlest manner with rose-coloured marble. And then the figures,—so light and graceful in pose and in their flowing draperies, so charming and joyous in expression, and so strongly individualized. I could run on about them for pages if I only had time.

I am so glad to think that Jessie will not miss these particular treats, since they and many other beautiful things in Perugia can be seen from a carriage. The train for Florence leaves here at seven A. M. & it is a hard journey so when we do start from here we will drive to Perugia & spend perhaps two days there.

Jessie has been getting several letters lately from her schoolmates greatly to her delight,—but none yet from Margaret & Nellie! Mary Scott[4] quoted the lines in the faculty-song about Stockton which greatly pleased us.[5] I am *perfectly delighted* to hear that the new course of study went through so smoothly. Delighted not only for the sake of the reform itself, but because it proves so conclusively that you have a united & loyal faculty behind you,—and that the Hibbens raised a false alarm on that score early in the year. I am perfectly well & as happy as a woman can be who drags a lengthening chain that separates her from her husband!—and who is going to miss his bachelaureate,—*that* is the crowning blow of all. I am not able to think about that with any degree of fortitude, and certainly not to write of it. Patience, patience! Jessie joins me in devoted love to all. I love you unspeakably, my darling, I won't try to say how much, nor what I feel about the further separation, and the necessity of adding to my dear one's cares and anxieties. Oh, how I hated to send the telegram today with that word "dipththeria" in it. But we decided it was better you should *know* that than *imagine* it was Roman fever. With love inexpressible

Your little wife,   Eileen.

ALS (WC, NjP).

[4] Mary Blanchard Scott, daughter of Professor William Berryman Scott.
[5] The stanza about Stockton Axson from the "Faculty Song" follows:

> Here's to Axton smooth as silk,
> With voice as soft and sweet as milk.
> Not too strick and not too slack,
> He's just as white a man as Jack.

The preceding stanza was about John Grier Hibben. *1904 Campus Songs* (n.p., n.d.), p. 8.

To Austin Scott

My dear President Scott: Princeton, N. J.   11 May, 1904.

Thank you for your letter of May 10.[1] I have received Mr. Leary's testimonials[2] and will put them on file for our consideration when the eligible list comes back from Oxford. Of course I will let you know as soon as it does come.

Indeed I do get tired, and about this time of the year the most natural refuge to think of is that of which you are about to avail yourself, namely a trip to England. I think the college presidents of the country might well form a recreation association.

With much regard,

Sincerely yours,   Woodrow Wilson

TLS (A. Scott Papers, NjR).
 [1] It is missing.
 [2] See Russel W. Leary to WW, May 9, 1904 ALS (WP, DLC).

To Henry Bedinger Cornwall

My dear Professor Cornwell: Princeton, N. J.   11 May, 1904.

I have learned from Professor Neher with the greatest gratification of the success of the chemical department in devising a capital scheme of instruction to fit into our new plans, and I wish to express special satisfaction that you are to take part both terms in the laboratory work in quantitative analysis. This is an arrangement which I have long regarded as most desirable and from which I expect the most satisfactory results to follow. I sincerely hope that you will make it a very important part of your work, and I feel confident that you will be rewarded by the outcome.

Very sincerely yours,   Woodrow Wilson

TLS (in possession of Richard R. Cornwall).

To Ellen Axson Wilson

[Princeton, N. J.]   12 May, 1904

Atherino Florence through Lyonnais Charcos Abbackung[1]

WWhw copy of cablegram (WP, DLC).
 [1] Wilson gives the sense of this cablegram in the letter which follows.

To Ellen Axson Wilson

My precious darling,   Princeton, N. J.   12 May, 1904

My poor, dear, precious pet! The cable reached us yesterday which told us that Jessie had had *diptheria*, and, though all you said of it in the admirably framed message was as reassuring as it could be in the circumstances, of course it has given us a dreadful shock, and has filled our hearts with quite unspeakable things. The shock to you, my pet, must have been awful, and the wait of anxiety intolerable, away from home and me and every familiar aid and comfort,—and my dear, my precious Jessie! I suppose her chief, unselfish thought that *she* was breaking up the plans and holding you and the others back from Florence and Venice and all the other pleasures of the trip! Bless her! She is *so* sweet and precious! May God keep you both, my sweet, sweet darling! This must *never* happen again. We must never have the sea between us again. We need each other too much. It is more than I can bear without actual unhappiness when everything goes prosperously and well; and when anything untoward happens it seems as if my heart would snap under the strain and tragedy of it. Ah, the anguish of not being at hand to help,—to help with love if with nothing else—and that, after all, is everything at a time like this, isn't it, my Eileen? Ah, darling *now*, if never before, I know how I love you, and how I love my darling Jessie. The threat of disease, the helplessness of separation uncover the heart's depths, and everything in the world seems dwarfed beside these that constitute the very life blood.

I hope that I have answered your cable for money in the best and most convenient way, and that the Blairs[1] have given the Crédit Lyonnais clear instructions how to send you at Florence the extra £100 which I directed them to send. But that will all be settled long before this letter reaches you.

Hard as the additional two weeks of separation will be to bear, it is most wisely decided on, my darling, and I shall be glad to have you escape the fatigue of Commencement. I dreaded it for you, coming, as it would have come, immediately after a long sea voyage. Madge can manage excellently well the '79 lunch and the Commencement reception. The Trustee lunch takes care of itself,—or, rather, is perfectly well taken care of by Holland.[2] You need not fear that you are neglecting anything, or that anything will be overlooked. Make your mind perfectly easy about us. We are *all perfectly* well. A letter received from Margaret to-day says her eyes are serving her excellently, as Nellie's are her. They have both of them been singularly fortunate in feeling no bad after effects whatever,—and Maggie seems equally well off. Are you not proud of us all? And what bricks the servants were,— Annie and Anna![3] They did not turn a hair. Maggie's sister, whom the college now employs, came in, to help in the kitchen, and everything went on as usual, without a hitch or a flutter. We really did not have any trouble or any anxiety even, except our anxiety about the effect the news of the measles would have on your spirits and enjoyment.

I have to be in New York to-night (my only remaining public dinner engagement),[4] but shall hurry back to-morrow morning to be near the base of news. I am not only well but strong, hearty, lusty. I pray God my darling is as well. I love you, oh, I love you, unspeakably. God bring us to each other's arms again and our precious Jessie to lovely health!

Your own   Woodrow

ALS (WC, NjP).
  1 Blair and Co., bankers, 24 Broad St., New York.
  2 John W. Holland, caterer.
  3 Annie M. McLaughlin and Anna Erickson.
  4 A news report of his address is printed at May 13, 1904.

From Henry Bedinger Cornwall

My dear Dr. Wilson,   [Princeton, N. J.]   May 12th 1904.

Your very kind letter was read with much pleasure, and I have been very glad to do what I could to further the plans for the new arrangement of the curriculum.

My only concern has been with reference to the Trustees and Alumni, and as the plan unfolds itself there is so much to commend it that I hope they will give it their support and approval, as I have no doubt they will. I can assure you that I heartily welcome the prospect of resuming supervision of quantitative laboratory work, and look for my reward in the stimulus of a higher plane of work than some of that to which the necessities of our present curriculum have seemed to confine me. This is equally true of the courses in Mineralogy, where I am expecting to resume work which I had to drop long ago.

Yours very sincerely,   H. B. Cornwall

ALS (WP, DLC).

From Harper and Brothers

Dear Sir: New York City May 12, 1904.

Your letter to our Mr. Harper regarding the sales of your "History of American People" has received great consideration. We are gratified to know that, in a way, our handling of your work has been satisfactory and that the advertising in the different literary periodicals in the country has been sufficient to have attracted your notice. It would seem that perhaps you may be in error regarding two things: one, the large sales of books reported by common rumor, the other, the organization which we have for sales of books by subscription.

There is no doubt that the report of sales of all kinds of books have been tremendously exaggerated by publishers and promoters for the purpose of influencing probable buyers. To such a degree did this exaggeration reach that, for the past several years we, in common with a few other large publishers, have consistently refrained from announcing to the public any figures regarding the sales of any books. We notice that more and more publishers are beginning to follow this example.

We believe that the sale of your great work has been as large as can be expected up to this time. The trade edition has done exceedingly well. The subscription edition sales have been as good as could be hoped for. As you probably know, we have recently prepared a new binding for the subscription edition with a view to re-interesting the people who handle subscription books and the buyers thereof. We have no doubt that we will sell many of this new subscription set.

For your information, we shall send, under another cover, circulars etc., which we are beginning to use. Besides our staff in the New York office, we have important branch offices employing scores and hundreds of agents whom we consider competent, in the following cities:

Boston, Mass.	Denver, Colo.	Memphis, Tenn.	Phila., Pa.
Butte, Mont.	San Francisco, Cal.	Milwaukee, Wisc.	Rochester, N. Y.
Chicago, Ill.	Detroit, Mich.	Washington, D. C.	St. Louis, Mo.
Cleveland, Ohio	Kansas City, Mo.	New Orleans, La.	St. Paul, Minn.

We think our subscription organization enables us to cover the country at least as well as any other house. This subscription department is a distinct department.

In view of all the circumstances, and the fact that we are about to start upon a campaign to sell the set in the new binding, we now ask you to withhold your judgment of our methods and ability to sell in this way, until a few months have elapsed, in which time we can have opportunity to report to you the result of our efforts.

With very kind regards, we are,

Very sincerely yours,   Harper & Brothers.

TLS (WP, DLC).

Notes for a Toast

Association of Bank Clerks   N. Y.   12 May, '04

Business and Politics

Their dangerously close association, especially in the case of banking, in the popular mind.

Their necessary association in connexion with the financial operations of governments.

The real foundation for the popular feeling:

The large operations of business do rest with a few, do maintain a close connexion with legislation. Modern business, conducted, as it is, on the grand scale, is a form of statesmanship.

The effects, the bitter effects, of change and disaster fall, not upon the masters of business, but upon the multitude whose view is narrowed to a livelihood, and to whom suffering comes direct and quickly.

Just business should, therefore, be based upon a study of affairs; and that study should breed a *spirit* of statesmanship, which is more honest and more serviceable than a spirit of pity (philanthropy) after the fact.

WWhw MS. (WP, DLC).

A News Report of an After-Dinner Speech

[May 13, 1904]

WOODROW WILSON ON BUSINESS AND POLITICS

Urges College Education at Bank Clerks' Dinner.
Country's Future Is Theirs

President Wilson of Princeton, as the principal speaker at the third annual banquet of the New York Chapter, American Institute of Bank Clerks, held last night at the Hotel St. Denis, responded to the toast, "Business and Politics," with an urgent plea for statesmanship in banking and business and a college education as a necessary preparation for the banker and business man of the future.

"I know we live in an age of technical education," said Prof. Wilson, "but I want to say to you frankly that ten years from now technical education will not mean all it means to-day. Already the world is so built that if I know only my own task I know practically nothing at all. It is becoming a necessity to-day, and will be more so in the future, for a man to know not only the ins and outs of his own profession, but also its relation to all other professions and pursuits if he is not to lose his way in this world of ours.

"You know that modern business is not what business used to be. Business no longer has local limitations or geographical boundaries. There is hardly any kind of business that does not send its tentacles to the end of the world; that is particularly true about banking. Because money is needed in every province of enterprise, banking touches every other profession."

Reverting to the subject of his toast President Wilson added:

"No majority ever rules anything. Majorities are manipulated. The concerting minority invariably determines what the majority shall do. You say you are self-governing. But did you ever choose the candidate you gave your vote? I think not, for candidates are selected by men whom you do not know and never met, and men whom perhaps you would not care to meet or know. And if you want to do any choosing yourself you must belong to that little coterie.

"Leaders in the world of finance manipulate the destinies of the Nation to-day. Sometimes they manipulate them to the detriment of the country, but that is always either through ignorance or corruption, and most frequently from ignorance. But on the other hand it is true that frequently the wise financier has come to the rescue of his country in the hour of its direst need.

"I do not predict or anticipate a revolution in this country, but if a revolution does come, social or economic, it will be because the leaders in finance have not been thoughtful enough or looked far enough ahead. I believe the majority of bankers in this country are men of the highest probity, but if temptation comes the banker should remember that he has in his hand the very nerves of the social organism, and that if he closes it cruelly the whole body politic will tremble and wince."

Printed in the *New York Times*, May 13, 1904; one editorial heading omitted.

To Winthrop More Daniels

My dear Daniels: Princeton, N. J.   13 May, 1904.

Allow me to thank you for your letter of May 11.[1] I think that on the whole I substantially agree with everything you say, and I am perfectly willing to accept your suggestion that I give the elements of jurisprudence instead of the elements of politics as the first term junior course. Will you not be kind enough to drop a line to Thompson[2] to that effect? The reasons you give are sufficiently conclusive to remove all doubt from my mind.

I think that an ultimate happy solution of the difficulty about the too specific character of Mr. Garfield's course on the government of dependencies would be to make that a pro-seminary course and give a lecture course in the elements of politics. That, however, does not affect next year when it would hardly be practicable for him to prepare a course of that nature. I will seek an early opportunity to have a conversation with him about it and see how the suggestion strikes him.[3]

With warm regard,

                 Cordially yours,   Woodrow Wilson

TLS (W. M. Daniels Coll., CtY).

   [1] It is missing.

   [2] Henry Dallas Thompson, Secretary of the Committee on Weekly Schedules and Examination Schedules.

   [3] The suggestion apparently did not strike Garfield favorably, for he taught his courses, Government of Dependencies and Government by Party in England and the United States, both of which were senior lecture courses, until he resigned in 1908 to accept the presidency of Williams College. However, proseminars were inaugurated in the autumn of 1905 in the Department of History, Politics, and Economics, with Garfield as departmental director.

A News Report of an Address to the Princeton Village Improvement Society

                                   [May 14, 1904]

ANNUAL MEETING

The annual meeting of the Princeton Village Improvement Society was held in the parlors of the Inn Tuesday evening. . . .

The evening's interesting proceedings closed with an address by President Woodrow Wilson, who said in part:

"Ladies and Gentlemen:—I think the most eloquent tribute which can be paid to this society is contained in the reports which have just been read.

"I was very much surprised to be asked to speak to this society to-night, for although I am a member of the society I fear no one would ever have known it from any work that I have done in connection with it. I do not think I am entitled therefore, on account of any activity in the work, to speak for the Village Improvement Society.

["]At the same time it is a matter of real gratification to be permitted to express in part the appreciation which the community feels for the work which the Society has done."

After suggesting the great difficulties with which the Society must have had to contend, he continued:—"I think the beauty of this sort of work shows itself most in a small community. This is due principally to the spirit with which the work is conducted. It is most interesting to see the bonds of sympathy grow strong in the community. This is by far the best thing about the labours of the Village Improvement Society. Their's is not a spirit of tolerance; it is not a spirit of condescension on the part of the more fortunate to those who are less fortunate. There is not in this place, so far as I can make out, any desire on the part of the better placed to patronize those less favoured. I believe the spirit which actuates this Society is that of down-right, honest, human sympathy; and also a distinct desire to draw the sympathies of the community together for the accomplishment of the common weal."

President Wilson here took occasion to say that very few people who had not served on the Borough council could appreciate the amount or the difficulty of the work necessary to carry on the borough government. Too many persons were apt to think that the Councilmen, as a rule, were negligent of their duties in relation to such work as the Society had undertaken, and were ignorant of the difficulties in the way. He then resumed:—"The members of this society in their association with the borough officials get a new sort of information; they get an interior knowledge of what the government of a Borough means, and they are surprised at the ready sympathy with which they are met. I am sure everybody has witnessed the splendid response of the Borough Council to the sort of aid and suggestion which the ladies of this Society have offered. The society consists in part of gentlemen, but it subsists on the ladies. Of course the men lend their willing countenance, but we must admit that of all the active work being done by far the greater part is being done by the ladies."

The speaker then commented on the work itself as follows:— "The work itself has been of a kind which is difficult to describe. . . .[1] I have caught glimpses of it, but that part which attracted my attention most was this: They have not wasted their time on ambitious plans or theories, but have accomplished in a practical way a very difficult undertaking. It is difficult to look in people's back yards, to peer over people's fences, to inquire about the condition of your neighbor's lots, and not be offensive. Yet, the proof of the success with which this has been done is proof also that it has been done with tact and has not caused offense. . . .

["]I suppose that the best thing the persons of comfortable circumstances do for those in less fortunate circumstances is to communicate to them new tastes. I take it that the difference between a cultivated person and an uncultivated person is more in the things he dislikes than what he needs and desires. One of the reasons why beauty, as for instance a touch of flowers, changes the morals, is that it changes the taste of the household. Order is more comfortable than disorder. The mere nurture of plants requires that sort of unselfish effort which, after all, is the best thing in anybody."

President Wilson then showed how the Society had encouraged this unselfish spirit, had implanted new thoughts, new ideas, and new tastes in the households of the less fortunate, and in so doing had brought into closer sympathy many persons of widely different circumstances, thus creating the genuine "community feeling." Continuing he said:—"I think I can say that this Society has created more community feeling in our town than it has ever had before. This is particularly gratifying, because of the fact that there is such an evident tendency to a too distinct separation of groups."

The population he said was made up of about half members of the University who did not feel the same sort of interest in the town which the non-University people felt,—and yet were as vitally concerned in its welfare. The Society had been the connecting link which bound together the entire community.

He concluded by saying: "I think it is a very fortunate circumstance that the ladies have this work in hand. I suppose the Board of Health would resent suggestions from men more than they dare resent suggestions from women. It is very awkward to refuse and much more pleasant to grant a lady's request or suggestion. So we are convinced that the work of the Society is being carried on by much the best part of the community—while it is in the hands of the ladies.

["]I think I have expressed in these few words what all think of the Village Improvement Society and I know I have succeeded in expressing my own opinion."

Printed in the *Princeton Press*, May 14, 1904.
    [1] This ellipsis and the following one are in the original text.

From Ellen Axson Wilson

My own darling,   Leone, Assissi, May 15 [1904]

Everything is going on with us just as well as it possibly could.
Jessie improves visibly and with a rapidity that exceeds our hopes.
She went out to *walk* a little today,—has been driving for four
days. It is really wonderful that she looks so little the worse for
such an attack, for it was very far from being a mild case before
the antitoxin was given. In fact it was the most dreadful looking
throat I ever saw, thickly covered all over with white, broken with
putrid spots. Now she is *well*,—practically. I shall have no hesi-
tancy in sending "charcos" for my next telegram—if nothing else
happens in the meantime! Of course she must be treated as if
made of glass for weeks yet,—indeed Dr Bull says she must be
extremely careful not to overexert herself all summer.

I am sorry, dearest, that you should have had the sensations
of having lost us,—of not knowing my address when you got my
long telegram. As a matter of fact the place is so small, that
there would be no trouble about a telegram finding me. But of
course you couldn't know that & I should have been more explicit.
But the telegram was already so *appallingly* long and expensive!

Mary left yesterday—in tears—for Florence where the Smiths
are still. How I miss her, especially to *talk* for me! It seemed quite
an ordeal to get off that cablegram myself yesterday and to regis-
ter my "steamer order" to Genoa. But I had no trouble after all.
The matter of the exchange is all arranged. I sail June 9 on the
"Konig Albert," stateroom 267. Oh how long it seems! And to
think that but for the change I should have been actually on the
way back to my own darling in ten more days. But it is weak to
dwell on that and I won't do it. Perhaps sometime or other I shall
be very glad indeed that Jessie *forced* me to say and see Florence,
—though I can't look at it in that light yet. And this waiting will
enable the dear child herself to see something of the pictures before we leave Florence if she continues to gain strength at her
present extraordinary pace.

I am getting very hungry for letters, for owing to the uncertainty of my movements, or rather to my plan for leaving here last
Friday, they have not been forwarded me. Your last received was
written on April 26, and this is May 15—my birthday! I hope that
you now have my letter written on the 1st telling the details of

Jessie's illness, for it will be reassuring to you. And of course you have *mine* of April 26—the day we left Rome. How strange it seems that I should have been rejoicing in it at getting Jessie safely away from Rome,—and she actually had diphtheria then. Your letter written the same day expresses your delight at getting "another 'charcos' "! The cable was sent that same fateful day.

Jessie is as happy as a lark now and we are having a very pleasant peaceful time together. I spend every morning from ten to twelve at San Francesco; we take a little drive every afternoon at five, and the rest of the day I read to her,—Anthony Trollope, "Pickwick" & Mark Twain's "Joan of Arc,"—all of which I had the Smiths send me from Florence for the purpose. We have a lovely balcony on our floor (the 1st floor fortunately,) and she is now getting much amusement from watching the life of the "piazza" below. My two hours a day at the church are a perfect delight to me. The two churches ("upper" and "lower,"—one built on top of the other,) are a museum in themselves of early Tuscan art,— both Florentine & Sienese. We see both schools at their best and it is most interesting to study carefully the differences. And not only is the *quality* of much of it *very* high, but the *quantity* is amazing, practically every portion of the wall-space of two huge cathedrals, with a dozen chapels to boot, are covered with frescoes. One could not exhaust the interest,—or the freshness of it in a month. I make some delightful new discovery every day; only yesterday I found a whole chapel that I had not seen before,— being usually locked—which was perfectly charming. The pictures were in the Sienese manner,—presumably by Simone Martini,—and while they havn't the vigorous and highly intellectual quality or the dramatic power of Giotto, there is mystical sentiment, great refinement both in feeling and execution, and exquisite purity and soft harmony of colour. Indeed as a whole,—a complete harmonious work of art[—]it is the most perfect thing in the two churches. Its windows too are among the best. You know one of the many delightful things about these wonderful churches is that they are *Gothic* cathedrals (completed in the 13th century) and as rich in early glorious stained glass as York or Chartres. Indeed the glass is much like that at York, much lighter in tone than the Chartres,—which is fortunate or one could not see the pictures. It is next to impossible, as it is, to see four of the most important;—Giottos four great allegorical paintings on the dome over the high altar. Three of them represent the vows of the Franciscan order[—]poverty, chastity, & obedience[—]and the fourth is the apotheosis of St Francis. Isn't it too bad that Jessie must miss all this; I am rather hoping that early Tuscan art is too much of an acquired taste to appeal to her! She is to go, by the doctor's consent, for a little while to the *upper* church which is perfectly warm & dry. The pictures there are not nearly so fine or worthy of study as those in the lower, but decoratively they are perfect, being delightfully soft and harmonious in colour and blending in perfectly with the beautiful windows. It is also rich in fine carving, both in wood and stone, and taking everything together is in *colour* the most beautiful Gothic interior I have seen anywhere. Colour as of course you know plays a very much more important part in Italian Gothic.

But it is time to dress for dinner & I havn't told you about our lovely drive (Mary's & mine) to Spello & Spolato to see the masterpieces of Pinturrichio & Lippo Lippi. Now it must wait till next time. We had a *beautiful* day. I wish you could see those delightful little rascally angels of Lippis. They were enchanting. One of them had his wings hitched on in front, which greatly puzzled us until I arrived at the obvious solution, which was that one of the others had been playing a trick on him. They were quite mischievous enough to do it. There were dozens of them all up to some game, while the solemn function of crowning the Virgin was proceeding.

Give our dearest love to the children, Madge, Stockton, & all friends. For yourself, sweetheart, "I would that my tongue could utter the thoughts that arise in me." I think of you all day & dream of you every night—& that at least is a comfort!

Your own   Eileen

ALS (WP, DLC).

To Ellen Axson Wilson

My own darling,   Princeton, N. J.   16 May, 1904

Now your own dear letter has come,—the one of May first, telling in detail your dreadful trouble in Assisi,—as well as the reassuring cablegrams, and I begin to see the whole thing as it happened. Surely, no letters could be more vivid, more compact of every quality that makes the things written of real, and yet at the same time makes the writer more real and vivid still, than these letters of yours. This particular letter nearly broke my heart,—because of my separation from the splendid, courageous, capable, ineffably sweet little lady who wrote it. Every line of it spoke courage, self-possession, resource, wisdom, capacity, and yet it throbbed so with the emotions and the deep anxieties excited by what had happened that it seemed to me like a cry for help coming from my own, the one person in the world whom I love absorbingly, entirely, and it seemed as if my heart must surely break. I cannot tell you how the dear letter intensified my admiration for you, my Eileen! You acted so exactly as you should have acted in every particular and with such wisdom and efficiency; and the account you give of it all is so clear, thorough, satisfying. It makes me feel as if I could not have known more (barring details) had I been there. How my heart goes out to you, my darling, my darling, at thought of the anguish and unspeakable anxiety you must have gone through. Now, I trust it is all over. In a few days you will be in the convent at Fiesole,—a place which the Hibbens describe with enthusiasm. Tram cars carry you to the heart of Florence,—and my darling will of course divert herself after all she has been through by seeing what she meant to see in Florence. Nothing will ever induce us to repeat this experiment, my sweet one, of putting the sea between us in such a way, and risking a heart-break at being separated by half the world when we need each other and love cannot stand the torment. The measles were a trifling thing, an amusing incident, compared with this distressing disaster to our precious Jessie; but even the measles made you unhappy,—and me unhappy because it was necessary that you should know of them,— and marred the thing I had planned for your happiness and refreshment.

Your letter of May 4, the second from Assisi, has come while I was writing, and has sent my spirits up a hundred per cent. with its cheerful tone and reassuring details of the dear, sweet patient. How good God has been to us, darling, in putting Mary Hoyt by your side and in surrounding you with such charming and helpful kindness, from doctor, land lady, all! I cannot express the profound thankfulness and joy I feel because of it.

A word of business. I cabled, through the Blairs, not £50, but £100, to be sent to you, by the Crédit Lyonnais, *to your Florence address*. I suppose the Smiths will see that it is forwarded to you at Assisi. I take it for granted, too, that you can pay Mary Hoyt out of it. If not, let me know and I will send the $100 as you direct. And *don't*, my love, worry about or apologize for expense. That is not to be thought of in a case like this,—and it hurts me a little that you should explain *to me*. I *love* to spend the money you need!

Bless you a thousand times for this sweet, sweet letter, with its precious flavour of yourself in all your sweetness and strength! We are all perfectly well (Margaret included) and literally everybody sends affectionate messages, full of genuine sympathy. With love that fills my heart to bursting

Your own   Woodrow

ALS (WC, NjP).

To Florence Stevens Hoyt

My dear Florence: Princeton, N. J.   18 May, 1904.

I am glad to say that you need give yourself no anxiety about the situation of the dear ones in Italy. The actual diptheria lasted only two or three days, and I have received a cable assuring me of the health of the whole party since the close of the period during which Mary or Ellen would have developed the disease if they had caught it. It has been a most distressing thing to have this happen to them so far away from home, but they have come out of it with extraordinary ease and I think I can assure you in all frankness that there is literally no longer any ground for anxiety.

Ellen wrote me that Mary did not wish you to know about it because she was afraid you would be anxious. I think that was probably a mistake, though a most amiable one, but at any rate no harm has been done now since the sky has cleared.

In haste,
Affectionately yours,   Woodrow Wilson

P.S. Their address until Saturday or Monday is Hotel Leone, Assisi, and after than [that] I feel quite sure it will be Pension Jennings-Riccioli, 37 Corso dei Tintori, Florence.

TLS (WP, DLC).

From Ellen Axson Wilson

My own darling,   Leone   Assisi, May 18 [1904]

We are actually about leaving Assisi! I am just up from lunch and in three hours we start for Perugia,—driving of course as it is almost as cheap and much pleasanter than the train. These Umbrian towns are all on such mountain tops, that one has a drive of ¾ hour from the station to the town in almost every case. So when they are close together it is much simpler to drive all

the way. It is 2¼ hours in this case and Jessie is going to enjoy
it immensely. We think a few days in Perugia will be a pleasant
change to us all;—and I shall be glad to get something to eat! I
have lived practically on bread & cheese & tea for the last three
weeks. The regulation dinner here is soup made of water &
cheese, boiled veal & greens, artichokes fried in oil, boiled kid
with lettuce, and a very alarming looking "sweet." But the bread
& butter & oranges were good so I have not suffered. She has
been very kind in getting necessary extras for Jessie,—fresh milk
from the campagna and, lately, chicken & rice. We cooked eggs
for her ourselves on an alcohol lamp, and got lovely meat jellies
& zwieback from Rome. So we have been very comfortable.

Mary writes that she has found me a very nice pension in
Florence. I cannot go to the "Jennings" because I must have one
with a "lift" and a garden for Jessie. It is the "Pension Trollope"—
will write more about it when I see it. Mary says Florence is much,
much the best of all, that she is simply beside herself over it. She
also says it is quite as cool as Assissi & begs me to hurry on as
soon as possible.

We drove Jessie to the door of the upper church yesterday and
let her go in and see it as we planned. I was so glad that she
should'nt miss it, especially the beautiful glass. Then in the afternoon we drove down to San Damiano, and peeped into the touchingly simple little church in which St Francis' ministry began &
which, with the tiny little convent adjoining was the home of
Santa Clara & her "poor Clares." One comes much closer there
to "the little poor man of Assisi" than in the magnificent San
Francesco built in his honour after his death. Yesterday we were
led through an absolutely plain little chapel,—no more than a
dimly-lighted stone cell,—in which the handful of monks & nov-
ices were holding vespers. The faces *all* expressed deep absorbed
feeling. It was the only Catholic service I have seen in Italy which
seemed to me solemn and moving,—not excepting the great celebration at St. Peters in honour of St. Gregory.

Nothing really has happened since I wrote last;—we have spent
three pleasant peaceful days & Jessie improves steadily. Nearly
everyone has drifted on, & for some days we have averaged only
four people at table. A young Cambridge (Eng.) man & myself
are the constant elements. He is very nice and gentlemanly; we
have exactly the same tastes in literature and art and are quite
chummy.

We both got a budget of letters which made us *very* happy.
Jessie had two from Margaret and one from Jessie. The first one

Nellie wrote seems to be lost, much to Jessies distress. She is very much shocked at Margarets "goings on,"—dinners, receptions, &c!

I was of course a good deal distressed to find that the crisis at home had been so much more acute than you in your kindness had let me know! It was not only Maggie's illness, but that the children were ill so much longer than I supposed;—Nellie a month and Margaret three weeks, she says! I did not know measles ever lasted so long. And now that we are all "out of the wood," it is hard not to be a little blue at the pecuniary side of it; the *frightful* expenses of this spring—trained nurse here & trained nurse there by the month, &c, *&c,* &c! The sum total of *my* doctors bills was $230.00! I am leaving here with $160.00 of the $1000.00. And of course I am taking the nurse with me, as I am told Jessie must not be left alone for a long time to come. But it doesn't help to brood over it! What *can* be the explanation of your cable to Rome failing to reach me! I left the "Rinaldi" for Assisi on the 26th, and you seem to have cabled on the 25th. It is too bad! The one from Florence was forwarded me by the Smiths. Your budget of news in this letter is *very* interesting. I had no idea Mr. Little was ill. Alas! you don't speak of his leaving anything more to Princeton; I fear that in this case "no news is bad news."[1] And so we *are* to have Bob Garrett! I think Dr. McEwen would be a good clerical trustee. He has shown great energy and executive ability in Pittsburg. It would be like having another business man,—a clergyman without the clerical disabilities. Then he is so sane, and understands men,—and would be *so* loyal to you.

I had no idea Mrs. Marquand was coming abroad; she would much better stay safely at home with those children! But other people don't seem to be pursued by such an unrelenting fate as we! How good it was to get these two dear letters! but the part about the sailing of the Princess Irene naturally broke my heart,—almost. Oh, my love, my love! I *want you*! You *can't* want me so much! I love you unspeakably,   Your own   Eileen.

ALS (WC, NjP).
[1] Her fear was well founded. Henry Stafford Little died intestate.

To Charles Williston McAlpin

My dear Mr. McAlpin: Princeton, N. J.   18 May, 1904.

I sincerely hope that you have returned in good shape, and feeling like yourself again. I shall hope to see you very soon.

I write to say that in view of the radical restatements which will be necessary in view of the new course of study, I have asked a sub-committee on the Course of Study, consisting of Professor West, Professor Magie, Professor Thompson, and Professor Neher, to act as a Committee on the Catalogue and prepare for your office all the statements of the courses and all matter pertinent thereto in the form in which it should be printed.

I know that this is in direct line with your own wishes and that it will in the long run save you a great deal of trouble and work.

Always,

Cordially and sincerely yours,   Woodrow Wilson

TLS (McAlpin File, UA, NjP).

To Ellen Axson Wilson

My precious darling,   Princeton, N. J.   19 May, 1904

No further news has come to us from over sea since my last letter was written, but that *must* be a good sign. I will take it as such and think all comforting things about my dear ones: that dear Jessie has long since got out for her drives and is getting her strength back fast in that salubrious mountain town; that my darling,—who grows more dear, more *terribly* dear, to me every day of my life,—is revelling in the Giottos; and that on Saturday, or Monday at the latest, your faces will be set towards Fiesole and the quiet convent, whence you can sally forth every day for a few hours to take possession of the beauties you were to make your own in Florence. It is sweet to think of peace after the storm, and of pleasure coming to you again,—the pleasure I covet for you with a sort of eager averice,—the pleasure I would sacrifice anything of my own to get for you in overwhelming measure!

Dear Nellie is not to miss the Ben Greet players, after all! Isn't that nice? They are to play to-morrow again, twice, on our lawn. The stage is up, just where it was last year. In the afternoon it is to be *Much Ado About Nothing* and in the evening *A Midsummer Night's Dream*. They mean to repeat *As You Like It* the next (Saturday) night; but I shall not go, I think. I would rather keep the impression of last year. Mr. and Mrs. Kennedy[1] (Miss Matthison) are staying with the Harpers, as usual. This being a slack season (as it seems) with them,—long intervals between engagements,—the company came last evening (Wednesday), and are very busy rehearsing. This evening I had the pleasure,—and it was a most genuine pleasure,—of taking dinner with the Harpers to meet the Kennedys and Mr. Greet. No one else was there, and so I saw them all at close range, and in a sort of intimate circle. They are like old friends with the Harpers now, and on that intimate and natural footing were wholly delightful. *She* is perfectly charming. I felt at once that I could be close friends with her. Mrs. Harper says "she rings true" to every test of fine womanhood, and certainly her charm is most penetrating. *Off* the stage, as on it, she is "natural, simple, affecting," and impresses you as a woman whose affections are noble, whose tastes are pure and elevated. I fear no *American* actress could be so natural and to one's taste off the stage. But I wont get again on my hobby, English simplicity!

Do not give yourself the least concern about the Commencement functions. Madge is making ready for them with a great deal of good sense and quiet capacity,—reminding me a little of your own dear self. After all, it's a most capable family! The '79 lunch on Saturday, the Trustees' lunch on Monday, and the Reception on Tuesday will go off all right and without worry to me, that is already evident,—so don't give them a thought.

What will they *not* lack of charm, though, in lacking you, my darling, my incomparable, noble little wife! Your grace and beauty and sweet, vivid interest in everybody and everything make you the life and centre of every function of that kind, and nobody can take your place even for the nonce,—and *I*,—well I am *more* than half reduced. I have nothing of my own that can take the place of what is lacking because you are away, and I get none of the usual *reflection* of grace and charm I sometimes take from you. Ah, well! I shall have you again some day, God willing; and shall again be able to pour into your ears the love, the unspeakable love of   Your own   Woodrow

All are perfectly well,—and all unite in unbounded love to all.

ALS (WC, NjP).
¹ Charles Rann Kennedy, dramatist, and his wife, Edith Wynne Matthison Kennedy, prominent actress.

To Isaac Henry Lionberger

My dear Mr. Lionberger: Princeton, N. J.   20 May, 1904.

I know that you will not deem me impertinent if I venture to call your attention to the present financial needs of the University. Unpalatable as it is, it is my plain duty to do so; and I feel confident that I can count upon your interest and your careful consideration of the matter I lay before you.

The University will, without increase of endowment, face this year, for the first time, a serious deficit; not because she has lost funds or suffered from any mismanagement, but simply because her growth has outrun her resources,—no undergraduate paying more than one third what it costs to give him what is offered in the catalogue, and every addition to the grounds or buildings meaning additional outlays for maintenance. The deficit will be from $6,000 to $10,000, and will undoubtedly recur from year to year unless provided for in some permanent way.

The Trustees have, therefore, determined to capitalize it by seeking subscriptions which will aggregate $100,000 a year for three years. This will enable them to spend $10,000 and invest $90,000 a year, securing an endowment by the end of the three years of $270,000, which will take care of the deficit. They have chosen the period of three years because that period seems likely to carry us beyond the present financial depression to a time when we may once more look for large gifts and a development by leaps and bounds.

They look to the alumni for this subscription because they seem the natural partisans and defenders of the University in every time of emergency. Seventy-five thousand dollars of the yearly $100,000 has already been subscribed, thirteen men pledging $5,000 apiece, others from $1,000 to $2,000 each, and almost all of these have promised to continue subscribers in the same amounts for the three years. The list already includes many names not on the usual subscription lists on such occasions, and we are confident that, when completed, it will show at any rate part of the true range and extent of the Umiversity's [University's] loyal clientage. The subscriptions will not be called in until the $100,000 fund is made up entire, at least for the first year, and there are no guarantors.

May I ask that, if possible, you will allow me to add your name to the list of subscribers, for as large a sum as you can possibly spare? We call this our emergency fund, because the emergency is real; and we feel that we must complete the subscription by the 1 July, the end of our fiscal year.

Pray pardon me if I have taken a liberty. The University has reached one of the most interesting stages of her development: the expectation of the whole country is that she will do something distinguished; and we dare not hold her back or hamper her.

With much regard,

Sincerely yours,   Woodrow Wilson[1]

TLS (President's Papers Coll., MoSHi).

[1] As the shorthand draft of WW to W. C. Procter, May 20, 1904 (WP, DLC), reveals, Wilson sent similar letters to William C. Procter, Charles P. Richardson, Samuel M. Shoemaker, Oliver Harriman, Jr., Lucius A. Lewis, and Frederick A. C. Perrine.

From Simon John McPherson

My dear Dr. Wilson: Lawrenceville, New Jersey   May 20, 1904

I am extremely sorry that the meeting of the Curriculum Committee is set for Saturday, May 28th, as it may be necessary for me to be away with the members of the school on that day. Would it be possible to put it on some other day than Wednesday or Saturday?[1]

I am extremely anxious to be present at this meeting in order to have the new course of study explained.[2] Of course I noted with great regret that history has been stricken out as an entrance requirement. I strongly object to that for three reasons: 1. It lowers the standard of Princeton in that department, setting it below that of almost every higher institution east of the Allegheny mountains. 2. It throws the boys in Lawrenceville, who are preparing for Princeton, out of line with those preparing for the dozen other colleges that receive boys from here. 3. It appears to me that Princeton, while she has strong men in the history department, has upon the whole an extremely weak course in that subject. Men in Princeton have none too great an opportunity, to say the least, to study history. Moreover, I am of the opinion that those who get no taste for history before entering college are far less likely to acquire a taste for it afterwards.

I was sorry, also, to observe that chemistry was omitted from the entrance requirements, and physics only was left as a science entrance requirement. Our experience here is that physics is decidedly harder than chemistry; indeed it is too hard for some of the boys who are immature. Chemistry has been found to be easier. If you will look at the results of the entrance examinations for physics last year you will see how few were admitted from any school. That also puts us out of line with other colleges.

There are certain other points that I should like to hear explained or discussed in the report. One in particular interests me, and that is the question of equivalency in the substitutes for Greek. I do not think that the substitutes represent an equal amount of work required for preparation in Greek. In that, however, I am very likely to be mistaken.[3]

Very sincerely yours,   S. J. McPherson.

TLS (WP, DLC).

[1] As WW to EAW, May 23, 1904, discloses, the Curriculum Committee did meet on May 28.

[2] McPherson was referring to a printed copy of the report of the Committee on the Course of Study, as amended and approved by the University Faculty and dated April 26, 1904.

[3] The report of the Curriculum Committee to the Board of Trustees printed at June 13, 1904, does not reveal whether McPherson's protests were discussed when that committee met. However, McPherson renewed his suggestions with some vehemence when the Board of Trustees met on June 13 (see Jenny D. Hibben to WW, June 28, 1904). The Board voted to add ancient history, or English history, or American history and civil government to the entrance requirements for A.B., B.S., and Litt.B. degrees and to permit students desiring entrance to the B.S. and Litt.B. programs to offer chemistry *or* physics as one of their entrance requirements. Wilson made these changes on his printed copy of the report of the Committee on the Course of Study (Trustees' Papers, UA, NjP), and they were included in the report that was spread on the minutes of the Board of June 13, 1904.

To Ellen Axson Wilson

My own darling,   Princeton, N. J.   23 May, 1904

Your letter of the 7th, belated, did not come till to-day, but, ah, it was worth while to wait for such a refreshing draught of good news and sweet comfort of love. Your letters are *wonderful*, my darling! Saturday (this is Monday) brought your cable from Florence with the blessed word "Charcos" again,[1]—meaning that the journey you had dreaded for Jessie is over and that you are happily settled for a stay of two weeks and more in one of the places you had most eagerly looked forward to visiting; the dear patient not hurt by the journey, and all well. So that I can read these dear letters with their details of all the earlier stages of the recovery with a mind already full of the happy issue. And, with a mind at ease, these wonderful letters seem to me the sweetest, the most moving ever written. My heart burns with love as I read them: a love for my darling Jessie more tender, more deep, more full of admiration and of joy that we should have so lovely a daughter than I know how to say (she must be wholly compounded of you!); and a love for my Eileen that seems the very breath of my life, so intimately does it reveal to me what she means to me. Dr. Bull is *right*, my pet,—you *did* save your sweet child's life "in acting immediately in right time and on the right way,"—you are the most wonderful combination of sweetness and strength, charm and capacity I ever knew of, and I shall not breathe right until I have you clasped safe in my arms again.

I cannot *think* anything but love, apparently, when I write to you these days,—and it is not necessary that I should. There is nothing to tell of. Nothing happens to us. We are well and happy, Margaret included; and that is all. The plays came off most successfully, Nell saw them all (they repeated *As You Like It* on Saturday) and was happy. She looks and is most vigorous. The routine of the close of the year is on us: to-morrow committee meetings of the Board in New York, and on Saturday a meeting of the Committee on the Curriculum to hear my exposition of the new course of study.[2]

I am at work on my baccalauriate, and my! it does go hard; but I shall work out *some* sort of homily

Our preacher on Sunday was Dr. Cecil of Richmond,[3] a most attractive gentleman, a genuine Southerner, and an excellent preacher, of the old fashioned type no longer, I fear, very much appreciated in this latitude. He came Saturday *morning*, but took care of himself and gave us no trouble. Saturday afternoon, *Jessie* will be interested to learn, we beat Pennsylvania 7-4, with ease and great satisfaction!

This being my budget of news, easily exhausted, may I not come back to the only thing I can really think about,—my love and admiration for you. I have only one complaint against you,—your repeated explanations of the *expense* you have been put to, and your words of half apology *as if I would care*. Why, darling, the money has come in from the *History*: there is plenty; and I send it to you with joy! Don't be a goose! What difference does *that* part of it make. Don't I know that you manage much better than I could? Don't I know that the sweetest thing in the world is to be *able* to send you what you want? It is a positive luxury to have *some* way in which I can help a little,—something to do besides using *words* merely to express my love and devotion to you. You are all the world to me; it is inexpressibly sweet that you, the loveliest woman in the world and the finest, should be mine, and that I should be, for my salvation,

Your own   Woodrow

All send love to all

ALS (WC, NjP).
   [1] This cablegram is missing.
   [2] There is a WWhw outline of his "exposition," dated May 28, 1904, in WWP, UA, NjP.
   [3] The Rev. Dr. Russell Cecil, pastor of the Second Presbyterian Church of Richmond, Va.

Two Letters from Ellen Axson Wilson

My own darling,   Florence   May 23, 1903 [1904]

Here we are safe in Florence, four whole days before the earliest time we had thought of coming! Perugia was not a success from the convalescent point of view. It was an excellent modern hotel, yet it was harder to get the special things we needed for Jessie than in the little inn at Assissi. Then there was no garden; and the weather was very dry; there were great clouds of dust constantly in the air so that there was no comfort in taking her either to drive or to walk. So as the sister thought there was no doubt about her being strong enough for the journey we left Perugia after one day and reached here Friday afternoon. Jessie did not seem tired *at all*. She told the Smiths that she was *"perfectly* well only she couldn't get anyone to believe it"! As for me instead of being happy and excited at finally reaching Florence I was unreasonable enough to be *miserable* because I had put off our sailing *two* weeks when *one* would have sufficed, and to get in concequence a perfectly desperate attack of homesickness! I spent my time on the journey planning to open the whole matter anew with Jessie & the steamship company, and get the passage changed to June 2. But I am afraid now I haven't the courage to begin all over again with the company,—and make myself rather absurd I suppose. If it were only unsettled,—if I had a free hand— how speedily it would be decided for June 2! I believe Mary Hoyt thinks I am crazy, because finally when we were alone together I broke down and wept bitterly,—at "having to stay in Florence two weeks" she says! She is thankful she is not married or in love if it makes people so perfectly ridiculous!

Jessie is so very *very* well that there is evidently no further need of a nurse; the sister is *quite* sure of it herself, so she is to go back to Rome tomorrow. I am delighted to be able to save any further expense on that score. Mary will come to us instead and stay until Thursday week. Of course, I shall insist on paying the difference in cost to her,—which in this case is 5½ fr. a day (!) for she, alas! is staying at a cheap "girls home" for 3½ francs a day & I had to come to a 9 fr. place in order to get the necessary "lift" & garden for Jessie. Mary wanted,—begged *hard*,—to stay with me until the end & put us on the steamer at Genoa, (She goes anyhow from here to Genoa.) but of course I wouldn't hear to that. As it is,—leaving here on the 2nd—she has but two weeks for the Italian lakes & Switzerland, for she must be in Holland on the 16th when her ticket expires. *Isn't* she sweet and unselfish? I can never forget her goodness to me through all this time.

I have had hard luck getting a letter written & I must cut this rather short or it may miss the mid-week steamer. I went to San Marco with Mary yesterday morning, meaning of course to write my letter just after lunch. But a Miss Young from Danville Ky.[1] sent up her card just as I came up stairs and made me a *long* visit. Then the Smiths came & spent the rest of the afternoon. And I have yet to find the pension where one can write at night; we are very swell here with our "electric light,"—one tiny bulb right up in the ceiling; more impossible than candles to read or write by. I am writing this now at break-neck speed for I wanted to have an Eng. doctor look Jessie over, give a tonic if necessary, & advise me about a number of points,—& I had to take her before writing so as to catch him in his office hours. He was a Dr. Gerry, & proved *very* nice and satisfactory. He says he knows this place well,—comes here constantly,—& from the point of health it is *everything* that could be desired, and that it will not be too late or too hot for her in Florence up to June 9th—I was suffering from misgivings on that point. He also says it won't do her the least harm to go sight-seeing for an hour or so a day. And he found her throat in a *perfectly* healthy condition. So I feel very cheerful and reassured about her. The place is really charming,— it has not only its own garden, but is surrounded by other *beautiful* ones, and is only five minutes walk to the loveliest & largest park I ever saw, stretching along the banks of the Arno. The food too is *delicious*,—really the very best *American* cooking. It is a famous old place—this "Villa Trollope."

The Smiths left early this morning for Venice! They seem to have had a glorious two weeks here; in fact Lucy was so extremely effervescent and excited that she was rather overpowering to poor me who am naturally in a slightly subdued frame of mind. It was a relief to have them go. Marguerite & her mother are also here & will stay on for some time "to be with" me. But I *must* stop, —will write again almost immediately & tell you what we are seeing & doing. Oh, I must mention one thing: this is the anniversary of the burning of Savonarola; there is a bronze plate on the spot in the piazza, & on this day the Signoria go and decorate it elaborately with flowers; (though not in sack-cloth & ashes as they should.) Then the citizens & strangers follow suit. We went with *our* offerings and found it a very interesting scene. Of course we saw his cells yesterday at San Marco. I have never found any place more solemn & moving than those cells; and indeed the whole convent, with the lovely faded old pictures by Fra Angelico —one in each cell. Think of each monk having a heavenly vision like that all to himself!

With love to all my dear ones, and love *unspeakable* for my own darling from his devoted little wife,   Eileen.

ALS (WP, DLC).

1 Either Eugenia or Sara Lee Young, unmarried daughters of the Rev. Dr. John Clarke Young, President of Centre College, 1830-57. They were traveling in Italy at this time with their sister, Zillah Young (Mrs. Robert P.) Jacobs.

My own darling,   Villa Trollope   May 25, 1903 [1904]

This is our fourth day in Florence; we are well settled and having a "beautiful time" in spite of the sad fact that we should have been on our way to Genoa today. Jessie is *very* well and happy. She has been driving about the city and seen the *outside* of everything; we havnt begun yet to take her really sight-seeing. Yesterday we had a perfectly glorious drive to San Miniato, a beautiful old church on a high hill just beyond the city. The church is a noble & interesting old basilica with wonderful sculptures and mosaics in the interior, but the chief thing is the *drive* itself, between enchanting gardens & villas, and the view,—above all the view! take it all in all the most glorious, the most *perfect* I have ever seen. It would be impossible to exaggerate the beauty of the city as it lies below one with its Duomo "like a dim red crown," the grand tower of the Palazzo Vecchio,—"noblest symbol of liberty the world has ever seen," Giotto's campinile, lovely beyond *all* words, and all its lesser towers and domes and palaces. Then there is the shining Arno with its lovely valley, the ivy-covered wall of Michel-Angelo, the dark slope of Mount Morello, the cypress-crowned height of Fiesole, and beyond all the mountains,—ridge beyond ridge, peak above peak of ever fainter purple. Of course there are other rivers & valleys and mountains as lovely, but surely no where else in our modern world is there such another city in such a setting! It realizes ones highest dream of what nature and art may do to aid each other.

I have been to three of the great galleries,—four counting San Marco—the Ufizzi, the Pitti and the Bella Arti,—but as for really seeing any of them yet!—they are simply inexhaustible! I am left gasping, overwhelmed,—almost dismayed at the feast spread before me. Everywhere I turn there is some masterpiece that I have longed to see all my life, and I rush from one to another and am so overcome with rapture and excitement that I end by holding my head with both hands in a sort of despair. This morning it was the "Pitti"—the best I have seen as a *whole*,—it is a much smaller collection than the Ufizzi and there is less winnowing of chaff to be done as one goes along. (Though in *all* of them there is surprisingly little that is not good,—being in that respect a great contrast to the Roman galleries.) The Pitti palace itself is a nobly beautiful building, so that the pictures have there an especially fine setting. The only disappointment one has is that many pictures at the Ufizzi and a few at the Pitti have been more or less ruined by "restorations." Of course I *knew* that but hadn't quite *realized* it, I suppose;—at any rate I was not prepared to find in the case of some of the "masterpieces" such hot disagreeable colour laid on by those imbeciles. Perhaps I am a little spoiled by my Umbrian experience;—by dwelling so long and lovingly on the soft, dusky or tender tones of the old frescoes at Assisi, Spoleto, Spello. But after all the spoiled one[s] are the exception. How I wish you could see the great Giorgione![1] It is as lovely in tone & colour as in every other respect. I mean of course the three men with the "monk at the clavichord" that you like so much. It is *perfectly* beautiful; I could scarcely tear myself from it. How I should like to copy it! It seems rather bold to speak of even copying such a wonder but I *could* do it,—for I *feel* the expression of that face down to the bottom of my soul.

But I must stop my ravings, for we are to take the other chief drive this afternoon,—to the Certosa,—& must make a rather early start. We are having glorious weather for such purposes,—a thunderstorm Monday afternoon cooled the air & laid the dust and now it is just right, for Americans at least. The English complain—unreasonably—of the heat. There is a strong & cool breeze all the time, and not a particle of heaviness in the air. Dear Jessie has been reading "The Cardinal's Snuff-box,"[2] a charming little book the scene of which is laid in Italy, and she seems to think she has had as nice a morning as we had. I can't help feeling "bad" at leaving her alone and going off to enjoy myself, but I know she is having a better time than with the sister who is a perfect angel but *would* talk all the time about her former "cases," —like all other nurses. Just now Jessie has a visitor, a nice little English girl who, oddly enough, is also named "Jessie" and is only one month older than our Jessie. She and her Aunt sit opposite us at the table. They are very nice people; her father is a barrister & a "F.R.S," and they live at Chester in one of those villas beyond the town overlooking the Dee. Her older sister is named Marjory, & is a graduate of an Oxford college.

But I *must* stop abruptly. Give my dear, dear love to all. I am perfectly well and very happy, and I love you, *love* you, *love* you; I am with you in spirit always, dearest, day & night,—I am in every heart-throb   Your own   Eileen.

ALS (WC, NjP).
[1] "The Concert," now generally attributed to Giorgione's disciple, Titian, who was strongly influenced by him.
[2] Henry Harland, *The Cardinal's Snuff Box* (London and New York, 1900).

To Ellen Axson Wilson

My own, precious darling,   Princeton, N. J.   27 May, 1904

To write this last letter that can reach you before you sail seems like saying utter good-bye to you for two, nay, for four long weeks,—till the 22 of June, the day the König Albert is expected to arrive in New York! Alas! it seems to give an additional stab to my heart to think of it. Fortunately your letters will be coming all the while,—those incomparable letters which seem to speak in the very tones of your own dear voice and to make me part of what you are doing and experiencing,—and *you* will be coming nearer and nearer to me (how my heart beats to think of it!); but somehow the correspondence does not seem complete unless I am taking my part in it. I feel so near to you when I am trying to put my heart into words which you are to see and keep by you. It is almost like nestling close to you as I am so fond of doing when work lifts a little and I have a little space of freedom in which to be wholly happy. But these letters will be coming to you till the last, till you sail, and you will know by cable that we are well the very day you embark, and I can think of *that*, of these words, meant to be a pure pouring out of my heart's life to my darling, following you and making you *conscious* of me. I want them to make you realize every moment of your journey how my thoughts hover about you, night and day, with a tenderness, a pride, a joy, and yet a longing which I have spent twenty years in the vain attempt to put into words and which, God willing, I shall spend all my life trying to put into acts of love and devotion.

The last letter from you, darling, was the one written on your birth-day. It came yesterday; I found it waiting for me when I came back from Hartford, where I spent Wednesday attending the inauguration of Dr. Mackenzie[1] (our Muskoka friend who preached for us in February, you remember), and where I was rewarded with as fine, sincere, constructive an address as I ever had the good fortune to hear,—delightful in form as well as in matter.[2] Last night I took dinner at the Armour's, with an odd party,—the Huttons, Mr. and Mrs. Jesse Carter, and Mr. [Stephen Squires] Palmer. To-morrow, Saturday, night Madge and I dine at the Owens[3] to meet the Legh Reids.[4] I am looking forward to that with a great deal of pleasure. I shall enjoy talking to Mrs. Reid and I *know* that the topic of conversation will be *you*,—my favourite topic!

We are all *perfectly* well. Nell is catching up with her work in school (missed because of the measles) without distress or over-strain; all good news comes from dear Margaret; and everything is serene. Your discipline of anxiety is over, and you can loll on the decks with all sweet thoughts,—thinking (could there be anything sweeter to think of?) of the joy you are taking to those you love best. *Is* is [it] not sweet, my darling, to think of the happiness you have given, and give every day of your life? You are all the world to me; love follows you everywhere you go,—the love of every one who gets so much as a glimpse of the loveliness that is in both your heart and your mind; and you carry a sort of peace and gladness which it would be impossible to describe into every life you enter,—the atmosphere of your own nature is so pure and so stimulates all that is best and most truly pleasurable in others. And you are coming back to my arms, and we shall be happier than ever,—separation over, vacation come with all its sweet leisure. Ah, Eileen, Eileen, my darling, how *can* I wait?

Unbounded love to *precious* Jessie, our treasure. All love you both and overwhelm you with messages, and I am

Your own   Woodrow

ALS (WC, NjP).
    [1] The Rev. Dr. William Douglas Mackenzie was inaugurated as President of the Hartford Theological Seminary on May 25, 1904.
    [2] "Is a Constructive Theology Possible?," printed in *Services at the Inauguration of William Douglas Mackenzie, D.D. as President of The Hartford Theological Seminary* . . . (Hartford, Conn., 1904), pp. 26-46.
    [3] Elizabeth Sheldon Owen, widow of Henry James Owen and sister of Wilson's classmate, Edward W. Sheldon. Mrs. Owen lived at 10 Mercer St. with her daughter, Isabella Sheldon Owen.
    [4] Their old friends, the Legh Wilber Reids. At this time, Reid was Associate Professor of Mathematics at Haverford College.

Two Letters from Ellen Axson Wilson

My own darling,   Florence   May 29, Sunday [1904]

At last Jessie & I have been made happy by a budget of letters, —long hoped for, long delayed. It seems to us that the Crédit

Lyonnais are very remiss in attending to such matters. We expected to find them when we reached Florence at French and Lemin's;[1] but there was nothing there. I wrote at once to Paris and only yesterday they arrived, yours of the 6th, 10th & 12th, one from Mrs. Hibben, & three for Jessie. Your dear, *dear* one of the 16th sent directly to Florence made splendid time & reached me on *Friday*,—also Nellie's to Jessie. Oh, *how* glad I was to get them!—how your sweet tender words of sympathy and love seemed to bridge the gulf between us and make me feel your dear heart beating as it were against my own! I walked as on air for forty-eight hours! In fact I would be doing so still but that this little difficulty about the cabled money has brought me with a bump down to the hard earth. I am chiefly annoyed at having to trouble you further about it, my darling. The letter from the Crédit Lyonnais disclaiming all knowledge of it came just before lunch & Mary has gone, (on her way to the Boboli gardens,) to send you a cable about it.[2] How I hate to do it! but I don't know what else to do. We went Sat., a week ago yesterday, to French & Lemin expecting to find the money there,—they knew nothing about it but said it was probably at the Bank of Italy. As soon as possible,—that is on Monday, we went there,—place closed,—festa. Went again Tuesday,—no money,—they sent us, in vain, to two other banks. I wrote the same day fully to the Crédit Lyonnais, & as I said received the enclosed answer this morning.[3] Yesterday afternoon, being tired of waiting for a letter, I telegraphed them, but had no answer;—the telegram probably reaching them after office hours. I cannot imagine what is wrong unless indeed some confusion arose from the fact that I wrote them that you had sent 50 pounds when the real sum was 100. But of course a detail like that ought not to matter when I mentioned Blair, &c. &c. giving all the names dates &c. But enough of this—of course it will all come right in a day or so, and I am not suffering for the money: I can still borrow Mary's hundred if necessary, and I have seventy odd of my own though my hotel bill here is unpaid from the first. I had hoped by saying in my long cable that my money would suffice until I reached Florence to save you the expense of *cabling* the remittance,—but alas! I did not tell you *when* I would reach Florence! It is difficult to be very explicit in a cablegram.

Jessie really seems as well and almost as strong as ever; though of course it is difficult to judge about the strength, we are so very careful of her. She looks perfectly lovely, and enjoys everything

---

[1] French, Lemon & Co., Bankers, Via Tornabuoni 2, Florence.
[2] This cablegram is missing.   [3] Her enclosure is also missing.

extremely: we took since I last wrote the drive to the "Certosa,"—another high hill just out of the city with another beautiful view, —though not *so* beautiful as San Miniato. The Certosa itself is a very interesting ancient Carthusian monastery, with good old frescoes, tombs by Donatello, &c. &c. Jessie of course went there; and also Thursday aft. to the Boboli gardens perhaps the largest and most wonderful of all the *famous* "Italian gardens." (Tell Nellie she will find pictures of it in one of last winters "Century's") It is connected with the "Pitti Palace" once the home of the Medici, now the home of the famous "collection" and of the king when he visits Florence. I greatly regret to say that he is just about to visit it,—will arrive on June 2nd. It grows to be a real grievance with me that these crowned heads insist upon following me about so! In Southern Italy it was the German Emperor and Queen of Holland, in Rome it was Loubet & now it is the King of Italy,—and always they bring such crowds and confusion,—and raise the price of cabs!

But besides taking drives Jessie is now beginning to do a little sight-seeing. We all went to the Bargello Friday morning, where we saw sculpture—Michel Angelos, Donatellos, Luca della Robbias, &c &c. the first grandly beautiful, the others full either of vivid life and charm of expression or of exquisite sweetness. There was one little alto-relievo of a dead saint by Beneditto da Rovezzano, which I had never seen reproduced in any form and which is wonderful and beautiful beyond description. It had all the spirituality of the acetic type without any loss of beauty,—any painful meagerness,—the saint is still a man. But oh! the expression,—the *glorified peace*!—"My peace I give unto you,—not as the world giveth, give I unto you." The grand old building we found quite as beautiful and interesting as any of its contents. Jessie was perfectly enchanted with it; and indeed it does look as if it came out of a fairy tale. It absolutely satisfies one['s] dream of a medieval castle-palace; with its deep embrasured windows, the noble old ceilings, the stone walls hung with priceless tapestries and above all the wonderful court with its loggias & staircase, and traceried windows and carven work. And thoughts of the wonderful history of which it has been the centre adds the last charm to it.

Yesterday morning we went with Jessie to see the Michel Angelo's at the Medeci Chapel, Peruginos masterpiece at an old convent, and Bonozzo Gozzoli's masterpiece in the Riccardi palace. We had a beautiful morning,—just one (or two) superlatively fine things in each place and plenty of time to sit and study them quietly,—without fatigue. Our plan is to take Jessie out for a time in the morning[,] then come home to rest & read to her until four. Then Mary & I go out to "do" a church or two, (they are closed from 12 to 4.) at six we are back & starting with Jessie for her little drive.

Words cannot express how full and rich the week has been, or what a wealth of beautiful memories it has given me for the rest of my life. There is no other place to *compare* with Florence— from the artists standpoint—not even Rome. I need not say that I am enjoying it all *intensely* in spite of the drawback which I will not mention again,—being heartily ashamed of saying so much about it last Sunday! That melancholy letter was enough to give you the blues, and I beg your pardon for sending it. And yet after all when I talk of being "homesick" you know right well that what I really mean is that I am beside myself with longing for *you*,—that "home" simply means *your* arms,—and *that* need not make you *very* unhappy after all! Do you think so? I am perfectly well and strong. I hate to make myself ridiculous yet I must— unselfishly,—repeat an absurd speech of my opposite neighbours at table because it will furnish you such convincing proof that I am not worn out by what I have been through. They say I am the very image of Titians "Flora," & express great surprise that no one ever told me so before! I am about as much like Giottos tower, but that even a pair of idiots could compare me to that radiant creature at least proves that I am in fairly good condition. Those poor creatures came here for four days and planned to spend half of one going to see Egyptian *mummies*! Isn't it pitiful!— in a place more full than any other in the world of things eter- nally *alive* and young and beautiful. One of them took me aback tonight by asking me—at table d'hote—if I "knew the story of Leda and the goose"! But I managed to hide my embarrassment and simply say that it was supposed to be Jupiter in the shape of a *swan*. But the other at once explained to her friend in a lower voice that it was a "very improper story & she ought not to ask about it." Wasn't it dreadful?

Give dearest love & kisses to darling Nellie & all. I love you my precious one with all my heart and soul,—tenderly, passionately, entirely.   Your own   Eileen.

They have sent up my hotel bill & I have paid it (on Sunday!) since I began this—and I still have $30.00. I feel encouraged,— with Mary's hundred to fall back upon.

My own darling,   Florence, June 2 1904

I am writing my midweek letter a day later than usual,—and why do you suppose—because I have been to *Venice*! Now I know you *are* surprised! I went Monday at eleven, stayed two days and got back today at four. The whole crowd, Jessie, Mary & the Smiths, had been begging me to go, ever since we reached Florence; and finally Jessie seemed so *perfectly* well that I consented to leave her with Mary as they wished and join the Smiths there for two days. I did not mention it in my Sunday letter because I thought when writing it that the plan would have to be given up on account of the trouble about your remittance, which had just reached an acute stage; but finally I let myself be convinced that it would be a shame to miss Venice for life, for a difficulty so surely temporary. Of course I did not think of giving it up for *want* of the *money*, but because I thought I ought to be here to answer possible telegrams or letters; but we decided Mary could do that as well as I;—she it was who sent you the cable saying the British Linen Co. had it. (I rather think you had discovered that at the other end of the line & that the cable was unnecessary.) I havn't the money yet but expect to have it by Saturday. And I still have *nine* dollars! What could have possessed Blair to disregard instructions & send the money to *London*. The Linen Co. has *never* had my address, so calmly kept the money all three weeks & did nothing.

Dear Mary has just gone off in tears; I shall miss her horribly, but have been getting so nervous about her sacrificing so much on my account, that I am glad and relieved to see her go! I had a real struggle to get her off;—had to begin all over again at the last minute because my money was not actually in hand, and it made her unhappy to leave me with only nine dollars;—for of course I wouldn't borrow from her when I expect my funds so soon.

I found another dear letter from you and *such* a sweet one from Stockton awaiting me; they made me very happy; besides which my heart is beginning to dance within me at the near approach of the sailing time;—only six more days now. I am so excited at the thought that I can hardly keep still.

But I havn't said a word about Venice,—and I cannot say much tonight for of course I am tired after my *seven* hour journey and getting Mary off on the night train delayed my writing. Venice must wait until Sunday—suffice it to say that the whole trip was the most *brilliant success*. Very few creatures have ever seen so thoroughly so many things in two days before,—and with so little fatigue,–thanks to the goldola [gondola] system! And oh how glorious it all was–both the place and the pictures. It surpassed my every dream,–it was "all a wonder and a wild delight." It made my heart ache that dear little Jessie was so near and yet so far; of course such an imaginative child would have liked it better than anything else. And she is so *wonderfully* sweet and fine about it & everything. The Smiths are keeping house there with two American girls who were with us in Rome & with them here in Florence,–extremely nice cultivated women and *old* travellers. One is from Boston one from Brooklyn; they are as practical as they are artistic and wonderful economists. So they are settled for three weeks in the house on the Grand Canal in which W. D. Howells lived, get their own breakfast and luncheon and take dinner at all sorts of charming places,–out of door restaurants. It is simply fascinating, and costs them next to nothing, except for the gondola. I couldn't get a room in their house but had bed & breakfast at a little hotel near by & then was with them all day until bedtime. I wasn't even alone at the hotel but with some lovely old ladies from Danville Ky.[,] daughters of Pres. Young of Centre College; friends whom *I* made at this pension but who know *your* family well.

We are both perfectly well & we love you all with all our heart. I love *you* my own darling to *distraction*. In every heart-throb,

Your own   Eileen

Though Mary has gone I am still not entirely alone! Marguerite Walbridge is still here with her mother staying on expressly to be with me for the next five days. She will be a great comfort as well as pleasure to me for she has picked up not a little Italian. The English speaking concierge here will see me off with my trunks & I shall write to the English hotel in Genoa, to send one to meet me there & help me get them to the steamer. I shall have no trouble at all.

ALS (WC, NjP).

From James Hay Reed

My Dear Dr Wilson   Pittsburgh.   June 3 1904

I had intended to write to you about your emergency fund but put it off hoping to be able to do better. I have some pretty large engagements on hand and I do not feel that I can at present promise you the full amount viz $5000 annually. If you can make use in your plan of a subscription of $2500 annually for three years I will be glad to make the subscription. When I get through with my present undertakings I shall try to make up for it in some way. I tell you this frankly & *confidentially*

Yours Truly   J H Reed

ALS (WP, DLC).

From Ellen Axson Wilson

My own darling,   Florence   May [June] 5, 1904

At last, at last we are really reaching the end,—I fear it would be more correct to say the *beginning* of the end—of this long separation! Only two more whole days before we start for Genoa! The last Sunday, the last letter! How delightful it is to dwell on these facts! And the money has come at last and all is well with us in every respect. When I finally got it yesterday afternoon I had just $1.80 left! I should have been in a fine panic but for Marguerite Walbridge! She stood ready to supply not only my immediate needs, but if the worst came to the worst to furnish the wherewithal for paying my bill here & for reaching the steamer! Of course I did not *expect* to call upon her but it was certainly a comfort to have some one in the background. And the banks *have* been so extraordinarily dilatory that one did not know what to expect of them. I think I will celebrate with a mild shopping spree tomorrow afternoon. The Florentine shops are the most wonderful in Europe for their dainty artistic trifles suitable for gifts, and selling for a song;—solid silver pins, for instance, set with real turquoise for 20 cts; antique solid silver coffee spoons for 30 cts. &c. &c.! The Smiths and even Mary Hoyt lost their hearts and almost their heads at them!—naturally I have not been into them yet! But there is still time,—to be even extravagant!

I have had two busy delightful days since I last wrote you,—in the morning revisiting the chief galleries,—this time with dear Jessie,—in the afternoon going to various churches with Marguerite to see special masterpieces enshrined within them, or perhaps a Donatello pulpit or tomb, or a Luca della Robbia, or a wonderful antique "ambone." Yesterday I was especially interested in the Massaccio chapel at the Carmine. Massaccio, you know, was the "marvellous boy" who, dying long before he was thirty, had yet time to almost revolutionize art by his profound study of its underlying *principles*, and his extraordinary success in their application. Giottos Chapel at Padua, this one in Florence, and the

Raphaels & Michel Angelos in Rome mark the three great epochs in Italian painting. Such a manifestation of genius seems to me peculiarly wonderful in a young man, because it could not come by instinct; in the nature of the case it implies in addition to "the seeing eye" the deepest investigation of scientific principles. It was rather thrilling to think that on the spot where I stood to see these pictures, Michelangelo, Raphael,—*all* the later great masters of Italian art had stood to study them day after day, week after week. Massaccio himself lies buried under the pavement, as it [is] fitting; his own works forming his most noble monument.

Which reminds me of our last excursion of the afternoon. We all three drove, just before dinner, to the little Protestant cemetary to see Mrs. Browning's grave and to lay on it a sheaf of white lilies. It is the most beautiful little (modern) tomb I ever saw. The exquisite little capitals to the small columns are carven with lovely conventionalized white lilies. So I choose the right flower! Just beside it is the almost equally beautiful tomb to Holman Hunt's[1] young wife[2] who died in the first year of their marriage, and to whom, like Browning, he was forever faithful.[3] The inscriptions upon it are most touching. "When thou passeth through the waters I will be with thee, and through the deep waters they shall not overwhelm thee"; and on the other side, "Many waters cannot quench love" &c. Altogether it is a most fitting place for a lover's pilgrimage.

I promised to tell about my visit to Venice today,—but it seems almost too large a subject to begin upon now;—for of course I am already beginning to feel the impatience of pen and ink which always overtakes one when a separation draws near its end. But here is a brief outline;—I arrived at seven P. M. was met by the Smiths, jumped—oh *no! gracefully glided!*—into their gondola and proceeded up the Grand Canal, stopping a moment at their *palace* to wash my face. We then went to a little restaurant on a pier just outside the house Ruskin lived in, where we had our dinner and also a view over the lagoon. We meant of course to glide about & watch the moonrise, but a thunderstorm coming up cut the evening short, so I went to my hotel which had, I think, the finest situation in Venice. It was on the Grand Canal but *just* at its end, so that I could see at once up the canal and across the open waters of the lagoon. I had a front room and from my window watched first the magnificent storm effects over the city

---

[1] William Holman Hunt, English Pre-Raphaelite painter.
[2] Fanny Waugh Hunt, who died in 1865.
[3] Actually, Hunt married Marion Edith Waugh, sister of his first wife, in 1875.

blending with its innumerable brilliant lights and their still more brilliant reflections. I finally managed to go to bed but was too excited to sleep much. At two o'clock I was up again, for by that time the moon was riding high in the velvety *blue* Italian sky;—all the lights were out and the scene was of course utterly indescribable. But I managed to go to bed and to sleep again,—until half past four! Then I was aroused by the dawn, and watched the sunrise deepen from rose to gold, the moon still in the midst a globe of shining silver! *Ah!* I did have another nap however & started out feeling perfectly fresh at nine o'clock. We, of course, saw the grand piazza first, then "did" the inside of the Ducal Palace—Bridge of Sighs & all. After lunch we spent two hours inside of St. Marks. (I shall make no further comments, not even exclamation points,—have neither the time nor "the langwidges,"—this is a mere catalogue.) Then we went to four churches[—]one for Palma Vecchio's great St. Barbara, two for Bellinis, and one for Ruskin's—and, incidentally, *Carpaccio's*—delicious St George series.⁴ Then we rowed across the Lagoon to the Lido for dinner, which we had out of doors of course, with Venice just opposite us in a sunset glow looking like Turners pictures, "only more so." Try to imagine the return to Venice *in* that sunset! If you "covet pleasure" for me, dearest, you surely have your desire. After that we glided about the lagoon until half past ten watching the moonrise and listening to the singing in the boats. They have regular "concert boats" and "all the world" is crowded about them. The lagoon is almost *too* gay and spectacular on a clear night with its "flash-lights," operatic music &c, &c. I like best to watch it from a long way off.

I was a good girl and actually slept that night, only getting up at sunrise for half an hour. The next day I was at the Bella Arti from nine until three when it closed, coming out ¾ of an hour for lunch. Then we went to four more churches in each of which we saw *perfectly* glorious Titians, Bellinis or Tintorettos[,] some of the greatest masterpieces of all. Then we had dinner at another charming place after which I went straight to the hotel & was in bed by nine. The next morning I returned to Florence as aforesaid!

Your dear, *dear* letter of the 23rd reached me yesterday,—I wonder if it will be the last! I fear it will; but something sweeter

---

⁴ She referred to a series of nine paintings by Vittore Carpaccio in the Church of San Giorgio degli Schiavoni. They are described in Chapter XI, "The Place of Dragons," in John Ruskin's *St. Mark's Rest: The History of Venice* . . . (London, 1884). The chapter was actually written by Ruskin's pupil, James Reddie Anderson, and was edited by Ruskin for inclusion in his volume.

than even your letters is soon to follow. The thought of it makes my heart flutter almost painfully. I hardly dare let myself dwell on it much but try to live in the present. Oh how I pray that never again we may have the ocean between us! I don't need to "pray" that *I* may never again be on the wrong side of it without you! But no more of this! You may imagine how constantly my thoughts have been with you today reading and re-reading as I have done that precious letter, and feeling that it is the last message from my love until I am in his arms. How constantly I shall think of you on the steamer, and of all you are about, and of the bacca-lauriate, and oh! how I shall groan in spirit that I shall be missing it. Next Sunday I shall be with you in spirit and in sympathy every moment. Give devoted love to darling Margaret & Nellie, to Stockton & Madge and to all friends. May God in, His mercy, bless us all, dear one, and give us a happy home-coming. I love you with all my heart, my darling, *my darling*!

Your little wife   Eileen.

ALS (WC, NjP).

To Robert Bridges

My dear Bob: Princeton, N. J.   6 June, 1904.

I do not know what your preference will be about lodging in Princeton at the reunion, but I write to beg that you will be my guest at Prospect so that the old gang[1] may have their individual reunion as before.

I would have written long ago, if I could have sooner made sure that I was not to be obliged to have official guests. I now know that I shall be free and I have quite set my heart on having you come to Prospect. We have room enough to make the whole crowd comfortable.

Affectionately yours,   Woodrow Wilson[2]

TLS (WC, NjP).
  [1] He referred to his close friends in the Class of 1879—the "Witherspoon Gang" —members of which had roomed in Witherspoon Hall.
  [2] Identical letters, *mutatis mutandis*, are WW to R. R. Henderson, June 6, 1904, TLS (WC, NjP), and WW to C. A. Talcott, June 6, 1904, TLS (WC, NjP).

From John Grier Hibben and Jenny Davidson Hibben

T.S.S. Statendam

My dear Woodrow   [New York, c. June 8, 1904].

We left you with a sad heart—& we carry away with us the loving memory of you & of all your goodness to us.

We will think of you constantly—& I hope you will have smooth sailing the coming commencement

Ever your devoted friend   Jack

Dear love & good-bye—& *try* to be careful of your self through this trying week. How lovely & good you are to us!

Ever devotedly yours,   J.D.H.

ALS and ALI (WP, DLC).

From James Laughlin, Jr.

My dear Sir—   Pittsburgh   June 8th 1904

It is my wish to increase the *fixed* endowment to the John H. Page Classical Fellowship to Ten thousand dollars ($10,000.00.) after the present term, and I authorize you to say to the Finance Committee that the addition[al] Five thousand dollars ($5000.-00) in cash, will be at their disposal, upon call.

Also, in order that an income of $600.00 will be assured to the recipient of the Fellowship for the coming year, I will guarantee any deficit that might occur; should the income in the investment of the Fund, at going rate of interest, not reach that amount. I expect to be in Princeton after Commencement—& will see you personally

With kind regards to the Board of Trustees & yourself

Yours Sincerely—James Laughlin Jr.

Present address—Care Jones & Laughlin Steel Co—No. 722 Penn Arcade Building   Broad & Market   Phila.

ALS (WP, DLC).

To Robert Bridges

My dear Bobbie: Princeton, N. J.   9 June, 1904.

I haven't the least criticism of your preference to sleep in the building; the sentiment is natural and delightful, and I am only disappointed that we cannot have you.

Woods, Mitchell, Webster, Talcott, and Henderson have all accepted my invitation.[1] Does that interfere with your arrangements for the North entry? After what you said, I began to fear that I had played hobs with your arrangements.

I suppose you will be here on Friday afternoon with the rest. Can't you take most of your meals with us at any rate?

Always,   Affectionately yours,   Woodrow Wilson

TLS (WC, NjP).
[1] Their letters are missing.

To Franklin Murphy

Princeton, N. J.

My dear Governor Murphy: 9 June, 1904.

I am sincerely sorry that you cannot be present at the Commencement meeting of the Board. It is always most gratifying to have you present, but I of course recognize the imperative force of the reason for your absence, and thank you very much for your kind letter.[1]

I sincerely hope that your trip abroad was most refreshing to you in every way, and that you find your strength and spirits restored.

I heartily re-echo your sentence about Mr. Cleveland. I wish with all my heart that it might fall out in that way.[2]

Faithfully yours,   Woodrow Wilson

TLS (F. Murphy Papers, Nj).
  [1] It is missing.
  [2] That is, probably, that the Democrats should nominate Cleveland for the presidency at their national convention in St. Louis, scheduled to open on July 6.

From Wilson Farrand

My dear President Wilson: Newark, N. J.   June 9, 1904

Thank you for your note.[1] No, indeed, I did not misunderstand you the other evening.[2] I was not in any way seeking an opportunity to have the case re-opened, for frankly I do not see how that can be done. Reopening the case would only mean a very unpleasant fight that could result in only one way, but that would cause feeling and bitterness, and might do serious injury to the University. There is a stronger feeling than you have any idea of, in favor of Cameron, among the Alumni, as well as among the undergraduates. If the matter is pressed and Cameron summarily dismissed, there will be, I fear, a manifestation that will surprise you, and that will do harm. My object is to check this manifestation, and I am sure it can be done if there is no summary dismissal.

I did not understand either from Cameron or from you that he had *rejected* your proposition. The simple point seemed to be that in his excitement he had said things which should not have been said, and which might make the continuance of relations impracticable. The action which a gentleman should take under such circumstances, it seems to us, would make possible, without vital sacrifice on your part, his remaining for the year which you originally gave him. It would be an act of magnanimity to him, and it would make it possible, I believe, to have the whole matter settled in comparative quiet.

The best guarantee of Cameron's behavior during the year will be the guardianship of his friends—a better guarantee than his own assurance.

I hope that you do not misunderstand my attitude and spirit. I am a friend of Cameron's, and I am extremely sorry that he is to leave Princeton, but I do not propose to fight for him, knowing the situation as I do. It will be unfortunate for Cameron and for Princeton if the matter is pressed now, and it can be handled much more smoothly if your original proposition can be carried out. You, of course, cannot move in the matter, but I want to urge you to take advantage of any opening that may occur.

Sincerely yours,   Wilson Farrand

ALS (WP, DLC).
  [1] It is missing.
  [2] When they had discussed Wilson's decision to dismiss Arnold Guyot Cameron. About this whole affair, see WW to A. G. Cameron, Nov. 18, 1903, n. 1.

From Richard Townley Haines Halsey[1]

Dear President Wilson: [New York, c. June 10, 1904]

A number of the alumni, who have Princetons interests at heart, are greatly disturbed by the news of the position you have taken in the Cameron matter and feel that you have been strangely misled in regard to Camerons scholarship[.] While we know that the man is eccentric, yet his influence over those in his classroom has created a "literary enthusiasm" in his students, which in many cases has caused them to keep up their interest in French Literature after leaving college, an influence which is woefully lacking at Princeton and one which you are most anxious to have flourish[.] While we in no way can condone Camerons handling of the present unfortunate affair and one which bids fair to result in much needless suffering to those dependent upon Cameron for support, we must be lenient and take into consideration the fact that he (and a number of others) has been aware of an apparent attempt to belittle his scholarship and thereby take away his only means of supporting those dear to him. On these grounds his actions are explainable to those of us who know the personality of Guyot Cameron.

We feel that Princeton owes a debt to Arnold Guyot[2] and to Guyots (C) father,[3] both of whom gave their lives to Princeton, a debt which will be ill repaid by the removal of their sole representative, for unworthy cause. Another distressing situation may arise and which will be unfortunate for Princeton University, as in case Cameron is forced to leave his Alma Mater, much ill feeling will be caused among the students and younger alumni with whom Cameron is most popular.

There is always a chance that this indignation may be voiced in the press, and must necessarily cause unfavorable criticism of an administration which all Princeton men are eager to support   Yours respectfully   R. T. H. Halsey '86

ALS (WP, DLC).
  [1] Princeton 1886, classmate of Arnold Guyot Cameron; New York banker and member of the Board of Governors of the New York Stock Exchange.
  [2] Arnold Henry Guyot, Blair Professor of Geology and Physical Geography, 1854-84, and great-uncle of Arnold Guyot Cameron.
  [3] He referred, of course to Arnold Guyot Cameron's father, Henry Clay Cameron, who taught Greek at Princeton from 1852 until his retirement in 1902.

A Sermon

[June 12, 1904]

BACCALAUREATE ADDRESS, June 12, 1904.

"And they shall fight against thee: but they shall not prevail against thee: for I am with thee, saith the Lord, to deliver thee." Jer. I., 19.

YOUNG GENTLEMEN: Not all of your life is before you. Much of it is passed: the part in which your motives find their most intricate rootage, the part in which your strength has been formed and determined. That is a shallow view of life which makes youth no essential part of it and represents the years in which you must follow your callings and earn your livelihood and obtain your final place of influence in the world as the only period in which you really live and establish yourselves among men. You have already lived more than a third of the time alloted you,— some of you have lived quite half, some nearly all of it. Those of you who go the longest journey in the world will find, ere the full tale of your years is told and the end come, that the fountains you draw refreshment from are still the fountains you drank of in your youth: that the things which stir you are the same that stirred you in the long, dreaming days of expectation when you were boys. No one of you will ever shake off the personality he has now already made for himself or wholly lose the naive impressions of the days in which he has come to maturity.

"I have no patience," says Ruskin, in one of those passages in which he shows himself so penetrating a moralist: "I have no patience with people who talk about the 'thoughtlessness of youth' indulgently. I had infinitely rather hear of thoughtless old age and the indulgence due to *that*. When a man has done his work and nothing can any way be materially altered in his fate, let him forget his toil, and jest with his fate, if he will: but what excuse can you find for wilfulness of thought, at the very time when every crisis of future fortune hangs on your decisions? A youth thoughtless! when all the happiness of his home forever depends on the chances, or the passions, of an hour! A youth thoughtless! when the career of all his days depends on the opportunity of a moment! A youth thoughtless! when his every act is a foundation-stone of future conduct, and every imagination a fountain of life or death! Be thoughtless in *any* after years, rather than now,—though, indeed, there is only one place where a man may be nobly thoughtless,—his deathbed. No thinking should ever be left to be done there."[1]

The years shorten as they multiply, though you do not yet know how much. The next ten years will seem to you incomparably shorter than the last ten: the ten that follow will hurry past you with yet quicker pace; and so, decade by decade, the end of your life will seem to be thrust back upon the beginning. There are no years for length like those of the boy: only children know the majestic span of a long decade or the mists that rest upon the far distant heights of fifty towards which every lad and every youth us [is] climbing.

There is a deep significance in the length of those years, when the seed gropes its way upward through the dark soil towards the plain daylight and the sights of the workday world. Who shall ever set you forth in veritable analysis how the saps of the great world work in the blood, or decipher for you the boundless map of children's minds: their countries of romance, their broad waters of discovery and free adventure, their rivers and forests which only heroes ever see, their distances without end? The child is absorbed by no interest, makes no barter for leave to live, but stands upon a place apart, a little spectator of the world, before whom men and women come and go, events fall out, years open their slow story and are noted or let go as his mood chances to serve them. The play touches him not. He but looks on, thinks his

[1] From John Ruskin, "War," Lecture III in *The Crown of Wild Olive*.

own thought, and turns away, not even expecting his cue to enter the plot and speak. He waits,—he knows not for what. The days tell upon him like rain and air and the succession of the seasons, and seem long, very long, to his dreaming senses.

The dream is not stayed or ended at the portals of the college: the lad seems still to stand outside the plot of life. But the dream changes and is near to the hour of waking. It passes from the unreal to the real, and the man at last stands up to graduate, awake. At least it is high time he were awake. A university like this which we love is no child's dreaming place, but a veritable part of the world itself. Look at the buildings about you. There are more dormitories and society rooms and places of free and voluntary assembly than lecture rooms and places where pupils meet instructors: more places for living than for formal exercise. We are not a mere body of teachers and pupils met for occasional instruction and formal intercourse, but an independent community whose various life fills every moment of the day; governed by our own laws, shaped by our own separate customs, curiously compounded out of the habit, sometimes out of the playful whim, of the generations, the brief four-year generations, which have gone before us. We are busy with affairs as well as with studies, like men of the world, affairs which in their transaction seems as important to us as any affairs of the nation itself, and which are in fact as powerful in the moulding of our characters and the forming or confirming of our capacities. The play of life is on, and we are in the thick of it. Our thoughts take shape, our passions play along the line of action; our hopes and fears lay hold upon actual experience: we are men and act upon our own initiative.

Here, in this little world, this little state, this little commonwealth of our own, which has grown to maturity as naturally as any member of the family of nations, which is touched with the spirit of democracy, kept always fresh, spontaneous, eager, blithe by the constant youth of its citizens, we enact life beforehand, in four short years which are yet long and full of pith and action. It is chiefly what we have learned here, of whatever kind it be, that we are to carry with us as our make-up and capital into the world where we are to trade for success and happiness and power. It behooves us to take stock of it and know what we start withal.

Just because we have lived here in a community of free men, and have been something more than boys sitting under schoolmasters, we have learned many things very definitely about the world's work, by experience as well as by reading and precept.

We have all of us, willingly or unwillingly, read a good deal about the world's transactions: and we have learned that thought itself is of the stuff of action hardly less than the barterings of the marts of business. We have seen Science ply the quiet tasks which give the world its means of material progress. We have explored ideas and climbed the slow hill of thought from whose higher slopes, now lying about us, men have come to conceive as they do of nature and themselves. At the same time we have freely lived our own lives,—much more freely than we shall have leave to live them in the years now at hand,—much less under the constant direction, less trammeled with fixed hours and prescribed tasks, less watched and criticised and bidden, more like men who have made their place in the world than like youngsters. And so we have seen government and license, the making and unmaking of laws, the respect and the breach of order: have made and maintained organizations, created and combated opinion, struggled, won, and lost, made sacrifices and achieved enjoyments entirely of our own will and motive,—so that we shall not be surprised when these same things show themselves upon a bigger scale elsewhere, and these same faculties that we have used here are challenged to undertake more momentous things.

Here, in the diplomacy, the statesmanship, the politics of the campus, and in all the life, private and public, which fills the days so familiar to us, you have had occasion to see conduct and comradeship, whether in action or in mere friendly intercourse, as variously displayed, as nicely determined as you shall see them hereafter. And you have seen them close at hand and in almost their whole variety. You have, moreover, had more leisure to observe and note what you have seen than you will have when caught in the rush of professional business, sucked into the maelstrom of the world that surges beyond the boundaries of this our little commonwealth. The book of life has been opened before you in epitome. You are not likely to forget what you have read in it since you were Freshmen. You have here seen things whole and at short range which you will see hereafter only piecemeal and amidst the confusing movements of a stage the whole of which you can never see at any one time.

And so motive and the standards, true or false, which sanction or condemn conduct have been all the while lying before you for your study. When the scene and the stage itself change these things will not change. What has been honorable here will be honourable there; what has dishonoured, besmirched, debauched here will work the self-same sad havoc of life and hope there as well. The great world of action which lies beyond graduation is made mean or noble by the same things that have heartened or dismayed us while we were yet undergraduates. Have we not heeded how such matters ran? Have you not assessed each other, and forecast what shall befall the heedless, the idle, the reckless; the steadfast, the courageous, the true, the manly? Your expectation will not in many cases go far astray. Our little commonwealth has taught its lessons of conduct, of honour, of capacity very plainly day by day: and we are not so young as to imagine that the world has not already begun with us.

How, then, does the map of life look to us? It is too late, gentlemen, this is not the age for debate upon the question where we got the judgments which we have so confidently applied to our own conduct and the conduct of our fellows. They are based, beyond dispute, upon spiritual, not material, reckonings. The spirit of morality was changed and established once and for all by the coming of Christ into the world. Men of our kind and training do not doubt where the essence of character lies or in what scales it is to be weighed. Whether you are all of you aware of it or not, the air you have breathed here is Christian, saturated with influence and the traditions of men who have followed the divine master and sought to learn of Him. The commonest precepts of honour, of faithfulness, and of happiness amongst us are illuminated by texts out of the Old Testament and the New as if these were documents drawn at their birth to explain and authenticate them. There are our own judgments written of old, persistent, inevitable.

It is this that I would have you note. If you have taken stuff of character from this place, what is it? Lay its elements apart; examine them; do not fail to note whence they came and what they are. We boast that we breed a type of men here distinguishable from the rest of the world for manliness, a sense of duty and of honour, a serviceable way of life and a happiness in doing the ordinary parts of the Day's work, as well as the extraordinary, and doing them well: men morally noticeable. These men are better than the average, we say, less servile, more individual, full of an energy which is of the heart as well as of the mind. We send a new class forth with the confidence that they have entered into the type, that they have received the strength and caught the spirit which will separate and distinguish them. To each man, as he goes, we say "Be of good courage; do not fear the men you shall face and compete with or doubt to withstand those who would drag you back. They shall fight against thee: but they shall

not prevail against thee.'" Why? What virtue is in these men
that is not in others? What patent have they to go free of dismay
and failure? By way of reply, we are fain to finish the text and
say, "for I am with thee, saith the Lord, to deliver thee." That is
the inexplicit element in our thought. What we believe is, that
the spirit of right is in this place for her sons to drink of and be
strong: the spirit of right created by generations of christian men.
And this is none other than the spirit of God.

Is this true? I am no theologian. I shall not expound to you
anything not written on the face of life and of providence. But I
would have you note what it really is that we now speak of. There
is only one thing that sets a man forever free from defeat, and
that is a true knowledge of his own heart and its destiny. He can
be quit of failure only if he love and seek the right things. Then,
indeed, and of a certainty the Lord will be with him to deliver
him: and then only. And the right thing to love is not himself,
or even his own soul, but the things which are higher and greater
than himself, which are the inspiration of all the best instincts
and movements of his soul: the causes that cleanse and better
the world; truth in all her beauty, and knowledge for truth's sake;
and purity of heart, that the mind of man may be truth's fit
dwelling place.

The long reckonings of the world itself square with these precepts as if history were a book of morals. The fame that shines
pure, serene, and permanent upon her records is not the fame of
what brawn or cunning or any brutal mastery have *done*, but the
fame of what men of exalted spirit have *been*, for the guidance
and deliverance of their fellows, for justice and right living and
straight thinking in the world. The sheer force and conquering
might of mere righteousness and fortitude and unselfish fearless
devotion is written upon every page of history that has any gleam
of light upon it. The fruits of a college life lived as we try to live
it here and lift it from age to age are not knowledge merely and
the sort of superiority which a man gets by knowing more than
his fellows. They are more various than knowledge; and knowledge is only one of their many compounds. The college man ought
to see more in the life about him than others see; ought to have
access to sources of refreshment and of confidence that other
men have not found; ought to see values and know very clearly
the ways of lasting satisfaction.

The vast accumulation of wealth, the vast material equipment
of civilization in our day ought not to mislead us into supposing
that this is an age gross and material beyond precedent; more

debauched by greed or intoxicated by material power than any that has gone before it. It is not. Though its spiritual impulses and conceptions and undertakings do not run exclusively along the old, hallowed, and familiar ways of religion as in some noted days gone by,—particularly some days that shine bright and illustrious in the early annals of our own nation, the spirit of man has waxed as strong in our time as has his hand, and has given itself to works as mighty and as influential. It is said that we have given birth to no new ideals since Science ushered in the modern march of wealth; but it cannot be said that charity or any healing art or the study and ardent pursuit of any hopeful means of social betterment has lagged behind us in the crowded way. Men's consciences are awake and crave conquests which are attempted in the spirit of religion if not in its name and under its elder organization.

It is difficult, it is almost impossible, amidst the crowding hosts marching to and fro upon the city streets, amidst the smoke of chimneys and the rush of loaded vans, amidst the confusing calls of a thousand competing interests and the deafening noises of bustling and multifarious industry to see where these silent forces move or make out the method of their subtle victories.

> This tract which the river of Time
> Now flows through with us, is the plain.
> Gone is the calm of its earlier shore.
> Border'd by cities, and hoarse
> With a thousand cries is its stream.
> And we on its breast, our minds
> Are confused as the cries which we hear,
> Changing and shot as the sights which we see.
>
> And we say that repose has fled
> For ever the course of the river of Time.
> That cities will crowd to its edge
> In a blacker incessanter line;
> That the din will be more on its banks,
> Denser the trade on its stream,
> Flatter the plain where it flows,
> Fiercer the sun overhead.
> That never will those on its breast
> See an ennobling sight,
> Drink of the feeling of quiet again.
> But what was before us we know not,
> And we know not what shall succeed.

Haply, the river of Time—
As it grows, as the towns on its marge
Fling their wavering lights
On a wider, statelier stream—
May acquire, if not the calm
Of its early mountainous shore,
Yet a solemn peace of its own.

And the width of the waters, the hush
of the gray expanse where he floats,
Freshening its current and spotted with foam
As it draws to the Ocean, may strike
Peace to the soul of the man on its breast—
As the pale waste widens around him,
As the banks fade dimmer away;
As the stars come out, and the night-wind
Brings up the stream
Murmurs and scents of the infinite sea.[2]

Who should descry that eternal sea sooner, to whom should its murmurs and scents bring more authentic tidings of peace and happy fruition than the man nurtured as we have been. To whom should the forces of the modern world sooner show themselves for what they are? They deploy upon a field, indeed, where no eye but that of the man fit to command them can follow them with full comprehension. Not every man bred in a college can comprehend or be sure of the innumerable ways in which they display themselves. But every college man worthy of the name ought to be aware of their existence and of the right standards by which to measure them and fix their value, and ought to go forth to his work feeling that he is of necessity among the sponsors and champions of the influences that make for light and peace and purity.

For every college man ought to know that the full pulse of life is in nothing but the things that satisfy his spirit. Men's fortunes may be torn away from them: there is no material weapon with which they can fight misfortune and be sure to prevail. Only the spirit of man in [is] unconquerable. Many pretty books and homilies have been written for us of late in advocacy of the simple life, and beneath their sentiment lies a very noble and enlightening truth. There is no virtue in a plainly furnished room: a little circle of employments, a little group of friends is no certain means of grace. The simple life may be very mean and bare

---

[2] From Matthew Arnold's "The Future."

and unrewarding; what is worse, it may be very selfish and belittling. The kernel of the moral is simply that our life is greater than the things that we handle and that our life is in us, not in our possessions or our social and business engagements.

Turn back, with that conception in your thoughts, to the days which stretch through the four years behind you, and to those still more distant days which we have never yet assessed, which run back through our boyhood to the nursery and the very first faltering steps that we took. What have we been nurturing? Ourselves. Not our fortunes, but our power to live quite as much as our power to get. There is often honour in poverty, and happiness withal in a quiet spirit; there is sometimes dishonour in wealth and bitterness in the midst of plenty; that is an old story enough. The essence of the matter is in ourselves, and we count permanently in the world in proportion as we keep that essence pure. We are not in quest of distraction and mere absorption, but of happiness and the satisfaction of our powers.

Purity of heart, moreover, is not a mere native perfection, given only to children and young girls and saints as a natural endowment of innocence. It can be had also, and best had as a permanent and sure possession, by knowing and expelling the impurities of life; and knowledge is of its perfection. The innocence, the purity, the grace and integrity of heart to which God promises his prevailing strength is that which is learned of Him, —not the mere negative innocence of the child, against which craft may easily prevail, nor even the innocence of the saint alone, who has closed his affections against the world, but the innocence, rather, of deliberate steadfastness against the evil which is known and faced. There is heroism and the zest of conquest in no other kind. "They shall fight against thee: but they shall not prevail against thee; for I am with thee, saith the Lord, to deliver thee,"—to deliver that which is essential in thee, that which is heroic in thee, that which recognizes temptation, fears it, and resists it, that which has turned thy heart unto Me and made thee the comrade of those who are undismayed amidst the buffets of fortune and the change of circumstance.

It is our modern philosophy that virtue is not for the cloister and the convent but for the open field and the dusty road and every place of work and intercourse: for the cleansing of the world and the deliverance of those who toil in it. God is abroad, not shut up behind conventicle walls; and the college man ought to be the best man among the men of God, because by training and enlightenment a citizen of the world of good and evil. It is

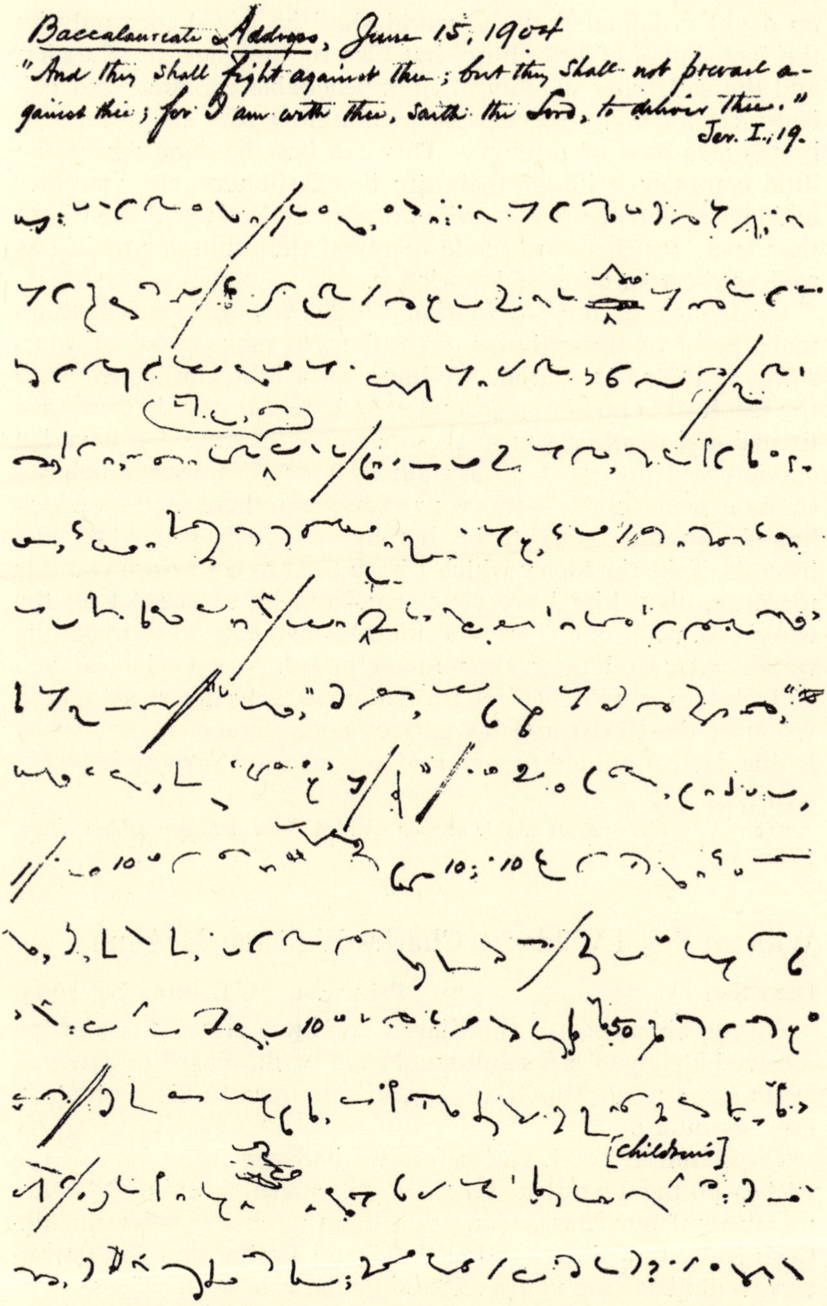
Baccalaureate Address, June 15, 1904
"And they shall fight against thee; but they shall not prevail against thee; for I am with thee, saith the Lord, to deliver thee."
Jer. I, 19.
[childrens]

The first page of Wilson's shorthand draft, curiously misdated, of his baccalaureate sermon on June 12, 1904.

no doubt ordained that the world shall be saved, not only by the foolishness of preaching, but also by the courage of action and the satisfying nobility of unimpeachable conduct; and colleges cannot make serviceable men unless they make men of brains also men of principle. This can best be done where the little commonwealth of their life breeds honourable character and gives influence to men who purpose the good of those whom they lead: for there are made manifest the fountains of life as well as the fountains of knowledge.

Gentlemen of the Graduating Class: You are sent forth to make proof of these things, or, rather, to make proof of yourselves in their illustration. We have not a little confidence as to the result. It is no idle or formal compliment to say that we have trusted and admired you in an uncommon degree. You have led opinion and governed affairs amongst us in a way which we shall not soon forget. It was your example in these matters which brought to my thought the homily to which you have just listened. Take the ideals which I have tried to lay before you this morning,—thay [they] are your own,—and let us see, let all the world see, what one class of Princeton men can do to make the world better and their alma mater proud. May God bless you and give to you in perfect revelation as your lives advance a vision of the Christ and his perfect saving grace. A great trust is this day committed to you, and a great transforming hope.[3]

T MS. (WP, DLC).
[3] There is a WWsh draft of this sermon entitled *"Baccalaureate Address*, June 15, 1904," in WP, DLC.

William Royal Wilder to Charles Williston McAlpin

Dear Sir: Princeton, N. J., June 12, 1904.

On March 16, 1904, the Class Committee of the Class of '79 received a copy of a resolution adopted by the Board of Trustees at its meeting on March 10, '04, in reference to the naming of our Dormitory.

On March 2, 1904, and before we had any intimation of the wishes of the Board of Trustees, we mailed a circular to the members of our Class, requesting them to choose between "McCosh Hall" and "Seventy-nine Hall," and stating that the Dormitory would bear the name selected by the vote of the Class.

One hundred and twelve contributors have voted. The returns show that seventy-one (71) favor calling the building "Seventy-nine Hall" against forty-one (41) who favor "McCosh Hall."

We request that you submit the foregoing facts to the Board at its meeting.

Very sincerely yours, Wm. R. Wilder Secretary

TCL (Trustees' Papers, UA, NjP).

To the Board of Trustees of Princeton University

REPORT OF THE COMMITTEE ON THE CURRICULUM, June 13, 1904.

THE BOARD OF TRUSTEES OF PRINCETON UNIVERSITY.

Gentlemen:

Your Committee on the Curriculum beg leave to report as follows:

They recommend that the title of Assistant Professor Covington be changed from Assistant Professor of Oratory to Assistant Professor of English.

That Professor Rankin's title be changed from Professor of Invertebrate Zoology to Professor of Biology, and that the President be authorized, upon consultation with the several professors concerned, to change the titles of the other members of the Department of Biology upon the principle suggested in the recommendation with regard to Professor Rankin.

That Professor William K. Prentice be allowed leave of absence from the 1 February, 1905, for a half academic year, for the purpose of taking part in the Syrian expedition which is to be sent out under the auspices of the University.[1]

That the following instructors be appointed for the ensuing year.

In English, Mr. Hardin Craig, Mr. Augustus White Long, Mr. Horace Meyer Kallen, and Mr. William Harry Clemons.

In Latin, Dr. David Magie, Jr., Dr. Edwin Moore Rankin, Mr. Howell North White, Mr. Robert Patton Anderson, and Mr. Donald Wm. Richardson.

In Greek, Mr. Fred LeRoy Hutson, and Mr. John Porter Hall.

In Civil Engineering, Mr. Ford Cushing Smith.

In Architecture, to do part of the work of Mr. Howard Crosby Butler, Mr. Aymar Embury.

That to fill the place for one year of Professor Jesse Carter, granted leave of absence, Professor Grant Showerman, of the University of Wisconsin, be appointed Professor of Latin.[2]

Your Committee further recommends that the following report of the action of the University Faculty, with regard to the systematic revision of the courses of the University at present embraced under the course for the Bachelor of Science and the degree of Bachelor of Arts, be adopted as the action of the Board of Trustees, and that the list of courses thereto appended, which has been suggested by the several departments in conformity with that scheme, be approved and authorized.[3]

TR (Trustees' Papers, UA, NjP).

[1] The Princeton Expedition to Syria of 1904-1905 was sponsored by graduates and friends of the university and led by Professor Howard Crosby Butler, who was in charge of art and architecture, accompanied by Dr. Richard Ludwig Enno Littmann in charge of epigraphy and Frederick Albert Norris '95 as cartographer. Professor William Kelly Prentice joined them in Damascus on March 1, 1905, to work on classical inscriptions. With the exception of Norris, this same group had participated in the American Archaeological Expedition to Syria in 1899-1900, which had as its objective the exploration of as large an area as possible in central Syria.

There was an air of urgency about the work of the Princeton Expedition to Syria, for the areas to be explored were rapidly being occupied by Circassian immigrants who, in their search for building materials, were laying waste to large numbers of ancient ruins.

Outfitted in Jerusalem in September 1904, the Princeton Expedition began work in Syria early the next month. "In the desert region," Butler later wrote, "we visited many deserted ancient cities, towns, and Roman military posts, our collection of inscriptions increased into the hundreds, maps were made of un-surveyed districts, and plans, elevations and restorations were made of a large number of buildings of different kinds. The material thus collected, in the shape of copies of inscriptions, and measured drawings and photographs, together with paper impressions and copious notes, is all of interest and importance to history, epigraphy and art. The historical periods represented are the Seleucid Greek, of the 2nd century B.C., the Nabataaen of the 1st century B.C. [-] A.D., the Roman of the 2nd and 3rd centuries A.D., and the Christian period of the 4th, 5th and 6th centuries. The classes of buildings studied include temples, baths, churches, tombs, private residences in great variety, towers and fortress-es." H. C. Butler, "Princeton Expedition to Syria," *Princeton Alumni Weekly*, VII (Jan. 12, 1907), 240.

Eventually, several hundred photographs and drawings were made and more than two thousand inscriptions copied. A large collection of Syrian antiquities was brought back to Princeton, including pottery, bronze ornaments, coins, glass, inscribed stones, and paper impressions of many inscriptions and architectural details. Contrary to expectations, publication of the work of the expedition was delayed for many years, and the first volume did not appear until several years after Butler's death in 1922. Ultimately, a full description, together with photographs, drawings, and facsimiles, was printed under the general title of *Syria: Publications of the Princeton University Archaeological Expeditions to Syria in 1904-5 and 1909* (9 vols., Leyden, 1930-49). The first volume opens with a lengthy and interesting account of the 1904-1905 expedition written from the notes of Frederick A. Norris.

[2] Showerman had been Assistant Professor of Latin Literature at Wisconsin since 1900.

[3] The report, with the amendments detailed in S. J. McPherson to WW, May 20, 1904, n.3, was approved by the Board of Trustees.

Henry Burchard Fine to the Board of Trustees' Committee on Morals and Discipline

Gentlemen: PRINCETON UNIVERSITY, JUNE 13, 1904.

Since the last meeting of your Committee only three students have been reported to me for intoxication, and of these only one had been previously reported for this offense. He was suspended for six weeks. I have no other serious breaches of college discipline to report.

At its April meeting the University Faculty adopted the revised regulations respecting conditions and absence from examinations to which I have referred in previous reports. A copy of these regulations is submitted herewith. I may direct special attention to the following provisions:

I, 2 "A student who has unexcused absences amounting to more than one-sixth of the exercises of any course shall be excluded by the Instructor from the examination in that course."

Hitherto the rule has read "may be excluded" instead of "shall be excluded," with the result that the penalty of exclusion from examination has been applied very unequally.

I, 3 "Absence from an examination, due to whatever cause, is counted as a condition if the term grade in the subject is below the passing mark."

Of course this rule can be applied to those courses only in which term work is required of a student and a record kept of this work, but it is to be hoped that these conditions will soon prevail in all our courses. The rule is meant to reach that class of students who completely neglect their work in term time, and then escape the penalty for their idleness by a feigned illness or the accident of an actual illness. The rule has been in operation in the Academic Department since February of last year and I find in it one of the principal causes for the great improvement in term work and attendance at examinations since that time. The attendance at the recent examinations has been very remarkable. Thus of the 190 Sophomores, not one was absent from the examination in Mechanics, and of the 200 Freshmen, but one was absent from the examination in Algebra.

The provisions II, 1-5 enumerate the possibilities open to a student when dropped from his class. It will be found that wherever practicable an arrangement is provided which will make it possible for the student to meet the requirements for his degree by the February after the graduation of his class. I have referred to this provision in previous reports. So far as it has been tested it has worked satisfactorily. The same may be said of the provision which requires a student to withdraw from college for a half year when dropped before resuming his studies.

I recently requested the Registrar to give me a list of the names of students who had withdrawn from college voluntarily for one cause or another during the present year. I found that the number of such students has been 35, of whom 10 were Academic students, and 25 were members of the School of Science. It will be seen that the loss in the School of Science is far greater than in the Academic Department. Indeed the percentage of loss is between three and four times as great in the one department as in the other. No doubt this is mainly due to the same cause that operates to make the loss through dropping greater in the School of Science than in the Academic Department, namely the inferior preparation of its students. Happily this cause may be expected soon to cease to exist when our new course of study, which provides for equivalent entrance requirements in the two departments, goes into operation.

Respectfully submitted,

H. B. Fine   Dean of the Faculty.

TRS (Trustees' Papers, UA, NjP).

To Austin Scott

My dear President Scott: Princeton, N. J.   14 June, 1904.

The list from Dr. Parkin and your letter concerning a meeting of our Committee on the Oxford Scholarship[1] came to me in the midst of the business connected with Commencement and I have been simply unable to think about the arrangement for a meeting of the Committee.

Only two of the men examined qualified, namely R. W. Leary, who is I think one of your men, and B. M. Price, a member of our graduating class.

I wonder if it would be convenient for you if Professor Fine and I were to come over to New Brunswick on Friday, June 17, in the afternoon at about (say) two o'clock? I have not had time to see Professor Fine about this, but I take it for granted that he could come with me at this time.[2]

With warm regards and sincere thanks for your kind words,

Cordially yours,   Woodrow Wilson

TLS (A. Scott Papers, NjR).
[1] The list and letter from Scott are missing.
[2] Russel Woodward Leary, Rutgers 1902, lost out to Benjamin Marsden Price '04 when the committee met on June 17. Price attended Oxford from 1904 to 1907, received the B.C.L. degree in the latter year, and returned to Princeton as Instructor in Jurisprudence and Politics for the academic year 1907-1908. He later practiced law in Pittsburgh and Chicago.

From John Heman Converse

Dear Sir: Philadelphia, June 14, 1904.

My election as a Trustee of Princeton University, is an honor which I highly appreciate. No institution in the country has a higher place in my regard than Princeton.

I do not feel, however, that it is at all possible for me to accept the place. As I am already a Trustee of Princeton Seminary; of my own Alma Mater, the University of Vermont; and one of the managers of Girard College, my time and energies in the direction of educational interests are fully occupied. I have felt, therefore, that there is no alternative except a declination of the high honor conferred upon me.[1]

Very truly yours,   John H. Converse

TLS (WP, DLC).
[1] No further nominations for Life Trustees were made until the Board of Trustees met on December 8, 1904, when the Rev. Dr. John De Witt and Archibald Douglas Russell were nominated. They were qualified and took their seats at the Board meeting of March 9, 1905.

An Address

[[June 14, 1904]]

THE REVISION OF THE COURSES OF STUDY

President Wilson's Address at the Alumni Luncheon
in the New Gymnasium, Tuesday, June 14, 1904

The matter which is most in the thoughts of those who are interested with [in] the government of the University at present is a systematic revision of the courses of study, which we have undertaken and just completed.

It was high time that the various courses of the University should have some sort of co-ordination and sequence. We could not go back to a fixed course of study; the modern variety of studies is too great; and we would not yield to the modern tendency toward absolutely free electives, because we have never yet been ready to admit that older men were less able to judge of the real worth of studies than very young men. We have never yet been able or willing to admit that experience and study counted for nothing. We believe that in study as in everything else there must be guidance by those who have had experience, and submission to guidance by those who have had none.

You understand, gentlemen, that we are for liberal culture, and that we also stand by preference for classical culture. We believe that the old methods are excellent methods; but we do not believe that the more modern methods are not also excellent. And yet we have for some years past been introducing the more modern schemes of study in a way which has come to us to seem not entirely frank. For example, we have permitted men without any restraint whatever to enter as candidates for the degree of Bachelor of Science and yet pursue purely humanistic studies. It so happened because of the accidents of growth that about three years ago there was more science open to the candidates for the A.B. than there was open to the candidates for the B.S. The B.S. men could not get as much science if they wanted to. And it also came about and is still true that the candidate for the B.S. could get practically as much of the A.B. studies as he wanted, with the single exception of Greek. Therefore a large majority of the men who are candidates for the degree of Bachelor of Science are really pursuing academic studies. Now that, I say, is not frank to the public. If we are to give men a humanistic training of this type, without Greek, we must give them the right label. They are not Bachelors of Science.

One of our propositions, therefore, is to institute a third degree, namely, that of Bachelor of Letters; for the purpose, the perfectly valid purpose, of preserving the historical significance of the Bachelor of Arts. It stands for something the significance of which has not been altered since the middle ages. The Bachelor of Letters is a label very much in use elsewhere; it is a label for those men who want a humanistic training without Greek. Why there should be so universal a desire to escape Greek I don't know except that there is a well known universal desire to escape difficulty. There is a well known instinct of the mind to follow the lines of least resistance, and because of that instinct this exquisite language is avoided by many men in preparation for a liberal training. The men who put themselves through the Greek training put themselves through the training that produced the intellectual movements of the modern world. The man who takes Greek puts himself through the process that produced the modern mind. The modern world does not have to be convinced that the sciences, taught as sciences, taught in their purity, taught as a body of principles, taught as exhibitions of the way in which nature manifests herself, are nowadays indispensable parts of a liberal training.

It is our hope, therefore, to see three groups of men, B.S., Litt.B., and A.B.; and in forming the course which they shall take we have set out to do a new thing—I mean new for us. We have tried to unify the University. Every opportunity offered by the University will be open to everyone who enters, whether he enter by the Litt.B., the B.S., or the A.B. door, with the single exception that the men who enter without Greek cannot pursue it afterwards. . . .[1] All the bill of fare of the University is open to everyone.

Upon what plan? This simple plan. The first year will remain a disciplinary year of required studies. The discipline of the University is different from the discipline of the schools. Moreover, the men who come to us come from all over the country, from schools of every kind, with preparation of every sort, and they have to be licked into shape, into the same shape. They have all of them to be put into the mill that enables them to do the things that have to be done after freshman year.

In sophomore year we try to introduce a great deal more elasticity, but with this boundary, this limitation, that the choice is among fundamental studies. A man is not to be allowed to begin at the top. He has got to go by some logical sequence in the studies of sophomore year, and prepare himself fundamentally for the studies of junior and senior year.

At the end of sophomore year we offer the student his choice among twelve departments of study. The University, as some of you may not know, has within the last twelve months been reorganized administratively. We have now drawn the several chairs in related subjects of study into departments, and there are now organized in the University twelve departments,[2] with departmental organization, for the purpose of studying the correlation of courses. Now, building upon that, we have divided the University into departments, and the departments into divisions. There is a Division of Philosophy, which includes philosophy, and history and politics. There is a Division of Art and Archaeology; a division of Language and Literature; a Division of Mathematics and Science, including all the mathematics and all the scientific studies. This division will hereafter constitute our School of Science.

When a man reaches the end of sophomore year he can concentrate his attention upon any of the twelve departments grouped within these four divisions. We limit the number of junior courses in each department, so that a man cannot take more than two. There are only two to take. And we allow him

[1] Elision in the original text.

[2] Wilson's memory betrayed him here. At this time, there were only eleven departments. See the memorandum printed at Nov. 20, 1903, and n. 3 to Wilson's Annual Report printed at Dec. 10, 1903.

to take five courses instead of seven as at present, increasing the number of hours devoted to each course from two to three, so that on a fifteen hour schedule he has five courses of study,— two in the department of his choice, a third he is advised to take in some properly related and supporting study, a fourth he is required to take outside the department and outside the division of his chief choice. His fifth elective is free to him to select as he pleases.

When he comes to the end of his junior year he is at liberty to re-choose his department, to all intents and purposes. He needs only two courses to qualify him for any one department in senior year; and he can so arrange his choice in junior year that he will be qualified for either of two, or, it may be, three departments in senior year. So that a man can reserve his final choice until he is about to enter senior year; and then he specializes in the department of his final choice.

We seek to distinguish after senior year the men who are after honors and the men who are not after honors. I do not mean extreme and uncanny excellence, but I mean a decent and self-respecting attention to business; because in order to qualify himself for general honors a man is obliged to stand in the sum total of his studies above the middle of his class, provided he does better, a little, in the particular department he chooses. But we distinguish these men as candidates for honors, and we grant them privileges which we don't grant to others. Among his chief privileges, the honor man can graduate into manhood, and take a course which is modeled in character after graduate courses, a course in which he is set at work of his own with a free hand, under the guidance of an experienced teacher. That is the method of graduate study everywhere. He will in most instances be held to but one hour of attendance upon the exercise of a course of this character. He is given more time to do his independent work, and given the sensation of standing on his own feet.

We have been trying to think of other privileges and tempting distinctions which we could confer upon the men who are candidates for honors, because after all they are the men who ought to wear the University P; they are the best players on our scholarship team. It is the pride of Princeton that year after year there are men upon our athletic field who would be entitled upon either standard to wear the University P. No university that I know of has so much reason to be satisfied with the scholarship of the men on the athletic teams. What we are trying to do is not to discredit the athletic team, but, to put it plainly, to give the scholar as good a standing as the athlete. The athlete has the popularity, the fame, the temptations to inflated thought, which the other men are denied, who go about with bowed heads and closed mouths and wonder where the reward is going to come in. We are seeking and would welcome suggestions. We are seeking rewards, temptations even, for the men who go in for honors.

Printed in the *Princeton Alumni Weekly*, IV (June 18, 1904), 604-606.

To Robert Bridges

My dear Bobbie: Princeton, N. J.   16 June, 1904.

I was extremely sorry that I had to run away from the alumni luncheon just after your delightful speech,[1] in order to be at Prospect to receive the guests at my reception, and so missed the opportunity of saying good-bye to you. I am to be in New York next week to meet Mrs. Wilson at her landing, and hope that I shall be able then to tell you how much I enjoyed the speech, how much it was admired, and how beautiful we all thought the poem with which it concluded.

Always,   Affectionately yours,   Woodrow Wilson

TLS (WC, NjP).
[1] See the news reports printed at June 18, 1904.

To John Henry DeRidder[1]

My dear Mr. DeRidder: Princeton, N. J.   16 June, 1904.

I very warmly appreciate the kind invitation of the New York State Banker's Association, conveyed by your letter of June 13,[2] and wish most sincerely that it were possible for me to accept it; but I am sorry to say that at that time[3] I shall be far away in the wilds of Canada,[4] and that it will not be feasible for me to avail myself of the opportunity you offer me.

Pray express to your Committee my warm appreciation and sincere regret.   Very truly yours,   Woodrow Wilson

TLS (WC, NjP).
[1] Cashier of the Citizens National Bank of Saratoga Springs, N. Y., President of the New York State Bankers Association, and father of John Howard DeRidder of the Class of 1905.
[2] It is missing.
[3] On July 14 and 15, 1904, when the New York State Bankers Association was to meet at Bluff Point, Lake Champlain, N. Y.
[4] The Wilsons planned to leave for Judd Haven, Muskoka, Ontario, about July 7.

From John Grier Hibben

My dear Woodrow,   T.S.S. Statendam [at sea]. June 16 1904

We are nearing the end of our voyage which has been an exceedingly stormy & rough passage. The Doctor tells me that it is the most trying voyage which he has made during the year & a half of his connection with this line. We have all been sick—Jenny & Beth have been in the depths & have suffered in mind & body for eight days. Yesterday afternoon we ran into sunshine & a smooth sea, and every one seemed to forget his woe. The Dutch band played & there was dancing in the evening on deck. Today everything is bright & lovely, with the coast of England in view & the prospect of reaching Boulogne late tonight, & disembarking at 6 o'clock in the morning. We are eager to cross the channel & come to our destination as soon as possible; therefore we have decided to leave Boulogne at once & not linger there to rest as we had at first planned[.] Our tedious hours have been brightened by following you in our minds & conversation through the various stages of Commencement—stopping to calculate for a moment the difference of time & then announcing that now such and such an event is in progress! I hope that you had smooth sailing in every way (observe the tendency to nautical metaphor.) You were so good to us in your many kind & thoughtful offices before our sailing. Your brandy was most delicious and in the darkest hours flowed freely. We will look eagerly for more word from you. With much love from us all.

Your affectionate friend   Jack

ALS (WP, DLC).

From Jenny Davidson Hibben

My dear Mr. Wilson—   [At sea, June 16, 1904]

We are in the blessed English Channel, after a voyage that baffles description! It will take weeks of quiet, *green* lovely country places to make up for it. Until to-day I never walked to the end of the deck! When this reaches you "Ellen" will be with you & peace & comfort in your heart after your days of trial, & know you are both happy. Give my love to her—& to all your children, but especially dear Nellie. She was so sweet this spring & Beth & I have talked about her many times. I feel as if months had passed since we said good-bye to you & Will & Daisy.[1] A sea voyage cuts us off completely from our former world for a time.

Jack & I appreciate all your lovely last kindnesses to us—& we can not thank you enough.

I shall be much put out if you do not tell us further of Guyot Cameron's course to-ward you. I am sure that Commencement was successful and everything much brighter about it than you thought it would be. Occasional thoughts of our dear home & the wild Laurence Young's[2] have floated through my sick head. If you see Latourette[3] will you beg him to water my window-boxes *constantly*—& if some time when you are uptown you would ask Mr. Robinson to send the Princeton Press to us. We forgot it before we left & I dote on it. Jack laughs at me for wanting it. I hope with all my heart that now you will begin to have a lovely summer. I know Mrs. Wilson will make you take care of yourself—after all your hard experiences you need a happy time. Forget the College if you can. There are sea gulls, & fishing boats & a heavenly breeze & sunshine outside & every thing brightens. We go directly to London & that we shall enjoy. Jack, I hope, stays a week with us. Until to-day I actually have not felt that we were going to England, but now that I see I believe.

With love for you,
Believe me   Ever yours,   Jenny Davidson Hibben.

I have written with such an absurd pointed pen & *so* painstakingly!

ALS (WP, DLC).
  [1] Her brother, William Newcomb Davidson, and her sister, Daisy Davidson (Mrs. Leonard Everett) Ware.
  [2] They are unknown to the Editors.
  [3] William Latourette, gardener, of 22 Charlton St.

From Richard Townley Haines Halsey

Dear President Wilson: New York, June 16, 1904.

I wish to express my thanks to you for replying so explicitly to my letter. The suspicion that Cameron's scholarship was being belittled was obtained from three trustees with whom I have talked concerning the matter.

I do hope for the sake of Princeton as well as Cameron himself that after a good rest that the latter will return to his work determined to make amends for his past indefensible conduct.

Thanking you again, I remain
                              Sincerely   R. T. H. Halsey

ALS (WP, DLC).

From Wilson Farrand

My dear President Wilson: Newark, N. J.   June 17, 1904.

I write simply to express my appreciation of your action in the matter of Professor Cameron, and to say that I am sure it will prove the wisest plan. I am quite positive that there will be no trouble during the next twelve months, but if there should be, a hint of some of us who are his friends will, I think, prove sufficient.

I have been perfectly frank in telling you the impression that I have formed of Cameron's work, and in expressing my regret at the necessity of dismissing him from the University. I wish sincerely that even at present some way out of the difficulty could be devised, for I believe that he could yet be made an effective member of the teaching force. At the same time, in candor, I must admit, as I already have in conversation, the extreme difficulty, if not impossibility, of making him a harmonious member of the faculty; and I must recognize the fact that you are in a far better position than any outsider to judge of the value of his lectures.

I presume that there will be more or less agitation of the subject, and possibly some direct pressure, but I think that any open manifestation has been avoided, and that the opportunity for deliberate consideration of both sides of the case will make possible a quiet settlement of the whole matter.

Sincerely yours,   Wilson Farrand

TLS (WP, DLC).

From Abram Woodruff Halsey

My dear Wilson: New York   June 17, 1904.

This is just a line to express to you my appreciation of the generous hospitality you gave to the members of the class during our reunion. I think we all appreciated that in the midst of many and onerous duties you gave us a large portion of your time and strength. We enjoyed hearing you and much more seeing and talking with you.

I can assure you that the loyalty of the class for the University has only been intensified by the events of the quin-vicennial reunion. I wish you great success in the broad and statesmanlike plans which you have projected for the future of the University.

It ill becomes me to suggest to a man of your literary culture the advisability of publishing anything, but personally I should greatly like to see your baccalaureate address in print, and I trust you will see your way clear to giving it a more permanent influence that [than] the mere passing hour of its deliverance.

I wish also, as President of the class, that you would express to Mrs. Wilson our universal regret that she was not able to be with us at the time of our reunion.

Faithfully yours,   A. M. Halsey.

TLS (WP, DLC).

Two News Reports of the Dedication of Seventy-Nine Hall and the Reunion of the Class of 1879

[June 18, 1904]

NEW '79 DORMITORY.

Formally Presented to the University on Saturday.

The exercises in connection with the presentation of the new Dormitory by the Class of 1879 at their twenty-fifth reunion, were held at noon, Saturday [June 11], on the steps of the dormitory.

After the opening song the key of the dormitory was formally presented to President Wilson by the Reverend A. W. Halsey, D.D., President of the Class of 1879. In opening, Doctor Halsey gave a brief account of the history of the new dormitory which was given by the class as a token of love for their Alma Mater. The idea, he said, met with the cordial approval and co-operation of every member of the class from the beginning, and the building now marks the fruition of their hopes.

The dormitory fund consists of $110,000, which had been subscribed and paid by the class; the building now at its dedication being entirely free from debt.

Continuing, Doctor Halsey spoke more directly to President Wilson and in handing over the key to him charged him to regard the building as a sacred trust. He further charged that the building be held not as a mere dormitory but as a place where friendships could be made and fostered. It is these friendships which have made Princeton what it is and are responsible for that mysterious influence known as the "Princeton spirit." In closing the speaker said that it was the highest aim of the class that this spirit might be transmitted and preserved in the gifts of the Alumni.

President Wilson in a short address accepted the key in behalf of the University. He spoke of the happy accident that a member of the class should be President of the University to accept the gift, and said that his first thoughts were as a member of that class. As President, however, he could realize that the gift means the most notable exhibition of class loyalty that has ever been given in America.

Continuing, he said that a university was governed by two means—by the opinion of the students and by the authority of the faculty; and the relations of the students and faculty had changed much in the last few years, in that the opinion of the students has increased in importance.

In accepting the key he realized the responsibility and acknowledged the influence of the "Princeton spirit."

Following President Wilson's address occurred the presentation of a silk flag given by the ladies of the class. In this connection Doctor E. P. Davis briefly addressed the class.

At the conclusion of this address the members of the class joined in singing the Class Ode,[1] which was written by Robert Bridges '79.

The exercises were concluded with a prayer and benediction by Reverend William T. Elsing.

Saturday evening the class dinner was given in the class room in the dormitory. The speakers included President Wilson, Reverend William T. Elsing, Mr. Adrian Riker, Honorable Charles A. Talcott, and Mr. Edward W. Sheldon, all of whom are members of the class of 1879.

The class has tendered to the University the use of the "Tower Room," as an office of the President.

Printed in the *Princeton Press*, June 18, 1904.
[1] "Class Ode of '79," words by Robert Bridges, with music from "The Lone Starry Hours" adapted by Henry Eleutheros Cooke, John Harris Orbison, and Alfred James Pollock McClure, all members of the Class of 1879. It is printed in *Fifty Years of the Class of 'Seventy-Nine Princeton* (Princeton, N. J., 1931), pp. 312-13.

[June 18, 1904]

This was the 25th anniversary of the great Class of '79 and one of the notable features of the week was the dedication of the new '79 Dormitory. At the conclusion of his address on behalf of the class at the alumni luncheon, Mr. Bridges recited the following poem, which we are enabled to reproduce here with the author's consent:

THE PLEDGE OF SEVENTY-NINE

We have builded it
Out of the dreams of our past and our youth,
From the hopes of our Springtime, the vision of Truth,—
The prize that escaped us, the race that we lost,
The mountain not climbed and the desert not crossed;
Yea, from our failures we've builded the towers,—
The turrets from castles that never were ours;—
This but the sign of the splendor that gleamed,
The shadow that's cast by the glories we dreamed!

We have builded it
Out of the fellowship forged in these halls,
From the faith that our friendship is stronger than walls;
That fairer and finer than building or Art
Is the loyal affection that rests in the heart.
We believe in the honors that never are sold,
In the wealth that's not counted by silver and gold;
In the learning that's part of an omniscient plan
When only it's learning that's backed by a man!

We have builded it
Here where the vision was woven and caught
In the loom of our minds, and our young souls were taught
To look in a man for the germ of the best,
And leave to the cynic the search for the rest.
We have builded a pledge that the vision was true—
That Time has but brightened and broadened the view;
That our faith is confirmed by the answering years—
For it's stronger than death and it's deeper than tears.

June, 1904.   Robert Bridges.

Eighty-six members of the class of '79 attended their Quinvicennial, with headquarters in the new '79 Dormitory. The building was formally dedicated at noon on Saturday, the presentation address being made by the Rev. Dr. A. W. Halsey '79, President of the class, and the address of acceptance by President Wilson, who, as all the alumni know, is a member of this distinguished class. The exercises also included the presentation of a silk flag by the women of the class, an address by Dr. E. P. Davis '79, the singing of the Class Ode, composed for the occasion by Mr. Bridges, and the benediction by the Rev. W. T. Elsing '79. On Saturday evening eighty-four members of the class were present at the Quinvicennial Dinner in the tower of the new dormitory, and nearly sixty members remained over for a very successful smoker at the same place on Monday evening. There are at present 145 members of this class living, of whom 118 subscribed to the $110,000 expended in building and equipping the new dormitory. The liberality of '79 is also illustrated by the fact that while engaged in the construction of this handsome building, they contributed to the new Gymnasium fund over $25,000; and the Treasurer of the class, C. C. Cuyler, reports that the gifts of '79 men to Princeton have aggregated over $425,000 since their graduation. In addition to President Wilson, this class now has three members on the Board of Trustees,—C. C. Cuyler, Cyrus H. McCormick, and Cleveland H. Dodge. Princeton has conferred the degree of Doctor of Divinity upon three of its members, the Rev. A. W. Halsey, the Rev. Professor John D. Davis, and the Rev. Chalmers Martin; and at this Commencement the degree of Doctor of Laws was conferred upon another member, Robert H. McCarter, Attorney-General of New Jersey. The class has voted to turn over to President Wilson, for use as his business office, the Tower Room of the '79 Dormitory, except when it is needed for the reunions and dinners of the class.

Printed in the *Princeton Alumni Weekly*, IV (June 18, 1904), 600-601.

A News Report

[June 18, 1904]

THE 157TH ANNUAL COMMENCEMENT

Besides all its other honors, the Class of '04 is the largest ever graduated from Princeton. At the 157th annual Commencement in Alexander Hall on Wednesday, June 15th, 273 degrees were conferred upon members of '04, which beats last year's class by fifty, and which is twenty-four more than the former largest class graduated, namely '02. The Class of '04 numbered 371 when it entered college four years ago, or just two short of one hundred more than the number graduated last Wednesday.

The degrees conferred upon the graduating class were divided as follows: 188 Bachelors of Arts, 64 Bachelors of Science, and 21 Civil Engineers.

Alexander Hall was comfortably filled, and the new plan of allotting nearly all the seats to members of the graduating class worked satisfactorily. Marshalled by Captain Libbey '77 and headed by President Wilson '79 and the Honorable Grover Cleveland, LL.D., '97, the academic procession marched from the front campus to Alexander Hall, filling the platform and all the ground-floor seats and overflowering into the horseshoe. Mr. Cleveland sat on the platform next to the baldichino, where the President presided. . . .

In his Commencement address the President complimented the graduating class on the unusual record they have made as under-graduates, and referred with especial praise to their handling of the delicate situation that arose during the past year in connec-tion with the violation of the spirit of the Honor System in exam-inations. He also spoke briefly concerning the revision of the course of study.

Printed in the *Princeton Alumni Weekly*, IV (June 18, 1904), 606-608.

A News Item About Summer Plans

[June 18, 1904]

President Wilson '79 will spend the summer resting in Canada. On June 30th he is to address the banquet of the Pennsylvania Bar Association at Cape May, on The University and The Law.[1] He expects to leave Princeton for Canada about July 7th.

Printed in the *Princeton Alumni Weekly*, IV (June 18, 1904), 603.
[1] A news report of this address is printed at June 30, 1904.

To Austin Scott

My dear Dr. Scott: Princeton, N. J.   18 June, 1904.

I send you the latest circular concerning the Rhodes Scholar-ships. It was received this morning. The only question in it ap-parently which we are expected to answer is that contained in the fourth paragraph. I would be very much obliged to you if you would give me your opinion upon the matter therein broached.

Dean Fine and I came away from our visit to New Brunswick very much delighted with the pleasure you had given us.

With much regard,

Cordially yours,   Woodrow Wilson

TLS (A. Scott Papers, NjR).

From Edward Augustus Woods

My dear Dr. Wilson: Pittsburg   June 18, 1904.

We were delighted to receive word this morning that my nephew, Mr. Price, '04, has secured the Cecil Rhodes scholarship.

I imagine from the fact that you and Dean Fine were members of the Committee with [the] President [of] Rutgers, that you have been placed in an embarrassing position in deciding between the two rival candidates, and I wish to thank you for the assistance you may have been properly able to exert in his behalf.

I can well imagine that during the first two years of the incumbency of your new position you have had such troubles as a new head of an institution and responsible for its efficiency, should have, not to speak of sickness at home added to your anxiety, and I assure you that, being as I am in close touch with Princeton, not only in this city, but elsewhere, though unfortunately not one of you, you have loyal and enthusiastic support in your good work from those familiar with the situation. I believe that under your administration the University will make substantial progress along lines most satisfactory to all who know what Princeton does stand for and always has stood for, and your influence in withstanding the tendency to short terms and elective courses fills all who really care for Princeton, I am certain, with pride that you have so much charge of her destiny.   Yours very sincerely,   Edward A. Woods,

TLS (WP, DLC).

From Martin Jerome Keogh[1]

My Dear Mr Wilson   Brooklyn, N. Y.   June 21st [1904]

I am convinced that any subject you may select for your address before the Peoples Forum at New Rochelle on Sunday February 5th will be both interesting and instructive to our audience.[2] Yet as you were kind enough to ask me to suggest a subject I may say that our audiences are made up mostly of working men who have shown their greatest interest in practical questions, such as The effect of strikes on the condition of the working man, Combinations of capital and of labor, The right of labor, under American institutions and so on. Of course, I need scarcely say that we are only too willing to leave the matter to your own pleasure and convenience. You will further oblige me by letting me know the subject as soon as you have decided upon it[3]

Thanking you very much I am very
faithfully yours   Martin J Keogh
(New Rochelle   N. Y.)

ALS (WP, DLC) with WWT notation at top of first page: "Subject: 'The Individual and the Organization.'"

[1] A Justice of the Supreme Court of New York, 2nd District.
[2] Their earlier correspondence is missing.
[3] See M. J. Keogh to WW, July 16, 1904, n. 1.

To Thomas Nelson Page

My dear Mr. Page: Princeton, N. J.   June 24, 1904.

I am most willing to serve you to the best of my ability in the matter of a definition of the powers of the President of the University of Virginia; but I am afraid that the task is a little too difficult for me.[1]

I received a letter the other day from Dr. Peters of the University[2] asking for our code defining the powers of my own office, but I was obliged to reply to it that we have no such body of rules. My powers are nowhere defined; they rest on a single sentence in the charter which confides to me the "immediate care of the education and government" of the students of the University. The charter also makes me, in the absence of the Governor of the State, ex-officio Chairman of the Board of Trustees. For the rest, the powers of the Presidency here are based upon a mere body of precedent, the insensible growth of a hundred and fifty odd years.

Perhaps I can best furnish you with what may serve as a basis for rules by stating in a few sentences what we here consider the office of President really to be. I think that the office may be regarded as as normal here as anywhere, standing midway between the autocratic presidency and the presidency which is a mere chairmanship of the Faculty.

We regard the President, who is both a member of the Board of Trustees and a member of the Faculty, as the representative and spokesman of both bodies. We expect him in the Board to represent the real views of the Faculty upon strictly educational matters, and in the Faculty to represent and enforce the views of the Board with regard to the administrative management of the University. He is not, of course, bound to confine his recommendations in educational matters to those things which have been accepted by the Faculty; he may, of course, even antagonize their views there: but it is against the traditions of the place for him to do so, inasmuch as his function is conceived to be one of leadership in which it is expected that he win the support of the Faculty for his measures before seeking the acquiescence of the Board.

The appointment of all instructors and the nomination of all permanent members of the staff of instruction, that is, assistant professors and professors, rests with the President. If he is wise, he, of course, seeks the full counsel of his colleagues in the Faculty with regard to this critical and important matter; but he is not bound to take their advice in the selection he makes, and his nominations are practically equivalent to election by the Board. I have never heard of any instance in which the Board rejected a nomination made by the President.

The President represents the University on all public occasions of whatever kind; is, of course, spokesman of the Board in the conferring of degrees and of the Faculty in the announcement of educational policy.

He has also, that is just because, I suppose, of the wide interpretation which may be put upon the sentence of the charter, a sort of vague residuary power which makes him a sort of court of the last resort in all matters. Every one who feels aggrieved by anything which the Faculty has done or any of its committees feels at liberty to resort to him by way of last appeal; but it is confidently expected of him by his colleagues that he will not intervene or rescind the action appealed from, but only, if he disapproves of it, seek conference with those who are responsible for it and bring about a change, if he deems a change necessary, by a conference and not by sheer authority.

On the business side, he is, unfortunately, made chief beggar. His plans for the material development of the University are the plans which the committees of the Board consider and act upon, and his taste and choice are expected to be the chief factors in material as well as in intellectual development of the University.

I believe that I have covered in these general statements the position and authority of our President here. If we were to formulate a code, we should, undoubtedly, formulate it along these lines. I do not know how safe it would be in the case of the University of Virginia to begin with a single general provision like that of our charter and leave the development to the wisdom of the men concerned and the processes of history; but our own feeling here is that an unwritten constitution is better than a written constitution, provided the right men are chosen in the early stages of the process.

I sincerely trust that these notes will be of some service to you,[3] and I hope with all my heart that if Mr. Alderman accepts,[4] he will serve the University with some such enthusiasm for it as you or I would feel.

With warmest regard,

Sincerely yours,   Woodrow Wilson

TCL (T. N. Page Papers, NcD).
[1] The letter to which this was a reply is missing.
[2] This letter from William Elisha Peters, Professor Emeritus of Latin at the University of Virginia, is also missing.
[3] Philip Alexander Bruce, *History of the University of Virginia, 1819-1919* (5 vols., New York, 1920-22), v, 62-66, summarizes the statement of the definition of the powers and duties of the President adopted by the Board of Visitors of the University of Virginia on September 15, 1904. This statement bears a striking resemblance to Wilson's definition of his own powers and responsibilities.
[4] Edwin Anderson Alderman, President of Tulane University, did accept the presidency of the University of Virginia, took up his post in September 1904, and was inaugurated on April 13, 1905.

From Julius Tutwiler Wright[1]

My dear Sir: Mobile, Ala.   June 24, 1904.

I write to invite you to deliver the annual commencement oration of Friday, May 26, 1905. We have been twice disappointed about having you with us, and this time I hope you can come.[2] As I wrote before, I desire for many reasons to make Princeton one of the especial goals of our preparation, and your presence on such an occasion would greatly aid me in this effort. If you accept, I shall ask the Hon. P. J. Hamilton, the most prominent Princetonian in Mobile, to deliver the diplomas to the graduating class and we will have a "Princeton" commencement. The School has established an annual fund of $100 to provide for the commencement address, and this, it will be a pleasure to hand you for the expenses of your trip.

Faithfully yours,   Julius T. Wright.

TLS (WP, DLC).
[1] Principal of the University Military School of Mobile.
[2] See J. T. Wright to WW, July 1, 1904.

From Jenny Davidson Hibben

My dear Mr Wilson—   Winchester. June 28, 1904.

Two letters from you in one day have made me feel as if you had really been talking to me—& I hasten to send you a reply. From having had just *three* letters from home in all the time we have been here, today we have *numbers*, & newspaper clippings & we have fairly revelled in them. Now you are settled I hope, for a happy summer at your dear lake—with all your family about you. (Beth & I were convulsed to-night at reading in the Princeton Press that *Madge* was Mrs. Stockton Axson!) I am sorry that Dr. McPherson behaved so badly—it must have pained you deeply.[1] I suppose he has a bad temper & those cowardly men in the faculty stirred him up. Many thanks for the account of our house. Mrs. Guide[2] must have hailed you with joy. Thanks for all your interesting items. I have forwarded one set of letters to Jack— & the others shall go to-morrow.

We had a perfect ten days in London, I think the very happiest I have ever known. Jack was in the gayest spirits & we did all the things we wished to. We went to the theatres & saw Sir Chas. Wyndham[3] (a most delightful actor), & Beerbohm Tree & Ellen Terry,[4] & into the galleries to see the pictures we were fondest of, & to lovely services at Westminster, & we cast all care aside. Jack went up to Oxford twice—once to secure a man he very much wanted for his series, Dr. Bussell of Brasenose College,[5] & he succeeded to his delight, & to meet the Master of Balliol,[6] & again for Commemoration which he said was the most brilliant thing imaginable, with Oxford in bright sunshine & filled with a gay throng. Now he is in Edinburgh, & Beth & I are here. We came down yesterday & go to Salisbury to-morrow. The house where we are stopping was recommended by the Harpers, & is *like them*. Its the most picturesque & wonderful old house, filled with marvellous dark oak beams & panelling, with a fascinating outlook but not as comfortable as one might wish.

Were you & Mrs Wilson here long? It seems to me the loveliest of cathedrals—perhaps it is because it is my first, but surely no interior could be more beautiful. This morning Beth & I went out to the Church of St. Cross, & walked home, a mile through the pretty meadows by the river—& this afternoon we went through Winchester College & to service in the Cathedral. I bought a gift for you, & we hadn't time to take it back to the house, so the brown paper package went into the lovely choir stalls where we sat & was consecrated by the service! Beth looked like a lily in her white dress with the dark oak carving behind her. After tea, not content, I climbed a hill back of the town, & had it all at my feet—the meadows—the ruined palace—St. Cross—the College—& the grey Cathedral. Now I am quite tired out! Beth I had stay at home & rest & she is quite rosy to-night.

Jack still did not look well, when he went North, & I have twinges of uneasiness about his health; & I do hope the strong Scotch air will help him. It's a dreadful wrench to be away from him, but I try to make myself believe that as well as being necessary, it will do him good to have no care. I must write on foreign paper the next time, & I beg you to pardon the blot, it's so untidy. Dear love to Mrs. Wilson & to you. I think it would be lovely if your "Ellen" would write to me. Beth sent you a postal to-day but directed it to Princeton. Our house is like the Stevenson story you read to Nellie when she was ill—["] the Lieut de—'s Door."[7]   Ever yours,   J. D. H.

As you say some of my sentences wouldn't parse!

ALI (WP, DLC).
  [1] See S. J. McPherson to WW, May 20, 1904, n. 3.
  [2] The Editors have been unable to identify her; perhaps she was renting the house while the Hibbens were abroad.
  [3] He was playing the lead in "The Liars," by Henry Arthur Jones, at the New Theatre.
  [4] They shared top billing in "The Merry Wives of Windsor" at His Majesty's Theatre.
  [5] Frederick William Bussell, D.D., Fellow and Vice-Principal of Brasenose College, 1896-1913.
  [6] Edward Caird, Master of Balliol College, 1893-1907, and author of a number of works on Kant and Hegel.
  [7] "The Sire de Malétroit's Door," a short story by Robert Louis Stevenson.

To Robert Garrett

My dear Mr. Garrett: Princeton, N. J.   29 June, 1904.

I am glad to tell you that the subscriptions to our emergency fund amount to $101,000.00, and we are therefore in a position to close the matter up as a business arrangement.

I find that I have forgotten what you said to me as to the time at which it would be convenient for you to pay your own subscription. I write, therefore, to beg that you will do so at your convenience, understanding that this is really meant and is not a form asking you to pay it now. It is merely a form of letting you know that the fund is completed.

You would do me a real service by consulting your brother[1] as to the time at which he would wish to pay his own subscription. Perhaps he has already arranged with you about the matter.

I hope that you are all in good health and I also sincerely hope that you are looking forward to a most agreeable vacation.

With warm regard,

Cordially and sincerely yours,   Woodrow Wilson

TLS (Selected Corr. of R. Garrett, NjP).
  [1] John Work Garrett '95.

To Benjamin Wistar Morris III[1]

My dear Mr. Morris: Princeton, N. J.   29 June, 1904.

Professor Harris[2] has supplied me with the profile maps you desire, and I send them to you under another cover.

I am sorry to say that he did not have complete data. You will see, therefore, that some of his grades are marked "proposed." When I consulted him, moreover, he told me that at the original laying out of the field[3] it was found that an extension of some 80 or 100 feet at the southern end, the end farthest away from the power house, would make it possible to lay out three football gridirons, and so complete the proportions of the field as a playground. He has assumed, therefore, such an extension of the field in these drawings. This would apparently make the north-and-south lines of the projected buildings, running along the inner side of the Avenue, quite 900 feet long; the other arm extending at right angles to the Avenue (here called "Prospect Drive") would extend about 350 feet, if carried no farther than the present farm house, whose position on these drawings, by the way, is only approximately established.

A complete resurvey and regrading to carry the ground by a slight rise to the buildings at the south of the field would not involve a change from the grades given on this sketch of more than a foot or two at the outside. We have, therefore, assumed that these provisional drawings would be sufficient for your present purpose. I sincerely hope that they will be.

Cordially and sincerely yours,   Woodrow Wilson

TLS (WC, NjP).

[1] A New York architect who had designed Seventy-Nine Hall and had recently been engaged to draw the plans for a long dormitory to run along the eastern side of Brokaw Field, south of the gymnasium. The projected Alumni Dormitory was to constitute the central portion of the larger structure.

[2] Walter Butler Harris, Professor of Geodesy at Princeton.

[3] Brokaw Field.

From Jesse Benedict Carter

My dear Mr. Wilson—   [New York]   June 29. 1904.

In the rush of the last ten days in Princeton I found it absolutely impossible to give myself the pleasure of greeting Mrs. Wilson on her return, and of being able to see you face to face once more before our departure. I was especially sorry for this because I had hoped that the hour of departing might bring with it a liberty of expression which would not seem to you presump-

tuous or extreme—and I wanted to thank you very heartily for
you[r] great goodness to Mrs. Carter and me. What you did was
big enough in itself—but the *spirit* of it was infinitely bigger.[1] I
trust that in some way I may be able to do something in return
—something even more direct and tangible than the *sacred use*
of these two years. It is not so very long ago that I wrote you my
promise of support at the beginning of your presidency.[2] The
expression of my *admiration* in that letter was entirely sincere.
If however I were writing it today—I would add irresistibly an expression of *affection*. My intellectual admiration has been quick-
ened into a *spiritual* thing—and it is not only for Princeton's sake
but for your own as well that I look forward with joy to the next
two years in which the thought and effort of these last two years
are to produce their *inevitable* good fruit. I wish I felt as sure
of everything in the world as I do of the ever increasing success
of your work.

Please forgive me for what may seem an impertinent expression—and remember that it is the *sincere* expression of a very
grateful person.

With very cordial remembrances in which Mrs. Carter joins—
to Mrs. Wilson & yourself, I am
Faithfully yours   Jesse Benedict Carter

ALS (WP, DLC).
[1] The Board of Trustees, on Wilson's recommendation, had granted Carter
a two-year leave of absence so that he might accept a post as Professor of the
Latin Language and Literature at the American School of Classical Studies in
Rome. The trustees had also voted to award Carter a stipend of $500 for the
coming academic year.
[2] J. B. Carter to WW, June 28, 1902, Vol. 12.

Joseph Smith Auerbach[1] to Moses Taylor Pyne

Dear Mr. Pyne: New York, June 29, 1904.

I shall be happy to subscribe $500 for the next three years.
I am sorry the amount is so small, but for reasons which I will
explain when I see you, it is all that I feel free just now to subscribe.

I should like very much to have a talk with you some time generally about the financial condition of Princeton. I believe, unless there is some other plan more certain of success, that the
Memorial College idea of which I gave you an outline, might
with modifications perhaps be adopted with good results.

I saw Mr. DeLancey Nicoll[2] the other day, and he authorized
me to say that he too would subscribe $500.
Very truly yours,   Joseph S. Auerbach

TLS (WP, DLC).
 ¹ Member of the New York law firm of Davies, Stone and Auerbach, prominent
in the civic and social affairs of New York, and father of John Hone Auerbach
'05.
 ² Princeton, 1874, prominent New York lawyer with offices at 31 Nassau St.

To Cleveland Hoadley Dodge

My dear Cleve: Princeton, N. J.   30 June, 1904.

I know that you will be glad to hear that the subscriptions to
our emergency fund are now complete, aggregating $101,000.
I think we all feel that in the circumstances and in view of what
you had done for the 79 building, it was particularly generous
in you to contribute.

I am writing, at the request of the Finance Committee of the
Board, to ask when it would be convenient for you to pay your
subscription to the Treasurer of the University.

With warmest regard and appreciation,

Cordially yours,   Woodrow Wilson

TLS (WC, NjP).

Notes for an Address

Cape May.   30 June, '04
Pa. State Bar Ass'n Dinner.

The Universities and the Law.
   Big subject,—big and little dueller
   A learned profession? "De Lawd told Moses to come fo'th, and
      he come fif and lost de race."
   The leadership of business and affairs, as formerly?
      Bread and butter ⎫
      Mastery   ⎬   The old antithesis and temptation
                     ⎭
   The future to be threaded by knowledge, principle, intellec-
      tual mastery.
   The Universities should contribute
      Knowledge of society and the field of affairs
      The temper, apparatus, outlook, method of *learning.*
   A school of Jurisprudence
      Historical study of the law
         The law of real property.

WWhw MS. (WP, DLC).

A News Report of Remarks to the Pennsylvania State Bar Association

[June 30, 1904]

LAW NO LONGER LEARNED PROFESSION, SAYS WILSON

Cape May, N. J., June 30.—Declaring that the law is no longer the learned profession it once was, President Woodrow Wilson, of Princeton, to-night told the Pennsylvania Bar Association at its closing session that in the university spirit applied to the study of law lay the remedy for the situation.

"I ask you if you believe you now belong to a learned profession?" he said. "I do not believe that any man can become a learned lawyer by merely reading cases. When we see students put into a laboratory to make experiments laid down in books I know they are not learning chemistry. There is a bread and butter pursuit of the law and another, possibly less remunerative, but leading to intellectual mastery.

"The country must be saved from many things by legal arrangement, and lawyers are bound in conscience and patriotism to supply the greater part of the solution. You are not going to find any precedents in law to cover the situation in the Philippines. I am not sure that we understand what political liberty is, but if we can give people institutions more suitable to them than ours are, we have given them liberty, if not the law.

"I do not believe that it is safe to conduct a law school outside of the limits of universities.

"Sometimes I have thought that the best way to train law students is to put them in the middle of a desert, inaccessible to courts.

"We owe it to ourselves to restore the university spirit to the study of the law."

Printed in the Philadelphia *Press*, July 1, 1904; two editorial headings omitted.

From Francis Fisher Kane[1]

My dear Sir: Philadelphia.   July 1st [1904].

I desire to thank you for the noble speech you made at the dinner last night of the Pennsylvania Bar Association. In the midst of the sordid commercialism in which I live, your address was like the fresh air of the mountains to one dwelling in a low-lying swamp. Our pride in Princeton and her President was never greater than when you concluded—and that is saying a great deal.   Yours sincerely,   Francis Fisher Kane.

ALS (WP, DLC).
 ¹ Princeton 1886, a prominent lawyer and politician of Philadelphia.

From Uzal Haggerty McCarter

Dear Doctor Wilson: Newark, N. J.   July 1st, 1904.

I have received your letter of June 30th and congratulate you upon the successful result of your efforts. You may notify the Finance Committee that I will send you a check for $5000. on or before the 26th inst., when I expect some money in, which will preclude the necessity of my borrowing the amount.

Again congratulating you upon your success, I remain,
                              Very truly yours,   Uzal H. McCarter

TLS (WP, DLC).

From James Henry Lockhart

My dear Dr. Wilson: Pittsburgh, July 1st, 1904.

Your favor of June 30th has been received and noted, and I am very glad to learn that you have been successful in securing subscriptions for the complete Emergency Fund. It will be convenient for me to pay my subscription at once, and I will forward same to the University Treasurer today.

Every Alumnus of Princeton cannot help but be proud of her past and present progress, and we all feel sure that with you at the helm, our dear Alma Mater is going to go on to even greater things as the days go by.

With very kindest regards, and wishing you a pleasant Summer sojourn, I am,
                              Yours very sincerely,   James H. Lockhart.

TLS (WP, DLC).

From Julius Tutwiler Wright

My dear Sir: Mobile, Ala.   July 1, 1904.

I regret deeply that we cannot hope to have you with us at any commencement season, but I appreciate fully your reasons for being unable to absent yourself from Princeton at that time. Can you not visit Mobile in the course of your next year's Southern tour, and deliver an address under the auspices of our school? I believe it would do much to establish our closer relations with Princeton—a result which I greatly desire. If you find it possible to do this, can you not notify me a few weeks before your arrival in Mobile?[1]

With warmest good wishes, I am

Faithfully yours,   Julius T. Wright.

TLS (WP, DLC).

[1] Wilson's trip to Alabama in 1905 included visits to Marion on April 20 and to Selma and Montgomery on the following day, but he was unable to go to Mobile. See the news reports printed at April 21 and 22, 1905, Vol. 16.

From Edward Field Goltra

My dear Mr. Wilson: St. Louis, Mo.   July 2, 1904.

Replying to yours of the 30th ultimo: Beg to say I will pay my own subscription to the University Treasurer whenever you desire. Kindly notify me your wishes, and state to whom you wish the cheque made payable.

Very sincerely yours,   Edward F. Goltra

TLS (WP, DLC).

To Winthrop More Daniels

My dear Daniels,   Princeton, N. J.   4 July, 1904.

Thank you most sincerely for your letter.[1] I greatly appreciate your willingness to write the article;[2] but, unhappily, a letter just received from Mr. [Walter Hines] Page, to whom I wrote at the same time that I wrote to you, names the September number for the article and demands copy by the 20th. of July. I would hardly dare wait, therefore, till the fifteenth for the determination of the matter.

I have fallen back, in the circumstances, on Harper, who I am sure will do the thing finely, and who is going to try to have it in Page's hands by the twentieth.[3]

Do you think that the editors of the Evening Post would be willing to have further notice taken of the new scheme in their columns, and somewhat at length? If you could do that about the time people are thinking of the opening of college it would be of material service to us.[4]

I hope that you will get thorough refreshment out of your little outing at Greensboro [Vt.]; and I wish you most heartily, what I am sure you will have, a complete success in your editorial work.[5] I have no doubt you will enjoy it, too, especially in the midst of a presidential campaign.

I wish I had brought the suggestion about an article on the course of study to your attention sooner. I seem to think slowly in such things

With warmest regard to you both,

Cordially and faithfully Yours,   Woodrow Wilson

WWTLS (W. M. Daniels Coll., CtY).

[1] It is missing.

[2] About Princeton's new plan of study.

[3] For some reason, Harper's article never appeared in *World's Work*, if, indeed, he ever wrote it.

[4] A long editorial by Daniels, "Princeton's New Curriculum," appeared in the New York *Evening Post*, Sept. 20, 1904. It was highly laudatory.

[5] Daniels had recently become a contributing editor of the New York *Evening Post*.

From Robert Garrett

My dear Mr Wilson: Princeton, New Jersey   4 July, 1904

I desire to acknowledge in writing your letter of the 29th ultimo. As I said to you yesterday I shall endeavor to send to the treasurer of the University some time during August a check to the amount of my subscription to the Emergency Fund. I think that it will also be possible for me to send with it a check covering my brother's subscription. I am exceedingly glad that you have been successful in the undertaking.

Very sincerely yours,   Robert Garrett.

TLS (WP, DLC).

To Robert Garrett

My dear Mr. Garrett,   Princeton, N. J.   5 July, 1904.

Thank you most sincerely for your letter of yesterday, embodying our conversation of Sunday. The arrangement you suggest about the payment of your subscription is perfectly satisfactory.

I hope that you are going to find time for some irresponsible enjoyment this summer, and that you will keep well.

With warmest regard,

Faithfully Yours,   Woodrow Wilson

WWTLS (Selected Corr. of Robert Garrett, NjP).

From David Benton Jones

My dear Doctor: Chicago   July, 5th., 1904.

I am in receipt of your letter of June 29th., and Herbert[1] and I both appreciate very much your good wishes on our behalf. Herbert is making very rapid and extremely satisfactory progress. He hopes to be out during the last part of this week.

I am more than delighted to know that the Emergency Fund has over-reached the $100,000.00 limit. As the field has not been carefully canvassed, it certainly can be pushed to considerably higher figures. I do not recall the name of Mr. Charles R. Smith of Menasha, Wisconsin.[2] He was a candidate for Alumni Trustee, nominated by those who had graduated from the Scientific School. He is abundantly able to contribute, and after his fashion, very much interested in Princeton. I also understand that the McCormicks are not down for anything as yet. Cyrus told me that he was not, owing to the "Burden of the '79 Dormitory" this year, but that next year he expected to join the procession.

The response to this appeal has convinced me that it is not a mere spasm that will pass away, and I hope that those who will be called upon to consider its disposition, will have courage to lean upon it to a very large extent, to meet the larger current expenses which the growth and development of the Institution will impose.

Most of the subscribers, I think, would feel a certain stimulus from knowing that from year to year, they were actually carrying on work at the University which otherwise could not be done. This stimulus would hardly operate if they felt they were merely piling up a comparatively small endowment fund. I realize that there is a danger in using it too freely for current expenses; that is, a danger that it may possibly fail before a permanent endowment can be secured. I think this danger is small.

If you could look upon this fund with reliance, and in proportion improve the efficiency of the work of the Institution, it would save anywhere from three to five year's time, (and that in the present state of Princeton, would be an incalculable gain). It would also have a tremendous influence in imparting to the situation an impetus, which would of itself be the greatest possible assistance to you in securing a permanent endowment.

It is by reason of all these things, that I hope a Committee with Mr. Cadwalader as Chairman, will be formally appointed to take this whole matter into very careful consideration; that is, the extension of the fund beyond the present limit and its wisest disposition. I of course, believe in caution, but I also believe in courage, especially in matters connected with Princeton.[3]

And now as to my brother's and my relation to the fund: It would suit our convenience much better and in no serious way affect the situation, if we could make our payments on the first of March of each year. We are prepared, of course, to make it for the full period of three years now contemplated, if the fund remains intact for that length of time, even though our last payment should be made after all other subscribers have paid up their three year's subscriptions. Our subscriptions would merely fall in a little belated. We have had large demands upon us this year in various directions, and should like to begin this subscription on the first of March. If this is satisfactory to those having it in charge, we can be entered as making our first payment fall due on March 1st, 1905.

I hope you will excuse the length of this epistle, but I shall miss for a year or so, the pleasure of considering, and concerning myself with, affairs relating to Princeton.[4] Long before I became a member of the Board, I found my interest in Princeton growing every year and with every subsequent visit to the place, and I hope it will continue long after my connection with the Board has ceased.

As this letter is already over-long, I might as well add a word as to the term of Alumni representation on the Board. I drew two years for the first term. I am entirely convinced that an Alumni trustee who has served five years, can promote the special interests which Alumni representation is supposed to promote, by absolutely declining re-election. To have a certain constituency represented for ten years by one man, will to a large extent, take away the interest of the Alumni. I hope very much therefore, that each Alumni trustee, as his term approaches conclusion, will decline re-election after he has served the first full five years. I gave Mr. Cadawalader my views on this subject at our last meeting, and he quite agrees with me that this will tend to keep alive the general interest in Princeton by the Alumni.

Hoping that you will have a most successful and satisfactory year, I remain,   Very sincerely yours.   David B Jones.

TLS (WP, DLC).

[1] His eldest son, who had been ill. He was graduated from Princeton in 1910.

[2] Charles Robinson Smith '76, president of the Menasha Wooden Ware Co.

[3] As documents in this volume and in Volume 16 will show, Wilson implemented this suggestion with great vigor and success in late 1904 and early 1905.

[4] Jones was soon to depart on an extended visit to Europe. He was absent from the meetings of the Board of Trustees on October 21 and December 8, 1904, but returned in time to attend the meeting of March 9, 1905.

From Cleveland Hoadley Dodge

Dear Mr. President: New York July 5th, 1904.

I have been away over the Fourth of July holidays and just have your good letter of June 30th and enclose my check for $2500. I hope another year to be able to do more than this for the Special Fund, but am particular that what I give in this way should go directly to the uses of the University and not be put to the Endowment. I feel very strongly that we are so sure of getting a large sum every year for the current expenses of the University that we can wisely expend at least half of the $100,-000 and you will then have a large sum each year to be used for the development of the University.

With warm regards, trusting that you will have a delightful summer   Yours sincerely,   C. H. Dodge

TLS (WP, DLC).

From Edward Thomas Devine[1]

The City of New York
My dear President Wilson: July 5, 1904.

As a special feature of the School of Philanthropy to be opened in this city in the autumn, we are planning a mid-winter workers' conference at which we have reason to expect the presence of a picked body of those who are taking an active part in practical social work of various American cities, North and South.

Professor Simon N. Patten, of the University of Pennsylvania, Dr. Felix Adler, and others, are giving morning courses of lectures in Theory. During the fortnight that the conference is in session, in the afternoons, ther[e] is to be a series of round-table conferences led by its various members in turn. Supplemental to these, courses and conferences, we are planning an evening series of ten lectures to which the public will also be invited. In these, each of the more prominent professions and callings will be presented by one who will be asked, not only to describe what contribution is made to real social progress by those who are engaged in the calling which he represents, but also to offer advice and suggestions as to the manner in which the co-operation of those who represent that calling can be secured in forward social movements.

The list of those who are first to be invited to give these lectures, so far as it has been completed, is as follows:

The Prophet, Dr. Felix Adler: the Teacher, President Charles W. Eliot; the Physician, Dr. S. Weir Mitchell; the Lawyer, Elihu Root; the Public Man, Woodrow Wilson; the Social Observer, John Graham Brooks; the Army and Navy Administrator, Captain Mahan. A series of ten will be completed by selecting three from the following: the Missionary, the Labor Leader, the Preacher, the Business man, the Artist, the Writer.

We are especially anxious that you should take part in this course, and should speak on the Public Man. Dates have not yet been arranged, and even the order is elastic. We can, therefore, probably make a date to suit your other engagements without difficulty. While we would not have the hardihood to ask you to come for a purely formal lecture, we hope that it may be both agreeable and possible for you to aid in the workers' conference from which we would expect real results.[2]

Faithfully yours,   Edward T. Devine

By the Public Man, I mean the Man in Public Life, which, I think, is a better title.

TLS (WP, DLC).

[1] Prominent social worker and writer, at this time General Secretary of the Charity Organization Society of New York City and Director of the New York School of Philanthropy, which was to train men and women for social work as professionals or volunteers.

[2] Wilson did not participate in the conference.

From John David Davis

My dear Dr. Wilson: St. Louis   July 6th 1904.

I am delighted to learn from your letter that subscriptions to the emergency fund now aggregates the sum of $101,000/00.

In reply to your inquiry as to when it will suit my convenience to pay my subscription of one thousand dollars, would say October first, but if for any reason an earlier payment is needed, I will make the payment when desired by the Finance Committee.

I heartily congratulate you upon your success in raising the required $100,000/00.

Very sincerely yours,   Jno D Davis

TLS (WP, DLC).

From John Lambert Cadwalader

My dear Mr. Wilson: New York, 7 July, 1904.

I am very glad to have your note—as I am in town for a day or two and just as I am departing for the other side—to the effect that Mr. Pyne had announced that the subscription to the emergency fund was complete, aggregating $100,000. I cannot dispose of the subject as far as I am concerned, probably, in a remaining day or two before I sail for Europe. I should rather suppose that subscribers, before the payment of their subscriptions, would desire to know, first, that there is a subscription—I mean something which the various parties have signed which fixes their liability; second, that it should be understood distinctly the amount to be raised, whether for one year or more, and the purpose to which the fund is to be applied; whether a part—and, if so, what part—of the principal is to be used to pay the yearly deficiency, or whether the whole is to be invested and simply the income applied to the deficiencies. In other words, it may be that all this has been worked out and that some distinct plan exists, but I doubt it; I have never heard of any distinct plan, nor do I really know whether a single amount is to be raised for one year or whether subscriptions are for several years. If the expectation is that the people who subscribe are to pay three years in succession, I should not be able to subscribe a full five thousand; on the other hand, if we are paying for a single year, I should arrange to do so. I can hardly straighten it out before I go, but will do so on my return.

Yours faithfully,   John L. Cadwalader

TLS (WP, DLC).

From Alexander Van Rensselaer

My dear President: Fort Washington Pa.   July 9 [1904]

I am much gratified to learn of the completion of the emergency fund—and will send you half my subscription this month & the balance later on. We all missed you at the wedding, which had quite a touch of the Princeton spirit![1]

With kindest regards to Mrs. Wilson

Always   Most truly yours   A. Van Rensselaer

ALS (WP, DLC).
[1] He was probably referring to the marriage of his nephew, Dr. Edward Blanchard Hodge, Jr., '96, to Gretchen Greene in Philadelphia in February 1904.

From John Grier Hibben

My dear Woodrow   Christ's College, Cambridge.   July 11/04

I am here after my far wanderings in the North & I am having a most delightful time. Mr. Shipley[1] my host is most thoughtful in providing not only for my comfort, but for my pleasure in affording me opportunities of meeting the Cambridge men. He gave a dinner "in Hall" Saturday night, also last night, & after dinner last night he had a number of men drop in to spend the evening. Tonight I am to dine at Kings with Professor Sorley, the successor of Sidgwick in the Moral Philosophy Chair.[2] Yesterday I saw the St. Johns gateway which I enclose.[3] You will be interested in seeing how closely it resembles the one we selected.[4] The eagles are most imposing & add greatly to the effect. The gateway at the end of the *Lyme Walk* is wholly of iron with no stone pillars. I am enjoying your letters immensely as Jenny forwards them to me from time to time. I am very much disgusted with Dr. Patton. I can scarcely believe it & yet it is wholly in character with much of the past. If George is not to assist in Logic & Psychology[5] I should be glad if Fogel[6] can be worked in. I am sure he would do the teaching work better than George.

I have so far succeeded in securing four men for the philosophical series. Dr. Bussell, the Vice-Principal of Brasenose for "Neo-Platonism & Christianity," Dr. [James] Adam, Fellow of Emmanuel College Cambridge, & Gifford Lecturer at Aberdeen, for the "Stoic & Epicurean," Baillie[7] for the "Post-Kantean Idealism," & Professor Pringle-Pattison[8] for "Evolution & its Philosophical Bearings." Tomorrow I go to Oxford for a day or two, & then on to Lynton where I am to join Jenny & Beth. I had a most charming visit with Baillie, also with Professor Pringle-Pattison at Selkirk. I went rabbit shooting with the latter, not a philosophical diversion. I hear from all sides that Baillie is looked upon here as one of the coming men in philosophy. He has a most delightful personality too. We should not have made a mistake, had he gone to Princeton. I hope that you are refreshed & strengthened after the many worries & anxieties of the year. Give a great deal of love to Mrs. Wilson & the children

Affectionately yours   John Grier Hibben

ALS (WP, DLC).

1 Arthur Everett Shipley, Fellow, Tutor, and Lecturer in Natural Science in Christ's College.

2 William Ritchie Sorley had succeeded Henry Sidgwick as Knightbridge Professor of Moral Philosophy at Cambridge University after Sidgwick's death in 1900.

3 It is missing.

4 He referred to what would become the Fitz Randolph Gateway and Fence along Nassau Street in front of Nassau Hall.

5 George Stevenson Patton had been asked to assist in logic and psychology courses during the coming academic year. Taking umbrage at this increase in his duties, he had complained to his father, who had intervened successfully on his behalf with Wilson. For further comment on this matter, see J. G. Hibben to WW, Aug. 13, 1904.

6 Philip Howard Fogel, who had just received the Ph.D. from Princeton, was appointed Instructor in Logic and Psychology for 1904-1905.

7 James Black Baillie, Professor of Moral Philosophy at Aberdeen University since 1902.

8 Andrew Seth Pringle Pattison, Professor of Logic and Metaphysics at the University of Edinburgh since 1891. None of the four men mentioned completed volumes for Hibben's series.

To Robert Bridges

My dear Bobby,

"The Bluff," Judd Haven, Muskoka District, Ontario, Canada. 13 July, 1904.

Your letter, with the enclosure from McClure,[1] came the day before we left home, and I brought it along with me to answer here.

My feeling is entirely with McClure, but my judgment swings wide. Scott[2] seems really impossible. We have had reason to fear, even, that he was unworthy in money matters. Every sympathetic man of means within reach of Princeton has done something for him, first or last, and all have dropped him. My own thought with regard to what ought to be done is hopelessly at sea. The value of his work is indisputable, but that is all that can be said: the man is abnormal and very dangerous indeed to deal with. I do not think that he will be suffered to starve, of course, but the University cannot keep him. It never has kept him, indeed, since our own undergraduate days. His recent connection with it arose altogether out of arrangements made by the Garretts which imposed no responsibilities and no promises on the University,—always, I think, a questionable piece of policy. If Garrett drops him, you may depend upon it any one would drop him.[3]

I am sending Chang[4] our address to-day. I hope the weather continues enjoyable in your latitude. Take care of yourself for the sake of those who love you.

Always   Affectionately Yours,   Woodrow Wilson

WWTLS (WC, NjP).

1 Bridges' letter and the enclosure from Professor McClure are missing.

2 William Earl Dodge Scott, Curator of the Department of Ornithology.

3 The Garretts may, indeed, have withdrawn at least full support from Scott, for, although he retained his position with the university until his death in 1910, it was on a part-time basis. In October 1904, he joined the staff of the Charles C. Worthington Society for the Investigation of Bird Life as director of the buildings and equipment erected on Worthington's estate in Shawnee, Monroe County, Pennsylvania. Scott lived at Shawnee and commuted periodically to Princeton to attend to his duties there. See the *Daily Princetonian*, Oct. 12, 1904, and the *Princeton Alumni Weekly*, v (Oct. 15, 1904), 42.

4 William Brewster Lee '79.

From Charles Fishburn Zimmerman[1]

My dear Dr. Wilson: Steelton, Pa.   July 13, 1904.

As an alumnus of Princeton and as a friend of her President, I want to take up with you a matter of deep concern to myself. I feel assurance of your judicious interest. I refer to the deferred and perhaps forgotten matter of a convenient plan by which Mr. ——, 'o1 might be able to secure his degree. Mr. ——, you will recall, obtained the McCosh prize in his Junior year by using an oration which was in large part a plagiarism. This was of course during the administration of Dr. Patton. It was my privilege to have been in touch with Mr. —— when the news of his deception was spread abroad in the public prints. I determined then to hold to him and have continued to do so. Since that time I have learned much of the underlying motives of his life, and have arrived at such honest hearted convictions of his genuineness of character that I cannot refrain from making to you a personal—and at the same time, unsolicited—appeal in his behalf.

Appearances often deceive, and if anyone believes that Mr. —— through cold calculation took the McCosh prize, such a one is indeed deceived by appearances. That was farthest from his mind. On the contrary, at no time did he think he stood any chance whatever for securing a prize in the contest. In unthinkingly appropriating at the last minute an old schoolmate's oration on the same subject, his action was prompted by his thorough dissatisfaction with his own production and by his desire to make a good showing. And when the prize was announced, none could have been more surprised than Mr. —— himself. This he told me at a time when he had nothing to conceal.

Yes, it was a grave offense and because of it we saw the fair name of Princeton trailed in the mire the following February. There was not a Princeton man but felt sorry about the whole occurrence,—for anyone of a generous and charitable turn of mind could readily understand what innocent guilt might have caused the situation. It was a most unfortunate outcome of a thoughtless though none the less wrongful act.

But I do not wish to base my appeal merely on the sentiment of the case. I realize and understand the contingencies, and having summed them all up, I plead justice also:—justice to a man who has proven to my entire satisfaction that his mistake was not premeditated. While in a sense the injury done to Princeton is irreparable, in another very significant sense it is as a passing shadow. Take the act itself and its intent in their worst form, and I ask you, is not the punishment already meted out to Mr. —— commensurate with the offense? He has lived these years with the stigma of his disgrace resting upon his shoulders from the day he left Princeton; and he has lived courageously in the town of his birth in the very presence of his harshest critics. He has sought to redeem himself before the world by burying himself in business; and the energy and faithfulness and success that have characterized his career have fully justified him to those who have watched him.

But he is not a happy man. Only the other day in talking with him over his outlook he seemed encouraged, only he said: "But Zim, it is awful hard to think that I am growing old without being a graduate of Princeton." He could hardly control his feelings, for the same love of the place that we all feel, burns in his heart. From early boyhood he had worked hard towards the goal he missed.

Doctor Wilson, there is something intensely tragedic in it all. I have come to you because I believe in you. Should you accept this letter in confidence and should you see your way clear to become aggressive for Mr. ——'s reinstatement, I can assure you that you will receive the unending gratitude of a concientious man, and at the same time will conserve what I believe to be Princeton's best and highest interests.

I await a thoughtful reply at your convenience.

Very sincerely yours,   Charles F. Zimmerman, 1900.[2]

TLS (WP, DLC).

[1] Princeton 1900, employed by the Steelton, Pa., Trust Co.

[2] The subject of this letter was not reinstated and never received a degree from Princeton.

From Cornelius Cuyler Cuyler, with Enclosure

My Dear Woodrow: New York, July 14/04

Pyne and I have had several interviews with Murray and Imbrie representing the Alumni Dormitory matter and I think we have got things up to a satisfactory point except as to the choice of an architect. Apparently there is some misunderstand-[ing] about this[.] I enclose Murray's letter which fully explains how the matter stands. I am leaving for Bar Harbor tomorrow night & shall probably be away for several weeks, although if I decide to sail for Europe on the 27th I shall be here for a day or two before that. In any event Mr. Bell[1] will advise Murray of the substance of any communication you wish to make should you prefer not to write Murray direct. I am sorry to bother you with business on your holiday but thought the matter important enough to lay before you now. Hoping you are enjoying your vacation & with kind regards, I am

Yours sincerely,   C C Cuyler

ALS (WP, DLC).
¹ His secretary, Alexander Bell.

E N C L O S U R E

Harold Griffith Murray to Cornelius Cuyler Cuyler

My dear Mr. Cuyler: New York, July 13, 1904.

At the conference yesterday between you, Mr. Pyne, Mr. Imbrie and myself, relative to the construction of the Alumni Dormitory, I made the statement that the members of the Alumni Dormitory Committee had always taken it for granted that we should have something to say with regard to the choosing of an architect, and the deciding of what the dormitory was to be like, provided it met with the approbation of the President of the University, and the trustees. We did not, of course, expect to erect anything on the campus which would be unsatisfactory to them, or out of harmony with any plan for the development of the campus which the University authorities might have in mind. In proof of this, I stated that President Wilson had some time since in writing agreed that Mr. [Pennington] Satterthwaite, '93, should be given an opportunity to submit plans for the dormitory, and it would seem to me that if he gave Mr. Satterthwaite an opportunity to submit plans, it would be only fair that every man who is an architect and a member of one of the contributing classes should be given a similar opportunity.

On June 17, 1903, over a year ago, Mr. Satterthwaite wrote to Dr. Wilson asking that he might be given an opportunity to submit plans for the dormitory.¹ Mr. Satterthwaite tells me that he addressed the President at that time because the Alumni Committee had not then been formed, and that any arrangements that he might make towards submitting plans would have to be made to each class separately, and he felt that in addressing the President it would be the most direct way to reach those in authority.

Dr. Wilson, on June 20, 1903, wrote to Mr. Satterthwaite that he has read his letter with a great deal of interest and "you may be sure it will have the most careful consideration of the Committee on Grounds and Buildings. When the time for considering plans comes, I shall certainly lay your letter before the Committee on Grounds and Buildings, and I feel confident that they will give it their most careful consideration."

I have endeavored to get Mr. Fraser[2] on the 'phone today, and ask him to make a statement to me as to what conversations he had with President Wilson on the matter of Mr. Satterthwaite submitting plans. He told me yesterday over the 'phone hurriedly that he had had several conversations with Dr. Wilson on this subject, and I understood him to say, and I do not think I am mistaken, that the President had promised that Mr. Satterthwaite should have the opportunity he desired. Mr. [James MacNaughton] Thompson, '94, on June 24th this year wrote to Dr. Wilson asking that Mr. Satterthwaite and Mr. Benthuysen, '94,[3] be given an opportunity to submit plans and sketches.[4] Dr. Wilson wrote as follows:

"My dear Mr. Thompson:

The Committee on Grounds and Buildings has generally been averse to architectural competition, and therefore, before receiving your letter, I had asked an architect[5] to submit a study for the new dormitories. I assured him that his sketches would not be put into competition with others, and it was on that condition that he agreed to try his hand on it, on the understanding, of course, that we would reject his sketches entirely if we did not like them. I would, of course, be very glad to have Princeton men who are architects have a hand in the development of the campus, but I am afraid, in this instance, we must wait and see what comes of our present arrangements before we can consider the suggestion in your letter of the 24th."

On April 14th of this year, I wrote to Dr. Wilson to the effect that although he had from time to time received communications relative to the Alumni Dormitory from different classes, who desired to contribute toward the erection of this building, that it was only at this time that a definite and permanent organization had been formed, with Mr. Imbrie, '95, as Secretary, and myself, as Chairman. This was the first official notification that Dr. Wilson received from the Alumni Dormitory Committee as such. Previous to this, any communications which he had received had been with individual classes, and not from any Committee as a whole.

I asked Dr. Wilson at the time to let me have as full and complete an expression of his ideas on the subject as possible. I received from him under date of April 19th a letter in which he says:

"I am extremely gratified to hear of the satisfactory progress you are making in the matter of the Alumni Dormitory, and I can assure you that you will have every assistance that we can offer you at each stage of the business."

The President then goes on in his letter to give an outline of the development of the campus, and then says:

"We are quite confident that the plan for the Alumni Dormitory can be worked in with this plan in a way which will be satisfactory to all concerned."

Nothing was said at any time by the President as to his deciding who the architect was to be, and his letter, therefore, to Mr. Thompson was a complete surprise to the Alumni Committee, the more so as Mr. Thompson is not a member of the Committee, and if President Wilson had any such ideas on the subject as he expressed to Mr. Thompson, we should, of course, have been glad to have been notified officially.

We all realize, I know, that the President is a busy man, and that in June his manifold duties are greatly increased, and it is not strange that certain details which appear to us important might escape his mind, but it is very much the spirit of the Alumni Dormitory Committee that Princeton men who are contributing toward the erection of this dormitory, and who are architects, should be given a chance to submit plans. It seems to me in keeping with the Princeton spirit, and decidedly with the temper of the Committee, and I shall esteem it a great favor on your part if you will present these facts to the President, so that he may understand the Alumni Dormitory Committee's views on this subject.

I am very sorry that I have not been able to get a hold of Mr. Fraser, as his conversations with President Wilson are of importance, but as he is gone out of town on a trip, and I failed to get his office on the 'phone, I shall be obliged to let the matter rest as it stands before you.

Mr. Imbrie and myself both desire to express to you and Mr. Pyne on behalf of the Alumni Dormitory Committee our appreciation and thanks for the courtesy which you have both shown us in the matter. We will endeavor to reciprocate in every way possible.   Yours very truly,   H G Murray '93

TLS (WP, DLC).
[1] Satterthwaite's letter is missing.
[2] George Corning Fraser, also of the Class of 1893.
[3] Boyd Van Benthuysen.
[4] Thompson's letter is missing.
[5] Benjamin Wistar Morris III.

From Bayard Henry

My dear President Wilson,   Philadelphia   July 14/04

In reply to your polite favor would say, I shall hope to pay $500. in October, and remaining $500. shortly after 1st of next year.

If I can conveniently ante-date these times, I shall be most happy to do so.

I am glad you are off on yr well earned vacation:

You have my best wishes for a jolly good time.

I was much disappointed not to hear you at Cape May, but professional engagements called me to Buffalo for same day.

Everyone who heard you was delighted. We go to North East Harbor Maine for August and the first two weeks in Sept and altho the weather is most comfortable here, I shall be glad when the time comes for *"running off."* Sir Wm. Mather is distressed on a/c of his inability to be with us in October.

He has had to undergo a serious surgical operation.

We will hope he can put in an appearance next year. With best regards to Mrs. Wilson and your daughters believe me ever,

                              Yours sincerely,   Bayard Henry

ALS (WP, DLC).

From Martin Jerome Keogh

Dear President Wilson: New Rochelle, N. Y.   July 16th 1904.

I thank you very much for your most polite and welcome letter of July 13th.

The subject which you have chosen for your address before the New Rochelle People's Forum on Sunday afternoon February 5th "The Individual and the Organization" is a most admirable one, and is just the one that in your hands will be made most attractive to our audience.[1]

With warmest regards, and thanking you for your kindness, I remain   Very Faithfully Yours,   Martin J. Keogh

ALS (WP, DLC).
[1] The address was postponed to February 26, 1905, because of Wilson's illness. A news report of the speech is printed at Feb. 27, 1905, Vol. 16.

To Harold Griffith Murray

Judd Haven, Ontario, Canada.

My dear Mr. Murray,   21 July, 1904

Mr. Cuyler, being on the point of leaving for Bar Harbor when your letter of the thirteenth of July reached him, has forwarded it to me, as the person principally concerned.

I need not tell you that I am sincerely sorry that any, even the least, misunderstanding should have arisen in regard to the plans for the class dormitory. I feel that I ought to say at once, and very frankly, that it never occurred to me that the selection of an architect was a question falling within the sphere of the Committee representing the classes; and you may be sure that no discourtesy of any kind was intended. In replying to Mr. Satterthwaite and in all that I have done or said about that matter I have acted on the principle, which, I must say, seems to me the only sound and tenable one, that the selection of an architect was a matter which the responsible representatives of the Trustees must handle and decide.

There is in this particular case the most imperative argument for that policy. The proposed dormitory must of necessity be an integral part of a series of buildings, much more extensive than it, and as intimately connected as Little Hall and the Gymnasium. Though the central part of this series, the part which will give it distinction and which will always seem to us the chief part because of the sentiment attached to it, will be the part contributed by the associated classes which your Committee represents, the series as a whole will be at least three times the extent of that portion, and two-thirds of it will be paid for entirely out of the funds of the University itself. I am sure that the Committee agrees with me that the architectural development of the campus must of necessity be in the hands of the Board of Trustees; and that, therefore, the only question now at issue is, the method of choosing the person to whom shall be entrusted the execution of the plans which the Board sanctions.

Here again I must say that it did not occur to me as appropriate or practically feasible to draw the Committee of the classes into the determination of that matter. My promise to Mr. Satterthwaite was fulfilled. In consultation with members of the Board's Committee on Grounds and Buildings it was agreed that a competition would be very undesirable; that we could not, as you say, invite one Princeton man to offer plans without inviting all others who should wish to be considered; and that the embarrassments of such a course would be very serious indeed,

especially if we should feel obliged to reject all of the plans submitted. It was deemed the wisest plan to do what was done:
namely, to put the matter, at any rate tentatively, in the hands
of some architect with whom we had already had satisfactory
dealings and who was already completely informed as to our
ideas and plans and see whether he could produce something
that would satisfy us. That course I pursued, and from the
pledges I have made to the architect consulted I cannot now
withdraw.

I am glad to make this full explanation. It was certainly due
your committee, in view of your letter to Mr. Cuyler. As I have
said, until I read that letter, I did not know that the Committee
expected officially to be consulted; and I must say again, with
all respect, that I do not regard such consultation as a wise or
feasible plan of business; but I am none the less glad to have an
opportunity to set the whole thing forth in detail, and with the
most cordial desire to act in close confidential relations with the
representatives of the classes who are doing this generous thing.

Please express to your Committee my sincere regret if I have
seemed in any way to fail in courtesy towards them, and assure
them that any mistake of that kind that I have made has been
made through entire inadvertence, and not, of course, by intention.

With much regard,

Sincerely Yours,   Woodrow Wilson

WWTCL (WP, DLC).

To Frank Johnston Jones[1]

My dear Sir,   Judd Haven, Ontario, Canada.   22 July, 1904.

I deeply appreciate the honour done me by the Board of Directors of the University of Cincinnati in inviting me to be one
of the guests of the University and one of the speakers at the
inauguration of Dr. Charles W. Dabney as President on the six-
teenth of November next, and very keenly regret that engagements already made render my acceptance impossible.[2] Both my
personal regard for Dr. Dabney and my esteem for the work done
by the University of Cincinnati render it hard for me to decline,
and nothing but the necessity of the case leads me to do so.

Pray express to the Board of Directors my warm appreciation
and sincere regret.

Very truly Yours,   Woodrow Wilson

WWTLS (Jones Coll., OCHP).
1 Prominent lawyer and businessman of Cincinnati and, at this time, chairman of the Board of Directors of the University of Cincinnati.
2 The letter to which this was a reply is missing; for a second declination, see WW to F. J. Jones, Oct. 24, 1904.

To James Harlan Cleveland[1]

Judd Haven, Ontario, Canada.

My dear Mr. Cleveland,   22 July, 1904.

I wish most sincerely that I could accept the invitation of the University of Cincinnati to be present at Dr. Dabney's inauguration.[2] I fully appreciate the interest of the occasion and the advantage of having Princeton represented. But, unhappily, I cannot. I have work cut out for me at Princeton and in the South, where I am overdue (having had to cancel engagements in the Spring) which make it impossible for me to undertake the Cincinnati address.

I am very sorry. I am sincerely obliged to you for your kind interest in the matter, and regret, not the least in this connection, that I am missing another opportunity to see Mrs. Harlan and you.

With warm regard,

Sincerely Yours,   Woodrow Wilson

WWTLS (Jones Coll., OCHP).
1 Princeton 1885, at this time Professor of Law at the University of Cincinnati.
2 The letter to which this was a reply is missing.

To John Grier Hibben

My dear Jack,   Judd Haven, 23 July, 1904.

My hand has done as much as it will with the pen in writing the eight pages I have just finished to Mrs. Hibben,[1] and I must, perforce, fall back on the machine. Perhaps, with the present uncertain movement of my pen, she would find my letters more legible if I were to use the machine in writing to her.

It was a great pleasure to get your letter from Cambridge, which has just reached me. To hear of all the enjoyment you are having, and all the propitious success with regard to your series, is as good as having them myself. I can imagine few things more delightful than going about, as you have been, on some real business and yet among men of the most stimulating and enjoyable kind, whom it is a privilege to know: men of your own stamp, pursuits, standards, tastes, whom you can enjoy and who can enjoy and justly appreciate you. What a pity that the water should hold such acquaintanceships back from becoming intimate friendships: for I cannot help thinking that the scholars on the other side are a little broader and more human men, a little more like all-round gentlemen, a little more marked by refinement and a broad and catholic taste for the most excellent things of scholarship and conduct, than the typical man of our faculties. I think what Prentice and one or two others said about [Samuel Henry] Butcher has stuck in my craw and made it difficult to esteem our scholars as I esteem those of Oxford and Cambridge and Edinburgh and St. Andrews. Culture is a word that it is easy to drawl and make too mawkish distinctions about: but it represents a splendid thing, after all, which is too hard to find on [in] America. I would not make a fool of myself about it, as Charles Eliot Norton,[2] for example, does: but our men would be more perfect gentlemen and better teachers if they had more of it. And I quite envy you your now various acquaintance with men of the sort I most admire and enjoy. I know they must have liked you as much as you liked them.

I have forgotten how many men you hoped to get out of Scotland and England for the series, but I should think that you must have got most of those you were gunning for: and I congratulate you with all my heart. Mr. Scribner, for one, will not fail to mark the contrast between sending a genuine and sending a false man upon such an errand. How delightful it will be get the detail of your summer from you, bit by bit, as we talk next winter. And, after this going about and this zest of success, how delightful it will be for you to join Mrs. Hibben and Beth again and begin the dolce far niente.

I hope with all my heart that next winter will hold more calm for us than last! I find my spirits, so to say, quite worn out by the strain of it,—particularly by the acute culmination at Commencement.

Had I told you in any letter that the Guarantee Fund is complete? It amounts to about $103,000, and every one concerned seems very happy about it. It does not "set us forward" an inch, but it at least removes some very embarrassing difficulties from our financial way.

Thank you for the picture of the St. Johns gate. It certainly is singularly like the one we have planned, and I think, very beautiful and satisfactory. What a pleasure it will be to see ours go up in the autumn. If the directions I left are carried out, I should think the work might be well under way before winter puts a stop to masonry.

I hope that you hear from as many persons as think constantly of you on this side the sea, and realize how you are loved and trusted and believed in.

As always, and with warmest love for all three of you,

Affectionately Yours,   Woodrow Wilson

WWTLS (photostat in WC, NjP).
    1 It is missing.
    2 Professor Emeritus of the History of Art at Harvard University. He spent a prolific lifetime seeking "to reconcile the antagonistic claims of 'democracy' and 'culture' in American Society." Kermit Vanderbilt, *Charles Eliot Norton, Apostle of Culture in a Democracy* (Cambridge, Mass., 1959), p. 1.

From Moses Taylor Pyne

My dear Woodrow   Princeton, N. J.   July 23/04

I don't want to bother you, but I want your views. The accounts are up now for the year. The deficit instead of being $12,000 as we hoped is $24,800. Against this we have the interest on the Jesup Fund[1] and the Alumni Fund[2]

          amounting to   5,300

          leaving a balance of   19,500

Then using $10,000 of the Emergency Fund we get it down to $9,500.

Now one of the extras comes from the five years insurance premium of $900 per year, all of which had to be paid this year. I think it perfectly proper to spread this charge over the five years so I have arranged to borrow the four coming years' premiums viz: 3,600

This brings the deficit down to $5,900

I am willing to contribute a great part of this myself but I think others should join. I feel this deeply since it leaves the debit balance of $24,000 carried over from last year uncared for. This was made up as you remember out of accounts such as the following:

          Coal b't at high price during the strike   11,000
          Bal. due on Infirmary Annex   2,500
              "   "   " Lavatories   7,500

and similar matters.

I cannot see how we can without dishonoring one old promise to the givers, let this debit balance run on much longer. Can you suggest anyone who will be willing to assist. I am ready to contribute $5,000 more toward this year's deficit, but if my subscription can draw more money I think it better to apparently hold back until others come forward & then I am ready to give the whole $5,000.

Do you approve the spreading of the Insurance premiums over the 5 years?   Sincerely yours   M. Taylor Pyne

ALS (WP, DLC).

1 An endowment fund established in 1900 by Morris Ketchum Jesup, the New York lawyer. The Morris K. Jesup Fund was worth $50,000 at this time.

2 An old endowment fund worth about $40,000 at this time.

From Harold Griffith Murray

My dear Dr. Wilson: New York, July 25, 1904.

I have just received your very full and complete letter setting forth your reasons why you do not consider it feasible to throw open for competition to Princeton architects the plans for the Alumni Dormitory. I feel the matter is one of such importance that it would be unwise for me to say anything further in the matter until I have submitted your letter to the Alumni Dormitory Committee, which has a meeting on the 28th of this month. I will be glad to forward you a report of this meeting as far as it bears on this question immediately after the meeting, which will be a further answer to your letter.

Thanking you for your courtesy in replying at such length to my letter to Mr. Cuyler, I remain,

Yours very sincerely,   H. G. Murray.

TLS (WP, DLC).

From Moses Taylor Pyne

My dear Woodrow: New York   July 26, 1904.

I have your letter enclosing your copy of the reply to Murray regarding the architects. I am sorry that any feeling should have arisen in the matter. Judging from what Murray told me, he understood that you had agreed to let his Class have something to say about the architect, but I feel sure he is mistaken in this matter. The question of the selection of an architect is always a very difficult one, because competition is extremely unsatisfactory, while when you have an architect chosen you are not sure that he is the best that could be picked out. Morris is very good, but he falls short I think, of Cope, and certainly of Stewardson,[1] in his ideas. I hope that by carefully going over his plans and making suggestions, and by letting him have plenty of time to finish them up, we can get him to give us something that is very high class, as this building must be.

We are still in Princeton and expect to remain another week. The weather has been delightful. We have not had a hot night and most of the days have been cool and clear. I shall see Cuyler next week at Bar Harbor and talk to him about the matter.

Very sincerely yours,   M. Taylor Pyne

I return your copy of your letter

TLS (WP, DLC).
  [1] Either Emlyn L. Stewardson or his brother, the late John Stewardson, both of Philadelphia and partners of the late Walter Cope.

To Benjamin Wistar Morris III

Judd Haven, Ontario, Canada.
My dear Mr. Morris,   30 July, 1904.

Your letter of the twenty-sixth of July has been forwarded to me here.[1] I must admit I am a little at a loss what to think about sending the drawings to this out-of-the-way place. I am exceedingly anxious to see them, and, if they can be sent without risk to them, I hope that you will send them.

One trouble is, the wretched tariff question. They would have to pass through the Canadian customs. I take it for granted they are not dutiable, however. Perhaps the Agent of Adams Express in New York can tell you whether they are or not, and how to mark them so as to show their exact character and prevent their being opened. Aside from that they ought to come through safely enough, by the hands of the Canadian Express; but they have to [be] handled by boatmen and ought to be as securely protected as possible.

Thanking you for your expedition in this important matter,
As always,   Cordially Yours,   Woodrow Wilson

WWTLS (WC, NjP).
  [1] It is missing.

From Moses Taylor Pyne

My dear Woodrow   [Princeton, N. J.]   July 30/04

Thanks for your favor of the 26: It is pleasant reading but I cannot make your estimates agree with mine & Duffield's.

You are correct in thinking that a large part of the deficit was due to the bad management of the Curator[1]–$10,000. But a good deal came from other causes. For example $1,500 is for preachers[,] $1000 for Scott's assistant.[2] Grading around '79 Bldg = $1832.18. Current library expenses = $2315.88. ($1000 of this however has been paid by my sister[3] & myself) Extra cost of gymnasium. Increase of light & heat owing to Mac Thompson's wretched mismanagement of the Power plant. Binding &c. in library $1700. (This will not be renewed.) &c. &c.

Duffield & I have gone over the accounts & while we may be too conservative, we don't see one way at present to reduce the estimated deficit for next year below $15,000–altho' I must say that that ought to be the maximum.

The Emergency Fund amounts to	$103,365.71
Of this we must invest	90,———
	————
Leaving a balance for current expenses of	13,365.71

Humphrey's[4] statement regarding the Alumni Fund must have referred to last year when we received not only the income but also the principal of all sums paid during that year. This year we can only figure on the interest.

This is, I believe, the exact state of affairs:

Deficiency for 1903/4 including '79 grading and library deficit not reported before, but deducting $3600 insurance premiums		$24,431.47
Offset in part by		
Emergency Fund	13,365.71	
Alumni Fund	1,687.78	
Jesup Fund	3,375.——	
Cash on hand	256.19	18,684.68
	————	
Net deficit		5,746.79
Of this I agreed to contribute		5,——
		————
Leaving still a balance of		746.79

which must be raised to close books free of debt.

Last year we carried over a deficit of over $24,000 still unpaid. If we can raise $105,000 again for the Emergency Fund, which we ought to do we should be free & clear of next year's charges. We can count for the reduction of the old deficit on the following:

Jesup & Alumni Funds	4,——
79 Dormitory	4,
Investments of Emergency Fund *say*	2,000

————

10,000

I figure this by estimating 4% on so much of the Emergency Fund as will not be required for the new Dormitory viz: 30,000 of which 4% would be   1,200 and allowing $800 for accumulations of interest on the balance until needed for the dormitory. But we must keep this deficit ever before us until it is wiped out.

I appreciate your kind expressions regarding my interest in the work. I am trying to do what I can, in a small way, towards building up the University and in this I am only one of several— I wish I could say of many. But you & I & C. C. & Bayard & a few others have the laboring oar. I can only say that what you say of me is pleasant as coming from you & that I can repeat it to you, as a "honeyman," only in a greater degree. It is a wonderful relief to feel that we have a man at the helm who is a Princeton man himself and is willing to work for Princeton, not merely to accept what she offers without return.

We are still here. The weather continues clear cool & bright. As I write 1 P.M. Saturday July 30 the thermometer stands at 74 Fahr. on my front porch. There is not a cloud in the sky. Princeton never looked so beautiful as it does this summer. The Russells, Bayard Henrys & ourselves leave August 2nd for North East Harbor Maine our address "Kimball House." C. C. is at Bar Harbor so we shall see him. I hope you are all enjoying yourselves. With kind regards to Mrs. Wilson & the girls in which Mrs. Pyne joins me I am, as ever.

Yours vy sin   M T Pyne

ALS (WP, DLC).
[1] James MacNaughton Thompson, Curator of Grounds and Buildings until his sudden resignation on March 5, 1904.
[2] Gilbert Van Ingen, Assistant in Geology and Curator of Invertebrate Paleontology.
[3] Albertina Pyne (Mrs. Archibald Douglas) Russell.
[4] Theodore Friend Humphrey '94, lawyer of New York.

From M. S. Commissariat[1]

Dear Sir,   Bombay, India   30th July 1904.

It will be a matter of legitimate satisfaction to you to hear that your excellent work on "The State" has found its way as a text book in the Bombay University for students preparing for the highest degree in Arts conferred by that University. I myself have gone through it with the greatest pleasure and interest and the work is a valuable help for the study of Comparative Politics.

The chief question of historical interest at present is the war going on in the Far East and attention is naturally turned to the Constitutions of the belligerent countries. You have in your introduction to your book mentioned your inability to include Russia for fear of increasing too much the size of the book. I would thank you to let me know if you have published or written anything on Russia recently.

I think it would greatly add to the value of your book by adding to it a chapter on Japan also, seeing that the modern Constitution of that country has been based on the Constitutions of European nations.

Believe me,

Yours very faithfully,   M. S. Commissariat.

ALS (WP, DLC).
[1] Fellow of St. Xavier's College, Bombay University.

An Introduction to *The Handbook of Princeton*

[*c. Aug. 1, 1904*]

Everyone who knows Princeton feels that it has an atmosphere and a spirit of its own, and I suppose that the ideal introduction to a book of this sort would contain an analysis of that distinctive charm and character. But, long as I have felt that charm and acknowledged affectionate allegiance to Princeton, I should despair of giving its character adequate interpretation. The spirit of a place, however distinctly felt, is too subtle a thing to be caught in words. It can be perceived only in its effects, realized only in the life which it produces. It is easy enough to state the ideals upon which the life of Princeton is based: they are manifest to all who stand inside her walls; the subtle thing which escapes analysis lies in the processes by which those ideals are sought in action.

At the heart of the influences which have made the place there undoubtedly lies the love of sound and liberal learning, a very manly reverence and enthusiasm for those things which prepare the spirits of men for the tasks and fortunes of life, making them quicker than their fellows to catch the outlooks of their journey and perceive the essential values of what falls in their way. The average undergraduate carries himself with a careless freedom which has very little in it of the pose of the thoughtful student. His love is for sport and good comradeship and the things that give zest to the common life of the campus. You would not think him, in passing, a man who cared for books or learning; and generally he is not,—not, at any rate, in any such sense as that in which his teachers and preceptors are lovers of the written page and the processes of quiet study. There are undergraduates whose chief care is for these things, indeed, and if they are a minority, they are a very large and important minority; but the ordinary undergraduate is not educating himself, as these men are; he is being educated. He knows it, and has a certain strong, even if unconscious, respect for the thing that is happening to him. He knows that it is the essential power and distinction of the place, where for long generations together men have been held to intellectual tasks; that the welfare and advancement of the nation somehow depend upon these processes, and certainly the greatness and permanence of the University which he loves. There would be no dignity in his pleasure, no distinction in his life with genial comrades, were the University and all that is done in it not lifted above all ordinary levels by tasks and ideals which are of the mind and spirit.

It is in much the same way that a strong and manly religion plays its part in ruling the spirit of the place. And yet here the motive force proceeds from the undergraduates themselves rather than from older men, their teachers, in the class room and laboratory. The University may be said to be rooted and grounded in religious conviction. She was established and has throughout all her life been maintained by men whose performance of their duty took its zest and vigour from their clear religious faith, and with whom the care of religion was as high and sacred an object as the care and furtherance of learning. But religion cannot be handled like learning. It is a matter of individual conviction and its source is the heart. Its life and vigour must lie, not in official recognition or fosterage, but in the temper and character of the undergraduates themselves. That religion lies at the heart of Princeton's life is shown, not in the teachings of the class room and of the chapel pulpit, but in the widespread, spontaneous, unflagging religious activity of the undergraduates themselves, in voluntary organization, and above all in the fact that men of all sorts, not serious students alone, but men out of every group and every sport and every interest of the various little community as well, take their active part in promoting faith and the right living

that springs out of it. Sound and liberal learning and equally
sound and liberal religion lie together at the foundation of all
that her sons most admire in the University.

The place has its free air of pleasure and of good fellowship
because its love of letters has never been belittled into pedantry
and the mere love of books. Letters have been for it an expression
of life, interesting because the utterance of men, the record of
what is real and of actual deep consequence wherever men would
act upon reason and not upon mere blind instinct. It has always,
so far as we can discover, been a place which chiefly loved men,
and loved books because they were the servants of men, lifting
his spirit and clearing his vision for the work of the world's day.

It has been a sign and evidence of this that affairs have always
so quickly and easily affected it. It has always been quick to think
of the country and take up the themes of first consequence to it.
It first showed this temper and disposition at the Revolution,
when, under the leadership of John Witherspoon, the great Scots-
man who did so much to give it character, it gave its best life to
the cause of the revolted colonies and bred both lawyers and
statesmen for the young republic; and it has never lost the spirit
of that time; has never been local or shut in or confined to a
single interest, but has felt that it belonged to the country in its
entirety,—patriotic in the best sense, knowing no other allegiance.
To this every true son of the place testifies. His horizon is that
of the nation itself, his sense of privilege and responsibility as
strong in the field of politics as in the field of letters.

It would be hard to say whether the free comradeship and
democracy of Princeton life is cause or effect in relation to these
things. No doubt it has been of deep consequence to her that
her life has been formed in a place apart, where no city dominated her and she herself constituted an independent community. The village of Princeton, though spread abroad over a great
area on either side the old highway upon which the original set-
tlers found it most convenient to lay out their farms and place
their homes, has less than four thousand inhabitants. Its life
centres in and depends upon the life of the University. It has,
indeed, time out of mind been the place of residence of a few
prominent families whose interests connected them with the
affairs of the commonwealth, not with the affairs of the University. Their homes, placed amidst broad lawns and pleasant
gardens, have always constituted a chief part of the beauty of
the town. And in later years other handsome residences have
been built and the green acres about them smoothed and beauti-

fied, as graduates of the University and other, newer friends, attracted by the quiet and dignity of the place, have been drawn to it by natural choice or inclination; so that it has become more than ever a place of stately homes and of interesting circles of people without official connection with the University. But it is unquestionably the life created by the University that has drawn these families to the town. Every one remarks its academic tone and atmosphere and feels the domination of the ancient institution at its centre whose broad campus and stately buildings give character and distinction to the town.

The life of the campus goes forward almost without heed of the life of the town. Its own affairs absorb it: it is a separate community, observing laws and customs of its own. It cherishes its own traditions, its own standards of taste, its own ideals of conduct and mastery,—some of them very whimsical and bearing evident traces of the fact that its men have not entirely ceased to be boys, but quite as many sober, elevated, well considered, the outcome of a great deal of serious observation and a long experience of university life. A university generation is only four years: within that short space of time the entire undergraduate body changes; but the tradition is unbroken, is kept alive by class after class, in most cases with very jealous care, and the continuity of the life is not interrupted. Only one class graduates at a time; only one is added at a time; the new class is each year quickly and thoroughly instructed in its duty.

The most influential Seniors govern their own class and the University in all matters of opinion and of undergraduate action. They are the leading citizens of the little community. They are self-selected. They lead because they have been found to be the men who can do things best, the men who have the most initiative and seem best to embody the spirit of the place in the way they look at things and determine mooted questions of action. "Leading citizens" are everywhere selected in the same way,— not by formal election, but by their own qualities and natural gifts of leadership; and by the time classmates have reached their senior year there is never any doubt as to who are the leading characters among them. Their intimate life together, their close comradeship and observation of each other, have thoroughly tried out their several qualities and capacities. Student life at Princeton depends upon the compact and intimate organization of classes which is so characteristic of the place. Each class is an organized body and acts as a unit in all the chief transactions of university life; and among the classes the senior class occupies a place of natural leadership and initiative. The university authorities consult the leading Seniors as a matter of course upon every new or critical matter in which opinion plays a part and in which undergraduate life is involved. They feel the counsel of these men to be indispensable. They know that it will be seriously given and that its chief motive will be love of the University, a care for its best interests, a desire to see its life bettered in every possible way for which opinion is ripe or can be ripened.

It is this community feeling and action, this natural constitution of leadership, this sense of close comradeship among the undergraduates, not only but also between the undergraduates and the Faculty, that constitutes the spirit of the place and makes its ideals and aspirations part of thought and action. It naturally follows, too, that graduates never feel their connection with the place and its life entirely broken, but return again and again to renew their old associations, and are consulted at every critical turn in its affairs. Such comradeship in affairs, moreover, breeds democracy inevitably. Democracy, the absence of social distinctions, the treatment of every man according to his merits, his most serviceable qualities and most likeable traits, is of the essence of such a place, its most cherished characteristic.

The spirit of the place, therefore, is to be found in no one place or trait or organization: neither in its class rooms nor on its campus, but in its life as a whole. Hence its love of men and of affairs, its preference for practical religion, in which initiative rests with its own volunteers, its patriotic feeling for the country as a whole, its predilection for the sort of learning which gives men horizon in their thinking and schools their wits and spirits for the tasks and changes of life. It lives and grows by comradeship and community of thought: that constitutes its charm; binds the spirits of its sons to it with a devotion at once ideal and touched with passion; takes hold of the imagination even of the casual visitor, if he have the good fortune to see a little way beneath the surface; dominates its growth and progress; determines its future. The most careless and thoughtless undergraduate breathes and is governed by it. It is the genius of the place.

                                        WOODROW WILSON.

March 27, 1905.[1]

Printed in John Rogers Williams, *The Handbook of Princeton* (New York, 1905), pp. xi-xvii.
[1] Undoubtedly inserted at the time that *The Handbook of Princeton* went to press. J. R. Williams to WW, Aug. 8, 1904, indicates that Wilson composed his introduction about August 1, 1904.

From Moses Taylor Pyne, with Enclosure

My dear Woodrow   Princeton, N. J.   Aug. 1/04

I enclose letter not to carry out the suggestion therein, but to show you that care must be taken not to irritate unnecessarily some good workers for Princeton. All is coming on well & coming out well, but it is advisable in working with the Globe Wernicke Committee[1] to use plenty of tact. They mean well but cannot understand.

Yours very sincerely   M Taylor Pyne

[1] See n. 1 to the news report printed at April 16, 1904.

E N C L O S U R E

James MacNaughton Thompson to Moses Taylor Pyne

Dear Mr. Pyne: [Princeton, N. J.]   7/30/04

Your good letter of the 26th at hand. If you can conveniently do so, do drop Dr. Wilson a hint to make some tack in the Alumni Dormitory matter concerning the Architect. Dr. Wilson wrote me that he had asked Mr. Morris to prepare plans with the understanding that there would be no competition but that Morris' plans could be discarded if not satisfactory.

I'm more than sorry that this trouble has come but as a rank outsider of an ordinary alumnus, I do hope that Dr. Wilson can be made to realize that there are breakers ahead. I've heard some pretty hard talk about "high-handed," "obstinate," "whole show" etc. and such talk is not a healthy sign. I know very well that Princeton has suffered from abortive architecture but is it reasonable to suppose that a Committee of Alumni would want some freak?—and moreover the G. & B. Com. would be the court of last resort, so to speak. All I'm after is to head off this ominous hot-air. Don't think me an alarmist but there's considerable smoke in sight and the fire ought to be smothered in its incipiency.

With kindest regards to Mrs. Pyne and yourself, in which Mrs. Thompson joins most heartily, believe me,

Faithfully yours,   J. MacN. Thompson

(Don't bother to answer this)

ALS (WP, DLC).

From Harold Griffith Murray

My dear Dr. Wilson: New York, August 4, 1904.

On Friday, the 28th ult., the Alumni Dormitory Committee met, and I submitted to them your letter from "The Bluff" relative to the Alumni Dormitory. The Committee, as a whole, expressed their desire to do everything to aid and assist you in the development of Princeton's Campus along lines which would be satisfactory to all, and they empowered Mr. Imbrie, the Secretary of the Committee, and myself, to confer with Mr. Cuyler and Mr. Pyne about the matter.

The Committee, however, expressly stipulates that the Dormitory shall be one of ten entires [entries], no entry to be more costly than another, and the whole Dormitory to cost not more than $120,000 or $125,000, and that the Dormitory shall always preserve its individuality as a unit, and at no time to be connected with any other Dormitory, and while it may be a part of the general scheme for the development of the campus, it is not to be connected with any other building, and only the ten classes from 1892 to 1901, inclusive, shall contribute to the Dormitory.

I trust that these facts will be acceptable and agreeable to you, as the Committee intends they shall be. The Committee desires me to thank you for your hearty expressions of good will towards us in the work we are undertaking.

I have written to Mr. Cuyler asking him to set a time and place when it will be agreeable for him and Mr. Pyne to meet Mr. Imbrie and myself to confer further about the matter.

                    Very sincerely yours,   H. G. Murray

TLS (WP, DLC).

To Harry Augustus Garfield

                    Judd Haven, Ontario, Canada.
My dear Mr. Garfield,   5 August, 1904.

It was very pleasant to see your handwriting again.[1]

I find, on examining the new schedule, which has just been sent me, that your lectures (three hours a week, under the new plan) come on Thursdays, Fridays, and Saturdays at noon. They therefore begin on Thursday, September 22nd.*

It is very unfortunate that the sessions of the Congress[2] should have been put just when they will most interfere with college appointments. A great many of us are affected by it. I shall have to leave St. Louis the very night I speak,[3] in order to get back for the opening of the University, and Fine has had to decline the part in the Congress offered him. I do not see which of the colleges escapes the inconvenience of the arrangement.

I hope that you are all very well and that you are having a thoroughly refreshing time. Please give our regards to the Adriances.[4]

All join me in cordial messages, and I am, as always,
Cordially and faithfully Yours,   Woodrow Wilson

* If the classes can be so soon organized. Probably on Friday, or Saturday.

WWTLS (H. A. Garfield Papers, DLC).
  [1] Garfield's letter, to which this was a reply, is missing.
  [2] That is, the Congress of Arts and Science of the Universal Exposition in St. Louis.
  [3] Wilson's address, "The Variety and Unity of History," is printed at Sept. 20, 1904.
  [4] Perhaps the Rev. Harris Ely Adriance and his wife, Sarah Holmes Adriance. Adriance was a graduate of Williams College (1883) and of Princeton Theological Seminary (1889). He was a social worker in New York as well as the founder and pastor of the Church of the Son of Man in that city.

To Charles Williston McAlpin[1]

Judd Haven, Ontario, Canada.
My dear Mr. McAlpin,   5 August, 1904.
Will you not be kind enough to let me know whether anything has yet been heard fro[m] M. Labori[2] about his coming to Princeton for a degree in October?[3]
Faithfully Yours,   Woodrow Wilson

WWTLS (McAlpin File, UA, NjP).
  [1] Actually, the McAlpins were in Europe at this time, and John Rogers Williams, historical editor and author of works on Princeton and Princeton University, was handling the business of the Secretary's office, facts which Wilson had momentarily forgotten.
  [2] Fernand Gustave Gaston Labori, French lawyer and legal scholar (1860-1917). Best known as the junior counsel for the defense at the trial of Alfred Dreyfus in 1899, he also edited, with Émile Schaffhauser, the Répertoire encyclopédique du droit français (14 vols., Toulouse, 1889-1910).
  [3] The Board of Trustees had voted on June 13, 1904, to confer the LL.D. degree upon Labori at the Commemoration Day ceremonies on October 22, 1904. For Labori's reply, see F. G. G. Labori to WW, Aug. 14, 1904.

From Moses Taylor Pyne

My dear Woodrow   North East Harbor [Me.], Aug 6 1904
Your kind letter recd. I have seen Cuyler who leaves tomorrow for Duluth & Canada to return about Sept 1st. I think we can

handle the debit balance in two years & that as long as we endeavour to pay it off our obligation to the givers is only slightly tainted—not broken. We must next Fall work up the Alumni Fund as well as the Emergency Fund—one for small, one for large subscriptions. We ought to get a new secretary who will give up his time & brains to it.

Bayard Henry & I shall be here until September. I hope you are following up the FitzRandolph Gateway as well as the Dormitory.

With kind regards to all from all I am as ever

Yours very sincerely   M Taylor Pyne

ALS (WP, DLC).

To Harold Griffith Murray

Judd Haven, Ontario, Canada.

My dear Mr. Murray,   8 August, 1904.

Allow me to thank you for your letter of August fourth, informing me of the actions of the Alumni Dormitory Committee on the twenty-eighth of July.

Your letter reached me yesterday morning, and I have thought over its contents very carefully. I am sure that every member of the Committee on Grounds and Buildings will be anxious to meet the st[i]pulations of your Committee, if it prove possible to do so. I will myself cooperate most willingly towards that end. But I hope that your Committee will postpone all final conclusions until we can have a full comparison of views, and that, meanwhile, it will take the following considerations up for very careful debate:

1. It is going to be very difficult indeed to find a site for a separate building which will compare with that which had already been provisionally fixed upon,—if indeed, it prove possible; and I fear that a separate building running for the length of ten entries at an unbroken height and without variation of mass will prove very hard to give distinction to, architecturally.

2. The stipulation that no additional entries shall be attached and that no other classes but those from 1892-1901 shall contribute is a serious disappointment to me and makes the scheme of less benefit to the University than it at first promised to be. When the plan was at first suggested,—not of course by your committee, which was not then formed, but by Mr. Imbrie, Mr. Prentice, and the men who, I believe, first gave it shape,—the strongest and to my mind the most attractive argument urged was

that the ten classes first associated could begin a building to which other classes, stimulated by their example, could from time to time add. It was upon this supposition that the site by the Brokaw Field was selected, a site not suitable for separate buildings, but only for an unbroken line like that of the Littles and the Gymnasium. Several classes had already asked if they could come in, and the thing at first hoped for had seemed at hand. This is, in my mind, a very serious consideration indeed, and I feel confident that your committee will not dismiss it lightly. It involves the interest of the University very deeply.

These are matters, however, which ought to be most thoroughly canvassed, and I hope most heartily that your committee and the committee of the Board will have,—will take,—ample time to discuss them when we all get once more within reach of one another in the autumn.

Thank you most sincerely for the kind expression of your letter.   Very truly yours,   Woodrow Wilson

WWT and WWshLS (WP, DLC).

From John Rogers Williams

Dear President Wilson: [Princeton, N. J.]   8 August, 1904.

I have just returned from my vacation in Virginia and find your letters of the 27th. ultimo[1] and the 5th. inst. In reply to the latter I beg to say that I am unable to find any answer from Maitre Labori and do not believe that such a reply has been received.

I wish to thank you for your splendid introduction to the Handbook. I thoroughly appreciate the trouble you have taken in the matter and want to thank you again for your invaluable assistance. . . .

Very sincerely yours,   [John Rogers Williams]

CCL (McAlpin File, UA, NjP).
[1] It is missing.

From Moses Taylor Pyne, with Enclosure

My dear Woodrow   N. E. Harbor Me   August 10/04

Your letter recd. I agree with you thoroughly & would not have sent Mac Thompson's letter except that I tho't it better to have the full knowledge of the feelings of all the people. I enclose a statement of the deficit which I have made up & which is, I think, very clear.

All are well. This is, as you know, a delightful spot & we are enjoying it & gaining health & strength daily. Bayard [Henry] & I have been taking long walks over the hills. Dr [Charles] Wood is here, so with C C [Cuyler] & D C Blair at Bar Harbor we have 5 trustees on hand.   Sincerely yours,   M T Pyne

ALS (WP, DLC).

E N C L O S U R E

Financial Statement of Princeton University

STATEMENT.

1903-1904.

EXPENSES.

	Estimated	Actual
Salaries,	$137,610.00	$134,326.67
Grounds & Buildings,	25,000.00	35,177.58
Incidental,	7,000.00	9,037.42
Taxes,	3,200.00	3,393.37
Catalogues,	2,500.00	2,504.53
Servants,	14,200.00	14,321.25
Steam Heat,	5,000.00	435.20
Water Supply,	3,000.00	1,592.66
Gymnasium,	4,000.00	1,452.38
E. M. Museum,	2,800.00	3,225.61
President's Ent. Account,	2,000.00	2,000.00
President's Secretary,	500.00	453.50
Commencement Expenses,	900.00	871.63
Astronomy,	600.00	1,033.07
Ass't. Librarians,	5,000.00	5,000.00
Evening Attendants,	1,500.00	1,500.00
Salary, Ass't. in Geology,	1,500.00	1,500.00
Librarian's Fund,	1,265.00	1,260.00
Library,	2,400.00	2,412.00
Insurance,	1,200.00	916.31
Dickinson Prize,	60.00	60.00
Classical Fellowship,	60.00	58.34
Janitor, Hist'l. Laboratory,	420.00	420.00
Infirmary,	1,500.00	1,424.45
Registrar's Ass'ts.	1,880.00	1,880.00

	Estimated	Actual
Light and Heat, Tutor's Rooms,	750.00	782.00
Chem. Apparatus,	150.00	145.16
Philo. "	200.00	118.32
University Library,	3,600.00	3,600.00
Chapel Music,	1,550.00	1,550.00
Sanitation,	500.00	339.67
Expenses. Clerk of Faculty,	50.00	27.21
Salary, A/C, S. S.	1,700.00	1,700.00
Ass't. Patagon. Reports.		1,000.00
Pulpit Supplies		1,150.00
Univ. Light & Heat,		6,500.00
Bayles Farm,		176.58
Library, Book Rests & Bind. '03,		850.00
" " " " '04,		850.00
Grading around '79 Building,		1,832.18
Library (Current expenses)		1,315.88
Estimated Expenses,	$233,595.00	
Actual expenses,		$248,192.97

INCOME.

	Estimated	Actual
Interest, Gen. Fund,	$ 27,084.87	$ 27,678.68
Blair Prof.	2,250.00	2,250.00
President's Fund,	3,655.00	3,655.00
Stewart $100,000 Fund	6,359.40	5,750.97
Chair of Politics,	4,000.00	2,000.00
Converse Fund,	370.00	370.00
Edwards' Chair Am. History,	2,000.00	2,000.00
Prof. Moral Philosophy,	1,840.00	2,000.00
McCormick Prof.	4,065.00	4,065.00
McCosh Prof.	2,080.00	2,500.00
Murray Prof.	4,000.00	4,000.00
Musgrave Prof.	2,548.05	2,548.04
Fund to Inc. Prof. Salaries,	692.00	692.00
Int. on N. Y. Deposits,	2,000.00	1,589.82
Entrance Fees,	945.00	974.00
Tuition Fees,	104,000.00	102,136.28
Room Rents,	45,000.00	45,344.57
Wallace Scholarship,	250.00	250.00
Wood "	100.00	100.00
Lenox Fund,	2,000.00	2,000.00

	Estimated	Actual
Diplomas,	500.00	1,200.00
A. G. Agnew Gift.	100.00	100.00
School Philos. Fund,	11,320.00	9,200.00
Charitable Fund,		356.60
Glass & Keys,		1,000.00

Estimated Income,	$227,159.32	
Actual Income,		223,761.50

(Estimated Expenses	$233,595.00	)
(		)
(Estimated Income,	227,159,32	)
(		)
(Estimated Deficit,	6,435.68	)

Actual Expenses,	$248,192.97
Actual Income,	223,761.50

Deficit,	24,431.47

Less

Emergency Fund,	$13,365.71	
Jesup "	3,375.00	
Alumni "	1,687.78	
M. T. Pyne,	5,000.00	
Miscellaneous	256.19	23,684.68

	746.79

DEBIT BALANCE 1902/3.

Steam Boilers,	$ 3,350.00
Dormitory Lavatories,	5,830.00
Fuel,	11,700.00
Gas,	630.00
Infirmary Annex,	2,490.00

	$ 24,000.00

T MS. (WP, DLC).

To Frank Thilly

Judd Haven, Ontario, Canada.

My dear Professor Thilly,   12 August 1904.

It was a real pleasure to see your handwriting again[1] and to know that you were once more on this side the water. I hope

your four months in Europe brought you genuine rest and refreshment.

Your courses next year, under the new scheme of study, are
to be: Advanced Psychology, with the Juniors, three hours a
week, first term, and Psychology (elementary), with the Sophomores, three hours a week, second term. This second term course
is to be required of all the Sophomores, and we shall of course
arrange to have you assisted in the recitation work.

When do you expect to get to Princeton with Mrs. Thilly and
your household gods? I hope you found her and the children
well. Mrs. Wilson and I expect to be back in Princeton by September tenth. We are all well, and all unite in the most cordial
messages to you all. We shall look forward to our intercourse
of next winter with the keenest satisfaction.

Faithfully Yours,   Woodrow Wilson

WWTLS (Wilson-Thilly Corr., NIC).
¹ Thilly's letter, to which this was a reply, is missing.

From Moses Taylor Pyne

My dear Woodrow   No. East Harbor, Me   Aug 12/04

Yours of the 8th recd regarding the Globe-Wernicke building.
I raised this very point with the Committee & both Cuyler & I
told them that such a building would have to be part of a long
row & not an isolated building. They did not answer this point
positively—in fact seemed rather favorable to our suggestion that
new classes should come in—such as the class of '80—and I
thought there would be little trouble about it. Evidently that point
in their letter to you is their conclusion. But I agree with you perfectly & the matter will have to go over to next Fall as we are all
away.

I fear my letters are a trifle incoherent. I have to write in our
common sitting room and am continually interrupted by conversation around me, interspersed by a running fire of questions
addressed to me.   Sincerely yours   M Taylor Pyne

ALS (WP, DLC).

From John Grier Hibben

My dear Woodrow,   Brussels   Aug 13/04

After a very delightful ten days in Paris we are now in our old
quarters in Brussels,—at the same comfortable Pension where we

were four years ago. I received your letter while in Paris & appreciated its warm words of friendship, & of interest in my undertakings concerning the Philosophical Series. Since writing to you at Cambridge, I have secured one other Oxford man, a Dr. Webb of Magdalen[1] who has consented to do the Mediaeval Period. He is the one person mentioned by the Oxford & Cambridge men alike for the period. I have still one other man who is uncertain & who is taking the matter under consideration—that is Mr. J. A. Smith of Balliol, who is regarded as the leading Greek scholar in Great Britain. I have had a long interview with him & hope that he will decide to do the Aristotle.[2]

I have just received a letter from Prof. Smith of Lake Forest[3] who has asked me to recommend some young man in Philosophy to take his place for one year during his absence abroad. I naturally think of Fogel for the place & yet if George Patton is not to assist in Logic & Psychology next year we would need Fogel in Princeton. I shall write to Smith giving Fogel's name for I feel I owe it to Fogel to give him the chance. I know however he would rather be in Princeton next year & would do the work of an instructor if needed for a very small salary. I am interested in the whole Patton situation & I think it is very inconsiderate of Dr. P. to put you in such an embarrassing situation. We met Charles & Mrs. McAlpin in Paris—also Allan & Mrs. Marquand,—dining one night with the McAlpins & the next day taking luncheon with the Marquands. The McAlpins were in regal apartments, once occupied by the Prince of Wales when he was in Paris—also by Napoleon. The latter I doubt. Paris was most fascinating. We had two most memorable excursions, to Fontainbleau and to Versailles—the only drawback was the heat which however was broken during the last two days of our stay. We are gradually working our way to Holland as we have decided to sail from Rotterdam instead of Boulogne. We will go from here to the little corner of Holland where Flushing is. We heard from a man who was on our steamer & who was born near Flushing that this part of Holland is rarely visited by tourists & preserves much of its original simplicity. On our way to Flushing we are planning to spend a day at Bruges which has not yet lost its mediaeval setting & atmosphere.

I took great comfort in meeting Charlie McAlpin. We had a long Princeton talk on Sunday afternoon. He is a very loyal friend of yours & a man upon whom you can depend implicitly. I am delighted to hear that the emergency fund has been completed, with the measure pressed down & running over. It will not be long now until we set our faces again to the west, & it will be a most delightful experience to meet our dear friends after so long a separation. It hardly seems possible that our summer is almost a thing of the past. We have had a most delightful time & I feel profoundly thankful for the success which I have had in securing such excellent authors for the series. In addition I feel it a great privilege to meet so many interesting men who have devoted their lives to the service of a pure scholarship & yet who are so human in their varied interests and sympathies. We will have much to talk over when we meet & settle to the work of a new year. I hope that for you especially it will be a year of smooth sailing in every respect. With much love to you all

Your affectionate friend   Jack

Henry van Dyke has added to his list of visits, one to Carnegie & one to Lord Tennyson. He breaks the record!!

ALS (WP, DLC).
  ¹ Clement Charles Julian Webb, Junior Dean of Arts and Classical Tutor. He never completed his volume for Hibben's series.
  ² John Alexander Smith, Classical Tutor and Librarian; Jowett Lecturer in Philosophy. He did not contribute a volume to Hibben's series.
  ³ Walter Smith, Professor of Philosophy at Lake Forest College since 1890.

From Henry van Dyke

Skibo Castle,¹ Dornoch, Sutherland.

My dear President Wilson: August 14, 1904.

Your very kind letter reached me in Edinburgh three days ago, but I've carelessly mislaid it and must answer a little in the dark, not remembering precisely the dates you mentioned. In regard to September 25th I sincerely wish that I could take the chapel service then. But there is a reason, (confidentially!) which makes it impossible. My wife will be in New York, waiting for the arrival of a little stranger, who is expected about September 27th; and naturally I want to be with her during as much of that week as possible.²

By shifting things a little I could arrange to preach on Dec. 6th or 11th,—on Jan. 15th or 22d,—and *possibly* on Oct. 16th. So will you just choose the day which suits you best, (if any of them is convenient,) and I will try to do the rest.

You may be sure that I count it a privilege to do anything in my power to help on with the work of Princeton, but I have very serious doubts about my power. It is not easy to preach.

I hope you are having a good summer. We are coming home on the Oceanic, sailing the 7th of September; and though we are having a jolly time among the grouse and the trout, right glad shall we be to see America again.

Faithfully Yours   Henry van Dyke

ALS (WP, DLC).
[1] Andrew Carnegie's recently constructed castle in Scotland.
[2] Their ninth child, Katrina Trask van Dyke, was born on October 1, 1904.

From Fernand Gustave Gaston Labori

Sir,   Paris   August 14th, 1904

I am deeply touched at the invitation extended to me by the Trustees of Princeton University for October 22nd to receive the honorary degree of Doctor of Laws.

I have been compelled to give up my trip to the States this year being obliged to remain in France during the month of September on account of a very important affair which I have to transact for a client & which can only be followed up at that time.

The honour done to me by the Trustees of the Princeton University makes me doubly regret the impossibility I am in of visiting America this year. I beg you to be good enough to transmit to them & to receive yourself my sincere thanks

Believe me, Sir, with high esteem

Yours very truly   Labori

ALS (WP, DLC).

To John Rogers Williams

Judd Haven, Ontario, Canada.

My dear Mr. Williams,   15 August, 1904.

Yes, Part IV. of the catalogue, "System of Undergraduate Study," will be furnished by Professor Thompson's committee.

In spelling such words as "Honours" I was only following my own habit.[1] I do not think that it would be well just now to alter the spelling hitherto used in the catalogue.

Please return a polite No to Mr. Cresse's letter,[2] thanking him for his interest in the matter, but telling him that, after careful consideration of the matter, the authorities of the University have thought it best not to use the Fair as an occasion for advertising.   Sincerely Yours,   Woodrow Wilson

WWTLS (McAlpin File, UA, NjP).
[1] Wilson had earlier sent him a nine-page WWT "Memoranda: Rearrangement and Revision of the University Catalogue," McAlpin File, UA, NjP. It not only

provided a new format for the catalogue but also included numerous literary emendations and extensive revisions bringing the catalogue up to date.

2 Cresse's letter concerning the possibility of a Princeton exhibit at the Universal Exposition in St. Louis is missing. As John D. Davis to M. T. Pyne, Dec. 2, 1903, makes clear, the Board of Trustees—at Wilson's insistence—had earlier decided against such a project.

From Herbert Hollingsworth Woodrow[1]

My dear Cousin: Grenoble, Aug. 16, 1904.

I am in Grenoble trying to acquire a little more fluency in French than I at present possess, with the idea of entering the university of Paris this fall, to specialize in psychology. I did not decide upon this course until after leaving Ann Arbor, and so have not had the opinion of any one in a position to know what is advisable. I wish to spend two years studying in Europe besides one, either my second or third, in the United States. I wish to ask you whether Paris offers as good advantages for the study of psychology as any of the universities in Germany. From what I know, I think it is the best place in Europe, but I will be very greatly obliged to you if you will tell me what you think about the matter. I am undecided whether I ought to go to Paris or to some German university, as I have considered Munich, Leipsic, and Berlin. If you will have the kindness to give me your advice, it will enable me to decide what to do, without the feeling of uncertainty that I (as well as the rest of family) would otherwise have.[2]   Very Sincerely Yours,   Herbert H. Woodrow.

ALS (WP, DLC).

1 Son of Thomas Woodrow and Helen Sill Woodrow of Chillicothe, Ohio. He had received the A.B. degree from the University of Michigan in June.

2 Wilson's reply is missing. Woodrow went to the Sorbonne, 1904-1905; studied at the University of Michigan, 1906-1907, and at Princeton, 1907; and received the Ph.D. from Columbia in 1909. After teaching in several universities, he served as Professor of Psychology and Chairman of the Department at the University of Illinois, 1928-50. He was the author of numerous works on educational psychology.

From Benjamin Wistar Morris III

My dear Dr. Wilson: New York   Aug. 16, 1904

I am sending you by express a roll of sketches[1] which form a suggestion of the treatment of the Buildings below the Gynmasium [Gymnasium.] A plan at a scale of 100 ft. to the inch is indicated in pencil on the light green paper print, which also indicates in a very rough way what I understood to be your idea of the future development of the grounds southeast of your own residence.

The tower of this group of buildings is located approximately on the spot indicated by you, as far as southeast and northwest dimensions go, but I find in studying the elevation that what was a comparitively small difficulty in the '79 Dormitory is magnified considerably in the great length of this new Building.

Beginning at the end nearest Dod your suggestion of turning the terminating pavilion at an angle with the main southeast and northwest stretch works out easily and I think is a happy thought. Then the southwest facade of the building continues on parallel with the road and trees to the point at the southeastern end of this stretch where it forms the angle with the wing at the eastern corner of Brokaw field and stretches out in a southerly direction. This stretch of the main southwest front is so long that the necessity is apparent of breaking it up in order to avoid monotony and this has been accomplished with a recessed court or quadrangle on the axis of which the tower rises. This court is approximately 120 ft. from southeast to northwest and is recessed in a northeasterly direction from the main southwest front about 56 ft.

At first I felt disposed to combat your idea of using the Magdalen Tower at this point but after making a number of thumbnail sketches, it seemed to me to be so appropriate and to compose so harmoniously with the buildings whose character is necessarily determined by their site, that I feel it can be used in a very successful way.

I know that you will appreciate that this drawing is hardly worthy of being called a sketch on account of its roughness of presentation, yet the amount of drawing necessary is so great to present an adequate idea of the design that I feel very anxious for your opinion of the suggestion which it makes, in order to avoid a large amount of what might prove to be useless labor.

I have been saturating myself with books and illustrations relating to the architecture of this period and becoming as intimate as possible with the ways and means by which its beautiful effects are produced and while I think the scheme of composition has distinctly the atmosphere of the Tudor period nothing has been taken directly from any example with the exception of the Tower and here I would make this suggestion: Is it not the mass and graceful proportions which will produce the effect you desire from the grounds of the University? If this is the case I would suggest that that part of the Tower which rises highest and dominates the neighborhood be a reproduction of the original so far as is practicable but that the gateway and lower portion be altered as may prove necessary to harmonize with the Buildings at its base.

Compton Wynyates, Moyn's Park, Kentwell Hall, Littlecote and Stoneleigh Abbey have all been drawn upon for their inspiration but I hope without robbing their architects and owners of anything properly belonging to them.

The chiaroscuro, which is lacking in this drawing, I know your imagination will supply and it is of course, next to the scheme of composition, the most important thing to be considered. I have kept it constantly in mind and if you find that this scheme has promise in it it will of course be developed and presented graphically.

The wing which stretches in a southwesterly direction from the end of the gymnasium has been turned at an angle to widen the opening and to give a more welcoming prospect to those approaching Princeton by train and the angle has been determined by the amount necessary to make it place inversely to the gymnasium as regards the central axis of the tower running at right angle with the main stretch of the Building.

Hoping that there may be something in these drawings which will interest you and assuring you that I await your comments with great interest,[2] I am,

Faithfully yours,   Benjamin W Morris Jr

TLS (WP, DLC).
  [1] They are missing.
  [2] As B. W. Morris III to WW, Dec. 12, 1904, discloses, Morris completed final plans for this dormitory complex in early December 1904. Only the central portion, then called the Alumni Dormitory and later named Patton Hall, was ever constructed.

From Joseph Smith Auerbach

Dear President Wilson: New York.   August 17, 1904.

Your letter of the 22nd of July, concerning my subscription to the Guarantee Fund, unfortunately was placed among some accumulated correspondence of Mrs. Auerbach which awaited her return from the mountains. It has only now been handed to me.

It will be convenient for me to pay my subscription whenever you desire, and I have no doubt a similar arrangement will be acceptable to Mr. Nicoll. While awaiting your reply I shall speak to him.   Very sincerely yours,   Joseph S. Auerbach

TLS (WP, DLC).

To Benjamin Wistar Morris III

Judd Haven, Ontario, Canada.

My dear Mr. Morris,   22 August, '04.

Pray do not think that I am neglecting your letter of the six-teenth, or that it did not reach me. It came in due course of mail. But the drawings have not yet turned up, and I am waiting for them. They are so extremely suspicious of all packages that cross their borders up here, and so slow in apprizing those to whom they are addressed of their advent at the customs office, that it is a tedious and vexatious business. No doubt at their con-venience I will be asked to say what the package contains, and then, when they get ready and happen to think of it, it will be forwarded. Meanwhile, I dare say it is safe enough!

With much regard,

Faithfully Yours,   Woodrow Wilson

WWTLS (WC, NjP).

From James Bryce

Hindleap, Forest Row,

My dear President Wilson   Sussex.   Aug 22/04

I am much honoured by your invitation to be your guest at Princeton on Oct. 22nd & deliver the annual address there: and should with great pleasure accept it could I count on being able to come at that time to Princeton. But I have already formed en-gagements which may make it difficult or impossible for me to come on that day: and in any case it would be quite out of my power now to find time to prepare an address fit to be delivered to a Princeton audience, for I have promised lectures to Columbia, Harvard & the Lowell Institute which it will take me all my time to compose: and all my strength to deliver.

However I do trust that I may have the pleasure of seeing you while I am in the U. S., & if I can make time to run down to Princeton for a night I will most gladly do so.[1]

Believe me   Very sincerely yours   James Bryce

ALS (WP, DLC).
[1] See J. Bryce to WW, Oct. 8, 1904, n. 1.

To Frank Thilly

Judd Haven, Ontario, Canada.
My dear Professor Thilly,   25 August, 1904.

I congratulate you with all my heart! It is delightful news that your letter[1] brings, of the birth of a little son.[2] I am much more interested than I was in the birth of a poor little heir to the throne of Russia.[3] Mrs. Wilson joins me in the most cordial messages of pleasure to you both, and in the hope that everything is going well with mother and child.

It was a real pleasure to hear from you. Thank you for your letter. I shall expect to arrive just as you do, at Princeton.

Always,   Faithfully Yours,   Woodrow Wilson

WWTLS (Wilson-Thilly Corr., NIC).
[1] It is missing.
[2] Frank Thilly, Jr., born on August 22, 1904.
[3] Tsarevitch Alexis, born on August 12, 1904.

To Benjamin Wistar Morris III

Judd Haven, Ontario, Canada.
My dear Mr. Morris,   25th August, 1904.

The drawings have come, and I have been studying them. It seems to me that they will furnish a basis for what we want. It is a peculiarly hard thing to give variety to so long a row of buildings, and I think you have done remarkably well. The part that seems to me most to need modification is that which constitutes the steps down hill, just beyond the initial mass; and I have some suggestions to make which I hope will solve the problem.

I am going to take the liberty of keeping the drawings until my return home. I am obliged to leave to-morrow for Toronto on business, and may be gone some ten days. In about two weeks we shall all be starting for home. It is so hard to get the drawings over the border, unless personally conducted and so impossible to say what I have to say in a letter, that we will, if you please, take the matter up after my return to Princeton.

Meanwhile let me congratulate you on so promising a beginning, and express the hope that the other members of the Committee will like it as much as I do.

Faithfully Yours,   Woodrow Wilson

Have you happened to study "Alton Towers," the seat of the Earl of Shrewsbury near Stoke-upon-Trent? I have recently come upon a picture of it and find it full of suggestions for us. One feature fits, I think, our present problem of masses.

WWTLS (WC, NjP).

Charles Follen McKim[1] to Junius Spencer Morgan

Dear Sir,   New York.   August 26, 1904.

I beg to submit for your consideration the following estimates for the Fence and Gates at Princeton University:

MASONRY:	BLUE LIMESTONE:	BUFF LIMESTONE:
		(deduct)
Wm. R. Matthews,	10,883.00	982.00
Tide-Water Bldg. Co.,	11,280.00	1,040.00
Norcross Bros.	20,650.00	1,500.00

METAL WORK:		
John Williams,	6,250.00	
Wm. H. Jackson & Co.,	8,125.00	
Tiffany Studios,	8,928.00	

The above estimates do not include the carving of the eagles on the two main fence posts. I feel that unless these eagles are modeled and executed by the ablest talant [talent] available, the result cannot be otherwise than commonplace, and I should, therefore, strongly recommend that the sum of $1,000 be set apart to enable you to secure the services of a sculptor of repute, who shall make the models and supervise the execution. I also strongly recommend that the eagles be executed in stone rather than in bronze.

With reference to the electric conduit work, the estimates include the drilling of the posts ready for the drawing of the wires, but do not include bringing the conduits from the source of supply, wherever it may be, to the posts. Furthermore, the estimates do not include the making of any roads, paths, sidewalks, or changes in the curb that may be found necessary.

It will be noted that in the masonry work alternate estimates are furnished for the substitution of buff limestone for blue limestone. The saving in cost, however, is relatively so little that I would strongly advise the use of the blue Indiana limestone, which, in my judgment, is far superior to the buff.

I would recommend the acceptance of Mr. Matthews' estimate of $10,883, and of John Williams' estimate of $6,250.

Until the commencement of the work on the University Cottage Club, I had no knowledge of Mr. Matthews, but he has conducted that work in a thoroughly workmanlike manner, and I have every confidence that he may be safely entrusted with this work. I think we are also fortunate in securing so low an estimate from John Williams, inasmuch as he has done so much work of this character for me, and disregarding the amount of his estimate, he would be the man to whom I should prefer to give the work.

On the basis of the above recommendations, the total cost would be as follows:

MASONRY	Wm. R. Matthews,	$10,883.00
METAL WORK	John Williams,	6,250.00
ALLOWANCE FOR EAGLES		1,000.00
		$18,133.00
Architects' Commission, 10%,		1,813.30
		$19,946.30

I hand you herewith a copy of the working drawing and the specifications, and will await your further instructions.

Yours very truly,   Charles F. McKim   B. L. F.

TLS (WP, DLC).
[1] Distinguished New York architect, member of the firm of McKim, Mead and White, who had drawn the plans for the Fitz Randolph Gateway and Fence.

A Draft of an Article[1]

[c. Aug. 29, 1904]

PRINCETON'S NEW PLAN OF STUDY.

Princeton has undertaken to construct a system of study out of the modern miscellany of university courses. The old college

[1] This was Wilson's initial response to John Brisben Walker, "What Is Education? The Studies Most Important for the Modern Man. Who Should Study Science," *Cosmopolitan*, XXXVII (Aug. 1904), 401-403, a reprint of which the author, editor of the magazine, had sent to Wilson on August 23, 1904, along with an invitation to Wilson to write an article in reply (see WW to J. B. Walker, Aug. 30, 1904). Walker's article scathingly denounced Princeton's new plan of study for its neglect of science in the curriculum at the very time when such studies ought to be more than ever stressed. The article went on to denigrate the study of Latin and Greek and, implicitly, other liberal studies and to argue that students in all fields needed more rather than less grounding in the technical and practical aspects of science.

As the next document reveals, Wilson asked Stockton Axson to read his article. Axson correctly observed that Wilson had not met Walker's arguments directly but had gone on the defensive and been too abstract in defining his own philosophy of unified studies. Impressed by Axson's comments, Wilson set his article aside and wrote the letter to Walker printed at August 30, 1904.

curriculum, confined to Greek, Latin, and Mathematics, with a dash of philosophy and of natural science for flavor, is now out of the question. Undoubtedly our fathers got out of its slow and careful digestion very robust and serviceable mental fibre; but the world has changed since their day. We are now too rich in various subjects of study to confine our young men to that ancient narrow round, excellent as the discipline was that was got out of it. And yet the very richness and variety of the modern field of study is itself a serious embarrassment. The lad cannot traverse all of it, and there has been much confusion of counsel of late years, and much disappointing failure, in attempting to give him access to selected parts of it. Princeton, though she has been hospitable to every new subject of study and has varied and enriched her programmes with the rest, has never, as it happens, broken with the principle that university study is not for information and variety but for discipline, for the release of the faculties for anything that may come: to teach men how and where to use their minds, and not merely to take them upon a tour amongst modern bodies of knowledge. She has had, therefore, a certain advantage in reconsidering her plans,—the advantage of always having kept a fixed purpose, however much her practice may have varied or gone astray.

In the first place, just because the things a man of the modern world must study are so complex and varied and the tasks for which he must discipline himself so intricate and difficult, it is held at Princeton that four years is not only not too long a time to devote to university processes, but is all too scant. Time is of the essence of the process. It is not a question of how much ground a student covers,—if that were all to be considered, he might be permitted to cover it at as breathless a pace as he chose, —but a question of how thoroughly he covers it and with how intimate a comprehension. He is not rushing through an encyclopaedia, but submitting himself to a process of training. Four years seems the minimum limit of thorough saturation. The freshman is a boy; the sophomore is adolescent; the junior is staggering for his sea legs; the senior finds them. Perhaps a small college which draws its students from a narrow local area can have an understanding with the schools which feed it; but the freshmen of a great university which draws its students from all quarters of the continent come from schools of every name and grade and quality and are as diverse as their origins. During their first year their variety must be unified; they must be forced into the university mould, by disciplinary studies like those which they have had at school but advanced a step further and pursued in the university spirit: the spirit, not of those who are repeating lessons, but of those who are consciously reading themselves into the thoughts and methods and ideals of men who look upon knowledge as a means of life, a medium of vision. The sophomore, if he be given this preliminary year of training and enlightenment, will have had his year of introduction, but he will not be ready for an immediate plunge into the deeper waters of university study which are to be found in the specialized courses and laboratory investigations of the upper years. He must first be given a thorough grounding in one or both of the fundamental physical sciences, physics and chemistry, and in the fundamental philosophical studies. He must also be given an opportunity to choose among the general studies, not hitherto brought within his reach, like the higher mathematics, general history, additional courses in science, and more advanced courses in the languages, ancient and modern, which will lead him to the special and more concentrated studies of his third year, whether in science, in history, in politics, in language, in philosophy, or in art. But he is not yet to specialize: his election is still among general, fundamental subjects. In junior year he is ready to choose a particular field of study, but ought not to confine himself to it. He has not yet won the full freedom of the world of studies. If he chooses a literary field of study, he ought also to choose something from the field of science, if a scientific field something from the group of literary or philosophical studies, wherewith to salt his specialty, in order that he may not lose the liberalizing influence to be got from a more various view. Only the senior should be permitted to confine himself to a single line, or a small number of closely related lines, of reading and investigation.

Such are the principles upon which the new plan at Princeton is based. To set the scheme forth here in detail would be to run into technicalities which would blur the outlines. The general reader would have to call a university specialist to his aid to understand what he was reading. But one side of the matter is worth looking at more closely. Hitherto, at Princeton as at many other universities, the two sections of the University, the School of Science and the Academic Department, have been somewhat sharply separated and contrasted,—a reminiscence of the day when scientific studies were added to the old group of classical, literary, and philosophical studies, but were set apart as courses to be separately administered; not received into the ancient, exclusive circle of accepted subjects but put upon trial by themselves. The new plan at Princeton will have the effect of doing away with this difference and unifying the curriculum of the University on the theory that the new humanities which centre in the laboratories are to be embraced in schemes of study on the same footing as the old.

But this is necessarily upon the assumption that the science taught is pure science, not applied science. These new humanities of modern study are humane only if studied in the spirit of the old, as bodies of knowledge and for their own sakes, not as means of practical skill merely and for the sake of a livelihood. They have no legitimate place in a university curriculum when studied in the spirit of manual training, as mere methods of work. To say this is not to discredit technical schools. They are as necessary as universities: it would be impossible to carry on the processes of the modern industrial world without them. The more they are multiplied and strengthened the more certain we shall be to have the vast number of master mechanics we need. But they are not universities. They are not even what they used to be, successful training schools for engineers, except in so far as they have changed their one-time character and approached the character of universities in their methods of scientific study.

The world has changed by leaps and bounds in these matters during the last generation,—during the last decade. Modern business has got too large for the old methods of preparation. The engineer nowadays, if he would rise to the top of his profession, must be something more than a mechanical expert; must be ready to become a master of industry and of men, to assume charge of great undertakings in any quarter of the globe, under the most various and unlooked for conditions of law, of climate, of labor. His resources will be tried to the utmost, and he must have resources. He must be fit for more, much more, than he has been directly taught: must be in some real sense a master of the sciences underlying the great constructive processes which he superintends. He needs the education of a general officer in the world's army of workers: no sort of training or information will come amiss. Native sagacity and natural adaptability will carry him a long way, but these he must have in any case, and they will not carry him so far as he could go with the added assistance of a definite and sufficient grounding in pure science and the general training of a university man.

This is doctrine preached now by the representatives of every modern profession that is based upon educational training,—as what modern profession is not? The representatives of the electrical engineering profession tell you that the special training hitherto thought sufficient for their tasks is no longer adequate: that the electrical engineer ought to have the training, first, of a general engineer, and turn to the specially intricate and difficult tasks of the electrical engineer only if he has proved himself fit and has got, besides, the special knowledge of electricity and of general physics that he will need. He must be a specially fit man selected out of the general engineering body by peculiar aptitude and exceptional training. The representatives of the general engineers tell you, in their turn, that the training of the mechanical and civil engineer has hitherto been too narrow and technical, too much that of the mere master mechanic; that he is too slightly grounded in the study of pure science: that the engineers trained in most of the technical schools are apt to be little more than mere rule of thumb experts. The better technical schools are, therefore, giving more and more time to the teaching of pure science, for its own sake, and less to the teaching of mere processes of application and manipulation. The plain implication of their change of practice is, that every engineer ought first, if he can possibly afford it, to be a university man before he attempts to become an engineer.

Nor is this new doctrine and advice confined to those who would promote the skill and mastery of the engineering professions. The doctors and lawyers sing the same tune,—and even men engaged in general commerce. The modern world, whether of knowledge or of action, is too complex to be mastered by blind experiment; it is not safe for any man to try his hand at its affairs in ignorance of their sweep and significance. The physician must work through a broad field of science, and work very thoroughly, in the spirit of the student of pure science, if he would go beyond the rudiments in his practice and depend upon anything better than crude experiment. The lawyer must know not only the law, itself a product of complicated circumstance running far back into history, but also the peculiar conditions of modern legislation and the social, circumstantial, economic foundations of business. The merchant must know the ends of the earth, understand the posture of international politics, trade in markets no ordinary traveller ever visits. Every profession demands men of general culture, whose training has awakened their minds to all the conditions of modern life.

This sweeping excursion through medicine, manufacture, law, commerce, and engineering may seem an unnecessarily grandiose justification of the simple proposition that the proper function of universities is to teach pure, not applied, science. But the modern university is a part of the world. It is no longer a place cloistered and set apart, for men who wish to separate themselves from the world and ponder the things, not of time, but of eternity. Its immediate object is not, indeed, business; but it is enlightenment, the preparation of at least a certain number of men to see life and its affairs with a comprehensive and comprehending view. Undoubtedly pure science deserves study for its own sake. Applied science would itself stand stationary and helpless if pure science did not walk before it showing the way, and yet not thinking of the mechanic arts but only of nature and the lurking secrets of the laboratory. But it heartens the man of science in the midst of his investigations, nevertheless, to know that he is playing into the hands of those who push forward the material progress of the age; that his pupils will carry power away with them, and capacity for helpful practical service; that the university is the laboratory of action. His conviction grows clear and steadfast that the university is not, as such, a place for the mechanic arts, but a place where their liberalization and fertilization are to be efficiently provided for. Technical schools may very well be connected with universities and so put within the influence of university atmosphere and method; the connection certainly benefits them; but the university cannot itself be a school of mechanic arts. Its function is distinct and indispensable. It becomes every year more and more imperatively necessary that engineers, doctors, lawyers, bankers, merchants should first of all be men of university training.

The Princeton plan is based upon this assumption; and also, by necessary inference, upon the assumption that, inasmuch as all the subjects on its programme are to be pursued in the university spirit, as means of culture in the broadest and sanest meaning of that much abused word, they should all be put upon the same footing and made as nearly as possible of equal educational value by the way in which they are taught and handled. The freshman is to be given a preliminary schooling in university methods of thorough study; the sophomore to be put in the way of getting a view of his studies which will broaden to modern horizons; the junior to be given choice of his chief field of study without discrimination between subjects new and old; the senior to be accorded the rights of those who know at last where they stand in the domain of knowledge and wish to get a firm, final grip upon a few things.

There is something else to be said by way of comment,—something which ought to be said with a great deal of emphasis. The last thing to be desired in the development of higher education in America is that all our universities should be alike and follow the same methods. It is to be desired, rather, that every university,—at any rate every university that has a distinguishing history or genius of its own,—should give leave to its individuality in plan and action. Our tendency is too much imitative in all things. We are too much inclined to duplicate success by imitation of method rather than by energy and independence of character. It is undoubtedly the democratic fault. Richness of power, abundance of strength, come by variety, in the field of education as in every other field of endeavor. There is nothing but impoverishment to be got by imitation and mere reproduction. Our lads should not all be forced into the same pattern, subjected to the same processes, irrespective of their individual needs and characteristics. For every candidate for an education there should be a choice as between universities, if he is to have the chance he should have to release his faculties after their kind. Uniformity reduces opportunity to a minimum, here as everywhere else.

But more than that. There ought to be a reasonable and natural differentiation between universities not only, but also a more candid and thorough differentiation between the several kinds of education, the professional and the non-professional, the technical and the general. However universities may differ, they should be alike in offering their baccalaureate, first degrees for general, not for technical, studies. The question is not Which is the better? Which is the more worth while, the general education or the particular technical training? but simply, Which is the one and which is the other? They are not and cannot be alike either in character or in purpose, and to confuse them is to lessen the value of both. In many of our universities they have in recent years been thoroughly confused. Purely technical studies have been included without hesitation in undergraduate programmes, and students who were supposed to be undergoing a general training in arts and science have been encouraged to devote a large part of their time to studies entirely practical and professional. The bachelors' degrees given them at graduation represented a training which was neither the one thing nor the other, but mixed of all kinds and fully effective in none.

The argument for a different and more reasonable practice may be very briefly and plainly put. Our national education must be all inclusive, but it ought not to be confused. There must be schools of manual training for the mass of the country's workers;

there must be thoroughly equipped schools as well as thoroughly equipped shops in which the master mechanic can fit himself; there must be technical schools in which all the mechanic arts upon which our industrial strength and progress depend shall be taught in their utmost detail and perfection. In all of these skill, the mastery of processes, will be the chief object always, as now: the thorough command of tools, of method, of manual and mechanical means, the use of the hands and of machines as instruments of perfect workmanship; and that skill cannot be acquired without a knowledge, also, of mechanical principles and the facts of science upon which it must always depend. But those who take the higher places, direct the larger undertakings, captain the greater enterprises, and put a new face on mechanic industry must know and be more, must have the university training behind them,—the training that makes them free of the general world of knowledge, that is as necessary for engineers as for statesmen, that makes them educated as well as skilful men. Only men whose view is wide and who are determined to make their opportunity full may seek this broad and fundamental training; but it must be made as free and accessible as possible. Many must have it if the world is to go forward; and it should be kept distinct and perfect for their use.

But notwithstanding the plain reasonableness of the process at once of unification and of differentiation by which such a plan as Princeton's is produced and the numerous courses of a modern university put upon a footing of equality, it does not follow that it would be wise to graduate all who study under it without any effort to group and distinguish them according to the route they have taken to graduation, the studies they have chiefly emphasized in making their several choices. It would lead to sad confusion to use a single blanket degree to cover all graduates, however diverse and contrasted their courses of study. The Greek language seems to be at the bottom of the trouble. There has been a widespread revolt in our day against the study of Greek: why it would be hard for any one who understands the merits of the question to say. Greek literature unquestionably underlies modern culture; and the Greek language in its perfection constitutes a medium of thought not only clear beyond comparison but also itself yielding a sort of radiance and beauty to be found in no other tongue ancient or modern. But the merits of the question have little to do with the matter. The trouble lies rooted in the difficulty of the Greek language. The modern tendency to follow short cuts and lines of least resistance is explanation enough of what has happened. Of the two classical languages Latin happens to be written in our own alphabet, to contain scores of words which we have borrowed, and to have a grammatical structure not too complex to be easily mastered; while Greek hides itself behind a strange alphabet, is less intimately connected with English in its vocabulary, and has many forbidding difficulties of verbal and grammatical construction. At any rate, more and more pupils in our schools are studying Latin as the years go by; while the numbers who study Greek stand still or diminish. And yet the full measure of thoroughness which universities must require in their literary courses cannot be filled up without Greek. Moreover, if only for the sake of keeping methods of culture clearly distinguished and preserving the established meaning of an ancient designation, the old Bachelor of Arts degree ought to stand now as before for the full circle of literary study upon which the accomplishments of distinguished men in so many generations have been grounded.

Men who enter the University without Greek, therefore, are not to be admitted at Princeton to the degree of Bachelor of Arts; though those who enter with Greek are to be permitted, in sophomore and junior year, to turn which way they will in their choice of studies. A full modicum of Latin is to be required of all candidates for entrance, and those who enter without Greek must offer as much French and German, as much elementary physics and additional mathematics, as will stand for the amount of study which would have been necessary for preparation in Greek. All those who enter without Greek will go the journey of freshman year, of preliminary drill, together, but will have the choice in sophomore and junior year whether they shall turn towards the degree of Bachelor of Science, which will mark the predominance of scientific studies in their course, or towards the degree of Bachelor of Letters (Litt.B.), which will mark the predominance of literary and philosophical, of what it has been the habit to call humanistic, studies in the courses which they have chosen. The modern languages will, of course, be available to all students, whatever their special plan of study, but they will naturally play a more prominent part in the studies of candidates for the degrees of Bachelor of Science and Bachelor of Letters than in the studies of candidates for the degree of Bachelor of Arts, and in the course of those who are candidates for the degree of Bachelor of Letters they will serve as substitutes for Greek. Perhaps in this way it will be possible to assess the relative values of these several courses of study, some old, some new; in any case, graduates will be labelled and put upon the market according to their kind, and there need be no confusion of values. The men graduated will have differentiated themselves, by natural processes of self-selection, and the University will have put no artificial obstacles in their way, guiding and directing them only in the interest of system and thoroughness, of a somewhat rounded and liberal training after the older models.

Elastic as this plan is, and is intended to be, it has not the disordered freedom of the elective system which has been adopted in the majority of our American universities during the past generation. Under the free elective system the student himself determines, except with regard to a very few fundamental or indispensable subjects, just what he shall study and what shall be the sequence of his studies: his own inexperienced judgment is put in charge of his university training, and he is more apt to follow his whims than his judgment. The dangers and mistakes of that system have shown themselves at Princeton as plainly as elsewhere; and it is the object of the new Princeton plan to obviate and correct them. It is of the essence of that plan, therefore, that the full body of fundamental studies is given its place in undergraduate training, and that the sequence of studies is determined even in the period of free election which comes with junior and senior year. It as carefully postpones specialization, too, and requires each student to keep the circle of his studies broad, by restricting the number of courses that can be taken in any one department of study and making it necessary that other subjects shall be combined with them.

At the same time, though the Princeton authorities confidently believe that experience will prove this new plan both sound and serviceable, they of course do not think that it is the only plan by which order can be got out of the modern multitude of studies. They believe that it is thoroughly correct in principle and that it is as elastic as is consistent with system; and they know that it is the legitimate and characteristic product of the genius of Princeton. Conservative, but not illiberal, Princeton has always stood for system as against miscellany in studies. Her instinct is for organization, and that instinct is admirably expressed in the new plan, which is not a scheme wrought out of any one man's mind but a thing produced by common counsel, after the true American fashion: the product of many minds and yet not a compromise. So far as Princeton is concerned that is enough to say for the present. It is prudent to stop this side prophecy.

Woodrow Wilson

WWT MS. (WP, DLC).

A Memorandum by Stockton Axson

[c. Aug. 29, 1904]

As you wanted me to find fault with it, I should say that possibly as a whole it is a little too much in the form of an argument and deals a little too much in abstract philosophy of education—this merely from the point of view of a popular presentation of the scheme in a magazine. Possibly a statement of the scheme, with the reasons given briefly and incidentally, might be better for a first announcement of the plan to the public.

I think the statement of courses leading to the 3 degrees (or rather the differentiation of the courses)—as given on pp. 14, 15.—should be amplified somewhat. I am not sure that there is enough of it to be clear to the casual reader.

As a matter of fact, I think the article is capital and only "on compulsion" have sought flaws.

Hw memorandum (WP, DLC).

To John Brisben Walker

Dear Sir: Judd Haven, Ontario, Canada, August 30, 1904.

Your letter of August twenty-third has just reached me here.[1] The article it encloses distresses me very much because of the gross injustice it does to Princeton. I do not know what statement you may have seen in the press, but the facts are just the opposite of the statement you have accepted as true.

By the recent changes at Princeton, Science has, for the first time there, been put upon a footing of perfect equality with all other studies; and the elective choice, so far as from being withdrawn, has been made of such a character as to open a liberal scientific training to every student such as was never offered him there before. The only change is that the choice is between *kinds* of study (scientific, literary, political, etc.) and not between individual courses of lectures. It is a systematic liberalization. I hope that you will see the justice of correcting the very serious misapprehension created by your article. Had I seen it sooner I would have written to call your attention to the matter.

You will see, therefore, that there is no ground for your invitation that I should write an article to defend Princeton's position. *It is perfectly consistent with the principles of the article to which you have given such wide currency* and which so seriously misrepresents it. No man in his senses or with any real learning would in our day wish to create a reaction against Science.

Pardon the emphatic terms of this letter, if they seem to you over emphatic. I feel that it is a very serious matter to have the recent action of Princeton taken for the opposite of what it really was.   Very truly yours,   Woodrow Wilson.

Printed in the *Cosmopolitan*, xxxvii (Oct. 1904), 741-42.
  [1] It is missing.

From Gertrude Macrum Woods[1]

Hotel Champlain   Clinton Co.   N. Y.
First September, Nineteen hundred and four.
My dear Dr. Wilson:

We have read in a Pittsburg paper that you are to be one of the speakers at the meeting of the State Sunday School Association to be held in Pittsburg on October twelfth.

It would be a very great pleasure for Mr. Woods and for me if you could arrange to stay with us during your visit to Pittsburg.

It has been many years since we first looked forward to a visit from you. The pleasure in anticipating meeting you has been increased with each visit of yours, and by each visit made by us to Princeton.

We shall indeed be disappointed if we cannot have you with us this time.

Mr. Woods joins me in warm regards to Mrs. Wilson and to you.   Very sincerely yours   Gertrude Macrum Woods.

ALS (WP, DLC).
  [1] Mrs. Edward Augustus Woods.

To Benjamin Wistar Morris III

Judd Haven, Ontario, Canada.
My dear Mr. Morris,   2 September, 1904.

I quite agree with the suggestion you make,[1] that we had better confer with regard to the drawings, and make such changes as may be necessary to perfect them before submitting them to the judgment of other members of the Committee. At this stage, as

I am sure the other members of the Committee would agree, the fewer minds the better.

We are starting for home next Thursday, and I shall hope to be able to see you, bringing the drawings with me, early the following week.

With much regard,

Cordially Yours,   Woodrow Wilson

The view of Alton Towers that attracted my attention was that towards the lake.

WWTLS (WC, NjP).
¹ Morris's letter, to which this was a reply, is missing.

To John Rogers Williams

Judd Haven, Ontario, Canada.

My dear Mr. Williams,   2 September, 1904.

I think that the reply you suggest is the proper one to make to Mr. Douglas's question.¹ I would say that, while there is nothing in the law of the University to prevent a negro's entering, the whole temper and tradition of the place are such that no negro has ever applied for admission,² and its seems extremely unlikely that the question will ever assume a practical form.

Sincerely Yours,   Woodrow Wilson

WWTLS (McAlpin File, UA, NjP).
¹ His letter is missing.
² Wilson meant that no Negro undergraduate had ever applied, and he was probably correct, although John Chavis, the distinguished North Carolina minister and educator, and several other free Negroes had studied privately under President John Witherspoon. An unknown number of Negroes took graduate courses at Princeton while students at Princeton Theological Seminary from President James McCosh's time down into the twentieth century. The first to receive a degree from Princeton was Irwin William Langston Roundtree, A.B., Lincoln University, 1886; A.M., 1889; B.D., Drew Theological Seminary, 1889. Roundtree took graduate work at Princeton while a special student at Princeton Theological Seminary from 1892 to 1894 and was awarded the A.M. degree by the former institution in 1895. The second Negro to win a degree from Princeton was George Shippen Stark, A.B., Lincoln University, 1899, and B.D., Princeton Theological Seminary, 1902, who received the A.M. degree from Princeton University in 1906. Arthur Jewell Wilson, Jr., who was graduated in June 1947 on an accelerated program as of the Class of 1948, was the first Negro to receive an undergraduate degree from Princeton.

From John Brisben Walker

Irvington-on-Hudson, New York.

Dear President Wilson,   September 3, 1904.

I am as much pleased with your letter stating the position of Princeton as if it had meant to me a personal benefit. I could not understand how a man of your marked ability could occupy the position given in the newspapers, but seeing no contradiction, I concluded that there had been influences in the governing board of which I knew nothing. I shall of course, take great pleasure in publishing your letter, and making a very humble apology for my mistake.[1]

I came back from St. Louis profoundly discouraged in regard to American educational work. I found that Germany had ninety-six percent of its children in the schools, and Japan ninety-two per cent in its public schools. In the marvellous perfection of the exhibits of those two countries the scientific trend of mind was shown in every direction. With forty percent of illiterates in Alabama, and Louisiana spending *fifty-eight cents per capita* on education, where will America be with reference to Germany and Japan in the next twenty years?

Whenever you have anything to say on the subject of education, I hope you will use the Cosmopolitan. We have not the largest circulation of any of the magazines, but we claim—we believe truthfully—that it is the "largest clientelle of intelligent, thoughtful readers reached by any periodical in the world." I hope that you may preserve your fullest strength of mind and body for your great work.

Yours faithfully,   John Brisben Walker

TLS (WP, DLC).

[1] Walker's "very humble apology" consisted of the following signed statement printed at the end of Wilson's letter (*Cosmopolitan*, xxxvii [Oct. 1904], 742):

"It is with very great pleasure that I make this correction with reference to the position at Princeton, of whose policy President Wilson writes, '*It is perfectly consistent with the principles of the article to which you have given such wide currency.*' That was the article on 'The studies Most Important for the Modern Man: Who Should Study Science?' the list including: the Engineer, the Clergyman, the Lawyer, the Manufacturer, the Merchant, the General Business Man, the Farmer, the Doctor, the Artist and the Literary Man."

From James Waddel Alexander

My dear Dr. Wilson,   N. Y.   Sep. 8, 1904.

I hope, if I occasionally drop you a line about administrative matters at Princeton, you will only regard it as an evidence of the interest I feel in your success and not attribute it to a meddlesome disposition.

Something is occasionally said or done which comes under my notice, & I feel like passing along to you for your own use in your own way the impressions that are made on my mind.

It is in this spirit, that I occupy an idle hour in writing to you about the Guyot Cameron episode.

Cameron has undoubtedly stirred up a good deal of a smell, & it is with a desire to prevent its doing real harm that I give attention to it. Guyot himself has left me severely alone since I told him that his line of argument (an assault on you & your motives) had better be altered when he talked with other trustees, because it would not have the effect he intended. But Prof. H. C. Cameron tackled me at Princeton & earnestly protested against what he called an "outrage." Mrs. Cameron waylaid me outside of Alexander Hall and to use a classical phrase, "gave it to me in the neck," as a trustee—and I may add, she did not spare *you*. Mrs. McCosh asked me about the matter, but expressed no opinion. She let me gather, however, that the town was talking. Sympathy was evidently being aroused, and those having no responsibility can always be very merciful. I have heard too of the feeling among the students & on the part of Cameron's own class. All goes to show that a hostile sentiment has been stirred up. And the question in my mind is how to handle the thing so that harm will not be done.

A night or two ago, Mr. [Richard T. H.] Halsey, of Cameron's Class, engaged me in conversation on the subject. I think he was less sure of his ground after our discussion, but he, if convinced at all was convinced against his will. I asked him if he did not think the President should try to put the various teaching departments in a satisfactory shape. He said he did. I asked him if sympathy for the individual should prevent his taking the necessary steps. He was not ready to take that position. But he said the President had "hounded" and "persecuted" Cameron until he had become excited & almost beside himself. I told him that those were general terms; & asked him to specify the acts which he called "hounding" and "persecuting." He said you had attacked Cameron's scholarship. I asked him to specify how you had attacked it. He said by talking about it. I told him that if you had talked it was because you had been attacked by Cameron & because Cameron had stirred up a false set of rumors about his treatment & the motives for it. I ventured to doubt whether you had attacked his scholarship. I imagined that you had adversely criticised his teaching capacity & had recognized that he was an "impossible" man personally. He averred that the *results* of his teaching were good & said you could not know because you had not attended his exercises. I asked him if *he* had. He said, no. I asked him how *he* knew. He knew from [Wilson] Farrand. I asked him how Farrand knew. He said the boys who went from his school told him. I called his attention to the fact that all his information was hear-say, and asked him whether he supposed for a moment that the President of the University, charged with the chief responsibility, and whose reputation as a scholar & executive was at stake, had formed his opinion without much greater investigation that [than] it was within the power of Farrand to make, an opinion backed by the unanimous judgment of the solid members of the faculty. I can't remember that he had an answer for that. I asked him if it were conceivable that the President could tolerate in the faculty a man who persistently circulated allegations to the discredit of the good faith and justice of the President himself. He admitted that Cameron had put himself in the wrong, but he said he had apologized & that magnanimity demanded that he should be forgiven. I asked him what he would advise the President to do. He said he & his classmates would "jump on" Cameron & insist that he not only apologize, but refrain from all acts incompatible with a loyal performance of his duties under you & that he endeavour so to frame his method of teaching as to conform to a proper standard. If he did this & continued to do it throughout his term of service, he thought the President should extend his time & treat him leniently. If the President, under these circumstances, did not do so, he & his class would take no further interest in Princeton. Then, I said, you and your classmates would desert Princeton because the President refused to let sympathy interfere with his organization of the French department, so that it would be a credit to the University instead of a disgrace? He denied that such organization required the dismissal of Cameron. I asked him to state candidly whether or not he would feel proud to have Cameron held out to the scholars of other institutions, as the head of our French Department. He candidly admitted that he would not. But he thought he was an interesting & instructive lecturer, who produced results, & who had enthusiasm—a quality lacking in the Princeton Faculty.

Well, the sum of the whole matter is that Cameron's clan are agitating against what you have undertaken, and that Cameron & his family are agitating in the little Princeton community. There is perhaps a friendly feeling for Cameron among the students. All these ingredients, constantly stirred up, are making a mess, which evil human nature may increase in size, extent &

capacity for harm—not so much in the particular case in hand but in the general situation—weakening your influence in certain quarters & making a division of sentiment possible even among those responsible. In this unfortunate state of affairs, what ought to be done? If possible, "from the nettle danger snatch the flower safety." As a mere tentative suggestion, for your own good judgment, would it not be well for you to bring the whole matter promptly and decisively to a head, by stating the case to the Board, in its true light & getting it definitely on record; arraigning Cameron 1st for his incompetency to teach & 2nd for his contumacious acts; letting him be heard, if necessary, by a special committee; and then defining and recording such an exact state of facts, that the rumors of the gossips and the unsupported complaints of sympathizing friends, could be answered conclusively? After such a trial and judgment, you would be in a strong position—either, to insist on your first demand, without being misjudged, or to modify it with clemency, without being stultified, as the case seemed then to require. Cameron is trying to put *you* on the defensive in the forum of College opinion. Your strategy, it seems to me, is to put *him* on the defensive, before the same court.[1]

I repeat, that all this is mere suggestion. You are in a position to judge more wisely than I what course is the best, & perhaps have formulated one far better than mine. I do think you should endeavour to help the town, the alumni, & the students, to see your action in its true light. It is wise to be discreet as well as firm and brave.

I ask pardon for such a harangue. It all comes of my intense interest in Princeton & in yourself as its head & as my friend.

Faithfully Yours,   James W. Alexander

ALS (WP, DLC).
[1] If Wilson "stated his case to the Board," he did so at its meeting in June 1905. However, Wilson's remarks, if he made them, never became a matter of record, and there was no arraignment or trial of Cameron. See WW to A. G. Cameron, Nov. 18, 1903, n. 1.

From Annie Wilson Howe

My darling brother,   Markham, Va.   Sept. 8th, 1904.

I feel very badly because I have not answered your last letter and thanked you for your offer to pay Annie's tuition for the winter. As you know I am more obliged to you than I can say, but I cannot let you do it, dear. We will probably spend the winter at Chapel Hill, if I can find a cheap boarding house there.

I am ashamed to write these days, even to you, because we have so many troubles to relate. I am sure a good day is coming some time. . . .

We leave Markham tomorrow morning for Chapel Hill.

Warmest love to you all from   Your devoted Sister

ALS (WP, DLC).

From Thomas L. Snow

The Bluff, Judd-Haven,

My dear Dr. Wilson   Lake Rosseau, Muskoka   Sep 13/04.

My intention is to sell out of our property "The Bluff" and also out of the adjacent lands belonging to Dunn, over which I hold the option of purchase at any time during the next three years.

Therefore, should the opportunity present itself to you, of refering to us any capitalist desiring a site for a private house, or other purpose, will you very kindly hand him my address.

It is improbable that any offer will reach a figure that will tempt us to part with two properties that embrace between them a splendid lake frontage, and on one of which a valuable business connection has been reared: yet the proposition is worth the penning and, I trust, your time in reading it.

Dunn's property contains about 290 acres: ours 130.

Several days of perfect September are descending on Muskoka as generally is the case when so few are left to enjoy them.

Do not, pray, encroach on your precious time by formally replying to this: but if anything should turn up in connection with the subject, then, all well and good.

With kind regards to Mrs. Wilson and her daughters and yourself

Very faithfully yours   Thos. L. Snow.

ALS (WP, DLC). Enc.: Handrawn map of the Muskoka region showing the location of Wilson's property and the other tracts mentioned by Snow.

From Junius Spencer Morgan

My Dear Wilson: New York.   Sept. 14/04

I went on Monday afternoon to McKim, Mead & White's office and they made note of certain suggestions for changes and treatment, of which you asked me to tell them.

Mr. McKim likes the idea of the inscription as indicated on the blueprint and wishes, before you make your decision against it, to give a larger detail of this feature.[1]

I have been spending the last two or three days with Harry Osborn at Garrison, and last night took up to his house the blueprint and showed it to him. He makes one or two suggestions which I submit to you for your consideration: First, that the urns on the secondary posts of the main gate do not go well with the eagles. He suggests in their place a ball on a larger scale and perhaps with a little different treatment—but a ball such as we have on the two end gates.[2] Secondly, (and this idea I think well of), he thinks that on the two posts should be put:

on the left,—the arms of the Fitzrandolphs,
on the right,—the arms of the college of New Jersey,
and in the centre above these two, in the iron work and (perhaps) in colors the arms of Princeton University.[3]

He also brought up the question as to whether the main gate is quite wide enough.

Should you wish me to take up any of these points with McKim please let me hear from you to that effect and I will do so. I send herewith the blueprint which you gave me, in case you have not received the other one from McKim, Mead & White.

Yours sincerely, J. S. Morgan

I believe in getting help from anyone who can give it, but I think Solomon *meant* to say "in the multitude of counsellors there is confusion."

ALS (WP, DLC).
[1] The date "1905" appears below the University coat of arms on the archway, followed by the inscription: "Gift of Augustus Van Wickle to Commemorate Nathaniel Fitz Randolph of Princeton Donor of the Original Campus."
[2] The urns were retained.
[3] The coats of arms were added as Osborn suggested.

To Hugo Münsterberg

Princeton, N. J.

My dear Professor Münsterberg: 15 September, 1904.

I am very much obliged to you for your kind letter of September 14th[1] and am most unaffectedly sorry to find that I am already promised for the evening of October 8th. I am on that evening to address the School Masters' Club of New York.[2]

I shall look forward with pleasure to seeing you in St. Louis[3] and cannot sufficiently regret that my visit must be only a flying one.   Very sincerely yours, Woodrow Wilson

TLS (Münsterberg Papers, MB).
[1] It is missing.
[2] Notes for this address are printed at Oct. 8, 1904.
[3] That is, when Wilson was to speak before the Congress of Arts and Science at the St. Louis Universal Exposition on September 20, 1904. About Münster-

berg's role in the organization of the Congress, see WW to H. Münsterberg, March 18, 1903, n. 1, Vol. 14.

To Benjamin Wistar Morris III

My dear Mr. Morris: Princeton, N. J.   15 September, 1904.

I had only myself to blame for not finding you the other day. I went into the city without having had time to let you know that I was coming.

Now I am sorry to say I must postpone seeing you until after the opening of the University. I am about to leave for St. Louis to deliver an address and must rush back to open the University. I will make an appointment with you as soon as possible after my return.

In haste,   Sincerely yours,   Woodrow Wilson

TLS (WC, NjP).

From Charles Follen McKim

Dear Sir,   New York.   September 15, 1904.

At the request of Mr. J. S. Morgan, I beg to submit herewith revised estimates for the Fence and Gates of Nassau Hall. The figures, as originally submitted to you were, for the masonry, on the basis of blue Indiana limestone, Stony Creek granite, and with the eagles omitted, ... $10,883.00

By your instructions buff limestone is to be substituted for the blue limestone, at a saving of $982.00

In the effort to select a granite which will harmonize best in color with the limestone, I have found a granite which I should prefer to the Stony Creek, and its use would make a saving of 1,014.00

Making a total credit of $1,996.00

As you know, it is proposed to omit from the general contract the carving of the eagles; but I have thought it best to include in the general contract the rough stone, ready for the carving. This will cost an additional sum of 55.00

Making a net saving of   1,941.00

Thus making the total cost of the masonry   8,942.00

The estimate for the iron work was $6,250.00

After further consideration I would strongly recommend (and in this recommendation Mr. Morgan
concurs), that the iron should be galvanized before
it is painted, thus avoiding, in a large measure, the
danger of rust stains upon the stone work. This
would involve an additional expenditure of 800.00

Making the total cost of the iron work 7,050.00

On the basis of the above recommendations, the
total cost of the work would be as follows:

Masonry—William R. Matthews, ... 8,942.00
Metal Work—John Williams, ... 7,050.00
Allowance for Eagles, ... 1,000.00

16,992.00

Architect's commission, 10% 1,699.20

$18,691.20

which is a total saving of $1,225.10 over the figures as originally
submitted.

I have the contracts prepared, with the exception of the prices,
and if these suggestions meet with your approval, will you kindly
let me know, in order that the work may proceed immediately.[1]
Both Mr. Matthews and Mr. Williams have agreed to complete
their work before the first of January next.

Yours very truly,   Charles F. McKim,   B. L. F.

TLS (WP, DLC).
[1] Work began the following month.

To Thomas L. Snow

My dear Mr. Snow: Princeton, N. J.   16 September, 1904.

I have received your letter of September 13th and read it with
some concern. I am sincerely sorry to hear that you wish to sell
"The Bluff" property. I will, of course, take advantage of any opportunity that may offer itself to commend the property to the
attention of anyone who may be able to buy it and yet I cannot
help having a hope that you will retain the property and that we
shall have the pleasure of being with you again as your guests.

We reached home very well and not too tired and have settled
very naturally to our usual occupations. Mrs. Wilson and my
daughters join me in warmest regards to you all.

Cordially and sincerely yours,   Woodrow Wilson

TLS (photostat in RSB Coll., DLC).

From Jacob Ridgway Wright[1]

Hotel Imperial New York

Dear old Doctor Tommy Wilson,   September 16, 1904.

I have been ill and have been kept in my bed here for some five weeks, by "Jap" Garmany.[2]

I have forwarded to John [Constine] Coons, of Wilkes Barre, a note of introduction, to hand to you upon his entrance as a new student at Princeton, which I doubt not he will promptly present at the earliest opportunity. There is much I wanted to say to you regarding him that cannot be said in that same letter. The boy is the eldest son of Joseph C. Coons, Esq., a leading member of Luzerne County Bar, whose sterling character and strong professional qualities are attested by all his colleagues, and notably by McClintock, Fuller, Atterton, Dunning, Welles, Bedford,[3] and all the other Princeton men who are practicing law at the Luzerne bar. But my own knowledge of and interest in Mr. Coons is of a personal character. We have been associated in business relations and have had adjoining desks in the same rooms for many years. He is my warmest, closest friend. And he is a Jew of such prominence that he has for ten years been a member of the Executive Committee of the B'nai B'rith, the greatest Jewish philanthropy the world has ever known. You may call to mind that he was one of the committee who presented to President Roosevelt the petition to the Czar of Russia anent the Kisheneff masacre.

Now to the point I wish to make. The boy is very like his father in temperament and mentality. He is bright, studious, alert, honest and fond of the better things, especially music (playing the violin and viola); he may try to make one of the college orchestras. If he should merit a place, and chance favors his winning on his merits, I do not want him to be "thrown over" in this or any other direction because of his religious belief. Both you and I know that it is the fashion to look at the Jew unsympathetically, simply because he is a Jew. But I cannot be wrong in my belief that you would not allow this boy, or any other boy, in fact, to be discriminated against because of his race, color, belief or otherwise. Therefore, because the boy's father is my dearest and best friend, and because I know the boy so well, I am going to ask you to see to it that John Coons is not "held up" or discriminated against for these reasons. I want him to have a fair and even chance with the other fellows, and I know you will keep your eye on him and see that he is protected without permitting him to know it.

I have been quite ill and am still so, and vastly weak,[4] but felt that I must let you know what I have been worrying about, and that, you can judge from the foregoing letter.

I have not been home for months and did not know that John Coons had even passed his examinations, but have learned so from his father's letter to me a few days ago, and since then I have, so to speak, worried over this case, because I want you to know it and understand it thoroughly. Knowing me as you do, you can appreciate the fact that I would not put myself out to this extent had I not a most warm, personal interest in the case.[5]

And now, with the warmest and sincerest wishes for your success, not only now by [but] in the future, when I shall have the pleasure of voting for you as the Democratic nominee on the national ticket, for President, I am,

Most sincerely yours,   J. Ridgway Wright '79.

TLS (WP, DLC).

[1] Wilson's classmate; a prominent businessman and political leader in Wilkes-Barre, Pa.

[2] Their classmate, Jasper Jewett Garmany, M.D., Clinical Professor of Surgery at the Medical College of New York University.

[3] Andrew Hamilton McClintock '72, Henry Amzi Fuller '74, Thomas Henry Atherton '74, Henry White Dunning, Class of 1882 but not graduated, Henry Hunter Welles, Jr., '82, and Paul Bedford '97.

[4] He died on January 20, 1905.

[5] Coons was graduated with the A.B. degree in the Class of 1908.

An Address on the Nature of History[1]

[[Sept. 20, 1904]]

THE VARIETY AND UNITY OF HISTORY

We have seen the dawn and the early morning hours of a new age in the writing of history, and the morning is now broadening about us into day. When the day is full we shall see that minute research and broad synthesis are not hostile but friendly methods, coöperating toward a common end which neither can reach alone. No piece of history is true when set apart to itself, divorced and isolated. It is part of an intricately various whole, and must needs be put in its place in the netted scheme of events to receive its true color and estimation; and yet it must be itself individually studied and contrived if the whole is not to be weakened by its

[1] Delivered before the Division of Historical Science of the International Congress of Arts and Science of the Universal Exposition in St. Louis (about this Congress, see WW to H. Münsterberg, March 18, 1903, n. 1, Vol. 14) on September 20, 1904. Wilson had been asked (N. M. Butler to WW, Dec. 22, 1903) to "deal with the inner unity of the general subject-matter included under the division."

imperfection. Whole and part are of one warp and woof. I think that we are in a temper to realize this now, and to come to happy terms of harmony with regard to the principles and the objects which we shall hold most dear in the pursuit of our several tasks.

I know that in some quarters there is still a fundamental difference of opinion as to the aim and object of historical writing. Some regard history as a mere record of experience, a huge memorandum of events, of the things done, attempted, or neglected in bringing the world to the present stage and posture of its affairs,—a book of precedents to which to turn for instruction, correction, and reproof. Others regard it as a book of interpretation, rather, in which to study motive and the methods of the human spirit, the ideals that elevate and the ideals that debase; from which we are to derive assistance, not so much in action as in thought; a record of evolution, in which we are not likely to find repetitions, and in reading which our inquiry should be of processes, not of precedents. The two views are not, upon analysis, so far apart as they at first appear to be. I think that we shall all agree, upon reflection and after a little explanation of the terms we use, that what we seek in history is the manifestation and development of the human spirit, whether we seek it in precedents or in processes.

All of the many ways of writing history may be reduced to two. There are those who write history, as there are those who read it, only for the sake of the story. Their study is of plot, their narrative goes by ordered sequence and seeks the dramatic order of events; men appear, in their view, always in organized society, under leaders and subject to common forces making this way or that; details are for the intensification of the impression made by the main movement in mass; there is the unity and the epic progress of *The Decline and Fall*, or the crowded but always ordered composition of one of Macaulay's canvases; cause and effect move obvious and majestic upon the page, and the story is of the large force of nations. This is history embodied in "events," centering in the large transactions of epochs or of peoples. It is history in one kind, upon which there are many variants. History in the other kind devotes itself to analysis, to interpretation, to the illumination of the transactions of which it treats by lights let in from every side. It has its own standard of measurement in reckoning transactions great or small, bases its assessments, not upon the numbers involved or the noise and reputation of the day itself in which they occurred, so much as upon their intrinsic significance, seen now in after days, as an index of what the obscure men of the mass thought and endured, indications of the forces making and to be made, the intimate biography of daily thought. Here interest centres, not so much in what happened as in what underlay the happening; not so much in the tides as in the silent forces that lifted them. Economic history is of this quality, and the history of religious belief, and the history of literature, where it traces the map of opinion, whether in an age of certainty or in an age of doubt and change.

The interest of history in both kinds is essentially the same. Each in its kind is a record of the human spirit. In one sort we seek that spirit manifested in action, where effort is organized upon the great scale and leadership displayed. It stirs our pulses to be made aware of the mighty forces, whether of exaltation or of passion, that play through what men have done. In the other sort of history we seek the spirit of man manifested in conception, in the quiet tides of thought and emotion making up the minor bays and inlets of our various life of complex circumstance, in the private accumulation of events which lie far away from the sound of drum or trumpet and constitute no part of the pomp of great affairs. The interest of human history is that it is human. It is a tale that moves and quickens us. We do not approach it as we approach the story of nature. The records of geology, stupendous and venerable as they are, written large and small, with infinite variety, upon the faces of great mountains and of shadowed cañons or in the fine shale of the valley, buried deep in the frame of the globe or lying upon the surface, do not hold us to the same vivid attention. Human history has no such muniment towers, no such deep and ancient secrets, no such mighty successions of events as those which the geologist explores; but the geologist does not stir us as the narrator of even the most humble dealings of our fellow men can stir us. And it is so with the rest of the history of nature. Even the development of animal life, though we deem its evolution part of ours, seems remote, impersonal, no part of any affair that we can touch with controlling impulse or fashion to our pleasure. It is the things which we determine which most deeply concern us, our voluntary life and action, the release of our spirits in thought and act. If the philosophers were to convince us that there is in fact no will of our own in any matter, our interest in the history of mankind would slacken and utterly change its face. The ordered sequences of nature are outside of us, foreign to our wills, but these things of our own touch us nearly.

It is the honorable distinction of historical writing in our day that it has become more broadly and intimately human. The instinct of the time is social rather than political. We would know not merely how law and government proceed but also how society breeds its forces, how these play upon the individual, and how the individual affects them. Law and government are but one expression of the life of society. They are regulative rather than generative, and historians of our day have felt that in writing political and legal history they are upon the surface only, not at the heart of affairs. The minute studies of the specialist have been brought about, not merely by the natural exigencies of the German seminar method of instruction, not merely by the fact that the rising tide of doctors' theses has driven would-be candidates for degrees to the high and dry places, after all the rich lowland had been covered, but also by a very profound and genuine change of view on the part of the masters of history themselves with regard to what should be the distinctive material of their study. Before our modern day of specialization there was virtually no history of religion, or of law, or of literature, or of language, or of art. Fragments of these things were, of course, caught in the web of the old narratives, but the great writers of the older order looked at them with attention only when they emerged, gross and obvious, upon the surface of affairs. Law was part of the movement of politics or of the patent economic forces that lay near the interests of government. Religion was not individual belief, but as it were the politics of an institution, of the church, which was but the state itself in another guise. Literature concerned them only as it became the wind of opinion beating upon the laboring ship of state, or when some sudden burst of song gave a touch of imaginative glory to the domestic annals of the nation which was their theme. Art came within their view only when it was part of the public work of some Pericles or became itself part of the intricate web of politics, as in the Italian states of the Renaissance. Language concerned them not at all, except as its phrases once and again spoke the temper of an epoch or its greater variations betokened the birth of new nations.

And all this because their interest was in affairs of state, in the organized and coördinated efforts of the body politic, in opinions and influences which moved men in the mass and governed the actions of kings and their ministers of state at home and abroad. In brief, their interest was in "events." It is curious and instructive to examine what we mean by that much-used word. We mean always, I take it, some occurrence of large circumstance,—no private affair transacted in a corner, but something observed and open to the public view, noticeable and known,— and not fortuitous, either, but planned, concerted. There can, properly speaking, be no "event" without organized effort: it is not a thing of the individual. Literature is excluded, by definition, and art, and language, and much of religion that is grounded in unobserved belief, and all the obscure pressure of economic want. A history of "events" cannot be a history of the people; it can only be a history of the life of the body politic, of the things which statesmen observe and act upon.

The specialist has taught us that the deepest things are often those which never spring to light in events, and that the breeding-ground of events themselves lies where the historian of the state seldom extends his explorations. It is not true that a community is merely the aggregate of those who compose it. The parts are so disposed among us that the minority governs more often than the majority. But influence and mastery are subtle things. They proceed from forces which come to the individual out of the very air he breathes: his life is compounded as the lives of those about him are. Their lives play upon his, he knows not how, and the opinion he enforces upon them is already more than half their own. And so the analysis of the life of the many becomes part of the analysis of the power of the few—an indispensable part. It is this that the specialist sees. He sees more. He sees that individual efforts as well as aggregate must be studied, the force that is in the man as well as the air that is in the community. The men who give voice to their age are witnesses to more things than they wot of.

Mr. Ruskin, in the preface to the little volume on Venetian art to which he has given the name *St. Mark's Rest*, propounds a theory which will illuminate my meaning. "Great nations," he says, "write their autobiographies in three manuscripts,—the book of their deeds, the book of their words, and the book of their art. Not one of these books can be understood unless we read the two others; but of the three the only quite trustworthy one is the last. The acts of a nation may be triumphant by its good fortune; and its words mighty by the genius of a few of its children; but its art only by the general gifts and common sympathies of the race. Again, the policy of a nation may be compelled, and, therefore, not indicative of its true character. Its words may be false, while yet the race remains unconscious of their falsehood; and no historian can assuredly detect the hypocrisy. But art is always instinctive; and the honesty or pretense of it are therefore open to the day. The Delphic oracle may or may not have been spoken by an honest priestess,—we cannot tell by the words of it; a liar may rationally believe them a lie, such as he would himself have spoken; and a true man, with equal reason, may believe them spoken in truth. But there is no question possible in art: at a glance (when we have learned to read), we know the religion of Angelico to be sincere, and of Titian, assumed."

Whether we agree with all the *dicta* of this interesting passage or not, the main truth of it is plain. It is to be doubted whether the "genius of a few of its children" suffices to give a nation place in the great annals of literature, and literary critics would doubtless maintain that the book of a nation's words is as naïf and instinctive as the book of its art. Here, too, the sincere and natural is easily to be distinguished ("when we have learned to read") from the sophisticated and the artificial. Plainly the autobiography of Benjamin Franklin is separated by a long age from the autobiography of Benvenuto Cellini, and the one is as perfect a mirror of the faith of the man and the manner of the age as the other. But these questions are not of the present point. Undoubtedly the book of a nation's art and the book of its words must be read along with the book of its deeds if its life and character are to be comprehended as a whole; and another book, besides,—the book of its material life, its foods, its fashions, its manufactures, its temperatures and seasons. In each of these great books the historian looks for the same thing: the life of the day, the impulses that underlie government and all achievement, all art and all literature, as well as all statesmanship.

I do not say that the specialists who have so magnified their office in our day have been conscious of this ultimate synthesis. Few of them have cared for it or believed in it. They have diligently spent their intensive labor upon a few acres of ground, with an exemplary singleness of mind, and have displayed, the while, very naïvely, the provincial spirit of small farmers. But a nation is as rich as its subjects, and this intensive farming has accumulated a vast store of excellent food-stuff. No doubt the work would have been better done if it had been done in a more catholic spirit, with wider sympathies, amidst horizons. The broader the comprehension the more intelligent the insight. But we must not ask for all things in a generation or expect our own perfection by any other way than the familiar processes of development.

Perhaps we are near enough the time of synthesis and coördination to see at least the organic order and relationship of the several special branches of historical inquiry which have been grouped in this Division of our Congress. All history has society as its subject-matter; what we ponder and explore is, not the history of men, but the history of man. And yet our themes do not all lie equally close to the organic processes of society. Those processes are, of course, most prominent in political and economic history, least prominent, perhaps in the history of language. I venture to suggest that the organic order is: Politics, economics, religion, law, literature, art, language. So far as the question affects religion and law, I must admit that I am not clear which of the two ought to take precedence,—in modern history, certainly law; but most history is not modern, and in that greater part which is not modern clearly religion overcrows law in the organic, social process.

I know that the word religion, in this connection as in most others, is of vague and mixed significance, covering a multitude of sins; but so far as my present point is concerned, it is easy of clarification. Religion, as the historian handles it, involves both a history of institutions, of the church, and a history of opinion. As a history of opinion it perhaps lies no nearer the organic processes of society than does the history of literature; but from the beginning of recorded events until at any rate the breaking up of foundations which accompanied and followed the French Revolution, it concerns the church as an institution as definitely as the history of politics, with its various records of shifting opinion, concerns the state, and the organic life of the body politic. In such a view, religion must take precedence of law in the organic order of our topics. From the remotest times of classical history, when church and state, priest and judge, were hardly distinguishable, through the confused Middle Age, in which popes were oftentimes of more authority than kings and emperors, down to the modern days, when priests and primates were, by very virtue of their office, chief politicians in the plot of public policy, the church has unquestionably played a part second only to the state itself in the organization and government of society, in the framing of the public life.

Law occupies a place singular and apart. Its character is without parallel in our list. It has no life of its own apart from the life of the state, as religion has, or literature, or art, or language. Looked at as the lawyer looks at it, it is merely the voice of the state, the body of regulations set by government to give order to the competitive play of individual and social forces. Looked at from the historian's point of view, it consists of that part of the social thought and habit which has definitely formed itself, which has gained universal acquiescence and recognition, and which has been given the sanction and backing of the state itself, a final formulation in command. In either case, whatever its origin, whether in the arbitrary will of the law-maker or in the gradually disclosed and accepted convenience of society, it comes, not independently and of itself, but through the mouth of governors and judges, and is itself a product of the state. But not of politics, unless we speak of public law, the smaller part, not of private, the greater. The forces which created it are chiefly economic, or else social, bred amidst ideas of class and privilege. It springs from a thousand fountains. Statutes do not contain all of it; and statutes are themselves, when soundly conceived, but generalizations of experience. The truth is that, while law gets its formulation and its compulsive sanction from the political governors of the state, its real life and source lie hidden amidst all of the various phenomena which historians are called upon to explore. It belongs high in the list I have made, because it so definitely takes its form from the chief organ of society.

To put literature before art in the organic order I have suggested, is not to deny Mr. Ruskin's *dictum*, that art more than literature comes "by the general gifts and common sympathies of the race," by instinct rather than by deliberation; it is only to say that more of what is passing through a nation's thought is expressed in its literature than in its art. As a nation thinks so it is; and the historian must give to the word literature a wider significance than the critic would vouchsafe. He must think not merely of that part of a nation's book of words upon which its authors have left the touch of genius, the part that has been made immortal by the transfiguring magic of art, but also of the cruder parts which have served their purpose and now lie dead upon the page,—the fugitive and ephemeral pamphlets, the forgotten controversies, the dull, thin prose of arguments long ago concluded, old letters, futile and neglected pleas,—whatever may seem to have played through the thought of older days.

Of the history of language I speak with a great deal of diffidence. My own study of it was of narrow scope and antedated all modern methods. But I know what interest it has for the historian of life and opinion; I know how indispensable its help is in deciphering race origins and race mixtures; I know what insight it affords into the processes of intellectual development; I know what subtle force it has had not only in moulding men's thoughts, but also their acts and their aspirations after the better things of hope and purpose. I know how it mirrors national as well as individual genius. And I know that all of these data of organic life, whether he take them at first hand or at second, throw a clarifying light upon many an obscure page of the piled records that lie upon the historian's table. I fancy that the historian who intimately uses the language of the race and people of which he writes somehow gets intimation of its origin and history into his ear and thought whether he be a deliberate student of its development or not; but be that as it may, the historian of language stands at his elbow, if he will but turn to him, with many an enlightening fact and suggestion which he can ill afford to dispense withal. It is significant, as it is interesting, that the students of language have here been definitely called into the company of historians. May the alliance be permanent and mutually profitable!

My moral upon the whole list is, that, separated though we may be by many formal lines of separation, sometimes insisted on with much pedantic punctilio, we are all partners in a common undertaking, the illumination of the thoughts and actions of men as associated in society, the life of the human spirit in this familiar theatre of coöperative effort in which we play, so changed from age to age and yet so much the same throughout the hurrying centuries. Some of the subjects here grouped may stand high in the list of organic processes, others affect them less vigorously and directly; but all are branches and parts of the life of society. In one of the great topics we deal with there is, I know, another element which sets it quite apart to a character of its own. The history of religion is not merely the history of social forces, not merely the history of institutions and of opinions. It is also the history of something which transcends our divination, escapes our analysis,—the power of God in the life of men. God does, indeed, deal with men in society and through social forces, but he deals with him also individually, as a single soul, not lost in society or impoverished of his individual will and responsibility by his connection with the lives of other men, but himself sovereign and lonely in the choice of his destiny. This singleness of the human soul, this several right and bounden duty of individual faith and choice, to be exercised oftentimes in contempt and defiance of society, is a thing no man is likely to overlook who has noted the genesis of our modern liberty or assessed the forces of reform

and regeneration which have lifted us to our present enlightenment; and it introduces into the history of religion, at any rate
since the day of Christ, the master of free souls, an element
which plays upon society like an independent force, like no
native energy of its own. This, nevertheless, like all things else
that we handle, comes into the sum of our common reckoning
when we would analyze the life of men as manifested in the
book of their deeds, in the book of their words, in the book of
their art, or in the book of their material arts, consumption,
needs, desires; and the product is still organic. Men play upon
one another whether as individual souls or as political and economic partners.

What the specialist has discovered for us, whether he has
always discovered it for himself or not, is, that this social product which we call history, though produced by the interplay of
forces, is not always produced by definite organs or by deliberation: that, though a joint product, it is not always the result of
concerted action. He has laid bare to our view particular, minor,
confluent but not conjoint influences, which, if not individual,
are yet not deliberately coöperative, but the unstudied, ungen-
eraled, scattered, unassembled, it may be even single and individual expression of motives, conceptions, impulses, needs, desires,
which have no place within the ordered, corporated ranks of such
things as go by legislation or the edicts of courts, by resolutions
of synods or centred mandates of opinion, but spring of their
own spontaneous vigor out of the unhusbanded soil of unfenced
gardens, the crops no man had looked for or made ready to reap.
Though all soils from which human products suck their sustenance must no doubt lie within the general sovereignty of
society, and no man is masterless in our feudal moral system,
these things which have come to light by the labor of those who
have scrutinized the detail of our lives for things neglected have
not been produced within the immediate demesnes of the crown.
Historians who ponder public policy only, and only the acts of
those who make and administer law and determine the relationships of nations, like those who follow only the main roads of
literature and study none but the greater works of art, have therefore passed them by unheeded, and so, undoubtedly, have missed
some of the most interesting secrets of the very matters they had
set themselves to fathom. Individuals, things happening obscure
and in a corner, matters that look like incidents, accidents, and
lie outside the observed movements of affairs, are as often as not

of the very gist of controlling circumstance and will be found when fully taken to pieces to lie at the very kernel of our fruit of memory.

I do not mean to imply that the work of the specialist is now near enough to being accomplished, his discoveries enough completed, enough advertised, enough explained, his researches brought to a sufficient point of perfection. I daresay he is but beginning to come into his kingdom: is just beginning to realize that it is a kingdom, and not merely a congeries of little plots of ground, unrelated, unneighborly even; and that as the years go by and such studies are more and more clarified, more and more wisely conceived, this minute and particular examination of the records of the human spirit will yield a yet more illuminating body of circumstance and serve more and more directly and copiously for the rectification of all history. What I do mean, and what, I daresay, I am put here to proclaim, is, that the day for synthesis has come; that no one of us can safely go forward without it; that labor in all kinds must henceforth depend upon it, the labor of the specialist no less than the labor of the general historian who attempts the broader generalizations of comment and narrative.

In the English-speaking world we have very recently witnessed two interesting and important attempts at synthesis by coöperation in Mr. H. D. Traill's *Social England* and Lord Acton's *Cambridge Modern History*, the one now complete, the other still in course of publication. We have had plans and proposals for a somewhat similarly constructed history of the United States. Mr. Justin Winsor's *Narrative and Critical History of America* hardly furnishes an example of the sort of work attempted in the other series of which I have spoken. Aside from its lists and critical estimates of authorities, it is only history along the ordinary lines done in monographs, covering topics every historian of America has tried to cover. Mr. Traill's volumes, as their general title bears evidence, run upon a wider field, whose boundaries include art, literature, language, and religion, as well as law and politics. They are broader, at any rate in their formal plan, than Lord Acton's series, if we may judge by the three volumes of the *Cambridge Modern History* already published. The chapter-headings in the Cambridge volumes smack much more often of politics and public affairs than of the more covert things of private impulse and endeavor. Their authors write generally, however, with a very broad horizon about them and examine things usually left unnoted by historians of an earlier age. The volumes may fairly be taken, therefore, to represent an attempt at a comprehensive synthesis of modern historical studies.

Both Mr. Traill's volumes and the *Cambridge Modern History* are constructed upon essentially the same general plan. The sections of the one and the chapters of the other are monographs pieced together to make a tessellated whole. The hope of the editors has been to obtain, by means of carefully formulated instructions and suggestions issued beforehand to their corps of associates, a series of sections conceived and executed, in some general sense, upon a common model and suitable to be worked in together as parts of an intelligible and consistent pattern; and so uniform has been our training in historical research and composition in recent years, that a most surprising degree of success has attended the effort after homogeneous texture in the narrative and critical essays which have resulted; a degree of success which I call surprising, not because I think it very nearly complete, but because I am astonished that, in the circumstances, it should have been success at all and not utter failure.

It is far from being utter failure; and yet how far it is also from being satisfactory success! Allow me to take, as an example of the way in which these works are constructed, my own experience in writing a chapter for the volume of the *Cambridge Modern History* which is devoted to the United States.[2] In doing so I am far from meaning even to imply any criticism upon the editors of that admirable series, to whom we are all so much indebted. I do not see how, without incredible labor, they could have managed the delicate and difficult business intrusted to them in any other way; and I am adducing my experience in their service only for the sake of illustrating what must, no doubt, inevitably be the limitations and drawbacks of work in this peculiar kind. I can think of no other way so definite of assessing the quality and serviceability of this sort of synthesis. I was asked by Lord Acton to write for his volume on the United States the chapter which treats of the very painful and important decade 1850-1860, and I undertook the commission with a good deal of willingness. There are several things concerning that critical period which I like to have an opportunity to say. But I had hardly embarked upon the interesting enterprise, which I was bidden compass within thirty of the ample pages of the Cambridge royal octavos, before I was beset by embarrassments with regard to the manner and scope of treatment. The years 1850-1860 do not, of course, either in our own history or in any other, constitute a

---

[2] It is printed at Dec. 20, 1899, Vol. 11.

decade severed from its fellows. The rootages of all the critical matters which then began to bear their bitter fruitage are many and complex and run far, very far, back into the soil which I knew very well other writers were farming. I did not know what they would say or leave unsaid, explain or leave doubtful. I could take nothing for granted; for every man's point of view needs its special elucidation, and he can depend upon no other man to light his path for him. I therefore wrote a narrative essay, in my best philosophical vein, on the events of the decade assigned me, in which I gave myself a very free hand and took care to allow my eye a wide and sweeping view upon every side. I spoke of any matter I pleased, harked back to any transaction that concerned me, recking nothing of how long before the limiting date 1850 it might have occurred, and so flung myself very freely,—should I say very insolently?—through many a reach of country that clearly and of my own certain knowledge belonged to others, by recorded Cambridge title. How was I to avoid it? My co-laborers were not at my elbow in my study. Some of them were on the other side of the sea. The editors themselves could not tell me what these gentlemen were to say, for they did not know. The other essays intended for the volume were on the stocks being put together, as mine was.

I must conjecture that the writers for that volume fared as I did, and took the law into their own hands as I did; and their experience and mine is the moral of my criticism. No sort of cunning joinery could fit their several pieces of workmanship together into a single and consistent whole. No amount of uniform type and sound binding can metamorphose a series of individual essays into a book. I may be allowed to express my surprise, in passing, that some individual historians should have tried to compound and edit themselves in the same way, by binding together essays which were conceived and executed as separate wholes. The late Mr. Edward Eggleston furnished us with a distinguished example of this in his *Beginners of a Nation*, whose chapters are topical and run back and forth through time and circumstance without integration or organic relation to one another, treating again and again of the same things turned about to be looked at from a different angle. And if a man of capital gifts cannot fuse his own essays, or even beat and compress them into solid and coherent amalgam, how shall editors be blamed who find the essays of a score of minds equally intractable? No doubt the Cambridge volumes are meant for scholars more than for untrained readers, though Mr. Traill's, I believe, are not; but even the docile scholar, accustomed of necessity to contrast and variety in what he pores upon and by habit very patient in reconciling inconsistencies, plodding through repetitions, noting variations and personal whimsies, must often wonder why he should thus digest pieces of other men's minds and eat a mixture of secondary authorities. The fact is, that this is not synthesis, but mere juxtaposition. It is not even a compounding of views and narratives. It is compilation. There is no whole cloth, no close texture, anywhere in it. The collected pieces overlap and are sometimes not even stitched together. Events—even events of critical consequence—are sometimes incontinently overlooked, dropped utterly from the narrative, because no one of the writers felt any particular responsibility for them, and one and another took it for granted that some one else had treated of them, finding their inclusion germane and convenient.

But if we reject this sort of coöperation as unsatisfactory, what are we to do? Obviously some sort of coöperation is necessary in this various and almost boundless domain of ours; and if not the sort Mr. Traill and Lord Acton planned, what sort is possible? The question is radical. It involves a great deal more than the mere determination of a method. It involves nothing less than an examination of the essential character and object of history,— I mean of that part of man's book of words which is written as a deliberate record of his social experience. What are our ideals? What, in the last analysis, do we conceive our task to be? Are we mere keepers and transcribers of records, or do we write our own thoughts and judgments into our narratives and interpret what we record? The question may be simply enough asked, but it cannot be simply answered. The matter requires elaboration.

Let us ask ourselves, by way of preliminary test, what we should be disposed to require of the ideal historian, what qualities, what powers, what aptitudes, what purposes? Put the query in another form, more concrete, more convenient to handle: how would you critically distinguish Mommsen's *History* from a doctor's thesis? By its scope, of course; but its scope would be ridiculous if it were not for its insight, its power to reconceive forgotten states of society, to put antique conceptions into life and motion again, build scattered hints into systems, and see a long national history singly and as a whole. Its masterly qualities it gets from the perceiving eye, the conceiving mind of its great author, his divination rather than his learning. The narrative impresses you as if written by one who has seen records no other man ever deciphered. I do not think Mommsen an ideal historian. His habit as a lawyer was too strong upon him: he wrote history too much as if it were an argument. His curiosity as an antiquarian was too keen: things very ancient and obscure were more interesting to him than the more commonplace things, which nevertheless constitute the bulk of the human story. But his genius for interpretation was his patent of nobility in the peerage of historians; he would not be great without it; and without it would not illustrate my present thesis.

That thesis is, that, in whatever form, upon whatever scale you take it, the writing of history as distinguished from the clerical keeping of records is a process of interpretation. No historical writer, how small soever his plot of time and circumstance, ever records all the facts that fall under his eye. He picks and chooses for his narrative, determines which he will dwell upon as significant, which put by as of no consequence. And that is a process of judgment, an estimation of values, an interpretation of the matter he handles. The smaller the plot of time he writes of, the more secluded from the general view the matters he deals with, the more liable is he to error in his interpretation; for this little part of the human story is but a part; its significance lies in its relation to the whole. It requires nicer skill, longer training, better art and craft to fit it to its little place than would be required to adjust more bulky matters, matters more obviously involved in the general structure, to their right position and connections. The man with only common skill and eyesight is safer at the larger, cruder sort of work. Among little facts it requires an exceeding nice judgment to pick the greater and the less, prefer the significant and throw away only the negligible. The specialist must needs be overseen and corrected with much more vigilance and misgiving than the national historian or the historian of epochs.

Here, then, is the fundamental weakness of the coöperative histories of which I have spoken by example. They have no wholeness, singleness, or integrity of conception. If the several authors who wrote their sections or chapters had written their several parts only for the eye of one man chosen guide and chief among them, and he, pondering them all, making his own verifications, and drawing from them not only but also from many another source and chiefly from his own lifelong studies, had constructed the whole, the narrative had been everywhere richer, more complete, more vital, a living whole. But such a scheme as that is beyond human nature, in its present jealous constitution, to execute, and is a mere pleasing fancy—if any one be pleased with it. Such things are sometimes done in university seminars, where masters have been known to use, at their manifest peril, the work of their pupils in making up their published writings; but they ought not to have been done there, and they are not likely to be done anywhere else. At least this may be said, that, if master workmen were thus to use and interpret other men's materials, one great and indispensable gain would be made: history would be coherently conceived and consistently explained. The reader would not himself have to compound and reconcile the divergent views of his authors.

I daresay it seems a very radical judgment to say that synthesis in our studies must come by means of literary art and the conceiving imagination; but I do not see how otherwise it is to come. By literary art, because interpretation cannot come by crude terms and unstudied phrases in writing any more than pictorial interpretation can come by a crude, unpracticed, ignorant use of the brush in painting. By the conceiving imagination, because the historian is not a clerk but a seer: he must see the thing first before he can judge of it. Not the inventing imagination, but the conceiving imagination,—not all historians have been careful to draw the distinction in their practice. It is imagination that is needed, is it not, to conceive past generations of men truly in their habit and manner as they lived? If not, it is some power of the same kind which you prefer to call by another name: the name is not what we shall stop to discuss. I will use the word under correction. Nothing but imagination can put the mind back into past experiences not its own, or make it the contemporary of institutions long since passed away or modified beyond recognition. And yet the historian must be in thought and comprehension the contemporary of the men and affairs he writes of. He must also, it is true, be something more: if he would have the full power to interpret, he must have the offing that will give him perspective, the knowledge of subsequent events which will furnish him with multiplied standards of judgment: he should write among records amplified, verified, complete, withdrawn from the mist of contemporary opinion. But he will be but a poor interpreter if he have alien sympathies, the temperament of one age when writing of another, it may be contrasted with his own in every point of preference and belief. He needs something more than sympathy, for sympathy may be condescending, pitying, contemptuous. Few things are more benighting than the condescension of one age for another, and the historian who shares this blinding sentiment is of course unfitted for his office, which is not that of censor but that of interpreter. Sympathy there must be, and very catholic sympathy, but it must be the sympathy of the man who stands in the midst and sees, like one within, not like one without, like a native, not like an alien. He must not sit like a judge exercising exterritorial jurisdiction.

It is through the imagination that this delicate adjustment of view is effected,—a power not of the understanding nor yet a mere faculty of sympathetic appreciation, or even compounded of the two, but mixed of these with a magical gift of insight added, which makes it a thing mere study, mere open-mindedness, mere coolness and candor of judgment cannot attain. Its work cannot be done by editorship or even by the fusing of the products of different minds under the heat of a single genius; its insight is without rule, and is exercised in singleness and independence. It is in its nature a thing individual and incommunicable.

Since literary art and this distinctive, inborn genius of interpretation are needed for the elucidation of the human story and must be married to real scholarship if they are to be exercised with truth and precision, the work of making successful synthesis of the several parts of our labors for each epoch and nation must be the achievement of individual minds, and it might seem that we must await the slow maturing of gifts Shakespearean to accomplish it. But, happily, the case is not so desperate. The genius required for this task has nothing of the universal scope, variety, or intensity of the Shakespearean mind about it. It is of a much more humble sort and is, we have reason to believe, conferred upon men of every generation. There would be good cause to despair of the advance of historical knowledge if it were not bestowed with some liberality. It is needed for the best sort of analysis and specialization of study as well as for successful synthesis, for the particular as well as for the general task. Moreover, a certain very large amount of coöperation is not only possible but quite feasible. It depends, after all, on the specialists whether there shall be successful synthesis or not. If they wish it, if it be their ideal, if they construct their parts with regard to the whole and for the sake of the whole, synthesis will follow naturally and with an easy approach to perfection; but if the specialists are hostile, if their enthusiasm is not that of those who have a large aim and view, if they continue to insist on detail for detail's sake and suspect all generalization of falseness, if they cannot be weaned from the provincial spirit of petty farmers, the outlook is bad enough, synthesis is indefinitely postponed.

Synthesis is not possible without specialization. The special student must always garner, sift, verify. Minute circumstance must be examined along with great circumstance, all the background as well as the foreground of the picture studied, every part of human endeavor held separately under scrutiny until its individual qualities and particular relations with the rest of the human story stand clearly revealed; and this is, of necessity, the work of hundreds of minds, not of one mind. There is labor enough and honor enough to go around, and the specialist who puts first-rate gifts into his task, though he be less read, will not in the long estimate of literature earn less distinction than the general historian. It is a question of the division and coöperation of labor: but it is more; it is also a question of the spirit in which the labor is done, the public spirit that animates it, the general aim and conception that underlies and inspires it.

As a university teacher I cannot help thinking that the government of the matter is largely in the hands of the professors of history in our schools of higher training. The modern crop of specialists is theirs: they can plant and reap after a different kind if they choose. I am convinced that the errors and narrownesses of specialization are chiefly due to vicious methods and mistaken objects in the training of advanced students of history in the universities. In the first place, if I may speak from the experience of our American universities, students are put to tasks of special investigation before they are sufficiently grounded in general history and in the larger aspects of the history of the age or nation of which they are set to elaborate a part. They discover too many things that are already known and too many things which are not true,—at any rate, in the crude and distorted shape in which they advance them. Other universities may be happier than ours in their material, in the previous training of the men of whom they try to make investigators; but even when the earlier instruction of their pupils has been more nearly adequate and better suited to what is to follow, the training they add is not, I take the liberty of saying, that which is likely to produce history, but only that which is likely to produce doctors' theses. The students in their seminars are encouraged, if they are not taught, to prefer the part to the whole, the detail to the spirit, like chemists who should prefer the individual reactions of their experiments to the laws which they illustrate.

I should think the mischievous mistake easy enough of correction. It is quite possible to habituate students to a point of view, and to do so is often, I daresay, the best part of their preparation. When they come to the advanced stage of their training, at which they are to be set to learn methods of investigation, they should not be set first of all to the discovery or elaboration of facts, to the filling in of the hiatuses easily and everywhere to be discerned, by their preceptors at any rate, in the previous study of detail. They should, rather, be set to learn a very different process, the process of synthesis: to establish the relations of circumstances already known to the general history of the day in which they occurred. These circumstances should not all be political or economic or legal; they should as often concern religion, literature, art, or the development of language, so that the student should at once become accustomed to view the life of men in society as a whole. Heaven knows there is enough original work waiting to be done in this kind to keep many generations of youngsters profitably employed. Look where you will in the field of modern monographs, and it is easy to find unassociated facts piled high as the roofs of libraries. There is not a little fame as well as much deep instruction to be got out of classifying them and bringing them into their vital relations with the life of which they form a part. It were mere humanity to relieve them of their loneliness. After they had been schooled in this work, which, believe me, some one must do, and that right promptly, our advanced students of history and of historical method would be ready to go on, if it were only after graduation, after the fateful doctor's degree, to the further task of making new collections of fact, which they would then instinctively view in their connection with the known circumstances of the age in which they happened. Thus, perhaps thus only, will the spirit and the practice of synthesis be bred.

If this change should be successfully brought about, there would no longer be any painful question of hierarchy among historians: the specialist would have the same spirit as the national historian, would use the same power, display the same art, and pass from the ranks of artisans to the ranks of artists, making cameos as much to be prized as great canvases or heroic statues. Until this happens history will cease to be a part of literature, and that is but another way of saying that it will lose its influence in the world, its monographs prove about as vital as the specimens in a museum. It is not only the delightful prerogative of our studies to view man as a whole, as a living, breathing spirit, it is also their certain fate that if they do not view him so, no living, breathing spirit will heed them. We have used the wrong words in speaking of our art and craft. History must be revealed, not recorded, conceived before it is written, and we must all in our several degrees be seers, not clerks. It is a high calling and should not be belittled. Statesmen are guided and formed by what we write, patriots stimulated, tyrants checked. Reform and progress, charity and freedom of belief, the dreams of artists and the fancies of poets, have at once their record and their source with us. We must not suffer ourselves to fall dull and pedantic, must not lose our visions or cease to speak the large words of inspiration and guidance. It were a shame upon us to drop from the ranks of those who walk at the van and sink into the ranks of those who only follow after, to pick up the scattered traces of the marching host as things merely to pore upon and keep. We cannot do this. We will return to our traditions and compel our fellow historians of literature to write of us as of those who were masters of a great art.[3]

Printed in Howard Jason Rogers (ed.), *Congress of Arts and Science*[,] *Universal Exposition, St. Louis, 1904* (8 vols., Boston and New York, 1905-1907), II, 3-20.
[3] There is a WWhw outline and a WWsh draft of this address in WP, DLC. Although his transcript is missing and the outline and shorthand draft bear no composition dates, several letters from the Hibbens in WP, DLC, not printed in this series, make it clear that Wilson composed "The Variety and Unity of History" during the summer at Judd Haven, Ontario.

A News Report

[Sept. 23, 1904]

THE UNIVERSITY OPENS.

Formal Exercises Were Held in Marquand Chapel Yesterday Afternoon.

The opening exercises of the University were held at three o'clock yesterday afternoon, in Marquand Chapel. The Trustees and members of the Faculty in academic costume formed at the Library, and entered the chapel in a procession.

President Wilson, who presided, opened the exercises with prayer. After the reading of the First Psalm, President Wilson made a short address.[1] He spoke of the deaths of Mr. Laurence Hutton and Dr. Charles Woodruff Shields,[2] and gave a few words of welcome to the entering men. The President concluded with the announcement that, through the generosity of Mrs. Humphreys, the University would be given, during the coming winter, two musical entertainments.[3] The exercises closed with a benediction by the Reverend Dr. Henry van Dyke.

Printed in the *Daily Princetonian*, Sept. 23, 1904.
[1] There is a brief WWhw outline of this address entitled "Opening of University" and dated Sept. 22, 1904, in WP, DLC.

2 Hutton died in Princeton on June 10, 1904, Shields in Newport, R. I., on August 26, 1904.

3 Mary Prince Humphreys, widow of Willard Cunningham Humphreys of the German Department, had given the university $10,000, the income from which was to be used annually for two recitals at Princeton, the first to consist of folk songs, the second of classical songs. Each recital was to be accompanied by a lecture "of such character," to quote the bequest, "as to enable the hearers to listen more intelligently to the songs in the programme." The performances were to be called the Anne M. Loomis Recitals in memory of Mrs. Humphreys' mother.

From Alexander Henry

Dear Dr. Wilson,   Philadelphia, Sept. 23, 1904

It gives me pleasure to send you a program[1] of our coming state S[abbath]. S[chool]. Convention in Pittsburgh. The prospects for the Convention are of the brightest character, and we confidently expect this *40th* Convention to be the best.

You will note that we are going to ask you to preside at the conference on Thursday afternoon[2] which will be opened by Floyd W. Tomkins of Philada.[3] We took it for granted that you would be in Pittsburgh by that time, and felt that it would add much to the interest of the Conference if you should preside.

I feel sure that you will be interested in our Educational S.S. Exhibit. Nothing equal to it in connection with S.S. work has ever been attempted. It is the result of months of work on the part of Dr. C. R. Blackall of Philada.[4]

We greatly appreciate your willingness to assist us in making this convention helpful to our Penna S.S. workers.

Yours sincerely,   Alexander Henry.

ALS (WP, DLC).

1 It is missing.

2 As the news report printed at Oct. 14, 1904, discloses, Wilson did preside over a session for pastors in the afternoon of October 13. That evening, he delivered a major address, "The Young People and the Church," the text of which is printed at Oct. 13, 1904.

3 The Rev. Floyd Williams Tomkins, pastor of the Protestant Episcopal Holy Trinity Church in Philadelphia.

4 Chairman of the Administration Committee of the Pennsylvania State Sabbath School Association.

A News Report

[Sept. 26, 1904]

FRESHMAN RECEPTION

Class of 1908 Entertained by Philadelphian
Society Saturday Evening.

The annual reception of the Philadelphian Society to the Freshman class, was held in Murray-Dodge Hall from 7.30 to 10 o'clock Saturday evening. Dumont Clarke, Jr., 1905, president of the Society, welcomed the entering men and briefly explained the working of the organization. . . .

The speaking was concluded by President Wilson, who made the address of the evening. He spoke of Princeton spirit and its power of making men of distinction. Following the lines of thought of the former speakers, President Wilson described the opportunities for development in Princeton and explained [that] the curriculum work was after all the most important in that it trains men to think. He stated as his ambition for Princeton that it should be permanent and immortal, permanent through the spirit that gives it life and immortal by the immortal men it produces.

Printed in the *Daily Princetonian*, Sept. 26, 1904.

From William Church Osborn

My dear President Wilson: New York.   September 26, 1904.

I have your note of the 23rd, and will send you in a short time my check for $1500. for use in the English Department. I am sorry that my letter last spring, in reply to your letter, failed to give you a positive idea that I expected to renew this subscription.[1] I thought that I had stated it clearly so that you could rely on the money and make your plans accordingly. I have read your address to the Alumni on the new curriculum,[2] and the plan seemed to me to be both wise and progressive.

With best wishes for your success for the coming season, I am,
          Very cordially yours,   Wm. Church Osborn

TLS (WP, DLC).
[1] See W. C. Osborn to WW, April 28, 1904.
[2] It is printed at June 14, 1904.

A News Item

[Sept. 27, 1904]

CAMPUS IMPROVEMENTS.

Owing to the recent retirement of Mr. J. MacN. Thompson as Curator on August 1, Mr. Bunn,[1] the present holder of this office, has scarcely had time in which to carry out many improvements on the campus. A most noticeable improvement, however, is the iron fence surrounding Prospect. It runs along the south side of of McCosh walk, enclosing the space just this side of the '79 dormitory, and when completed will add considerably to the appearance of the President's grounds.

Printed in the *Daily Princetonian*, Sept. 27, 1904.
1 Henry Conrad Bunn, who had been Assistant Treasurer of Princeton University since 1902.

From Burton Alva Konkle[1]

My Dear Sir: Swarthmore, Pa.   27 Sept 04

Probably you do not remember a letter I wrote you some half-dozen years ago, expressing my appreciation of your essay on Sir Henry Maine in the *Atlantic*.[2] I do not believe much in letter-writing by the unknown to the well-known, for in most cases it is liable to misconstruction however worthy and genuine the motive which prompted such letters.

I think though when I have been able to say of a man, as I have of you for many years, that he has been the spokesman of my best thought in the field of history and politics, that I am justified in my desire to tell you so, and offer you the tribute of a volume of my own final contribution in the same fields, as I do by this mail, in the form of a study of the great contest in Pennsylvania over the single and double-legislature constitutions. Please accept this life of Judge Smith, who was a leading actor in that contest, as an expression of my appreciation of your helpfulness to me in your writings and addresses.[3]

I have not had the courage to send it to you before, although it was out last February, but when, on August 18th, so great an authority as the *Nation*, used a couple of columns in saying it was worth while, I thought the "worthwhileness" would justify me.

Your addresses on the history of politics at Philadelphia ought to be heard by every voter in the world.[4]

Sincerely   Burton Alva Konkle

P.S.—"Spokesman of *my* best thought" sounds rather funny—but let it go.

ALS (WP, DLC).
1 A former public school teacher and Presbyterian minister, who had settled in the Philadelphia area in 1897 and devoted himself to the writing of history.
2 See B. A. Konkle to WW, Oct. 20, 1898, Vol. 11.
3 Burton Alva Konkle, *The Life and Times of Thomas Smith, 1745-1809* (Philadelphia, 1904). This volume is in the Wilson Library, DLC.
4 Konkle was referring to six lectures on great leaders of political thought, which Wilson gave in Philadelphia in early 1901 under the auspices of the American Society for the Extension of University Teaching. About these lectures, see the news item printed at Jan. 12, 1901, Vol. 12.

A News Report of a Religious Talk

[Sept. 29, 1904]

PHILADELPHIAN SOCIETY.

First Weekly Meeting of the Year
Addressed by President Wilson.

President Wilson addressed the first regular meeting of the Philadelphian Society in Murray Hall at 7 o'clock last evening. He read parts of the eleventh and twelfth chapters of Ecclesiastes and chose as his text "Rejoice, Oh young man, in thy youth, remembering that for all these things thou shalt be called to judgment," and "Fear God and keep his commandments for this is the whole duty of man." The speaker said in part:

"The most important thing in the beginning of an undertaking is to establish ideals. If a man does not do so, he is like a wanderer and always astray. What is it that a man comes to college for? There is no profit in mere knowledge. You do not want your mind to be a storehouse or a curiosity shop. What you put into your mind is absorbed, and becomes part of your life. What goes into your mind ought to be carefully scrutinized and chosen, for it will leave a permanent trace on your life. A man ought to ask himself just what he wants to put in, and what he wants to do with it. The difference between a college man and one who has not received a college education, is that the college man's mind is trained, regulated, and chastened. A man's spiritual make-up determines his power, and that is the reason that the Philadelphian Society is of such vital importance to Princeton. Princeton is now practically governed by the students, and this has been made possible because the Christian system is practiced here.

"First we must convince ourselves what law we must follow, and then we must go ahead in spite of everything. Now is the time is [to] establish our ideas, for by and by it will not be so easy, since we become hardened and less plastic. How much better it is to do good at the start. If we do, we will become more and more useful to our fellow-men, and will be a greater power among them. The force of Christianity is the force of comradeship, and this with the wish for the best things in the world, we would feign [fain] believe is the 'Princeton Spirit.' "[1]

Printed in the *Daily Princetonian*, Sept. 29, 1904.
[1] For this address, Wilson used the notes printed at Nov. 15, 1900, Vol. 12.

A Commemorative Address[1]

[[Sept. 29, 1904]]

PRESIDENT RAYMOND,[2] LADIES AND GENTLEMEN:

It gives me peculiar gratification to bring the greetings of Princeton to Union on this occasion. We are very proud to have bred so many good colleges, and we count it a singular honor that we should, in some sense, have originated Union College.[3]

It is pleasant to be a college president for some reasons, although not so pleasant for others. It is a very peculiar profession. The chief duty of it seems to be to go about and talk about subjects you only partially understand. (Laughter.) But one of the things which we do understand is the comradeship between institutions of learning, and no function of a college president is more grateful than this which I happen to be illustrating at this moment, the carrying of fraternal greetings to other institutions engaged in the same work, not by way of rivalry but by way of comradeship, the competition being only as to which shall do the work best.

The peculiar interest of an occasion like this, to my mind, is that it is the celebration of the achievements of an individual. It is very difficult, indeed, to conceive of the achievements of an institution. It is very difficult to warm the cockles of the heart over an event, unless you can see some real personal force dominating that event. No one has ever loved an institution in the abstract or admired an event in the abstract. The devoted attachment which alumni have to their Alma Mater is not in the air; it is not the love of a thing which they have never seen. It is the throb which will never cease until they die because of the old companionships[,] the intimate contacts which they have had there. They feel the touch of the shoulder with the men with whom they went through the old place; and it is the place, the image of things, the touch of persons that is upon them until they die. The image of their Alma Mater is there; the image of their classmates, and of their fellows of whatever class, as they went through the happy days. If they got any inspiration aside from their comradeship, they got it from individuals in the teaching chair whom they well remember. Every time that a man takes

---

[1] Delivered in the First Presbyterian Church of Schenectady, N. Y., at a ceremony commemorating the centennial of the assumption of the presidency of Union College by Eliphalet Nott.

[2] Andrew Van Vranken Raymond, President of Union College.

[3] Union's first two presidents were Princeton men. The first, John Blair Smith, Class of 1773, served from 1796 to 1799. The second, Jonathan Edwards, Jr., Class of 1765, served from 1799 to 1801.

fire, he takes it from fire; and no weak individuality ever per-
petuated itself or touched another heart to make it strong. So
that the best way to image an institution for yourself is to image
it in the terms of a particular life which happens to stand in
the history of the institution most conspicuous.

Of course, the long life, the distinguished service, which you
now celebrate, brings many sorts of images to the mind; the
image of the man; the image of the teacher, and the image of
the minister of the Gospel: the man whose activities were of
many kinds, but whose individuality was of one kind; and his
pupils were touched and governed by that. We suppose sometimes in this day of combined and organized effort that the individual is sunk. But do you know of any organization now vital
which is not touched by the personal force of some one man who
organized it, or who now conducts and dominates it? Did you
ever know of an age in which the power of individual thought
told for more than it does in this day? Organization is not the
mere multiplication of individuals; it is the drawing of individuals together into a net formed by the conceptions of a single
mind, and the greater the organization, the more certain you
are to find a great individuality at its origin and center. The
business which is now handed on from father to son in our day
cannot be handed on unless the son is like the father, unless he
has the some power of keeping the threads of an intricate organization in his hand, and putting the force of an original mind into
the changing circumstances of a business which never stands
still, and is every day transformed by the changing circumstances of the day. There never was a time when such drafts
were made upon individual power as are made in this day of organized industry and organized effort upon every hand. Let us
not make the mistake of supposing then that we can dispense
with the idiosyncrasy of being ourselves. A man has nothing else
to contribute to the world except himself; and that is the principal argument for keeping himself efficient, and keeping himself
pure; because there will be a seed of decay in him if he does not.

It is very wholesome, therefore, in celebrating the history of an
institution to celebrate it in the form of memorials and stories
and in scattered recollections of great individuals. I suppose that
every teacher has had the same experience that has come to me.
It happens that almost every time I have had the delightful experience of being thanked by some man for what I did for him
when he was in college, it turned out upon inquiry that it was
something I did for him outside the class room. Rather humili-

ating to the lecturer! But it means this, that when you are talking to a room full of men, you are not touching any one of them particularly; it is outside the class room that the individual man comes to you for direct counsel, to have some individual problem straightened out for him, or some problem of conduct. Then, if you have any heart under your jacket, you give him all the best things that are in you, and you give them for the particular purpose for which he needs them; if he gets anything out of it, that is what he remembers for the rest of his life. When your name is mentioned he doesn't remember the lecturer, he doesn't remember the man who has written books, and gotten this sort and the other sort of fame; he recollects the man; the genuine grip of his hand on a particular occasion, when he really put his heart alongside of his in order to help him. And this is the greatness of the man whose memory we celebrate to-day; that he took pains to lay his mind and heart alongside of the individual minds and hearts with which he dealt; and, thereby transmitted the power that was in him, and the purity and elevation of aim.

I sometimes wonder if some of the public men amongst us realize how much they are wasting their time,—men who take color from their surroundings, who wait to ascertain what their views shall be upon a particular occasion. I wonder if they realize that they might just as well be the thin atmospheric air which they are breathing, so far as any influence is concerned, or so far as any power is concerned. Every nation that does its own thinking loves nothing so much as a brave man; loves nothing so much as a man who has opinions which he does not fear in any circumstances to declare.

I think that one of the embarrassments of being a college president is that you have to stop to ask yourself a demoralizing question. You are asked your opinion about something, and you remind yourself, before replying, that you are two persons—the individual A.B. and the representative of an institution; and there is the sneaking temptation to hide the cowardice of the individual behind what is politic for the institution; is it wise for the president of the university to express himself on that subject? That is one of the most subtle temptations of the devil. (Laughter.) The devil is a very astute person, and he knows how to manage a college president as well as anybody else. (Laughter.) And I take it that when you get hold of a strong individuality like the individuality of Dr. Nott, the beauty of it is that it does not make any difference whether he remembers he is president of anything or not, just so he makes the impression that he himself is consistent with his own principles, and with the rectitude of his own character. You know that you give singular men leave to say very singular things. And really if men wanted to have the greatest degree of liberty in the world they would take pains to be singular; then if they said erratic and impossible things their friends would only shrug their shoulders and say, "You know what kind of a fellow he is." If you could add to singularity purity, singularity is a fine capital to trade with. Dr. Nott was a singular man, who like our own Dr. McCosh, of Princeton, added power to his singularity; Dr. Nott, like Dr. McCosh, was a man whom you could laugh at every day, and yet never for a moment despise. Think what an asset that is in a man's character! We all do something every day, I dare say, that is so very laughable and ridiculous that most of us have to conceal it because we would be despised if we were laughed at. Here were men who could be laughed at every day, and never for a moment despised. I dare say that if you take a splendid piece of machinery, and look at it from the point of view of mere gracefulness of motion, you will find some very silly little cogs going around in a very ridiculous fashion; but that would not make you think the machine without dignity in its power. The great splendid united motion of it is what strikes you, and you do not look into the detail of the silly little cogs going around in their excited fashion. There is beauty in anything that is big enough in its proportions to hide the disproportions of the minor details; and there is not beauty in anything that is not regulated and chastened and brought into splendid complete form.

You know Ruskin's beautiful illustration of that. He says: "Compare a river which has escaped its banks with one that is governed by it: the shapeless expanse of water, and the quiet stream between the green banks, and which is the more beautiful? Compare the clouds spread over the whole surface of the heavens with those which the wind has governed and builded into castles, or made to scud along it like fleets of ships upon the deep blue, and you will see that the thing that is governed, that is swept into shape, that moves in mass and volume and power, is the thing of beauty";[4] and that the reason that these eccentric lives are beautiful is that they bulk big, and move with a sort of careless majesty, which is the majesty of nature itself, governed by the wind that blows where it listeth, which only the mind of God directs and the ear of God hears; the minds which are care-

[4] Wilson was paraphrasing Sect. 2, Chap. 7 of *Seven Lamps of Architecture*, which he had used several times before in speeches. See the notes for a public lecture printed at Dec. 18, 1894, Vol. 9, and n. 2 to that document.

less of what others plan, so they move with the great forces that made them. It takes the imagination, it quickens the pulse, to think of great men; and great institutions are always compounded of great men.

I think that the chief cause of my gratification is, not only that I bring most cordial greetings from Princeton to Dr. Raymond, and Union, but that I have the opportunity to stand here and pay a tribute to the memory of that sort of force which is the only sort that will ever quicken young men and advance the education of the country. (Great applause.)

Printed in *Union University Quarterly*, 1 (Nov. 1904), 181-86.

From James Bryce

Dear President Wilson,   New York City   Sept. 29/04

You were kind enough to ask me to come to Princeton for Commencement & to deliver an address. I found that with all the other things I was already bound to do it would be impossible for me to prepare an address, and I have had, & have in prospect, so much public speaking that I was, and am really unable to undertake any more. But I should very much like to see you and to see Princeton while I am in America; and if it were convenient to you that I should run across to you there from New York while I am there (Oct. 10-22) without any public speaking but just to see the place & talk to you, I would gladly do so.

I shall be from Oct. 2 till Oct. 5 at The Grange, Toronto, Canada, staying with Goldwin Smith.[1] My general address is as above.   Yours very truly   James Bryce

ALS (WP, DLC).
[1] Resident of Toronto since 1871, prominent English historian and lecturer, and recipient of the LL.D. at the Princeton Sesquicentennial Celebration in 1896.

A News Item

[Oct. 1, 1904]

President Wilson '79 returned to Princeton in excellent health, having spent most of the summer with his family in Canada. His first out-of-town fall engagement was an address at Union College, Schenectady, N. Y., on September 29th, on the occasion of the exercises commemorative of the administration of President Nott. Among his other engagements for the near future are an address before the Schoolmasters' Club of New York, at Hotel St. Denis, on October 8th, and an address before the State Sunday School Association of Pennsylvania, in Pittsburgh on October 13.

Printed in the *Princeton Alumni Weekly*, v (Oct. 1, 1904), 8.

To Winthrop More Daniels

My dear Daniels: Princeton, N. J.   1 October, 1904.

Of course every subscription such as the one you speak of does, in a way, interfere with the collection of funds for the University, but at the same time it seems to me really a private thing and one in which it would not be right for me to intervene at all.[1]

I am none the less obliged to you for asking the question.

I find that the editorial in the Evening Post is attracting the widest and most favorable attention.[2]

    Cordially and sincerely yours,   Woodrow Wilson

TLS (W. M. Daniels Coll., CtY).
  [1] The Editors have been unable to discover any information about this matter.
  [2] Daniels' editorial, "Princeton's New Curriculum," in the New York *Evening Post*, Sept. 20, 1904.

To Benjamin Wistar Morris III

My dear Mr. Morris: Princeton, N. J.   1 October, 1904.

It is singular how impossible I have found it to get to New York. I ought to be able to manage it by the end of next week, but if you are coming this way during the week it would give me great pleasure to see you. I am pretty sure to be found on Monday, Tuesday or Wednesday.

    In haste,   Cordially yours,   Woodrow Wilson

TLS (WC, NjP).

From Robert Erskine Ely[1]

My dear Dr. Wilson: New York   October 1, 1904

In your letter to me of May 20th last,[2] you were so good as to say that you were disposed to accept the invitation of the League for Political Education to be one of our lecturers this season. You suggested that I write you about October 1st.

We would like very much to have you address the League on one of the following Saturday mornings at 11 o'clock.

Nov. 12, 26; Dec. 3, 10; Feb. 18, 25.

If equally convenient for you, one of the earlier dates would be preferable. If you could select two dates which would be possible to you, allowing us to choose between them, that would be advantageous.

As to subject, any subject within the field of political and social science, or relating to education or public affairs would be very acceptable. It would be no disadvantage if you were to repeat an address already prepared and delivered elsewhere than in New York or even here.

Other lecturers expected in our Saturday morning course are: Andrew D. White, Edward Everett Hale, Booker Washington, John Graham Brooks, etc.

The lectures are held in the theatre in this building[3] and the audience numbers usually upwards of five or six hundred. Many of them are of the distinctly well-to-do class. In fact the audience is apt to represent much that is influential in the life of this city. You may be assured that you will find it a wise investment of time to address the League, as others have found it. Otherwise it would be immoral to give you this invitation.

One feels in the atmosphere unmistakeable indications of the steady progress of Princeton under the present administration. I was greatly interested in the account in the Evening Post editorial, of the changes in the courses of study. How admirably you have combined required foundation work with opportunities for specialization.

With much appreciation of your kindness in being willing to do the League and the cause it represents this service—in which Dr. Gould,[4] Professor Clark[5] and our other officers join me—and with pleasantest anticipations of hearing you,[6] I am,

Sincerely yours, Robert Erskine Ely

TLS (WP, DLC) with WWhw notation on top of first page: "The Univ. and the Nation."

[1] See R. E. Ely to WW, March 14, 1902, n. 1, Vol. 12.

[2] Ely's second letter to Wilson and Wilson's reply of May 20, 1904, are both missing.

[3] At 23 West 44th St., New York.

[4] Elgin Ralston Lovell Gould, economist and authority on the social conditions of the working classes.

[5] John Bates Clark, Professor of Political Economy at Columbia University and author of many works on economics. Both Gould and Clark were old friends of Wilson's.

[6] See the news announcement printed at Dec. 3, 1904.

An Editorial from the *Daily Princetonian*

[Oct. 3, 1904]

The action of some men in removing on Friday night,[1] a portion of the fence surrounding Prospect, is to be severely condemned by every one. There are some excellent reasons on both sides of the question of erecting the fence, but such action as this makes all argument in the matter useless. No matter if the authorities are almost generally criticized for the erection of the fence, disapproval can never be an excuse for vandalism.[2]

Printed in the *Daily Princetonian*, Oct. 3, 1904.

  [1] September 30, 1904.

  [2] Many students had in fact been highly upset by the construction of the fence. As the *Daily Princetonian* editorialized on October 1, 1904, they believed that the fence was both "unnecessary and unsightly" and that it detracted from the beauty of McCosh Walk, "a spot which has been the pride of undergraduates since the days when it was customary to see President McCosh taking his daily walk there." The editorial accepted the administration's explanation that some kind of barrier was necessary to permit the development of the gardens of Prospect and eliminate the increasing intrusions by "excursionists from Trenton" and other trespassers, especially during the spring and summer. However, it suggested the use of a temporary, portable fence during these seasons and the addition of a special watchman.

From Robert Edwards Annin[1]

Dear Dr. Wilson: New York, Oct. 3–1904.

I was much gratified to receive your very kind note of Sept. 28th accepting the Association's invitation to be their guest at their Annual dinner on Nov. 10th,[2] and due notice of any portion of the program that you ought to know, will be sent to you in ample time.

I am not certain whether, in my letter to you, I invited you to be my guest over night; if not, I take this occasion of saying that it would afford Mrs. Annin and myself great pleasure to entertain you, and that you would find it quite convenient to return to Princeton via Newark if you wished to get back Friday morning. I will make arrangements to have you met and taken to my house, where you can dress, and it is then a very pleasant drive over to East Orange, where the dinner will be held.

Again thanking you for so fully meeting our wishes, I remain—
                    Sincerely yours,   R. E. Annin.

TLS (WP, DLC).

  [1] Princeton 1880, founder and President of the Princeton Alumni Association of the Oranges. A descendant on his mother's side of Jonathan Edwards, Annin was a member and eventually a partner of the New York export firm of R. W. Forbes & Co. His *Woodrow Wilson, A Character Study* (New York, 1924) was a very hostile biography. He died in 1935.

  [2] See the news report printed at Nov. 26, 1904.

To Robert Edwards Annin

My dear Mr. Annin: Princeton, N. J.   4 October, 1904.

I am sincerely obliged to you for your kind letter of the third. It will give me the greatest pleasure to be your guest on the occasion of my visit to Orange. When the date approaches, I will send you word of the train I expect to take, and I shall look forward to the occasion with the greatest interest.

    Always,   Cordially yours,   Woodrow Wilson

TLS (FTU).

To Winthrop More Daniels

My dear Daniels: Princeton, N. J.   5 October, 1904.

I write to beg that you will continue to serve as head of your department during the present university year.

    Your continued service will greatly oblige,

                    Yours most sincerely,   Woodrow Wilson

TLS (W. M. Daniels Coll., CtY).

To the Board of Trustees of Princeton University

                    Princeton University, 7 October, 1904.
            For the Information of the Board of Trustees.

    There will be no formal exercises on Commemoration Day this year. It was expected that Maitre Labori, Mr. John Morley, and Sir William Mather would be present to receive the degrees voted them by the Board; but it has unfortunately proved impossible for them to be in Princeton in October. An invitation was extended to Mr. Morley to deliver the address on Commemoration Day, but he was unable to accept; and invitations subsequently extended to Sir William Mather and Mr. James Bryce proved equally unavailing. For these reasons, it has proved impossible to arrange for the exercises, which it had been expected would be held on the twenty-second.   WOODROW WILSON.

T MS. (McAlpin File, UA, NjP).

From Cyrus Hall McCormick

My dear Woodrow: Chicago.   October 7th, 1904

I regret more than I can tell you that I shall be unable to be at the October meeting of the Trustees. The fact is there is a most unfortunate conflict between the date of the Northwestern Ry Directors' meeting, which occurs here on Thursday, and the Princeton meeting on Friday. I had supposed that the Northwestern Directors' meeting was to be in New York, and was congratulating myself on my ability to make both of these appointments so easily; but now that I find the Directors' meeting is in Chicago, I must attend, as it is an annual meeting.

The only thing of importance that occurs to me which may be acted upon at this meeting is the question of the name of the '79 Building. Has any progress been made and is it likely that the question will be settled now? What is the feeling, so far as you know, and how does the matter stand now, as compared with last June?[1]

I am   Very sincerely yours,   Cyrus H. McCormick.

TLS (WP, DLC).
[1] The question was, in fact, settled by the trustees on October 21, 1904, when they accepted the name "Seventy-Nine Hall," which had been approved by the Committee on Grounds and Buildings. See H. C. Bunn to C. C. Cuyler, Oct. 18, 1904, printed as an Enclosure with C. C. Cuyler to the Board of Trustees, Oct. 21, 1904.

Notes for an Address[1]

8 Oct., 1904

Schoolmasters Club. Hotel St. Denis

Educational Ideals:

I *speak of the University,* wh. I know, not of the School, wh. I never served.

The *University for a Minority,*—none the less a minority because self-selected,—free, not 'privileged'—

For the Majority, Common Schools
                      Technical   "
                      Industrial   "   } Information—Skill.
                      Agricultural   "

For the Minority—What?

The capacity to { See
                  Judge
                  Lead
                  Combine

Insight—Comprehension—Appreciation
Dr. Ward's lecture[2]
Mr. Chesterton's function of Poetry[3]
Mr. Bryan's "Without regard to any other country"[4] and
The utilitarian's "Without regard to any other century or
    any mere abstraction."
  The function of the University, to make Idealists
    Imagination and Progress.

WWhw MS. (WP, DLC).
  [1] No New York newspaper reported on this address to what was probably the
dinner meeting of the Schoolmasters Association of New York and Vicinity on
October 8, 1904, nor was Wilson's address mentioned in any of the published
proceedings of that organization.
  [2] A reference to the first of three lectures on "The Relations of Science and
Philosophy" given by Professor James Ward, Professor of Mental Philosophy
and Logic at Cambridge University, in Murray Hall at Princeton University in
October 1904. Wilson introduced Ward at the opening lecture on October 5. In
this lecture, Ward characterized current philosophy as idealistic and said that
it was necessary to relate religion to the practical realities of the day. *Daily
Princetonian*, Oct. 6, 1904.
  [3] A somewhat obscure reference. Perhaps Wilson was referring to Gilbert K.
Chesterton's argument that poetry should deal with contemporary, practical
problems.
  [4] That is, William Jennings Bryan's argument that the United States could
adopt the bi-metallic standard without reference to the monetary policies of
other countries.

From James Bryce

Dear President Wilson   New York City   Oct. 8/04
  I should much enjoy spending a quiet Sat. to Monday with
you, and I think that next Saturday would be an available day
for me[.] Subject to my finding when I reach New York on Monday that my friends there have made some engagement for me
for it, which is quite unlikely, I shall venture to consider that as
the arrangement, as you suggest it; should it be still suitable for
you.
  My wife who is with me would be greatly interested in accompanying me to see Princeton, should that be quite convenient
to you   Very truly yours   James Bryce

  I will write from New York at once if it should turn out that
an engagement has been made there for me for Saturday. I am
engaged for the *forenoon* of that day, but could come by an afternoon train, and think tis but a 70 minutes run[1]

ALS (WP, DLC).
  [1] The Bryces did visit the Wilsons on Saturday, October 15, and remained
through the weekend. See J. Bryce to WW, June 30, 1907, Vol. 17.

A News Item

[Oct. 9, 1904]

STUDENTS JEER DR. WILSON.

Princeton's senior class had its annual "horse peerade" yesterday. Led by a brass band and dressed in absurd costumes, the grotesque procession filed on the university field, where a baseball game was being hotly contested.[1] The costumes represented everything from a grewsome representation of death to very red cheeked country maidens. Owing to the general disapproval of the students over the fact that Dr. Wilson, president of Princeton University, has recently put up an iron fence in front of his residence, several seniors, well disguised, bore huge cloth placards before and behind, on which was pictured an iron fence, lettered with such injunctions as "Keep out" and "Keep off the grass."[2]

Printed in the *New York Herald*, Oct. 9, 1904.
[1] The annual Sophomore-Freshman baseball game, which ended in a 1 to 1 tie.
[2] The spirit of protest aroused by the Senior P-rade was to go beyond words and banners. During the night following the parade, as the documents will soon reveal, unknown persons—undoubtedly students—vandalized Seventy-Nine Hall.

From Richard Heath Dabney

My dear Woodrow: [Charlottesville, Va.]   9 Oct., 1904.

Although Dr. Alderman has already begun his work here as our first President, a formal inauguration will take place on April 13th, (Jefferson's birth-day,) at which representatives of other leading institutions will be requested to be present. I suppose it will be some time before the official invitations will be sent out; but I am not going to delay a moment my private & personal request that you be my guest on the occasion, and that you make your stay with us as long as your official duties will permit you to be absent from Princeton. As the years flit by, I feel more keenly the separation from genuine friends which the necessities of life make inevitable, and I am therefore greedy for every moment I can get with such a friend. Do not fail, therefore, to come, and to stay as long as you can. Mrs. Dabney & I agreed that it will not do to postpone this request. For, if we do, there is danger that some one else will get ahead of us.[1]

By the way, can you send me a copy of the programme of ceremonies at your own inauguration? I think our committee of arrangements will want to study a number of such programmes.

Alderman has made a good impression here, & I believe he will achieve success. The Board of Visitors came near choosing more than one objectionable man in addition to the preposterous Miles,[2] and we were therefore much relieved at Alderman's election.

The "Jeff" & "Wash" societies[3] are considering the plan of arranging for a debate between representative students of the U. of Va. & those of Princeton. Do you think it can take place? One of our students asked me to find out what you thought about it.[4]

Yours faithfully   R. H. Dabney.

Please give my kindest regards to Mrs. Wilson.

ALS (WP, DLC).
  [1] Wilson was not able to attend Alderman's inauguration. Edgar Odell Lovett represented Princeton University.
  [2] About the "preposterous Miles," see WW to R. H. Dabney, Nov. 10, 1902, n. 4, Vol. 14. For the names of several other men considered for the presidency of the University of Virginia, see Dumas Malone, *Edwin A. Alderman: A Biography* (New York, 1940), pp. 166-67.
  [3] That is, the two literary and debating societies at the University of Virginia, the Jefferson and the Washington.
  [4] This debate apparently never took place.

From Cornelius Cuyler Cuyler

My Dear Woodrow: New York. Octo. 11/04

I have been thinking a good deal about our conversation of Sunday afternoon. I little knew then that an attack had been made on the '79 Dormitory.[1] I am advised by Bunn that financially it amounts to very little fortunately—almost nothing—but it is the general temper shown by such an act which has disgusted me.

Pyne and I had a long talk this morning and we think that in view of the loud complaints from our prominent alumni who have lately been in Princeton it would be well to remove the fence[2] some distance from in front of the '79 Building before the Yale game.[3] Bunn tells me that if it meets with your approval he can put on a force of men at once and do the whole thing by that time. So many of our old men will be back that day that I do not want anything to mar the occasion for them as I fear would be the case if the fence were to remain in what all seem to regard as an unfortunate location. Furthermore I do not want you to be bothered about the matter any more and in addition I am some what selfishly desirous of relieving myself from further criticism as Chairman of Grounds & Buildings

Your warmest friends like Thompson, Dodge, Pyne, Bayard Henry and others all agree that the fence is most appropriate but think it a mistake to have put it where it now is. If any slight modification in the choice of a new location for it is desired Bunn will readily fall in with your wishes in this respect but it should certainly be a considerable distance away in order to relieve the present ugliness of the situation and when this is once done I think all trouble will be over as far as this particular matter is concerned.   Yours sincerely,   C C Cuyler

ALS (WP, DLC).
  1 See the following document for a description of this attack.
  2 That is, that portion of the fence around Prospect separating it from Seventy-Nine Hall and that portion skirting close along McCosh Walk. Cuyler's suggestion was followed, apparently much to the satisfaction of students and alumni. The Committee on Grounds and Buildings of the Board of Trustees also sought to draw criticism away from Wilson by inserting a notice in the *Daily Princetonian*, Oct. 22, 1904, which read: "The placing of the fence around 'Prospect' was the act of the Grounds and Buildings Committee and was authorized by the Board of Trustees. C. C. Cuyler Chairman."
  3 Played on November 12, 1904, Yale winning by the score of 12 to 0. There were no reports of vandalism or protests at this time.

An Editorial from the *Daily Princetonian*

[Oct. 13, 1904]

It is almost a disgrace to the name of Princeton that on two occasions within two weeks the necessity should arise of mentioning acts of vandalism which have been committed on the campus. The removal of a portion of the fence surrounding Prospect was bad enough but on last Saturday night [October 8] some unknown persons broke the glass in several windows of the '79 Dormitory, tore down a chandelier, and chipped the steps in one of the entries from top to bottom. To say that such actions arouse the indignation and surprise not only of the generous alumni who presented this building to the University, but also of all true Princeton men, graduates and undergraduates, but mildly expresses the sentiments which these acts of vandalism arouse. Whether the damage is done by graduates or undergraduates, there is absolutely no excuse for such lawless conduct and every effort possible should be made to bring the guilty parties to justice. We speak for the undergraduate body when we say that such acts are to be condemned in the strongest possible terms and it is the energy of this spirit which should be turned with all its force not only toward the discovery of the guilty parties in this instance but also toward the prevention of such lawlessness in the future. Undergraduates are much more able to handle such matters than the University authorities and the remedy lies in the force of the public opinion of the student body.

Printed in the *Daily Princetonian*, Oct. 13, 1904.

An Address on Christian Education[1]

[[Oct. 13, 1904]]

THE YOUNG PEOPLE AND THE CHURCH

We bear a relationship to the rising generation whether we will or not. It is one of the principal tasks of each generation of mature persons in this world to hand on the work of the world to the next generation. We are engaged even more than we are aware in molding young people to be like ourselves. Those who have read that delightful book of Kenneth Graham's entitled "The Golden Age," the age of childhood, will recall the indictment which he brings against the Olympians, as he calls them,—the grown-up people,—who do not understand the feelings of little folks not only, but do not seem to understand anything very clearly; who do not seem to live in the same world, who are constantly forcing upon the young ones standards and notions which they cannot understand, which they instinctively reject. They live in a world of delightful imagination; they pursue persons and objects that never existed; they make an Argosy laden with gold out of a floating butterfly,—and these stupid Olympians try to translate these things into uninteresting facts.

I suppose that nothing is more painful in the recollections of some of us than the efforts that were made to make us like grown-up people. The delightful follies that we had to eschew, the delicious nonsense that we had to disbelieve, the number of odious prudences that we had to learn, the knowledge that though the truth was less interesting than fiction, it was more important than fiction,—the fact that what people told you could not always be relied on, and that it must be tested by the most uninteresting tests.

When you think of it, we are engaged in the somewhat questionable practise of making all the world uniform. We should be very sure that we are very handsome characters to have a full heart in the undertaking of making youngsters exactly like ourselves. There is an amount of aggregate vanity in the process which it is impossible to estimate. Moreover, you will notice that

[1] A news report of the convention in Pittsburgh at which Wilson delivered this address is printed as the following document.

there are very whimsical standards in this world. We speak of some persons as being normal, and of others as being abnormal. By normal we mean like ourselves; by abnormal we mean unlike ourselves. The abnormal persons are in the minority, and therefore most of them are in the asylum. If they got to be in the majority, we would go to the asylum. If we departed from that law of the Medes and Persians which commands us to be like other persons, we would be in danger of the bars. The only thing that saves us is that the abnormal people are not all alike. If they were, they might be shrewd enough to get the better of us, and put us where we put them.

And we are engaged in rubbing off the differences. We desire not to be supposed to be unlike other persons; we would prefer to abjure our individuality, and to say, as Dean Swift advised every man to say who desired to be considered wise, "My dear sir, I am exactly of your opinion." We try to avoid collisions of individuality, and go about to tell the younger people that they must do things as we have always done them, and as our parents made us do them, or else they will lose caste in the world.

There are two means by which we carry on this interesting work of making the next generation like the last. There is life itself, and that is the most drastic school there is. There is no school so hard in its lessons as the school of life. You are not excused from any one of its exercises. You are not excused for mistakes in any one of its lessons. We say a great many things that are harsh, and deservedly harsh, I will admit, about college hazing; but there is a more subtle hazing than that. The world hazes the persons that will not conform. It hazes after a manner that is worse than hazing their bodies,—it hazes their spirits, and teases them with the pointed finger and the curl of the lip, and says, "That man thinks he knows the whole thing." That, I say, is a very much more refined torture than making a man do a great many ridiculous things for the purpose of realizing that he is ridiculous, and so getting out of conceit with himself. I do not believe in hazing, but I do believe that there are some things worse than hazing. And I have suffered worse things from my fellow-men since I got out of college than I suffered while I was in college.

Life is a terrible master to those who cannot escape its more trying processes. The little urchin in the slums of the city knows more of the prudences of life when he is five than most of us knew at five and twenty. He knows just how hard a school he lives in, and just how astute he must be to win any of its prizes, to win even the tolerance of the powers that conduct it, even to live from day to day. He knows how many cars of Juggernaut must be dodged on the streets for the mere leave to live, and the keenness of his senses, his shrewdness in a bargain, is such as would predict him a man successful in commerce, would mean that some day he was going to overreach his fellow-man as now life seems to be overreaching him, and imposing upon him, and snatching every coveted thing from his grasp. The process of culture, the process of civilization, and the processes that can be bought by wealth, are largely processes of exemption from the harder classes of the school of life. Some young gentlemen brought up in the lap of luxury seem to have escaped all lessons, seem to know just as little about the world as it is possible for a person to live nineteen years and know. I have sometimes thought that if we could get a whole college of youngsters who had spent their boyhood in the slums, where they had to have wits in order to live, we would make extraordinary progress in scholarship; whereas, when in our discouraged moments,—I mean discouraged moments in our teaching,—we take some grim comfort in saying, as a Yale friend of mine said, that after teaching twenty years he had come to the conclusion that the human mind had infinite resources for resisting the introduction of knowledge. But you cannot resist the introduction of the knowledge that life brings. Life brings it and unloads it in your lap whether you want it or not.

The other means we have of indoctrinating the next generation and making the world uniform is organization. The individual process is not enough, we think, the process of working upon each other individually so that a miscellaneous set of influences prick each of us like so many currents of electricity. We think we must organize as a body to have a given, definite predetermined effect upon others. So we take unfair advantage of a youngster in organizing a whole school so that he cannot escape having certain impressions made upon him. We tax the public in order to pay for the schools which will make it impossible for him to escape. And there are various instrumentalities which are organic. In the first place, there is the home; then there is the school; then there is the church; then there are all the political means, the means which we call social in their character, by which to mold and control the rising generation. All of these have their part in controlling the youth of the country and making them what we deem it necessary that they should be.

What do we wish that they should be? If forced to reason about it, we say they ought to be what we have found by experience it is prudent and wise to be; and they ought to be something more,—they ought to go one stage beyond the stage we have gone. But we cannot conduct them beyond the stage we have reached. We can only point and say, "Here are the boundaries which we have reached; beyond is an undiscovered country; go out and discover it. We can furnish you with a few probabilities; we can supply you with a few tendencies; we can say to you that we think that wisdom points in this direction; but we cannot go with you; we cannot guide you; we must part with you at the opening of the door, and bid you Godspeed. But we want you to go on; we do not want you to stop where we stopped."

What capital, after all, is it that we supply them with? I take it that knowledge is a pretty poor commodity in itself and by itself. A ship does not sail because of her cargo. There is no propulsion in that. If the captain did not know his port, if he did not know his rules of navigation, if he did not know the management of his engines, or have somebody aboard who did, if he did not know all the powers that will carry the ship to the place where her cargo will have additional value, the cargo would be nothing to him. What is his purpose? His purpose is that the cargo should be used. Used for what? For the convenience or the enlightenment, whatever it may be, of the people to whom he is carrying it.

And so with knowledge. The knowledge you supply to the little fellow in the home is not merely conveyed to him in order that he may be full; the knowledge that is supplied to him in school is not put in him as if he were merely a little vessel to be filled to the top. My father, who was a very plain-spoken man, used to use a phrase which was rough, but it expressed the meaning exactly. He said, "My son, the mind is not a prolix gut to be stuffed." That is not the object of it. It is not a vessel made to contain something; it is a vessel made to transmute something. The process of digestion is of the essence, and the only part of the food that is of any consequence is the part that is turned into blood and fructifies the whole frame. And so with knowledge. All the wise saws and prudent maxims and pieces of information that we supply to the generation coming on are of no consequence whatever in themselves unless they get into the blood and are transmuted.

And how are you going to get these things into the blood? You know that nothing communicates fire except fire. In order to start a fire you must originate a fire. You must have a little spark in order to have a great blaze. I have often heard it said that a speaker is dry, or that a subject is dry. Well, there isn't any subject in the world that is dry. It is the person that handles it, and the person who receives it that is dry. The subject is fertile enough. But the trouble with most persons when they handle a subject is that they handle it as if it were a mere aggregate mass meant to stay where it is placed; whereas it is something to be absorbed into the pores, to have the life circulation communicated to it, and the moment you communicate that to it, it itself becomes a vehicle of life. Every one who touches a live thing knows he has touched living tissue, and not a dead hand.

So that no knowledge is of any particular consequence in this world which is not incarnate. For example, we are taught the knowledge of the laws of hygiene, but what earthly good are the laws of hygiene to us if we do not live in obedience to them? Presently disease springs upon us, and Nature says, "Thou fool. You knew these things. What profit is it to you to know them and not to regard them in your way of life? They were never yours. They were never part of you. You never possessed them." The moral of which is simply this, that the truths which are not translated into lives are dead truths, and not living truths. The only way to learn grammatical speech is to associate with those who speak grammatically.

And so of religion. Religion is communicable, I verily believe, aside from the sacred operations of the Holy Spirit, only by example. You have only to ask yourself what is the effect of a profession of religion on the part of a man who does not live a religious life. You know that the effect is not only not to communicate religion, but to delay indefinitely its influence. It is certainly true that we are not to judge religion by those who profess it but do not live it. But it is also true that if those who profess it are the only ones we live with, and they fail to live it, it cannot be communicated except by some mysterious grace of the Holy Spirit himself. So that no amount of didactic teaching in a home whose life is not Christian will ever get into the consciousness and life of the children. If you wish your children to be Christians, you must really take the trouble to be Christians yourselves. Those are the only terms upon which the home will work the gracious miracle.

And you cannot shift this thing by sending your children to Sunday-school. You may remedy many things, but you cannot shift this responsibility. If the children do not get this into their blood atmospherically, they are not going to get it into their blood at all until, it may be, they come to a period of life where the influences of Christian lives outside of the home may profoundly affect them and govern their consciences. We must realize that the first and most intimate and most important organization for the indoctrinating of the next generation is the home, is the family. This is the key to the whole situation. That is the reason that you must get hold of the whole family when you get hold of the children in your Sunday-school work; that your work will not be half done when you merely get the children there, and it may be, their mothers. You must include the fathers, and get your grip upon the home organization in such wise that the children will have the atmospheric pressure of Christianity the week through.

We are constantly debating and hearing it debated, How will the church get hold of the young people? You cannot answer that question unless you have a philosophy of the matter. And it seems to me that the inevitable philosophy of the matter is this: There are only a certain number of things that impress young persons, only a certain number that impress old ones, or, for that matter, that impress anybody. The things that impress the young person and the old are convictions and earnestness in action that looks like business, and a certain dignity and simplicity that go along with being in earnest. You will notice that when a man is going about his business he does not study his gestures, he does not consider his poses, he does not think how he looks when he is sitting at his desk in his chair. There is a directness and simplicity of approach in the thing which shows an utter lack of self-consciousness. He is not thinking about the machinery by which he is acting; he is after the thing.

When we say, therefore, that the way to get young people to the church is to make the church interesting, I am afraid we too often mean that the way to do is to make it entertaining. Did you ever know the theater to be a successful means of governing conduct? Did you ever know the most excellent concert, or series of concerts, to be the means of revolutionizing a life? Did you ever know any amount of entertainment to go further than hold for the hour that it lasted? If you mean to draw young people by entertainment, you have only one excuse for it, and that is to follow up the entertainment with something that is not entertaining, but which grips the heart like the touch of a hand. I dare say that there is some excuse for alluring persons to a place where good will be done them, but I think it would be a good deal franker not to allure them. I think it would be a great deal better simply to let them understand that that is the place where life is dispensed, and that if they want life they must come to that place.

If they believe that you believe what you say, they will come. If they have the least suspicion that you do not believe it, if they have the least suspicion that you are simply playing a game of social organization, if they have the notion that you are simply organizing a very useful instrumentality of society for moralizing the community, but that you don't after all believe that life itself lies in the doctrine and preaching of that place and nowhere else, you cannot keep hold of them very long. The only thing that governs any of us is authority. And the reason that it is harder to govern us when we are grown up than when we are young is that we question the authority, and you have to convince our minds of the reasonableness of the authority. But the young mind yields to the authority that believes in itself. That is the reason that consistency of conduct is indispensable to the maintenance of authority. You cannot make the young person do what you do not do yourself. You cannot make him believe what you do not believe yourself.

I have known some parents who had very deep doubt about some of the deeper mysteries of revelation, but who, nevertheless, tried to communicate those deep mysteries to their children, with an absolute lack of success that was to have been expected. They did not believe them themselves. Did you never have the uneasy experience of going into the presence of a child who did not care to speak to you? There are two beings who assess character instantly by looking into the eyes,—dogs and children. If a dog not naturally possessed of the devil will not come to you after he has looked you in the face, you ought to go home and examine your conscience; and if a little child, from any other reason than mere timidity, looks you in the face, and then draws back and will not come to your knee, go home and look deeper yet into your conscience. There is no eye so searching as the eye of simplicity. And you might as well give up the attempt of trying to wear a mask before children, particularly the mask that you are so desirous of wearing,—the mask of hypocrisy. It does not work, and it is a very fortunate thing that it does not work. If it did, we would make our children as big hypocrites as we are. You must believe the things you tell the children.

Have you not seen the flicker of the child's eye when he first asked you if there was really any Santa Claus, and you told him yes? He knows something is the matter. He may not be shrewd enough or thoughtful enough to know what is the matter, but after that he has his doubts about Santa Claus, simply because, by some electric communication that you cannot stop, your doubts about Santa Claus have been communicated to him. If you are a positivist, he will be a positivist; if you believe, he will believe.

It is all in the atmosphere. Sometimes it seems to me that nine-tenths of what we give other persons is in our personality. The value of one man contrasted with another is that some men have no electricity in them. They might be in the room or out of the room; it doesn't make any difference. Other men come into the room, and the moment they come into it something happens, either attraction or repulsion. I cannot sit in a railroad station comfortably, because men will come in whom I want to kick out, and persons will come in whom I want to go up and speak to, and make friends with, and I am restrained because when I was small I was told that was not good form, and I would not for the world be unlike my fellow-men. So I sit still and try to think about something else, and my eye constantly wanders to some person whom it would, I am sure, be such fun to go and talk to, who I know has something I would like to have. And yet, as for nine-tenths of the persons in the room, they do nothing but vitiate the atmosphere, and you would rather have their breathing room than their presence.

And it is thus all through life. A man comes to you to press a piece of business upon you, and he goes away, and you say to yourself, "No, I won't go into that."

And some one else says, "Why not? Don't you believe in him?"

"No, I don't believe in him."

"Do you know anything wrong that he ever did?"

"No."

"Didn't he verify his statements?"

"Yes."

"Then why don't you go in with him?"

"Well. I don't know. I won't do it. I don't like his looks. There was something about him that made me think it was not all straight, and, at any rate, I will look into it, and hear about it from somebody else before going any further."

We are constantly having that feeling. And that is the feeling which illustrates my thought, though I have gone pretty far afield to illustrate it,—that it is conviction, authority, simplicity, the directness of one who is going about his business, and goes about it with genuineness, which governs young people. The moral of that is, that you are going the wrong way about accomplishing what you seek when you try to make that entertaining which, in the nature of things, though engrossing, is not entertaining in the ordinary sense of the word.

To tell a human being of the things that affect his eternal salvation I should say is decidedly under-described if you call it entertaining. It is not entertaining in any reasonable sense of the word to tell him of the things that most profoundly affect his welfare in this world and in the next. I know that there are ways of telling men the truth which repel them; I know that too many men are tried for by efforts which merely frighten. I believe that too much effort is made to get people to believe for fear of the consequences of unbelief. I don't believe any man was ever drawn into heaven for fear he would go to hell. Because, if I understand the Scriptures in the least, they speak a gospel of love. Except God draw you, you are not drawn. You are not brought in by whips, you are not drawn by a frowning face, you are not drawn by a threatening gesture. You are drawn by love, you are drawn by the knowledge that if you come you will be received as a son. Nothing but yearning draws you. Fear never drew you anywhere.

You must realize that it is all a question of personal relationship between man and his Maker, and a personal relationship founded upon love. For love is the only thing that I know that ever led to self-abnegation. Ambition does not lead to it; no use of power for power's sake leads to anything but self-aggrandizement. Can you name me any motive in the world that ever led a man to love another life more than his own except the motive of love? And yet what we are working for in the young people, as in the old, is to show them the perfect image of a Man who will draw all the best powers of their nature to Himself, and make them love him so that they will love him more than they love themselves, and loving him so, will love their fellow-men more than they love themselves. Everything heroic, everything that looks toward salvation is due to this power of elevation. It is a noteworthy thing that we reserve the beautiful adjective "noble" for the men who think less of themselves than of some cause or of some person whom they serve. We elevate to the only nobility we have, the nobility of moral greatness, only those men who are governed by love.

You cannot create love by entertainment, but you can make love by the perfect exhibition of Christ-like qualities, and, with the assistance of the Holy Spirit, by the withdrawal of the veil which for most men hangs before the face of our Lord and

Saviour. Our whole object, it seems to me, in church work is simply this: to enable all to see him, to realize him, and if we devote ourselves to that purpose with singleness of heart and without thought of ourselves, we shall suddenly find the seats filling, because where there is fire thither men will carry their lamps to be lighted. Where there is power, men will go to partake of it. Every human soul instinctively feels that the only power he desires, the only power that can relieve him from the tedium of the day's work, the only thing which can put a glow upon the routine of the day's task, the only thing that can take him back to the golden age when everything had a touch of magic about it, when everything was greater than the fact, when everything had lurking behind it some mysterious power, when there was in everything a vision and a perfect image,—is this thing which he sees enthroned upon the shining countenances of those who really believe in the life and saving grace of their Lord and Master.[2]

Printed in Woodrow Wilson, *The Young People and the Church* (Philadelphia: Sunday School Times Co., 1905).

[2] For this address, Wilson used the notes printed at Feb. 23, 1904. Although correspondence about the matter is missing, a stenographer undoubtedly recorded this lecture, and Wilson edited his transcript before it was printed.

A News Report of a Religious Address

[Oct. 14, 1904]

CROWDS HEARD WOODROW WILSON

President of Princeton University Addresses
State Sabbath School Convention.

Three immense meetings gathered under the auspices of the State Sabbath School association convention were addressed last night by Dr. Woodrow Wilson, president of Princeton University; the Rev. Dr. William Patterson of Philadelphia[1] and Dr. Joseph Clark.[2]

The largest gathering was in the auditorium of the Sixth United Presbyterian church, where upward of 4,000 people tested the seating and standing capacity of the room, while many were perched on tables in front of the pulpit platform. Another gathering of over 2,000 congregated in the Sunday school room, while an overflow of some 1,200 persons gathered in the Emory Methodist Protestant church, a half square away, where it was also necessary to turn people away. The meetings were addressed simultaneously, the speakers being escorted from one meeting to the other, delivering the same address to each. . . .

Dr. Wilson spoke on "The Young People and the Church." Referring to college life, he pointed to hazing as a necessity, in a way, toward introduction to life's mysteries and declared he had suffered worse from men of the world than he did as a student. He held that knowledge was a poor commodity unless digested by use, and that the same applied to religious instruction. He asserted that the home was the key to all religious sentiment, and unless it had Christian atmosphere the child would lose the inspiration imparted by the Sabbath school. He stated that it was not only necessary to get the child in the Sabbath school, but the parents as well; that it was the spirit of earnestness alone that would draw people into the church, and it was the truth that held them. He said it was not a fear of going to hell that drew people into the church, but it was the love for Bible teachings, and strongly advocated the impression of fear in religious teachings be superseded by the spirit of love. . . .

Four simultaneous conferences were conducted during the afternoon. Dr. Wilson presided over a session for pastors; President Wanamaker[3] was in charge of a conference for superintendents; H. J. Heinz conducted a session for teachers, and teachers of elementary grades were shown practical illustrations in tuition in Bethany Lutheran church, a square away, where children's classes were in operation.

Printed in the *Pittsburgh Gazette Times*, Oct. 14, 1904.
  [1] Pastor of the Bethany Presbyterian Church of Philadelphia.
  [2] General Secretary of the Ohio State Sabbath School Association.
  [3] The Philadelphia merchant who at this time was president of the Pennsylvania State Sabbath School Association.

From Thomas L. Snow

"The Bluff" [Judd Haven, Ont.]

My Dear Dr. Wilson   Oct 16/04.

The notices have been nailed up about the shore of your island: six in number, painted legibly in black on white background: and worded exactly like the form you gave me. The charge is two dollars and a half.

We probably leave on the long projected trip to England about beginning of November. To me, the prospective joy thereof promises to be far from unmixed, since after having spent twenty consecutive winters in this, almost, Siberian solitude, the change of existence will be so radical and abrupt as to seem at every turn intolerable and galling. It is, however, my wife's treat: and having, three years ago, promised her and the boys that I would permit myself to be taken with them to England when their joint savings had reached a certain figure, I am now cornered, and faced with the terrific reality. Only yesterday, I was ambushed into a sort of dress rehearsal by Mrs. Snow, and compelled to squirm into a violent construction of starch and things, and in that state I was shrieked at and danced round by the boys. A rash promise is a bad scrape to get into, Goodness knows, but there are worse devices for repenting in than sackcloth and ashes.

Nevertheless, although it is tolerably certain that, after a respite of yet a week or two, razor and starch will convert me into a dismal travesty of the past, yet I stoutly hope to be spared to once more drive the cattle home across the breezy uplands, and to again see some of the familiar and good faces that last summer sent us.

Since I last left what is known as civilization, the phonograph has come forth; so have the telephone, the electric trolley, the electric lighting & things known to me by hear-say only. Imagine the scope for impressions! that lies ahead!

Our very kind regards go with this to Mrs. Wilson, her daughters, and yourself, and, hoping,—in this instance—to elude the deserts of egotism,

Believe me   Very faithfully yours   Thos. L Snow.

ALS (WP, DLC).

From Henry John Heinz

Dear Doctor Wilson: Pittsburgh. October 19, 1904.

So many times have I heard your excellent addresses in Pittsburgh last week praised that I feel all the more keenly my personal loss in not having heard you. This pleasure I had promised myself, but other meetings at the same hour claimed my time and presence, thus depriving me of a privilege I had fully expected to enjoy. But having had a small part in arranging for your presence at the Convention, I wish to extend to you my personal thanks for your able addresses,—the feature of the Convention,—as many have denominated them, through which you contributed much toward making our convention the success it was. While the over flow meeting laid upon you additional labor, I am told by those who heard you in both rooms that the last was even better than the first.

Our plan of putting sixty-seven men at work in the sixty-seven counties of the state was not fully consummated, but it is not improbable that our Executive Committee at its first meeting in November will complete it.

Yours very truly,   H. J. Heinz

TLS (WP, DLC).

To Abel McIver Fraser

My dear Dr. Fraser: Princeton, N. J.   20 October, 1904.

I had promised myself with a good deal of confidence that I could attend the Celebration of the Church which you are planning for the 30 October; but I now find to my great disappointment that official duties will keep me at home.

I know how great a pleasure I am missing, and I assure you that I am acting against my inclination. Pray express to the Committee in charge of the Celebration my warm appreciation of their invitation and my sincere regret at being obliged to decline.

With much regard,

Cordially and Sincerely yours,   Woodrow Wilson

TLS (WP, DLC).

To Fannie Bayle King[1]

My dear Mrs. King: ·   Princeton, N. J.   20 October, 1904.

I greatly appreciate your kind letter of the 18th and wish very much that it were in my power to accept the invitation which it brings. I have promised myself that it would be possible for me to attend the Centennial Celebration of the Church; but official duties have crowded upon me too thick and fast, and I am obliged greatly against my will to decline.

I none the less appreciate most deeply your wish that I should be your guest, and hope that the pleasure of making your acquaintance is only postponed.

My apology for using the typewriter must be that I find real difficulty now-a-days in using the pen, because of an immoderate use of it in the past.

Most sincerely yours,   Woodrow Wilson

TLS (Fannie King Coll., ViU).

[1] Mrs. William Wayt King of Staunton, Va., whose husband was connected with Mary Baldwin Seminary.

To Thomas L. Snow

My dear Mr. Snow: Princeton, N. J.   20 October, 1904.

I take pleasure in enclosing a postal order for $2.50 to pay for the signs you were kind enough to put up on our island. I wish I could think of a more convenient way to send it.

We are all deeply interested to know that the time is actually set for your projected visit to the old country, and we hope most sincerely that you will enjoy it much more than you anticipate. At any rate, you will certainly, as you say, bring back with you the vivid impressions which must come from a changed world. I dare say the wilderness will seem to you more attractive than ever, after the rush and fever of the modern city; but the delight of seeing your people again and the memories of what you see and hear will make a fine store of pleasant recollections for the long winters in Canada. It is very delightful, too, to think of the pleasure that Mrs. Snow and the boys will derive from the trip.

Mrs. Wilson joins me in wishing you the most prosperous passage and the best that can be got from the trip.

Always,   Sincerely yours,   Woodrow Wilson

TLS (photostat in RSB Coll., DLC).

Henry Burchard Fine to the Trustees' Committee on Morals and Discipline

Gentlemen: PRINCETON UNIVERSITY, OCTOBER 21, 1904.

I beg leave to submit the following brief report:

No undergraduate has been reported to me for intoxication since the term began. Three students were reported to me for this offense in connection with the Freshman parade last Commencement and they were suspended until after the Sophomore-Freshman Base Ball Game this Fall.

So far as I can learn there has been no serious case of hazing thus far this Fall. There has been the usual "horsing" of the Freshmen, but this come [came] to an end, according to undergraduate custom, the day of the Sophomore-Freshman Base Ball Game.

The number of students dropped last June for deficiencies in scholarship was 47, of whom 36 belonged to the School of Science and 11 to the Academic Department. The number dropped last February was 72, of whom 58 were School of Science men and 14 were Academic. As was to be expected, the strict enforcement of the rules of scholarship is lessening the number of men who fall below the passing mark.

In this connection it may be of interest to observe that of the 72 men dropped last February, 38 have re-entered college this Fall. A considerable number of the rest were not at liberty to return. A careful examination of the record will show that over two-thirds of those who were at liberty to return have done so.

The new course of study seems already to have increased the seriousness and industry of the students in their college work. This is particularly noticeable in the Sophomore and Junior classes.

The total number of new students enrolled this year and now present in Princeton is 443, as against 435 last year. They are distributed into classes as in the following table in which I have given the corresponding figures of last year:

		1904	1903
Freshman Academic		148	167
B.S.		136	131
C.E.		75	75
		359	373
New Specials Acad.		17	14
" " S. S.		44	27
" Seniors Acad.		6	5
" " S. S.		4	1
" Juniors Acad.		1	4
" " S. S.		2	1
" Sophomores Acad.		9	6
" " S. S.		1	4
Grand total		443	435

About 40% of the Freshmen are Presbyterians and about 25% Episcopalians. There are 30 Methodists, 13 Congregationalists, 12 Catholics, 11 Baptists. The rest are scattered among some twelve different denominations, except 19 who seem to be attached to no church. About three-fourths of the Freshmen are communicants of the churches with which they are connected.

The Registrar informs me that the average age of entrance of the Freshman class is 18 years 11 months and 16 days.

Respectfully submitted,   H. B. Fine

TRS (Trustees' Papers, UA, NjP).

Cornelius Cuyler Cuyler to the Board of Trustees of Princeton University, with Enclosure

Gentlemen: Princeton, N. J., October 21st, 1904.

As Chairman of the Committee on Grounds and Buildings I beg to submit the Curator's report hereunto attached which was read and adopted at the meeting of the Committee on Tuesday last, October 18th, 1904.

Very respectfully,   C C Cuyler,
Chairman Com. of Gds. & Bldgs.

ENCLOSURE

Henry Conrad Bunn to Cornelius Cuyler Cuyler

Dear Sir: Princeton, N. J., October 18th, 1904.

Since assuming the duties of Curator, August 1st, 1904, I beg to report the following work executed in the department of Grounds and Buildings:

GROUNDS

The contract for the iron fence around "Prospect" was awarded to David Pettit, of Philadelphia, for $2194. The erection of the fence has been done by Wm. R. Matthews at a cost of about $400, and is now about completed. . . .

The following recommendation was added at the meeting of the Committee on October 18th:

"Upon motion of Dr. Wilson which motion was carried, the Committee recommended to the Board of Trustees that the dormitory presented to the University by the Class of '79, should be known as " '79 Hall."

H. C. Bunn   Curator

TLS (Trustees' Papers, UA, NjP).

The Committee on Finance to the Board of Trustees of Princeton University

[c. Oct. 21, 1904]

During the early part of the past winter it became very evident to your Committee that the present amount of Annual Income to be counted upon, would not suffice for the current expenses of the University. To bring the Grounds and Buildings up to date, has required, for the past three years, very large sums over and above the amount provided for in the Budget. Then again, there were a large number of other proper expenses, such as salaries, pulpit supplies, Library maintenance, etc., which had been paid by private yearly subscriptions, liable to be terminated at any time, or else by small donations raised by the personal efforts of the President and many others. So numerous have these latter become, that, in the case of some of the more generous of our Alumni, hardly a week passed during the course of which they were not solicited more than once for some gift to the University. The situation was showing signs of becoming intolerable and the President devised a scheme to obviate the necessity of the numerous applications for assistance, which were not only irritating the warmest friends of the University, but were keeping larger gifts from being made.

His scheme was essentially as follows:

(1) That we no longer permit this indiscriminate appeal for small subscriptions and that we place on our Budget many of these items of expense now carried by private gift.

(2) That we encourage subscription to the Alumni Fund and try to increase that to a larger Annual amount.

(3) That we endeavor to get Twenty (20) men who will agree to contribute $5,000 each for three years. Of this $100,000 per annum we are to use $10,000 for current expenses, and invest the remaining $90,000. At the end of three years, therefore, if we can carry out this scheme, we should have $270,000 invested, producing at 4%, an Annual income of $10,800.

It was to be understood that while we were glad to have subscriptions running over three years, yet, unless distinctly stated by the subscriber, no one was to be bound for more than one year at a time.

During the past Academic year however, only Thirteen (13) persons could be found willing to become subscribers of $5,000 each to this Fund, viz:

S. S. Palmer,	$5,000
P. R. Pyne,	5,000
D. C. Blair,	5,000
R. Garrett,	5,000
J. W. Garrett,	5,000
D. B. & T. D. Jones,	5,000
J. H Converse,	5,000
J. L. Cadwalader,	5,000
J. H. Lockhart,	5,000

A. Van Rensselaer,	5,000	
U. H McCarter,	5,000	
J. Laughlin,	5,000	
M. Taylor Pyne,	5,000	

making a total of only $65,000
But the following other subscriptions were received:

C. H. Dodge,	$2,500	
Judge Reed,	2,500	
Mrs. A. D. Russell,	2,500	
N. B. Ream,	2,000	
J. D. Davis,	1,000	
J. J. McCook	1,000	
E. F. Goltra,	1,000	
W. B. Hornblower,	1,000	
T. N. McCarter,	1,000	
Bayard Henry,	1,000	
H. B. Thompson,	500	
B. F. Jones, Jr.,	500	
J. S. Auerbach,	500	
Pliny Fisk,	500	
D. Nicoll,	500	
S. B. Dod,	200	
J. S. Dennis	100	

                                                             18,300
and Mr. M. K. Jesup generously gave us a donation of   15,000

                                                             $98,300

The unusual expenses of the past year however,
left a deficit of $19,112.50
After setting aside for investment of the $90,000,
there remained in the Emergency Fund $8,300.00
With accrued interest of   65.71
To which was added, by your
Chairman,   10,000.00   18,365.71

Reducing the deficit to $746.79
[M. T. Pyne, Chairman]

From the Minutes of the Board of Trustees
of Princeton University

[Oct. 21, 1904]

COMMITTEE TO RAISE FUNDS TO ERECT RECITATION HALL

On motion of Mr. Bayard Henry, duly seconded, the following resolution was adopted:

RESOLVED that the President appoint a Committee of twenty with power to increase its membership to one hundred, to secure plans, and raise the necessary funds to erect a recitation hall, to be known as McCOSH HALL.[1]

[1] For further action by the Board concerning this committee, see the extract from the Minutes of the Board of Trustees printed at Dec. 8, 1904.

From William Royal Wilder

My dear 'Tommy,'   New York   October 21st. 1904.

You will be pleased to note that the 'Smoker' of the "Oldest Living Graduates," notice of which you will discover herewith, is sure to eventutate [eventuate] on the 3rd prox.[1]

Simons[2] writes me that there will be at least thirty '82 men present, and Dix[3] threatens a very large attendance on the part of his Class. I sincerely hope both you and [William F.] Magie will be on hand, also [John D.] Davis.

I cannot express to you the gratification I feel in regard to the naming of the Building, and more especially the way in which Cuyler states it has been done.[4]

I am frank to say that the enjoyment of the Commencement Season was in a measure spoiled for me, for I was in constant dread of having an issue forced by some of the men at a time when any discussion would have been both profitless and disastrous.[5]

One of these days and when in a reminiscential mood, and you care to hear it, I will tell you of two or three mighty narrow escapes we had both Saturday and Monday nights.[6] I am glad it is all over.

Bob Bridges and I are going to get up a circular to the Class in regard to the Smith Farm,[7] the deficit caused by the Commencement Exercises and the furnishing of the Tower Room.

Would you object to having a statement in the circular to the effect that on your motion, the Committee on Grounds and Buildings voted to name the Building '79 Hall?

If it were not for the fact that my family was still in the country, I would come down Sunday to 'talk it out' with you. I have a notion that we do not quite understand each other, possibly it is due to this very matter. You and any man in your position needs the loyal support of every Princeton man, and no stone should be left unturned to secure it.

It is needless to say that you have had and shall ever have mine so long as you are President of the College, despite our disagreements on matters of policy or principle.

When next in town, and if convenient, I wish you would lunch with me.   Very sincerely yours,   Wm. R. Wilder

TLS (WP, DLC).

1 For an account of this informal gathering of the members of the classes from 1878 through 1882, see the news report printed at Nov. 19, 1904.

2 Edwin Sidney Simons, Princeton 1882.

3 Edwin Asa Dix, Princeton 1881.

4 That is, that Wilson himself had introduced the resolution to name the building Seventy-Nine Hall.

5 He was referring to the intense controversy over the naming of Seventy-Nine Hall.

6 Wilder had probably succeeded in heading off open denunciation of Wilson for insisting that the new hall be named for President McCosh.

7 The circular is not among the materials on the Class of 1879 in UA, NjP. The "Smith farm" was located near Monterey, Mass., and had been purchased in 1895 through the contributions of twenty-eight members of the Class of 1879 for the support of Herbert Boughton Smith '79 and his family.

To Bliss Perry

My dear Perry: Princeton, N. J.   24 October, 1904.

I greatly appreciate your kindness in sending me a copy of your volume "The Amateur Spirit,"[1] and have already dipped into it with the greatest pleasure. I peculiarly appreciate and value the kind words which you have written on the fly-leaf.[2] It is very delightful indeed to find you believing such ideal things about me, and I pledge you my best efforts to play the part with consistency.

I am delighted to hear from Hibben that you are coming here to speak.[3] It will be like old times to hear you again.

Mrs. Wilson joins me in warm regards to you all,

Always,   Faithfully yours,   Woodrow Wilson

TLS (B. Perry Papers, MH).

1 Bliss Perry, *The Amateur Spirit* (Boston and New York, 1904).

2 The inscription in the volume, now in the Wilson Library, DLC, reads: "To Woodrow Wilson, a pattern of the qualities which it is the aim of this little book to praise, from his former colleague Bliss Perry October, 1904."

3 The *Daily Princetonian*, Oct. 21, 1904, had announced that Perry would deliver the first Trask lecture of the academic year, "probably . . . in the first part of December." Perry spoke in Alexander Hall on December 8, 1904, on the subject, "Literary Fashions." *Daily Princetonian*, Dec. 9, 1904.

To Frank Johnston Jones

My dear Mr. Jones: Princeton, N. J.   24 October, 1904.

I had hoped most sincerely that it would be possible for me to come to Cincinnati to attend the Inauguration of President Dabney, but circumstances at home have so shaped themselves that it is really impossible for me to do so.

My feelings towards President Dabney are so cordial, my wish for his success so genuine, that it would give me the greatest gratification if I could be present and extend to him my congratulations and good wishes in person; and inasmuch as I must deny myself this pleasure, I hope that you will convey to your Committee a very cordial expression of my feelings to [of] appreciation and regret.   Very sincerely yours,   Woodrow Wilson

TLS (F. J. Jones Coll., OCHP).

To Robert Bridges

My dear Bobbie: Princeton, N. J.   25 October, 1904.

Wilder writes me that in a circular you and he are planning to get out about completing and furnishing the tower room, you had thought of mentioning the fact that it was upon my motion in the Committee on Grounds and Buildings that the name of '79 Hall was recommended to the Trustees. I know the generous purpose you had in the matter, but I am very much afraid that not the true but an unfavorable construction would be put upon my motives in the matter by many of the class,[1] and I should very much prefer that no mention of me should be made in this circular.

I know that you will understand my feelings in the matter, and will not think me too sensitive in asking this.

Always,   Affectionately yours,   Woodrow Wilson

TLS (WC, NjP).
[1] That is, that they would conclude that he had yielded in the controversy under pressure.

From Elijah Richardson Craven

My Dear Dr Wilson: Philadelphia, Pa.   October 28/04

Your very grateful letter of the 21st instant, for which I thank you, was not received by me until Saturday morning. But for the unexpected visits of one of my daughters and another relative I should have returned an immediate answer.

I must acknowledge that my request that another should be elected in my place as Chairman of the Committee on the Curriculum was to me a sore trial. I had been Chairman of that Committee from its establishment, and the request to be relieved from the office seemed to be the cutting off of one of my links to life. But it was *right* that I should make the request to be relieved & it was *right* that the Committee should accede thereto.

Dr. Jacobus[1] will make an admirable Chairman, & he is the man I should have recommended as my successor had I deemed it proper to make a recommendation.

With renewed thanks for your kind letter, I remain as ever,
Yours most truly   E. R. Craven.

ALS (WP, DLC).
[1] The Rev. Dr. Melancthon Williams Jacobus, Professor of New Testament Exegesis and Criticism and Dean of the Faculty at Hartford Theological Seminary.

To Benjamin Wistar Morris III

My dear Mr. Morris: Princeton, N. J.   29 October, 1904.

I am in receipt of your letter of October 28, and would say in reply that I shall take pleasure in calling at your office at about 3 o'clock in the afternoon of Thursday, the 3 November, to look over your new studies for the dormitory plans.

Thanking you for letting me know about them,
Very sincerely yours,   Woodrow Wilson

TLS (WC, NjP).

From John De Witt[1]

Dear Dr Wilson,   Princeton, N. J.   29th Oct 1904

I have just now read in the *Alumni Weekly* that in the University there are less students by fifty one than there were last year.[2] Any one who has lived close to the University & watched it from the outside must have expected a falling off in numbers as the first result of the great reform in the curriculum inaugurated this year. Great reforms have to be paid for. And I think that the intelligent friends of Princeton who study its movements with care will be disposed to congratulate you, as I do heartily, that the loss in numbers has been so slight. Surely—and I do not believe slowly—the change will commend itself to Princeton's public, as it has already justified itself to those who have examined it; and the gains will be far greater than the present apparent loss.   Very Sincerely yours   John De Witt

ALS (WP, DLC).
[1] Princeton 1861, Archibald Alexander Professor of Church History at Princeton Theological Seminary.
[2] *Princeton Alumni Weekly*, v (Oct. 29, 1904), 76.

From Charles McLean Andrews[1]

My dear President Wilson:

Bryn Mawr, Pa.
October 30, 1904.

When in England during the last year I had occasion to examine the unbound papers in the Privy Council Office I came across the enclosed petition from "The College of New Jersey commonly called Nassau Hall," and as I thought it interesting and worthy of preservation I had it copied together with other papers that I was having copied for other purposes.

I now send it to you with my compliments, hoping that it may not be known to you already. If it be familiar then I am but sending my coals to Newcastle, but if it be not then I think that you will find something in it of interest for the history of Princeton University.

With very kind regards, believe me,
                    Yours very truly,   Charles M. Andrews.

TLS (WP, DLC). Enc.: TC of petition from the College of New Jersey to George III, June 25, 1766 (WP, DLC).
[1] Professor of History at Bryn Mawr College.

To John Grier Hibben and Jenny Davidson Hibben

My dearest Friends,   Princeton, 8 Nov., 1904.

I called at the house at five this afternoon to take you my congratulations,[1] but had the deep disappointment of finding neither of you at home. Perhaps I can say what I wish to say,—what I have again and again tried to say,—better with my pen than by word of mouth,—because with less self-consciousness.

It is as delightful as it is rare to see two persons crowned as you are with the sort, and the abundance, of happiness which their perfect gifts of mind and heart and their lives above reproach make them most worthy of and most capable of enjoying,—their deep love and admiration for each other not only, but also the unstinted love and admiration of a whole community,—so that they do not have to count and hoard their friends but may see everywhere the evidence of what, nothing adventitious, but only their own fine qualities have won for them. I wish I could express my own love and admiration for you both in words which would be adequate and yet not seem touched with exaggeration. I congratulate you from the bottom of my heart, and Ellen joins her own warmest and most affectionate messages to mine.

Can you not go as my guests to New York on Saturday, the 19th, to go to a matinee? Drop me a line to say what you would rather see. I may not be able to find either of you again before next week,—the finding time of this week having passed.

Always Your devoted friend,   Woodrow Wilson

ALS (photostat in WC, NjP).
[1] Upon their seventeenth wedding anniversary.

A News Item about Columbia University's 150th Anniversary Celebration

[Nov. 12, 1904]

President Wilson '79 and Dean West '74 attended the ceremonies of Columbia's sesquicentennial celebration[1] (a term introduced, we believe, by Professor West, when Princeton observed its 150th anniversary in 1896) and Mayor George B. McClellan '86 responded to the toast "Columbia and the City," at the alumni banquet held in connection with the occasion.

Printed in the *Princeton Alumni Weekly*, v (Nov. 12, 1904), 109.
[1] Wilson and West were Princeton's academic delegates at the University Convocation on October 31 celebrating the founding of King's College in 1754. The term sesquicentennial was not used at Columbia.

From Benjamin Wistar Morris III

My dear Dr. Wilson   New York   Nov. 15th 1904.

I have your letter of the 14th instant and am glad to be able to answer that it seems both possible and desirable to arrange for apartments in the Tower[1] and without in anyway interfering with the fenestration. I enclose a rough sketch[2] showing a possible arrangement of plan. In the panel next over the arch there is height enough for two stories which can be lit by tall mullioned windows of the well known type.

Your suggestion of the additional recessed part at the north end has given me an additional idea which I am now studying

& it promises to be a great improvement: at the southerly end of the recessed part I have disconnected the buildings; not much, but just enough to make an attractive opening with a view to the south east; a cloister joins them & the whole composition is enriched & improved in my opinion. There are possibilities in the by-product also: it gives an opportunity to name or individualize a part of the big structure, without changing the general scheme in any essential particular.

I saw Mr. Cuyler at the University Club last evening & he said he was coming in soon with Mr. Pyne to have a look. As planned now, this part of the building will accommodate 104 students & will cost according to a rough approximate $175000.00[.] The '79 Dormitory, figuring the Tower section as equivalent to two, has 8 sections of 8 men each or 64 students housed at a cost of $108000, which gives $1682 as cost per man in new building and $1687 "   "   "   "   " '79 Hall.
The $175000 is based on 32 cents per cubic foot, the cost of '79 Hall, *everything* included. I dont think the Tower can be built for $50000.00[.] I think it will exceed that amount by $5000.00 designed as you wish it, and I think the total group will cost as at present contemplated not over $600000 complete & ready for occupancy, including Architect & all other luxuries. The capacity of the entire group will be from 285 to 300, which is about $2000 per man. If a suite of two rooms and study are rented at $320 per annum, which I understand is the average of the '79 Hall the gross income will be $4800 or 8%, which after deducting expenses & fixed charges should easily net between 4 & 5 per cent.

The scheme of separation of the Globe-Wernecke sections[3] means, that if the ten classes give $100000 only, that the balance must be assumed by the University.

Sincerely yours,   Benj. W Morris Jr

ALS (WP, DLC).
[1] See B. W. Morris III to WW, Aug. 16, 1904.
[2] It is missing.
[3] See n. 1 to the news report printed at April 16, 1904.

To Benjamin Wistar Morris III

My dear Mr. Morris: Princeton, N. J.   17 November, 1904.

Thank you very much indeed for your letter of November 15th; it gives me just the information I desired.

I am interested in your suggestion about introducing a break between the two portions of the building at the southern end of the recess which we had planned for the northern part of the building.

I am expecting, unless a heavy cold continues to hold me at home, to be in New York on Saturday. Would it be convenient for me to come in at half past two to see you? If not just drop me a line and I can make it some other time.

Always cordially and sincerely yours,

Woodrow Wilson

TLS (WC, NjP).

To Frank Thilly

Princeton, N. J.

My dear Professor Thilly: 18 November, 1904.

In a conversation the other day with the Treasurer of the University he happened to mention to me the fact that you had not presented to him any statement of your expenses in removing from Columbia to Princeton and I have had a sort of fear that you felt some delicacy about the matter.

I hope very much that you will send a statement of the full amount of the cost of the transfer, including not only the expenses of transferring your furniture and household effects, but also, of course, the travelling expenses of yourself and your family in making the transfer. The Finance Committee of the Board very fully and cordially approve of this charge and the Treasurer will pay it immediately upon your presenting the statement.

Always cordially and faithfully yours,

Woodrow Wilson

TLS (Wilson-Thilly Corr., NIC).

A News Report of an Alumni Affair in New York

[Nov. 19, 1904]

THE '78-'82 REUNION

The Weekly is indebted to the Rev. Dr. John H. Kerr '78, who is Publishing Secretary of the American Tract Society, for the following report of the recent reunions of the classes of '78 to '82:

It was a happy thought which led to the bringing together of the classes of '78, '79, '80, '81 and '82 at the new Astor House in New York on Nov. 3rd, first, for separate class dinners in adjoining rooms, and then later in the evening for a joint smoker in the College Trophy Room. Ninety-two members of these classes responded to the announcement sent out, and none of those who came regretted that he had done so, for the evening was spent most enjoyably in the renewal of old class and college ties.

Of course a gathering of '79 men, as indeed of any Princeton men, would be a lame affair without President Wilson, and so he was there, and the event of the evening was one of his characteristic speeches, bubbling with humor and packed with information concerning the new curriculum. When the President sat down we all felt that our Alma Mater was indeed in safe hands under his wise and progressive administration.

Printed in the *Princeton Alumni Weekly*, v (Nov. 19, 1904), 130-31.

A News Report of a Lecture in New York on Americanism

[Nov. 20, 1904]

WILSON SAYS ELASTICITY SAVES THE CONSTITUTION

Made to Help, Not to Hinder,
Asserts Princeton's President.

The first of a series of lectures on Education under the auspices of the Lecture Bureau of the Department of Education was delivered in Cooper Union last night by President Woodrow Wilson of Princeton University, who chose for his subject "Americanism." The hall was crowded when he was introduced by Dr. Henry M. Leipziger, the Supervisor of Lectures in this city, and the applause that greeted the lecturer was loud and frequent. Dr. Wilson spoke for over an hour and without making reference at any time to notes.

"The processes of the development of our country in the present," he said, "are not the processes of the past. Our development heretofore has been marked by century periods. Our first century was devoted to getting a foothold on the continent; the second was used up in getting rid of the French, and the third was occupied in the making of the Nation, and now we are in the fourth century of our development.

"We feel that we do not have to prove that we are the greatest country in the world, but, like the lawyer in the story, we admit it. Heretofore we have been in the process of making; we have just come out of our youth, and we are imbued with all the audacity of youth, and sometimes, I fear, with some of its indiscretions. We have had three centuries of beginnings, and what we need now is not the original strength, but the finished education."

During the course of his address he referred to the Constitution of the United States, and said that much had been written lately as to its interpretation in these days, the cry being that it was not held in the esteem and veneration of years ago.

"If that means," said Dr. Wilson, "that it is not interpreted by the Supreme Court of the United States as it was interpreted when the fathers had just framed it, then the critics are right. There is no reason why it should be so interpreted. The Constitution was not made to fit us like a strait-jacket.

"In its elasticity lies its chief greatness. There were blank pages in it, into which could be written passages that would suit the exigencies of the day. It is constructed like one of our great modern buildings, where the nuts and bolts are so formed that they give sufficiently to the strain put upon them.

"As Kipling writes in his story of 'The Ship That Found Herself,' the different parts of the machinery cry to each other to give just a little under the tremendous pressure, until finally she sails into port a great and harmonious whole, with every part working smoothly with every other part, because the construction had been such as to allow it. The Constitution was not made to hinder us, but to help us. If it were not so, we would long ago have snapped the cords."

Speaking about the typical American, Dr. Wilson said that if he were asked for a definition of him he would have said that he was such a man as could live on our frontier. "I would name Benjamin Franklin rather than Alexander Hamilton," he said, "for Hamilton, much as I admire him, was a transplanted European in his way of thinking. He was not such a man as could have formed a vigilance committee, but Franklin was the man for the frontier. If there wasn't any way to live, he would have invented one.

"To-day our mapmakers say they could mark no frontier on the map of the United States. Since 1898 our frontier has been moved across the Pacific, and we can find uses for it, no doubt, just as we used the old frontier for the restless spirits who feel hemmed in by present restrictions.

"What we need to-day is not irregular strength; we want tested and schooled strength. We have principles enough and ideals enough; what we need now is the method to apply our principles. We have been tolerably good mechanics, and we are now in the way to become skilled artists. Our task is to round off the product, to show it in its finished state.

"Any man can be a reformer. It is easy enough to get into this chronic state of finding fault with existing conditions, but it is quite another thing to put forth an applicable remedy. If you want to make the reformer understand this, ask him to frame a bill, and after he has worked at it night after night he will be likely to tell you that he knows just exactly what he wants, but he'll be hanged if he knows how to express it.

"I consider that it is nothing less than immoral for a man to advocate pulling a structure down when he cannot tell you what to put up in the place of what he has or would destroy.

"The difficulty of approaching a subject from the broad standpoint, from the unselfish view, is aptly illustrated by the story of the Englishman who said that it was perfectly absurd for the French to call bread 'pain.' He was told that it was no more absurd than for the English to call it 'bread' to which he replied, 'But it is bread.'

"The man of to-day must have a programme. Take this trust question, for instance. If our efforts are to be confined to 'trust busting' we must approach the matter not only from the standpoint of wanting to wipe out a thing because it hinders us or because it grips us here or there. That is the essence of selfishness, and we shall never arrive at anything by that route.

"That subject, like all others, must be considered in a spirit of fairness; fairness to capital as well as to labor. We should no more seek to deprive a man of his accumulated wealth than to deprive the laborer of the fruits of his labor. If you want me to consider you witty, I may ask you to make a joke; if you want me to consider you wise, I will ask for some other show of that wisdom than your mere claim to it. If we are groping to-day, we are groping not for principles but for a way to apply those principles which we have in plenty.

"It isn't Americanism to know my job better than you know yours, but to help you with my knowledge to make you know your job better. We have plenty of men who are skilled and selfish. What we need are men who are skilled and patriotic.

"If we need one thing more than anything else, it is to rid ourselves of our provincialism. Local pride is only a pleasant way of referring to local provincialism. I remember some years ago, when I was at that stage that I felt as if I had arrived. I made my first trip to the West and I found out that there were few things they could not tell me there better than I could tell them myself. I came back with a broader conception of Americanism.

"To rid our young men of provincialism, I would have every young man of the North educated in the South and every young man of the South educated in the North. I would have every young man of the West educated in the East, although that is manifestly impossible, and to carry out the matter to its conclusion, every young man of the East educated in the West.

"The man who travels across the Continent in an express train does not see the country or know it. He must feel the people, feel the community, feel the country to know it, and your so-called traveled man has his erudition largely on the surface. I must look at a map of the United States every week to feel sure that the Mississippi River is in the middle of the country. That may arise from the fact that I have only crossed it twice, and it seems to be so far away that it is almost impossible to believe that the Pacific is quite as far from it as is the Atlantic.

"We to-day are in the position of arriving, and we will arrive all the sooner and will do our work better when we are free from that provincialism which now mars us."[1]

Printed in the *New York Times*, Nov. 20, 1904; several editorial headings omitted.
[1] There is a WWhw outline of this address, dated Nov. 19, 1904, in WP, DLC.

To Edgar Fahs Smith[1]

My dear Dr. Smith: Princeton, N. J.   25 November, 1904.

You may be sure that I am willing to acquiesce in anything that will insure the success of the Franklin Celebration;[2] and if you find that it is necessary for the completion of our plans to invite the President to deliver the main address, I heartily concur.[3]

Cordially and sincerely yours,   Woodrow Wilson

TLS (Archives, PPAmP).
[1] President of the American Philosophical Society and Vice-Provost of the University of Pennsylvania.
[2] That is, the celebration of Franklin's bicentennial in 1906. Wilson was a member of the Franklin Bicentennial Committee of the American Philosophical Society. See WW to I. M. Hayes, April 8, 1903, Vol. 14.
[3] If President Roosevelt was invited, he was unable to attend.

An Address of Welcome to the Association of Colleges and
Preparatory Schools of the Middle States and Maryland[1]

[[Nov. 25, 1904]]

Mr. President:[2] It is with very great pleasure that I welcome
you to Princeton. Princeton lies a little off the main lines of
travel. We do not often have the pleasure of seeing so many of
our friends here; and yet I would like very much to see Princeton regarded as on the main lines of travel for visits of this kind.
Nothing gratifies us more than to have assemblies of this sort
come to Princeton, both to confer with us and to criticise us;
and then it affords something to talk about after they have gone
away.

It seems to me that the value of a conference like this (and
I am sure you will agree in the judgment) is not so much the
discussion of subjects and methods of study as a certain adjustment and accommodation of points of view and the fostering
of community of spirit and of principle. The reason we come
together is that we may understand each other better and that
our differences of opinion may be accommodated by knowing
the needs that lie behind them, and the points of view from
which they have been taken; and ever since I began the study
of the history of this country it has seemed to me that there
is no region of our country in which this sort of thing ought to be
easier to do than the region represented by this assemblage. The
Middle States have always seemed to me the most typically
American part of the United States—typically American in the
fact that they were mixed of all races and kinds from the
first: not pure in blood, like New England and the South, not
given over to any special point of view, but from the first containing the complete American mixture.

This has given them a greater elasticity of mental movement,
has given them more ability to see from more points of view,
than any other region of the country. I should not like to say
how few points of view have obtained in New England; as a
Southerner I should not like to say how exclusive the views of
the South have been. I am content, now, merely to dwell upon
the variety of view which has obtained in the Middle States. It
ought to be possible, therefore, for us, by conference, to do a
better service in American education than is open to some other

[1] This association met in Murray Hall on the Princeton campus, November
25-26, 1904. See the news item printed at Nov. 29, 1904.
[2] Truman Jay Backus, President of Packer Collegiate Institute of Brooklyn.

assemblages of the day; because here we feel more of the American spirit of the double sort: not only this newness and this mixture, but the oldness which connects us with the old world. There is a certain value in breathing the salt air of the Atlantic, which brings us the flavors out of an old age to which we also belong, as well as in being stimulated always in a new continent, reminding us of the new tasks that belong to us. It ought to be the more easy for a conference of this sort to take the point of view with regard to education which should be acceptable to the whole country; and I do not see, for my part, how educational conferences of any kind are to make any progress, unless we come to a common point of view with regard to education. It ought to be possible at any rate for a body like this, representing a homogeneous constituency, to come to a common point of view. I say "homogeneous," because we by our very title represent the colleges of the Middle States, and the schools preparatory to college: not the colleges and the schools, but the colleges and the preparatory schools. It is a question of what leads up to higher education, and a question of what higher education is, which we are concerned in discussing; and therefore it seems to me that we ought to come at some common principle as to what education is for.

Now I am not going to attempt to make sail upon that great ocean: I am not going to attempt to instruct you as to what education is; but I want to offer one suggestion which does not contain too philosophic a content and is not too disputable. I want to make this suggestion: that we should regard education, not as a means of enabling the pupil to find an occupation, but as a means of enabling the pupil to find himself.

Just as our own sense of identity depends upon our knowledge of who we were yesterday and what we were yesterday; and our own knowledge of our place in the physical universe depends upon our knowing where the other things in the universe are, so that we can get our bearings with regard to them: so, it seems to me, the object of education is to enable us thus to orient ourselves—to determine which is the East and which is the West, to determine our geographical position in the history of human life and the human mind; to know how we are related to the thinking that has been done and the thinking that is being done—to the things that have been done and the things that remain to be done.

That, it seems to me, is the common object of education—to release the faculties for any use they may turn out to be serviceable for; so that we are dealing not with the fortunes of our pupils but with their spirits, with their understandings, with their apprehensions. If that be the object of education—why, then, every question of study, of the subject-matter of study, and of the group studied, has some standard by which to be judged, as far as we have any standard; because the standard of practical serviceability is so various that it is not one standard but a thousand, and unless we have some one standard we have no single means of assessment and judgment in respect of the subjects or the methods of study.

Now in Princeton this is our conception of education; and the service that you will do us will be the service of enabling us to judge by your discussions just where we all stand with regard to a common task; because we are here in a period of inquiry and we believe, at any rate, that we have the open mind. While we are sure of our object I believe we are entirely teachable as to the means of attainment. We have a conviction as to what we are about; but we are very modest in respect of our judgment as to whether we are going after it in the right way.

You may easily conceive, therefore, that it is with peculiar pleasure that I welcome to this place, in the name of the University, a body of men and women who can give, out of a rich experience, the suggestions which will enable us to know which is the road to the place we seek. I therefore extend to President Backus and to the association through him, the freedom of the place—knowing by your looks that you will not make too free— and hope that you will regard us and it as at your disposal throughout your session.[3]

Printed in *Proceedings of the Eighteenth Annual Convention of the Association of Colleges and Preparatory Schools of the Middle States and Maryland . . .* (n.p., 1905), pp. 5-8.
    [3] There are WWhw notes for this address, dated Nov. 25, 1904, in WP, DLC.

A News Report of an Alumni Dinner in East Orange, New Jersey

[Nov. 26, 1904]

The Orange Alumni Association held its first annual dinner at Berkeley Hall, East Orange, on Nov. 10. . . .

President Wilson brought the oratory of the evening to a fitting climax by a response to the toast of "Princeton University," which held his audience spellbound for thirty minutes. This speech should be published in full, for no extracts can do it justice. Following is a portion of his remarks:

"The real tonic there is in an occasion like this is that we are all bound together by the spirit which runs through the veins of every man from the class of '32 to the men of '04. Surely there is something definite we mean when we speak of the Princeton we love, and I think we discover it when we say that Princeton is not a place where a man goes to find a profession, but a place where he goes to find himself. There is laid before him something like the map of life. He knows the road that men have traveled in carrying the world forward. He measures himself with the great undertakings of the human mind. Our belief in a general and disciplinary education is a belief that it means the ennobling of man, that it enables him to find his relative place in the world. A university is the place for a man to get the ideas which serve life. In making a course of study there is no argument so conclusive in regard to the length of the course as the argument that it takes time for the process of saturation to complete itself. It cannot complete itself in less than four years.

"We are not engaged in a small matter in this question of education. We are engaged in nothing less than in determining what the next generation shall be. It is a sobering thought, having to construct the curriculum of a university. In the construction of the new curriculum at Princeton we have done one notable thing. We have excluded all study of applied science and devoted ourselves to pure science—that is, the study of the principles which underlie all the processes of nature. This is an age, beyond any age that men ever saw before, based on a knowledge of principles.

["]Moreover, unless we enable men to find themselves, their soul's relation to other men, we shall not be faithful citizens of a free country. When you are preparing students you are preparing history for future generations. While it is true that the work of our hands produces all the material triumphs of the age, it is also true that the only thing permanent is the spirit of man. Nothing differentiates America from any other country in the world so much as this, that America has set up more ideals than any other nation; that it has dreamed more dreams. America is great because of the spirit of its thinkers, and not because of the monuments of its manufacturers. At heart, every man who succeeds is a dreamer. He is pursuing an invisible theory, and unless the vision is pure a taint will come into the blood. There ought not to be any limit to the resources or the confidence with which we conceive the ideals toward which we push on. Some day, I predict with great confidence, there will be an enthusiasm for learning in Princeton."

Printed in the *Princeton Alumni Weekly*, v (Nov. 26, 1904), 141, 144-45; one editorial heading omitted.

To Bayard Stockton[1]

Princeton, N. J.

My dear Mr. Stockton: 26 November, 1904.

Allow me to thank you for letting me see the enclosed letter.[2] I have read it with a great deal of interest and also with a great deal of pleasure, for I am sure that we all feel that Dr. Shields was worthy of the admiration and friendship he excited. I hope with all my heart that his writings will some day find their proper place. I do not myself feel capable of assessing their value, but I know the fine spirit and devotion of the man who wrote them.[3]

    Always,

        Cordially and sincerely yours,   Woodrow Wilson

TLS (TxU).
    [1] He practiced law in Trenton and was the last direct descendant of Richard Stockton, the signer of the Declaration of Independence, to make the ancestral estate of Morven his permanent home. Bayard Stockton was married first to Charlotte Julia Shields and then to Helen Hamilton Shields, both daughters of Charles Woodruff Shields. Shields had purchased Morven from the trustees of the Estate of Samuel Witham Stockton in 1891; both of his daughters resided there during their marriages to Bayard Stockton and, upon Shields's death in 1904, the property passed to the surviving daughter, Helen Shields Stockton, and her stepsons and nephews, Richard and Bayard Stockton. See Alfred Hoyt Bill, *A House Called Morven: Its Role in American History, 1701-1954* (Princeton, N. J., 1954), pp. 149-56.
    [2] It is missing.
    [3] Perhaps Stockton or the writer of the missing enclosure had asked Wilson to contribute a prefatory statement or biographical sketch to the third volume of Shields' *Philosophia Ultima, or, Science of the Sciences* (3 vols., New York, 1885-1905), which was published posthumously with a biographical sketch of Shields by William Milligan Sloane.

To Simon Gratz

My dear Sir: Princeton, N. J.   28 November, 1904.

I have carefully examined the old letters which you so thoughtfully and generously sent me the other day, and find them of unusual interest and value with regard to several items in the history of Princeton.[1] I wish to express my very great appreciation of your kindness and generosity, and am sure that in doing so I express the feeling of all the authorities of the University. We shall value these documents very highly.

One of the longest and most interesting lacks its final pages, and therefore its signature and date. Is it possible that the remaining page, or pages, is still among the collection of papers from which you took the letters? If so, it would add greatly to our obligation if you would complete your kindness by sending it.[2]

With warmest regard and renewed expressions of appreciation,   Very sincerely yours,   Woodrow Wilson

TLS (Gratz Collection, American Historians, PHi).
  [1] The most important of these documents is described and printed in the *Princeton Alumni Weekly*, v (March 11, 1905), 369-71.
  [2] Further correspondence about this matter is missing, but the remaining page or pages were never found.

A News Item

[Nov. 29, 1904]

EDUCATIONAL CONVENTIONS.

Two Associations Held Meetings in Princeton Last Week.

The eighteenth annual convention of the Association of Colleges and Preparatory Schools of the Middle States and Maryland was held last Friday morning in Murray Hall. . . .

President Woodrow Wilson opened the convention on Friday morning with an address of welcome to the delegates. . . .

The annual meeting of the Association of teachers of Mathematics was held in the Chancellor Green Library at 10.30 o'clock, Saturday morning. President Woodrow Wilson opened the meeting with an address of welcome, which was followed by several learned and interesting papers by prominent delegates.

Printed in the *Daily Princetonian*, Nov. 29, 1904.

A Newspaper Report of an Address on the South and the Democratic Party

[Nov. 30, 1904]

STRONG APPEAL TO THE SOUTH

Woodrow Wilson Would Have It Stand
for Real Democracy

Backing the Men Whose Conservatism Alone Balks the Party
  Wreckers—No Good, He Says, Can Come From a Sectional
  League—Virginian Diners Cheer

The third annual dinner of the Society of the Virginians, given last evening at the Waldorf-Astoria, was one of the largest and one of the most successful reunions the society has held. More than 100 members of the society and invited guests sat at table. The speakers, beginning with James W[addel]. Alexander, the Governor, as the president of the society is called, included President Woodrow Wilson of Princeton University, William B. Hornblower, F. Hopkinson Smith, and ex-Attorney General William A. Barber of South Carolina. Others who sat at the Governor's table were Vice.-Gov. H. R. Bayne, Col. A. G. Dickinson, Edward Owen, Robert L. Harrison and James A. Patterson. . . .

The feature of the evening was President Woodrow Wilson's speech, which was almost exclusively devoted to politics. President Wilson said that while it did not become him, as a person in an academic position such as he held, to discuss politics from a partisan point of view, he felt that he might well say something on general lines about matters affecting the country as a whole. He began with an incident of the campaign. He said:

Among my colleagues at Princeton is a son of James A. Garfield. Mr. Garfield came to me a little while before election and said: "They are asking me to go and make some political speeches. I did not know how it would impress you, and I thought I would ask you."

I told him that the only objection I had was that I was on the side against which he would speak, but that his being a member of the faculty of Princeton University did not destroy his privileges as an American citizen, and to go ahead and make all the speeches he wanted to. I do not believe it is the right thing for a Virginian to keep his mouth shut.

I feel that I am where I belong among you here. There was once a rather unsophisticated old woman who went to one of those side shows where they have marvellous pictures on the outside of things that are not to be seen on the inside. And in the show she saw a man who read a newspaper, or pretended to read a newspaper, through a two-inch plank.

"Come right along out of here, Silas," the old lady said to her husband. "This is no place for me with these thin clothes on!" (Prolonged laughter.)

Now, I have no such feelings here among you to-night. I feel that I am of you: that I belong here.

We Americans know a good deal, undoubtedly, about self-government. We understand each other when it comes to that subject. Yet, I fear we have not come to quite as free and cordial an understanding as we ought.

When we find out that all the best governed cities in the world are not American cities, it causes us to be "sickl[i]ed over with the pale cast of thought." I remember once, after a disaster at a municipal election here in New York, a gentleman was bemoaning to me the result, when it occurred to me to ask him if he had voted.

"Well, no," he replied, "I did not."

Then I replied that I did not see what he had to complain of; that he had done all he could to bring about the result that he much deplored.

Going on to discuss the political future of the South, President Wilson said:

No one can justly wonder at the present impatience of the Southern political leaders at finding themselves without real independence or influence in the politics of the country; the only section of the country which did not make a real choice of its political actions in the recent elections. But the only remedy suggested would put the Southern States in a still worse position.

To act independently of old party affiliations, as some of their leaders have recently proposed that they should act, would be to make them, if they still hung together and acted in concert, a third party in the politics of the country, and not a party of principle at that, but a geographical party, a sectional party, which would act in isolation and draw upon itself afresh old enmities and suspicions.

The real opportunity of the South is of another sort. It has now a unique opportunity to perform a great national service. As the only remaining part of the Democratic party that can command a majority of the votes in its constituencies, let the South demand a rehabilitation of the Democratic party on the only lines that can restore it to dignity and power.

Since 1896 the Democratic party has permitted its name to be used by men who ought never to have been admitted to its counsels, men who held principles and professed purposes which it had always hitherto repudiated.

By themselves and under their proper designation as populists and radical theorists, contemptuous alike of principle and of experience, these men could never have played any role in national politics but that of a noisy minority. Since they forced themselves into the councils of the party and got the use of its name, every doubtful State has been turned into an enthusiastic supporter of the Republican party. Until it has read them out of the party as an alien faction there will be no doubtful States again.

It is now high time that the South, which has endured most by way of humiliation at the hands of this faction, should demand that it be utterly and once for all thrust out of Democratic counsels; that the men of New York, New Jersey, Connecticut, Massachusetts, Indiana and the prosperous States beyond the Mississippi who wish for reform without loss of stability should join with it to reassert the principles and return to the practices of the historic party which has always stood for thoughtful moderation in affairs and a careful use of the powers of the Federal Government in the interest of the whole people of whatever class or occupation.

There is no longer any Democratic party either in the South or in any Northern State which the discredited radicals can use. The great body of one-time Democrats that musters strong enough to win elections has revolted and will act with no organization which harbors the radicals—as the radicals themselves did not in fact act with the organization they themselves had discredited in the recent campaign, when the whole country felt that the Democratic party was still without definite character or make-up.

The country, as it moves forward in its great material progress, needs and will tolerate no party of discontent or radical experiment; but it does need a party of conservative reform, acting in the spirit of law and of ancient institutions. Hosts of voters are waiting and ready to flock back to the standard of such a party when once they see it come upon the field properly purged and authenticated.

The old Democratic party stood by the South through good report and ill; the South has now an opportunity to requite its thankless services by recalling it to its old counsel and spirit. To do this would be to render a real national service conceived in the interest of the whole country of whatever opinion; for the politics of the nation cannot go normally and healthfully forward without the stimulation and contest of two parties of principle.

President Wilson's speech was greeted with one of the most remarkable demonstrations of approval that has been manifested at a public dinner in this city for a long time. He was time and again overwhelmed with applause as he was speaking and had to wait until the handclapping ceased long enough to permit his voice to be heard before he could go on. When he closed, in a voice impressive and earnest in its tone, the applause broke loose like a pent-up torrent, and he was called to his feet to bow his acknowledgments to the extraordinary ovation tendered him.[1]

Printed in the New York *Sun*, Nov. 30, 1904.
[1] There is a WWsh draft of the main portion of this address in WP, DLC, which he apparently prepared as the basis of a press release.

A News Report

[*Nov. 30, 1904*]

ACCEPT CARNEGIE GIFT.

Princeton Obtains Land for Rowing Lake.

Princeton, N. J., Nov. 30 (Special).—The first definite confirmation of the report that Andrew Carnegie is to build a lake for Princeton was obtained to-night, when a well known alumnus of the Orange and Black, who is closely identified with the project,[1] assured a correspondent of The Tribune that such a lake had been planned and provided for and was to be constructed through Mr. Carnegie's generosity.

Mr. Carnegie's proposition, made some time ago, was that if Princeton obtained the land he would provide the money with which to carry out the construction of a water course which would give to Princeton men the facilities for boating now enjoyed by the students of all the other big universities. The land necessary for the lake has altogether been obtained or held on option and contractors are now figuring on the work of excavation and bank building.

The lake is to be more than three miles long and about a thousand feet wide at its greatest breadth. It will extend along the west bank of the Delaware and Raritan Canal from Princeton to Kingston. Most of the first mile is Princeton land, as the campus is but a scant half mile from the canal's edge. This will make the southern end of the lake border on the Princeton campus.

Extending northward toward Kingston a large portion of the land necessary for the construction of the lake has been given by Edward Howe, sr., the Princeton banker, who has given a strip one thousand feet long, and by the Gulick estate.[2] It is understood that a number of wealthy alumni have interested themselves in the purchase of the rest of the land.

Mr. Carnegie became interested in the project through Howard Butler, his legal adviser and right hand man in New-York. Mr. Butler is a Princeton graduate and a relative of the Howes, who live on the outskirts of the town and are among the most active alumni of the Orange and Black.[3]

Printed in the *New York Daily Tribune*, Dec. 1, 1904.
  [1] Howard Russell Butler. About Butler and the subsequent development of Lake Carnegie, see ns. 1 and 2 to the news item printed at Nov. 29, 1903.
  [2] A reference to a gift of land made by Alexander Reading Gulick, Princeton 1889, lawyer of New York. Gulick, along with Howard R. Butler, attended to many of the details of the acquisition of the land and the building of the lake.

From George Foster Peabody [1]

Brooklyn Heights   New York
My dear Doctor Wilson: Dec. 1st, 1904.

I have not had, I believe, the actual pleasure of meeting you but doubtless you will have some consciousness of who I am and therefore will forgive me so far intruding as to enclose to you this editorial from today's "World" and the communication respecting the Democratic party.[2] I do this because you will perhaps be inclined to think my recent association with the campaign[3] may justify me in having some thought on the subject matter which you dealt with in your recent address before the Virginia Association. I find myself in very complete sympathy with the editorial in the "World"[4] and, speaking generally, should be inclined to say that the suggestion you make, as I understand it, would be not unlikely to lead to two results[:] First, the continuance of the Republican party in power for a longer period and next, to have as its successor in the administration of the Government a party of ultra radicals without business experience.

My own fairly close observation as a banker in Wall Street for more than twenty years leads me to the conclusion that Mr. Bryan and other radicals are right in their contention as to the tremendously serious tendency of present conditions, particularly as regards the "money power" as they call it. I cannot, of course, but believe that their lack of experience and knowledge of business makes their proposed remedies lack in soundness—in justice also, in some respects; but I think no greater evil can befall the future of this country and its great mission to the world than that leaders of thought, upon whom a great responsibility is placed, should indicate a lack of sympathy with the hopes and desires of the honest minded and sincere hearted of these radical leaders. I cannot believe that you are without sympathy with what they wish to accomplish but I feel that the impression made upon all of them by the newspaper reports of your address will be that of an utter lack of sympathy on your part.

As a native of Georgia, not coming North until after the Civil War, my thought is that the imperative duty now resting upon the South in a political sense, is to reaffirm its loyalty to essentially Democratic doctrines, and the first of these is the firm adherence to a righteousness of the platform assertion that "protection is robbery of the many for the benefit of the few" and next, that the traditional position of the party under the leadership of Andrew Jackson, in connection with the contest with the United States Bank, should be reasserted in its due relation to the present conditions of banking and exchange in this country.

I rely upon your recognizing that I take the time to write this to you only as a matter of what seems to me public service, for I can see no political necessity greater now than that the Democratic party should be made a really democratic party—that is seeking only for the true welfare of the great masses of the people whose prosperity is seriously limited by the unquestioned control exercised by corporate aggregations of capital in all branches of Government—Municipal, State and Federal. I think in a large sense that the people of the world are to suffer or gain as the future of the Democratic party in the United States shall be during the next two decades.[5]

Very truly yours,   George Foster Peabody

TLS (WP, DLC).

[1] New York investment banker and philanthropist, especially active in the field of southern education.

[2] He enclosed clippings of "A Small and Select Democracy," New York *World*, Dec. 1, 1904, and Samuel E. Moffett to the Editor, *ibid.*

[3] He was Treasurer of the Democratic National Committee in 1904.

[4] "A Small and Select Democracy," the text of which follows:

"President Woodrow Wilson of Princeton thinks the Democratic party, though in a minority of above 2,000,000, is still too large. He would have it read out the 'discredited radicals.' He urges the South to demand that this element be 'utterly and once for all thrust out of Democratic counsels.'

"It appears that a good many radicals have not waited to be thrust out. They have thrust themselves out, leaving a little gap of not quite 305,000 votes to be filled in Illinois, one of nearly 100,000 in Indiana and similar shortages in other states. Perhaps after driving out the rest of them it may be possible to pick up votes enough between Trinity Church and the New York Sub-Treasury to balance the loss.

"President Wilson says that the country 'needs and will tolerate no party of discontent or radical experiment.' If the country wants no party of discontent, of course it must be contented with existing conditions. In that case why not stick to the party that stands for those conditions? What use or excuse can there be for any party but the Republican?"

[5] Wilson's reply is missing in the Papers of George Foster Peabody, DLC.

An Announcement

[Dec. 3, 1904]

LECTURE BY PRESIDENT WILSON.

Dr. Woodrow Wilson, president of Princeton University, will address the League for Political Education, No. 23 West Forty-fourth st., this morning at 11 o'clock. His subject will be "The University and the Nation."[1]

Printed in the *New York Daily Tribune*, Dec. 3, 1904.
   [1] No New York newspaper carried a report of this address.

To Zephaniah Charles Felt[1]

My dear Felt: Princeton, N. J.   December 6, 1904.

I am sorry to have been so long about replying to your letter of Nov. 26,[2] but have been rushed day after day and have not felt that I had time to do it justice.

It is very disappointing to me that I cannot get out to Denver this Winter to meet the Alumni there at their Annual dinner, but I hope that you will convey to them my warmest greetings.

I think they can rest assured that Princeton is going a very normal course towards an increase of power and influence. The commercial spirit of the age has touched almost everything, and has of course touched Princeton among the rest, but not below the surface. I do not think I am deceiving myself in believing that, while wealth and social distinctions are showing themselves in the University as elsewhere, the heart of the place has not been touched, and that its spirit is still wholesomely democratic.

It of course gives us a little concern to see the University growing into so numerous a community and it is agreed by some of us that it might be wise before very long to limit the number to be admitted to (say) 2000 undergraduates, in order that we might provide in the best possible way for them and at the same time guard against impairing the homogeneity of the place and preserve for it the democratic character which has always been its chief charm. But this is a question which does not have to be immediately determined. There is nothing as yet about the University which old graduates could not endorse and believe in, and I think that every member of the Faculty would agree with me in saying that the moral tone of the place has steadily improved for years together, with the increase of a governing opinion among the undergraduates.

Please express to the members of the Association my warm appreciation of their greetings and give them heartiest assurances of my loyalty and regard.

Cordially and sincerely yours,   Woodrow Wilson

TLS (WC, NjP).
[1] Wilson's classmate, at this time in the real estate business in Denver.
[2] It is missing.

Charles Augustus Young to the Board of Trustees of Princeton University

GENTLEMEN: PRINCETON, N. J., Dec. 6th, 1904.

I present herewith my resignation of the chair of Astronomy, to take effect at the close of the present academic year, when I shall have completed a professorial service of forty nine years, twenty eight of them in Princeton.

I take the step with sincere and deep regret as breaking a long and, to me, very happy association during which I have received unvarying consideration and kindness from yourselves and from my colleagues in the Faculty. And I do it the more regretfully just now because I am so heartily in accord with the recent reforms in the curriculum and administration, which seem to promise a still more brilliant future for the University.

But the inroads of chronic disease, and the infirmities and limitations of advancing age, make me increasingly and painfully conscious that I am no longer able to render such service as is rightfully demanded from the occupant of my professorship, especially in the Graduate department and in the Observatory. While I might perhaps carry on the routine classroom work of the undergraduate course a little longer, (with the liability, however, of a sudden and final interruption at any time), I feel keenly that this is not sufficient. The interests of the Institution require that the work should pass into younger and stronger hands.

May I venture to add in closing that it would be a great gratification to me if, in my retirement, I might still retain a place upon your rolls as Professor Emeritus: I would like as long as I live to remain "a Princeton man."

With the highest respect and regard I remain

Yours sincerely   Charles A. Young.

TLS (Trustees' Papers, UA, NjP).

To the Board of Trustees of Princeton University

[Princeton, N. J.] DECEMBER 8, 1904

GENTLEMEN OF THE BOARD OF TRUSTEES:

I am happy to be able to report the University in a very whole-some and satisfactory condition. A steady access of seriousness and thoroughness continues to show itself from term to term in the work of the class rooms and laboratories, to the great encouragement of the instructors in every department, and cases of discipline seem to grow fewer and fewer. The work of instruction goes forward with greater zest this year than last and with greater satisfaction to both instructors and classes, chiefly because of the improvement wrought in every respect by the new regulation and arrangement of studies, of which I shall speak at length presently, but also because the students of the University have responded in the best spirit to the more rigorous and consistent application of the standards of scholarship. The decrease in the number of cases calling for discipline is undoubtedly due in large part to the admirable personal influence of the Dean of the University, whose character tells for stimulation and restraint no less than his unhesitating use of his authority. The steady, if insensible, growth of opinion and of self-government among the undergraduates plays an important part in bringing about the same salutary result. The life of the student body tends in matters of personal conduct to purify itself.

The Dean of the University is chairman of the Committee of the University Faculty on Examinations and Standing, questions of scholarship seeming to the Faculty to lie at the root of most questions of conduct among the undergraduates. The number of cases in which it has proved necessary to drop men from their classes for failure in study has not as yet decreased. The numbers for 1903 were, fifty-five in February, thirty-nine in June, a total of ninety-four; the numbers for 1904, seventy-two in February, forty-seven in June, a total of one hundred and nineteen, an increase of twenty-five. Quite two-thirds of the men thus dropped return to college and enter the next lower class, which they are generally permitted under the rules to do, but the number dropped amounts to from seven to nine *per cent.* of the whole number of undergraduates, if the two semi-annual series of examinations be taken together. This is by no means an extraordinarily large percentage as compared with the figures of like kind shown in other institutions where the rules of scholarship are carefully and systematically enforced; but it is higher than we like to have it, and we confidently look forward to its material reduction. The number of men dropped from their classes in the School of Science has, so far, been more than twice as great as the number dropped from the classes of the Academic Department. So soon as the new uniform entrance requirements begin to tell upon the preparation of the students sent to us this disparity may be expected to show a noticeable decrease. The recent reorganization of studies, moreover, has so increased the advantages of the School of Science and so completely done away with any hindrances that may have existed to its consistent development along with the general body of the University that there is every reason to believe that candidates for the degrees in science and engineering will not much longer be distinguishable from candidates for the degrees in letters in their work and discipline.

The chief means of reducing the number of failures, namely an increased force of teachers and better facilities for instruction, will be available only when our endowment is materially added to; but improved methods we have already adopted, and they will, without doubt, yield us improved results. The recent reorganization of studies is unquestionably a long step in the direction of efficiency. The student will be better trained and his chances for success in the examination will be materially improved.

The following table shows the number admitted to the University as undergraduates this year as compared with last:

	1903			1904		
	Acad.	S.S.	Total	Acad.	S.S.	Total
Freshmen without conditions, .	60	61	121	54	34	88
" with conditions, . . .	114	160	274	100	188	288
Specials, ...	12	37	49	24	41	65
Seniors, ...	5	1	6	7	4	11
Juniors, ...	4	1	5	2	2	4
Sophomores, ...	6	3	9	10	1	11
	201	263	464	197	270	467

Of the freshmen admitted upon examination in 1903, fifteen, for one reason or another, did not come, and of the freshmen admitted in 1904 nineteen did not come; so that the corrected figures for the two years are, 1903, 449; 1904, 448. This shows a falling off of one from the entrance figures of this year as compared with those of last year. To these statistics the following should, for the full information of the Board, be added:

	1903			1904		
	Acad.	S.S.	Total	Acad.	S.S.	Total
Examined, but not admitted, . .	26	43	69	24	41	65
Preliminary and partial exams., .	225	260	485	269	302	571

The only comment which these figures suggest is that the increase in the number of preliminary examinations, that is, partial examinations looking to entrance next year, is remarkably large. It has increased eighty-six; and the total number of preliminary examinations greatly exceeds—exceeds by more than one hundred—the total number of admissions this year. Since the examinations represent almost altogether applications for admission to the freshman class and the total number examined this year, including both those admitted and those rejected, amounts to 496 (specials also included) the prospective increase as indicated by the preliminary examinations is seventy-five.

The total undergraduate enrollment of the University is 1292 as compared with 1317 last year, a falling off of 25. Most of the larger eastern Universities have this year shown a falling off in their total enrollment, for reasons not yet clearly explained. Princeton seems to have been less affected than the rest, except that the figures in her graduate school have fallen from 114 to 91—a decrease of 23. This decrease in the number of graduate students arises chiefly from the fact that fewer students of the Theological Seminary than usual are availing themselves of the opportunity to pursue graduate courses in the University. The number of students devoting themselves wholly to graduate work has not fallen off, and the quality of the men enrolled is excellent. Why fewer Seminary students are pursuing graduate courses we can only conjecture. The character of the work being done in the class rooms and laboratories and seminaries of advanced instruction would seem to indicate that some part of the reduction of numbers, perhaps both on the undergraduate and on the graduate side, has been due to sifting processes which have strengthened and not weakened the student body as a whole. No doubt, too, conditions outside the University and affecting the life of the country as a whole cause a slight ebb and flow in numbers. It is seldom possible to see at once the causes which bring about such changes.

It is my sad duty to report the death of the Rev. Professor Charles Woodruff Shields, Professor Emeritus of the Harmony of Science and Revealed Religion, and of Mr. Laurence Hutton, A.M., lecturer on English literature. Neither Dr. Shields nor Mr. Hutton was actively engaged in teaching at the time of his death. Mr.

Hutton had been for many months in too delicate a state of health to permit of his lecturing, and Dr. Shields had been for a year upon the retired list as professor emeritus; but the loss of such men is not to be measured by the work they were doing as the last days closed about them.

Dr. Shields was graduated from Princeton in 1844 and was appointed to his chair in the University in 1865, under the presidency of Dr. John Maclean. His connection with the University had, therefore, extended over a period of thirty-nine years and he had come to seem a part of it, a very gracious and venerable part, reminding younger men by his courtly manners and the unmistakable flavour of distinction in all that he uttered of the graceful courtesy and literary taste of an age less hurried and less blunt of speech, more punctilious also and more given to the broader kinds of cultivation, than our own. Many generations of graduates will remember his lectures, his polished sermons, and his gentle personal dealings with them with unaffected admiration and affection. He had seemed to the very last to carry lightly his accumulated weight of years. He was happily conscious of his long and honorable record as a servant of the University and of his church, and looked back upon it with honorable pride. Death came very quietly upon him (August 26), almost without warning, and took him only at the end of a life rounded and complete.

Mr. Hutton was but sixty-one years of age and seemed only just arrived at the complete maturity of the many fine qualities which made him so universally beloved. It was his personality even more than his love of letters and his zeal for the finer things of conduct, his disinterested love of men rather than his addiction to books and study, that endeared him to us and has made his loss seem irreparable. His generosity and constancy in friendship were beyond all praise; his good fellowship was from his heart, perfect in its genial simplicity and unaffected sympathy. A more wholesome and cheering memory we shall not have than of him.

◊

It is pleasant to turn from loss to gain and record the additions to our teaching body. Professor Frank Thilly has assumed the duties of the Stuart chair of Psychology to which he was elected at the meeting of the Board in March, 1904. For the past eleven years he has been Professor of Philosophy in the University of Missouri, whither he went fresh from graduate studies in Berlin, Heidelberg, and Cornell, and where he distinguished himself both as a teacher and as a writer. He has entered upon his duties here with characteristic enthusiasm and is already a noteworthy addition to the force and momentum of our distinguished Department of Philosophy.

Professor Grant Showerman, Assistant Professor of Latin in the University of Wisconsin, has generously consented to undertake Professor Jesse Carter's work here for the present academic year, having been granted leave of absence from Madison for the purpose, and has put us under obligation to him for thus giving us the use of his experience in work which it was very undesirable to entrust to untried teachers.

The minor additions to the teaching force are reported in the annual catalogue.

◇

The subject which at present most engages our attention in the administration of the University is the operation of the new course of study. It is of course too early to form any definite or comprehensive judgment concerning its merits or influence in execution. It has been set afoot with singularly little difficulty and has seemed already to strengthen and simplify the work of the University at every point. The principles and ideals which it involves have been recognized in every quarter as of capital significance and importance, and deserve to be set forth with some degree of particularity, some detail of exposition. It is worth our while, now at the outset, to set forth very clearly the objects and methods to which we have devoted ourselves and the resources of the University.

The desire of all who in recent years have undertaken the reform of college studies in this country has been to find some plan by which to give consistency to the selection of studies which the undergraduate is now-a-days called upon to make among the multitude of courses and subjects of modern instruction. That is the object of our plan, and we hopefully expect it to answer its purpose. Its object is organization: to present for the use of the student an organic body of studies, conceived according to a definite and consistent system and directed towards a single comprehensive aim, namely, the discipline and development of the mind.

In order to accomplish this, and because the students who come to us and to all the larger universities of the country come with the most various and unequal preparation, it was deemed necessary to make the first, the freshman, year a year altogether of prescribed studies and both freshman and sophomore years years devoted to subjects elementary and fundamental in character: the languages ancient and modern, mathematics, physics, chemistry, logic, psychology, history, and the outlines of English literature. Every student is required to take mathematics, physics, logic, psychology, a modern language, and one or both of the ancient classical languages, as well as some drill in the language of his own English tongue. His addition to this of chemistry, history, and the outlines of English literature, or of a second modern language, as well as the number and thoroughness of his courses in mathematics and the languages, depends upon the election of studies he intends to make in his third year, when his attention will begin to be concentrated upon a few subjects.*

At the beginning of his third, or junior, year the student is called upon to make his individual choice of his subsequent course of study. He does not choose, however, from a miscellany of studies, but picks from a scheme of related subjects. In order

---

* The following scheme shows the arrangement of studies for the first two years. In their Freshman year candidates for the A.B. degree take the following studies:

Freshman Year

	Hours per week
English	2
Latin	4
Mathematics	4
French or German of entrance 2 ⎱ Greek 4 ⎰	6
	—
	16

Candidates for the degree of B.S. or Litt.B. the following:

	Hours per week
English	2
Latin	4
Mathematics	4
Physics (3) with French (3) or German (3) ⎱ or ⎰ French (3) and German (3)	6
	—
	16

In their Sophomore year candidates for the A.B. degree take as required studies physics, logic, psychology, Greek and Latin, and choose two elective courses from the following list: Latin (additional to required), Greek (additional to required), chemistry, mathematics, history, outlines of English literature, French, German. Sophomore candidates for the degree of Litt.B. or B.S. take as required studies, physics, logic, psychology, mathematics or Latin, and choose two elective courses from the following: Latin (unless Latin is taken as a required study), chemistry, mathematics or (in case mathematics is taken as a required subject) graphics, history, the outlines of English literature, French, German. See the report of the Committee on the New Course of Study appended to this report.

to systematize his choice the undergraduate studies of the University are grouped in Divisions and Departments as follows:

I. Under the Division of Philosophy, the Department of Philosophy and the Department of History, Politics, and Economics.

II. Under the Division of Art and Archaeology, a single Department of Art and Archaeology.

III. Under the Division of Language and Literature, the Departments of Classics, of English, and of the Modern Languages.

IV. Under the Division of Mathematics and Science, the Departments of Mathematics, Physics, Chemistry, Geology, and Biology; Astronomy being included in the Division but not erected into a separate department.

Each department, except that of History and Politics, offers in the junior year two courses; the Department of History, Politics and Economics, because of its tripartite make-up, offers three. The junior is required to choose five courses: all the courses of some one department, in order to give concentration and consistency to his studies, and, in addition to these, one additional course from another department in the same division; one course outside the division in which the department of his choice lies, so as to broaden the subject-matter of his studies; and one as he pleases, though necessarily, because of the limitation of the number of courses in any one department, outside the department to which he is chiefly devoting himself.

The courses of junior year in such subjects as politics, economics, art, archaeology, geology, biology, and astronomy, which have not been dealt with in freshman and sophomore years, are general and expository in character, laying the foundation for the more specialized study of senior year; the courses in English and the modern continental languages lay the foundations of literary criticism, sketch the history of the typical periods of the literatures dealt with, and give a systematic introduction to philological study, the historical development of the several languages. The object throughout junior year is not only to broaden the view of the student in the subjects he has chosen but also to lay the foundations of exact scholarship. It is a year of liberalization but also a year of definite aims and of processes intended to give the student a comprehensive acquaintance with the particular field of study he has selected.

In senior year the student is required to continue his studies in a department whose general courses he has taken in junior year. Inasmuch as there are in almost every case but two junior courses given in any one department and the student is left to choose two of his five courses in another department, he may easily qualify himself for either of two cognate, or even contrasted, departments in his senior year. This is an elastic feature of the scheme which seems to me of great value. The student is not obliged at any point of choice from entrance to graduation to confine himself to any single department. Even in the Department of History, Politics, and Economics, in which three of his five junior courses are prescribed, he can choose both of his other two electives outside that field and so qualify himself for any cognate department.

In senior year three of his five courses must be within a department for which he is qualified, and no department offers more than three, so that he is obliged in making choice of his other courses, which he may choose where he will, to give breadth and variety to his studies.

At no point in the plan, therefore, is there opportunity for narrow specialization, and at no point a chance to disperse the attention over a miscellany of unrelated subjects, while throughout any choice is permitted that has some smack of system and consistency about it. There is, moreover, a progressive order in the courses taken. They are related to each other by definite sequence. The courses of senior year are more specialized, detailed, particular than those of any preceding year, and are meant to draw the general training of the earlier years to as definite a completion as may be along particular lines. The movement of courses the four years through is from general to special, and the drill of freshman and sophomore years is as important to the senior as the liberalization and the introductory view of large subjects offered him in junior year.

It will be observed that the plan is frankly based throughout upon the fact, which is now a fact of general experience, that the undergraduate student is not likely to make a systematic choice of studies unless aided by more mature judgments than his own, and upon the assumption that the knowledge of men more mature than himself is a safer guide to a consistent and serviceable choice than his own untested tastes and preferences. He exercises his preference, but he exercises it with the sort of intelligence and consistency which the plan itself prescribes. It is a system of assisted election.

Some features stand out as of the very essence of the plan. Its fundamental principle is, that the object of undergraduate study is general training rather than specialized skill, a familiarity with principles rather than the acquisition, imperfect at best, of a mass of miscellaneous information,—that the acquisition of information is, indeed, not education at all; that education is a training necessary in advance of information, a process of putting the mind in condition to assimilate information and know what to do with it when it is acquired: that ideas, principles, schemes of thought, and methods of investigation govern facts and determine their place and value.

It is in pursuance of this fundamental conception with regard to the matter and method of education that courses in applied science have been excluded from the plan. Courses in applied science usually consist merely of drill in practical processes of test, analysis, or mechanical construction which are known to be serviceable in modern manufacturing and industrial undertakings. There was a time when these processes were neither very numerous nor very complex, and there was then time and opportunity to teach them in connection with theoretical courses in the class room and laboratory; but that time has long since passed. The processes of modern manufacture are innumerable, and time would fail to teach them all, even in the technical schools whose business it is to prepare experts. In the technical schools, moreover, no less than in the colleges, it is becoming evident, not to men of science only, but also to men who speak from a direct practical knowledge of industrial undertakings, that much more than mere skill in practical processes, learned by precept and example in the laboratories and workshops of the training schools, is necessary for the equipment of the men who are to take charge of the mechanical and chemical processes of our present industrial world. New processes must be found and used at every turn of the rapid movement of modern industry, and nothing but a very clear-cut and definite mastery of the principles of science, and of the more recondite principles at that, will supply them. Even old and familiar processes will go astray or stand unimproved in an age of improvement unless the men of skill be also men of broad theoretical knowledge in the sciences from which every process springs. Practical science gets all its sap and vitality from pure science; and the business of the colleges is plain. There is little enough time as it is in the four years of undergraduate study to teach the pure science which is fundamental: there is none in which to teach a few processes picked from the mass and inadequately supported by theory.

Pure 'Science,' indeed, in the broadest sense of the word, is at all points the business of undergraduate instruction. The progress and excellence of the practical professions no less than the fundamental things of culture depend upon this preliminary pursuit of knowledge without immediate regard to its practical uses. Some men, for lack of time or of means, must hurry into their professional work without this first orientation in the general field of study; even the so-called 'learned' professions must no doubt be crowded with men who are mere experts in a technical business, with no scientific knowledge of the principles they handle, and with no power, consequently, to lift their work to the levels of progress and origination; but some, fortunately, may approach their life tasks more slowly, by a more thorough way of preparation, and it is in the interest of society that these be as many as possible. It is our deliberate purpose to minister to these men and not to those who skimp and hurry and go half trained into their professions. And not to these only but also to those who seek or may be induced to take the general training of character which is to be had by means of the contacts and comradeships of a vital college life, the general training of mind and perfection of quality to be had from studies whose outlook is upon the broad field of all that the world thinks and does. There is no school of character and ambition comparable with that which breeds generous rivalries in an atmosphere permeated with the love of science and of letters.

Such things, it is true, are produced rather by the influence of men than by the compulsions of study; but studies vitally combined and pursued, as nearly as may be, in the natural sequence by which they spring the one from the other contribute not a little to the awakening and quickening both of mind and purpose, and it is one of the main objects of our new plan of courses to furnish and stimulate method and sequence in study. The limitation of the number of courses given in any one department is of interesting use in bringing about the desired result. If but two courses can be given in junior year in any one department and but three in senior, the years of concentration upon particular lines of study, these five chief bodies of study must be chosen for their central and preponderant importance, must be the five best calculated to give the student an insight into principles and processes. The best and most solid parts of each great branch of thought and each great field of natural phenomena must be picked out, and not such assorted fragments as the tastes or the convenience of the pupil or instructor may have suggested; and by such choice the teacher is no less stimulated and put to his paces than the pupil. The baccalaureate degree is again made to stand for a definite, ascertainable body of training. It seems to be a practicable way of getting something like the old definiteness and discipline out of the modern multitude of studies,—for each man a definite body of training, though not the same for all.

The entrance requirements put at the basis of the new scheme were chosen with the same principles and ideals in view. We were hampered in this part of our task by the fact that we were obliged to take what we could get, what the schools were willing and able to give us. But, so far as such limitations permitted, we have sought to reduce the entrance requirements to a very simple list. And in choosing the subjects to be incorporated we have found ourselves inclined to concentrate as much as possible on subjects from which we knew that discipline really was to be got in the schools. Old subjects are, generally speaking, taught with more efficiency than new subjects. Teachers of the classics and of mathematics have an assurance and a perfection of method in every way more serviceable than the ways and means of training now at the disposal of—at any rate the ways and means of training now actually used by—teachers of the modern languages. The elements of such sciences as physics and chemistry are not taught in the schools with as much thoroughness and success as has been attained in the teaching of mathematics; and we would rather have well trained students than students merely versatile and variously informed, whatever the means or the medium of their training.

The question of requiring or not requiring Greek did not detain or distress us. We were assured by experience that students drilled in the full classical training came to us better prepared for success in college tasks than those who had studied only Latin and substituted a modern language for Greek; and we were clear in our judgment that the old historical degree of Bachelor of Arts, the only degree that ever has been stamped with something like a definite significance, ought not to be wrested to strange meanings, to the obliteration of all definition in the labels of graduation. We therefore retained Greek as of course as a requirement of all those who should enter as candidates for the Arts degree. But we knew what the schools were doing and what a new age was demanding and were perfectly willing to attempt courses of liberal, humanistic training without Greek. We had long been doing so, indeed, but under a misleading plan and label. We had long been permitting candidates for the degree of Bachelor of Science to pursue courses in which science was at a minimum and the literary and philosophical studies at a maximum, and great numbers of them had come to following programmes of study not to be distinguished, at any rate in junior and senior years, from those taken by candidates for the degree of Bachelor of Arts, except for the exclusion of Greek. We now offer such men the degree of Bachelor of Letters and thus distinguish them from the men who are really pursuing scientific courses.

And, because we have made all our courses in science courses in pure science, we have put them in the same category with literary, philosophical, and general humanistic studies as means of liberal training. We have obliterated the line which was once so sharply and so arbitrarily drawn between the 'literary course' and the 'scientific course,' between the "Academic Department" and the "School of Science," not in organization, of course, but in spirit, object, and method. We have still our School of Science, resting upon the separate foundations of plan and endowment so wisely and generously given it by the great family the name of one of whose most distinguished members it bears; but its courses are not now set apart from the other courses of the University in artificial isolation. Science is as open to the candidate for the degree of Bachelor of Arts as literature, philosophy, art, and history are to the candidate for the degree of Bachelor of Letters, and the Bachelor of Arts does not lose his claim to that title by turning to science in the years of his concentration within a definite department of study. Until the close of sophomore year, moreover, candidates for the degrees of Bachelor of Science and Bachelor of Letters keep company in their studies without distinction: they are all alike simply men who have entered without Greek. It is when they make their choice of a special department of study at the beginning of junior year that they part company, those who select a scientific department turning towards the degree of Bachelor of Science, though they may have A.B. men as their comrades in the choice, while those who select literary or philosophical subjects, art, or history, turn their faces towards the degree of Bachelor of Letters.

Such is the scheme, alike in its system and in its elasticity. It is as yet too early to speak of its operation, except to say that it has been most cordially received even by that arch conservative the undergraduate himself. Apparently it is not a harness that galls or that too much restrains his liberty of movement. The ease and absence of friction and the general satisfaction with which it has been put into operation have surpassed our most sanguine expectations, and seem to give safe augury of its immediate success.

The effect it will have on the graduate courses of the University and on the development of the Graduate School interests us deeply, but is as yet hardly more than a matter of speculation. Though it has reduced, by systematizing, the number of courses offered to the undergraduates, it has not reduced, but rather increased, the amount of undergraduate work required of each member of the teaching force, because the number of hours per week devoted to each course given has been increased fifty *per cent.*,—from two hours to three. It is likely, therefore, that if these changes have any effect at all upon the amount of graduate work we can do with our present Faculties, the amount will be diminished rather than added to. This makes us the more anxious to obtain the means to increase the force which we can devote to graduate instruction, which ought not to suffer but to be greatly fostered.

But there is one feature of the new scheme, which I have not yet touched upon, which seems likely to operate by way of direct stimulation of graduate study. In order to put a premium on careful study, the new plan provides for the establishment of what we have called "pro-seminary" courses in senior year for students who have earned a more than ordinarily creditable standing in the studies of their department during junior year. The pro-seminary is thus a class of honour men. They meet but one hour a week, instead of three, and meet, not to hear a lecture or to report on common tasks assigned, but to present individual pieces of work, whether of analysis, recapitulation, or investigation, allotted them by the instructor in charge of the course. The methods of the pro-seminary, if not its subject matter and materials, are the methods of the graduate seminar: independent individual work and not the mere conning of work already prepared by the professor or by authoritative text writers. Men trained in this way will be much more likely to acquire a taste and zest in study which will carry them on to graduate work than will the men who follow the ordinary routine of class training. The pro-seminary will undoubtedly be the seed-bed of the seminar and tend constantly to recruit the ranks of serious graduate students. A Graduate College becomes more than ever, therefore, the necessary crown and completion of the curriculum.

◇

Material growth must necessarily go hand in hand with the development of studies and the perfection of methods of work. The material growth of the University has already seriously lagged behind its actual development in work and energy. I am not now speaking directly of the lack of money, but of the lack of dormitories, laboratories, and class rooms. Dormitories are necessary to our life, not only because the town is small and affords inadequate accommodation for the men for whom there is no room in the college buildings, but also because the characteristic life of the place, the things which give vitality alike to its intellectual and to its social character, centre in the campus associations, in the close daily contacts which make the undergraduate body a consciously corporate community. The solidarity and democracy of that community are at once its strength and its hope of continued distinction. There are now nearly four hundred undergraduates who must room in the expensive, scattered, inadequate lodgings of the town; and the dormitories are improperly crowded. Dormitories ought to be built for the accommodation of the entire body of undergraduates, as nearly as possible, to say nothing of the many graduate students who seem thrust out of the life of the place altogether because lodgings must be denied them in the college dormitories. These things must certainly be done, and done soon. And it is plain that, what with new dormitories, new recitation halls, laboratories, museums, and graduate schools of one sort and another, which we wish presently to be adding, it is an imperative counsel of prudence and forethought that we should take immediate steps for the preparation of a comprehensive architectural and landscape plan for the development of our campus, a plan which will have not the next decade merely, but the next fifty years in view, if we must be so long about it,—whatever length of time may turn out to be necessary for making Princeton what she now demands to be made in respect of her material equipment and development.

The careful study beforehand of matters like this is not a mere dictate of convenience; it affords invaluable assistance in working out purposes which are not material but of the spirit of all our hope and endeavour. This is the concrete way to express our plans for the intellectual, social, and moral life of the University, and to set our thoughts upon definite objects. When we have once, in our imagination, seen Princeton what we mean to make her, or to enable those who come after us to make her, we have made every vague purpose definite, and have clarified our perception of the means by which they are to be attained. I hope that funds will be provided for making such a plan at once. It will be both a guide and a safeguard.

The report of the Treasurer of the University, printed with this report, shows how greatly our endowments must be added to if we are to go forward with the great undertakings we have set before ourselves, or even maintain the University efficient in its present work. This is the first time that a financial statement of the condition and resources of the University has been made public. It is by your direction that the Treasurer's report is now published, and I think the step very wise and very significant. There is a sense in which every university, whatever the circumstances of its establishment or the plan of its government, is a public institution. Princeton, certainly, though privately endowed and governed as a close corporation, was conceived and has always served as an institution of the state and the nation. Her endowments have been drawn from men of all interests and connections, and her claim for additional endowment is made upon grounds, not of special or of local, but of general and national interest. It is eminently proper, therefore, that a public statement should be made concerning her property, her annual expenditures, her investments, and all her sources of income.

It will be matter of no small surprise to those who have known her history and the distinguished work she has done to learn upon how slender a capital she has conducted a great and successful business. The total invested funds of the University amount at par value to but $2,705,500, yielding, an income of $185,261.65. The total income of the University, from all sources, is but $460,863.20, the balance over and above income from investments being derived chiefly from tuition and other fees ($188,763.26), room rents $45,344.57, and from annual gifts $39,219.99. The expenses of the University sum up quite $482,122.26, which represents the most economical possible administration of its affairs. The budget shows, therefore, for 1904-5, an estimated deficit of nearly $18,000. There was an actual deficit during the fiscal year 1903-4 of $17,280.32, which was covered by generous gifts of money made for the purpose, as, apparently, the current deficit of the present year will have to be.

This represents the growth of the University and the continuous expansion of its work without any proportionate increase in its endowment. To borrow, and pervert, a phrase of the political economists, her life is seriously pressing upon the means of subsistence. The University never showed greater vitality. Her growth cannot be stopped except by processes which would sap that vitality. The plan for increasing her endowment which your Committee on Finance presents to you at this meeting is, therefore, the business which most presses for your immediate and careful consideration.[1] There is more hope than anxiety in these evidences of the University needs. They mean that she is springing forward from one stage of life to another; but they mean also that our efforts to supply her with means must be proportioned to her opportunities and capacities.

Respectfully submitted, WOODROW WILSON.[2]

Printed document (WP, DLC).
[1] The plan was presented orally by the committee's chairman, Moses Taylor Pyne, and led to the adoption of the resolution printed in the following document.
[2] There is a WWsh draft, dated Dec. 8, 1904, and a brief WWhw outline of this report in WP, DLC.

From the Minutes of the Board of Trustees of Princeton University

[Dec. 8, 1904]

On motion of Mr. Pyne, duly seconded, the following resolution was adopted:

RESOLVED that a committee of twenty be appointed to take into consideration the matter of providing funds for the University; with power to the Committee to increase its membership to one hundred.[1]

In accordance with this resolution, the President of the University appointed the following committee:

Cleveland H. Dodge '79, Chairman
John L. Cadwalader '56
John W. Aitken '69
John D. Davis '72
Charles Scribner '75
Bayard Henry '76
David B. Jones '76
James R. Macfarlane '78
Cyrus H. McCormick '79
Edward W. Sheldon '79
Pliny Fisk '81
Uzal H. McCarter '82
William C. Osborne '83
William B. McIlvaine '85

Joseph B. Shea '85
James H. Lockhart '87
Charles W. McAlpin '88
C. Ledyard Blair '90
Albert G. Milbank '96
Robert Garrett '97 . . .

◇

APPOINTMENT OF COMMITTEE TO SECURE FUNDS FOR MC COSH HALL RECONSIDERED

On motion of Mr. Bayard Henry, duly seconded, the following resolution was adopted:

RESOLVED that the action taken at the last meeting of the Board providing for the appointment of a committee of twenty to secure funds for the erection of McCosh Hall be reconsidered.

COMMITTEE ON NEW LECTURE HALL

On motion of Mr. Pyne, duly seconded, the following resolution was adopted:

RESOLVED that the President appoint a committee of five, including himself, which shall have power to determine upon and settle a site for a new lecture hall and which shall be empowered to have architectural plans and specifications prepared and to obtain estimates of cost, provided the expenses thereof shall not be a charge upon the finances of the University, which Committee shall report at the March meeting of the Board of Trustees.

In accordance with this resolution the following committee was appointed: Trustees Cleveland H. Dodge, M. Taylor Pyne, C. C. Cuyler, Henry W. Green and the President of the University. . . .[2]

INFORMAL MEETING OF TRUSTEES AND FACULTY

On motion of Mr. Bayard Henry, duly seconded, the following resolution was adopted:

RESOLVED that the President be requested to arrange for an informal meeting of the Board of Trustees and the members of the Faculty upon the evening immediately preceding the October meeting of the Board of Trustees.

[1] The activities and progress of this group, soon expanded into the Committee of Fifty, will be disclosed in considerable detail in following volumes.
[2] See the news report printed at March 4, 1905, Vol. 16.

To Robert Bridges

My dear Bobby: Princeton, N. J.   December 9, 1904.

I will be very glad to write a letter to the Admissions Committee of the University Club in Wood. Halsey's behalf.

I am going to try to see you next week for a few minutes. I am going into the hospital next Thursday to have the matter straightened out that I told you about, and shall probably be there about four weeks. You need give yourself no concern about the operation: it promises to be a very slight and safe affair.[1]

Always affectionately yours,   Woodrow Wilson

TLS (WC, NjP).
[1] Wilson was entering Presbyterian Hospital in New York on December 15 for an operation for a hernia to be performed by Dr. Andrew J. McCosh '77. His recovery was delayed by the onset of phlebitis in one leg. See EAW to Anna Harris, fragmentary letter, Feb. 12, 1907, Vol. 17.

From Charles Augustus Young

Princeton, N. J.   Friday Eve
My dear President Wilson   Dec. 9th [1904]

I have just received your letter announcing the acceptance of my resignation by the Trustees and their generous liberality in the matter of my salary as Professor Emeritus.[1]

My heart is full: I hardly know how to express my profound gratitude for the kindness with which I have been treated; but it is mingled with sincere, almost painful, regret at the cutting of my moorings here: I do not go away because I wish to, but because I see clearly that I ought.[2] And thanks to you and your associates in the Board, I can look forward to an unanxious, quiet evening of life. With warmest regard

Yours sincerely   C. A. Young

ALS (WP, DLC).
[1] The Board of Trustees had elected him to an emeritus professorship at an annual salary of $2,000.
[2] He was planning to return to his childhood home in Hanover, N. H., upon his retirement in June 1905.

To Charles Williston McAlpin, with Enclosure

My dear Mr. McAlpin: Princeton, N. J.   December 12, 1904.

I inclose the Minute concerning Professor Young which the Board instructed me to prepare for the minutes of its last meeting.

Cordially yours,   Woodrow Wilson

TLS (McAlpin File, UA, NjP).

A Tribute and Farewell

Princeton, N. J.   December 12, 1904.

The Board, in accepting the resignation of Professor Young, direct that the following minute be entered: The Board do not feel that they can consent to sever Professor Young's active connection with the University without expressing their grateful appreciation of the distinguished services he has rendered both to science and to the University. His connection with Princeton has added to its fame and to its influence in the intellectual world; his teaching has given generation after generation of students a true conception of the mission and the greatness of science; his personal qualities have been a true image of the poise, the modesty and the clear-eyed sincerity of true learning. He has won the perfect confidence and affection of his associates by his unusual graces of character, as well as their unstinted admiration by his extraordinary gifts of mind. He leaves behind him in his retirement an example of achievement and devotion which should challenge every teacher in the University to chasten his ambitions and to put only what is pure and of high purpose into his work; and the Board would have him feel that their affectionate good wishes follow him to the old home where his years of well earned rest are to be spent.[1]

T MS. (Trustees' Papers, UA, NjP).
[1] This tribute was spread on the Minutes of the Board of Trustees, Dec. 8, 1904.

To Charles Williston McAlpin

My dear Mr. McAlpin: Princeton, N. J.   Dec. 12, 1904.

I hand you herewith the committees which the Board directed me to appoint.

I: Committee to consult with the officers of the Pennsylvania Railroad: Mr. Cleveland, My [Mr.] Cadwalader, Hon. Wm. J. Magie, Mr. M. Taylor Pyne, and Mr. Bayard Henry.[1]

II: Committee to choose site for McCosh Hall: Mr. C. H. Dodge, Mr. M. Taylor Pyne, Mr. C. C. Cuyler, Mr. H. W. Green, the President of the University.

III: Com. on procuring funds for the University:
Mr. C. H. Dodge '79, Chairman.
J. L. Cadwalader '56; John W. Aitkin '69; John D. Davis '72; Bayard Henry '76; David B. Jones '76; A. J. McCosh '77; Jas R.

Macfarlane '78; R. H. McCarter '79; C. H. McCormick '79; E. W. Sheldon '79; Pliny Fisk '81; W. C. Osborne '83; Jos. B. Shea '85; J. H. Lockhart '87; C. W. McAlpin '88; C. Ledyard Blair '90; Stanley R. McCormick '95; A. G. Milbank '96; and Rob't Garrett '97.

Be kind enough not to have these committees immediately recorded in the Minutes, because in the case of the first one I have not yet obtained Mr. Cleveland's consent to serve as chairman, and in the case of the last one I should like to have time to modify it upon conference with Dodge, Pyne and Cuyler.

Cordially and sincerely yours, Woodrow Wilson

TLS (McAlpin File, UA, NjP).
[1] Wilson was acting in response to the following resolution adopted by the Board of Trustees on December 8, 1904: "Resolved that a committee of five be appointed to confer with the officers of the Pennsylvania Railroad Company looking to the improvement of the railroad facilities between Princeton and the Junction." All of the men named by Wilson accepted appointment. Pyne, chairman of the committee, reported to the trustees on June 12, 1905, that the committee had had a conference on June 1 with the president and other officials of the railroad, adding: "An informal talk was had and the ground gone over. Engineers have since been at work on the right of way and radical improvements are promised for the near future."

From Benjamin Wistar Morris III

My dear Dr. Wilson: [New York]   Dec. 12, 1904

I understand that you are to address a meeting of the committee of the ten classes at the Princeton Club on Wednesday evening next and intend explaining the drawings to them. Mr. Pyne and Mr. Dodge called to see them on Friday afternoon on their way up town and showed their interest in a very practical way by volunteering to pay the bill if I could get Mr. Jules Guerin to render the drawing. I was delighted and accepted their offer most thankfully and Guerin is now I hope making a very beautiful picture of the Building.[1] I will have the drawings delivered to the Princeton Club on Wednesday afternoon about 6 O'clock addressed to you. Trusting this meets with your approval, I am,

Yours very sincerely   B. W. M. Jr.

CCLI (WC, NjP).
[1] It now hangs in one of the small dining rooms on the second floor of Prospect, the faculty club of Princeton University.

To Benjamin Wistar Morris III

My dear Mr. Morris:　　　　Princeton, N. J.　Dec. 13, 1904.

Allow me to thank you for your kind letter of the 12th inst. I am delighted to hear that Mr. Guerrin is to make a perspective of the building and that it will be at our conference on Wednesday evening. That suits me exactly.

　　　　Cordially and sincerely yours,　Woodrow Wilson

TLS (WC, NjP).

To Charles William Kent

My dear Charles:　　　　Princeton, N. J.　Dec. 13, 1904.

I very much appreciate your kind letter of Dec 9th, and wish with all my heart that it were possible for me to be present in April when Alderman is inaugurated, but it is really out of the question.

I am going almost immediately into the hospital for an operation which, though slight, will, the doctors say, take the strength out of me very much and they are very insistent that I make as few speaking engagements for the Spring as possible. I know you will see how unusually good these reasons are, and trust you will explain to all my personal friends that the matter is really beyond my choice.

I deeply appreciate your invitation to stay with you and hope that the visit to the University is only a pleasure deferred.

　　　　Always faithfully yours,　Woodrow Wilson

TLS (Tucker-Harrison-Smith Coll., ViU).

A Desk Diary

[Jan. 1-Dec. 31, 1905]

Year Book Your Memory in Cloth Covers 1905 with WWhw entries of engagements and appointments.

Bound desk diary (WP, DLC).

A Pocket Notebook

[c. Jan. 1-Dec. 31, 1905]

Inscribed (WWhw) "Woodrow Wilson Jany 1905," with WWhw and WWsh names and addresses (often of potential donors to Princeton University), reminders, incidental accounts, bibliographical references, notes for letters, etc.

Pocket notebook (WP, DLC).

Ellen Axson Wilson to Charles Williston McAlpin

My dear Mr. McAlpin,   New York, Jan 3 [1905]

Mr. Wilson has today received a note from Mr. Cleveland declining to serve on the committee to confer with Penna. railroad authorities.[1] He therefore begs that you will send him at your early convenience a list of the members of the board who are on this committee, that he may lose no time in considering what is best to be done in regard to its chairmanship.

Mr. Wilson is still on his back, thanks to the "phlebitis,"—in every other respect he seems really well.

With kind regards from us both,

Yours very sincerely,   Ellen A. Wilson.

ALS (McAlpin File, UA, NjP).
[1] This letter from Grover Cleveland is missing.

From John Rogers Williams

[Princeton, N. J.]

My dear President Wilson: January 4, 1905.

I beg to acknowledge receipt of Mrs. Wilson's favor of the 3rd inst. addressed to Mr. McAlpin and in reply would say that the committee of five appointed to confer with the officers of the Pennsylvania Railroad Company consists of the following members:

Grover Cleveland
John L. Cadwalader
William J. Magie
M. Taylor Pyne
Bayard Henry.

Respectfully yours,   [John Rogers Williams]

CCL (McAlpin File, UA, NjP).

A News Report

[Jan. 6, 1905]

WORK ON THE LAKE BEGUN

Authoritative announcement was made on Wednesday that the contract for the construction of the Carnegie Lake has been awarded. The project includes the construction of a concrete dam at Kingston, twenty-seven feet in height and six hundred and fifty feet in length to back up the combined waters of Millstone River and Stony Brook. This will form a lake which will extend nearly to the Princeton branch of the Pennsylvania Railroad, a distance of three and three-quarter miles. The width of the lake, as determined by the topography of the land will be four hundred feet wide in most places, although at one point it will measure one thousand feet across. The lake will cover about five hundred acres of the marsh lands on both sides of the Millstone River, three hundred and fifty of which have already been purchased.

The district has been surveyed during the past two years and options on the land have been secured. The work of clearing the meadows and marshes for the bed of the lake has already been begun, and the construction work should be completed in two years. A boulevard will probably be built along the northern shore of the lake and it is expected that in addition to the increased facilities for aquatic and winter sports which the lake will furnish the University, the lake will do much to make Princeton a popular inland resort. Boat houses will be built, and it is expected that the Pennsylvania Railroad will construct a station at the shore of the lake.

Printed in the *Daily Princetonian*, Jan. 6, 1905.

From Charles Williston McAlpin

My dear Mrs. Wilson: [Princeton, N. J.]   January 6, 1905.

President Wilson asked me to call on Mr. Cleveland this morning and I am taking the liberty of sending you the result of my conversation with him in order that you may tell the President if you think best.

Mr. Cleveland expressed his willingness to remain on the Committee in conference with the officials of the Pennsylvania Railroad as a member in compliance with President Wilson's request.

Very sincerely yours,   [C. W. McAlpin] Secretary.

CCL (McAlpin File, UA, NjP).

A News Item About an Operation

[Jan. 7, 1905]

President Wilson '79 left Princeton a few days before the Christmas vacation began, for a slight surgical operation, which was performed at the Presbyterian Hospital in New York, by

Dr. Andrew J. McCosh '77. On account of the operation, the President will not return to Princeton for a few weeks.

Printed in the *Princeton Alumni Weekly*, v (Jan. 7, 1905), 213.

A News Item

[Jan. 7, 1905]

PRESIDENT WILSON CONVALESCING.

President Wilson, who was operated on at the Presbyterian Hospital, New York City, on December 16, has been progressing slowly but favorably and the physicians in charge of the case expect him to be able to sit up to-day. Provided his improvement continues, President Wilson expects to leave in a short time for the South where he willl remain until he has completely recovered.

Printed in the *Daily Princetonian*, Jan. 7, 1905.

A News Report

[Jan. 14, 1905]

ALUMNI DORMITORY.

Architect's Plans Have Been Accepted.
Ground to be Broken in Spring.

The plans for the Alumni Dormitory to be presented to Princeton by the classes of '92 to 1901 inclusive, have been drawn by Mr. Benjamin W. Morris, Jr., the architect, and accepted by the Alumni Dormitory Committee and the trustees of the University. The new dormitory will run along the east side of the Brokaw tennis courts and is the first of a handsome group proposed by the trustees to be erected on the east and south sides of Brokaw Field. It will be a separate and distinct building, but architecturally harmonious with the proposed group, with which it will be connected by an arcade. The style is the Collegiate Gothic, similar to Blair, Little and the New Gymnasium. . . . The total length of the building will be 284 feet and its greatest depth 80 feet. Each class is to contribute $13,000 and the entire building is to cost $130,000. There will be ten separate entries, one named for each class. The building will vary in height from two to five stories, the higher portion providing for two entries, the other eight entries being in two story sections flanking the higher portion.

Printed in the *Daily Princetonian*, Jan. 14, 1905.

A News Report

[Jan. 19, 1905]

CARNEGIE LAKE.

Detailed Account of the Plans and Progress of the Work.

The new Carnegie Lake is now in the first stages of construction and the work will be pushed steadily forward to completion. A general outline of the plan and construction of the lake is here given.

The lake will be formed by the construction of a dam across the Millstone River about eleven hundred feet south of the Kingston mill. This dam will flood the country to the south of it, which is adjacent to the canal, and the lake will extend southward to the Princeton branch of the Pennsylvania railroad, a distance of three and one-half miles.

The land extending from the proposed dam to the Aqueduct is by nature fitted for a lake and here the width will be from six hundred to one thousand feet. The excavating will begin at the Aqueduct and a channel will be dug extending south to the Princeton branch. This channel will have a width of from three hundred to eight hundred feet and will be excavated to a depth of from six inches to three feet. The natural depth of the lake will vary from four to twelve feet. The lake will also back up the Millstone valley for about one mile so that the stream itself will be broadened and deepened for that distance.

The lake will extend almost directly north and south. Steep slopes mark the westerly shore so that little filling will be necessary. The easterly shore follows the bank of the canal. At the southern extremity near Washington Road embankments of considerable height will be constructed on the University property, the intention being to make observation grounds.

The dam at Kingston will be a concrete re-enforced dam of the buttress and curtain type. The design is a novel one: a siphon or hooded section being built at the west end of the dam giving opportunity for making hydraulic experiments on the flow through siphons, also for determining the run-off of the one hundred and sixty-seven square miles of water-shed tributary to the lake. The dam will have two forty-eight inch sluice gates for floods and also for drawing off the water in dry weather if necessary.

A boulevard will be constructed along the western shore of the lake extending from Washington Road to the dam. The drive will be elevated and shaded by trees, most of its length being through a wooded park. Bridges over the lake will be constructed at Washington and Harrison Streets. These bridges will have four spans of one hundred feet each. The roads about the town of Aqueduct will be raised above the level of the lake.

All the land for the lake has been purchased and the main body of the lake has been purchased and the main body of water will comprise about four hundred and fifty acres with an addition of one hundred acres up the Millstone. Visitors may reach the lake by the Kingston branch of the Pennsylvania Railroad at the northern extremity of the lake, or by the Princeton branch at the southern end. Boats may travel from New York on the Raritan river to New Brunswick and from thence down the canal to the lake; likewise, boats from Philadelphia may come up the Delaware River to Trenton and from thence via the canal to the lake.

The contract for the entire construction has been awarded by Mr. Howard Russell Butler, who acts for Mr. Carnegie, to the Hudson Engineering and Contracting Company of New York City. The chief engineer is Mr. J. James R. Croes, who prepared all the plans of the lake and is superintendent of the construction. Mr. Croes has a splendid record as an engineer having at different times served on the New York Water Board and being at one time President of the American Society of Civil Engineers. Mr. John M. Mackenzie is the resident engineer in charge of the work and Mr. W. A. Mackenzie is the assistant engineer.

The contract demands that the lake be completed at the expiration of one year, which will be about November or December, 1905. Work has already been started upon the clearing of trees and removal of stumps from the lake basin. Fifty men are at present at work but in the course of a month two hundred men will be added. The excavation of the channel at the southerly end of the lake will then start.

The plans of the lake are as yet incomplete but as the work progresses, definite designs will be finished and the work will be described more in detail.

Printed in the *Daily Princetonian*, Jan. 19, 1905.

A News Item

[Jan. 21, 1905]

President Wilson '79 left the Presbyterian Hospital in New York this week, for Palm Beach, Florida, for a brief rest before returning to Princeton. Meantime, the alumni will read with interest the final installment of the President's annual report to the trustees, which appears on another page.[1]

Printed in the *Princeton Alumni Weekly*, v (Jan. 21, 1905), 249.
  [1] Wilson's Annual Report to the Board of Trustees appeared in the *Princeton Alumni Weekly*, v (Dec. 17, 1904, and Jan. 7 and 21, 1905), 195-98, 215-20, 252-56.

To Benjamin Wistar Morris III

The Breakers, Palm Beach, Fla.

My dear Mr. Morris,   27 Jan'y, 1905

One thought I find coming to me every time I think of, what we will call, provisionally, the Decennial Dormitory. I pass it on to you. It seems to me that it will be, artistically, very risky to put chimney stacks on the tower at the southern end. If their tops cannot be brought down to the level of the crenulations, I think they had better be left off altogether. The rooms below can very well dispense with fire places and get along with the steam heat.[1]

And I am not altogether easy about the composition of roof line and chimney tops on the four-storey mass just south of the two entries with which the building is to begin at the north. Could you, without too much trouble, send me (here, if it can get here by the 9th of Feby, or to Princeton, if not) a rough perspective sketch of the upper part of that portion of the building,—the lower part merely indicated without detail?

I feel quite like myself already, but must wait a couple of weeks on my "game" leg.

With warm regard,

Sincerely Yours,   Woodrow Wilson

ALS (WC, NjP).
  [1] The tower at the southern end was erected without chimneys.

To Charles Williston McAlpin

My dear Mr. McAlpin: Palm Beach, Fla., Feb'y 6th, 1905.

I have made the most excellent progress in getting back my strength and am planning to be in Princeton by Wednesday the 15th.

Won't you give my regards to all my friends and believe me, with warmest gartitude [gratitude] for all you have done to protect me from business,

Faithfully and cordially yours,   Woodrow Wilson

TLS (McAlpin File, UA, NjP).

ADDENDA

To Daniel Moreau Barringer

Princeton, New Jersey.

My dear Moreau: 2 February, 1903.

It was certainly a generous impulse which led you to write me
your kind letter of January 28th,[1] and I want to assure you that
it went straight to my heart. I know how strong your feeling is
with regard to your own father:[2] I know, therefore, how keenly
you can sympathize with me in the loss I have just suffered. I
believe that like yourself sentiment of this kind plays a larger
part in my life than in that of most men; and there is no sympathy I would rather have than that of a man who feels an even
chivalric devotion to his father and to all the honorable things
that his father stands for. I send you in return my warm love and
appreciation.

As ever,   Affectionately yours,   Woodrow Wilson

TLS (WC, NjP).
  [1] Barringer's letter of condolence upon the death of Wilson's father is missing.
  [2] Daniel Moreau Barringer (1806-73), prominent North Carolina politician,
Minister to Spain, 1849-53.

To Granville Stanley Hall[1]

Princeton, New Jersey.

My dear President Hall: 30 October, 1903.

I am afraid that I do not clearly understand the exact purport
of the questions you put in your letter of the 27th,[2] but I am
most willing to reply to them as I understand them.

I think that non-professional university fellowships and scholarships are undoubtedly useful in providing good students with
a means for carrying on advanced study. They seem to have been
clearly serviceable to scholarship.

American University students are so many of them from families which cannot afford to pay their full expenses that it does
not seem to me practicable unless we deliberately limit our student bodies to those who have means to derive any larger portion
of the income than is now derived from students' fees. Invested
endowment must at best carry the greater part of the burden.

I do not think that graduate departments in a philosophical
faculty can be expected to bring in any income at all from students, except possibly by way of dormitory rentals.

Very sincerely yours,   Woodrow Wilson

TLS (G. S. Hall Papers, MWC).
  [1] President of Clark University.
  [2] It is missing.

INDEX

NOTE ON THE INDEX

THE alphabetically arranged analytical table of contents at the front of the volume eliminates duplication, in both contents and index, of references to certain documents, such as letters. Letters are listed in the contents alphabetically by name, and chronologically within each name by page. The subject matter of all letters is, of course, indexed. The Editorial Notes and Wilson's writings are listed in the contents chronologically by page. In addition, the subject matter of both categories is indexed. The index covers all references to books and articles mentioned in text or notes. Footnotes are indexed. Page references to footnotes which place a comma between the page number and "n" cite both text and footnote, thus: "624,n3." On the other hand, absence of the comma indicates reference to the footnote only, thus: "55n2"—the page number denoting where the footnote appears. The letter "n" without a following digit signifies an unnumbered descriptive-location note.

An asterisk before an index reference designates identification or other particular information. Re-identification and repetitive annotation have been minimized to encourage use of these starred references. Where the identification appears in an earlier volume, it is indicated thus: "*1:212,n3." Therefore a page reference standing without a preceding volume number is invariably a reference to the present volume. The index supplies the fullest known forms of names, and, for the Wilson and Axson families, relationships as far down as cousins. Persons referred to in the text by nicknames or shortened forms of names can be identified by reference to entries for these forms of the names.

A sampling of the opinions and comments of Wilson and Ellen Axson Wilson covers their more personal views, while broad, general headings in the main body of the index cover impersonal subjects. Occasionally opinions expressed by a correspondent are indexed where these appear to supplement or to reflect views expressed by Wilson or by Ellen Axson Wilson in documents which are missing.

INDEX

WOODROW WILSON

AND ELLEN AXSON WILSON